KT-563-795

STRODE'S COLLEGE
LIBRARY

EXPLORING

Abnormal

PSYCHOLOGY

Richard S. Perrotto, Ph.D.

Joseph Culkin, Ph.D.

*Queensborough
Community College
of the City University
of New York*

HarperCollins
CollegePublishers

Acquisitions Editor: Catherine Woods
Developmental Editor: Bob Nirkind
Project Editor: Susan Goldfarb
Assistant Art Director: Lucy Krikorian
Text Design: Delgado Design, Inc.
Chapter-opening Art: Eve Olitsky
Cover Design: Lucy Krikorian
Cover Illustration: Eve Olitsky
Photo Researcher: Sandy Schneider
Production Manager: Willie Lane
Compositor: Waldman Graphics, Inc.

About the Artist: Eve Olitsky received a B.F.A. in set and costume design from New York University's School of the Arts and an M.F.A. in creative writing from Columbia University. Her work in fine art and illustration has been exhibited throughout the New York area. Ms. Olitsky is an assistant professor in the Fine Arts Department of Montclair State College and an instructor in the Illustration Department of the Parsons School of Design.

For permission to use copyrighted material, grateful acknowledgment is made to the copyright holders on pp. 475–476, which are hereby made part of this copyright page.

EXPLORING ABNORMAL PSYCHOLOGY

Copyright © 1993 by Richard Perrotto and Joseph Culkin

All rights reserved. Printed in the United States of America. No part of this book may be used or reproduced in any manner whatsoever without written permission, except in the case of brief quotations embodied in critical articles and reviews. For information address HarperCollins College Publishers, 10 East 53rd Street, New York, NY 10022.

Library of Congress Cataloging-in-Publication Data

Perrotto, Richard S.
    Exploring abnormal psychology / Richard S. Perotto, Joseph
Culkin.
        p.   cm.
    Includes bibliographical references and indexes.
    ISBN 0-673-46413-X
    1. Psychology, Pathological.   I. Culkin, Joseph.   II. Title.
RC454.P425   1993
616.89—dc20   92-5274
                                                                     CIP

    95 9 8 7 6 5 4 3

Contents
IN BRIEF

Contents IN DETAIL

Special
Features

xxiii

*P*reface

In our years of teaching we have come to recognize that abnormal psychology textbooks do not meet the needs of our students. Most are too long to be covered in a one-semester course, and they emphasize unnecessarily detailed research methodology. Such texts appear too scientific to most students, intimidating them and distracting them from the fundamentals. Educating our students has required that we adopt a more accessible approach. Feedback from other instructors in the field of abnormal psychology across the country has consistently substantiated these concerns and has stimulated the development of our own text.

OUR APPROACH

We believe that students need a concise yet comprehensive text that covers the major topic areas without overwhelming the reader with unnecessary detail and jargon. To this end, we have developed *Exploring Abnormal Psychology*. The book is necessarily brief (substantially shorter than most competing texts), but it emphasizes pedagogy; the writing style is straightforward, but it is not patronizing. As community college professors and practicing psychologists, we are able to write in a style appropriate for most students and to draw from actual clinical work in order to provide real case studies as examples. Our goal has been to strike a balance between theory and real-world psychological problems. We hope that our text will both inform students and pique their interest in the fascinating field of abnormal psychology.

KEY FEATURES

1. Rather than being driven by a particular theoretical slant, this text emphasizes contemporary research and the balance between psychology and the neurosciences. Whenever data permits, current knowledge about the integration of psychology and the neurosciences is presented in describing etiology and treatment.
2. Principles of theory and therapy are integrated into Chapters 2 and 3. This is an important feature of the book. Specific details of each therapy are described in the context of our discussion of individual mental disorders, providing a continuity of thought. This approach is in dramatic contrast to that of other books that present major theoretical perspectives early in the text and discuss therapy near the end. Our approach eliminates the need for specific therapy chapters, sparing the student the need to jump from chapter to chapter in order to integrate information. This also effectively reduces the length of the text without omitting content.
3. Chapter 12, on eating and impulse control disorders, and Chapter 15, on family violence and divorce, discuss topics heretofore uncovered in other texts. Considering the prevalence and magnitude of these problems, we believe they deserve special attention. These chapters add to the practical, real-world dimension of this book.
4. The guiding diagnostic system in this text is the DSM-III-R. However, we have anticipated the DSM-IV and have included an appendix based on available DSM-IV literature published to date.

PEDAGOGY

Pedagogical elements incorporated into this program help students grasp concepts and terminology and expand students' peripheral knowledge of abnormal psychology.

1. A detailed chapter outline appears at the start of each chapter.
2. A numbered list of learning objectives follows the chapter outline.
3. At the beginning of each chapter, a vignette introduces a real case relating to the topic covered in that chapter. The vignette acquaints readers with one aspect of the chapter's content and also presents a ''teaser'' in that the case analysis is not revealed until that particular subject is discussed within the chapter. As the case is developed in subsequent vignettes, students learn about diagnostic issues and etiologic and treatment possibilities.
4. Brief case examples, most taken from the authors' files, are presented throughout the text to illustrate particular clinical issues, etiologies, and possible treatments.
5. Terms introduced in the narrative are defined in the margins, with phonetic pronunciation guides where appropriate.
6. Boxed ''Close-up'' features highlight interesting issues—such as ''Stress and Infection'' in Chapter 6 and ''Obesity and Socioeconomic Status'' in Chapter 12—related to the chapter topic.
7. Each chapter features a ''Profile,'' a biographical sketch that provides readers with insight into the professional and personal lives of famous individuals who have made significant contributions to the discipline of abnormal

psychology, such as Albert Bandura (Chapter 3) and Bruno Bettelheim (Chapter 11).

8. Numbered chapter summaries recapitulate key concepts covered in each chapter.
9. At the end of each chapter, "Terms to Remember" lists terms defined within that chapter, along with the page numbers where they are defined. These terms also appear in the Glossary at the back of the book.
10. "Suggested Readings" provides a list of supplementary readings pertinent to chapter topics.
11. Each chapter ends with a feature titled "Legal and Ethical Issues." These sections focus on subjects pertaining to the chapters' content.

SUPPLEMENTS

Instructor's Manual

Written by Frank Prerost of Western Illinois University, this manual, organized by text chapter, provides an abundance of teaching aids, including chapter outlines, learning objectives, key terms, abstracts, readings, discussion and lecture ideas, activities and projects, and film references.

Test Bank

Based on the tests we give to our own students, the Test Bank contains approximately 150 multiple-choice questions per chapter (more than 2300 in all), as well as 10 essay questions (150 total). The Test Bank is available in printed form and on floppy disks for most popular desktop computers. For more information, please call your HarperCollins representative.

Study Guide

Written by Matthew E. Lambert of Texas Tech University, this guide helps students grasp the concepts in the text. Included in the Study Guide are chapter introductions, vocabulary exercises, two sets of practice tests, and study tips.

Brief Casebook in Abnormal Psychology

Developed by Judith Rosenberger of Hunter College and Edith Gould of the Psychoanalytic Institute of the Post-Graduate Center for Mental Health in New York, this casebook contains 13 cases that cover a wide range of psychological disorders. Each case, written from the perspective of the person with the disorder, is followed by a clinical discussion and "case questions" that encourage students to develop their critical thinking skills by applying what they have learned to actual clinical settings.

Computerized Case Simulations

This new interactive software program, developed by Matthew E. Lambert, offers students the opportunity to take the role of therapist, assessing, diagnosing, and treating fictional patients in four separate computerized case simulations. Each simulation involves extensive data, along with a number of variables and reactions to treatment that students can follow over time. Available for IBM PC and compatibles.

The World of Abnormal Psychology Video Series

Produced as part of the Annenberg/CPB Collection, this acclaimed 13-part video series offers ideal support for lectures and discussions. The program contains enlightening interviews and commentary from academics, clinicians, and people suffering from various psychopathologies, as well as outstanding animation of physiological processes. The tapes are available to eligible adopters of *Exploring Abnormal Psychology*.

ACKNOWLEDGMENTS

The development of a book depends on the hard work, diligence, and scrutiny of many people. We wish to gratefully acknowledge the contributions of the following reviewers, whose considerable efforts, suggestions, ideas, and insights helped us through the realization of our first textbook:

Sara Ashcroft, Monroe Community College
Ileana Arias, University of Georgia
Chris Auman, Richmond Community College
Gladys Baez-Dickereiter, St. Phillips College
Francis Battisti, Broome Community College
Barbara Brackney, Eastern Michigan University
Peter Brady, Clark State Community College
T. L. Brink, Crafton Hills College
Gary Brummer, Jackson State Community College
Lorry Cologey, Owens Technical College
Roger DeWitt, Aims Community College
Donald Eland, Macomb County Community College
Stanley Feist, State University of New York College of Technology at Utica/Rome
Mark Fine, University of Dayton
Peter Flynn, Northern Essex Community College
John Foust, Parkland College
Stan Friedman, Southwest Texas State University
Judy Gentry, Columbus State Community College
Eric Graf, Ithaca College
Jo-Anne Haber, Stark Technical College
Bruce Hinrichs, Lakewood Community College
April Hollenhorst, Indian Hills Community College
Sharon Hott, Community College of Allegheny County
Kevin Keating, Broward Community College
Joan Kerr, College of Lake County
Michael Klein, J. Sargeant Reynolds Community College
Dennis Kreinbrook, Westmoreland County Community College
Carol Lamon, Houston Community College
Angela La Salla, Community College of Southern Nevada
Gary Lesniak, Portland Community College
William Levy, Manchester Community College
Paul Lewan, Green River Community College
Emma Lou Linn, Saint Edward's University
Gary McClure, Georgia Southern College
Ralph Moorehead, San Juan Community College

Mark Morey, State University of New York College of Oswego
Patricia Owen, St. Mary's University
Martin Pearlman, Middlesex County College
Christopher Potter, Harrisburg Area Community College
Carroll Price, Penn Valley Community College
Carol Riechenthal, Merrimack College
Kathleen Rusch, Marquette University
Jack Sandler, Olympic College
John Sempowski, Monroe Community College
John Shepherd, New Mexico Junior College
Pamela Stewart, Northern Virginia Community College
Carol Thompson, Muskegon Community College
Mike Toutanzhi, American River College
Mike Witmer, Skagit Valley College

When we began writing this book, we knew that it would be a challenge. Little did we know how Herculean a task it would be. We quickly realized that despite our expertise as psychologists and professors, much more goes into writing a psychology book than a knowledge of psychology. The team of professionals at HarperCollins came to the rescue by guiding us through every step of the development process.

We would like to extend special thanks to sponsoring editors Don Hull, who saw great promise in our crude sample chapters; Laura Pearson, who began our project with us and contributed many ideas; and Catherine Woods, who stepped in down the stretch and saw us through to the end.

Once the project was under way, development editor Bob Nirkind and his assistant Wade Olsson guided us through every phase of the manuscript's preparation. Although Bob's critical eye forced us to write and rewrite sections of every chapter, there is no doubt that the final product is much better for it. For this we are greatly indebted.

Thanks are also extended to Leslie Hawke for her help in developing the supplements to accompany this text and to Susan Goldfarb, project editor; Lucy Krikorian, assistant art director; Willie Lane, production manager; and Sandy Schneider, photo editor.

Finally, we would be remiss if we did not give special thanks to our families for their patience and support.

RICHARD S. PERROTTO
JOSEPH CULKIN

About the Authors

RICHARD S. PERROTTO received his Ph.D. in psychology from the University of Delaware in 1979. Since 1978 he has been on the faculty of the Department of Social Sciences, Queensborough Community College of the City University of New York. During these years he has taught courses in abnormal, physiological, and introductory psychology as well as personality. Professor Perrotto is a New York State–licensed psychologist with postdoctoral training in behavioral psychotherapy. He has extensive experience in the evaluation and treatment of diverse client problems. He has published scientific articles in the areas of abnormal psychology and brain-behavior relationships. Professor Perrotto is a member of the American Psychological Association and the Queens County Psychological Association.

JOSEPH CULKIN received his Ph.D. from the Graduate Faculty of the New School for Social Research in 1980. He has been on the faculty of the Department of Social Sciences, Queensborough Community College of the City University of New York, since 1979. Professor Culkin is a New York State–licensed psychologist with postdoctoral training in behavioral psychotherapy and marriage and family counseling. He has taught courses in abnormal and introductory psychology as well as psychological disorders of childhood and personality. His research interests and publications include nonverbal communication, depression, gender roles, and family psychopathology. Professor Culkin is a member of the American Psychological Association, Eastern Psychological Association, and Queens County Psychological Association.

EXPLORING

A
bnormal

PSYCHOLOGY

Chapter ONE

Introduction to Abnormal Psychology

OBJECTIVES

1. Identify the four meanings of the term *abnormal behavior*.
2. Compare naturalism and supernaturalism and their views of abnormal behavior.
3. Trace the important events in the rise of the modern scientific attitude toward mental disorders.
4. Outline the research strategies for investigating abnormal behavior.
5. Discuss the limitations of research methods in abnormal behavior.
6. Describe the ethical principles governing research in abnormal psychology.

*A*t the age of 34, after three years in a high-pressure technical position with a defense contractor, Tom suffered what he described as "a complete breakdown." Although he was a brilliant engineer, he became incapable of performing even the smallest assignment. He felt intense anxiety when he awoke on weekdays and was morbidly fearful of making mistakes on the job.

Over several months Tom's condition worsened. He began to suffer attacks of anxiety during which he was sure he was losing his mind. He grew severely depressed and began to experience chronic insomnia. During his last month at work he was sleeping only about two hours per night and was performing his job poorly.

Consequently Tom was placed on disability leave by his employer, and several months later he was laid off. After losing his job, Tom became even more depressed and anxious. He spent most of his days either in bed or pacing nervously around his living room. For the next six months he was almost totally dependent on his wife's care. In this chapter we will refer to the case of Tom to illustrate the different meanings of abnormal behavior.

abnormal psychology
The scientific study of abnormal behavior and mental disorders.

Since ancient times, people have attempted to understand and treat abnormal behavior. **Abnormal psychology** is the scientific study of abnormal behavior and mental disorders. In this chapter we explore the alternative definitions of abnormal behavior and trace the history of abnormal psychology from its ancient roots to modern times. Finally, we examine the contemporary research methods used to investigate abnormal behavior.

1-1   WHAT IS ABNORMAL BEHAVIOR?

It is certain that most of us will observe, if not experience, some abnormal behavior during our lives. From a depressed relative to an alcoholic co-worker or a mentally retarded neighbor, examples of abnormal behavior are everywhere. Yet no simple, universally accepted definition of abnormal behavior exists. At best we can understand abnormal behavior in terms of degrees of psychological adjustment. If we accept that "normal" and "abnormal" are different parts of the same dimension of adjustment, then there is no absolute boundary between normal and abnormal behavior. The meanings of normal and abnormal behavior are determined by common standards from which four definitions of abnormal behavior emerge:

1. Abnormal behavior as statistical deviation
2. Abnormal behavior as violation of social norms
3. Abnormal behavior as maladaptive behavior
4. Abnormal behavior as personal distress

Abnormal Behavior as Statistical Deviation

statistical deviation   A rare or uncommon event, such as abnormal behavior.

One way of evaluating behavior is to determine how common it is. According to a **statistical deviation** definition of abnormal behavior, behavior is abnormal if its occurrence is rare or uncommon. For instance, all people eat, but few force themselves to vomit after eating. Using a statistical deviation definition, we say that those individuals who self-induce vomiting after eating are showing abnormal behavior.

Many exceptional people, such as retired U.S. Supreme Court justice Thurgood Marshall, entertainer Madonna, and hockey superstar Wayne Gretzky, exhibit statistically deviant behavior but are not necessarily abnormal psychologically.

Statistically deviant behaviors are not necessarily signs of psychological disturbances. Many rare behaviors are quite desirable and healthy—for example, artistic creativity, mathematical genius, leadership, and athletic excellence. To view these behaviors as abnormal just because they are uncommon would be absurd—otherwise we would label as abnormal many of society's most talented individuals. Consider that in their own unique ways Wayne Gretzky, retired Supreme Court justice Thurgood Marshall, and Madonna all have exhibited statistically deviant behavior.

Tom's condition was statistically deviant. Although most of us feel sad or anxious at times, we do not as a rule experience these emotions to the extreme degree that Tom did. In the United States about 20 percent of the population suffer from some form of depression, and another 4 to 8 percent suffer from serious anxiety problems (W. Smith, 1989).

Abnormal Behavior as Violation of Social Norms

social norms
Conventional rules of conduct in a society.

Every society sets norms or standards for behavior. **Social norms** are conventional rules of conduct for a society, and whoever violates them may be identified as abnormal. Once we recognize the social origin of these rules, we see that the term *abnormal behavior* cannot have a universal meaning. Definitions of abnormal behavior vary from one society to another, so what one group labels abnormal may be acceptable behavior to another.

When Western standards are imposed on people from other cultures, many of their behaviors seem strange and abnormal to us. In some countries, people eat insects, practice sorcery, and encourage sex play among children. While these behaviors might be viewed as abnormal by us, many people in the world would view as abnormal American behaviors such as birth control, having one spouse, unchaperoned dating, and bottle-feeding infants (Butcher & Bemis, 1984; Opler, 1959).

The enormous variety of human social traditions, dress, beliefs, and behavior indicates that no absolute norms are available to judge everyone.

Even within American society there are numerous conflicts over what constitutes "normal" behavior. Ethnic, racial, and religious groups often express divergent beliefs based on their own values and traditions. Today the standards of professionals in abnormal psychology do not necessarily conform to the beliefs of all members of society. For example, the controversy over whether homosexuality is abnormal behavior or an alternative sexual lifestyle illustrates one area of conflict between the mental health professions and widespread public sentiments. Although homosexuality is no longer considered a mental disorder by most mental health professionals, it is still seen as an extreme norm violation by many other members of society.

What social norms did Tom's behavior contradict? He broke no laws, but his behavior did violate some of our society's unwritten rules: do your job well; provide for your family; maintain control of yourself. Tom's emotional condition made it difficult for him to obey these social rules. Not only was he unforgiving of himself for not working—he was further stung by the negative judgments of others. Even members of his own family criticized him for not "pulling himself together."

The severe alcoholism of skid row residents has significantly interfered with their ability to adapt successfully to the demands of everyday life.

Abnormal Behavior as Maladaptive Behavior

maladaptive behavior
Behavior that interferes with everyday coping.

Maladaptive behavior is behavior that interferes with a person's ability to meet everyday responsibilities and cope with the everyday demands of family, work, and social life. Adjusting to the problems and circumstances of day-to-day living is essential to everyone's mental health. Most of us experience problems in adjustment from time to time, but we usually manage to overcome them. In practical terms, the difference between ordinary adjustment problems and maladaptive behavior depends on the degree of impairment.

Maladaptive behavior can result from attempts to cope with problems. Unfortunately, such attempts often turn out to be self-defeating. For example, some people use drugs like alcohol and cocaine in an attempt to control emotional distress, but in the long run this behavior will cause more problems than it solves.

Many of us feel "down" in times of stress, but we continue to meet our daily responsibilities. Tom, however, had such severe emotional distress that he could no longer function on the job. His anxiety, poor concentration, and lapses of memory made working impossible. He also neglected his family obligations. For weeks he was so distraught that he could not leave his home; on some days he could not even leave his bed.

Abnormal Behavior as Personal Distress

personal distress criterion A definition of abnormal behavior in terms of unpleasant emotional states.

Our final definition of the term *abnormal behavior* considers the individual's subjective emotional state. According to the **personal distress criterion**, abnormal behavior is associated with unpleasant emotional experiences. Painful feelings such as fear, guilt, and depression are a common feature of psychological disturbances. Since complex relationships exist between emotions and behavior, personal distress is sometimes both a cause and a consequence of abnormal behavior.

As with our other definitions, personal distress is not always a reliable indicator of abnormality. Emotional distress is often a normal and healthy reaction to life events. For example, mourning the death of a loved one is not abnormal.

A lack of personal distress may even indicate a serious psychological disturbance—consider a psychopathic criminal like Charles Manson, who expressed no guilt or remorse over his role in several gruesome murders (see Chapter 13).

To say Tom was depressed and anxious is to simplify his emotional condition. He was plagued by feelings of guilt over losing his job, having no income, and depending on his wife. His self-esteem was very low, and he saw himself as a hopeless, miserable failure. At the same time, Tom was both ashamed of losing control of his emotions and enraged at his family for their lack of sympathy. His anxiety kept him awake many nights, and as a result he became physically, as well as emotionally, "burned out." At the urging of his wife, Tom finally sought help, and after nearly a year of treatment combining therapeutic drugs and psychotherapy, he began to work again in a less stressful occupation.

Our four definitions of abnormal behavior are neither universal nor absolute. You should consider them flexible guidelines for evaluating behavior, keeping in mind that human behavior is usually more complicated than mere labels. Since none of our definitions provide a completely satisfactory meaning for abnormality, caution is necessary in using them to judge people. Ultimately, the difference between normal and abnormal behavior depends as much upon our imperfect ideas about behavior as on the behavior itself.

1-2   HISTORICAL OVERVIEW

Although every culture has its own ideas about what constitutes abnormal behavior, modern abnormal psychology is primarily the product of Western philosophy and science. In this section we will examine its history within these cultural traditions.

Supernaturalism

supernaturalism The belief that gods, demons, spirits, and magic influence behavior.

Accounts of abnormal behavior are found in the myths, religious writings, and historical records of many cultures. Descriptions thousands of years old indicate to us that many familiar mental and behavioral problems have long existed. In ancient times, most explanations of mental and physical abnormalities were grounded in **supernaturalism**, which is the belief that our behavior can be influenced by gods, demons, spirits, and magic.

Supernaturalism also generated practices that attempted to cure abnormal behavior. Exorcism and magic are spiritual rituals intended to drive out demons thought to be controlling a person's mind and body. Archaeological discoveries suggest that some ancient healers cut or pounded holes in their patients' skulls, perhaps to set free evil spirits. We cannot prove that this technique, known as *trephination*, was really a treatment for spirit possession. It may have been a religious ritual or a primitive surgery for head injuries (W. B. Maher & B. A. Maher, 1985).

Supernaturalism and religious notions about abnormal behavior dominated Western thought throughout the Middle Ages. The mentally ill were thought to be possessed or sinful, and this often led to their rejection and persecution within society. A tragic result of this attitude was the witch-hunting frenzy of the sixteenth and seventeenth centuries. In 1486, two Dominican priests wrote a book called *Malleus Maleficarum* (*The Hammer of Witchcraft*), which served

CLOSE-UP
The Malleus Maleficarum *on Demonic Possession and Extracting Confessions from Witches*

"From this it is concluded that, since devils operate there where they are, therefore when they confuse the fancy and the inner perceptions they are existing in them. Again, although to enter the soul is possible only to God Who created it, yet devils can, with God's permission, enter our bodies; and they can then make impressions on the inner faculties corresponding to the bodily organs . . . the devil can draw out some image retained in a faculty corresponding to one of the senses. . . . And he causes such a sudden change and confusion, that such objects are necessarily thought to be actual things seen with the eyes. This can be clearly exemplified by the natural defect in frantic men and other maniacs." (Sprenger & Kramer, 1968, p. 100)

. . .

"And while she is being questioned about each several point, let her be often and frequently exposed to torture, beginning with the more gentle of them. . . .

"And note that, if she confesses under torture, she should then be taken to another place and questioned anew, so that she does not confess only under the stress of torture.

"The next step of the Judge should be that, if after being fittingly tortured she refuses to confess the truth, he should have other engines of torture brought before her, and tell her she will have to endure these if she does not confess." (Sprenger & Kramer, 1968, pp. 218–219)

for over a century as the official guide to the identification and punishment of witches (Sprenger & Kramer, 1968).

Most alleged witches were women whose unusual behavior spurred suspicion of satanic influence. Today the behavior of these "witches" might be seen as symptomatic of mental disorders. Most likely, these so-called witches were guilty of nothing more than eccentricity that aroused fear in their neighbors. Thousands of people were tortured and executed during the witch hunts. The last witch trials in colonial America were held in Massachusetts in 1692, but in Europe and Latin America they continued well into the 1700s. Great Britain's Witchcraft Acts were not repealed until 1736 (Zilboorg, 1941).

The supernatural view of abnormality is not just a historical curiosity. Despite progress in the scientific understanding of human behavior, many people still believe in the role of spiritual forces in abnormal behavior. In many societies the shaman, priest, or spiritual healer is responsible for treating abnormal behavior through prayer, magic, and ritual. Supernaturalism is a characteristic of most religions and is certainly not restricted to traditional non-Western cultures (J. D. Frank, 1974).

This sixteenth-century drawing of a witch riding off with the devil represented a common belief that witches consorted with the forces of evil.

Modern-day supernaturalism is found throughout the world in many groups who use religious and magical rituals for healing mental and physical ailments.

One example of modern supernaturalism appears in segments of New York's Hispanic community, where *spiritism* flourishes. In the spiritist belief system, physical and mental disabilities are caused by several sources, including *brujería* (sorcery) and *mala influencia* (evil influence). A medium intervenes with the spirit world to remove the supernatural forces that disturb the patient. A *despojo* (exorcism) ritual might be performed as follows:

> The despojo is performed by a medium who fumigates the person being exorcised with cigar smoke and then runs his or her hands along the back of the sufferer's head and neck (the cerebro, considered to be the place where spirits enter) and then down along the person's shoulders and arms. . . . The medium then takes hold of the client's hands, raises them above the client's head, and throws them down abruptly. (Harwood, 1977, p. 96)

Early Naturalism

naturalism The view that disorders have natural physical causes.

Ancient Greek physicians were the first in the Western tradition to propose alternatives to supernaturalism. **Naturalism** is a point of view that explains disorders of body and mind in terms of natural, physical processes. An early advocate of the naturalist view was Hippocrates (460–377 B.C.), often called the "father of medicine," who attributed physical and mental diseases to various biological causes. His **humoral theory** explained disease as an imbalance of four bodily fluids, or *humors*—blood, phlegm, black bile, and yellow bile. In the following passage, Hippocrates describes his view of two mental disturbances, phrenitis (a thought disorder) and melancholy (depression):

humoral (*hue*-mor-ul) **theory** Hippocrates' theory of bodily fluids, or humors, in diseases.

> Patients with phrenitis most resemble melancholics in their derangement, for melancholics too, when their blood is disordered by bile and phlegm, have this disease and are deranged—some even rage. In phrenitis it is the same, only here the raging and derangement are less in the same proportion that this bile is weaker than the other one. (Hippocrates, Trans. Potter, 1988, p. 179)

Today Hippocrates' theory seems primitive. However, he took a step in the direction of modern scientific theory by stating his ideas in terms of natural processes, so that they could be tested and eventually disproved. In fact, the testability of ideas is an important feature of scientific explanations, distinguishing them from other nonscientific and supernaturalistic views.

During the time of the Roman Empire, the physician Galen (circa 138–201 A.D.) established principles that influenced European medicine for centuries. He borrowed some of his ideas from Hippocrates and others, but Galen emphasized the brain as the source of mental action, and he assumed that brain disruptions caused mental illnesses. For example, Galen thought that stomach vapors might invade the brain and cause a state of melancholy or depression.

By the Middle Ages, traditional Greek and Roman naturalism had largely been replaced by the religious beliefs of Christianity. The medical writings of Hippocrates, Galen, and others were preserved mainly through the efforts of Islamic scholars like the Persian physician Avicenna (989–1037), who continued the study and treatment of mental disorders. Some of the first mental asylums were opened in the Islamic world during the thirteenth century (Ellenberger, 1974).

Humanism and the Age of Reason

humanism A philosophy that stresses the value and uniqueness of individuals.

During the sixteenth century, European thinkers became more and more interested in science and philosophy. Artists, scientists, and philosophers began to loosen their ties with Christian dogma and examine the world in nonreligious, or secular, terms. **Humanism** emerged as a movement that stressed the value and uniqueness of individuals and sought to understand behavior in human, rather than supernatural, terms.

Although most people continued to think of abnormal behavior as a sign of spiritual or demonic influence, a few spoke out with more rational and en-

The English philosopher John Locke was a major figure in the development of empiricism.

In the sixteenth century, the German physician Johann Weyer criticized religious interpretations of abnormal behavior, favoring instead a medical perspective.

lightened ideas. In the mid-sixteenth century, a German physician, Johann Weyer (1515–1576), strongly criticized the prevailing spiritual interpretations of abnormality. He favored a biological and psychological view of mental problems, and his attacks on witch-hunting placed him in conflict with religious authorities. Weyer was an important figure in the early development of a medical perspective on abnormal behavior. He advocated an objective, rational attitude, as illustrated by his remarks on witches:

> The witches do not produce the diseases to which they confess to be the cause. And it is to be proven here that all that is told concerning them does not deserve to be considered as anything else than pure fable. Let us therefore speak now of that terrible state called nightmare, and look carefully and fully into what truth there is in it in order that the fantasy of false beliefs be removed forever, not only from the minds of the people, but also from the heads of some learned men. (Zilboorg, 1969, p. 156)

empiricism (em-*peer*-uh-sisum) A philosophy that emphasizes sensory experience and learning.

Science and philosophy flourished in the seventeenth century, the *Age of Reason*. **Empiricism**, an influential philosophy from that era, emphasized the role of sensory experience and learning in the development of an individual's ideas and behavior. John Locke (1632–1704), a leading empiricist philosopher, proposed that the mind at birth is a *tabula rasa* (blank slate) that acquires its ideas by the action of the senses. For Locke, "madness" was a matter of disordered ideas:

> [M]admen . . . do not appear to me to have lost the faculty of reasoning; but having joined together some ideas very wrongly, they mistake them for truths, and they err as men do that argue right from wrong principles. (Locke, 1963, p. 150)

rationalism (*rash*-un-ul-ism) A philosophy stating that innate ideas contribute to knowledge.

In contrast to empiricism, the philosophy of **rationalism** proposed that knowledge is due not just to sensory experience but also to inborn capabilities of thought. This doctrine of *innate ideas* was promoted by the French philosopher and mathematician René Descartes (1596–1650), who stressed the role of intuition in human understanding. Descartes coined the famous rationalist phrase "I think, therefore I am."

Debates between rationalists and empiricists set the stage for one of the

nature-nurture debate
The controversy over
whether behavior is due to
innate causes (nature) or to
experience (nurture).

most durable controversies in psychology, the **nature-nurture debate**. Is behavior due to innate causes ("nature") or experience ("nurture")? Today, questions about the origins of abnormal behavior reflect this philosophical puzzle.
Modern proponents of the "nature" side argue that abnormal behavior is caused
by innate biological or hereditary factors. Advocates of the "nurture" side point
to the role of the learning environment. As you will see in later chapters, there
is some support for both of these views on abnormal behavior.

Reform Movements

Neglect, suffering, and rejection have characterized the plight of the mentally
ill throughout most of history. By today's standards, conditions in early mental
asylums and hospitals were uniformly wretched. Patients were usually confined,
beaten, and physically restrained. The St. Mary of Bethlehem asylum in London
was typical of its time. The term *bedlam* derives from its name, and, as the term
suggests, the asylum's atmosphere was chaotic. For a small admission fee, visitors were allowed to watch the antics of the patients in Bedlam and similar
asylums.

   In the late 1700s the treatment of the mentally ill began to change. At a
Parisian hospital La Bicêtre, the psychiatrist Philippe Pinel (1745–1826) insti-
tuted sweeping reforms. Pinel removed the chains from his patients and offered
them humane treatment. He believed that the insane need decent living conditions in order to recuperate. This idea became known as **moral treatment**
(Pinel, 1806).

moral treatment An
approach that provided
decent, humane conditions
for the mentally ill.

   Gradually, moral treatment spread to other countries. In England, the physician William Tuke established a retreat for the insane that was based on a few
simple principles:

> Neither chains nor corporal punishments are tolerated, on any pretext, in
> this establishment. The patients, therefore, cannot be threatened with these

*The wretched conditions
in insane asylums like
the St. Mary of
Bethlehem Hospital
(Bedlam) in London
prompted the reform
movement of the
eighteenth century.*

severities; yet, in all houses established for the reception of the insane, the general comfort of the patients ought to be considered. (Hunter & Macalpine, 1963)

A staunch supporter of moral treatment in the United States was Dorothea Dix (1802–1887). Dix was a schoolteacher who became a powerful advocate for the mentally ill. She promoted the use of humane practices in mental hospitals and asylums, and her fund-raising and political efforts helped establish more than 30 mental institutions.

The Rise of Scientific Views

By the late 1800s, the study of abnormal behavior was being incorporated into the growing disciplines of psychiatry and psychology. During this period, two competing outlooks emerged. The biogenic and the psychogenic views differed in their attitudes toward the origins and treatment of abnormal behavior.

psychiatry (sye-*kye*-uh-tree) The branch of medicine that specializes in mental disorders.

biogenic (bye-oh-*jen*-ik) *view* The belief that abnormal behavior has biological causes.

The Biogenic View. Psychiatry is a branch of medicine concerned with the diagnosis and treatment of mental disorders. Modern psychiatry grew out of the work of nineteenth-century neurologists, whose discoveries indicated that mental illness might spring from physical diseases. Historically, psychiatry has promoted a **biogenic view**, which attributes abnormal behavior to biological causes.

Great excitement was generated by the discovery that the bacterium that caused syphilis could infect the brain and lead to a pattern of severe mental deterioration called *general paresis*. That a specific disease could explain the complex emotional, behavioral, and personality changes found in general paresis held out the promise of further medical explanations for abnormal behavior.

medical model The view that abnormal behavior reflects a bodily disease or disturbance.

During the 1800s, the study of abnormal behavior was dominated by the **medical model**, which assumes that abnormal behavior reflects an underlying disease or bodily disturbance. The medical model applies the language and perspective of medicine to abnormal behavior. Descriptions of abnormal behavior commonly employ adopted medical terms, such as *symptom* and *diagnosis*. Furthermore, the medical model classifies mental illness much as it does physical illness and proposes medical treatments to correct its assumed causes.

Wilhelm Griesinger (1817–1868), a German psychiatrist, assumed that mental and behavioral abnormalities reflected diseases of the brain, and he was one of the first to seek scientific evidence for his biogenic views. Griesinger was a pioneer in the use of postmortem brain dissections in searching for the neurological causes of psychiatric problems.

One outstanding figure of late-nineteenth-century psychiatry was Emil Kraepelin (1856–1926). Like Griesinger, he supported the use of scientific methods in studying abnormal behavior and promoted the belief that mental illness results from biological disturbances, especially in the brain. Kraepelin was instrumental in the development of modern methods of psychiatric diagnosis and classification (Kraepelin, 1923).

Another influential psychiatrist was the Frenchman Jean-Martin Charcot (1825–1893). Although Charcot believed mental illness was caused by biolog-

PROFILE
Emil Kraepelin (1856–1926)

Emil Kraepelin was a leading advocate of the medical model in late-nineteenth-century psychiatry. He set standards for the diagnosis and classification of mental disorders that are still influential today.

Kraepelin was born in a provincial capital in northern Germany. His father was an actor, and his older brother, Karl, became a well-known botanist. In Kraepelin's youth, the German states were unified into the German Empire. Like many in his generation, Kraepelin developed a strong sense of German nationalism, which he retained throughout his life.

In 1878, Kraepelin took his medical degree at Würzburg and began to specialize in neuroanatomy and neuropathology. For a time he studied physiological psychology with Wilhelm Wundt, who is often called the father of modern psychology, and he even considered a career in that new field. After working at universities in Estonia and Heidelberg, he became a professor of clinical psychiatry at the University of Munich in Germany, where he stayed from 1903 to 1922.

Kraepelin was a major figure in promoting the medical model of mental illness. He based his classification system on meticulous observations of the clinical picture (symptoms) and developmental course of mental disorders. Although Kraepelin believed in the biological causes of mental illness, he did not contribute much to their elucidation. In 1883, at age 27, he wrote his *Textbook of Psychiatry*, which was published in nine editions up to 1927 and served as the standard of reference for a generation of European and American psychiatrists.

In his personal and professional life, Kraepelin could be autocratic and intolerant. He disdained speculation and insisted on facts. However, he was a loving father of three daughters, and he espoused humane attitudes on many social issues. For example, in 1880 he wrote a book advocating the abolition of the death penalty. Kraepelin was an outspoken supporter of the alcohol abstinence movement—an unpopular position for a professor in Munich, a center of the German brewing industry. He died in Munich of heart disease in 1926.

ical factors, he showed that a psychological treatment, hypnosis, could eliminate symptoms of "hysteria," a disorder characterized by physical disabilities, such as arm paralysis, that had no physical cause (see "Close-up: Hypnosis" on page 17). Despite his allegiance to the biogenic view, Charcot was instrumental in the birth of the competing psychogenic view. He contributed through his own work with hypnosis and, indirectly, through the efforts of his most famous student, Sigmund Freud (Szasz, 1974).

psychogenic (sye-koh-*jen*-ik) *view* The belief that abnormal behavior has psychological causes.

The Psychogenic View. Along with the biogenic view evolved another perspective called the **psychogenic view**. This perspective attributes abnormal behavior to disruptions of psychological processes such as emotions, personality, learning, and thinking. In the late nineteenth century, the psychogenic view received support from both psychiatry and the emerging science of psychology.

Charcot's most famous student was a young Austrian physician, Sigmund Freud (1856–1939), who began his psychiatric career after studying hypnosis with Charcot in Paris. In his early years as a psychiatrist, Freud worked with his friend and mentor Josef Breuer (1842–1925). Breuer had found that his hysterical patients benefited when they were able to recall the upsetting events related to the onset of their disorders. One of his patients described the treatment as "chimney sweeping." It seemed to work by allowing the release of powerful emotions that fueled the symptoms.

psychoanalysis Freud's therapy for resolving unconscious conflicts.

Breuer's and Freud's work with hysterical patients was the basis for a *talking cure*, by which patients could unlock the memories and feelings that lay behind their symptoms. Freud later modified the talking cure into **psychoanalysis**, a treatment approach that attempts to uncover and resolve the unconscious conflicts which are assumed to cause abnormal behavior. Psychoanalytic theory and therapy are discussed more thoroughly in Chapter 2 (Fine, 1979).

Sigmund Freud, founder of the psychoanalytic movement, is shown in this 1885 photo with his future wife, Martha Bernays.

The Austrian physician Josef Breuer was a friend and mentor of Freud early in Freud's career. Breuer's approach to treating hysteria became the basis for psychoanalysis.

CLOSE-UP
Hypnosis

Hypnosis has long been one of the most curious treatments in psychiatry and psychology. The modern era in hypnosis began with the Austrian physician Anton Mesmer (1734–1815), who used hypnotic techniques called *mesmerism* to free his patients of their hysterical symptoms. Mesmer believed his cures depended on the transmission of physical energy, or "animal magnetism," to the patient's body. He was eventually discredited as a fraud because of his unorthodox and unscientific methods.

Despite the Mesmer scandal, psychiatrists resurrected hypnosis as a treatment in the 1800s. The term *hypnotism* is derived from the name of Hypnos, the Greek god of sleep, and is credited to an English physician, James Braid (1795–1860). Braid accurately distinguished neurohypnotism ("nervous sleep") from mesmerism, but he wrongly interpreted hypnosis as a kind of sleep state. Braid's technique of instructing the subject to concentrate on an object is still used today as means of creating a hypnotic trance.

In the late 1800s hypnosis was at the center of a controversy between two schools of French psychiatry. Despite his successful use of hypnosis, Charcot asserted that hysteria and other mental disorders had a biological basis. His opponents,

psychiatrists Liebeault and Bernheim, were leaders of the *Nancy school* of psychiatry, named for the French city. They also used hypnosis for treating hysteria, but, unlike Charcot, they assumed the disorder was a form of self-hypnosis.

Freud was trained in hypnosis by Charcot and employed it for a time early in his career. However, Freud was not a very successful hypnotist, and he soon abandoned hypnosis in favor of his own psychoanalytic methods. With the rise in popularity of Freudian psychoanalysis, hypnosis fell from favor in psychiatry and psychology for many years.

By the 1960s, however, hypnosis again appeared as a form of treatment. Experiments showed hypnosis was effective in pain control and memory enhancement. In addition, hypnotherapists like the psychiatrist Milton Erickson explored the many clinical uses of hypnosis in treating diverse emotional and behavioral problems. Although hypnosis is more popular today than ever before, it is not without its critics, who point out that not everyone benefits from hypnosis and believe that for some individuals it might even be hazardous (Dowd & Healy, 1986; E. R. Hilgard, J. R. Hilgard, & Kaufmann, 1983; E. L. Rossi, 1980).

During the second half of the nineteenth century, psychology began to emerge as an independent scientific discipline. In 1879, Wilhelm Wundt founded the first laboratory for psychological studies in Leipzig, Germany, and this event is generally identified as the birth of modern psychology. Although the first psychologists were mainly interested in physiological and sensory processes, others soon began to address psychological issues such as thinking, emotion, personality, and abnormal behavior.

By the late 1890s, clinical psychology was starting to develop as a distinct mental health discipline. **Clinical psychology** is a specialization within psychology that studies the causes and treatments of abnormal behavior. In 1896,

clinical psychology
A specialization in psychology that studies the causes and treatment of abnormal behavior.

psychologist Lightner Witmer established the first psychological clinic at the University of Pennsylvania. Witmer introduced a team approach to patient care, in which treatment required the coordination of psychologists, psychiatrists, and social workers. In the early 1900s the emerging *child guidance movement*, a forerunner of modern guidance counseling, furthered the development of clinical psychology. A milestone in this movement was the establishment in 1909 of a clinic for youths in Chicago in association with the juvenile court.

Another significant force that shaped early clinical psychology was the *mental testing movement*. Advances in mental aptitude testing, and especially the development of standardized intelligence tests, provided psychologists with measurement tools for conducting clinical research and assessment. The first psychological journal devoted to research on abnormal behavior, the *Journal of Abnormal Psychology*, was initially published in 1906 (Kendall & Norton-Ford, 1982).

Integrationism. The merits of the biogenic and psychogenic views of abnormal behavior have been debated since they were introduced over a century ago. In recent years the debate about whether biological *or* psychological factors cause abnormal behavior has diminished somewhat, and a new outlook, integrationism, has begun to appear. **Integrationism** merges biogenic and psychogenic explanations to provide a more comprehensive understanding of the biological *and* psychological roots of abnormal behavior. It assumes that neither biological nor psychological factors alone fully explain the origins of abnormal behavior.

Modern research provides some convincing evidence for both biological and psychological contributions to many mental disorders, and in later chapters we will attempt to present integrated views of specific disorders wherever possible.

integrationism The view that merges biogenic and psychogenic explanations of abnormal behavior.

1-3 ▒ INVESTIGATING ABNORMAL BEHAVIOR

Scientific research has revolutionized our understanding of abnormal behavior and mental disorders during the past century. The following section introduces the major research strategies employed in the field of abnormal psychology today.

▒ Epidemiology

epidemiology (ep-uh-deem-ee-*ol*-uh-jee, ep-uh-dem-ee-*ol*-uh-jee) The study of the distribution of disorders in the general population.

Epidemiology is the study of the distribution of disorders in the general population. Epidemiological studies describe two important statistics, the prevalence rate and the incidence rate. The *prevalence rate* is the percentage of a population or group that has a particular disorder. For example, the prevalence rate of schizophrenia is approximately 1 percent in the population at large. The *incidence rate* is the number of new cases of a disorder in a given time period, usually one year. Suicide, for example, has an annual incidence rate of slightly more than 12 persons per 100,000 in the United States, so there are approximately 25,000 suicides each year in this country.

TABLE 1-1 ▨ **PREVALENCE RATES OF DISORDERS AMONG PERSONS AGED 18 YEARS AND OLDER IN FIVE U.S. CITIES[a]**

	Prevalence Rates (%)				
Disorders	**A**	**B**	**C**	**D**	**E**
Alcohol abuse/dependence	3.0	4.3	2.0	2.4	3.2
Drug abuse/dependence	1.0	1.4	1.5	0.6	1.7
Schizophrenia	0.7	0.8	0.5	1.2	0.3
Manic episode	0.5	0.4	0.6	0.2	0.1
Major depressive episode	2.5	1.8	2.6	1.5	2.4
Anxiety disorders	6.1	12.5	5.1	12.2	5.9
Antisocial personality	0.3	0.5	0.8	0.4	0.4

[a]A = New Haven, B = Baltimore, C = St. Louis, D = Durham, E = Los Angeles.

Source: Adapted from "One-Month Prevalence of Mental Disorders in the United States" by D. A. Regier et al., 1988, *Archives of General Psychiatry, 45*, pp. 977–986.

Prevalence and incidence data help us explain mental disorders. When prevalence or incidence rates for a disorder differ among groups, group-related factors may help to explain the disorder. For example, the higher prevalence of disorders like schizophrenia among poor people suggests that socioeconomic forces may be associated with mental health problems. We must be careful in interpreting epidemiological research, however, because not all cases of mental disorders are reported.

The National Institute of Mental Health (NIMH) Epidemiologic Catchment Area Program collects data on mental disorders at several sites throughout the United States. Table 1-1 shows the prevalence rates for several major disorders as reported in five cities (Regier et al., 1988).

Behavior Genetics

behavior genetics The study of the hereditary basis of behavior.

Behavior genetics is a field that studies the hereditary basis of behavior. Long before the modern science of genetics developed, philosophers speculated about the influence of heredity on abnormal behavior, but no scientific underpinning supported such speculations until genetic transmission was discovered in the nineteenth century. Today, behavior genetics researchers assess the impact of heredity on abnormal behavior with three methods: *family studies, twin studies,* and *adoption studies* (Plomin, DeFries, & McClearn, 1980).

family study A method of assessing the occurrence of disorders in a family.

Family Studies. The **family study** is a method for assessing the prevalence of some abnormal behavior or mental disorder among members of the same family. The researcher begins by selecting a sample of *probands,* subjects who have a specific disorder. Next the investigator searches for the presence of the disorder among the probands' family members. If a mental disorder has hereditary roots, its prevalence rate should be higher among the probands' relatives than in the general population. Furthermore, the prevalence rate of the disorder should increase with the degree of relatedness.

Behavior genetics studies of identical and fraternal twins provide information about the influences of heredity on behavior and personality.

The interpretation of family studies is hampered because we cannot separate hereditary effects from environmental factors such as family stress. An above-average risk of a disorder among relatives hints at genetic causes but does not preclude environmental causes. Despite many practical difficulties in collecting family data, researchers using this method have found evidence of a hereditary basis for some major disorders, including depression and schizophrenia.

twin study A method of examining the occurrence of disorders among twins.

Twin Studies. A **twin study** is a method for examining the occurrence of the same abnormal behavior or mental disorder in twins. Genetically identical (*monozygotic*) twins develop from a single fertilized egg (a zygote). *Dizygotic* (fraternal) twins develop from two separately fertilized eggs, so they share half their genes. Twin studies estimate the percentage of twin pairs in which both twins have the same disorder, a statistic called the **concordance rate**.

concordance rate The percentage of twin pairs in which both twins have the same disorder.

The concordance rate for hereditary disorders is greater in monozygotic twins than in dizygotic twins, since identical twins have the same genetic makeup. Twin studies assume that both dizygotic and monozygotic twins encounter equally similar environments. However, environmental differences cannot be completely discounted, since even the most "identical" twins do not experience exactly the same environment. Environmental differences may arise because of prenatal, familial, and social variables, and a brother and sister who are twins will often be raised quite differently. Despite their limitations, twin studies have revealed the impact of heredity on several disorders, including schizophrenia, depression, and alcoholism.

Adoption Studies. A major flaw of both family and twin studies is their inability to separate the effects of heredity and environment. This problem is overcome in an **adoption study**, a method which studies people who have been raised not by their biological parents but rather by an adoptive family. If a disorder is hereditary, biological children of affected people will have higher-than-average rates of the disorder, despite being raised by unaffected adoptive parents. Adoption studies are especially informative when they examine monozygotic twins raised in different adoptive families.

Adoption studies are difficult to conduct because few adoptees are available as subjects and because of problems in obtaining the confidential adoption records. However, the adoption study method provides the most compelling support for genetic hypotheses of some disorders, such as alcoholism and schizophrenia.

Correlational Research

Correlational research is a method for estimating the strength of association or correlation between variables. Correlation is based on statistical formulas that yield numbers called *correlation coefficients*, which have values ranging from -1 to $+1$. The size of the correlation coefficient indicates the strength of the association, and the sign (positive or negative) indicates its direction.

A *positive correlation* means that two variables tend to change in the same direction. As one variable increases, so will the other. For example, alcohol use and antisocial behavior are positively correlated: high levels of one often accompany high levels of the other. A *negative correlation* exists when variables tend to change in the opposite direction. Depression and social activity are negatively correlated: the more severe the depression, the less social activity is present.

Prospective and retrospective studies are two important kinds of correlational research. In a **prospective study**, researchers monitor the subjects over an extended time period and note correlations between early and later variables. When there is a correlation between early and later variables, the early variables may be viewed as *risk factors* for the later ones. Risk factors increase the likelihood that a later abnormal behavior or mental disorder will occur. For example, antisocial behavior in childhood is a risk factor for social maladjustment in adolescence.

In a **retrospective study**, researchers collect information "after the fact" in order to assess the relevance of earlier developmental variables to some later behavior. For example, school records of adolescent suicide victims might yield evidence of some significant events that preceded the suicides.

Correlational research may inform us about important factors associated with abnormal behavior, but correlations do *not* reveal cause-and-effect infor-

adoption study
A method of studying disorders in adopted children and their biological and adoptive families.

correlational research
A method of estimating the strength of associations between variables.

prospective study
Research that monitors subjects over an extended time period.

retrospective study
Research in which information is collected after the fact.

mation. Although we may know that two variables are correlated, it is not certain which is the "cause" and which is the "effect." For any correlation, there might be one or more unobserved *third variables* affecting the relationship. For example, consider the negative correlation between social activity and depression. High levels of depression are typically correlated with low levels of social activity. However, the causal relationship is ambiguous. Social inactivity may cause depression; depression may inhibit social activity; or another variable, such as anxiety, may produce both depression and social inactivity.

Experimental Research

experimental research
A method of controlled manipulation for assessing cause-and-effect relationships.

In **experimental research**, the investigator manipulates variables in order to assess their cause-and-effect relationships. The experimenter manipulates or changes an *independent variable* and measures its effect on a *dependent variable*. Typically, two groups of subjects are employed in experimental research. The *experimental group* consists of subjects who receive the manipulation. The *control group* is not manipulated but serves as a standard of comparison to judge the effect of the manipulation.

Experimental and control groups should be as similar as possible in order to reduce the influence of other *extraneous variables*. Anything that may affect the dependent variable is considered an extraneous variable. In experiments, potential extraneous variables include many characteristics of the setting and the subjects (for example, age, sex, personality, social class, and intelligence).

To reduce the influence of extraneous variables, subjects may be assigned to the experimental and control groups in random fashion—someone may simply pick numbered slips from a box. *Random assignment* means that a subject has an equal chance of being placed in the experimental or control group. The *matched control* strategy reduces the impact of extraneous variables by matching the experimental and control subjects on all relevant variables, such as sex and age.

Even when such controls are used, problems may arise because the expectations of the experimenter and subjects can influence the outcome of the study. Expectation effects are reduced in a *"double-blind" study*, in which neither subject nor experimenter know whether the subject is in the experimental or control group. Furthermore, in a double-blind study the participants are kept "in the dark" as much as possible about the research objectives.

Suppose that we wish to test the effectiveness of a new drug for depression. To prevent preconceived beliefs about the drug's effectiveness from influencing the results, we make sure that neither the subjects nor the investigators know who has received the drug and who is in the control group. Otherwise, expectations about the drug might influence subjects' behavior and investigators' perceptions.

Practical impediments often limit what can be accomplished in an experiment, and researchers must sometimes create artificial conditions that mimic events in real life. Researchers use artificial experimental conditions in an *analogue study* to focus on specific events in a much more controlled fashion than would otherwise be possible. An experiment on a new therapy for animal phobias might enlist college students who have a fear of snakes to test the therapy in a university laboratory setting. Although analogue studies are generally well controlled, they are often lacking in realism.

Single-Case Research

single-case research
An experiment with one subject.

Single-case research is a type of experiment involving the manipulation of a single subject. Where group studies are impractical, or where they might not clearly reveal individual behavior, single-case studies can be quite informative. In single-case research, the subject serves as his or her own control group.

The *ABAB design* is a single-case strategy used in testing the effect of treatment procedures. An initial "baseline" period of observation, A_1, is followed by a treatment period, B_1; a second observation, A_2; and finally another treatment period, B_2. Figure 1-1 depicts the results of a single-case study that rewarded a student's attention to classroom tasks.

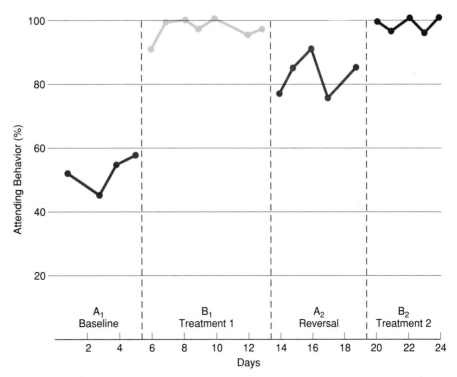

Key: A_1: Baseline condition—no reward for attending
B_1: Treatment condition—reward for attending
A_2: Reversal condition—no reward for attending
B_2: Treatment condition—reward for attending

Figure 1-1 ABAB design: results of reward on attendance behavior in a seventh-grade student.

Source: Adapted from "Modification of Arithmetic Response Rate and Attending Behavior in a Seventh-Grade Student" by F. D. Kirby and F. Shields, 1972, *Journal of Applied Behavior Analysis, 5,* pp. 79–84.

Case Study

case study   In-depth
examination of one
person's life and
development.

An in-depth examination of one person's life and development is known as a
case study. Historically, case studies have contributed significantly to our understanding of abnormal behavior. Early theorists like Freud relied heavily on
the case study method to illustrate their concepts and therapies. A good case
study yields rich, real-life information that reveals the complexities of an individual's personality, experiences, and psychological processes.

Although a case study provides detailed information about an individual, it
lacks control. Case studies are also subject to investigator bias. Investigators
may be so invested in their own perspectives that they overemphasize
"friendly" facts and neglect "unfriendly" ones. Prejudices and "pet" theories
can shape a researcher's observations of the case subject and lead to a biased
report. Even the most fair and balanced case study is difficult to generalize to
other individuals. No matter how much we know about the details of one person's life, their relevance to everyone else is questionable.

Ethics in Research

All research in psychology is guided by ethical principles developed by the
American Psychological Association (APA). The intention of these principles is
to ensure that researchers adhere to a code of ethical behavior that safeguards
the rights of subjects in research studies. Three major ethical principles govern
the activities of psychologists engaged in research: *informed consent, confidentiality*, and *welfare of subjects*.

Informed Consent. The principle of informed consent means that subjects
have the right to know the purpose of the research and that they must voluntarily consent to participate. Subjects cannot be tricked or coerced into participating in a study, and they have the right to withdraw from a study at any time
for any reason.

In order for subjects to give informed consent, they must be mentally competent to understand explanations of the research procedures and must be able
to make a reasonable decision about participating. *Informed consent* means
that subject participation is voluntary, not forced by the investigator or other
agents (such as an employer or family member). Further, informed consent
implies that the subject has been told about any potential risks or advantages
of participation and has weighed them in deciding to participate.

The issue of deception in research touches on the informed consent principle. Investigators sometimes find it necessary to conceal the purposes of their
study from subjects in order to establish proper control in the research, as in a
double-blind experiment. Deception is ethically permissible if the potential
value of the study is sufficient, no alternatives to deception are available, and
the subjects are provided with a correct explanation ("debriefing") afterwards.

Confidentiality. Research subjects have the right to confidentiality. Any information about the subjects must be kept strictly private, and the identities of
research participants are kept anonymous. Data collected in the course of a

study cannot be published in a way that compromises a subject's confidentiality. For example, the results of intelligence tests for specific subjects may not be revealed. Confidentiality can be broken only under special conditions—for example, if failing to release information would result in danger to the subject or to others.

Welfare of Subjects. Subjects participating in psychological research have the right to be protected from any harm or injury. This ethical principle restricts the use of manipulations or conditions that are potentially hazardous to the subjects. The welfare of subjects includes both their physical and psychological well-being. Procedures that may pose a physical or psychological risk to subjects are permissible only if *not* using the procedure might cause even greater harm to the subjects (American Psychological Association, 1990).

SUMMARY

1-1 The definition of abnormal behavior must take four points into account. First, statistical deviation points to the rarity of abnormal behavior. Second, abnormal behavior typically violates one or more social norms or conventions. Third, abnormal behavior is maladaptive. Fourth, personal distress is associated with abnormal behavior. No single definition is sufficient to cover all expressions of abnormal behavior.

1-2 Since ancient times, abnormal behavior has been explained as the product of supernatural forces like spirits and demons. Early Western thinkers like Hippocrates offered naturalistic explanations that emphasized physical causes of abnormality. The Age of Reason in Europe saw the rise of secular philosophies that offered nonreligious explanations for behavior. Humanism emphasized the value of individuals and explained behavior in human terms. According to empiricism, knowledge and behavior are shaped by sensory experiences. The philosophy of nativism proposed the role of innate ideas in human action. Reform movements of the eighteenth century insisted on humane, moral treatment for the insane. In the nineteenth century, the biogenic view attributed abnormal behavior to biological causes and the medical model viewed mental disorders as the result of underlying diseases. The psychogenic view in psychiatry and clinical psychology attributed abnormal behavior to psychological factors.

1-3 Many research methods are employed in abnormal psychology today. Epidemiologists study the distribution of disorders by assessing prevalence and incidence rates. Behavior genetics researchers study the hereditary basis of abnormal behavior using three strategies—family, twin, and adoption studies. Correlational research estimates associations between variables. Experimental research examines cause-and-effect relationships between independent and dependent variables and can involve groups or single-case designs. Case studies explore in depth the life of one individual. All research in abnormal psychology follows the ethical principles of informed consent, confidentiality, and protection of subject welfare.

TERMS TO REMEMBER

abnormal psychology (p. 4)
adoption study (p. 21)
behavior genetics (p. 19)
biogenic view (p. 14)
case study (p. 24)
clinical psychology (p. 17)
concordance rate (p. 20)
correlational research (p. 21)
empiricism (p. 12)
epidemiology (p. 18)
experimental research (p. 22)
family study (p. 19)
humanism (p. 11)
humoral theory (p. 11)
integrationism (p. 18)
maladaptive behavior (p. 7)

medical model (p. 14)
moral treatment (p. 13)
naturalism (p. 11)
nature-nurture debate (p. 13)
personal distress criterion (p. 7)
prospective study (p. 21)
psychiatry (p. 14)
psychoanalysis (p. 16)
psychogenic view (p. 16)
rationalism (p. 12)
retrospective study (p. 21)
single-case research (p. 23)
social norms (p. 5)
statistical deviation (p. 4)
supernaturalism (p. 8)
twin study (p. 20)

SUGGESTED READINGS

Kazdin, A. E. (1980). *Research design in clinical psychology.* New York: Harper & Row.

Plomin, R., DeFries, J. C., & McClearn, G. E. (1980). *Behavioral genetics: A primer.* San Francisco: Freeman.

Zilboorg, G. (1941). *A history of medical psychology.* New York: Norton.

LEGAL AND ETHICAL ISSUES: ETHICS IN ALCOHOLISM RESEARCH

A recent study solicited participation from families in which the father was an active alcoholic who was neither involved in nor seeking any treatment for his alcoholism. Families were paid $400 for taking part in the study, which required their involvement over a two-week period during which home observations and laboratory sessions were scheduled. During one laboratory session, alcoholic beverages were made available for consumption. The purpose of the study was to examine interaction patterns among members of alcoholic families (T. Jacob, Krahn, & Leonard, 1991).

Critics have raised several questions regarding the ethics of this study. Although subjects gave informed consent, the prospect of subtle coercion was raised by the amount of money paid to the families, particularly since nearly one-quarter of the alcoholic fathers who volunteered were unemployed. Four hundred dollars is a lot of money for an unemployed individual and might be enough to mitigate the voluntariness of participation. The principle of informed consent means that subjects must be competent to decide whether to participate in a study about which they have been given a reasonable understanding. Whether active alcoholics are fully competent to evaluate the risks and demands of a study in which they will be given alcohol is open to debate.

The principle of protecting subjects' welfare is also relevant to this study. By furnishing a setting in which alcohol use was fostered, the investigators may have supported an already existing pathological behavior. It is ethically questionable to officially sanction drinking by self-acknowledged alcoholics. Although the investigators did screen subjects for medical problems and retained the subjects in the lab until their blood alcohol levels were safe, the procedure did promote and reinforce alcohol use in problem drinkers.

In designing research with human subjects, investigators are ethically obliged to weigh the potential risks to subjects against the potential gains that might result from the study. This study's potential for yielding useful information about the dynamics of alcoholic families was considered sufficient justification. However, the study revealed no major differences between the alcoholic families' interactions and interactions in other nonalcoholic but distressed families. In hindsight, it may be asked whether the ends really justified the means (Beutler & Kendall, 1991; Koocher, 1991; T. Jacob & Leonard, 1991; Stricker, 1991).

Chapter TWO

Theoretical Perspectives: Focus on the Individual

OBJECTIVES

1. Explain the basic assumptions of the biological perspective on abnormal behavior.
2. Outline the biological causes of mental disorders.
3. Discuss the three types of biological therapy.
4. Explain the basic assumptions of the psychodynamic perspective on abnormal behavior.
5. Distinguish between Freudian and contemporary psychodynamic theories of mental disorders.
6. Identify the main techniques of psychodynamic therapy.
7. Explain the basic assumptions of the humanistic and existential perspectives on abnormal behavior.
8. Discuss the principles of humanistic theory and therapy.
9. Identify the themes of existential psychology as they relate to mental disorders.
10. Distinguish among the biological, psychodynamic, and humanistic/existential perspectives on abnormal behavior.

*S*everal weeks into his first term at college, Roy began to hear voices mocking him and accusing him of "perversion." At first he thought some students in his dormitory were playing a trick on him. He grew increasingly enraged and threatened to hurt his dormmates if they did not stop their harassment. One day he smashed his television and radio because he thought they were transmitting threatening messages. School authorities contacted Roy's mother, who took him home. At home the voices continued, and Roy became convinced that a satanic conspiracy was attempting to turn him into a homosexual. A few days after Roy's return home, his mother had him admitted to a mental hospital, where he was diagnosed as having paranoid schizophrenia.

Roy's condition is a severe mental disorder, and it influenced many aspects of his functioning. We will return to the case of Roy to illustrate the theoretical concepts and treatment strategies of the perspectives discussed in this chapter.

In this chapter we will examine three major views of abnormal behavior—the biological perspective, the psychodynamic perspective, and the humanistic and existential perspectives. These perspectives offer diverse explanations and treatments for abnormal behavior, but they all emphasize processes within the individual as the cause of abnormal behavior.

2-1 ■ THE BIOLOGICAL PERSPECTIVE

biological perspective
The view that abnormal behavior has biological causes.

The **biological perspective** attributes abnormal behavior to biological causes. This perspective is the modern heir to the naturalistic explanations and biogenic view discussed in Chapter 1. Its assumptions and language reflect a close relationship with modern psychiatry and the medical model of mental illness.

Basic Assumptions

The biological perspective attributes mental disorders to internal biological causes, including biochemical, neurological, and genetic mechanisms. The biological perspective emphasizes physical factors but does not necessarily deny the contribution of other, nonbiological variables.

Since the late 1800s, psychiatry has promoted the *medical model* of mental disorders, which conceives of abnormal behavior as an expression of some underlying disease. *Mental illness, symptom*, and *diagnosis* are just a few of the terms adopted from medicine and used in discussions of abnormal behavior. The biological perspective holds that mental problems have physical causes and assumes they are best treated by physical means. **Biological therapy** is a medical treatment approach that attempts to correct the physical disturbances presumed to underlie abnormal behavior. Later in this chapter we will discuss the role of several biological treatments for mental disorders.

biological therapy
Medical treatment intended to correct the physical causes of abnormal behavior.

Biological Causes of Abnormal Behavior

Disruptions in physical functioning, especially in brain activity, can lead to abnormal behavior. Three types of biological causes—*biochemical, neurological*, and *genetic*—are particularly influential.

TABLE 2-1 NEUROTRANSMITTERS AND MENTAL DISORDERS

Neurotransmitter	Related Mental Disorders
Dopamine (DA)	Schizophrenia; drug addiction
Norepinephrine (NE)	Mood disorders; anxiety disorders
Beta-endorphin	Drug addiction
Serotonin (5-HT)	Mood disorders
Gamma-aminobutyric acid (GABA)	Anxiety disorders

neurotransmitters
Chemicals used by neurons
to communicate with one
another.

Biochemical Causes. Our behavior and mental life depend on complex chemical interactions in the brain and body. **Neurotransmitters** are chemicals that neurons (nerve cells) use to communicate with one another. Many neurotransmitters have been identified, but we know of only a few that have proven associations with abnormal behavior (L. W. Hamilton & Timmons, 1990). Table 2-1 summarizes the relationships between some neurotransmitters and mental disorders (Andreasen, 1984; L. W. Hamilton & Timmons, 1990).

Some abnormal behaviors have been linked to disturbances in the *endocrine system,* which produces the body's hormones and regulates their activity. Complex interactions between the nervous system and the endocrine system control our moods, emotions, and bodily drives. For example, certain thyroid gland dysfunctions are associated with depression and other mood disorders (L. W. Reiser & M. F. Reiser, 1985; Sachar, 1976).

Studies on nutrition and diet have shown that nutrient imbalances can affect behavior. For example, the overconsumption of carbohydrates is linked to hypoglycemia (low blood sugar) and mood disturbances. The mechanisms are not clearly defined, but there is evidence that diet influences brain neurotransmitter levels. Despite much suggestive data, the importance of diet in specific mental disorders is still uncertain (Pelletier, 1979; Spring, Chiodo, & D. J. Bowen, 1987).

Neurological Causes. All mental functions are based on the activities of the nervous system. When the nervous system is damaged by disease, head injury, drugs, or infection, normal functioning is disrupted, and the resulting neurological problems can cause many psychological symptoms. Fetal alcohol syndrome, caused when a pregnant woman drinks excessively, illustrates the damaging effects of alcohol on the developing nervous system. Infants born with this condition often develop mental retardation and behavioral disturbances (see Chapter 8).

As you read in Chapter 1, the medical model was furthered by the discovery that the bacterium responsible for syphilis caused mental deterioration in people with general paresis. If syphilis goes untreated, some victims develop *neurosyphilis,* a brain infection leading to severe disruptions of thought, perception, and personality. Brain damage or disease are clearly responsible for some mental symptoms; such a condition is labeled *organic.* These problems are more thoroughly discussed in Chapter 14, "Organic Mental Syndromes and Disorders" (Lechtenberg, 1982).

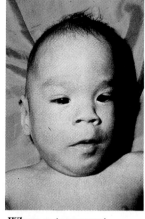

When a pregnant woman drinks alcohol excessively her child is at risk for fetal alcohol syndrome, a condition marked by intellectual impairment and distinct facial features

Genetic Causes. The inherited "programs" for the human body's structure and function are carried in our genes, which are located on 23 pairs of chromosomes. Genetic causes have been clearly identified for only a few mental disorders, but several others show signs of genetic influence. Behavior genetics research, discussed in Chapter 1, has revealed evidence of a hereditary basis for several major disorders, including schizophrenia, depression, bipolar (manic-depressive) disorder, and alcoholism.

Genetic and chromosomal abnormalities may be inherited or may be caused by environmental problems. In either case, such abnormalities often have adverse effects on brain development and consequently on psychological functions. One chromosomal disorder is Down syndrome, a form of mental retardation caused when an extra chromosome 21 is passed on to the zygote, usually because of an error in the formation of the mother's egg.

Genetic factors alone do not fully explain the development of mental disorders. However, a person with a particular genetic abnormality may be more vulnerable to certain disorders. The interactions of genetic vulnerabilities and environmental forces often determine whether and how a mental disorder appears (Rosenthal, 1970).

Biological Therapies

Biological therapies seek to correct the presumed physical disturbances behind abnormal behavior. Three types of biological therapy used today are drug therapy, electroconvulsive therapy, and psychosurgery.

Drug Therapy. The most common biological approach to treating abnormal behavior is drug therapy. For centuries, traditional healers and physicians have used chemicals in treating mental disturbances. The modern era of drug therapy started in the 1950s with the introduction of **psychotropic drugs,** which are used to change thinking, emotions, and behavior for therapeutic purposes. Since the 1950s the treatment of mental disorders has been revolutionized through the introduction of dozens of psychotropic drugs.

psychotropic (sye-koh-*trope*-ik) *drugs*
Therapeutic drugs that change thinking, emotions, and behavior.

Antianxiety drugs, also known as minor tranquilizers, control symptoms of anxiety, panic, stress, fear, and general tension. This group includes diazepam (Valium), chlordiazepoxide (Librium), alprazolam (Xanax), and others that suppress activity in the brain's emotional arousal systems. (Psychotropic drugs are identified by their generic chemical names, and the common trade names follow in parentheses.) These drugs relax and reduce tension in the patient (Gorman & Davis, 1989).

Antidepressant drugs elevate mood and mobilize depressed individuals, enabling them to experience more positive feelings about themselves and their environment. The antidepressants include *monoamine oxidase (MAO) inhibitors,* such as phenelzine (Nardil), and tricyclic and heterocyclic antidepressants, such as imipramine (Tofranil), amitriptyline (Elavil), and norpramin (Desipramine). A new antidepressant, fluoxetine (Prozac), chemically distinct from the others, has recently been hailed as more effective than the older medications in alleviating symptoms of depression for some people. As a group, antidepressant drugs appear to work by changing the activity of neurotransmitters, especially norepinephrine and serotonin, in the brain and body (Davis & Glassman, 1989).

The symptoms of severe psychotic disorders like schizophrenia are controlled by *antipsychotic drugs,* such as chlorpromazine (Thorazine) and haloperidol (Haldol). Antipsychotic drugs tend to reduce activity in the brain's dopamine neurons. Because of these drugs, thousands of people have been returned to an active life outside of mental institutions.

Of course, even the best therapeutic drugs have some side effects, and consequently, they must be used cautiously. Many of the side effects are insignificant, but others are serious and may even be life-threatening. For example, antianxiety drugs like Valium have proved to be especially addictive. The antidepressant Prozac has recently been suspected of causing aggressive and suicidal impulses, although the evidence for this is far from definite. Antipsychotic drugs, as well, have clearly proven debilitating side effects. They can cause serious disruptions of movement and lead to involuntary spasms of facial and body muscles, a condition called *tardive dyskinesia* (Davis, Barter, & Kane, 1989).

Electroconvulsive Therapy. In **electroconvulsive therapy** (ECT), commonly known as shock treatment, a controlled electrical current is delivered to the brain. This produces disorganized electrical activity called seizures. ECT is mainly used in the treatment of severe depression. The precise mechanisms of its therapeutic action are not known. Despite this uncertainty, ECT is widely used, though usually only after antidepressant drugs have proved ineffective.

The main potential hazard of ECT is memory impairment, but this has been reduced in recent years with improved technology. ECT may even be preferable to drug therapy, for some depressed individuals, especially when the patient cannot tolerate the drugs. ECT has the added advantage of providing immediate reduction of depression when a person's suicide potential is high, whereas antidepressant medications can take up to several weeks to work. Despite evidence of its usefulness for many depressed people, ECT remains a controversial treatment that many of its critics consider damaging and primitive (H. H. Goldman, 1988; Scovern & Kilmann, 1980; Weiner, 1989).

electroconvulsive therapy Therapy using electric current to produce brain seizures.

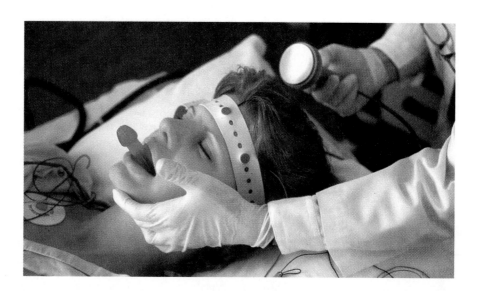

Depressed patients are often treated by ECT, a biological therapy involving the delivery of electrical shock to trigger brain seizures.

psychosurgery Brain surgery for mental disorders.

Psychosurgery. Brain surgery intended to correct the symptoms of mental disorders is called **psychosurgery**. In most cases in which psychosurgery is performed, there is no hard evidence of brain disease. This controversial therapy is reserved as a last resort for severely disturbed patients who do not respond to other, less risky forms of treatment.

In the 1930s, a Portuguese physician, Egas Moniz, introduced the *prefrontal lobotomy,* an operation that involved drilling holes in the skull and cutting the connections between the frontal lobes and other brain structures. Lobotomies were considered successful with some severely psychotic patients, but the procedure was dangerous and was sometimes even fatal.

The heyday of psychosurgery was in the era before psychotropic drugs were introduced, when alternative medical treatments were unavailable. Today, despite popular misconceptions, lobotomies are rarely done and, in fact, very few psychosurgical procedures are performed in the United States each year. The most common reasons for performing psychosurgical operations are to control severe treatment-resistant mood disturbances, obsessive-compulsive disorder, and aggression.

Since psychosurgery is irreversible, it is performed only when psychotherapy and drug therapy have failed. Technical advances in psychosurgery have led to operations that cause less brain damage and fewer side effects. Still, the risks include seizures, intellectual impairments, personality changes, and death (Donnelly, 1985; Valenstein, 1980).

Before his admission to the mental hospital. Roy had begun to threaten his mother, and he would not allow her to bring anyone into the house. He hardly slept and stayed up most of the night talking to and cursing at his hallucinated voices. In the hospital, Roy was given an antipsychotic drug, Haldol, and soon his symptoms diminished. He stopped hearing voices and grew less agitated, but he remained very suspicious and fearful. The diagnosis of paranoid schizophrenia indicated that Roy suffered from a psychotic disorder that severely impaired his reality contact. According to Roy's mother, there was a history of mental illness on his father's side of the family. Roy's paternal grandmother and one of her sisters had both suffered "nervous breakdowns" that required their hospitalization. The combined evidence of a good response to drug therapy and a family history of similar mental illness suggests that potent biochemical and genetic causes lay behind Roy's abnormal behavior.

The Biological Perspective: An Evaluation

The biological perspective has generated an enormous amount of research into the physical causes of mental disorders and has led to the development of some effective therapies. Historically, the medical model is important because it introduced a new way of viewing mental disorders and made abnormal behavior a subject of study in the biological sciences. Besides contributing to our understanding and treatment of mental disorders, this perspective has advanced the development of brain science.

There are also shortcomings to this perspective, however. Biological models do not completely explain psychological disorders. Furthermore, biological treatments are not always effective for mental problems. In "medicalizing" abnormal behavior, we may overlook relevant nonbiological causes and fail to treat them. Some critics of this perspective argue that complex psychological problems can never be reduced to biological causes (Szasz, 1974).

CLOSE-UP
The Antipsychiatrists

Many of the most outspoken critics of the medical model of mental disorders have come from within the ranks of psychiatry. Psychiatrist Thomas Szasz argues that so-called mental illnesses are not diseases or biological malfunctions but "problems in living" that are due to psychological and social causes. In Szasz's opinion, the concept of mental illness offers a false explanation for human problems. Although the concept of mental illness was developed to describe certain symptoms, it has come to be falsely regarded as the *cause* of those symptoms. According to Szasz, this concept is the modern parallel of the old idea of witchcraft:

> We now deny moral, personal, political, and social controversies by pretending that they are psychiatric problems: in short, by playing the medical game. During the witch hunts, people denied these controversies by pretending that they were theological problems: in short, by playing the religious game. (Szasz, 1974, p. 182)

Szasz believes that patients whose abnormal behavior is due to a genuine brain disease should be labeled as neurologically impaired and treated accordingly. However, labeling all abnormal behavior as mental illness extends an inadequate medical metaphor to conditions that are better understood in a social context.

The treatment implications of the medical model have also been attacked by some psychiatrists as unjustified and inappropriate. According to psychiatrist Peter Breggin, the biological treatments that follow from the medical model are most distinctive for their brain-disabling effects. Breggin has generated much controversy by encouraging people to abandon the use of psychotropic medications, which he regards as pharmacological lobotomies. In his view, biological therapies serve primarily to make patients more manageable in the psychiatric "storehouses" called mental hospitals (Breggin, 1980).

Szasz, Breggin, and other like-minded critics of the medical model are often called antipsychiatrists because of their antagonism toward mainstream biological psychiatry. However, they do not actually oppose psychiatry as a whole. They are advocates of an alternative view of psychiatry that does not reduce all abnormal behavior and mental suffering to medical terms.

2.2 ■ THE PSYCHODYNAMIC PERSPECTIVE

psychodynamic perspective The view that attributes abnormal behavior to internal psychic conflicts.

The **psychodynamic perspective**, which originated with the work of Sigmund Freud, attributes abnormal behavior to internal psychic conflicts among the forces of mental life, including drives, emotions, and personality. Since Freud's time the psychodynamic perspective has changed dramatically, and today it encompasses several divergent points of view. Modern psychodynamic theories often differ on specific issues, but they all share a few basic assumptions about abnormal behavior and its treatment.

Basic Assumptions

unconscious determinism An assumption that behavior is due to unconscious forces.

In the psychodynamic view, the forces responsible for behavior are thought to occur mostly at an unconscious level. This assumption, called **unconscious determinism**, implies that individuals have limited conscious awareness of and control over their behavior and mental activity.

The psychodynamic view further assumes that events in the early years of life are critically important to personality development and mental health. Problems in these early stages are thought to disrupt personality, social interactions, and emotional growth and to set the stage for later abnormal behavior. Although events in adulthood may trigger abnormal behavior, its roots lie in childhood.

Since mental disorders are thought to be caused by unconscious mental activity, psychodynamic therapies seek to uncover unconscious conflicts in order to restore the patient's health. Psychodynamic therapy is often called *insight therapy* because its goal is to enhance the individual's self-understanding.

Freud's Psychoanalytic Theory

In his long and remarkable career, Freud established the foundations of the psychodynamic perspective. His psychoanalytic theory was not just a view of mental disorders but a comprehensive explanation of the human condition. The core of psychoanalytic psychology is found in Freud's theory of personality.

Personality Processes. Freud identified three parts of personality, the id, ego, and superego, and he assumed that the mechanisms associated with these personality structures are the basis of all behavior, normal as well as abnormal.

id The primitive, unconscious, instinct-dominated part of personality.

The **id** is the primitive, unconscious part of personality dominated by two innate forces, the life and death instincts, which are primarily expressed as sexual and aggressive drives. The *pleasure principle* is the governing principle of the id. It motivates the id to seek relief from the unpleasant tension of the drives. *Primary process thinking* is the irrational, emotion-dominated activity of the id, expressed in dreams, fantasies, and impulses. The symptoms of mental disorders also reflect primary process thinking and serve unconscious id needs. Like dreams, symptoms are expressions of unconscious emotional impulses that satisfy the pleasure principle.

ego The personality structure associated with identity and adaptation to reality.

defense mechanisms Ego strategies for coping with conflicts and distress.

The personality structure called the **ego** is closely associated with personal identity. The ego also mediates between the individual and the external world, guiding the person's adaptation to reality. The *reality principle* governs the ego's activity and requires the ego to control id drives in the interest of adaptation. The ego also controls the **defense mechanisms**, strategies employed to cope with psychic conflicts and associated emotional distress. Table 2-2 describes some important defense mechanisms.

Ego activities, called *secondary process thinking*, include reasoning, judgment, and problem solving. These secondary process activities are used in the service of the reality principle to help the person function in everyday living. Mental disorders indicate the ego is not successfully coping with the demands of reality.

superego The moral part of personality, controlling conscience and ego ideal.

The **superego** is the moral part of personality that evaluates "good" and "bad." It begins with internalized parental values and expands to include the morals of other people and society. Two prominent aspects of the superego are the *conscience* and the *ego ideal*. The *conscience* is the punishing aspect that inhibits behavior through guilt and shame. The *ego ideal* is an idealized image that is the ego's standard of evaluation. We feel pride and self-esteem when we act according to our ego ideal (Freud, 1933, 1949, 1961).

TABLE 2-2 MAJOR EGO DEFENSE MECHANISMS

Defense Mechanisms	Clinical Examples
Denial inhibits one from facing facts or realities.	An alcoholic won't admit she has a serious drinking problem.
Displacement channels feelings to substitutes.	A frustrated father takes out his anger on his children.
Projection attributes repressed feelings to others.	A failing student blames her parents for her poor grades.
Rationalization gives false excuses for behavior.	A shy man claims that no woman is good enough for him.
Reaction formation turns feelings into their opposites.	A bully's aggression covers up his inferiority feelings.
Regression uses immature ways of expressing feelings.	A student reacts to failure by having temper tantrums.
Repression keeps ideas and feelings unconscious.	A sexually abused child has no memory of the abuse.
Sublimation expresses feelings in a socially acceptable manner.	A young man directs his anger into playing competitive contact sports.
Undoing symbolically "erases" feelings.	A teenager fearful of her sexual urges "purifies" herself by excessive washing.

Conflict and Anxiety. The conflicts at the root of mental disorders are inseparable from personality functioning. Freud described three types of conflicts and their associated anxieties. Conflicts between the rational ego and irrational id produce *neurotic anxiety*. When powerful id impulses threaten the ego, neurotic anxiety appears and the ego defense mechanisms are employed to contain it. For example, a woman who resents her controlling husband may feel threatened by her own anger and defend against the threat by repressing that anger. Through reaction formation, she becomes even more submissive to him.

Conflicts between the ego and the external world produce *reality anxiety*. The environment places demands on all of us, and sometimes these demands threaten our ego stability. Coping with work, school, family obligations, and money problems often generates reality anxiety. For example, an unemployed man who is struggling to find work and support his family may displace his frustrations into abusive behavior toward his wife and children.

When the individual's activity violates the superego's values, *moral anxiety* results. Moral anxiety reflects conflicts between the person's sense of right and wrong and the demands of id and ego. For example, a single mother who feels guilty about leaving her children in day care may use the defense of projection, unjustly accusing her sister of neglecting her own family.

Emotional conflicts in mental disorders usually involve many sources of anxiety. At the center of these conflicts is the ego, whose task it is to find a compromise solution. The ego employs defense mechanisms to resolve the con-

PROFILE
Sigmund Freud
(1856–1939)

Sigmund Freud was the founder of psychoanalytic theory and therapy. His views had far-reaching effects on modern psychology and psychiatry and the social sciences.

Freud was born in 1856 in Moravia, now a part of Czechoslovakia. He was the oldest of eight children of Jacob and Amalie Freud. His father was a merchant. In 1859 the family moved to Vienna, where Sigmund remained for most of his life. An ambitious and talented student, Freud excelled in science and philosophy. In the 1870s, he did some pioneering studies in invertebrate neurology, and he was one of the first scientists to investigate the effects of cocaine. Freud took his medical degree from the University of Vienna in 1881 and began to practice medicine. He married in 1886, and he and his wife Martha had six children. Their youngest child, Anna Freud, was later to become a famous child psychoanalyst.

Freud studied psychiatry with Jean-Martin Charcot in Paris in 1885, and that experience was a turning point in his career. Returning to Vienna, he collaborated with Josef Breuer in treating hysterical patients, but he soon began to formulate his own method of psychoanalysis. In those early years he was largely isolated from mainstream psychiatry and was often ridiculed for his novel ideas. He gradually attracted a circle of students, who formed the Vienna Psycho-Analytical Society, and before long psychoanalysis grew into an international movement.

Freud, genius and explorer of neurosis, was also a man with many neurotic tendencies of his own. In the course of his self-analysis, begun in the late 1890s, Freud conceived many ideas that he incorporated into his theory of neurosis: for example, his extreme devotion to his mother prompted the "discovery" of the Oedipus complex. He was often arrogant, demanding, and defensive, and he struggled for many years with depression and self-doubt. For a time during the 1890s, he even used cocaine regularly and found it to relieve his depression.

After living in Vienna for nearly 80 years, Freud fled to England in 1938 to escape the Nazis. Many in his family, including four of his sisters, were not so fortunate, and they perished in concentration camps.

The vice that proved fatal to Freud was his addiction to cigars. In 1939, after years of pain and numerous operations, he died of cancer of the jaw (Clark, 1980; Roazen, 1976).

flicts, but if the defense mechanisms are inadequate or excessive, then symptoms of mental disorders may appear. It is important to realize that conflict and anxiety do not necessarily indicate abnormality. In the Freudian view, conflict and anxiety are normal aspects of human life, and the difference between normal and abnormal behavior depends on how well the individual copes with conflict and anxiety (Freud, 1936).

libido The energy of the sexual instinct.

psychosexual development A theory of the stages of libidinal activity: oral, anal, phallic, latency, and genital.

Psychosexual Development. Freud thought personality development was determined by the expression of **libido**, the energy of the sexual instinct. Freud's theory of **psychosexual development** proposed that libido is focused on specific bodily functions at five different stages defined by distinctive patterns of pleasure-seeking activity: *oral, anal, phallic, latency,* and *genital stages.*

Events can interfere with psychosexual development and cause traumas, fixations, and complexes that predispose the individual to long-term maladjustment. A *trauma* is an intensely adverse experience that can disrupt normal development. The trauma of sexual abuse in childhood, for example, can produce persistent emotional distress that interferes with the victim's self-image and social development. Failure to satisfy developmental demands can produce *fixations,* or unresolved emotional problems that cause the fixated person to remain developmentally "stuck." Childhood experiences may also create *complexes,* powerful unconscious feelings organized around a specific theme or issue such as dependency or inferiority.

Roy's parents divorced when he was 3 years old, and he was raised by his mother. He had very little contact with his father, who lived nearby but showed almost no interest in the child. Roy often saw his father in the neighborhood and hoped for his attention, but he was repeatedly disappointed. Roy developed a complex based on his experience of rejection. He became quite insecure and usually anticipated that people would dislike or ignore him. Roy grew extremely dependent on his mother, to the extent that even in adolescence he found it hard to perform simple tasks for himself, such as buying a shirt.

In the *oral stage* of psychosexual development, the infant's pleasure seeking focuses on oral activity, such as sucking, feeding, and biting, and conflict arises in weaning the infant from the breast or bottle. Problems encountered in this stage can cause fixations that express themselves in habitual oral activity. For example, alcoholics, nail biters, smokers, and overeaters are said to have oral fixations.

During the oral stage of psychosexual development, infants seek pleasure through oral activities and stimulation.

During the *anal stage*, the focus of libidinal activity is transferred to the infant's elimination of feces. In toilet training, the infant is challenged by the social world to control a natural, reflexive bodily function. The child who experiences considerable anxiety during this time may react with aggressive defiance or by developing excessive self-control.

In the *phallic stage*, masturbatory behavior is the dominant expression of libido. The child's erotic self-stimulation is the first obviously sexual form of libidinal activity. According to Freud, the most influential events of this stage involve the *Oedipus complex*, in which a young boy feels sexual attraction to his mother and perceives his father as a hostile rival for her affection, and the *Electra complex*, its parallel in girls. In the Oedipus complex the boy's fear of the father's punishment takes the form of *castration anxiety*, a fear that he will lose his penis. Although castration anxiety is absent in girls, Freud believed the Electra complex was associated with *penis envy*, a girl's desire to have the male genitals.

In both boys and girls, these phallic-stage events are critical for personality development. The Oedipus and Electra complexes are resolved when the child represses his or her libidinal urges for the opposite-sex parent and identifies with the same-sex parent. The identifications during this stage have a powerful effect on the child's ego identity and superego. Disturbances in the resolution of Oedipus and Electra complexes can lead to many later problems—in particular, sexual disorders (Freud, 1953).

In his "Little Hans" case (1909), Freud outlined the role of the Oedipus complex in the phobia of a 5-year-old boy. Hans feared going out of his home because he thought a horse might bite him. In Freud's view, Hans's fear of being bitten by a horse was a symbolic expression of the castration anxiety he experienced as part of his Oedipus complex. Hans's fear of the horse was a displacement of his fear of his father, and feeling threatened by horses was a projection of his fantasy of being castrated by his father. (Freud, 1959)

After resolving the Oedipus or Electra complex, the child enters the *latency stage*, during which libidinal activity is repressed. As the name suggests, sexual interests are latent or hidden in this stage, and the child's attention is directed toward developing social relationships. The onset of puberty signals the beginning of the *genital stage*, when sexual interests reemerge to be directed toward more mature sexual activity.

Contemporary Psychodynamic Theories

The psychodynamic perspective has changed greatly since Freud's time. Today we find several influential theories derived from Freud's original concepts, among them analytical psychology, interpersonal theory, ego psychology, and object relations theory.

Analytical Psychology. An influential post-Freudian theory to emerge from psychoanalysis was the **analytical psychology** of Carl Gustav Jung (1875–1961). Jung was a Swiss psychiatrist who had studied schizophrenia under the tutelage of the eminent psychiatrist Eugen Bleuler and later found himself attracted to Freud's theory. For several years, Jung was Freud's most outstanding student and an important figure in the psychoanalytic movement.

analytical psychology
Carl Jung's psychodynamic theory of personality.

Carl Jung was an early colleague of Freud who eventually broke from the psychoanalytic movement and developed analytical psychology.

Jung's analytical psychology diverged from Freudian psychoanalytic theory, first, on the issue of libido. Jung did not accept the dominance of sexual motives in behavior and conceived of libido as a general psychic energy. Second, Jung divided the unconscious into personal (repressed) contents and the *collective unconscious*, a repository of inherited psychic structures shared by all people. These collective structures, or *archetypes*, are expressed in common myths and symbols of different cultures. For example, the *anima/animus* archetype represents what Jung assumed to be the inherent bisexuality of human nature; *anima* refers to the innate feminine quality and *animus* to the masculine quality.

According to Jung, mental disorders represent both a state of imbalance among aspects of personality and a potential way of correcting the imbalance. In contrast to Freud, Jung saw the unconscious as a source of healing and creativity, not simply as a collection of drives and repressed wishes. By emphasizing the spiritual, constructive, and goal-directed aspects of human nature, analytical psychology anticipated some of the ideas of the humanistic perspective discussed later in this chapter (Jung, 1982).

Interpersonal Theory. Attempts to include social factors in psychodynamic explanations of behavior led to the development of **interpersonal theory**, which views personality, development, and mental disorders in the context of social relationships.

interpersonal theory
A psychodynamic view that explains personality and behavior in a social context.

One of Freud's first disciples was Alfred Adler (1870–1937). For several years Adler was a member of Freud's inner circle, but in 1911 he split with Freud and formed an association for *individual psychology*. Adler viewed people as primarily social beings, and he emphasized the importance of social, as well as unconscious, motives for behavior. In his view, abnormal behavior reflected problems that originate in social or family activity. For example, children who are neglected may acquire negative attitudes and feelings about themselves (an *inferiority complex*) which result in persistent emotional distress (A. Adler, 1927).

Karen Horney was an advocate of interpersonal psychodynamic theory and an important figure in the development of the psychology of women.

Harry Stack Sullivan (1892–1949), an American psychiatrist, interpreted abnormal behavior in terms of interactions with "significant others," especially family members. He proposed that the personality, or *self-system*, develops from images the individual obtains from other people and internalizes. These images, called *personifications*, represent the positive ("good me"), negative ("bad me"), and repressed ("not me") aspects of personality. In working with schizophrenics, Sullivan came to believe that disturbed parent-child interactions cause severe problems in the individual's ability to form meaningful relationships (Sullivan, 1953).

Karen Horney (1885–1952) also believed mental disorders were a consequence of interpersonal disturbances. In her theory, neurosis begins with *basic anxiety*, a general feeling of insecurity resulting from an inadequate mother-child relationship. Defenses against basic anxiety involve three *neurotic strategies* that are expressed in social behavior:

- Moving toward others, as in extreme dependency
- Moving against others, as in aggression
- Moving away from others, as in social avoidance

Horney was also a pioneer in the psychology of women and a critic of the male bias in Freudian theory. For example, she viewed Freud's concept of *penis envy* as a distorted and chauvinistic notion. In Horney's view, women are more envious of a man's social power than of his genitals (Horney, 1937).

ego psychology
Psychodynamic theory that regards the ego as the central force in personality.

Ego Psychology. **Ego psychology** is a psychodynamic theory that views the ego as the central, integrating force in personality, which mediates conflicts within the individual and between the individual and the world. In Freudian theory, the ego was considered a "servant" to the id. In contrast, ego psychology attributes to the ego some functions that are independent of id activity, such as memory and problem solving. According to ego psychology, mental disorders are mainly caused by disruptions in ego functioning and development (Hartmann, 1958).

Erik Erikson (1902–1982) proposed the best-known theory of ego psychology, in which he described an eight-stage model of *psychosocial development* covering the life span from birth to death. At each stage, mastery of the developmental challenges provides the ego with important adaptive skills that establish a basis for further development. Erikson's ego psychology also reflects the themes of interpersonal theory insofar as it explains the development of *ego identity* within the framework of social behavior (Erikson, 1959).

Object Relations Theory. Like ego psychology and interpersonal theory, **object relations theory** assumes that personality is defined by early relations with other people, parents in particular. The "objects" in object relations theory are internalized images of others which establish a foundation for individual personality.

object relations theory
A psychodynamic view that emphasizes early social relations in personality development.

Margaret Mahler (1897–1985) assigned great importance to the early years of life, in which children experience a "psychological birth" as they grow more independent of the mother. Impairment of this *separation-individuation* process, she wrote, predisposes a child to later emotional and social maladjustments (Mahler, 1975).

Along with Roy's great dependency on his mother came a strong resentment of her power over him. During his childhood, Roy was terrified that his mother might abandon him as his father had. Despite his wish to be more self-reliant, he could not separate from her because he worried he could not survive without her. When his mother insisted that he attend an out-of-state college in order to mature, he felt that she was discarding him and he became very anxious.

Problems in the formation of early object relations result in inadequate personality organization, and the earlier in life such difficulties arise, the more severe the symptoms will be. Disturbances in internalizing object relations cause contradictory self-images, or *ego states*, to appear. The individual's defensive attempts to overcome conflicting ego states often lead to inconsistent and unpredictable behavior. For example, people with certain severe personality disorders often have extremely unstable self-images and unstable relationships because of inconsistent ego states (Kernberg, 1976).

Psychodynamic Therapies

psychotherapy
Treatment with psychological methods.

Freudian psychoanalysis was the first modern form of **psychotherapy**—an approach to treatment that uses psychological methods, particularly patient-therapist dialogue, to overcome mental disturbances. Traditional psychoanalysis and other psychodynamic therapies assume that symptoms will be relieved when the patient gains adequate insight. Despite disagreements over specific techniques, psychodynamic therapists tend to share a common approach to treatment. The approach is called the **analytic attitude**. Its features are neutrality and openness, a desire to help, the use of interpretations, and providing a safe atmosphere for the patient (Schafer, 1983).

analytic attitude An approach emphasizing neutrality, openness, desire to help, and offering interpretations.

Psychoanalytic Techniques. In order to help patients uncover and work through unconscious conflicts, psychoanalysts employ several therapeutic techniques. The "golden rule" of psychoanalysis since Freud's time has been **free association**, which means that the patient reports any thoughts, feelings, im-

free association The rule by which patients report anything that comes to mind.

pulses, or memories that come to mind. Free association is intended to reveal important unconscious material. The psychoanalyst's role is to interpret the possible meanings expressed in the patient's stream of thought.

Freud considered dreams to be "the royal road to the unconscious," and he assumed that they reveal repressed wishes. *Dream interpretation* is a technique for uncovering unconscious feelings and desires in order to shed light on the patient's problem. For example, a severely depressed patient who dreams of visiting his or her recently deceased mother may be unconsciously expressing repressed suicidal feelings.

A central issue in psychoanalysis is the patient's **resistance**, a struggle against self-awareness and improvement. Because the unconscious roots of disorders are often painful to acknowledge and symptoms can provide relief from unconscious conflicts, the patient may not truly want to change. Resistance is shown in many ways, including ambivalence toward treatment, rejection of interpretations, missed appointments, reluctance to talk, and self-defeating habits. The therapist points out and interprets signs of resistance so that the patient can move beyond it toward self-understanding.

resistance
A psychoanalytic patient's struggle against self-awareness and improvement.

During her therapy sessions, Rose would talk about anything except her father. As a child, she was sexually molested by him on several occasions, and she had been terrified of him ever since. She freely expressed animosity toward her mother for not protecting her but admitted none for the man who had victimized her. Rose refused to discuss her father's actions and always changed the subject when asked about him.

transference (*trans*-fur-ents) The patient's projection of feelings onto the analyst.

Transference occurs when the patient redirects feelings held for parents, family members, or authority figures toward the therapist. Interpreting transference helps to clarify the role of the patient's relationships and associated feelings in the current problem. For example, a dependent, insecure man may be very passive in therapy, expecting the therapist to take control of his life for him. The dependency of such a patient may reveal a pattern of relating to authority figures, including his parents. **Countertransference** refers to the feelings and attitudes of the analyst for the patient. Transference and countertransference can have both beneficial and disruptive effects in psychoanalysis (Freud, 1963).

countertransference
Feelings and attitudes of the analyst toward the patient.

Ego Analysis. As we have seen, ego psychology assigns to the ego the central role in resolving psychic conflicts. **Ego analysis** is the use of strategies such as *ego support* and *ego building* to assist patients in effectively utilizing their ego resources. The therapist identifies successful areas of functioning and then helps the patient apply those skills to problem areas. This approach to therapy attempts to enhance the patient's adaptation, self-integration, and ego development (G. Blanck & R. Blanck, 1974).

ego analysis Strategies of ego support and ego building.

Short-term Dynamic Psychotherapy. **Short-term dynamic psychotherapy** (STDP) is a time-limited treatment designed to help patients recognize conflicts more quickly than in traditional psychoanalysis. STDP is more confrontational in style than other psychodynamic techniques. The STDP practitioner provokes intense emotional reactions by directly confronting patients' defenses, in the hope that this will help patients recognize their underlying

short-term dynamic psychotherapy Time-limited psychodynamic treatment.

conflicts and defenses. Supporters of STDP acknowledge that it is not suitable for everyone, but it is useful with patients who are not severely impaired (Davanloo, 1980).

The Psychodynamic Perspective: An Evaluation

Psychodynamic theory and therapy have often been criticized as imprecise and unscientific. Critics charge that little scientific evidence supports the psychodynamic approach and that its concepts are often impossible to test experimentally. Ideas like "libido" and "Oedipus complex" are difficult to translate into objective measurements. Most of the evidence for psychodynamic theory and therapy relies on the case studies and clinical inferences of psychodynamic therapists. However, some controlled research supports psychodynamic concepts of development, personality, and emotion (Kline, 1981; Masling, 1983).

Since its inception, the psychodynamic perspective has played a major role in the evolution of modern psychology. From this viewpoint have emerged complex and comprehensive explanations not only of abnormal behavior but also of personality and human development. Beyond its impact on psychiatry and abnormal psychology, the psychodynamic perspective has shaped other social sciences, such as anthropology and sociology.

2-3 THE HUMANISTIC AND EXISTENTIAL PERSPECTIVES

humanistic and existential perspectives
Viewpoints that value understanding of an individual's subjective experiences.

Most modern perspectives on abnormal behavior are modeled after the natural sciences, such as physics, in that they attempt to predict and control events. In contrast, the **humanistic and existential perspectives** value understanding the subjective experiences of individuals more than predicting or controlling people's behavior (Giorgi, 1970). Although the humanistic and existential perspectives differ in some ways, they are similar enough to discuss together. The four assumptions that define the main themes of these perspectives are freedom, personal responsibility, personal growth, and phenomenology.

Basic Assumptions

Freedom is a primary experience of human beings. We perceive ourselves as having voluntary control over our behavior. Traditional scientific theories deemphasize individual freedom, but the humanistic and existential perspectives place it at the core of human functioning. The concept of freedom implies that behavior is partly the result of the individual's choices. This notion of freedom does not mean that we consciously choose to exhibit abnormal behavior or mental disorders. It means that our decisions may lead us, ultimately, to psychological disturbances.

Since our actions originate in our choices, we bear *personal responsibility* for our actions and their consequences. However, the humanistic and existential perspectives do not propose that the individual enjoys complete freedom of choice and bears all responsibility for outcomes. Many circumstances beyond the individual's control need to be considered, especially in the development of abnormal behavior. Biology, family, and culture set limits on our freedom and personal responsibility.

self-actualization Prime motive or drive to fulfill individual potential.

phenomenology (fen-om-uh-*nol*-uh-jee) The study of individual subjective consciousness or experience.

Personal growth and development are central concerns of the humanistic and existential perspectives. The meaning of an individual's behavior is found in the goals toward which he or she strives. The prime motive in human growth and development is **self-actualization**, the inherent drive to fulfill our individual potential. When personal growth is disturbed, such as by the failure of a relationship, emotional and behavior problems may follow. The symptoms of mental disorders may reflect disruptions in, or inadequate attempts at, personal growth.

The humanistic and existential perspectives rely on **phenomenology**, which is the study of individual subjective consciousness or experience. Phenomenology is concerned with the subject's conscious thoughts, feelings, attitudes, and perceptions. This approach aims to understand individuals from an "inside" point of view undistorted by preconceived attitudes or theoretical suppositions.

Humanistic Theory and Therapy

The philosophy of *humanism* extends back several hundred years in Western philosophy. It assigns great importance to the uniqueness and individuality of each person. Modern humanistic psychology reflects these concerns, as shown in Maslow's need theory and Rogers's self theory. In therapies derived from humanistic theories, the main goal is to assist the individual in his or her efforts toward self-actualization.

need hierarchy An organized sequence of needs from lower to higher levels.

Maslow's Need Theory. Abraham Maslow (1908–1970) was a major figure in the birth of humanistic psychology in the 1950s. Maslow's view of behavior hinges on the concept of human needs. The **need hierarchy** is an organized sequence of needs in which satisfaction of the "lower" needs precedes satisfaction of the "higher" needs.

Abraham Maslow promoted a humanistic view of behavior and motivation in his need theory.

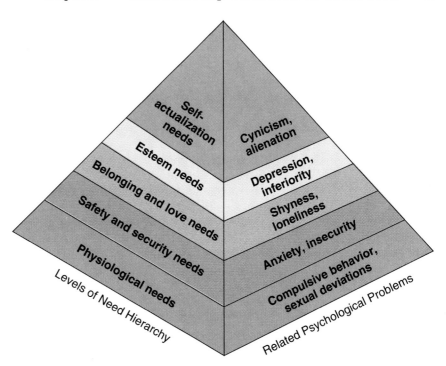

Figure 2-1 Maslow's need hierarchy and related problems.

For Maslow, personal development proceeds by the progressive fulfillment of higher-level needs. First are the *physiological needs* or bodily drives, such as hunger, thirst, and sex. Next, *safety and security needs* demand our protection from harm or danger. Next are *belonging and love needs* involving family, friends, and romantic relationships. The *esteem needs* indicate a desire for feelings of worth or self-esteem. The *self-actualization* or *growth needs* represent the highest level of development. Here we find the most complex and meaningful concerns, including spiritual, aesthetic, and intellectual needs that Maslow called the "farther reaches of human nature."

According to Maslow, self-actualization is reflected in the way individuals act to fulfill their needs. Frustration of this process inhibits personal development and can produce psychological problems. Abnormal behavior indicates a disturbance in need satisfaction. Figure 2-1 shows associations between need hierarchy levels and psychological problems (Maslow, 1970, 1971).

Rogers's Self Theory. One of the most influential modern psychologists was Carl Rogers (1902–1987). His **self theory** proposed that psychological well-being depends on a healthy self-concept. For Rogers, the **self-concept** is a sense of identity composed of the individual's self-perceptions and the values attached to those perceptions. A healthy or *fully functioning person* has a self-concept characterized by openness, flexibility, and trust. According to Rogers's theory, self-actualization is an inherent tendency of human nature that guides development in a positive direction.

Self theory attributes psychological disorders to impairments in self-concept and self-actualization. Inconsistencies between self-concept and personal experiences produce an unpleasant state called *incongruence*. For example, an

self theory Rogers's view that healthy self-concept is the basis of psychological well-being.

self-concept The sense of identity based on one's self-perceptions and values.

inhibited woman who sees herself as nonsexual, but nevertheless feels a strong attraction to a man, might be in a state of incongruence. Her experience (sexual feelings) does not fit her self-concept (nonsexual), and this mismatch may cause emotional distress.

Healthy development requires that a child receive *unconditional positive regard*—love and affection with "no strings attached." Sometimes parents assign conditions to their giving of affection. Such *conditions of worth* communicate that the parents' love is based on the child's meeting certain standards. For example, if parents convey to their daughter that their love depends on her obedience to them, she may feel she is "good" only while doing what she is told. Children who experience excessive conditions of worth have difficulty developing healthy self-concepts (C. R. Rogers, 1961; C. R. Rogers & Sanford, 1985).

As a child, Roy was well cared for by his mother, who worked to provide him with material comforts. He felt that she loved him, but he thought she was overly concerned with making rules and regulations for him. Although he was never physically punished for misbehavior, he knew when his mother disapproved of him by the way she withdrew from him emotionally. Roy's self-concept was shaped by the experience of such conditions of worth.

client-centered therapy
Rogers's nondirective therapy based on unconditional positive regard, empathy, and honesty.

Client-Centered Therapy. Rogers's **client-centered therapy** (CCT), often called *nondirective therapy*, is characterized by the therapist's attitudes of unconditional positive regard, empathy, and honesty. A CCT therapist does not instruct the client to act or think in a particular way. Instead, the therapist helps clients explore their own values and feelings and make their own decisions about how to act.

Carl Rogers made important contributions to the humanistic perspective with his self theory and client-centered therapy.

For Rogers, the client's subjective personal experience, called the *phenomenal field*, is the focus of therapy. Like psychodynamic therapy, CCT promotes insight or self-understanding. However, unlike psychoanalysis, the CCT approach attends more to the "here and now" concerns of the client rather than to childhood experiences. One technique used to enhance the patient's self-awareness is *reflection*, in which the therapist mirrors, restates, and paraphrases the client's thoughts and feelings (C. R. Rogers & Sanford, 1985).

The following dialogue between Rogers and a depressed client illustrates the method of reflection:

Client: Well now, I wonder if I've been going around doing that, getting smatterings of things, and not getting hold, not really getting down to things.

Rogers: Maybe you've been getting just spoonfuls here and there rather than really digging in somewhere rather deeply.

Client: M-hm. That's what I say—(slowly and very thoughtfully) well, with that sort of a foundation, well it's really apparent to me. I mean, it seems to be really apparent to me that I can't depend on someone else to give me an education. (Very softly) I'll really have to get it myself.

Rogers: It really begins to come home—there's only one person that can educate you—a realization that perhaps nobody else can give you an education. (C. R. Rogers, 1961, p. 120)

Gestalt (geh-*shtalt*) *therapy* An individual and group humanistic therapy that emphasizes "here and now" awareness.

Gestalt Therapy. Gestalt therapy, which was developed by Frederick Perls (1893 – 1970), is an individual and group therapy that emphasizes awareness of

Frederick (Fritz) Perls is best known for developing Gestalt therapy, a humanistic therapy that is widely used in treating individuals and groups

immediate present experiences as the means of achieving self-understanding. Gestalt therapists direct the individual's attention to "here and now" feelings and thoughts, stress personal responsibility for change, and encourage self-acceptance.

Like other humanistic therapies, Gestalt therapy relies more on the description of experiences than on explanation. The "what" and "how" questions are considered more important than the "why." A controversial aspect of this approach is the active, dramatic, and often confrontational involvement of the therapist. Gestalt therapy techniques range from empathic support to the provocative challenging of the client (Perls, 1969; Stephenson, 1975).

Existential Theory and Therapy

existentialism (eks-uh-*sten*-chul-isum) A philosophy concerned with subjective human existence.

Existentialism is a philosophy that explores the facts of subjective human existence as its utmost concerns. Since its origin in the late eighteenth century, existentialism has emerged as an influential force in psychology. No single dominant existential theory of abnormal behavior exists, but there are three common themes in the major existential theories and therapies: anxiety, alienation, and authenticity (Kaufman, 1975).

existential anxiety Apprehensiveness due to awareness of freedom and responsibility.

Existential Anxiety. A fundamental fact in human existence is anxiety, which the Danish philosopher Søren Kierkegaard (1813–1855) described as the "dizziness of freedom." **Existential anxiety** is the apprehensiveness that comes from our awareness of personal freedom and our confrontation with the responsibility for our own lives. Associated with anxiety is *existential guilt*, regret over missed chances and lost opportunities—"the road not taken." Existential anxiety and guilt are not abnormal, but if they become too intense they may lead to abnormal behavior.

The fundamental issues of life and death play a prominent role in the existentialist view of mental health. Death sets an absolute limit to our subjective existence, and our awareness of death provokes anxiety about our personal mortality. The psychiatrist Irving Yalom believes that such *death anxiety* is associated with many psychological problems.

Bruce was a middle-aged man who was always "on the prowl" for women. His sexual conquests numbered in the hundreds, though he never cared for any of the women. His interest was just to have an orgasm, and it was not unusual for him to go out searching for another partner afterward, sometimes minutes later. His sexuality was compulsive; he felt he had to "have" a woman, even if he really did not wish to. When alone, Bruce was overwhelmed with fears and fantasies of death, and his sexual pursuits helped to confirm that he was alive and warded off his death anxiety temporarily. (Yalom, 1980)

alienation A state of meaninglessness due to a lack of goals, values, or purpose.

Alienation. Existential theories assume that people need to have meaning in their lives. Austrian psychiatrist Viktor Frankl has described this as the *will to meaning*, an innate drive to create purpose in life. **Alienation** is the state of meaninglessness in which people find themselves when they lack goals, values, or purpose. Some existentialists attribute alienation to a breakdown in the social institutions that traditionally provided meaning in people's lives. Whatever its

Psychologist Rollo May has contributed to the theory of existential anxiety, authenticity, and freedom as well as to the development of existential therapy.

R. D. Laing, an existential psychiatrist, proposed that schizophrenia represents a split between the true and the false selves.

source, alienation contributes to many emotional disturbances because the alienated person is cut off from others and from opportunities for personal growth (Maddi, 1967).

authenticity Being responsible for one's own existence and integrity.

Authenticity. Rollo May, a psychologist and a major existential theorist, defines **authenticity** as "the modality in which a man assumes the responsibility of his own existence." A person who lives authentically lives with integrity in a manner consistent with his or her personal values. Authenticity requires honesty with oneself and with others and is necessary for mental health (R. May, Angel, & Ellenberger, 1958).

The consequences of inauthenticity were explored by the radical psychiatrist R. D. Laing (1927–1989) in his work with schizophrenics. Laing viewed schizophrenia as a state of inauthenticity caused by a split between the individual's "true self" (the real core of personality) and "false self" (the image shown to the world). Laing maintained that the true and false selves split in schizophrenia because the individual was unable to make sense out of the dilemmas and inconsistencies imposed by family and society (Laing, 1959).

The image Roy presented to the world was what he considered the "ideal son," who was obedient, needy, and passive. During adolescence, he anguished over his inability to stand up to his mother. He fantasized about defying her but could not bring himself to do so. Roy secretly blamed his mother for his shortcomings and problems. He told himself he couldn't have a girlfriend because his mother would object. He hated his mother for many reasons, but he would not express his negative feelings toward her, and he made a great effort to hide his inner life.

existential therapy An approach that helps people cope with the problems of existence.

Existential Therapy. Existential therapy is a treatment approach that helps individuals understand, confront, and cope with the problems of human existence. Although this approach is not easily defined, it is distinguished by what Rollo May calls the "context of therapy." In the existential context, therapy is a genuine encounter in which the therapist and patient both participate in seeking change. Symptoms are viewed not simply as signs of maladjustment but as attempts to preserve one's existence in the face of threats to it. The therapist's task is to relate to the patient as a real person, not as an example of some abstract theory.

In May's view, therapeutic techniques have value, but only when they follow from an understanding of the individual. Techniques such as dream analysis, however, should not be relied on to create that understanding. In existential therapy, the therapist is not a technician whose job is to "fix" the patient but is a collaborator in the person's self-discovery (R. May, 1983).

logotherapy (*loh*-goh-*ther*-up-ee) Existential therapy intended to activate the will to meaning.

Viktor Frankl developed the approach known as **logotherapy**, an existential treatment that seeks to activate the will to meaning, as defined by the individual's own values and beliefs. Frankl's experiences as a concentration camp prisoner during World War II convinced him that even the most horrifying events may be endured if a person can find a reason for living. Although not associated with a religious perspective, logotherapy emphasizes the importance of the spiritual dimension of life in creating mental health (Frankl, 1963, 1967).

The Humanistic and Existential Perspectives: An Evaluation

The humanistic and existential perspectives are not exactly the same. Although they share some philosophical roots and assumptions, they do not always present the same views of human nature. Humanists stress the basic goodness of people, while existentialists recognize both good and evil as fundamental to human nature. In addition, existential psychology is more closely allied with the psychodynamic tradition, because the major existential theorists, including May, Laing, and Frankl, were originally psychoanalysts.

The humanistic and existential perspectives have both been criticized for relying on vague, unscientific, and untestable concepts. Many critics consider these views more a philosophy of life than a scientific perspective. However, supporters of these views contend that the demands of scientific precision should not take precedence over attempts to understand and help other people cope with the problems of human existence.

Humanistic and existential theories have spawned both individual and group therapies which are widely used and accepted. The personal growth movement that began in the 1960s was drawn largely from humanistic and existential theories. Evaluating the scientific merits of these therapies is very difficult, because their concepts lack clear definition and their treatments are unstandardized. However, some studies of client-centered therapy show that the therapist's warmth and empathy are significant factors in treatment outcome. Even though experimental evidence is generally lacking, clinical case reports suggest that humanistic and existential therapies can be beneficial (Shlien & Zimring, 1970; C. R. Rogers, Gendlin, Kiesler, & Truax, 1967).

SUMMARY

2-1 The biological perspective attributes abnormal behavior to disturbances in biological processes, especially in the brain. These disturbances are influenced by biochemical, neurological, and genetic factors. Biochemical processes involve the major neurotransmitter systems, the endocrine system, and nutrition. Brain injury, disease, and drugs can impair neurological activity and cause abnormal behavior. Associations also exist between psychological problems and genetic and chromosomal processes. Biological therapies seek to correct abnormal behavior by altering brain activity through drugs, electroconvulsive treatment, and psychosurgery.

2-2 The psychodynamic perspective emphasizes unconscious emotional conflict and developmental problems as the cause of mental disorders. Freud's psychoanalytic theory explained abnormal behavior as an expression of personality processes in the id, ego, and superego. Defense mechanisms are attempts to cope with psychic conflict. Interpersonal theory stresses social relationships in the origin of personality and abnormality. Ego psychology puts the ego at the center of personality and mental life. Object relations theory views internalized parental images as the critical "objects." Psychodynamic therapies foster insight that will help the patient overcome problems. Psychodynamic techniques include free association, dream interpretation, the analysis of transference and resistance, ego support, and short-term dynamic psychotherapy.

2-3 Freedom, responsibility, and self-actualization are core concepts of humanistic and existential views. Maslow's need theory views abnormal behavior as a consequence of frustrated need satisfaction. Rogers's self theory regards psychological disturbances as a reflection of problems in self-concept. Humanistic therapies, such as client-centered therapy and Gestalt therapy, enhance attempts at self-actualization. Existential theory addresses three themes in human existence: anxiety, alienation, and authenticity. Existential therapy and logotherapy help people confront and cope with the problems of human existence and its meaning.

TERMS TO REMEMBER

alienation (p. 50)

analytical psychology (p. 40)

analytic attitude (p. 43)

authenticity (p. 51)

biological perspective (p. 30)

biological therapy (p. 30)

client-centered therapy (p. 48)

countertransference (p. 44)

defense mechanisms (p. 36)

ego (p. 36)

ego analysis (p. 44)

ego psychology (p. 42)

electroconvulsive therapy (p. 33)

existential anxiety (p. 50)

existentialism (p. 50)

existential therapy (p. 52)

free association (p. 43)

Gestalt therapy (p. 49)

humanistic and existential perspectives (p. 45)

id (p. 36)

interpersonal theory (p. 41)

libido (p. 39)

logotherapy (p. 52)

need hierarchy (p. 46)

neurotransmitters (p. 31)

object relations theory (p. 43)

phenomenology (p. 46)

psychodynamic perspective (p. 35)

psychosexual development (p. 39)

psychosurgery (p. 34)

psychotherapy (p. 43)

psychotropic drugs (p. 32)

resistance (p. 44)

self-actualization (p. 46)

self-concept (p. 47)

self theory (p. 47)

short-term dynamic psychotherapy (p. 44)

superego (p. 36)

transference (p. 44)

unconscious determinism (p. 35)

SUGGESTED READINGS

Andreasen, N. (1984). *The broken brain: The biological revolution in psychiatry.* New York: Harper & Row.

Fine, R. (1979). *A history of psychoanalysis.* New York: Columbia University Press.

Rogers, C. R. (1961). *On becoming a person.* Boston: Houghton Mifflin.

Szasz, T. S. (1961). *The myth of mental illness.* New York: Harper & Row.

LEGAL AND ETHICAL ISSUES: SEXUAL RELATIONSHIPS BETWEEN THERAPISTS AND CLIENTS

Mrs. Y, a former client of Psychologist M, charged him with having engaged in a sexual relationship with her over the course of 18 months, during which period he continued to see her in a client relationship, treating her for depression within the context of marital problems. (American Psychological Association, 1987, p. 80)

This case describes an increasingly common ethical and legal dilemma in modern psychology and psychiatry. Sexual relationships between therapists and their clients have long been a problem. Years ago, Freud recognized the intensity of the therapeutic relationship and warned of the potential danger of sexual attraction between patients and therapists. Although most therapists have heeded the warning, many have not. Only a minority of psychologists and psychiatrists are guilty of sexual misconduct toward clients, but surveys indicate that nearly 10 percent of male and 3 percent of female therapists have engaged in such activity. Most often, the offending therapist is a man and the client is a woman. In about one-third of the cases, the therapists are repeat offenders who have had relations with several clients (Ethics Committee of the American Psychological Association, 1988; Gartrell, Herman, Olarte, Feldstein, & Localio, 1986).

The ethical principles of the American Psychological Association and American Psychiatric Association strictly prohibit sexual intimacy with clients. Nevertheless, in recent years there has been a dramatic increase in the number of reported violations. In fact, sexual misconduct is the most common ethical violation reported against psychologists. Typically, therapist-client sexual relations are detrimental to the clients, often destroying their trust in therapy and intensifying their symptoms. Sexual misconduct has produced severe consequences for some clients, including depression, suicidal behavior, and hospitalization. One study found that 90 percent of clients involved sexually with their therapists suffered some psychological damage (K. S. Pope, Keith-Spiegel, & Tabachnick, 1986).

Psychology and psychiatry have addressed this problem by educating therapists about the dangers of sexual misconduct and assigning severe penalties for violations, including expulsion from professional organizations. Legally, sexual misconduct by therapists establishes liability in malpractice suits, and it has been ruled a felony offense in some states. Whether these sanctions will reduce the prevalence of this problem has yet to be demonstrated.

Chapter
THREE

Theoretical Perspectives: Focus on Interactions Between the Individual and the Environment

OBJECTIVES

1. Explain the basic assumptions of the learning perspective.
2. Outline the principles of classical and operant conditioning as they apply to abnormal behavior.
3. Distinguish among, and give examples of, the major techniques of behavior therapy.
4. Discuss the principles of social learning theory that are relevant to abnormal behavior.
5. Identify the strategies of cognitive-behavior therapy.
6. Explain the cognitive theory of abnormal behavior and its approach to therapy.
7. Apply the concepts of family systems theory to abnormal behavior.
8. Describe the theory, rationale, and strategies of family therapy.
9. Explain the role of sociocultural factors in abnormal behavior.
10. Distinguish among the learning, family systems, and sociocultural perspectives on abnormal behavior.

*A*fter her arrest for shoplifting several hundred dollars' worth of merchandise, Alicia was ordered by a judge into treatment for her drinking problem. At age 41 she had long been abusing alcohol and other drugs, including tranquilizers, cocaine, and marijuana. Although she drank a substantial amount of alcohol every day and had been arrested previously on several alcohol and drug charges, Alicia did not feel that her drinking and drug use were a problem. Along with her alcohol and drug abuse, she had a history of severe depression, four suicide attempts, and many self-destructive relationships with men. She was also a compulsive shoplifter who generally took things she neither wanted nor used. More often than not, she just gave away or discarded the stolen items. Like her emotional problems and substance abuse, Alicia's stealing had begun in early adolescence. As she began therapy, her goal was to stay out of jail, not to change her behavior.

Throughout this chapter, we will return to the case of Alicia to illustrate how her behavior was influenced by both her individual psychological characteristics and the features of her environment.

In this chapter, our focus shifts from an emphasis on the individual to interactions between individuals and their environments. The three major viewpoints we will consider are the learning, family systems, and sociocultural perspectives.

3-1 ■ THE LEARNING PERSPECTIVE

learning perspective
The view that abnormal behavior is due to faulty or maladaptive learning.

The **learning perspective** assumes that abnormal behavior is caused by faulty or maladaptive learning experiences. Three major learning theories offer distinctive ideas regarding the nature and origins of abnormal behavior: behaviorism, social learning theory, and cognitive theory. There are some important differences between these theories, but they share common assumptions regarding the importance of learning, they all use objective methods, and they are all based on a scientific philosophy.

Basic Assumptions

The learning perspective assigns the greatest importance to the individual's learning experiences in how abnormal behavior develops. Moreover, therapy is approached as a learning experience to help individuals overcome their problems and behave more adaptively.

The learning perspective is grounded in objective, scientific research methods, so careful observation and measurement are the hallmarks of this approach. Theoretical concepts are offered only if they can be translated into objective measures called *operational definitions*, which make the theories scientifically testable. The requirement of testability also extends to the therapies that are derived from this perspective.

determinism The idea that events obey laws of cause and effect.

The learning perspective is also based on **determinism**, the idea that events obey laws of cause and effect. Determinism originated in the natural sciences, where it was applied in an attempt to understand the physical world. The deterministic view assumes that human behavior is also governed by laws and thus is predictable and controllable. Learning theories accept the premise of determinism, but they do not always agree about the specific cause-and-effect mechanisms behind abnormal behavior.

Behaviorism

behaviorism The school of psychology stressing objective study of behavior.

Behaviorism is a prominent school of psychology that stresses the objective study of behavior. It began in the early 1900s with research on animal conditioning and grew into one of the dominant theories in modern psychology. Traditional behaviorism emphasizes the need for objective measurements and explanations of behavior and excludes unobservable mental processes from its analysis of behavior.

environmental determinism The belief that behavior is caused by environmental forces.

An essential idea of the behaviorist theory is **environmental determinism**, the belief that behavior is caused by forces in the environment rather than by inner feelings or thoughts. Thus, behaviorism discounts the causal influence of subjective mental processes on behavior. B. F. Skinner (1904–1990) was for many years the leading advocate of behaviorism. He rejected "mentalistic" explanations because he believed they obscure the analysis of environmental causes (1974).

Normal and abnormal behavior are thought to develop as a result of learning experiences. Two kinds of learning mechanisms, classical and operant conditioning, are essential to behavioristic explanations.

classical conditioning Learning new associations between stimuli and reflexive responses.

Classical Conditioning. **Classical conditioning** is one type of learning in which new associations between environmental stimuli and reflexive responses are acquired. The Russian physiologist Ivan Pavlov (1849–1936) first described this type of conditioning in his early studies with dogs. After repeatedly pairing a neutral stimulus, such as a bell, with a food stimulus that caused the dog to salivate, Pavlov found that the bell alone would cause the animal to salivate.

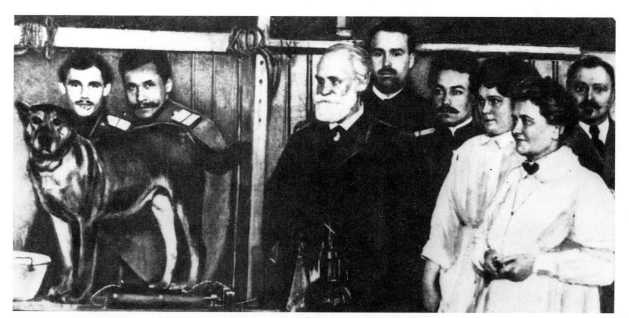

The classical conditioning experiments of Russian physiologist Ivan Pavlov (center, with white beard) provided a foundation for the development of behaviorism.

Behaviorists John Watson (with mask) and Rosalie Rayner (left) applied classical conditioning to elicit fear responses in the famous "Little Albert" study.

Procedure:

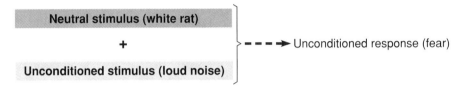

Figure 3-1 Classical conditioning: the "Little Albert" study.

Result:

Conditioned stimulus (white rat) ▸ Conditioned emotional response (fear)

Using Pavlov's ideas, John B. Watson (1878–1958), the founder of the behaviorist school, showed that classical conditioning could also explain the learning of emotional responses in humans. In 1920, Watson and his colleague Rosalie Rayner conducted their famous "Little Albert" study, in which a 9-month-old infant named Albert was conditioned to fear a white rat by being frightened with a loud noise while in the presence of the rat (see Figure 3-1).

The fact that Albert was not previously afraid of the rat suggested to Watson that phobias and other emotional disturbances might also be learned in this manner. Furthermore, after being conditioned, Albert demonstrated fear in the presence of other furry objects besides the white rat. This observation illustrated the principle of *stimulus generalization*, which states that stimuli similar to the conditioned stimulus (the rat) can also provoke the conditioned response (fear) (Watson & Rayner, 1920).

Conditioned emotional responses such as abnormal fears and other emotional reactions result from specific learning experiences. The following case excerpt illustrates how fears can be conditioned and generalized to many situations.

Bob sought treatment for a fear of heights at age 47. When he was 8 years old, he was critically injured in a fall from a third-story apartment window. After that he was terrified of heights and uncomfortable in any situation where he might fall. Bob could not bring himself to climb ladders, stand on balconies, fly in airplanes, cross bridges, or ride escalators. Even walking up steps generated anxiety.

Operant Conditioning. Classical conditioning is not the only way in which responses can be learned. In the early 1900s, psychologist E. L. Thorndike (1874–1949) described another type of learning governed by the consequences that follow a behavior. From his research, he concluded that animals learn to emit behaviors that are instrumental in attaining a goal or objective. For example, cats in a cage learn to open a door in order to get food. On the basis of his observations, Thorndike proposed the **law of effect**, which states that behaviors that produce satisfying effects are strengthened and those that produce dissatisfying effects are weakened (Hilgard & Bower, 1975).

law of effect The principle that satisfying effects strengthen behavior and dissatisfying effects weaken behavior.

operant (*op*-uh-rant) *conditioning* A type of learning through reinforcement and punishment.

On the basis of Thorndike's law of effect, B. F. Skinner elaborated the theory of **operant conditioning**, a type of learning in which instrumental behaviors, called *operants*, are strengthened or weakened by their consequences—reinforcement and punishment. A *reinforcer* is a stimulus that increases the probability that a response will be repeated, and a *punisher* is a stimulus that decreases the likelihood of a response. According to Skinner's (1969) theory, behavior is controlled by its reinforcing and punishing consequences.

There are two kinds of reinforcers, positive and negative. In *positive reinforcement*, a stimulus added to the environment strengthens the antecedent behavior. For example, someone who complains of feeling depressed may receive positive reinforcement for complaining if friends and family members express sympathy and pay more attention to him or her. In *negative reinforcement*, the removal of a usually unpleasant or aversive stimulus strengthens behavior. People with drug habits, for example, find drug taking negatively reinforced because it can eliminate unpleasant emotional states.

Alicia remembers being nervous and glum throughout her childhood, and in adolescence she became extremely moody and was often depressed. Feeling insecure about herself, she found it hard to interact comfortably with other teenagers, especially boys. After her first few experiences with drinking alcoholic beverages and smoking marijuana, she quickly became a regular user. Her drug use was powerfully reinforced because drugs relaxed her, made her less self-conscious, and opened up a new world of social activity for her.

According to behaviorism, drug use can become a powerful habit because its effects are strongly reinforcing.

Punishment can suppress or inhibit undesirable behavior.

Punishment, too, can be responsible for the development of abnormal behavior, because punishment tends to suppress or inhibit responses. When someone regularly receives punishment for a behavior, the behavior will diminish or perhaps disappear altogether. For example, a child who is often punished for trying to be independent may stop trying, and consequently never develop adequate self-help skills. In addition, people are motivated to avoid the situations in which they receive punishment. This *avoidance learning* is found in many phobias, wherein people avoid the circumstances they fear.

Behavior Therapy

behavior therapy
A treatment based on principles of classical and operant conditioning.

Behavior therapy is an approach to treatment that is based on classical and operant conditioning and applies these learning principles to replace maladaptive behavior with more effective responses. It fosters the development of coping skills and has been successful with a wide range of problems, including phobias, anxiety, stress, and depression.

systematic desensitization
A technique to reduce fear by gradual exposure to stimuli, plus relaxation.

Systematic Desensitization. Systematic desensitization, a technique for reducing fear and anxiety responses, is based on classical conditioning. Patients are gradually exposed to fear-producing stimuli in a step-by-step fashion while they relax to inhibit the fear. Desensitization may involve exposure to actual or imagined stimuli or both; it always begins with the least frightening stimuli and proceeds to more and more frightening ones (Rimm & Masters, 1979; Wolpe, 1969).

In treating Bob's fear of heights, a combination of actual and imagined situations was used, including mild ones like standing on a stool (actual) and extreme ones like flying in an airplane (imagined). For Bob and for many other people with phobias and anxiety problems, systematic desensitization has proved quite successful. This therapy is discussed more extensively in Chapter 5.

Flooding and Implosion. Flooding and implosion are behavior therapy techniques that expose patients to frightening stimuli in an intense fashion for a prolonged period of time in order to break down the fear response. These methods are based on the principle of *extinction*, according to which conditioned emotional responses weaken when a conditioned stimulus is not followed by an unconditioned stimulus. In **flooding**, the patient *directly* confronts the object or situation (conditioned stimulus) that provokes the conditioned fear response. For example, a person with an insect phobia might hold a jar of beetles. In **implosion**, the phobic person *imagines* a prolonged exposure to some intensely frightening stimulus, such as holding a jar of beetles (Stampfl & Levis, 1968).

Shaping. **Shaping** is the systematic use of reinforcement to encourage the gradual acquisition of new responses. Because reinforcers are applied to reward small changes in the direction of a goal or target behavior, shaping is often called the *method of successive approximations*. Sometimes complex behaviors must be broken into smaller units before rewards will work. For example, in shaping the speech of mentally retarded children, the therapist often needs to reinforce the pronunciation of individual syllables or sounds; later the children can learn to express words and sentences.

flooding Prolonged exposure to a feared stimulus.

implosion Imagined exposure to a feared stimulus for prolonged period.

shaping Reinforcement of successive approximations to a goal behavior.

In systematic desensitization patients overcome their fears by learning to relax while being exposed to frightening stimuli, such as snakes.

A wide range of applications for shaping behaviors in adults and children is found in clinical and educational settings. Some of the more successful uses to which shaping has been put are

- Teaching speech and self-control skills to developmentally disabled children,
- Improving sexual performance in individuals and couples with sexual dysfunctions,
- Promoting social and communication skills in people with depression, and
- Helping individuals with phobias to overcome their avoidance behavior (Rimm & Masters, 1979; Turner, Calhoun, & Adams, 1981).

contingency management
The use of reinforcers and punishers to modify behavior.

Contingency Management. Contingency management is a strategy that modifies behavior by manipulating its reinforcing and punishing consequences. A common example of this approach is the *contingency contract*, in which target behaviors are associated with predetermined rewards and punishments. For example, a classroom-based contract for a hyperactive child might provide rewards, such as extra playtime, for selected behaviors, such as staying seated during class and remaining in the room. *Self-management* is a variation of this technique in which people apply rewards or punishments to control their own behavior. Self-management programs are used to improve self-control in many areas, including overeating, smoking, and substance abuse (Karoly & Kanfer, 1982).

A *token system* is a special contingency management program that rewards behavior with symbolic reinforcers which the recipient can later exchange for other reinforcement. For example, a child may earn gold stars (symbolic reinforcers) for cooperation in class and later trade them for more tangible rewards like candy. Institutions in which a high degree of control exists are good settings for token systems. The most comprehensive institutional programs are called *token economies*. These programs have been employed in many psychiatric hospitals, prisons, and schools (Ayllon & Azrin, 1968).

aversion therapy
Treatment designed to eliminate behavior by associating it with aversive stimuli.

Aversion Therapy. Aversion therapy eliminates undesired behaviors by associating them with aversive (painful or unpleasant) stimuli. One approach, *aversive counterconditioning*, uses aversive stimuli to inhibit conditioned responses. A strategy used with child molesters reduces their deviant sexual response by pairing relevant sexual stimuli (e.g., fantasies of sex with children) with a painful electric shock (Adams, Tollison, & Carson, 1981).

Punishment can also be used as an aversion therapy. This is called *contingent aversive control*. For example, psychotic children are punished in order to eliminate extreme self-injurious behaviors, such as biting themselves. There are serious ethical and legal questions about the application of aversive control techniques, especially when physical punishment is involved. Nevertheless, when aversion therapy is used cautiously, it can be effective (Lovaas & Newsom, 1976).

Social Learning Theory

By the 1960s, learning theory had moved beyond traditional stimulus-response behaviorism to a point of view that considered unobservable mental processes in the explanation of behavior. Cognitions, such as thoughts, beliefs, and feel-

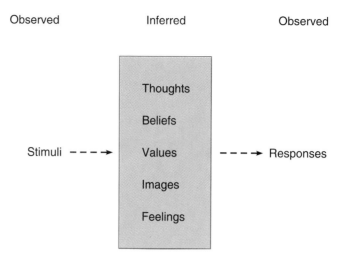

Observed   Inferred   Observed

Stimuli - - - → | Thoughts

Beliefs

Values

Images

Feelings | - - - → Responses

Figure 3-2 Cognitive mediating variables. *Cognitive behaviorism proposes that inferred cognitive variables mediate the associations between observed stimuli and responses.*

ings, were proposed to be *mediating variables*, the "bridges" between stimuli and responses (see Figure 3-2). *Cognitive behaviorism* seeks to integrate the objective methods of behaviorism with concepts that represent these inferred cognitive mediating variables.

social learning theory A cognitive-behavioral view that emphasizes interaction of cognitive and environmental variables.

Social learning theory is a cognitive-behavioral theory that emphasizes the interaction of cognition and environmental variables in causing behavior. Beginning with the work of psychologist Albert Bandura on observational learning and that of Julian Rotter on personality, social learning theory has developed into one of the dominant viewpoints in modern psychology.

observational learning Learning by observing and imitating modeled behavior.

Social learning theory places great emphasis on the acquisition of behavior through **observational learning**, a type of learning that requires the observation and imitation of modeled behavior. Bandura's early research showed that children do not need direct reinforcement in order to learn to imitate the aggressive behavior of adults. Children can learn aggression and other behaviors simply by observing the adult model's actions and their consequences. Many abnormal behaviors can be fostered by observational learning. Consider the way children learn to imitate their parents' maladaptive behaviors, such as antisocial behavior, overeating, fear, and alcohol use (Bandura, 1977).

Another distinctive feature of social learning theory is that it includes individual cognitive factors, or *person variables*, in explanations of behavior. Among these person variables are an individual's expectancies, values, interpretations, plans, and competencies. To illustrate the impact of person variables on behavior, consider the responses of two employees who are asked to report to their new supervisor's office. One employee becomes very anxious and angry because he sees the situation as a threat to his job security (interpretation) and he believes he will probably be fired (expectancy). The other employee approaches the meeting feeling confident because she is looking forward to making a good impression (plan) by using her effective communication skills (competency) (Mischel, 1973).

self-efficacy expectations Beliefs about one's ability to perform behaviors.

In his theory Bandura has emphasized the role of **self-efficacy expectations**, beliefs people hold about their ability to perform specific behaviors. People with high self-efficacy believe their actions will succeed, and they are more likely to act effectively. Those individuals with low self-efficacy believe

Figure 3-3 Reciprocal determinism. *Reciprocal determinism proposes that there are mutual cause-and-effect relationships between behavior, person variables, and the environment.*

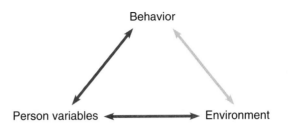

Behavior

Person variables ⟷ Environment

that their actions will be inadequate, and they are more apt to exhibit emotional distress and maladaptive behavior. For example, students who expect failure approach test taking with anxiety that interferes with their performance. As you will see in later chapters, self-efficacy expectations influence many emotional problems, such as anxiety disorders, depression, and stress reactions (Bandura, 1982).

An important distinction between social learning theory and behaviorism is in their views of determinism. As we have seen, the behaviorist theory assumes the concept of environmental determinism, which proposes that environmental variables cause behavior. In contrast, social learning theory promotes **reciprocal determinism**, the assumption that there are mutual causal influences among environmental variables, person variables, and behavior, as shown in Figure 3-3 (Bandura, 1984).

reciprocal determinism
The belief that mutual causal influences exist among environmental variables, person variables, and behavior.

A few concepts from social learning theory are illustrated in the case of Alicia. Her father and older brother were both alcoholics, and they provided powerful but unhealthy models whom she unfortunately imitated. Alicia's mother, who was often victimized by an abusive husband, was a passive and depressed woman who modeled attitudes of helplessness and fatalism for her daughter. Alicia, too, was subject to the emotional and physical abuse of her father. He demanded her respect and obedience, but in return he showed her little affection or interest. In all likelihood, exposure to the maladaptive influences of her family members engendered Alicia's low self-efficacy expectations and her associated depression. When she drank and used drugs, her emotional distress was temporarily subdued.

Cognitive-Behavior Therapy

cognitive-behavior therapy Treatment that alters maladaptive thoughts and behaviors, using learning principles.

Cognitive-behavior therapy seeks to alter maladaptive thoughts and behaviors with techniques derived from social learning theory and behaviorism. There is considerable similarity between the methods of behavior therapy and cognitive-behavior therapy, but unlike behavior therapy, cognitive-behavior therapy focuses on changing cognitions as well as overt actions.

modeling therapy
Treatment based on observational learning.

Modeling Therapy. In **modeling therapy**, a technique based on observational learning, individuals acquire more effective behavior by observing the adaptive behavior of models (Bandura, 1969). Several options are available in modeling therapy. In *direct modeling*, a therapist might demonstrate a behavior—for example, by showing a shy patient how to initiate a conversation. In *covert modeling*, the patient imagines observing someone enacting the behav-

PROFILE
Albert Bandura
(b. 1925)

Albert Bandura is the leading figure in contemporary social learning theory. His work provides an integrated viewpoint on behavior, learning, and motivation.

Bandura was born and raised in a small rural town in northern Alberta, Canada. He graduated from the University of British Columbia with a bachelor's degree in psychology in 1949, and he went on to earn his Ph.D. in clinical psychology in 1952 at the University of Iowa. Since 1953 Bandura has been on the faculty of Stanford University.

During his graduate studies Bandura was impressed with the experimental approach to learning. Throughout his career he has integrated this approach with many other aspects of psychology. Although he has shown a wide range of interests, he is best known for his work on observational learning, aggression, cognitive-behavior therapy, and self-efficacy theory. Bandura's social learning theory is one of modern psychology's most comprehensive viewpoints. It encompasses ideas from learning theory, social psychology, cognitive psychology, developmental psychology, and personality theory. In his research on modeling therapy, Bandura has developed the practical applications of social learning theory.

Beyond his scientific accomplishments, Bandura has contributed significantly to modern psychology as a teacher, advisor, journal editor, and leader. He is a past president of the American Psychological Association and a fellow of the American Academy of Arts and Sciences. He has also been the recipient of many awards, including the American Psychological Association's Award for Distinguished Scientific Contributions.

The most important of Bandura's books are *Social Learning and Personality Development* (written with Richard Walters, 1963); *Principles of Behavior Modification* (1969); *Social Learning Theory* (1977); and *Social Foundations of Thought and Action: A Social Cognitive Theory* (1986).

ior. In *participant modeling*, the patient actively imitates the modeled behavior, as in the following treatment for snake phobia:

1. Stroke the snake's midsection, then tail, then top of head.
2. Raise the snake's midsection, then tail, then head.
3. Grasp the snake gently but firmly a few inches from the head and about 6 inches from the tail, remove it from the cage. (Rimm & Masters, 1979, p. 126)

There is a broad range of applications for modeling therapy with adults and children. Successful outcomes with this treatment have been demonstrated for anxiety, phobias, depression, and interpersonal problems.

Self-instructional Training. *Self-talk*, which refers to those things we privately say to ourselves, can affect our behavior for better or worse. What we tell ourselves about the meaning of events around us and about our expectations can also determine our emotional responses. Modifying self-talk in order to improve an individual's behavior and emotional state is called **self-instructional training** (Meichenbaum, 1977).

self-instructional training Treatment that modifies private self-talk.

Among its many applications, self-instructional training has proved effective in teaching people to control their anger. The following self-talk statements can be used in anger control training:

> What is it that I have to do?
> I can work out a plan to handle this.
> Try not to take this too seriously.
> Easy does it. Remember to keep your sense of humor.
> As long as I keep my cool, I'm in control. (Novaco, 1975)

covert sensitization A technique designed to eliminate a behavior by imagining its aversive consequences.

Covert Sensitization. **Covert sensitization** inhibits or eliminates undesirable behavior by having the patient imagine unpleasant consequences. This strategy, a cognitive-behavioral form of aversion therapy, is used to control habitual behaviors like overeating and smoking. For example, a smoker might be asked to envision having a cigarette, then becoming horribly nauseated and vomiting repeatedly and uncontrollably. Covert sensitization is rarely employed as a sole treatment; it seems to work best when used as part of a broader therapy program (Cautela, 1973).

Both self-instructional training and covert sensitization were used in treating Alicia's impulsive shoplifting. In preparation for shopping, she rehearsed a plan to help her control her impulses to steal. She instructed herself to make a short list of items to buy, go directly to where the items were located, and proceed to the register immediately after finding the last item. In addition, Alicia was covertly sensitized to shoplifting by imagining herself being caught stealing, publicly ridiculed by store employees and patrons, arrested, handcuffed, and incarcerated.

Cognitive Theory

Within the last 20 years psychology has undergone a "cognitive revolution." A view of abnormal behavior has emerged which emphasizes the role of cognitive processes. **Cognitive theory** hypothesizes that people learn the faulty thinking patterns and attitudes that are intrinsic parts of psychological disturbances. However, maladaptive cognitions are not solely responsible for such disturbances. Like social learning theory, cognitive theory recognizes that both personal and environmental influences interact in causing abnormal behavior.

cognitive theory The view that faulty learned thinking patterns are the main causes of psychological disturbances.

Psychologist Albert Ellis proposes that emotional problems are largely due to self-defeating and irrational belief systems that people employ in interpreting events. Ellis's *A-B-C theory* describes the factors that operate in producing emotional disturbances. In this model, an activating event (A) engages an irrational belief system (B) which causes significant emotional consequences (C) (Ellis & Harper, 1975; Ellis & Whitely, 1979).

Ellis explained his A-B-C theory to a patient in treatment for marital difficulties and a drinking problem:

Albert Ellis proposes that emotional problems are the result of irrational thinking that can be overcome through rational-emotive therapy.

A . . . represents the fact that you've done badly and that your wife castigates you for your mistakes. And C . . . stands for the fact that you feel like a fool and keep drinking yourself into a stupor. . . . [B]etween A and C comes B—your Belief System about A. . . . And B stems from your general philosophy of life . . .—the philosophy that you should blame yourself (down or damn yourself as a total human) for doing the wrong thing. (Ellis & Harper, 1975, p. 119)

The theory of psychiatrist Aaron Beck points to inadequate cognitive processes in the development of emotional disorders. In Beck's view, three kinds of thinking problems are most prominent:

- *Cognitive errors* consist of illogical reasoning which leads to faulty conclusions or follows incorrect premises.
- *Cognitive appraisals* are misinterpretations of the meaning of events or behavior.
- *Cognitive sets* are assumptions or belief systems which are irrational and self-defeating.

These cognitive factors interact to produce emotional disorders like anxiety and depression. For example, a depressed person might operate under the assumption "I am a loser" (cognitive set), leading to the negative thought "This job is too hard for me" (cognitive appraisal) and the irrational conclusion "I'll never amount to anything" (cognitive error) (Beck, 1976; Beck & Emery, 1985).

Cognitive Therapy

cognitive therapy
Treatment designed to change faulty beliefs and assumptions.

Cognitive therapy is designed to change the faulty beliefs and assumptions that maintain abnormal behavior and emotional distress. Although its roots lie in diverse sources, such as phenomenology, psychodynamic psychology, and learning theory, modern cognitive therapy most closely resembles cognitive-behavior therapy. The boundary between cognitive and cognitive-behavior therapy is often fuzzy, since both seek to alter maladaptive cognitions. However, cognitive therapy assumes cognitions have a more central role and focuses treatment more directly at them.

The major objective of cognitive therapy is to change the patient's thinking by replacing maladaptive thoughts with more effective ones. This is called *cognitive restructuring*. Albert Ellis's **rational-emotive therapy** (RET) is an approach to cognitive restructuring that identifies, confronts, and eliminates irrational thoughts by using logical persuasion, argumentation, and reasoning. Ellis introduced RET in the 1950s as an alternative to behavior therapy and psychoanalysis, and it has since developed into a dominant school of cognitive therapy (Ellis & Dryden, 1987).

rational-emotive therapy
Cognitive therapy designed
to eliminate irrational
thoughts.

The cognitive therapy of Aaron Beck was initially applied in the treatment of depression, but it has been extended to anxiety, personality disorders, and many other problems. The cognitive therapist evaluates and challenges the patient's dysfunctional beliefs by questioning their validity, necessity, and usefulness. Three important questions are addressed in order to confront and correct dysfunctional beliefs:

- What is the evidence for the belief?
- What are other ways of interpreting reality?
- What are the consequences of the belief? (Freeman, Simon, Bentler, & Arkowitz, 1989)

The cognitive therapies of Ellis, Beck, and others recognize that processes other than faulty cognitions contribute to emotional disorders, but their treatment strategies focus primarily on changing troublesome cognitions. Table 3-1 summarizes a few faulty cognitions that are associated with emotional distress.

The Learning Perspective: An Evaluation

The learning perspective has been criticized on many grounds over the years. Because behaviorism does not directly address mental activity, critics see it as an overly simplistic and incomplete explanation of human behavior. Another objection is that behaviorism propogates a *mechanistic view* of people as robotlike responders to the environment. In addition, the concept of environmental determinism neglects the role of human consciousness, personality, and free will on behavior.

Social learning and cognitive theories overcome these criticisms somewhat by including mental processes in their explanations of behavior. Nevertheless, psychodynamic theorists contend that behaviorist, social learning, and cognitive theories neglect the unconscious and developmental causes of abnormal behavior. In opposition to the suggestions of cognitive theory, some researchers question the primacy of cognition in our emotional reactions, arguing that emotions are not simply the result of cognitive processes (Zajonc, 1980).

Because the learning perspective evolved from controlled studies, it rests on strong scientific foundations. Perhaps its most distinctive feature is that its theoretical concepts are posed in a testable manner. The scientific rigor of this perspective has made possible the development of laboratory models of abnormal behavior which have clarified our understanding of many disorders.

TABLE 3-1 ▮▮▮ **COGNITIONS RELATED TO EMOTIONAL DISTRESS**

* *Catastrophizing*: Thinking in extreme, catastrophic terms; thinking the worst will probably happen.
* *Dichotomizing*: Thinking in "black-and-white" terms; extremist, "all-or-nothing" thinking.
* *"Musturbating"*: Thinking in terms of "shoulds" or "musts" or "have to's"; placing unreasonable obligations on oneself.
* *Overgeneralizing*: Thinking that what happened in one situation will happen in others.
* *Personalizing*: Taking impersonal events personally; assuming personal responsibility for events without justification.
* *Prognosticating*: Thinking one knows what lies ahead; predicting future events or behaviors.

The therapies that have emerged from the learning perspective have proved successful in treating many types of abnormal behavior. Although some critics object to the degree of control exerted by cognitive and behavioral therapists, it is important to realize that they do not impose treatments on people against their will. On the contrary, the treatments are adapted to suit the individual needs and objectives of the patient (Kazdin & Wilson, 1980; Shapiro, 1985; Bowers & Clum, 1988).

3-2 ▮▮▮ THE FAMILY SYSTEMS PERSPECTIVE

family systems perspective The view that abnormal behavior is due to dysfunctional family interactions and relationships.

The **family systems perspective** conceives of abnormal behavior as an expression of dysfunctional interactions and relationships among family members. This perspective has its origin in biology's *general systems theory*, which defines a system in terms of its interacting parts. General systems theory has been extended from biological systems to social systems such as cultures, groups, and families. This idea of a system is captured in the statement "The whole is greater than the sum of its parts." A family system is composed of separate parts (family members), but the characteristics of the whole emerge in a unique way by virtue of the relationships among those parts (von Bertalanffy, 1973, 1974).

▮▮▮ Basic Assumptions

An obvious fact about families is that they consist of people whose interactions influence one another. The ongoing exchange of influences among family members shapes their thoughts, feelings, and behaviors. This interdependence defines the family as a system. Family relationships provide the primary context in which individual behaviors are developed and maintained.

The mutual effects that family members have on one another defy simple explanation. Systems theory relies on a *circular view of causation* rather than a traditional, linear (A → B → C), cause-and-effect model. According to systems theory, behaviors are embedded in circular patterns of interaction, such that

In the family systems perspective, relationships and communication among family members shape their behavior.

one person's behavior may be both the cause and effect of another's behavior. The following dialogue illustrates circularity in a dysfunctional family:

Mom: I'm depressed and angry because my husband is an alcoholic and my son uses drugs.

Son: I take drugs because I can't stand living with my parents, who always fight and criticize me.

Dad: I drink to escape from the aggravation of my nagging wife and good-for-nothing son.

homeostasis (ho-me-oh-*stay*-sis) The tendency for a family system to maintain a state of balance.

Homeostasis, a term initially used to describe physical systems, means that a system functions in a way that maintains a state of balance. This idea implies that families act to preserve their usual patterns of behavior, or the status quo, in family life. Ironically, the family's attempt to maintain homeostasis can cause abnormal behavior. For example, a child's aggression might distract parents from their marital conflict, thus saving the family from divorce. Abnormal behavior serves a purpose within the family system and is considered a feature of the system as a whole, not just of the family member who exhibits it. The meaning of abnormal behavior or symptoms is found in its role in the family system (Hoffman, 1981).

Aspects of Family Systems

Theories of family systems have developed from diverse clinical and research sources that emphasize many features of family life. In this section, we will discuss three major aspects of family functioning and their relevance to abnormal behavior: family communication patterns, family organization, and family development.

Family Communication Patterns. Beginning in the 1950s, the Mental Research Institute (MRI) group in California studied communication patterns in families that had a schizophrenic member, and from that work came concepts that have since been extended to other types of families. In systems theory, family relationships are defined and maintained by communications among family members, and abnormal behavior is seen as a deviant pattern of communication (Watzlawick & Weakland, 1977).

From the communication studies of the MRI group emerged the *double-bind hypothesis* of schizophrenia. In this view, schizophrenics are victims of a "no-win" dilemma in which they receive contradictory messages that they cannot refute but must respond to. For example, a mother's words convey a loving message when she tells her child to go to bed because he needs his sleep, but nonverbally she is telling him to get away from her because she is tired of him (Bateson, Jackson, Haley, & Weakland, 1956). (This hypothesis is examined further in Chapter 10.)

Since the early MRI studies on schizophrenia, other researchers have identified relationships between abnormal behavior and various types of deviant family communication. For example, defects in the clarity, consistency, and emotional content of communications among family members have been associated with schizophrenia and aggression, as well as some childhood disorders (Doane, 1980).

Family Organization. Relationships among family members define the family's organization or structure. The relationships, in turn, are defined by **boundaries**, the roles performed by family members and the rules of behavior that correspond to those roles. The concept of boundaries helps describe how activities of family members fit together to form the family system. Some roles are clearly defined and are performed by specific people. For example, though now much less common than they were at one time, the mother-caretaker and father-breadwinner are traditional complementary roles in the American family. Members of dysfunctional families often perform conflicting, erratic, and poorly defined roles. Individuals can develop psychological problems as a result of the roles they play in the family system.

> Until she was about 13, Alicia played the role of "parental child," the child who takes on adult responsibilities. She cared for her younger siblings after school and on many weekends while her mother worked and her father was out drinking. Her older brother, also an alcoholic, left home in his early twenties; after that her father's anger focused more on her than ever before. As Alicia became more independent and rebellious, her role changed to that of the scapegoat who got blamed for everything wrong in the family.

Families are typically organized into *subsystems* that include two or more family members allied with each other in some way. Subsystems often appear as coalitions among family members and are usually defined by some shared role or function. For example, the *parental dyad* is a subsystem responsible for "executive" functions of the family, including making important decisions, setting family rules, and planning family activities.

An important type of family structure is the **triangle**, a three-way relationship among individuals or subsystems. Triangles may be healthy and balanced, as when positive interactions prevail between mother, father, and children. However, in dysfunctional families imbalanced and unhealthy triangles often dominate (Minuchin, 1974).

boundaries Rules and roles that define relationships in a family.

triangle A three-way relationship among individuals or subsystems.

Inadequate communication patterns among family members are associated with problems in mental health.

Shortly after remarrying, Lisa was caught in a stressful triangle with her children and husband. The children and their stepfather competed fiercely for Lisa's time and attention. On top of this, the children's loyalty to their biological father was an enormous obstacle to building a new family order. The harder Lisa tried to appease them all, the more hostile they grew toward her and each other.

enmeshment A state of intense emotional and behavioral involvement among family members.

The degree of emotional and behavioral involvement among family members is another significant feature of family organization. The term **enmeshment** is used to indicate that family members are intensely involved with one another and have unclear boundaries between themselves. There are some advantages to enmeshment, including emotional support and closeness, but problems also exist when family members' roles and emotional conditions are too intertwined. The mother of a depressed adolescent concisely expressed their enmeshment by stating, "His pain is my pain."

At the other end of the spectrum is the disengaged family, whose members have little involvement with one another. These families live by the motto "Every man (or woman) for himself (or herself)." Researchers find associations between both of these extreme family patterns and abnormal behaviors like aggression, delinquency, and substance abuse (Olsen, Russell, & Sprenkle, 1979).

family life cycle Stages in the family's adaptation to life events.

Family Development. Like individuals, family systems grow and change. In its developmental progress, a family passes through stages as it confronts life's demands and opportunities. The **family life cycle** is defined by stages in structure and functioning as the family adapts to the demands of everyday life. The major *transitional events* in life, such as births, deaths, marriages, and illnesses, place stress on the family. Depending on how the family system is organized, these events may prove manageable or overwhelming (Carter & McGoldrick, 1980).

Consider a traditional two-parent family in which the woman has been the mother-caretaker and the man has been the father-breadwinner. Each has successfully adapted to a clearly defined role that is essential for the family's functioning. When their children have grown up and left home, the couple may find their familiar roles compromised and experience the so-called empty nest syndrome, characterized by loneliness and a sense of loss (McCullough, 1980).

Family development can also be viewed from a multigenerational perspective. Abnormal behavior sometimes evolves in the unique context of a family's history, and some families get stuck in dysfunctional patterns for several generations. Although heredity may play a part in multigenerational problems, psychological factors are also prominent. A family's attitudes, myths, habits, and values make up the psychological heritage passed from generation to generation, and this heritage can promote abnormal behavior. Violence is one problem that can extend over several generations as the victims of abuse grow up to perpetrate more abuse against their own children (Boszormenyi-Nagy & Spark, 1973).

Family Therapy

In recent years, family therapy has blossomed into a major treatment approach and several types of family therapy have evolved. However, here we will discuss only family therapies based on a systems view that share a few assumptions about treatment. No matter which individual in the family exhibits the abnormal behavior, the family system is the focus of treatment and all family members share the responsibility for change. The strategies of family therapy seek to alter dysfunctional family relationships that engender abnormal behavior.

family systems therapy Treatment designed to reduce emotional overinvolvement among family members.

Family Systems Therapy. Psychiatrist Murray Bowen (1913–1990) developed **family systems therapy**, a treatment approach that seeks to improve the family's ability to adapt to stress by reducing emotional overinvolvement among family members. Bowen's early work with schizophrenic patients convinced him that schizophrenia was due to an extreme "emotional stucktogetherness" of parent and child.

Family systems therapy promotes a psychological separation or *differentiation* of family members by defining and strengthening boundaries. Family members may be assigned specific chores or tasks to enhance their differentiation. For example, an overly dependent teenager will be instructed to shop for new shoes without her mother. Differentiation also has an individual meaning: people who confuse their thoughts and emotions lack differentiation. Bowen's therapy supports the dominance of thinking over feeling in behavior, and in that regard his approach resembles cognitive therapy.

Bowen speculated about the multigenerational transmission of disorders by a *family projection process.* He hypothesized that family dysfunctions are the culmination of problems, attitudes, and behavior patterns passed down from prior generations through psychological means. Family systems therapy confronts the significant issues which tie people to their families of origin in order that they can better understand their present behavior (Bowen, 1978; Kerr, 1981; Papero, 1983).

structural family therapy Treatment designed to correct family structure problems by changing rules and roles.

Structural Family Therapy. **Structural family therapy** seeks to correct problems in the family's structure, including dysfunctional roles, rules, and power balances. Psychiatrist Salvador Minuchin is the most influential figure in structural family therapy. In his extensive writings, Minuchin has described numerous therapeutic strategies for correcting the family's structural inadequacies. These strategies require the therapist to challenge the dysfunctional family's symptoms, structures, and view of reality.

The structural family therapist challenges the family's symptoms by interpreting them as "necessary" features of family functioning. This technique, *reframing,* informs family members that the real problem lies not in the specific symptoms but the relationships among family members. Reframing helps family members gain an understanding of their interdependence and enables them to perceive the connection between the reported problem and their interactions. For example, if a family seeks treatment for constant arguing, the therapist might reframe the problem by pointing out how the arguing helps family members stay at a comfortable emotional distance from one another.

A therapist can also challenge family structure by *unbalancing* the dysfunctional system. The unhealthy balance can be disrupted by defining new roles for family members and by clarifying the boundaries between members. Unbalancing the family challenges its view of reality and provokes its members to consider new and potentially better options for themselves. Consider a family in which the young son controls his mother by his temper and the father tacitly approves by blaming the wife for not disciplining the child. A structural therapist could unbalance the system by instructing the parents to switch roles so that the father takes responsibility for dealing with his son's temper flare-ups (Minuchin & Fishman, 1981; Minuchin, Rosman, & L. Baker, 1978).

strategic family therapy Treatment designed to change the dysfunctional homeostasis in a family.

Strategic Family Therapy. **Strategic family therapy** attempts to change the dysfunctional homeostasis that is responsible for the family's problems. This approach developed out of the MRI group's work on communication within dysfunctional families. Like other systems therapies, strategic family therapy attempts to modify the family system as a whole. However, unlike family systems and structural family therapies, strategic family therapy sets rather precise behavioral objectives for the family and is often limited to a small number of treatment sessions.

Strategic family therapy commonly uses *paradoxical techniques,* which involve advice or instructions that may seem contradictory or absurd. In one paradoxical technique called prescribing the symptom, family members are told to maintain the behavior which they are seeking to change. For example, the parents of a rebellious teenager are told to encourage the rebelliousness so that the child can continue to "rebel" only by being cooperative. Caution is impor-

In family therapy, family members learn to work together to communicate and interact more effectively.

tant in paradoxical intervention because of the risk that it may backfire and cause an increase in the abnormal behavior (Hoffman, 1981; Stanton, 1981).

The Family Systems Perspective: An Evaluation

Systems theory provides a broad framework for interpreting and treating abnormal behavior in families and individuals. Research on systems hypotheses has provided some evidence linking abnormal behavior to important aspects of family functioning. In addition, the success of family therapies has been demonstrated in many disorders, including addictions, eating disorders, and child behavior problems (Gurman & Kniskern, 1981).

However, systems theories are open to criticism on several counts. Most importantly, the systems perspective overlooks the influence of the individual family member's personality, attitudes, and emotional states on abnormal behavior. Family members are part of a system, but they are also distinct individuals with unique biological and psychological features.

Many concepts of systems theory have proved difficult to measure and test. Concepts like differentiation and homeostasis are ambiguous and defy objective measurement. The difficulties of objective testing and evaluation also apply to family therapies. Finally, systems theories can be criticized for offering descriptive metaphors of family life rather than scientific explanations for abnormal behavior.

3-3   THE SOCIOCULTURAL PERSPECTIVE

sociocultural perspective The view that abnormal behavior is due to social and cultural forces.

The **sociocultural perspective** is a point of view that explains abnormal behavior in terms of sociocultural forces and their impact on the individual. Although this perspective has not been as influential in psychology as in other social sciences, it does offer valuable ideas regarding abnormal behavior.

Basic Assumptions

The sociocultural perspective assumes that the meaning of abnormal behavior lies in the social interactions among individuals and groups. In Chapter 1 we saw that social norms are essential in evaluating abnormal behavior because a society's conventions, values, traditions, and institutions provide a framework that defines normality and abnormality. In addition, the development of abnormal behavior is influenced by aspects of the sociocultural environment, such as gender, race, and class. Traditional social theory considers mental illness and other forms of social deviance to be the result of social pathology and disorganization. It assumes that abnormal behavior in an individual reflects more general societal ills, such as poverty, discrimination, and a lack of social cohesion (Clinard & Meier, 1989).

labeling theory The view that society's labeling of deviant behavior defines mental disorders.

Labeling theory interprets mental disorders in terms of the effects of society's perceptions and labeling on those people who show deviant behavior. When people violate social norms, they are labeled in unfavorable ways—"crazy," "sick," and "mentally ill"—and these labels impose a specific social role on the labeled person. Like other roles, the role of "mental patient" is socially reinforced by others' perceptions of and interactions with the individual. A person labeled as mentally ill may internalize a self-image to match the label and thereby become trapped in the role. Furthermore, society typically places demands on people to maintain the roles to which they have been assigned. Thus, once a person is identified as mentally ill, it is difficult for him or her to change that label (Scheff, 1966).

Sociocultural Factors in Mental Health

Researchers have found significant associations between mental health problems and sociocultural factors. These associations suggest that social forces contribute to mental disorders. The **social stress hypothesis** proposes that people who experience severe social stress are most likely to develop abnormal behavior. For example, in the United States, disproportionately high rates of some mental disorders are found among the economically disadvantaged (see Table 3-2). Many of the most serious mental disorders, such as schizophrenia, depression, and alcoholism, are more common among impoverished individuals (Bruce, Takeuchi, & Leaf, 1991).

social stress hypothesis The belief that abnormal behavior is due to social stress, such as poverty.

Furthermore, social stress is correlated with both race and gender in the United States. Women and members of racial minorities are more likely to live in conditions of impoverishment, and consequently more likely to experience above-average amounts of social stress (Belle, 1990). Poverty and some of its attendant psychological disorders are significantly more prevalent within these groups than in American society at large.

Research generally indicates a modest positive correlation between socioeconomic status (SES) and mental health. This relationship also extends to children, whose overall psychological well-being is correlated with their parents' SES level. One well-known investigation, the Midtown Manhattan Study, found that mental health suffers and impairment increases as parental SES declines (see Figure 3-4). The complex SES–mental health relationship involves many variables that influence social, physical, and psychological well-being. Poverty increases the risk of mental health problems by exposing the individual to sig-

CLOSE-UP
"On Being Sane in Insane Places"

In 1973, David Rosenhan, a psychologist, published a study with the foregoing title, which appeared to support the view of labeling theory. With the cooperation of hospital administrators, Rosenhan arranged for healthy subjects to be admitted to several mental institutions. These "pseudopatients" falsely reported psychotic symptoms, such as hearing voices, in order to gain admission, and most of them were diagnosed as schizophrenic.

After they were admitted to the hospitals, the pseudopatients stopped reporting symptoms and started acting "normally." Nevertheless, they continued to be perceived as mentally ill by the staff. For example, the pseudopatients took notes on their observations of the staff and patients, and in some cases this behavior was interpreted by staff members as a symptom. Ironically, "real" patients were often more perceptive of the pseudopatients' normality than the doctors and nurses were. Within a couple of months, all the pseudopatients were released from the mental hospitals. At the time of their releases, most were described as having symptoms "in remission."

Although Rosenhan's study has not escaped criticism, its findings point to the influence of social perceptions on the meaning of abnormal behavior and suggest that perhaps it is not possible to be "sane in insane places." After the pseudopatients were diagnosed, their actions were perceived in ways that conformed with the mental hospital setting and the pseudopatients' assigned roles as mental patients. Rosenhan's conclusions are generally consistent with the assumptions of labeling theory:

> Once a person is designated abnormal, all of his other behaviors and characteristics are colored by that label. Indeed, that label is so powerful that many of the pseudopatients' normal behaviors were overlooked entirely or profoundly misinterpreted. . . . As far as I can determine, diagnoses were in no way affected by the relative health of the circumstances of a pseudopatient's life. Rather, the reverse occurred: the perception of his circumstances was shaped entirely by the diagnosis. (1973)

TABLE 3-2   **POVERTY AND THE PREVALENCE OF MENTAL DISORDERS**

	Six-Month Prevalence (%)	
Mental Disorders	**Poor**	**Not Poor**
Any disorder	15.2	9.0
Alcohol abuse/dependence	5.7	2.8
Drug abuse/dependence	1.0	0.6
Major depression	7.9	4.0
Obsessive-compulsive disorder	2.0	0.7
Phobia	4.4	3.0
Schizophrenia	1.5	<0.1

Source: Adapted from "Poverty and Psychiatric Status: Longitudinal Evidence from the New Haven Epidemiologic Catchment Area Study" by M. L. Bruce, D. T. Takeuchi, & P. J. Leaf, 1991, *Archives of General Psychiatry, 48*, pp. 470–474.

nificant stresses, including inadequate medical care, poor nutrition, unhealthy living conditions, crime, financial frustrations, and alienation from mainstream society (Dohrenwend et al., 1980; Myers, Lindenthal, & Pepper, 1974; J. J. Schwab & M. E. Schwab, 1978; Srole et al., 1978).

Since childhood, Alicia had lived in conditions of economic hardship. Her father was an unskilled laborer without a high school diploma, and that, combined with his alcohol problem, made for a limited earning potential. Her mother worked at various jobs but had no specific skills and was often unemployed. The family lurched from one financial crisis to the next, and Alicia experienced the typical stresses of a disadvantaged childhood, including family fights over money, disappointment, frequent moves, and social embarrassment.

Treatment Approaches

No specific therapy derives from the sociocultural perspective. What does emerge is an attitude that treatment must consider the realities of the social environment as well as individual behavior.

community mental health movement A union of the social reform movement, psychotherapy, and an ecological view of behavior.

The **community mental health movement** unites the social reform movement, psychotherapy, and an ecological view of human behavior. In this view, which appeared during the 1960s, mental health problems are addressed with an appreciation of the social contexts in which they arise. Social problems, such as joblessness, poverty, and powerlessness, are seen as the primary obstacles to mental health. The community mental health movement emphasizes prevention over treatment and seeks to empower people to cope with and change their social circumstances at a grass roots level (Heller et al., 1984).

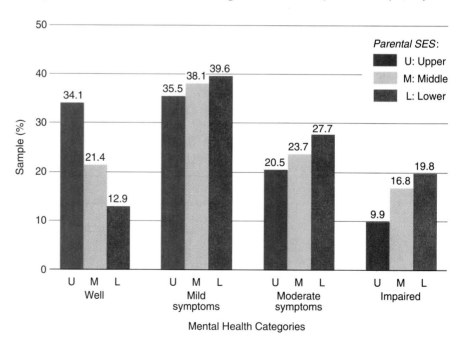

Figure 3-4 Mental health and parental socioeconomic status (SES): the Midtown Manhattan Study.

Source: Adapted from *Mental Health in the Metropolis: The Midtown Manhattan Study* by L. Srole, T. S. Langner, S. T. Michael, P. Kirkpatrick, M. K. Opler, and T. A. C. Rennie, 1978, New York: New York University Press.

Social psychiatry and *ethnotherapy* are related approaches that incorporate culturally relevant attitudes and activities into the treatment of abnormal behavior. These approaches insist that therapy must respect the cultural values and belief system of the patient in order to be effective (DeVos, 1974). One ethnically oriented approach is *cuento* (story) *therapy*, which employs traditional folktales in work with Puerto Rican children. The folktales convey culturally pertinent information, values, and skills to the children in order to help them better cope with their problems (Costantino, 1986).

The Sociocultural Perspective: An Evaluation

The sociocultural perspective takes into account important relationships between abnormal behavior and sociocultural factors. However, such associations do not prove that sociocultural factors cause abnormal behavior. According to the *downward social drift hypothesis*, individuals encounter social problems such as poverty and unemployment because they have psychological disabilities that prevent them from functioning adequately in modern society.

Critics of social labeling theory argue that it does not satisfactorily explain the origin of abnormal behavior. Labeling theory emphasizes the effects of labeling on people who violate social norms, but it does not say why they violated the norms in the first place. There is, in fact, little research evidence to support labeling theory's explanation of mental disorders (Gove, 1982).

The sociocultural perspective has contributed some valuable ideas about the prevention of mental health problems through social intervention and community self-help programs. Certainly the treatment of mental disorders can only be helped by an appreciation of the patient's cultural environment and values. As social psychiatry and ethnotherapy show, the patient benefits when treatment works along with cultural forces rather than against them.

SUMMARY

3-1 The learning perspective attributes abnormal behavior to learning processes, such as classical and operant conditioning and observational learning. Behaviorism rejects mental processes as causes and stresses environmental determinism. Social learning theory emphasizes cognitive variables, such as self-efficacy expectations. Cognitive theory attributes emotional disorders to faulty thinking. Behavior therapy modifies abnormal behavior by using learning techniques, such as shaping, aversive therapy, and contingency management. Cognitive-behavior therapy and cognitive therapy seek to change thoughts and beliefs associated with emotional disturbances. The learning perspective has contributed scientifically sound theories and therapies for a wide range of abnormal behaviors. Critics decry its mechanistic view and superficial explanations of complex behavior.

3-2 The family systems perspective assumes that the behavior of family members functions to maintain homeostasis and that abnormal behavior reflects systemic dysfunctions. Problems develop because the family has faulty communication patterns, organization, and adjustment to developmental changes. Family therapies treat the entire family and attempt to correct dysfunctional relationships. Family systems therapy, structural family therapy, and strategic family therapy are three effective types of family therapy.

The family systems perspective has generated useful therapies for many disorders, but it is limited because it neglects individual psychological and biological processes.

3-3   In the sociocultural perspective, social forces and institutions are considered the major causes of abnormal behavior. Labeling theory is concerned with effects that labeling deviant behavior has on the role of the individual. Socioeconomic status, race, and gender are social factors that are associated with mental disorders. Within the sociocultural view, the treatment of abnormal behavior must take the social and cultural context of the individual into account. The community mental health movement, social psychiatry, and ethnotherapy are treatment approaches that illustrate this perspective.

TERMS TO REMEMBER

aversion therapy (p. 64)
behaviorism (p. 59)
behavior therapy (p. 62)
boundaries (p. 73)
classical conditioning (p. 59)
cognitive-behavior therapy (p. 66)
cognitive theory (p. 68)
cognitive therapy (p. 69)
community mental health
    movement (p. 80)
contingency management (p. 64)
covert sensitization (p. 68)
determinism (p. 58)
enmeshment (p. 74)
environmental determinism (p. 59)
family life cycle (p. 75)
family systems perspective (p. 71)
family systems therapy (p. 75)
flooding (p. 63)
homeostasis (p. 72)

implosion (p. 63)
labeling theory (p. 78)
law of effect (p. 61)
learning perspective (p. 58)
modeling therapy (p. 66)
observational learning (p. 65)
operant conditioning (p. 61)
rational-emotive therapy (p. 70)
reciprocal determinism (p. 66)
self-efficacy expectations (p. 65)
self-instructional training (p. 68)
shaping (p. 63)
social learning theory (p. 65)
social stress hypothesis (p. 78)
sociocultural perspective (p. 77)
strategic family therapy (p. 76)
structural family therapy (p. 76)
systematic desensitization (p. 62)
triangle (p. 73)

SUGGESTED READINGS

Bandura, A. (1977). *Social learning theory.* Englewood Cliffs, NJ: Prentice-Hall.
Ellis, A., & Harper, R. A. (1975). *A new guide to rational living.* No. Hollywood, CA: Wilshire.
Hoffman, L. (1981). *Foundations of family therapy: A conceptual framework for systems change.* New York: Basic Books.
Scheff, T. J. (1966). *Being mentally ill: A sociological theory.* Chicago: Aldine.
Skinner, B. F. (1974). *About behaviorism.* New York: Knopf.

LEGAL AND ETHICAL ISSUES: THE DUTY TO WARN

In 1969, Tatiana Tarasoff was killed by Prosenjit Poddar, a graduate student at the University of California. Depressed over her refusal to date him, Poddar had expressed his intention to kill her during a session with his therapist at a university health facility. The psychologist notified the campus police, but on questioning Poddar the police found him rational and released him. After the crime Poddar was convicted of voluntary manslaughter in consideration of his impaired mental capacity due to paranoid schizophrenia.

Tatiana's parents sued the university, and the supreme court of California ruled in their favor, concluding that the therapist had been obliged to protect her by a warning. This "duty to warn" obligation has since been upheld in other states and has been extended to include potential danger even without explicit threats.

Prior to the Tarasoff case, the confidentiality of a client's communications to a therapist had been considered inviolable. But since the Tarasoff decision, a patient's confidentiality rights must be weighed against the public safety. Despite its good intentions, this ruling created dilemmas for both therapists and their clients. Knowing the limits of confidentiality, clients may hesitate to discuss any feelings of anger and hostility, and iron-ically, this may prevent any warning to their potential targets.

A difficult problem posed by the Tarasoff case is the prediction of violence. Therapy clients often voice threats; for example, a wife angered by her husband's infidelity may say, "I'm going to strangle him!" How seriously should such threats be taken? Studies show the unreliability of predicting violent behavior, and clinicians must rely on their assessment of the client's emotional state and thought processes (Appelbaum, 1986; Monahan, 1981).

Recently, questions about the duty to warn have arisen in other areas. One controversial area involves patients infected with the human immunodeficiency virus (HIV). Debate has emerged over therapists' duty to warn the sex partners of patients known to be HIV-positive. Given the fatality of AIDS, the disease caused by HIV, an infected person who engages in "unsafe" sex presents a clear danger to the partner. As yet, the relevance of the Tarasoff decision to the confidentiality of HIV-infected patients has not been clearly established. Therapists and the courts continue to struggle with these complex issues (Melton, 1988).

Chapter FOUR

Clinical Assessment and Diagnosis

OBJECTIVES

1. Explain the purposes of clinical assessment.
2. Outline the different types of assessment strategies used in clinical practice.
3. Describe the general principles and practices of psychological testing.
4. Distinguish between structured and unstructured interviews.
5. Differentiate among self-report inventories, projective tests, intelligence tests, and neuropsychological tests.
6. Discuss behavioral assessment and how it compares to other forms of psychological evaluation.
7. Outline and describe the types of physiological evaluation techniques.
8. Explain the purposes of diagnosis and the criticisms leveled against it.
9. Describe the DSM-III-R multiaxial diagnostic system.
10. Compare DSM-IV to DSM-III-R.

*D*orothy, age 50, entered treatment with symptoms of depression. She lacked energy, had trouble sleeping, and could not concentrate or work. Dorothy had little interest in life and was plagued by frequent suicidal urges. She reported having been depressed for periods of time throughout her teen and adult years, and she had been hospitalized several times for depression. She had a well-functioning and supportive husband. The challenge for the therapist was to determine the nature of her depression and recommend the most effective treatment. In this chapter, we will explore some of the assessment strategies available and see how they proved helpful in Dorothy's case.

4-1   CLINICAL ASSESSMENT

Clinical assessment is a systematic process of collecting information about an individual, family, or couple. This information is organized and used to make diagnoses, select treatments, and assist in the therapist's understanding of psychological problems. In addition, assessment information can be helpful in the resolution of legal matters, such as child custody disputes or insanity pleas. Assessment data is also used in differentiating problems that have a biological basis from those that arise mainly from psychosocial factors.

Many assessment tools are available to the clinician or mental health professional, who considers both the type of information needed and the assessment goals themselves in deciding which tools to use. For example, different evaluation techniques and assessment strategies are used to determine whether someone has a phobia, whether another person could benefit from psychotropic medication, and whether another has suffered brain damage.

The clinician's theoretical orientation can also influence the evaluation approach. For example, a psychoanalyst may try to assess unconscious processes, and a behaviorist would be more concerned with measuring observable behaviors. Finally, the assessment is also shaped by whether the subject under evaluation is an individual, a couple, or a family. The following sections describe the different types of assessment strategies used by clinicians in the mental health field today.

Interviewing

interview A method of gathering information about mental, emotional, and behavioral functioning.

The most commonly used method of gathering clinical information is the face-to-face **interview**, during which the mental health professional investigates mental, emotional, and behavioral functioning by asking probing questions and evaluating the patient's responses. The degree of structure to the interview can vary.

unstructured interview An unstandardized interview format.

Unstructured Interviews. The **unstructured interview** is rather free-flowing; it is conducted according to what circumstances require. The clinician chooses topics and asks questions judged to be relevant at the moment. Actually, the term *unstructured interview* is misleading, since it suggests a disorganized and haphazard approach. In reality, *unstandardized* is more descriptive. The clinician is not bound to cover specific topics, nor is there a predetermined way of rating the person's responses to questions. For example, a therapist may have an interview with a man who is disturbed because he discovered that his wife is having an affair. Instead of trying to assess the presence of a particular mental

86

Interviews are the most common method of gathering information about mental, emotional, and behavioral functioning.

disorder, the clinician focuses on the man's particular thoughts and emotional reactions. This approach helps to develop rapport between interviewer and client and enables the client to feel safe and supported. Under these conditions, people feel more at ease to disclose information and are more open to treatment.

Most interviews begin with a statement about the problems that prompted the person to come in for consultation. Dorothy, for example, said, "I feel depressed, I've been having trouble sleeping, and I'm anxious most of the day." Of course, Dorothy and many other people do not know precisely what the interviewer is looking for. All they know is that they are not feeling well and want help. So the clinician attempts to elicit information that will specify the patient's complaints as clearly as possible, and as this proceeds the interview takes on more structure. When Dorothy reported being depressed, the interviewer began asking questions designed to determine whether she was in fact depressed and what type of depressive disorder was present.

The initial specification of the problem is followed by a look at the patient's history, especially with respect to the factors leading to the problem's development. Important developmental factors include the quality of family life during childhood, child-rearing experiences, previous relationships, educational and employment experiences, and medical history. The clinician will also explore the possibility that the client has previously had the same or similar problems. Such information can help clarify current problems. For example, Dorothy indicated that she had been depressed on and off for most of her life, and she revealed that her mother and father fought constantly because of her father's womanizing. Moreover, her mother never gave her approval and frequently burdened her with her own personal problems.

Once historical factors have been explored, the interviewer investigates factors that currently contribute to the person's difficulties. These can include

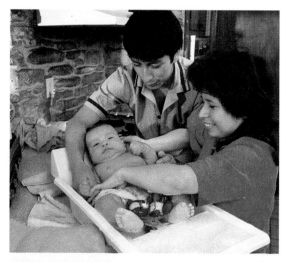

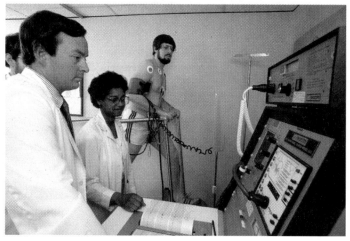

During the interview, the clinician evaluates the client's family life, childhood experiences, interpersonal relationships, and educational and employment history. A medical examination can also reveal physical factors that may be contributing to the client's problems.

drug or alcohol abuse, physical illness, legal or economic difficulties, or problems in an important relationship. Simple questions like "What can you tell me about your health?" or "How have you been getting along with your girlfriend?" can open a discussion of these issues. The clinician asks about available social supports, including friends and relatives, in order to better understand the problem. Sometimes these others can be recruited to help resolve the problem.

Personal strengths and assets, as well as a willingness to change, are also evaluated in the interview. As mentioned earlier, Dorothy's husband was quite supportive of her. However, he had recently lost his job. In contrast, Dorothy's mother was still criticizing her and provided little support. By now her father and sister were deceased, and her estranged son was a drug addict. These circumstances prompted her feelings of being alone and having no family to lean on.

Evaluation of Unstructured Interviews. Many critics argue that unstructured interviews introduce bias that can contaminate the conclusions drawn and thereby lead to the selection of inappropriate treatment. The clinician's attitudes, values, expectations, and other personality variables can shape the outcome of the interview as much as the client's presented problems. The therapist's theoretical orientation, gender, political beliefs, and cultural background can also be influential. For example, an interviewer in the midst of a serious marital problem may not fairly evaluate a client in a similar predicament.

structured interview schedules An interview method based on predetermined topics and questions.

Structured Interview Schedules. **Structured interview schedules** use predetermined questions and scoring methods. The goal is to enhance diagnostic consistency and reduce bias effects. The clinician begins with a specific assessment focus, such as determining the presence of schizophrenia, depression, or panic disorder. The clinician then asks predetermined questions and rates the patient's responses according to a preestablished numerical scoring system.

Assume a clinical researcher is conducting a study designed to compare the effectiveness of different therapies for panic disorder (see Chapter 5). The researcher must be certain that the subjects really have the condition. To determine this, he or she can ask specific questions that test for the presence of panic: "Do you have shortness of breath?" "Does your heart beat rapidly for no reason?" "Do you ever feel faint?" "Are you afraid that something terrible is going to happen?" The researcher then rates the intensity or frequency of affirmative responses and uses a scoring system to decide whether panic disorder is present. Some interview schedules can be administered and scored by computers.

The more commonly used structured interview schedules include the Schedule of Affective Disorders and Schizophrenia (SADS) (Spitzer & Endicott, 1978), the Diagnostic Interview Schedule (DIS) (Robins, Helzer, Croughan, & Ratcliff, 1981), and the Structured Clinical Interview for DSM-III (SCI) (Spitzer & J. D. W. Williams, 1986).

Evaluation of Structured Interviews. The use of structured interviews increases precision and consistency because each interview is conducted and scored in the same manner. This provides for greater confidence in diagnosis and thereby enhances our understanding and treatment of psychological problems. Also, the undesirable effects of the biased clinician's judgments are minimized. On the negative side, some flexibility may be lost.

In recent years, cultural factors in assessment have received increased attention because assessment techniques have been applied internationally. In the United States, clinicians serve a culturally varied population. Research indicates that cultural differences between clinician and client often result in misdiagnosis and in overestimation or underestimation of mental problems. This places a burden on clinicians to familiarize themselves with the needs and beliefs of people from other cultures (Butcher, 1987; Westermeyer, 1987).

Psychological Testing

In many cases, the interview provides sufficient information to make a diagnosis or to conduct research. However, psychological test data provides information about cognitive, emotional, social, and personality functioning that may be difficult to obtain from the interview. There are many circumstances in which additional information is required. For example, a clinician who is unsure about a client's potential for drug abuse or aggressive behavior can use test data to help improve predictions. Courts, schools, or government agencies often request test data. For example, test data about parents is sometimes required in order to resolve child custody cases. Dorothy's depression rendered her unable to work, and she applied for disability benefits. In determining whether she qualified for benefits, the state asked her therapist to provide test data to help substantiate his clinical impressions.

Elements of Psychological Tests.   The usefulness of any psychological test depends largely on its construction. Simply stated, the best test is one that is standardized. **Standardization** means that the test designers have clearly specified the conditions under which the test should be administered and scored. Specifications include test-taking instructions, time limits, and rules for scoring. Standardization also means that norms have been established. During its development, the test is administered to a large number of subjects representing the target population. The test designers then determine average test scores to use as a standard of comparison for individual test takers. In other words, a score on a particular test is meaningful only when we have an appropriate reference group for comparison. For example, a 12-year-old girl's score on an aptitude test is interpreted by comparing her score with scores of other children in the same age group. The comparison or reference group is known as the **normative group**.

Other important aspects of test construction are its reliability and validity. **Reliability** refers to the consistency of test scores obtained. *Test-retest reliability* means that repeated administrations of the same test give consistent results. Tests should also have *internal consistency*, meaning that there is reliability across different parts of the same test. *Inter-judge reliability* is concerned with consistency of scores when different people administer the same test.

Validity means that a test measures what it claims to measure—that is, it is accurate. Just as a thermometer should accurately measure temperature, an intelligence test should accurately measure intelligence. There are many types of validity. *Construct validity* is the degree to which a test measures a theoretical concept or construct. Introversion, ego strength, neuroticism, dominance,

standardization
A means of specifying conditions of test administration and scoring.

normative group
A comparison group used in test standardization.

reliability   Consistency of test scores.

validity   Test accuracy.

assertiveness, and aggression are some of the clinically relevant constructs measured by tests. *Predictive validity* is a measure of how well a test predicts some clinically relevant future event, such as suicide, drug abuse, or avoidance behavior. A test with good predictive validity allows clinicians to make these predictions with better confidence. Finally, *convergent validity* refers to how well a test correlates with other measures of the same variable or construct. For example, a test measuring intelligence should correlate with other tests claiming to measure the same aspects of intelligence (Anastasi, 1988).

self-report inventories Questionnaires in which the subject reports on aspects of psychological functioning.

Minnesota Multiphasic Personality Inventory (MMPI) A self-report test of personality functioning.

Self-Report Inventories. Self-report inventories are paper-and-pencil questionnaires that ask the subject to report about aspects of psychological functioning. The **Minnesota Multiphasic Personality Inventory (MMPI)** is the most widely used test of abnormal personality in clinical practice and research (Hathaway & McKinley, 1940). The MMPI was originally developed in the late 1930s to help in making psychiatric diagnoses for hospital inpatients. The MMPI has since been updated and restandardized in the MMPI-2 (Butcher, 1989).

The MMPI consists of 566 statements, and the MMPI-2 contains 567 questions. Respondents are asked to say whether the statements are mainly true or false about themselves. Scores are obtained on four validity scales and ten clinical scales (see Table 4-1). Over 500 special scales can also be derived if desired. The MMPI includes validity scales that determine the person's test-taking attitude. They measure cooperativeness, truthfulness, defensiveness, and faking. The test interpreter can use this validity information to determine whether the subject answered questions honestly and openly and whether scores on the clinical scales are meaningful. For example, many police departments use MMPI data to help select candidates. Some candidates may try to appear well-adjusted and hide certain information in order to get the job. Validity scales are sensitive

TABLE 4-1   DESCRIPTIONS OF TEN MMPI CLINICAL SCALES

Scale Label	Meaning of High Score
1. Hypochondriasis-Hs	Vague physical complaints; unhappy, whiny, demanding.
2. Depression-D	Low self-esteem, depressed mood.
3. Hysteria-Hy	Dependent, naive, dramatic.
4. Psychopathic Deviate-Pd	Antisocial, rebellious, impulsive; alcohol/drug use.
5. Masculinity-Femininity-Mf	Males: Sensitive, passive, feminine; females: masculine, rough, unemotional.
6. Paranoia-Pa	Suspicious, sullen, overly sensitive, mistrustful.
7. Psychasthenia-Pt	Worried, anxious, obsessive, tense, phobic.
8. Schizophrenia-Sc	Alienated, detached; bizarre thoughts, erratic moods.
9. Hypomania-Ma	Energetic, sociable, irritable, flighty, grandiose.
10. Social Introversion-Si	Introverted, shy, sensitive, overcontrolled.

Source: "Descriptions of 10 MMPI Clinical Scales" from *The MMPI: An Interpretive Manual* by R. L. Greene. Copyright © 1980 by R. L. Greene. Reprinted by permission of Allyn & Bacon.

to this kind of "faking good" test-taking attitude (Greene, 1980). The agency providing disability benefits was interested in whether Dorothy was "faking bad," that is, whether she was as disturbed as she claimed to be.

If the MMPI profile looks valid, statistical procedures can be used to generate a personality profile. Generally, diagnostic decisions are based on the two highest clinical scale scores, the *high-point pairs*. The test evaluator makes a clinical judgment by comparing the subject's profile to that of a reference group with a similar profile. Figure 4-1 presents Dorothy's MMPI profile.

Clinical Analysis Questionnaire (CAQ)
A self-report test of normal and abnormal personality.

The **Clinical Analysis Questionnaire (CAQ)** is a 272-item self-report inventory used to measure normal and pathological personality factors (Krug, 1980). The CAQ consists of 16 scales from psychologist Raymond Cattell's 16PF test, which measures 16 normal personality traits, and 12 "pathological" scales derived from the MMPI and other test instruments. Thus, the CAQ is an attempt to measure normal and abnormal personality factors in a single test. Table 4-2

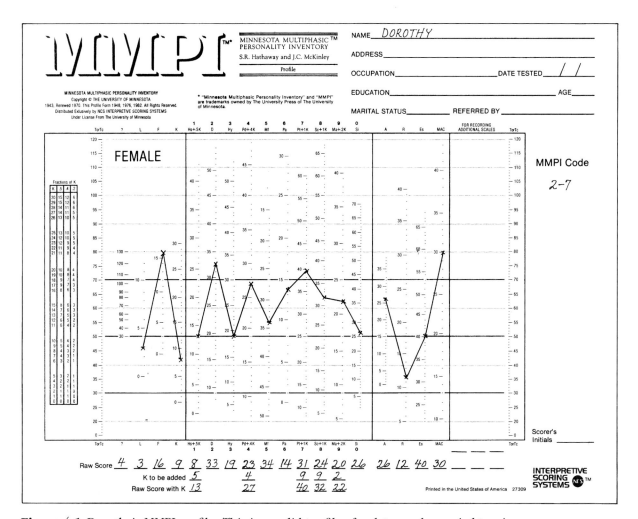

Figure 4-1 Dorothy's MMPI profile. *This is a valid profile of a depressed, worried person.*

Source: Minnesota Multiphasic Personality Inventory. Copyright © by the Regents of the University of Minnesota. 1942, 1943 (renewed 1970). This form 1948, 1976, 1982. Reprinted by permission of the University of Minnesota Press.

TABLE 4-2 ▦ OTHER SELF-REPORT INVENTORIES

Inventory	Author(s)	Description
IPAT Anxiety Scale Question (ASQ)	Cattell & Scheier (1963)	Trait anxiety
Million Clinical Multiaxial Inventory (MCMI)	Millon (1977)	Personality styles, pathological personality syndromes
State-Trait Anxiety Inventory (STAI)	Spielberger (1983)	Anxiety and anger as temporary emotional states or stable personality traits
State-Trait Anger Scale (STAS)	Spielberger (1988)	
Combined-STAXI	Spielberger et al. (1983)	
Beck Depression Inventory (BDI)	Beck (1978)	Depression
IPAT Depression Scale	Krug & Laughlin (1976)	Depression
Eysenck Personality Questionnaire (EPQ)	Eysenck & Eysenck (1969)	Introversion, extroversion, neuroticism, psychoticism

describes other self-report measures (Cattell, 1973; Cattell, Eber, & Tatsuoka, 1970; Cattell & Johnson, 1986).

Evaluation of Self-Report Inventories. Despite their popularity in clinical evaluation, self-report inventories are open to criticism. Beyond the usual concerns about standardization, self-report inventories are limited by the special problem of deception. Self-report data is more susceptible to faking because of the subject's freedom in answering questions. A person's test-taking attitudes ("set") can influence how he or she answers questions. People whose test-taking set puts a high value on social desirability are likely to provide answers that place them in the best light, so they may "fake good." Some critics also argue that self-reporting is not likely to tap hidden or unconscious aspects of functioning. Finally, there is the problem of motivation. It is difficult to ensure that patients consider the test important enough to cooperate and answer openly.

Because of its widespread use, the MMPI has been the focus of much criticism. One of the major complaints about the original version was that the sample on which the test was standardized, 1500 Minneapolis adults, does not represent the population at large. There have been complaints of poor reliability and low validity on some scales and high overlap between clinical scales, and there have been questions about the MMPI's relevance to other cultures and subcultures. This is particularly important in light of the cultural diversity among those taking the test. (Non-English versions are available.)

The MMPI-2 was designed to address some of these complaints, especially with regard to standardization. However, informal complaints are already coming in on several grounds. First, it is argued that the MMPI-2 is too new and its database too small to be accepted uncritically. Second, some of the questions have changed, so the same person could take the MMPI and the MMPI-2 and get a different profile, thereby creating diagnostic confusion.

projective tests Tests in which the subject projects psychological and emotional problems onto an ambiguous stimulus.

Projective Tests. In **projective tests**, the subject is asked to interpret ambiguous stimuli. According to the *projective hypothesis*, people "project" attitudes, feelings, and impulses into their interpretation of ambiguous stimuli. In a clinical situation, it is presumed that the test taker will project psychological and emotional problems onto the stimuli. Clinicians who subscribe to the projective hypothesis claim that data from projective tests are more likely to reveal unconscious processes and are less susceptible to faking (Schuerger, 1986). There are five types of projective testing techniques:

1. *Word association tests* present stimulus words, and the subject responds by saying the first word that comes to mind. The clinician makes evaluations on the basis of the subject's reaction time and how unusual the responses are compared to those of "normal" people.
2. *Sentence completion tests* present the first words of a sentence that the subject is asked to complete (for example, "My father . . ." or "I am concerned about . . .").
3. *Drawing tests* require the subject to draw a person; a family; or several figures, such as a house, a tree, and a person. Drawings are analyzed for their clinically significant features, including the relative sizes of the figures. For example, a large size discrepancy between male and female figures may reflect the relative importance the subject assigns to men and women. The

Figure 4-2 Samples of a drawing test. *Left: Drawing by an 8-year-old girl one month after parents' separation. Body parts are mobile, people are clothed, and there is sex-role differentiation. Right: Drawing by the same girl during the second year of parents' separation. Figures are less articulated and are flattened; movement has ceased; and father is positioned in lower-right-hand corner of picture, away from other family members.*

Source: From "The Difficult Divorce" by M. B. Isaacs and B. Montalvo, 1989, November/December, *Family Therapy Networker*, p. 49.

Drives, needs, and other psychological characteristics can be inferred from a client's responses to projective tests like the Thematic Apperception Test (TAT) pictured here.

Thematic Apperception Test (TAT) A projective picture story test.

Rorschach test An inkblot projective test.

position of the figures on the page, erasures, the positions of the limbs, the style of clothing, and details of body parts can also be revealing. Figure 4-2 presents one example of a drawing test.

4. *Picture story tests* have the subject view a picture and then tell a story about it. The most famous is the **Thematic Apperception Test (TAT)**, which consists of 20 pictures. The test taker is asked to tell complete, detailed stories about each of them. The examiner then interprets the responses in terms of psychological drives and needs, such as achievement, aggression, dominance, and autonomy (H. A. Murray, 1943).

5. *Inkblot techniques* require subjects to find some meaning in "meaningless" inkblots. The **Rorschach test**, first described by psychiatrist Hermann Rorschach in 1921, is the most famous inkblot test (Rorschach, 1942). The Rorschach consists of ten cards with a symmetrical inkblot on each. Five are in shades of gray and five are colored. Subjects view the cards and are asked what the blot looks like or what it reminds them of. The interviewer asks the subject how he or she arrived at that response and which part of the blot was most stimulating. Interpretive strategies, some computerized, have been devised for this test. Despite criticisms of the Rorschach's reliability and validity, it is probably the most widely used projective technique. Figure 4-3 shows the sort of inkblot that appears on a Rorschach card.

Evaluation of Projective Tests. Projective tests generally do not meet statistical criteria for standardization, reliability, and validity, and thus their interpretation may be too subjective. Furthermore, the projective hypothesis remains in dispute. Much evidence exists to show that a person's test responses are determined by factors other than "projections"—for example, recent experiences.

Figure 4-3 Sample inkblot. *This is an example of the kind of inkblot used to evoke responses in the Rorschach test.*

intelligence testing Tests of cognitive ability.

Stanford-Binet Intelligence Scale A test of cognitive ability.

Wechsler (*Wex*-ler) *Adult Intelligence Scale* Tests of cognitive ability.

Intelligence Testing. Intellectual ability is a fundamental aspect of mental functioning, and its measurement is a useful part of an overall clinical assessment. **Intelligence testing** provides information regarding a patient's cognitive ability, motivation, frustration tolerance, and concentration. The **Stanford-Binet Intelligence Scale** is one of the more widely used tests of cognitive ability for subjects from age 2 through adulthood. The recently revised scale consists of 15 subtests; it assesses verbal meaning, short-term memory, quantitative reasoning, and abstract visual reasoning (Delaney & Hopkins, 1987).

Another widely used individually administered intelligence test for adults is the **Wechsler Adult Intelligence Scale** (Revised Edition) (WAIS-R), which consists of verbal and nonverbal subtests of cognitive ability (Wechsler, 1981). The WAIS-R, developed by psychologist David Wechsler, measures intelligence as a deviation score. This means that a subject's test scores are compared to scores of other people from the same age group. Although this method of calculating intelligence was novel when it was first incorporated into the WAIS scales, it is the standard today.

The WAIS-R consists of 11 subtests, 6 verbal and 5 performance (nonverbal). Verbal and performance scores are determined, then combined to yield a full-scale intelligence score (Anastasi, 1988; Wechsler, 1981). Table 4-3 summarizes the WAIS-R subtests. Versions of the Wechsler scales are also available for children from ages 4 through 16.

TABLE 4-3 ▦ **DESCRIPTION OF WAIS-R SUBTESTS**

Scale Name	Ability Tested
VERBAL SCALES	
Information	General factual knowledge
Digit Span	Short-term memory for numbers
Vocabulary	Word knowledge
Arithmetic	Mental calculation
Comprehension	Understanding of sayings and situations
Similarities	Concept formation
PERFORMANCE SCALES	
Picture Completion	Perception of missing pieces
Picture Arrangement	Nonverbal reasoning
Block Design	Visual analysis and synthesis
Object Assembly	Ability to assemble a puzzle
Digit Symbol	Memory for symbols

Evaluation of Intelligence Testing. The use of intelligence tests is controversial. Critics argue that they discriminate against members of cultural minorities and do not consider real-world manifestations of intelligence. Although culture-fair intelligence tests have been constructed, they are used infrequently. Despite their limitations, intelligence tests are useful in measuring cognitive and perceptual ability and disability. They can be used not only to fill out the clinical picture of an individual seeking therapy but also to screen for brain damage, to determine levels of mental retardation, and to help in educational evaluations (Anastasi, 1988; Frederikson, 1986; Graham & Lilly, 1984).

Neuropsychological Testing. The assessment of abnormality relies primarily on an interview, perhaps with personality testing as well. In some cases, psychological problems may be caused by, or may simply coexist with, neurological disease. When there is suspicion of neurological disease, or when disease is already known, neuropsychological testing is necessary.

neuropsychological testing Tests designed to detect and measure brain damage and cognitive disability.

Neuropsychological testing is designed to detect and measure brain damage and cognitive disability. A collection of tests is known as a test battery. When a particular psychological function is of interest, individual psychological tests may be selected instead (Berg, Franzen, & Wedding, 1987). One of the most widely used test batteries is the *Halstead-Reitan Neuropsychological Test Battery* (Reitan & Wolfson, 1985). It consists of an MMPI; a WAIS-R; and tests that measure motor speed, attention, concentration, visual scanning, and language processing. The *Luria-Nebraska Neuropsychological Battery* consists of 269 items that measure motor, visual, and tactile functions. It also measures language ability, reading, arithmetic, and writing (Golden, Purisch, & Hammeke, 1985). The *Bender Visual Motor Gestalt Test* consists of nine cards, each displaying a design that the subject is instructed to copy. The Bender, as it is commonly called, is used primarily for the purpose of screening for brain damage (Bender, 1938).

CLOSE-UP
Predicting Dangerousness

On January 17, 1975, Joseph Kallinger and his son Michael were arrested for murder. They had broken into five suburban homes, and during the last entry they had held eight people hostage while Joe brutally murdered a woman with a knife. In his severe mental illness, Joe believed he could reach "godhood" by slaughtering all the people on earth through mutilation of their sexual organs. Could Kallinger's dangerousness have been predicted?

In 1972, Kallinger, a Philadelphia shoe-maker, tortured two of his children because they had "betrayed" him. He stripped his daughter and repeatedly pressed a heated spatula between her legs. Then he beat his son with the handle of a hammer. His children reported him to the police, and Kallinger was apprehended. While in custody, he was evaluated by two psychiatrists and tested by a psychologist using projective tests. They determined that he was psychotic. Kallinger was then sent to a prison forensic unit where he was evaluated more extensively. He was evaluated as disturbed but not psychotic, and as not likely to be a threat to people outside his family. Remarkably, the chief psychiatrist recommended that if Kallinger were released, he should enter

family therapy. On this basis, the judge gave Kallinger a suspended sentence with four years' psychiatric probation. How could the magnitude of his dangerousness have escaped detection?

Although the Kallinger case is a notorious one, there are many other examples of people who are judged not to be dangerous but who then commit gruesome crimes. Clearly, violence is not easy to predict. Predictability improves measurably if a person has a history of violent behavior. It is also easier to predict violence when a person is threatening and is acting out the threat. In other cases, psychologists have to make predictions on the basis of imperfect tests that mainly provide information about personality functioning. Information about environmental factors that could trigger violent behavior is often not accessible to the clinician, and therefore one big piece of the puzzle is missing. In retrospect, Kallinger's dangerousness should have been obvious; but then, in retrospect, we have the benefit of complete information. The case of the shoemaker serves to demonstrate that clinical assessment can be generally useful, but it is not a foolproof science (Schreiber, 1984).

Evaluation of Neuropsychological Testing. It is well-known that disease of the nervous system can cause psychiatric symptoms such as depression, apathy, hallucinations, and personality changes. Neuropsychological testing may help detect, specify, and localize the problem. When the existence of brain damage is already established, testing can help determine the type and degree of cognitive, emotional, or behavioral disability and can thereby aid in making decisions about rehabilitation (Anastasi, 1988).

Behavioral Assessment

behavioral assessment
Analysis and classification of behavior.

Behavioral assessment is the analysis and classification of behavior. It has always been closely tied to principles of behaviorism and behavior therapy. Traditional behavioral assessment was confined to an isolated problem behavior that could readily be observed and measured and did not deal with thoughts and feelings. However, as principles of behaviorism and behavior therapy have evolved, so has behavioral assessment.

Behavioral Analysis. The simplest behavioral analysis focuses on a single behavior rather than clusters of behaviors. The most common model of behavioral analysis is the **A-B-C model** (for *a*ntecedents, *b*ehavior, and *c*onsequences). An *antecedent* is a stimulus that appears immediately prior to the *behavior* and contributes to its appearance. For example, an automobile accident may act as an antecedent to the avoidance of auto travel. *Consequences* refer to the results of performing a particular behavior. In Dorothy's case, anxiety was often the consequence of contact with her mother.

Behavior Classification. Behavioral assessment also involves classification of behavior. Maladaptive behaviors may be classified in a number of ways. One way is to view behaviors as either excessive or deficient. A child who frequently cries at school displays a *behavior excess*; an adult who finds it difficult to ask for a date displays a *behavior deficit*. Other problem behaviors are a matter of poorly learned *discriminations*, so that sometimes a perfectly normal behavior is elicited in the wrong situation. Speaking in a normal tone of voice may be fine in conversation, but it is inappropriate in a library where others are trying to study (Goldfried & Davison, 1976).

Classification also focuses on how behavior is controlled by the consequences of its stimulus. The law of effect states that behaviors followed by satisfying effects tend to be repeated, whereas behaviors followed by unsatisfying effects tend not to be repeated (see Chapter 3). In the behavioral framework, psychological problems are assumed to be caused and maintained by inadequate or inappropriate *reinforcement systems*. Some people do not respond to consequences that are usually reinforcing, such as praise or affection; these reinforcements no longer control behavior. Other people respond to reinforcing stimuli that are also dangerous or socially unacceptable, such as using drugs or having extramarital sex (Goldfried & Davison, 1976).

Behavioral assessment has evolved to include consideration of cognitive elements, that is, unobservable mental activity. Many cognitive-behaviorists consider thoughts and feelings acceptable targets for inquiry, as long as they can be measured in some way. For example, a depressed client may be asked to record negative thoughts experienced each day (Barrios, 1988).

Behavioral assessment has also expanded beyond the single behavior to the level of the syndrome, that is, a cluster of behaviors. For example, many people like Dorothy feel fatigued, lack interest in usual activities, have trouble sleeping, and show a loss of appetite. These symptoms cluster together and help define clinical depression. By evaluating the syndrome rather than each separate behavior, assessment promises more accurate diagnosis and greater ability to predict behavior, and it may lead to more effective treatment (Barrios, 1988; Foster, Bell-Dolan, & Barge, 1988).

Methods of Behavioral Assessment. Methods of behavioral assessment include interviewing, observation, role playing, use of checklists, and self-monitoring. The behavioral interview follows the general interviewing strategies discussed earlier in this chapter. The difference here is the greater emphasis on

---

A-B-C model A method of behavior analysis.

Direct observation of behavior is the foundation of behavioral assessment.

direct observation
Observation and coding of behavior.

objective measurements of behavior. Direct observation of behavior has always been the backbone of behavioral assessment. **Direct observation** is a behavioral assessment strategy in which trained observers code and classify behavior. The observers work either in a natural environment, such as a classroom or home, or in simulated situations. Despite the valid criticism that subjects' behavior may be influenced by the presence of the observer, direct observation methods remain an important source of clinical assessment data.

In using direct observation there is great emphasis on developing a system to classify behavior. The coding system must identify target behaviors and must define ways for the coder to detect the occurrence of the behavior, then specify the frequency and duration of its occurrence. For example, if the problem behavior is lip biting, the observer first clearly defines the criteria that constitute lip biting. Then the observer determines how often lip biting occurred per time period, say 15 minutes. The observer could also look at how long a particular lip-biting episode lasted.

Family Interaction Coding System (FICS)
A behavior coding system.

Psychologist Gerald Patterson and his colleagues have used an excellent formal behavioral coding system in their work. Dissatisfied with parents' verbal reports about their children's problems and the effects of treatment, Patterson developed a system for coding family interactions by having trained observers enter classrooms and homes to evaluate aggressive children in a natural environment. His **Family Interaction Coding System (FICS)** is a 29-category system used to evaluate the effectiveness of treatment programs (Patterson, 1982). The coded categories include "Approval," "Crying," "Commands," "Destructiveness," "Negativism," "Play," "Talk," "Tease," "Whine," and "Compliance." A "physical negative," for example, might be a situation in which a mother grabs a child's arm and shoves her. A "command" might be a statement like "Johnny, it's time to pick up your toys." (Patterson, Reid, & Maerov, 1978).

PROFILE
David Wechsler
(1896–1981)

David Wechsler is one of the foremost names in the study of mental measurement. The youngest of seven children, Wechsler was born in Romania on January 12, 1896. When he was 6 years old, his family immigrated to New York City, where he received his bachelor's degree at the City College of New York in 1916 and his Ph.D. from Columbia University in 1925.

Preparing for his induction into the army in World War I, Wechsler helped score performance tests for thousands of army recruits. After he was inducted, he tested adults who needed individual assessment of their aptitudes and abilities. He noticed that the army's tests were inaccurate in assessing the abilities of people from diverse backgrounds. Many inductees were well-adjusted in their everyday lives but repeatedly failed standardized intelligence tests, so Wechsler concluded that the commonly accepted definitions of intelligence were limited.

In 1922, Wechsler accepted a job with a testing organization, the Psychological Corporation. One day, a reporter asked him whether there was a difference in intelligence between men and women. Wechsler tried to answer this question by testing dancers from the then-famous Ziegfeld Follies. Since many of the show girls were college educated, it came as no surprise that their scores were equal to or better than those of Columbia University freshmen. At about the same time, Wechsler devised tests for the selection of taxicab drivers in Pittsburgh.

Wechsler became chief psychologist at Bellevue Psychiatric Hospital in New York in 1932 and was appointed to the faculty at the New York University College of Medicine in 1933. During this time, he standardized his famous Wechsler Scales and his concept of measuring intelligence as a deviation score. Dissatisfied with the Stanford-Binet, he brought out the *Bellevue-Wechsler Scale* in 1939. This test battery was the forerunner of the *WAIS-R* and comparable tests for preschoolers and children. These tests are the most widely used individual tests of mental ability today.

David Wechsler's illustrious career was punctuated with numerous awards and honors including two of the American Psychological Association's awards: Distinguished Contribution to Clinical Psychology (1960) and Distinguished Professional Contribution (1973) (Matarazzo, 1981; Edwards, 1974).

Other Behavioral Assessment Methods. In *role playing*, the therapist and the patient enact a situation that illustrates the problem. The session is videotaped and reviewed according to prescribed assessment rules. *Behavior checklists* are easy to use; the subject simply checks off which behaviors apply. For example, a father may be asked to check and rate behaviors that apply to his child in the last month. The client may also be trained to observe his or her own behavior. This technique, known as *self-monitoring*, is commonly used with target behaviors that are easy to record, such as the number of cigarettes smoked or the number of calories or drinks consumed.

Neurophysiological Assessment

neurophysiological assessment Techniques designed to assess abnormalities of the nervous system.

Neurophysiological assessment studies structural and functional abnormalities of the nervous system. Evaluation of nervous system functioning has broadened our understanding of mind and behavior and of abnormality in particular. For some conditions, such as schizophrenia, mood disorders, anxiety disorders, and addictive disorders, it is now possible to correlate alterations in physiological functioning with specific psychological disturbances (MacKinnon & Yudofsky, 1986).

electrophysiological recording Testing that monitors activity of the ANS.

Electrophysiological Recording. **Electrophysiological recording** procedures are commonly used to measure the activity of the brain and autonomic nervous system, the part of our peripheral nervous system that controls physiological functions and "primitive" emotions. Electrophysiological recordings most often include measures of brain arousal, heart rate, blood pressure, muscle tension, and sweat gland activity. Table 4-4 presents some of these techniques and their clinical uses.

brain imaging Procedures that derive images of the brain.

Brain Imaging. Advances in technology have made it possible to study the living brain in remarkable detail. Sophisticated **brain imaging** procedures derive images of the structure and chemical characteristics of the brain. *Computerized axial tomography* (CT or CAT scan) is an X-ray technique used in detecting structural problems like lesions (cuts), hemorrhages, abscesses, and tumors. CT scans have also proved useful in discovering deterioration of cerebral tissue, which is sometimes found in the brains of schizophrenics (Lechtenberg, 1982; Andreasen, 1988). Figure 4-4 depicts a CT scan of a normal brain.

TABLE 4-4   TYPES OF ELECTROPHYSIOLOGICAL RECORDINGS

Physiological Measurement (and Device)	Response Measured
Electroencephalogram (EEG)	Brain wave activity
Electrocardiogram (ECG)	Electrical activity of the heart during contraction
Blood pressure (sphygmomanometer)	Pressure built up by resistance to blood flow in arteries
Skin temperature (thermometer)	Peripheral circulation
Electromyogram (EMG)	Electrical activity of muscle fiber contraction
Skin resistance (GSR, EDR)	Changes in sweat response

Magnetic resonance imaging (MRI) converts electromagnetic fields generated from brain activity into a picture of brain structure. MRI is considered to be superior to CT scans for imaging brain tissue. Although MRI has uncovered structural abnormalities in schizophrenia and autism, the technique is still in the basic research stages. It has little current value as a diagnostic tool in abnormal psychology (Andreasen, 1988; Garber, Weilberg, Buonanno, Manschreck, & New, 1988).

Positron emission tomography (PET) and regional cerebral blood flow (RCBF) techniques permit us to evaluate brain function. PET scans provide a false-color computer reconstruction of the brain, based on the way different regions utilize glucose. Thus, PET compares the metabolism of different brain regions and indirectly informs us about neurotransmitter activity. PET has already enhanced our knowledge of the chemical basis of some mental disorders, but it is prohibitively expensive and is primarily an experimental tool in psychiatry (Andreasen, 1988; Lechtenberg, 1982).

Regional cerebral blood flow (RCBF) techniques involve the tracking of

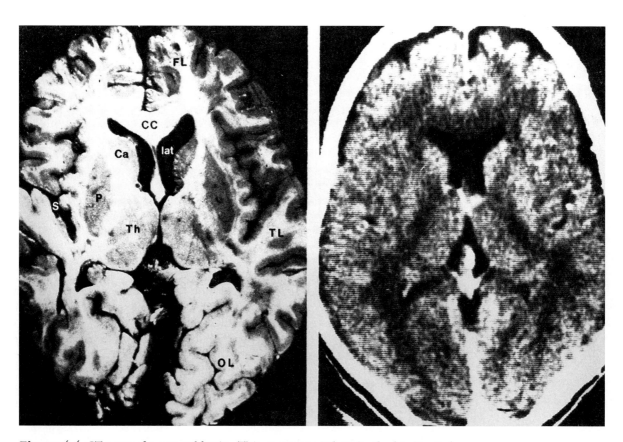

Figure 4-4 CT scan of a normal brain. *This scan was taken in the horizontal plane, which divides the brain into top and bottom sections.*

Source: From *The Psychiatrist's Guide to Diseases of the Nervous System* by R. L. Lechtenberg, 1982, New York: Wiley.

inhaled radioactive tracers throughout the brain's circulatory system. By comparing blood flow in different groups of subjects, scientists can derive RCBF measures of abnormality for many psychiatric disorders (Andreasen, 1988; Lechtenberg, 1982).

Evaluation of Neurophysiological Assessment. Presently, brain imaging techniques are research tools that may potentially expand our understanding of the neurological bases of mental disorders. However, their application in clinical practice is limited. When they are used, they are usually ordered to rule out other forms of brain disease and are unlikely to affect treatment options (MacKinnon & Yudofsky, 1986).

4-2   PSYCHIATRIC DIAGNOSIS

Observation and classification are basic to any science. Without a formal classification system, knowledge could not advance. By classifying mental disorders on the basis of mental activity and behaviors, clinicians can collect and organize information necessary to make a diagnosis. Moreover, the use of diagnoses helps in the prediction of future events and in the selection of the most effective treatments (Barlow, 1991).

The DSM-III-R

DSM-III-R A popular diagnostic system.

The most popular diagnostic system currently in use in America and internationally is the **DSM-III-R** (the Diagnostic and Statistical Manual of Mental Disorders, Third Edition, Revised) (American Psychiatric Association, 1987). The DSM-III-R defines a mental disorder as

> a clinically significant behavioral or psychological syndrome that occurs in a person and is associated with present distress (a painful symptom) or disability (impairment in one or more areas of functioning) or with a significantly increased risk of suffering, death, pain, disability, or an important loss of freedom. (American Psychiatric Association, 1987)

The DSM-III-R, the diagnostic foundation for this textbook, is a descriptive system that categorizes the prominent clinical features of mental disorders. Since the causes and treatments for mental disorders are either unknown or controversial, the DSM-III-R does not include such information as part of the diagnostic criteria. Instead, categories of disorders are determined by "expert group consensus" more than from facts derived from clinical research.

The DSM-III-R uses a multiaxial system that provides as much information as possible, thereby aiding in treatment planning. Under this system, a mental disorder is evaluated on five axes, or dimensions:

Axis I
• *Clinical Syndromes.* This category includes substance use disorders, schizophrenias, and anxiety disorders.

- *V Codes.* These conditions are not attributable to a disorder—for example, a marital problem, an occupational problem, an academic problem, or a "phase of life" problem.

Axis II
- *Developmental Disorders.* These include mental retardation and autism.
- *Personality Disorders.* These include antisocial, borderline, and paranoid disorders.

Axis III
- *Physical Disorders and Conditions.* These may be physical illnesses that account for some of the psychological symptoms. The illness may simply be worth noting even if there is no clear association with psychological symptoms.

Axis IV
- *Severity of Psychosocial Stressors.* This axis permits the clinician to describe the type and severity of contributing factors, including legal, financial, and family factors; physical illness; or injury. Stressors are rated on a 6-point scale, with 1 indicating no stress and 6 indicating catastrophic stress, such as the death of a child or suicide of a spouse.

Axis V
- *Global Assessment of Functioning Scale* (GAF). This scale permits the clinician to rate current and past-year functioning in psychological, occupational, and social areas. The GAF scale ranges from 1 to 90, with lower scores indicative of poorer functioning. For example, a GAF in the range 1 to 10 would describe a person who might be suicidal or homicidal or unable to manage simple hygiene.

The case of Dorothy provides a good illustration of how the DSM multiaxial system is applied. Diagnostic numerical codes have been omitted for simplicity.

- *Axis I*: Major depression, recurrent.
- *Axis II*: Borderline personality disorder.
- *Axis III*: Essential hypertension.
- *Axis IV*: Psychosocial stressors: financial problems from husband's loss of job; her inability to work; mounting credit card debt; and difficulties separating from mother. Severity: 4 (mix of acute and enduring circumstances).
- *Axis V*: Current GAF: 45. Highest GAF in past year: 60.

Toward the DSM-IV

DSM-IV The diagnostic system that will succeed the DSM-III-R.

In 1988, the American Psychiatric Association appointed a task force to start work on the **DSM-IV**, scheduled to be published in late 1993. The publication of the DSM-IV is intended to coincide with publication of the World Health Organization's International Classification of Diseases (ICD-10) and to provide correspondence between the two diagnostic systems.

Proponents of the DSM-IV argue that it will be a more scientifically based classification system than the DSM-III-R. Diagnoses will be based on comprehensive reviews of the scientific literature, analysis of accumulated and unpublished data, and field trials rather than on group consensus alone. *Field trials* apply tentative diagnostic criteria to actual patients in clinical practice. In this way, the reliability and validity of diagnostic criteria can be determined and refined as needed. Diagnostic criteria will be simplified in the DSM-IV, making it more "user-friendly." Many diagnostic categories will be refined and disorder subtypes added (Frances, Pincus, Widiger, Davis, & First, 1990; Frances, Widiger, & Pincus, 1989; Widiger, Frances, Pincus, Davis, & First, 1991).

Opposition to the DSM-IV was registered even before its publication. Critics complain that a new diagnostic system might confuse researchers and clinicians and might give the idea that diagnoses come and go, depending on the whims of psychiatry. Others say that changes are probably trivial and unnecessary. Response to these complaints awaits the final publication of the DSM-IV (Frances et al., 1989; Spitzer, 1991). The supposed advantage of DSM-IV over its predecessors is its foundation in scientific research. However, psychiatrist Robert Spitzer, who has been prominent in the development of the DSM system, believes that final decisions will ultimately be based primarily on expert group consensus.

For more on the DSM-IV, see the Appendix.

Evaluation of Psychiatric Diagnosis. The idea of diagnosing people's problems is controversial. From a purely scientific perspective, critics have questioned the reliability and validity of a diagnostic system based more on expert consensus than on psychological measurement theory. From a humane standpoint, critics argue that diagnoses label people, not conditions. They consider the use of diagnosis to be dehumanizing because it applies a stigma that the person may carry for life and it may do nothing to help relieve the person's distress.

Those who defend the use of diagnosis say that diagnoses are formulated to label conditions, not people, and that they are useful in clinical research as well as practice. If we are to find effective therapies, we must be certain that we are evaluating the same type of problem from study to study. The use of strict diagnostic criteria helps ensure this. The use of diagnoses also helps clinicians make better predictions about how people will behave in future situations. We accomplish this by studying large numbers of people who have been diagnosed to have the same disorder. Although resolution of these issues is awaited, psychiatric diagnosis remains influential in the field of abnormal psychology.

SUMMARY

4-1 Clinical assessment is a systematic process of gathering information about people. This information is used to help us understand the nature of mental disorders, in diagnosis, in selecting treatments, and in research applications. Assessment methods include structured and unstructured interviews, in which clinical information is collected in question-and-answer style. Psychological testing is often used to complement interview data or to provide information not available from the interview. Four types of psychological tests are used: self-report inventories, projective techniques, intelligence tests, and neuropsychological tests. Behavior analysis involves the classification of behavior and the identification and measurement of antecedent stimuli and consequences. Behavior assessment methods include interviewing, direct observation, role playing, self-monitoring, and coding systems. Physiological evaluation helps elucidate relationships between the brain and behavior. Such evaluations include measures of brain electrical activity and arousal of the autonomic nervous system. Brain imaging techniques such as PET scans, CT scans, MRI, and cerebral blood flow measures allow researchers and clinicians to look inside the living brain for signs of chemical or structural abnormality.

4-2 Classification is the cornerstone of science. Diagnosis in abnormal psychology must take thoughts, feelings, and behaviors into account. The use of a diagnostic system allows scientists to communicate more precisely in their efforts to learn more about mental disorders. The most popular psychiatric diagnostic system is the DSM-III-R. It is a descriptive, multiaxial system designed to classify disorders according to symptoms that cluster together. Work is currently under way for a DSM-IV to be published in 1993. The expected advantage of the DSM-IV over previous DSM systems is that it relies strictly on scientific evidence, rather than "expert group consensus," in the formation of diagnostic categories. Critics contend that the use of diagnostic systems is of questionable reliability and validity and that labeling patients is stigmatizing and dehumanizing.

TERMS TO REMEMBER

A-B-C model (p. 99)
behavioral assessment (p. 98)
brain imaging (p. 102)
Clinical Analysis Questionnaire (p. 92)
direct observation (p. 100)
DSM-III-R (p. 104)
DSM-IV (p. 105)
electrophysiological recording (p. 102)
Family Interaction Coding System (p. 100)
intelligence testing (p. 96)
interview (p. 86)

Minnesota Multiphasic Personality Inventory (p. 91)
neurophysiological assessment (p. 102)
neuropsychological testing (p. 97)
normative group (p. 90)
projective tests (p. 94)
reliability (p. 90)
Rorschach test (p. 95)
self-report inventories (p. 91)
standardization (p. 90)
Stanford-Binet Intelligence Scale (p. 96)
structured interview schedules (p. 89)

Thematic Apperception Test (p. 45)
unstructured interview (p. 86)
validity (p. 90)

Wechsler Adult Intelligence Scale
(p. 96)

SUGGESTED READINGS

Anastasi, A. (1988). *Psychological testing* (6th ed.). New York: Macmillan.

Andreasen, N. C. (1988). Brain imaging: Applications in psychiatry. *Science, 239,* 1381–1388.

MacKinnon, R. A., & Yudofsky, S. C. (1986). *The psychiatric evaluation in clinical practice.* Philadelphia: Lippincott.

Schreiber, F. R. (1984). *The shoemaker: Anatomy of a psychotic.* New York: Signet.

LEGAL AND ETHICAL ISSUES:
THE PSYCHOLOGIST'S ROLE IN LEGAL CASES

Over the past 25 years, more people have become embroiled in cases concerning child custody, delinquency, personal injury, and competency to stand trial. Many psychologists have evaluated clients involved in such legal disputes. Psychological assessment data can contribute to the disposition of a case and determine the welfare of a child, a defendant's innocence or guilt, or the amount of money awarded to a plaintiff. The following case illustrates a psychologist's role in a child custody dispute and considers the legal and ethical implications for psychologists.

An attorney requested that a psychologist evaluate three children while they were on a weekend visit at their father's home, because the father was suing for custody. During an interview, the father told the psychologist that the children were being sexually abused and exposed to drugs by the mother's live-in boyfriend. The psychologist reported this information to the state's department of child protective services, as required by law. Both parents were evaluated with interviews and MMPIs, and the children were assessed with interviews and observations of their play with each parent. The mother told the psychologist that no sexual abuse took place and that the husband was merely fabricating the story. The mother's boyfriend was not evaluated. The psy-

chologist sent a report based on the available evidence to both parents' attorneys, recommending that the mother retain custody. In light of this information, the court ruled in the mother's favor. The father then filed a complaint with the state psychological association's ethics committee.

After review, the ethics committee ruled that the psychologist had acted ethically in most, but not all, areas. First, the psychologist had no written request to report recommendations about which parent should have custody. Second, there was no *written* evidence that the psychologist had contacted the department of child protective services as required by law. Third, the ethics committee ruled that the assessment techniques used did not provide sufficient information to enable the psychologist to draw conclusions about which parent should have custody. The mother's boyfriend, accused of abuse, should have been evaluated.

This case shows that psychologists bear great responsibility in their work. Although they are not expected to be attorneys, they must be aware of and comply with ever-changing mental health laws through continuing education (Board of Professional Affairs, Committee on Professional Standards, 1988; American Psychological Association, 1990).

Chapter FIVE

Anxiety, Somatoform, and Dissociative Disorders

OBJECTIVES

1. Describe the main clinical features of anxiety disorders.
2. Differentiate among generalized anxiety disorder, panic disorders, phobia disorders, obsessive-compulsive disorder, and posttraumatic stress disorder.
3. Discuss the evidence for a hereditary basis for anxiety disorders.
4. Describe biochemical hypotheses and biological treatments for anxiety disorders.
5. Detail the major psychological explanations for anxiety disorders and discuss their corresponding psychological treatments.
6. Describe the somatoform disorders.
7. Outline the causes and treatments for somatoform disorders.
8. Differentiate the types of dissociative disorders.
9. Describe the causes of and treatments for dissociative disorders.

*K*aren was an attractive 26-year-old woman who came to the clinic because she was afraid to drive more than two or three miles from home. She was concerned that if she was driving alone she would become ill and nobody would be there to help her. If she had to travel, she tried to get a friend or her mother to go with her. On several occasions, even while accompanied, she had become nauseated and faint and felt that she could not swallow. She had insisted that the driver pull the car over until she felt better. Karen reported being nervous much of the time for no apparent reason, even when she was not traveling. During her nervous attacks, she trembled, her breathing was labored, and she felt that something bad was going to happen. Because of her fears, she had found an office job within walking distance of home, and she repeatedly turned down social engagements.

In her early twenties Karen had begun dating a young man and they had considered marriage. One Sunday afternoon they drove to visit her relatives upstate. When they arrived, and without apparent warning, her boyfriend informed her that the relationship was over and that he was no longer interested in her. Shortly thereafter, Karen's nervous attacks intensified, especially when she was traveling. Karen's problems illustrate many of the features of anxiety disorders we will explore in this chapter.

The anxiety, somatoform, and dissociative disorders were formerly classified together as neuroses. The term *neurosis* was first used in the eighteenth century to denote abnormal feelings and behaviors resulting from neurological problems. The belief in a physical basis for neurosis persisted into the twentieth century, but with the rise of Freudian theory, the causes were no longer viewed as neurological. Freud applied the term *psychoneurosis* to mental disorders based on repressed childhood conflicts. Freud used *neurosis* to describe a mental condition as well as to suggest a cause.

Since Freud's original conception, our understanding of neuroses has expanded, fueling controversy over the role of intrapsychic conflict. The controversy led to a reclassification of **neuroses** in the DSM-III as a purely descriptive term for a group of distressing symptoms that the person recognizes as unacceptable (ego-alien) (American Psychiatric Association, 1980). In the DSM-III-R, anxiety, somatoform, and dissociative disorders are placed in separate diagnostic categories. Today, the term *neurosis* is used merely as a synonym for *anxiety disorder* (American Psychiatric Association, 1987).

neuroses (new-*roh*-sees) Anxiety disorders.

5-1 ANXIETY DISORDERS

anxiety A negative emotional state comprised of fear, worry, tension, and physiological arousal.

Anxiety is a complex negative emotional state comprised of fear, apprehension, worry, tension, and physiological arousal. Table 5-1 lists many of the symptoms of anxiety.

Most of us experience anxiety at one time or another in our lives, but anxious people do not necessarily have an anxiety disorder. The diagnosis of an **anxiety disorder** requires the presence of symptoms of anxiety and a *persistent* set of thoughts, feelings, and behaviors that significantly affect normal functioning. There are two core features of anxiety disorders. First, there is an overestimation of danger or threat, and emotional reactions are out of proportion to the actual threat. To most people, the fears seem irrational. For example,

anxiety disorder Anxiety symptoms that affect normal functioning.

People with anxiety disorders experience symptoms of fear, worry, and apprehension. The woman in this photo is trying to overcome her fear of flying by sitting in an airplane.

TABLE 5-1   SYMPTOMS OF ANXIETY

Cognitive	Emotional	Behavioral	Physiological
• Apprehension	• Nervousness	• Restlessness	• Palpitations
• Foggy mind	• Tension	• Shakiness	• Tingling
• Self-consciousness	• Alarm	• Spasms	• Dizziness
• Preoccupation	• Uneasiness	• Avoidance	• Faintness
• Distractedness	• Worry	• Nail biting	• Lump in throat
• Confusion	• Terror	• Stuttering	• Dry mouth
• Memory problems	• Fearfulness		• Itching
• Hyperalertness			• Sweating
			• Vomiting
			• Headaches
			• Backaches
			• Flushed skin
			• Rashes

Source: Based on *Anxiety Disorders and Phobias* by A. T. Beck and G. Emery, 1985, New York: Basic Books.

a woman may sterilize all dishes out of fear that otherwise her children will get infected and die. Eating at a friend's house or a restaurant would elicit great anxiety because she cannot insist that the cups be sterile. Second, individuals with anxiety disorders avoid rather than cope with feared situations. For example, a person may alter the route to work to avoid crossing a bridge even though the change adds 20 minutes to the trip.

Types of Anxiety Disorders

Anxiety disorders are the most common mental disorders in the United States, affecting 4 to 8 percent of the general population each year. As much as 15 percent of us will have an anxiety disorder at some point in our lives. Anxiety disorders are more commonly diagnosed in women, in people with less education, and in younger rather than older adults (M. M. Weissman, 1985).

generalized anxiety disorder   Fear and chronic worry.

Generalized Anxiety Disorder. **Generalized anxiety disorder** (GAD) consists of persistent fear and chronic worry about two or more life circumstances, such as finances, friendships, or career. The fears are *free-floating—* that is, they are not associated with one specific stimulus. GAD is the most prevalent anxiety disorder, and it affects men and women with equal frequency. The typical age at onset of GAD is the twenties or thirties (American Psychiatric Association, 1987; M. M. Weissman, 1985).

Carla was a 23-year-old cashier at a local department store. She remembered she had always been nervous and recalled that even as a child she would awaken for school with nausea, vomiting, trembling, and a racing heart. She was afraid that something bad was going to happen even though logic told her that her fears were irrational. Carla graduated from college with honors, but she admitted she had almost had "nervous breakdowns" during her college years. She was so exhausted after graduating that she decided not to pursue a job in her chosen career. Instead, she took a cashier's job that would be far less demanding.

By the time Carla was 23, she had started taking sick days because of headaches, chronic fatigue, tension, and the persistent fear that something bad would happen. She grew increasingly tense in social situations and found herself repeatedly making excuses to avoid socializing. She spent much of her time worrying about her health and lack of money. At 25, she married a man who was apparently sympathetic to her plight, but the marriage soon became strained because of her worries. At that point she consulted a therapist to help her overcome her anxieties.

phobia disorders Intense fears of an object, activity, or situation.

Phobia Disorders. **Phobia disorders** are characterized by an intense fear of an object, activity, or situation and a powerful urge to avoid feared stimuli (American Psychiatric Association, 1987). However, not all fears necessarily indicate a phobia. What makes phobias different from ordinary fear reactions is that the fear is far out of proportion to the actual danger. Let's say you meet a tiger in the street and become terrified. This fear is not a phobia, since the presence of a tiger is a formidable, realistic danger. In fact, you would probably be abnormal if you were not terrified. However, if you refused tickets to the circus because of a fear that the tiger would maul you, then that would be phobic. Although the tiger could scale the barriers and tear you apart, the chances of that happening would be slim.

Phobias are classified according to the nature of the feared stimulus (American Psychiatric Association, 1987). **Simple phobias** are irrational fears of specific objects or situations, such as animals, germs, or injury. Many people have fear of dogs, snakes, insects, mice, heights, closed spaces, air travel, or seeing blood. Simple phobias can also generalize to other stimuli. For example, a serious bee sting in childhood may later generalize to a fear of any flying insect. Typically, impairment in other areas of life is minimal as long as the person can avoid the feared stimulus (American Psychiatric Association, 1987).

simple phobias   Fear of specific objects or situations.

Agoraphobic individuals fear being in situations from which they believe escape might be difficult. The woman shown here is trying to conquer her fear of escalators.

social phobia Fear of social evaluation.

Social phobia is a morbid fear of evaluation in social situations. Social phobics are reluctant to eat in public, use public restrooms, or speak publicly, for fear of embarrassment, shame, and humiliation. Most of all, the individual fears rejection and abandonment. Characteristically, the social phobic finds the anticipation of evaluation nearly as bad as the actual situation. Social phobia is apparently more common in males than females (American Psychiatric Association, 1987).

agoraphobia Fear of being in situations where escape may be difficult.

Agoraphobia is marked by an intense fear of being in places or situations in which the individual believes that escape is difficult. *Agoraphobia* derives from Greek words meaning "fear of the marketplace," but agoraphobic individuals actually fear leaving the safety of their homes unless accompanied by a friend or relative. They believe that if they leave home unattended, they will become disabled and nobody will be there to help. In severe cases, agoraphobics become dependent on the help of family and friends in meeting everyday responsibilities. Social activities become restricted, and relationships become strained. You may already recognize that Karen suffered from agoraphobia and also experienced generalized anxiety (Griest & Jefferson, 1988).

panic disorders Panic attacks, anticipatory anxiety, and avoidance.

Panic Disorders. **Panic disorders** (PD) are marked by recurrent panic attacks, anticipatory anxiety, and phobic avoidance. Panic attacks are experienced as intense fear that something terrible is about to happen—such as a heart attack, dying, going crazy, or losing control—along with strong physical symptoms, which come on unexpectedly and last for 10 to 30 minutes. Table 5-2 lists some of the symptoms experienced during a panic attack (American Psychiatric Association, 1987).

Someone who has experienced a panic attack is likely to anticipate having others. If the person associates the panic attacks with particular places, activities, or situations, he or she may develop agoraphobia. In fact, panic disorder includes agoraphobia in 80 percent of cases (American Psychiatric Association, 1987; Griest & Jefferson, 1988). Onset is most likely to occur during the stress of major life events, such as loss, separation, conflict, injury or illness, or facing

TABLE 5-2 ▬▬ **SYMPTOMS OF PANIC ATTACKS**

Physiological	
• Shortness of breath	• Flushes or chills
• Dizziness or faintness	• Numbness or tingling
• Rapid heart rate	• Chest pain
• Trembling or shaking	**Emotional**
• Sweating	• Depersonalization
• Choking feeling	• Fear of dying
• Nausea	• Fear of going crazy

TABLE 5-3 ▬▬ **COMMON OBSESSIONS AND COMPULSIONS**

Obsessions	Compulsions
• Germs	• Checking (locks, gas jets)
• Contamination	• Washing (hands, genitals)
• Illness	• Counting
• Doubting	• Touching
• Responsibility for someone's death or illness	

a new responsibility (Pollard, Pollard, & Corn, 1989). Adult agoraphobics often have a history of separation from significant others (Faravelli, Webb, Ambonetti, Fonnesu, & Sessarego, 1986; Hayward, Killen, & Taylor, 1989).

Karen suffered from panic disorder with agoraphobia, along with symptoms of generalized anxiety. Karen's history was filled with separations, starting when her father abandoned the family when she was a toddler. Throughout her childhood and teenage years, a succession of men dated and then left her mother, leaving Karen sensitive to rejection and abandonment.

obsessive-compulsive disorder Obsessive thoughts followed by an anxiety-reducing compulsive ritual.

obsessions Recurrent distressing thoughts.

compulsions Stereotyped anxiety-reducing rituals.

Obsessive-Compulsive Disorder. **Obsessive-compulsive disorder** (OCD) involves obsessions, compulsions, or both. **Obsessions** are recurrent, distressing, and intrusive ideas, images, or impulses that the person recognizes as senseless, repugnant, or unwanted. **Compulsions** are seemingly purposeful behaviors or rituals that are performed repeatedly, according to certain rules and in the same stereotyped way. Obsessions and compulsions interfere with a person's usual routine and impair occupational or social functioning (American Psychiatric Association, 1987). Table 5-3 lists some common obsessions and compulsions.

In a typical scenario, the person with OCD becomes extremely anxious because of the obsessive thought, then feels compelled to perform some behavior ritual to reduce the anxiety. The person may initially resist the compulsion but eventually gives in.

OCD usually lasts for decades. Its severity waxes and wanes; at its worst, it can become all-consuming and crippling. People with this problem tend to be quite secretive and are unable to admit their bizarre symptoms to others, and this secrecy probably hampers their chances of improvement. Not long ago it was believed that OCD was rare, affecting less than 1 percent of the general population. However, current estimates suggest a lifetime prevalence that approaches 3 percent (Karno, Golding, Sorenson, & Burman, 1988). There are apparently no gender differences.

Ralph was a 30-year-old man plagued by a long history of obsessions and compulsions. His current problem was an intrusive idea the he should kill people by running them over with his car. The urge was strong, and he became very nervous. He was terrified that he might already have acted on the impulse. His fear that he had actually murdered compelled him to drive repeatedly around the block to check for body parts or other signs of his crime. When he arrived at work he began to check his desk and the bathrooms for signs of his crime. He became so dominated by his obsessions and compulsions that he quit work and remained bedridden until seeking treatment three months later.

posttraumatic stress disorder Severe reactions to catastrophic events.

Posttraumatic Stress Disorder. Posttraumatic stress disorder (PTSD) involves a severe reaction to some catastrophic event beyond the realm of usual human experience (American Psychiatric Association, 1987). Events that can provoke PTSD include earthquakes, floods, avalanches, terrorist assaults, combat and concentration camp experiences, and rape. People suffering from PTSD experience phobic avoidance, difficulties in concentration, and guilt that they survived while others died or were more seriously victimized. Victims commonly reexperience the trauma in dreams and "flashbacks." They become numb to the world and feel detached from it.

Accounts of posttraumatic combat stress date back to the ancient Greeks. In recent years Vietnam war veterans have frequently been studied. They are

People with posttraumatic stress disorder suffer extreme emotional reactions to catastrophic events. The man shown here is witness to the aftermath of a tornado.

known to have a high incidence of psychological problems, including PTSD. A study conducted by the Centers for Disease Control in Atlanta indicated that 15 percent of Vietnam vets had had PTSD at some time since their service and that at least 2 percent were currently afflicted (L. Roberts, 1988). Another study showed that 81 percent of wounded vets met DSM-III-R criteria for PTSD (Pitman, Altman, & Macklin, 1989). Repetition of the traumatic experience in nightmares is quite common. In Vietnam vets, the dream closely replays the actual traumatic event and the person relives the fear of injury, threat, anxiety, rage, and fear of dying (R. J. Ross, Ball, K. A. Sullivan, & Caroff, 1989).

Second-generation Holocaust survivors also have a high rate of PTSD. One study showed that two to three years after the Israeli invasion of Lebanon in 1982, children of Holocaust survivors had higher rates of PTSD than other Israeli children (Z. Solomon, Kotler, & Mikulincer, 1988). Other studies have explored PTSD in school-age children exposed to sniper attacks. Researchers found a high rate of PTSD, and symptoms were most severe in children closest to the violence (Breslau, G. C. Davis, Andreski, & Peterson, 1991; Neder, Pynoos, Fairbanks, & Frederick, 1990; Pynoos et al., 1987; E. M. Smith, North, McCool, & Shea, 1990). Female rape victims can experience many PTSD symptoms. Rape also often ruins one's sense of autonomy and causes feelings of self-blame, shame, self-disgust, rage, and guilt. Often, rape victims become mistrustful and have relationship problems and sexual difficulties (Rose, 1986).

Many people who have suffered through catastrophic events do not develop PTSD. Some studies suggest that there are factors that increase the risk. The person most prone to PTSD is a male with a previous psychiatric history, little education, childhood conduct problems, and a history of separation from parents (E. M. Smith et al., 1990).

Causes of Anxiety Disorders

Historically, anxiety disorders were viewed as the psychological and emotional consequences of problems in early life. All the major theoretical perspectives on abnormal behavior have offered insights into the causes of anxiety disorders. Recent advances have increased our understanding of the causal role of biological factors. In the following section we investigate the more prominent biological and psychological explanations for anxiety disorders. The challenge for clinical researchers is to adequately account for the interactions of psychological and biological variables.

Hereditary Causes. Hereditary factors have been implicated in the etiology of anxiety disorders for over 100 years, since anxiety disorders run in families. This is particularly true of agoraphobia, OCD, blood injury phobia, and other simple phobias. In general, family studies show a higher incidence of these disorders in close relatives of the patient than in the general population. Twin studies also lend support to a hereditary explanation.

Biochemical Causes. Research into the causes of anxiety disorders has also revealed biochemical abnormalities that could have a genetic basis. One group of researchers has proposed a three-part explanation for the generation and maintenance of panic. First, it is known that caffeine, sodium lactate, and carbon dioxide induce attacks in people predisposed to panic. These substances may act by exciting electrical activity in norepinephrine-producing areas of the brain stem. Since the brain stem controls respiration and heart rate, subtle chemical changes may very well account for the physical symptoms reported by patients (see Table 5-2). Second, the model asserts that brain stem neurons excite the limbic system, a brain region known to regulate emotional states. Limbic stimulation is believed to account for the anticipatory anxiety observed in PD. Third, phobic avoidance, which is a learned phenomenon requiring significant cognitive ability in humans is attributed to the prefrontal cortex. Although the triggers for panic lie in the brain stem, the person must mentally connect the attacks with the situations in which the panic was experienced. Thus, we see that psychological and biological variables interact to produce panic (Carr et al., 1986; Charney, Galloway, & Heninger, 1984; Charney, Heninger, & Jatlow, 1985; Gorman et al., 1989; Gorman, Liebowitz, Fyer, & J. Stein, 1989; Greden, 1974; Hollander, Liebowitz, Gorman, J. M. Cohen, & D. F. Klein, 1989; D. F. Klein, Rabkin, & Gorman, 1985; M. A. Lee, Flagel, Greden, & Cameron, 1988; Liebowitz et al., 1986; Liebowitz, Fyer, & Gorman, 1984; Pitts & McClure, 1967; Redmond, 1985; Sanderson, Rapee, & Barlow, 1989; Uhde, Roy-Byrne, Vittone, Boulenger, & Post, 1985).

Karen connected her panic with driving away from home. She felt safer at home, so the mere thought of traveling produced anticipation of an attack. This raised her anxiety and probably helped trigger panic attacks.

Research indicates that OCD involves a dysfunction in the metabolism of the neurotransmitter serotonin in the brain (Modell, Mountz, Curtis, & Greden, 1989; Turner, Beidel, & Nathan, 1985; Yaryura & Bhaganan, 1977; Yaryura-Tobias, 1977). Generalized anxiety disorder has a biological basis in the underactivity of the GABA neurotransmitter system of the brain (Redmond, 1985). Physiological research on PTSD suggests that traumatic stress causes a chronic impairment of the brain's normal protection against excessive stimulation. The psychological consequences are the flashbacks, vivid nightmares, expressions of rage, and irritability seen in PTSD patients (Kolb, 1987).

Other Biological Factors. In some patients, panic is associated with cardiac abnormality and neurological defects of the inner ear (Jacob, Moller, Turner, & Wall, 1985; Liberthson, Sheehan, M. E. King, & Weyman, 1986). Obsessive-compulsive disorder is also associated with head injury, epilepsy, and amphetamine intoxication (Kettl & I. M. Marx, 1986; McKeon, McGuffin, & P. Robinson, 1984).

Psychosocial Causes. Psychodynamic perspectives on anxiety are rooted in the pioneering work of Freud. His theory of anxiety integrated several models he developed over the years. He viewed anxiety as a signal of conflict that induced the ego to construct defenses against uncomfortable memories and feelings. Freud thought that in GAD and panic disorders, which he called *anxiety neurosis*, the content of specific memories remains repressed and is expressed as apprehension and nonspecific fear. In phobias, repressed wishes are displaced onto a specific object or situation. The Freudian analyst interprets a feared stimulus as an external, symbolic representation of the repressed wish. For example, Freud believed that an agoraphobic woman's fear of venturing alone in public symbolically represented her unconscious wish to be seduced.

The classic psychoanalytic explanation for OCD is based on anal eroticism: obsessive-compulsive individuals are fixated at the anal stage of development. Their symptoms represent a tug-of-war between the sexual and aggressive urges of the id and the defense mechanisms of the ego, while the punishing superego intervenes.

Derek reported to his therapist that before going to bed he had to knock on the wall three times or else his father would die. In Freudian terms, Derek apparently repressed his unconscious hatred for his father, and the hatred was manifest as an intrusive thought of his father's death. He felt that if he did not perform the knocking ritual, he would be personally responsible for his father's death.

Modern psychodynamic theory takes into account certain physiological aspects of anxiety that are outside the territory of traditional psychoanalytic theory. Psychodynamic theory also recognizes factors other than separation, seduction, castration, and parental disapproval as important in the development of anxiety disorders. These factors include problems in interpersonal relationships, the integrative force of the ego, and object relations (see Chapter 2) (A. M. Cooper, 1985).

Behaviorists view anxiety disorders as the result of maladaptive learning. The earliest suggestion that anxiety disorders are learned came from Watson's demonstration of a conditioned emotional response in Little Albert. As described in Chapter 3, Albert learned to fear a white rat by associating the rat with a loud noise. On the basis of this and similar demonstrations, investigators concluded that many phobias were learned through classical conditioning (Watson & Raynar, 1920).

Some critics complain that behaviorists have traditionally explained anxiety disorders in humans by extending findings from animal conditioning experiments. Although conditioning may account for a limited range of fear reactions, laboratory demonstrations do not explain why some phobias are learned more readily than others. In fact, many phobic people fear stimuli that were dangerous for prehistoric people. For example, more people are afraid of animals than

Little Albert's conditioned fear of furry animals was the basis of the early behaviorist belief that phobias resulted from conditioning experiences.

Courtesy of Professor Benjamin Harris

preparedness theory
An explanation of phobias stating that certain fears contribute to species survival.

of hair dryers, even though there is a greater chance of being shocked by a malfunctioning hair dryer than of being mauled by a wild animal. In the view of **preparedness theory**, human beings have evolved biological tendencies to fear certain stimuli, such as snakes and darkness, because these fears had survival value to our species (McNalley, 1987).

Operant conditioning theory says that avoidance behavior is maintained by negative as well as positive reinforcement. Avoidance can evoke sympathy from certain others while providing relief from certain responsibilities. For example, an agoraphobic may be relieved of driving responsibilities and may receive the extra attention often given to an ill person.

Cognitive theories assert that anxiety reactions result from mental mistakes. These mental errors take the form of misinterpreting situations by appraising them as being more threatening than they really are. Individuals with panic disorder, such as Karen, misinterpret the bodily sensations of panic as a heart attack or seizure, and they expect to lose control (McNalley, 1990).

One prominent cognitive-behavioral theory is Albert Bandura's cognitive social learning theory. According to Bandura, fear and anxiety result from *negative self-efficacy expectations*, because people believe they cannot cope with potentially threatening situations (1982, 1977a, 1977b). Cognitive theorists, such as Albert Ellis and Aaron Beck, explain anxiety in terms of irrational or distorted thinking. Ellis contends that people experience anxiety because of irrational beliefs about social conduct, such as ''I must get love and approval from significant people'' or ''When I am frustrated I should view things as awful and catastrophic (A. Ellis & Harper, 1975). Such beliefs create a gap between what people expect to get and what they actually get in social situations. According to Beck, an individual may be overprepared for danger, so that ''he sees what he expects to see and not what is really present in the situation'' (A. T. Beck & Emery, 1985, p. 54). The person thus exaggerates danger.

From a cognitive perspective, Karen *expected* to lose control while driving, which helped trigger anxiety and panic. Having a panic attack then confirmed her belief that she could not cope with driving. In this manner, she was caught in a cycle in which her negative expectations helped produce the very emotional state she dreaded.

In the framework of humanistic psychology, anxiety is caused by a state of incongruence in which our personal experiences do not match our self-concepts. This means not moving toward self-actualization. Existentialists believe that anxiety arises because of our awareness of freedom and responsibility.

Treatments for Anxiety Disorders

Treatment for anxiety disorders is designed to alleviate symptoms of anxiety and help individuals cope with life situations that are anxiety-provoking. Biological treatment, usually psychotropic medication, is often recommended for individuals who experience debilitating anxiety or panic. Psychological treatments for anxiety disorders include psychotherapy and behavior therapy techniques.

benzodiazepines
(*ben*-zo-di-*az*-uh-peens)
Antianxiety drugs.

Drug Treatments. **Benzodiazepines**, the drugs most commonly used to reduce symptoms of anxiety, bind to specific neuronal receptors and raise the levels of the neurotransmitter GABA in the brain (Gelenberg, 1983). Buspirone

(Buspar), which is chemically unrelated to the benzodiazepines, is now being prescribed frequently for anxiety disorders because it has less sedative effect than the benzodiazepines, does not interact with alcohol, and is reportedly not addictive.

Symptoms of panic respond best to antidepressant drugs that influence norepinephrine (Gelenberg, 1983). Symptoms of PTSD are helped by antidepressants as well as benzodiazepines, but few carefully controlled studies have documented these observations (M. J. Friedman, 1988). Alprazolam (Xanax) is effective against both panic and anxiety. Symptoms of OCD are reduced by two relatively new antidepressant drugs, fluoxetine (Prozac) and clomipramine (Anafranil), which influence serotonin metabolism (Clomipramine Collaborative Study Group, 1991; Turner, R. G. Jacob, Bredel, & Himmelhoch, 1985) (see Table 5-4).

As part of her treatment, Karen's psychiatrist prescribed imipramine to help block her panic attacks. During the six months of medication treatment, Karen had very few panic attacks, and this helped her work up the courage to drive greater distances.

Psychotropic drugs rarely eliminate all the problems associated with anxiety or any other mental disorder. Medications can have troublesome or dangerous side effects, including drowsiness, mental depression, nausea, headache, weight gain, and skin rashes. Some people develop a tolerance to benzodiazepines, meaning that they require higher doses to get the same drug effect, and they become addicted. To minimize these undesirable effects, clinicians should follow certain guidelines in the drug treatment of any mental disorder. First, every patient should receive a comprehensive medical exam. Second, psychological treatments should be used when they are as effective as drugs and should be employed even during drug treatment. Third, drugs should be prescribed at the lowest possible dosage and for the briefest practical period of time (Schonover, 1983).

TABLE 5-4 ▦ DRUGS USED IN TREATMENT OF ANXIETY DISORDERS[a]

Benzodiazepines		Antidepressant Drugs	
Generic Name	Trade Name	Generic Name	Trade Name
Lorazepam	Ativan	Phenelzine	Nardil
Prazepam	Centrax	Imipramine	Tofranil
Chlordiazepoxide	Librium	Amitryptiline	Elavil
Clorazepate	Tranxene	Doxepin	Sinequan
Diazepam	Valium	Desipramine	Norpramin
Alprazolam	Xanax	Nortriptyline	Pamelor
		Fluoxetine	Prozac
		Clomipramine	Anafranil

[a]Benzodiazepines are most effective for symptoms of anxiety. Antidepressants are used for symptoms of panic and OCD. Buspirone (Buspar), which is chemically unrelated to the benzodiazepines and antidepressants, is prescribed for anxiety disorders.

Psychological Treatments. Psychoanalysis was the first form of psychological therapy used in the treatment of anxiety disorders. In classical psychoanalytic therapy the goal is to replace the irrational impulses of the id with the more rational processes of the ego through self-exploration. This requires that defenses and transference be analyzed to uncover the true sources of conflict found in the unconscious. As the person works through the conflict, the need to resort to neurotic coping behaviors is gradually eliminated.

Nelson experienced terrible anxiety whenever he took an exam. He would become dizzy and sweat profusely, and his writing arm would grow stiff and nearly immobile. The solution to his problems came from Nelson's awareness that the source of his test anxiety came from his repressed hatred for his father. His father, a university professor, stressed academic excellence and belittled Nelson's academic performance. Nelson's inability to take exams was a neurotic means of expressing his hatred. Once Nelson was able to accept his feelings toward his father, the way was cleared for him to resolve the conflict by exploring more adaptive ways of coping.

Modern analysts are more likely to focus on the adaptive capacities of the ego, and they sometimes encourage exposure to the feared situation. Psychiatrist Franz Alexander (1946) referred to this as a "corrective emotional experience." Short-term dynamic therapies have attempted to shorten the term of treatment by using a more direct and confrontational approach designed to provoke intense emotions and thereby help the person quickly recognize the source of the conflict.

exposure therapy
Behavioral treatment for anxiety disorders.

Exposure therapy is a behavioral treatment in which the individual is exposed to feared stimuli. Exposure therapy can be conducted by having the person face, or imagine facing, the feared stimulus. Exposure to real-life stimuli is known as *in vivo exposure*. Exposure can be accomplished step by step or all at once, and many of the exposure procedures may be practiced at home. Ironically, exposure therapy was suggested by Freud in 1919, when he stated that

> one can hardly ever master a phobia if one waits till the patient lets the analysis influence him to give it up. . . . One succeeds only when one can induce them through the influence of the analysis to . . . go about alone and struggle with the anxiety while they make the attempt. (Jones, 1955)

Systematic desensitization, a widely used exposure therapy, was developed by psychiatrist Joseph Wolpe in the 1950s (1958). This technique is based on a series of experiments that showed learned fear responses could be unlearned if the person confronted the feared stimulus or situation while relaxed.

In therapy, Karen was taught muscle relaxation. She learned to alternately contract and relax her muscles, beginning with the head, then the neck, arms, chest, back, abdomen, and legs. She was then asked to construct a hierarchy of her fears, first based on distance away from home. She used 3- by 5-inch index cards on which she described scenes of traveling away from home. She arranged the cards so each scene would provoke more anxiety than the previous one. For example, on card 1 she described herself awakening and getting ready for a car trip. On card 2 she was starting the car, on card 3 she was two blocks from home, and so on. On the final card, she was in the country, far away from home.

Exposure to feared stimuli is the basis of behavioral treatments for anxiety disorders.

The therapist described the scene on card 1 and asked Karen to relax until the fear reached tolerable levels. Scenes were then presented in order of increasing anxiety until she was consistently able to relax away the fear. The procedure was repeated using a familiarity dimension: first she traveled with someone familiar, and eventually she traveled alone. After 14 sessions, Karen's fears were significantly reduced.

Flooding (discussed in Chapter 3) is another exposure procedure effective in the treatment of more intense anxiety reactions. Generally, 90-minute sessions are most therapeutic. Briefer sessions sometimes sensitize, that is, make the condition worse (Marks, 1982).

Flooding with *response prevention* has proved successful in some patients with OCD. In this approach, the person is "bombarded" with the obsessive image and prevented from performing the compulsive ritual. The goal is to disconnect the image or thought from the anxiety-reducing act. The person learns that while the anxiety is initially intensified, it eventually wanes even though the compulsive act is not performed (Emmelkamp, 1982; Marks, 1982).

thought stopping
A therapy technique designed to reduce the impact of anxiety-producing thoughts.

Thought stopping is a therapy technique used to reduce the impact of anxiety-producing thoughts by having the person reproduce the thought and then dismiss it by shouting "Stop." The effect may be enhanced if the person wears a thick rubber band around the wrist and snaps it whenever the thought intrudes (Emmelkamp, 1982; Marks, 1982).

assertiveness training
A strategy to help people express feelings.

Assertiveness training is a behavioral strategy designed to help people express both positive and negative feelings in socially acceptable ways. Assertive action can help inhibit anxiety by increasing a person's chances of attaining highly valued goals. One way of conducting assertiveness training is to have the patient observe the therapist model assertive behaviors, then rehearse them in the therapy session and at home (Rimm & Masters, 1979).

PROFILE
Joseph Wolpe (b. 1915)

Joseph Wolpe has been one of the most influential figures in the history of behavior therapy. Raised in South Africa, he was greatly influenced by his grandmother, who tried to make him devoutly religious by having him read the works of many Jewish writers. But exposure to other philosophies brought him to a materalist view, in which human nature is seen in physical rather than spiritual terms. Since Wolpe viewed Freud as a materialist, he originally leaned toward psychoanalytic theory, but he soon questioned the ability of Freudian theory to account for all the facts. He was eventually drawn to Pavlov's research methods and materialistic ideology. The foundations were now laid for Wolpe's ideas on therapy.

In 1948, Wolpe received his M.D. in psychiatry from the University of Witwatersrand in South Africa, where he specialized in the study of fear reactions in animals. He moved to the United States and eventually went to Temple University, where he has remained since 1965.

Wolpe's claim to fame is that he developed a refined and systematic behavior therapy, *systematic desensitization.* This technique is based on fun-

damental behaviorist principles: behaviors are learned and can be unlearned, and fear and anxiety can be reduced by having the patient perform a behavior that is antagonistic to fear. (The latter is an application of a Pavlovian principle called *reciprocal inhibition.*) These scientifically based concepts stand in marked contrast to the traditional psychodynamic notion that the roots of abnormal behavior are to be found in the unconscious. Since its introduction in 1958, systematic desensitization has become the basis for many modern behavior therapies.

Joseph Wolpe has been influential in establishing behavior therapy as a major force in psychotherapy. He has been a leader in the Association for the Advancement of Behavior Therapy and has received many awards and honors, including the American Psychological Association's Distinguished Scientific Award for the Application of Psychology in 1979. His major works include *Psychotherapy by Reciprocal Inhibition* (1958) and *The Practice of Behavior Therapy* (1982) (C. S. Hall & Lindzey, 1985; Prochaska, 1984).

Cognitive therapy for anxiety disorders is designed to modify the distorted thinking that gives rise to anxiety. First, the therapist notes the presence of distorted thoughts and explains how they lead to anxiety. Next, the therapist challenges the distorted nature of the anxiety-provoking thoughts and explains how to restructure them with more adaptive thinking. The following illustrates the use of cognitive therapy in the treatment of GAD:

Client: If I don't get an A on the exam, I'll just die.
Therapist: I can understand your desire to do well, but don't you think that dying would be an extreme reaction to failing an exam?
Client: Well, I know I won't really die, but I don't know what I'll do if I fail.
Therapist: If you know that failing the exam won't kill you, then why express yourself that way? You feel so anxious because you have magnified the impact of failing a single exam. You can tell yourself instead that failing is not desirable, but if it happens you'll pick yourself up and do better next time.

The therapist can complement cognitive therapy by setting up activity schedules and homework assignments aimed at mastering problem areas of life, and the patient can practice coping using modeling procedures (Rimm & Masters, 1979).

Humanistic therapy attempts to alleviate anxiety by providing a genuine, empathic climate in which the person grows to accept the self, leading to self-actualization and reduced anxiety. The existential therapist attempts to understand the client's world as fully as possible. The therapist can teach the patient to assume responsibility for making decisions. The patient learns that anxiety is minimized as meaning is found in one's existence.

Evaluation of Psychotherapy for Anxiety Disorders. Over the years, some major clinical outcome studies have indicated that all psychotherapies are roughly equivalent in their effectiveness. Other studies have pointed to the

Humanistic therapists provide a warm and empathic climate within which the person can develop.

superiority of behavioral and cognitive therapies over more traditional insight-oriented approaches for the anxiety disorders. What can we make of these apparent contradictions?

Clinical outcome studies must be interpreted cautiously. It has been argued that they do not represent real treatment with real people having problems. Many of the earlier studies used student volunteers and brief treatments for anxiety problems defined by the results of paper-and-pencil questionnaires. In recent years, these criticisms have been addressed by using more stringent diagnostic criteria. Also, treatment effectiveness is now determined on the basis of statistical comparisons of different groups. However, even with methodological improvements, it is questionable whether statistical differences between one treatment and another have any clinical significance.

From these clinical studies we can conclude that psychotherapy works better than no treatment at all. In order to resolve questions about the effectiveness of specific treatments, it is imperative that future psychotherapy research be more consistent with the way psychotherapy is actually practiced (Kazdin, 1986; Persons, 1991; Stiles, Shapiro, & Elliot, 1986).

5-2   SOMATOFORM DISORDERS

somatoform disorder
Physical symptoms without organic cause.

The essential feature of a **somatoform disorder** is a physical symptom that suggests a physical disorder for which no organic cause can be found. In addition, there must be positive evidence, or at least a presumption, that the symptoms are linked to psychological factors. Unlike the case in *malingering*—the intentional production of false or grossly exaggerated physical or psychological symptoms motivated by external incentives, such as avoiding work or conscription—the presentation of the symptoms is not intentional: the symptoms are not under voluntary control. Since the symptoms cannot be explained by laboratory testing, these conditions are classified as mental disorders (American Psychiatric Association, 1987).

Types of Somatoform Disorders

In this section we discuss somatization disorder, hypochondriasis, somatoform pain disorder, conversion disorder, and body dysmorphic disorder. Somatoform disorders are intriguing, but they are far less common than anxiety disorders.

somatization disorder
Multiple physical symptoms without organic cause.

Somatization Disorder. Somatization disorder, also called *Briquet's syndrome*, is marked by multiple persistent physical complaints for which no medical cause can be found. Chest pains, nausea, vomiting, dizziness, genital pain, heart palpitations, and muscle weakness are just some of the many symptoms experienced. Throughout the more or less chronic course of the disorder, the symptoms are exaggerated and overdramatized. Frequently, individuals even subject themselves to unnecessary surgery (American Psychiatric Association, 1987).

Somatization disorder is more commonly diagnosed in women, especially those with a history of childhood sexual abuse (Morrison, 1989). However, recent research has shown the condition to be more prevalent in men than previously thought, especially in combat or disaster situations (Golding, R. Smith, & Kashner, 1991).

Denise was a 36-year-old divorced woman who entered the hospital emergency room complaining of severe abdominal distress. She said that shortly after supper she had felt nauseated and bloated, then vomited some undigested food. Shortly thereafter, she began suffering intense pain. As she calmed down and became more comfortable, she reported that she had suffered many similar episodes over the last 15 years, and she said that no doctor had been able to determine the cause. She had even undergone several surgical procedures to no avail.

More questioning revealed that she had episodes of dizziness, and she experienced chest pain that awakened her from sleep. She had trouble urinating and had low back pain. Denise admitted taking Valium four times a day for "nerves," phenobarbital four times a day for her stomach symptoms, and some pain pills as needed. Each medication had been prescribed by a different doctor. The results of a physical examination were normal, and the clinical picture led to a diagnosis of somatization disorder (Rowe, 1984).

hypochondriasis
Preoccupation with a minor symptom and fear it is sign of serious disease.

Hypochondriasis. In **hypochondriasis**, the patient is preoccupied with minor symptoms or diseases and misinterprets them as signs of serious disease. For example, the person may mistake a headache for a brain tumor or mild chest pain for a heart attack. The hypochondriac becomes phobic about the symptom (American Psychiatric Association, 1987).

somatoform pain disorder Pain in the absence of physical findings.

Somatoform Pain Disorder. In **somatoform pain disorder**, sometimes called *psychalgia*, the patient complains of pain but there are no physical findings. Sometimes this disorder involves muscle spasms and tingling of the hands and feet (American Psychiatric Association, 1987). The symptoms are believed to have symbolic significance. For example, a person's pain may mimic pain previously experienced by a deceased loved one (American Psychiatric Association, 1987; Purcell, 1988; Rowe, 1984).

conversion disorder
Loss or alteration of physical functioning.

Conversion Disorder. The classic somatoform disorder is **conversion disorder** (formerly called *hysterical neurosis*), which involves a loss or alteration of physical functioning (American Psychiatric Association, 1987). In common with the other somatoform disorders, the symptoms of conversion disorder mimic physical disease but there is no evidence of an organic cause. Symptoms are usually singular and make little anatomical sense. They can include convulsions, paralysis, muscle weakness, an inability to speak, lowered sensitivity to pain, absence of sensation, tingling, loss of hearing, blindness, choking, or "nervous coughing" (*tussis nervosa*). Some patients seem to be unconcerned about their impairment, a state called "la belle indifference" (American Psychiatric Association, 1987).

Conversion disorder was the condition suffered by Josef Breuer's famous patient Anna O., and it was the interpretation of this case that helped lay the foundation for Freud's psychoanalysis (see "Close-up: The Case of Anna O.") (American Psychiatric Association, 1987).

Conversion reactions appear suddenly during or after trauma and leave just as suddenly. They are more commonly diagnosed in women and patients in military hospitals, and they are usually seen first by neurologists and orthopedists. Some patients are ultimately found to have true neurological disease (Purcell, 1988).

Josef Breuer's treatment of Anna O. provided the impetus for the "talking cure" that formed the basis of Freud's psychoanalysis.

body dysmorphic disorder A strong, unfounded belief that a body part is defective.

Body Dysmorphic Disorder. **Body dysmorphic disorder**, a new DSM-III-R category, is characterized by a strong belief, in the absence of evidence, that a body part is defective or deformed in some way. Excess facial hair, deformities of the nose, wrinkles, skin spots, and facial swelling are commonly reported. The person may also be depressed and may exhibit obsessive-compulsive traits. The condition usually appears between late adolescence and the thirties and persists for several years (American Psychiatric Association, 1987).

Causes of Somatoform Disorders

The causes of somatoform disorders are poorly understood. Little data points to biological causes, such as hereditary predispositions or biochemical abnormalities.

Psychological Causes. Historically, the most influential views on the causation of somatoform disorders have been psychodynamic. In this view, somatization is described as the tendency to manifest psychological stress as a physical disability. Somatoform disorders are thought to arise from repressed Oedipus and Electra conflicts. Modern psychoanalytic thinking sees somatization as motivated by strong unconscious dependency needs, which produce conflict because of the person's self-image as a strong, self-sufficient person. To preserve the image, patients view their physical symptoms as beyond their control and responsibility. In other words, they do not believe that being incapacitated is their fault.

Other analysts view somatization symptoms as an interpersonal communication. In this view, somatization is not an illness but an attempt to nonverbally force another person to help. Playing the sick role will be rewarded with attention and sympathy (Ochitill, 1982).

CLOSE-UP
The Case of Anna O.

Anna O. came to Josef Breuer in 1880 at the age of 21. The only daughter of a well-to-do Viennese Jewish family, she presented a "museum of symptoms" after nursing her dying father. The symptoms relevant to conversion disorder were a persistent cough, headaches, and visual disturbances that were so severe she could not read. Anna hallucinated and thought that she was going blind and deaf. Also, her right arm and both legs were paralyzed. Since no organic cause could be found, Breuer diagnosed her as having "hysteria."

On one occasion Anna described how a particular symptom had developed, and, to Breuer's astonishment, the symptom disappeared. She proceeded to talk about one symptom after another, and many of them disappeared. Breuer continued to treat her by having her talk about her problems while under hypnosis, a technique she described as "chimney sweeping." At this time she had forgotten her native tongue, German, and could speak only in English. When asked to read from a book written in French or Italian, she read fluently in English.

After 18 months of treatment, Breuer pronounced Anna cured. That very evening, he was summoned to Anna's house and found her thrashing about and hallucinating black snakes. She was in the midst of an imaginary childbirth and asserted that Breuer was the father! Breuer fled. She remained ill for 6 more years and became a morphine addict, but by age 30 she had recovered completely and became a prominent feminist and social worker. She died of abdominal cancer at age 77.

Freud interpreted Anna's conversion symptoms as stemming from repressed sexual urges transferred onto Breuer, and he believed Breuer had developed a strong countertransferential reaction. Even Breuer's wife grew tired of hearing about Anna and became jealous. Disagreement between Freud and Breuer over this interpretation eventually led to their split, but Breuer's talking cure, or "chimney sweeping" technique, became the foundation for Freud's psychoanalysis (Breuer, 1989; Jones, 1981; Spitzer, Skodol, Gibbon, & Williams, 1983).

neuroticism Traits associated with somatoform disorders.

Traits of neuroticism are associated with the development of somatoform disorders. **Neuroticism** consists of self-consciousness, fear of impulses, vulnerability to stress, and a tendency toward anger, hostility, and depression. Individuals with these traits cope with the stresses of life by adopting a "sick role" which permits them to avoid family, social, and career responsibilities (Purcell, 1988).

Cultural factors are believed to contribute significantly to somatoform disorders as well. Somatization is a worldwide phenomenon and is particularly prevalent in cultures that discourage the expression of emotional turmoil. Finally, a strong relationship has been confirmed between early sexual trauma and somatization. In one study, a large percentage of women diagnosed with somatization had a history of being molested before puberty (Lipowski, 1988; Morrison, 1989).

Treatments for Somatoform Disorders

Few studies confirm the effectiveness of treatments for somatoform disorders. Antidepressant medication can be helpful for somatization problems that involve pain, and sedatives can reduce anxiety. However, sedative drugs must be prescribed cautiously since individuals with somatoform disorders are likely to become drug-dependent.

Psychoanalysis has traditionally been considered the treatment of choice for somatoform disorders. However, other forms of individual, group, and family therapies have been used. Since behavioral clinicians view somatization symptoms as the result of skills deficits or inhibitions, behavior therapy often involves teaching alternative skills so the individual no longer needs to maintain the maladaptive symptoms. In addition, the therapist can attempt to alter the environment so that avoidance of responsibilities is not reinforced and appropriate behaviors are reinforced. Being well becomes more rewarding than being sick. The participation of family members may be necessary, though little scientific evidence exists to support this idea (Ochitill, 1982).

Ari was a 27-year-old man who claimed to have injured his back in an industrial accident, resulting in paralysis and anesthesia in both legs. It was hypothesized that the patient had assumed the sick role in order to get disability benefits. In the country in which he lived, being sick also made it possible to avoid paying high taxes on a car.

The treatment began by telling Ari that he was not physically ill and therefore was not entitled to any benefits. Then he was told that an American doctor would arrive with a miraculous drug that had amazing curative powers. The patient was told that in order for the drug to work, he would have to go to bed at 8 P.M. every night. This was an extremely pleasant hospital, and it was hoped that forcing Ari to retire early would make being sick quite unpleasant. The drug actually used had an obnoxious odor, adding to the unpleasant atmosphere.

Within two days, Ari reported feeling in his legs and some movement of the toes. By the sixth day, he was walking perfectly. He kicked a soccer ball and did cartwheels to demonstrate his "miraculous" recovery (Goldblatt & Munitz, 1976).

5-3 DISSOCIATIVE DISORDERS

Dissociation is a psychological state in which certain aspects of mind are split off from consciousness. Of course, it is impossible to be aware of all the contents of our mind. We may momentarily forget something familiar, such as a frequently called phone number, or even forget our identity if suddenly awakened from a deep sleep. Such mental states are quite normal. The central feature of **dissociative disorders** is a sudden alteration of consciousness, identity, or memory that results in a severe disturbance of personality functioning and a disruption of the usual mental organization (American Psychiatric Association, 1987; Purcell, 1988).

dissociative disorders
Mental disorders involving alterations in consciousness, identity, or memory.

Types of Dissociative Disorders

Once considered extremely rare except in people who have been severely traumatized, dissociative disorders are now being diagnosed with greater frequency.

In this section we discuss psychogenic amnesia, psychogenic fugue, depersonalization disorder, and multiple personality disorder.

psychogenic amnesia
Sudden forgetting of important personal information.

Psychogenic Amnesia. In **psychogenic amnesia**, there is a sudden forgetting of important personal information (American Psychiatric Association, 1987). In one type of amnesia called *localized amnesia*, the person cannot recall events pertaining to a certain time period. For example, an individual who escaped from a terrible house fire in which many people died may not be able to recall anything about it for several days. This is the most common type of psychogenic amnesia. In an uncommon form called *generalized amnesia*, the individual may forget his or her entire life and may be found wandering in a state of confusion and disorientation.

psychogenic fugue
(fyoog) Unexpected travel and assumption of new identity.

Psychogenic Fugue. In **psychogenic fugue**, a person suddenly and unexpectedly travels away from home or work and assumes a new identity. The person in a fugue state is found wandering far from home, with no memory of his or her previous identity. The new identity is usually marked by more uninhibited personality traits than were typical of the former personality (American Psychiatric Association, 1987).

After learning of his wife's extramarital affair, Harvey, a 32-year-old schoolteacher, left home to go to work and disappeared. Two months later, one of his friends stopped for a meal in a restaurant in the next state and found Harvey washing dishes. Harvey did not recognize the friend, had no memory of the last two months, and had assumed a new name (Purcell, 1988).

depersonalization disorder A feeling of being "unreal."

Depersonalization Disorder. **Depersonalization disorder** is characterized by periods of feeling "unreal" or other alterations in the normal sense of self. A person may have the sensation that his or her arms have changed size; one might feel that one can see oneself from a distance. The person may feel mechanical or as if in a dream. As bizarre as this sounds, the person with this disorder realizes that these feelings are unnatural and is in touch with reality (American Psychiatric Association, 1987).

multiple personality disorder The existence of two or more distinct personalities.

Multiple Personality Disorder. A person in whom two or more distinct personalities exist is suffering from **multiple personality disorder** (MPD) (American Psychiatric Association, 1987), commonly known as "split personality." Each personality has its own memories, traits, beliefs, habits, and identity. The transition from one personality to another is quite sudden, and one personality may have little or no awareness of the others. At times, the personalities may be co-conscious (aware of one another). A person with MPD may report speaking with other personalities, and this may be mistakenly viewed as a schizophrenic hallucination (American Psychiatric Association, 1987; Purcell, 1988). Even though there is some similarity of symptoms, MPD should not be confused with schizophrenia (see Chapter 10).

Until quite recently, our understanding of MPD came primarily from clinical case reports. The use of structured interview scales is beginning to provide more scientific validation of the diagnosis, and MPD is being diagnosed with greater frequency. Most individuals with MPD have a background of sexual and physical abuse and family problems in childhood. In one study, 95 percent of patients had experienced physical and/or sexual abuse in childhood (Chu & Dill, 1990).

People with multiple personality disorder suffer from two or more distinct personalities. Billy Milligan, seen here, kidnapped and raped women while influenced by one of his 24 personalities.

Substance abuse, suicidal thinking, and self-abuse are frequent signs of the person's struggles with existence. Patients also experience intense headaches and unvalidated extrasensory experiences, including telepathy, clairvoyance, contact with ghosts, and knowledge of past lives (C. A. Ross et al., 1990).

In 1977, Billy Milligan, a man who had 24 distinct personalities, was arrested for the kidnap and rape of three women. Adalana was the personality responsible for the rapes. She was a lesbian who used Billy's body. Other personalities included Allen, the con man; Tommy, the escape artist; April, the bitch; Samuel, the wandering Jew; and Shawn, the deaf one. In the first court decision of its kind, Billy was judged not guilty of his crimes by reason of insanity. A letter written by Billy reflects some of the dissociation he experienced. The letter was written in fluent Arabic by Arthur, the personality who decided which member of the "family" controlled consciousness (Keyes, 1982).

> *Sometimes I do not know who or what I am. And sometimes I do not know the other people surrounding me. The echoes of the voices are still in my mind, but they have no meaning at all. Several faces appear to me, as if from a darkness, but I am feeling very fearful because my mind is totally divided. My (internal) family, in fact, is not in continuous contact with me at all, and have not been for a long time. . . . The events here in the last weeks were not very good. I am not responsible for it all. I hate everything that transpires around me, but I can't stop it, and I can't alter it. (Keyes, 1982)*

Causes of Dissociative Disorders

Little evidence links dissociative disorders with neurophysiological dysfunction. There is evidence that in MPD, brain activity does change, depending on which personality is conscious, but it is unclear whether the changes are causes or effects of the disorder. The electroencephalographic (EEG) changes observed in different personalities are probably manifestations of changing mental and emotional states found even in normal people. For example, it has been observed that normal people role-playing different personalities can show EEG changes even greater than those observed in patients with multiple personalities (Coons, Milstein, & Marley, 1982). Differences in cognitive ability have also been observed in multiple personalities. Five of Billy Milligan's personalities were tested, and different intelligence test scores were obtained (Keyes, 1982).

Psychodynamic views of MPD disorder are most prominent. They are based on the idea that dissociation is an attempt to protect the ego from some painful memory or impulse or from a traumatic experience.

Psychological evaluation revealed that Billy, his mother, and his siblings were severely sexually abused by the stepfather. In fact, Billy was repeatedly sodomized by his stepfather when he was 8 or 9 years old. It was the belief of the evaluating psychiatrist that such trauma directly led to the dissociative states (Keyes, 1982).

Behaviorists view dissociation as a complex learned response the patient constructs in order to avoid certain social or legal responsibilities. Therapists unwittingly may encourage patients to adopt the multiple personality role by providing official validation for different identities. In the course of the interview, the psychologist may ''suggest'' personalities that really do not exist, and the person may adopt multiple personalities because he or she believes it would be advantageous.

In 1977 and 1978, Kenneth Bianchi, known as the Hillside Strangler, raped and strangled ten California women. Charged with the murders, Bianchi submitted to hypnosis and displayed a second personality, Steve, which the defense used as evidence of a mental illness and grounds for an insanity plea. During the trial, the

Kenneth Bianchi, the Hillside Strangler, strangled ten women. His insanity defense, based on multiple personality disorder, was unsuccessful because it was determined that he had feigned the condition.

prosecution recruited psychologist-psychiatrist Martin Orne to disprove Bianchi's position. Orne suggested to Bianchi that if he really had MPD, he would probably have three personalities. Sure enough, when Bianchi was hypnotized, a third personality, Billy, appeared. Faced with this and other evidence against him, Bianchi dropped his insanity plea and plea-bargained for a life sentence rather than execution (Spanos, Weekes, & Bertrand, 1985).

Treatments for Dissociative Disorders

Psychodynamic therapies are designed to help the patient relive painful repressed experiences through hypnosis. While in trance, the person relives the trauma. When awakened, the person is kept talking and then realizes that he or she is recounting past events. The person gets in touch with the strong emotions that led to dissociation. This helps to fuse the personality. Barbiturate-assisted interviews have also been used with success. The person is given an injection of the drug sodium amytal and, under its influence, is better able to recall the forgotten material or even uncover other personalities. Despite some behavioral explanations for dissociative disorders, there is little impressive evidence that behavior therapy is an effective treatment (Combs & Ludwig, 1982).

SUMMARY

5-1 Anxiety disorders are the most common mental disorders in the United States. They are characterized by overwhelming tension, worry, apprehension, fear, physiological arousal, and avoidance behavior. Anxiety disorders include generalized anxiety disorder, panic disorders, phobia disorders, obsessive-compulsive disorder, and posttraumatic stress disorder. Biological explanations focus on hereditary predispositions and biochemical abnormalities. Psychological explanations follow traditional psychodynamic, behavioral, cognitive, and humanistic and existential theories. The most common biological treatments involve the use of psychotropic drugs. Psychological treatments are based on insight, exposure, cognitive restructuring, and self-acceptance.

5-2 Somatoform disorders present symptoms suggestive of a physical disorder, but they have no organic basis. They include somatization disorder, hypochondriasis, somatoform pain disorder, conversion disorder, and body dysmorphic disorder. Few convincing biological explanations have been advanced, and biological treatments have been confined to antidepressant and sedative drugs. Psychodynamic explanations have traditionally dominated thinking about causation, but behavioral and sociocultural explanations have recently been proposed. Psychological therapy can be psychodynamic, behavioral, or family-oriented, but few controlled outcome studies have been conducted in order to determine treatment effectiveness.

5-3 Dissociative disorders involve an alteration of consciousness, identity, or memory. They include psychogenic amnesia, psychogenic fugue, depersonalization disorder, and multiple personality disorder. Evidence for a biological basis for dissociative disorders is scant, and the more influential explanations and therapies have been psychodynamic.

TERMS TO REMEMBER

agoraphobia (p. 115)
anxiety (p. 112)
anxiety disorder (p. 112)
assertiveness training (p. 124)
benzodiazepines (p. 121)
body dysmorphic disorder (p. 129)
compulsions (p. 116)
conversion disorder (p. 128)
depersonalization disorder (p. 132)
dissociative disorders (p. 131)
exposure therapy (p. 123)
generalized anxiety disorder
   (p. 114)
hypochondriasis (p. 128)
multiple personality disorder
   (p. 132)
neuroses (p. 112)

neuroticism (p. 130)
obsessions (p. 116)
obsessive-compulsive disorder
   (p. 116)
panic disorders (p. 115)
phobia disorders (p. 114)
posttraumatic stress disorder
   (p. 117)
preparedness theory (p. 121)
psychogenic amnesia (p. 132)
psychogenic fugue (p. 132)
simple phobias (p. 114)
social phobia (p. 115)
somatization disorder (p. 127)
somatoform disorder (p. 127)
somatoform pain disorder (p. 128)
thought stopping (p. 124)

SUGGESTED READINGS

Beck, A. T., & Emery, G., with Greenberg, R. L. (1985). *Anxiety disorders and phobias.* New York: Basic Books.
Freud, S. (1909, 1963). *Three case histories.* New York: Collier.
Keyes, D. (1982). *The minds of Billy Milligan.* New York: Bantam.
Rachman, S. J. (1990). *Fear and courage* (2nd ed.). San Francisco: Freeman.

LEGAL AND ETHICAL ISSUES: THE INSANITY DEFENSE

"Not guilty by reason of insanity" is a jury verdict we are all familiar with. In actuality, the insanity defense is used in fewer than 2 percent of homicide cases and is successful in only a small fraction of those cases. Nevertheless, the insanity defense is controversial because criminal law is based on the assumption that people have free will and are therefore responsible for their own behavior. To prove insanity, the rule upon which criminal law is based must be broken.

Insanity as a legal notion is not based on DSM-III-R or any other criteria from psychology or psychiatry. Merely being diagnosed as having a mental disorder is not sufficient to prove insanity. The *M'Naghten rule* states that a person is insane if when the crime was committed, the perpetrator was so mentally defective that he or she could not understand the nature of the act or did not know right from wrong. The M'Naghten rule is widely used in the United States. The American Law Institute has proposed an insanity rule known as the *ALI* or *Brawner rule*. The first part of the ALI rule states that a person is insane and is not responsible if at the time of the crime, he or she was suffering from a mental disease or defect and lacked the capacity to understand the wrongfulness of the act or to conform to the requirements of the law. The second part of the ALI rule states that mental disease or defect cannot include any abnormality evidenced by repeated criminal acts.

In other words, being a criminal does not, in and of itself, prove insanity. Under both the M'Naghten and ALI rules, the clinician must judge in the present what a person was mentally capable of at some point in the past—certainly a difficult task.

The position of the American Psychological Association (APA) is that current standards for judging insanity are based on political and social pressures, rather than on scientific research that proves clinicians can accurately judge one's mental state in the manner required by law. According to the APA, there is little compelling scientific evidence that the behavioral sciences can provide informed decisions about whether a person could appreciate the wrongfulness of an act or could have the self-control to conform to the law (R. Rogers, 1987).

To date, two Vietnam veterans have been acquitted of murder charges on the grounds of PTSD. In 1975, a vet was convicted of stabbing murders and was executed in Florida's electric chair (Sparr & Atkinson, 1986). In the case of Billy Milligan, the judge used the ALI rule and concluded that "the doctors all testify that at the time of the acts in question, the defendant was mentally ill . . . and was unable to distinguish between right and wrong . . . and he did not have the ability to refrain from doing these acts (Keyes, 1982, pp. 110–111).

Chapter SIX

Stress-Related Disorders

OBJECTIVES

1. Identify three alternative definitions of stress.
2. Discuss three ways of measuring stress.
3. Discuss the relationship of stress to coronary heart disease, peptic ulcers, rheumatoid arthritis, headaches, and bronchial asthma.
4. Explain the psychological factors associated with each stress-related disorder.
5. Describe the relationships between the Type A behavior pattern, the hostility complex, and coronary heart disease.
6. Discuss the diathesis-stress hypothesis of psychosomatic illness.
7. Describe biological factors that affect the development of stress-related disorders.
8. Explain how personality factors are involved in stress-related disorders.
9. Describe how coping and social support are related to illness.
10. Discuss the role of psychotherapy and stress management techniques in the treatment of stress-related disorders.

L eonard, the 62-year-old president of a small company, went to his internist complaining of abdominal pains. Tests revealed an ulcer. One telltale sign that psychological factors contributed to Leonard's ulcer was that it took him six weeks to find the time to have the testing completed. He claimed he was just too busy to get away from work and could not afford to be sick because his company was all he had.

The doctor told him that he had to learn to take it easy, but all Leonard could do was comment that he was never one to take it easy. The doctor recommended a psychiatric consultation, but Leonard did not immediately consent. After several more days of pain, he finally agreed.

The attitudes expressed by Leonard are not uncommon in individuals with stress-related disorders. We will return to this case throughout the chapter to see how such conditions develop and what can be done to relieve them (Spitzer et al., 1983).

6-1 ▓ THE NATURE OF STRESS

Stress is a commonly used word in American culture. Stress seems to be everywhere, affecting everyone. We take stress tests in popular magazines, listen to discussions of stress on television talk shows, and even attend stress management workshops. The psychology and self-help sections of most bookstores are well stocked with books telling us how to recognize and cope with stress. But what *is* stress, and how can we measure it?

▓ Definitions of Stress

There is no universally accepted scientific definition of stress. Many experts define stress as the negative effects that stimuli have on us. Stress expert Hans Selye describes stress as a nonspecific change in body physiology, without reference to cause (1976). For example, taking an exam, driving a car in bumper-to-bumper traffic, or going on a first date can all be stressful if they produce adverse physiological changes. Other researchers define stress as any negative or positive life change (Holmes & Rahe, 1967). Events viewed as negative cause *distress* and events viewed as positive cause *eustress*. This definition focuses on the **stressor**, the stimulus that elicits stress, more than one's psychological or physiological reactions to the stressor.

stressor A stimulus that elicits stress.

The problem with these definitions is that they do not consider how people appraise their circumstances or how they perceive their ability to cope with stressors. A situation that is stressful for one person may not be stressful for another. Stress is not a property of the stimulus itself. Stressfulness depends on the personal meaning of the situation and on whether the individual believes he or she can handle that situation. Psychologists Richard Lazarus and Susan Folkman have advanced an alternative cognitive definition of stress, emphasizing the judgments we make about our ability to cope with stimuli. Lazarus and Folkman define **stress** as "a particular relationship between the person and the environment that is appraised by the person as taxing or exceeding his or her resources and endangering his or her well-being" (1984, p. 19). This is the definition we will use in this chapter.

stress A person-environment relationship appraised as taxing resources.

Stress is found virtually everywhere in American culture. For many people, working, taking an exam, or driving in bumper-to-bumper traffic can all be stressful.

Measurement of Stress

There are many ways to measure stress. One way is to use self-report questionnaires. The *Social Readjustment Rating Scale* (SRRS) measures stress in terms of positive or negative life change (Holmes & Rahe, 1967). Using the SRRS, subjects identify life changes they have recently experienced—for example, the death of a spouse, serving a jail sentence, being fired at work, having a son or daughter leave home, getting married, or getting divorced. "Stress points" are given for each life event, regardless of the subject's reaction, and weighted scores are tallied. In general, people with higher scores are considered more likely to develop a physical illness.

The SRRS has been an important tool for measuring stress, but it has been criticized for several reasons. First, the association between life change and illness is weak. Second, most psychologists believe that only events perceived as negative are stressful. Third, the SRRS does not consider the role of minor daily events.

The *Assessment of Daily Experience Scale* (ADE) addresses some of the criticisms of the SRRS by asking subjects to rate minor as well as major daily life experiences in terms of their psychological impact (Stone & Neale, 1982). Sample items about work-related activities include criticism or praise for job performance, socializing with co-workers, meeting deadlines, being promoted, or quitting a job.

Another way of measuring stress is to observe behavior. Stress can be manifest in facial expression, posture, activity levels, tone of voice, and other behaviors. However, such measures rely heavily on clinical inference and are not reliable when taken alone.

Finally, stress can be measured through its effect on respiration, blood pressure, heart rate, skin resistance, and other autonomic nervous system (ANS) indicators (see Chapter 4). Stress indexes that combine data from self-reports, behavioral observation, and physiological responses yield the most valid and reliable data.

Mind-Body Relationships

The idea that thoughts and feelings affect our physical health, which dates back several thousand years, is an expression of the ongoing philosophical dispute over the relationship between mind and body. Are mind and body separate, the same, or distinct but interacting? Ancient Greek and Roman physicians recognized a connection between mind and body and believed that physical problems could best be cured if the physician had a complete knowledge of the whole person. Thus, understanding the individual's mental and emotional state was an important part of the medical evaluation.

The notion of a mind-body connection lost popularity during the Middle Ages with a revival of religious explanations for mental and physical phenomena, but scientific interest was revitalized during the psychoanalytic movement in the late nineteenth and early twentieth centuries. We have seen that psychoanalysis was founded on the idea that repressed conflicts could be "converted" into physical symptoms, as in hysteria.

psychosomatic medicine
The study of relationships between emotions and disease.

The 1930s marked the start of the modern era of **psychosomatic medicine**, which is a medical discipline focused on the relationship between emotional conflicts and physical disease. A pioneer in this movement was psychoanalyst Franz Alexander (1891–1964), who proposed that suppressed emotional conflicts could be manifest as headaches, ulcers, high blood pressure, or arthritis, depending on which organ system was most vulnerable. Alexander believed that the organ most likely to be affected would be one weakened by previous illness, heredity, or other factors (H. I. Kaplan, 1985).

behavioral medicine
Integration of scientific disciplines in understanding illness.

Psychosomatic medicine also promoted research showing that emotions were accompanied by arousal of the ANS. As the study of stress became a distinct area of research, emerging scientific disciplines led to a greater understanding of how psychological factors relate to physical illness. One discipline, **behavioral medicine**, integrates medical knowledge, behavioral science, and

Psychoanalyst Franz Alexander was a pioneer in the field of psychosomatic medicine and the modern disciplines of behavioral medicine and health psychology. He proposed the theory that suppressed emotional conflicts could be manifested in physical symptoms.

behavior therapy and applies them to the understanding and treatment of physical illness. **Health psychology** applies psychological knowledge and principles to the understanding of health, illness, and the prevention of illness. In recent years, these two disciplines have overlapped in clinical practice (Rodin & Salovey, 1989).

health psychology
Application of psychology to the understanding and prevention of illness.

6-2   TYPES OF STRESS-RELATED DISORDERS

stress-related disorders
Physical ailments caused in part by psychological factors.

psychological factors affecting physical condition A DSM-III-R category for stress-related disorders.

cardiovascular disorders Abnormalities of heart and blood vessel function.

coronary heart disease Narrowing of coronary arteries.

Stress-related disorders are physical symptoms or ailments to which thoughts, emotions, and behaviors are believed to contribute. They were called *"psychosomatic and psychophysiologic disorders"* in the DSM system; they are now placed in a DSM-III-R category called **psychological factors affecting physical condition**, on Axis I (American Psychiatric Association, 1987).

Cardiovascular Disorders

Cardiovascular disorders involve abnormal function in the heart and blood vessels. Psychological factors are known or suspected to contribute to coronary heart disease and hypertension. **Coronary heart disease** (CHD) is marked by a progressive narrowing of the coronary arteries, caused by a buildup of fats. This condition, *atherosclerosis*, diminishes the oxygen supply to heart muscle cells and causes angina (chest pain). Atherosclerosis increases the risk of a heart attack as muscle tissue is destroyed.

CHD and the Type A Behavior Pattern. Modern studies of psychological factors in CHD date back to the 1950s. Cardiologists Raymond Rosenman and Meyer Friedman noted that their patients shared certain behavior and personality characteristics and that traditional risk factors, such as family history of CHD, diet, and sedentary lifestyle, could not adequately explain CHD. Their

Type A behavior pattern
Behaviors and traits associated with coronary heart disease.

ideas crystallized when a worker who was reupholstering chairs in their waiting room commented that it looked like their patients had been sitting on the edges of their seats. Spurred on by these observations, Rosenman and Friedman (1974) defined the **Type A behavior pattern** (TABP) as a cluster of behaviors and personality characteristics involving competitive striving for achievement, easily aroused hostility, aggressiveness, and time urgency. Eventually, a structured interview schedule was designed to assess TABP. Sample questions from the interview are presented in Table 6-1 (Rosenman, 1978).

Type A individuals try to squeeze 25 hours into a 24-hour day, and they are competitively immersed in several things at the same time. Their self-esteem depends on their accomplishments, and they are emotionally and physiologically aroused much of the time. Type A individuals are often irritable and angry, and they may express their anger outwardly in the form of forceful speech and vigorous body movements. Others turn their anger inward, seething and feeling on "edge." Two hard-driving Type A individuals who have suffered heart attacks are professional football coaches Mike Ditka of the Chicago Bears and Dan Reeves of the Denver Broncos. However, you do not have to be a football coach or be Type A to have a heart attack (M. Friedman & Rosenman, 1974; Rosenman, 1978).

Individuals with Type A characteristics such as those pictured here are extremely competitive, aggressive, hostile, and time-pressured. Type A characteristics are associated with an increased risk for coronary heart disease.

TABLE 6-1 ■■■ **SAMPLE QUESTIONS FROM THE BEHAVIOR PATTERN INTERVIEW**

---

1. Does your job carry heavy responsibility?
2. When you are angry or upset, do people around you know about it? How do you show it?
3. Is there competition on your job? Do you enjoy it?
4. Do you have children? When they were around the ages of 6 and 8, did you ever play competitive games with them, like checkers or monopoly?
5. Do you eat or walk rapidly? After you've finished eating do you sit around the table and chat, or do you get up and get going?
6. How do you feel about waiting in line at the bank, supermarket, or post office?

Source: From ''The Interview Method of Assessment of the Coronary-Prone Behavior Pattern'' by R. H. Rosenman. In T. M. Dembroski, S. M. Weiss, J. L. Shields, S. G. Haynes, and M. Feinleib (Eds.), 1978, *Coronary-Prone Behavior.* New York: Springer-Verlag.

Barry was 49 years old when he began having chest pains. Although he didn't know it at the time, this was the first signal of coronary heart disease and of the heart attack he would have later that year.

Barry was a busy dentist who had wanted to be a millionaire by age 40. He was always trying to expand his practice and would become angry when patients canceled appointments. He took only 20 minutes for lunch so he could squeeze in more patients, and he was always reminding his staff to ''pack'' his appointment book. When he wasn't working, Barry had trouble relaxing at home and always had to do something to keep busy. Often he would go to his office and rearrange furniture or check his dental equipment.

While driving to his office one day, Barry had a heart attack. He survived and is back at dentistry, but he is finding it difficult to change the behaviors and attitudes that contributed to his heart attack.

The Hostility Complex and CHD. Since it was first proposed, the TABP has been accepted as an important risk factor in coronary heart disease. However, further research suggested that the original TABP was too broad and that only certain elements of the TABP are relevant to heart disease. Now there is evidence that the active ingredient of the TABP is the **hostility complex**, described as frequent anger, competitiveness, and irritation at small things like waiting in line at the bank or waiting for someone to make a left turn at an intersection (H. S. Friedman & Booth-Kewley, 1988; K. A. Mathews, 1988; K. A. Mathews & Haynes, 1986; Williams & Barefoot, 1988; Wright, 1988).

hostility complex The active ingredient of the Type A personality.

Further clarification of the risk factors suggests five paths to CHD, four of which are related to psychological factors:

1. A family history of CHD
2. Self-imposed but not Type A behaviors, such as eating a high-fat diet, smoking, and following a sedentary lifestyle
3. Inability to ventilate anger (anger-in)
4. Persistent outward expression of anger (anger-out), in combination with feelings of time pressure and chronic ANS arousal
5. Traditional TABP, as measured by the Behavior Pattern Interview

Apparently, anger-in is the most accurate predictor of CHD. Some people who hold their anger in do not recognize their anger, and others recognize their anger but are either unable or reluctant to express it (Wright, 1988).

Mechanisms of CHD. We have discussed the relationships between Type A characteristics and CHD, but how do such characteristics actually lead to pathological changes in heart tissue? The best explanation is that Type A individuals exhibit overactivity in the sympathetic branch of the ANS when confronted with stressful situations (Krantz & Manuck, 1984). These "hot reactors" have a chronically increased heart rate, raised blood pressure, and high levels of stress hormones. Coronary-prone individuals also show hyperactivity in the *H-P-A axis*, a brain-body circuit involving the hypothalamus, pituitary, and adrenal glands. The long-term result is "wear and tear" on coronary arteries and a buildup of atherosclerotic plaque inside the arterial walls. Thus, the hostility reactions of Type A individuals can directly lead to heart disease (Williams & Barefoot, 1988; Wright, 1988).

hypertension   High blood pressure.

Hypertension, defined as blood pressure in excess of 140/90 millimeters of mercury, is a prevalent condition affecting between 10 and 30 percent of the adult population when mild hypertension is also considered (Inter-society Commission for Heart Disease Resources, 1970). Hypertension is a major risk factor for CHD, stroke, and kidney failure. Sixty-six percent of patients with CHD have a history of borderline or high blood pressure, and we have already noted that Type A people have increased blood pressure under stress (U.S. Department of Health and Human Services, 1984).

essential hypertension High blood pressure presumed to be related to psychological factors.

When the cause is unknown, high blood pressure is called **essential hypertension** and is presumed to be related to psychological factors. Essential hypertension comprises 90 to 95 percent of hypertensive cases. Evidence for a psychological component to essential hypertension comes from observations that individuals with the condition are tense, have Type A characteristics, and can often lower their pressure if they are able to relax (Inter-society Commission for Heart Disease Resources, 1970; U.S. Department of Health and Human Resources, 1984).

Peptic Ulcers

The term *ulcer* is almost synonymous with *psychosomatic disorder*. The stereotypic Wall Street broker or corporate executive gulps antacids like candy, and you have probably heard someone say, "This job is gonna give me an ulcer." A **peptic ulcer** is an open sore in the gastrointestinal (GI) tract, caused by digestive secretions, or stomach acids, eating through the GI lining and into the surrounding tissue. If located in the stomach, the sores are called *gastric ulcers*. Leonard, in our opening case illustration, had a *duodenal ulcer*, which is a sore located at the junction of the stomach and small intestine.

peptic ulcer   An open sore in the gastrointestinal tract.

Peptic ulcers are a major health problem, affecting 12 percent of men and 6 percent of women in the United States, and are responsible for more than 7,000 deaths, 400,000 hospitalizations, and 150,000 surgical operations each year. Ulcers cause lost work time and great personal misery. Some ulcers respond well to treatment, but many recur. Duodenal ulcers often present a life-long problem (M. M. Eisenberg, 1978; Oken, 1985).

Stress and Ulcers. In 1825, an army surgeon reported the case of a Canadian trapper who was shot in the abdomen. The gunshot produced a permanent

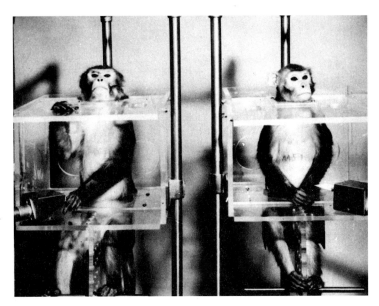

Brady's studies of "executive monkeys" were initially interpreted as evidence for a psychosomatic basis for ulcers. Although Brady's findings have been refuted, researchers have continued to seek a psychological link between psychological factors and ulcers.

hole through which the surgeon directly observed changes in stomach secretions when the man was afraid or angry (Oken, 1985). Numerous animal and human studies have since demonstrated a correlation between stress and the development of ulcers (J. M. Weiss, 1977). In an often-cited study, pairs of monkeys were restrained in chairs next to each other. An electrical shock was delivered, and one monkey could press a lever to terminate the shock for both monkeys. The second monkey, yoked to the first, was powerless to terminate the shocks. Thus, the first monkey, called the "executive," was responsible for "making decisions" about the welfare of both monkeys. The results showed that "executive monkeys" were more likely than their yoked counterparts to develop ulcers (Brady, 1958).

These findings were initially interpreted as evidence for a psychosomatic basis for ulcers, but the research could not be replicated. It was ultimately determined that the "executives" had been preselected on the basis of being more assertive and "take-charge," and this rendered the results meaningless. In fact, subsequent studies have indicated that ulcers are actually less likely to develop in subjects who are in a position of control, especially if the shock is predictable.

Researchers have demonstrated that prolonged restraint can also cause ulcers in animals, but such research cannot be conducted with humans because of ethical constraints. It is difficult to determine a clear causal relationship between stress and ulcers in humans (J. M. Weiss, 1977).

Leonard gave the appearance of being in control, but there was certainly enough in his background and current attitudes to suggest otherwise. Both he and his wife had been confined in Nazi concentration camps, where they witnessed many atrocities, during World War II. Leonard thought he would never get out alive and felt helpless. Upon coming to the United States, he struggled at various low-paying jobs until he began his business. He described his whole life as constant aggravation and was always on guard for fear that someone would take advantage of him and ruin his business. Leonard told his psychiatrist, "It's dog eat dog. The one who trusts loses" (Spitzer et al., 1983, p. 259).

Personality and Ulcers. The ulcer-prone personality was described by traditional psychodynamic theorists as an individual with intense unconscious conflicts over the need to be loved. The ulcer-prone individual overcompensates for dependency needs by acting self-reliant and independent. Since others usually take care of someone who is physically ill, this satisfies the individual's unconscious needs while allowing the appearance of independence. Alexander referred to this type of individual as "pseudoindependent." Although these ideas have generated much thinking and research, there is no scientific consensus on their validity, nor has any other distinct ulcer-prone personality type consistently been isolated (M. M. Eisenberg, 1978).

Rheumatoid Arthritis

rheumatoid arthritis
A chronic joint disease.

Rheumatoid arthritis (RA) is a chronic joint disease marked by stiffness, pain, swelling, and tenderness. As motion becomes restricted, there is some disability. Rheumatoid arthritis affects approximately 1 percent of the population and is three times more common in women than men.

Many factors have been implicated in the causation of RA, including infectious agents, heredity, and the immune system. Many researchers believe that RA is an *autoimmune disease*, meaning that the body's defenses go awry and it mistakenly assaults itself. Whatever the primary cause, RA ultimately causes injury to small blood vessels, joint inflammation, and a mobilization of antibodies that result in the destruction of joint tissue (Anderson, Bradley, Young, McDaniel, & Wise, 1985).

Personality and RA. The RA-prone individual has been described as depressed, dependent, and perfectionistic. Women with arthritis are often described as struggling with a conflict over the suppression and expression of anger. As yet, there is no compelling scientific evidence for an arthritic personality, nor are there any psychosocial factors that consistently distinguish arthritics from anyone else (Anderson et al., 1985).

We are beginning to identify physical pathways through which psychological factors may produce their effects on joints. For example, hormones whose levels change in response to stress also regulate joint activity. Furthermore, joints receive neural input from the ANS. These neural pathways may reveal mechanisms whereby stress could influence RA (Anderson et al., 1985; Silverman, 1985).

Headaches

Headache, one of the most common medical complaints, affects 80 percent of the American population. As many as 20 percent of the people seeking medical consultation complain of headache as the primary symptom. Headaches cause work impairment, sick days, and relationship problems, creating a financial burden for afflicted individuals and society as well. Two types of stress-related headache are migraines and tension headaches.

migraines Vascular headaches.

Migraines. Migraines are vascular headaches marked by a throbbing, stabbing sensation that is usually confined to one side of the head. Pain occurs because of excessive opening (dilation) of cerebral arteries, which send an increased blood flow to the brain. This produces pressure, tenderness, and swelling in the tissue surrounding the arteries. Nausea, vomiting, and sensitivity to light and sound are also common (Adams, Feuerstein, & Fowles, 1980; T. L. Thompson, 1985).

Changes in estrogen levels, caffeine consumption, and intake of monosodium glutamate (MSG—a flavor enhancer) are known to trigger migraines. Since migraines tend to run in families, a hereditary predisposition is suspected. Psychologically, migraine sufferers have been described by clinicians as perfectionistic, orderly, rigid, and preoccupied with moral issues, but scientific support for this or any other personality profile is weak (Adams et al., 1980; T. L. Thompson, 1985).

Lisa, age 32, had suffered from migraines since she was 13. Although the exact cause of her migraines eluded her and her doctors, it was evident that stress often helped trigger them. In adolescence Lisa often got headaches when she felt pressured in school or when her parents were arguing at home. Later her own marital discord often triggered attacks. Lisa's migraines usually began after a brief "aura" period during which her limbs on one side became weak and tingled. For several minutes her speech would be slurred and she would think she was having a stroke. Shortly thereafter, the headache would begin.

Tension Headaches. **Tension headaches** are characterized by contractions of head and neck muscles, producing a dull generalized ache. Sufferers report the sensation of having a band tightened where the back of the head meets the neck. Tension headaches usually start late in a stressful, duty-filled day. Individuals who get tension headaches tend to be tense, "keyed up," and competitive (Adams et al., 1980; T. L. Thompson, 1985).

tension headaches
Headaches involving muscular contractions.

Bronchial Asthma

bronchial asthma
A respiratory disorder involving constriction of airways.

Bronchial asthma, which affects 1 in 20 Americans, is a respiratory disorder involving swelling and excessive secretions within the bronchial passageways of the lungs, constriction of the airways, breathing difficulty, and wheezing. It is believed that the bronchial tubes of asthma patients are extremely sensitive to allergic agents (allergens). Some patients may be predisposed to asthma when they catch viral infections or encounter dust and fumes. Psychological factors can make the individual vulnerable to recurrent asthma attacks (H. S. Friedman & Booth-Kewley, 1987; H. Weiner, 1985).

Personality and Asthma. Most descriptions of the asthma-prone personality reflect psychodynamic ideas. According to this view, asthma-prone individuals are fundamentally infantile and unconsciously crave protection. Adult asthmatics raised by overprotective and dominating mothers may be dependent, immature, and prone to depression and feelings of helplessness. These individuals may suffer asthma attacks when their need to be protected is frustrated.

Asthma attacks can occur during periods of emotional excitement or in response to separation or loss. However, it is not clear how this happens. One possibility is that emotional states are accompanied by chemical changes in the lungs. This idea is based on evidence that the bronchial musculature is under the control of the ANS and is influenced by neurotransmitters known to be involved in physiological arousal and emotions (H. S. Friedman & Booth-Kewley, 1987; H. Weiner, 1985).

6-3 ▒ CAUSES OF STRESS-RELATED DISORDERS

psychosomatic hypothesis The idea that psychological factors contribute to physical disorders.

The **psychosomatic hypothesis** states that psychological factors play a role in the causation and maintenance of physical disorders. Despite a long history of speculation, anecdote, and research, support for the psychosomatic hypothesis is mixed. Some researchers even conclude that the presumed relationships between psychological factors and physical disorders are nothing but folklore (Angell, 1985). For people who subscribe to the psychosomatic hypothesis, the challenge has been to identify the relevant psychological factors and to show how these factors influence the structure and function of affected organs (Hurst, Jenkins, & R. M. Rose, 1976).

The consensus among clinicians and researchers is that the development of any disease is a multifactorial process that requires the interaction of biological and psychosocial variables. For example, a genetic defect can act as a primary cause of coronary heart disease. Hypertension could predispose, or make individuals more vulnerable, to CHD by aggravating the existing defect. Stress and Type A characteristics can act as trigger mechanisms for heart attack and may even be predisposing through direct effects on arteries. A sedentary lifestyle, smoking, and obesity may promote heart disease.

diathesis-stress hypothesis (dye-uh-*the*-sis) The idea that illness results from physical weakness and psychological stress.

This simplified explanation of the multifactorial causes of heart disease is an expression of the **diathesis-stress hypothesis** of psychosomatic disorders, which proposes that physical illness is the result of a physical weakness (diathesis) caused by hereditary errors, trauma, or prior illness, interacting with psychological stress. This means that stress, personality, lifestyle, emotions, and other psychological factors act in concert with an assortment of physical factors to produce disease. The role of psychological factors may be great in some people, less in others, and virtually nonexistent in still others. In this framework, stress may directly cause an illness, create a predisposition to it, or trigger or maintain it.

▒ Biological Causes of Stress-Related Disorders

Numerous physiological changes occur in our brains and bodies when we feel stressed. Years of research have detailed these alterations with greater precision. In short, it appears that distressing experiences may induce activity in brain circuits that are neurally and hormonally connected to the body's organ systems. Activation of these circuits is associated with pathological changes in the structure and function of internal organs (Axelrod & Reisine, 1984; Levinthal, 1990).

emergency theory The idea that stress disrupts homeostasis and activates the ANS.

Physiological Factors. In 1929, biologist Walter Cannon (1871–1945) proposed that biological systems strive to maintain *homeostasis*, a condition in which body functions are balanced in a way that makes the system work optimally. (The maintenance of body temperature is a good example of homeostasis. Regardless of external temperature, your body strives to maintain its internal temperature within narrow limits.) According to Cannon's **emergency theory**, stress disrupts homeostasis, thus activating the sympathetic branch of the ANS and prompting the secretion of stress hormones such as epinephrine. Cannon referred to these physiological changes as the "fight or flight" reaction that prepares the body to meet situational demands (Cannon, 1929).

general adaptation syndrome A three-stage model of stress response.

Cannon's ideas were expanded by Hans Selye, who proposed the **general adaptation syndrome** (GAS), a three-stage model describing the body's reac-

People who feel overwhelmed by work and other responsibilities often suffer from stress-related disorders. The woman pictured here is experiencing a job-related tension headache.

tion to stressors. The GAS was originally formulated to describe reactions of laboratory animals to physical stressors such as cold, heat, overcrowding, and food deprivation. In the GAS, the initial reaction to stressors is bodily arousal. If the person does not adequately cope with the problem, other physiological mechanisms go into action. Under prolonged stress, the body is no longer able to resist and protect itself, and this causes physical disease (Selye, 1976). Table 6-2 describes the GAS stages.

TABLE 6-2 ▓ **GENERAL ADAPTATION SYNDROME**

Stage	Physiological Features
Stage 1: Alarm	ANS arousal; secretion of epinephrine and norepinephrine
Stage 2: Resistance	Increased activity of hypothalamic-pituitary-adrenal axis; secretion of adrenal steroids
Stage 3: Exhaustion	Organ "breakdown" due to overburdened physiological systems

Source: From *The Stress of Life* by H. Selye, 1976, New York: McGraw-Hill.

PROFILE
Hans Hugo Selye
(1907–1982)

Hans Hugo Selye, one of the great pioneers of medicine, was the originator of a famous model of stress called the *general adaptation syndrome* (GAS). His revolutionary concept of stress led to many treatments for coronary diseases, kidney failure, arthritis, and ulcers.

Selye was born in Vienna, Austria, and was raised near Budapest, Hungary, in a large mansion converted into a clinic by his parents. His father was a surgeon and general practitioner in a long family line of physicians, so it was natural for Selye to lean toward medicine. He received his M.D. degree from the German University in Prague, Czechoslovakia, in 1929 and a Doctor of Science degree from McGill University in Montreal in 1942. It was at McGill that he began to form his concept of the GAS. Selye left McGill to become the first director of the Institute of Medicine at the University of Montreal, where he had the luxury of extraordinary laboratory space and worked with many prominent researchers from all over the world. It was here that his research efforts peaked.

Selye admitted that the greatest influence on him was the standard of excellence set by his family. At an early age he was taught to detest me-

diocrity and quitting. One event always stood out in his mind. When Selye was 9 years old his father bought him a black Arab pony. One day the horse jumped high and Hans fell off and broke his arm. As soon as his father had set the broken arm in plaster, he commanded Hans to mount the horse again immediately, fearing that his son would always be afraid of horses otherwise.

Selye was considered a superb lecturer. He had enormous energy, charm, intelligence, imagination, and an unyielding determination to succeed. His command of eight languages allowed him to cover massive quantities of research literature few others could manage. Although Selye seemed cool and distant to some younger colleagues, he was actually very warm in his relationships, especially those with his wife and four children.

Selye's productivity was staggering. He authored more than 1600 scientific articles and over 40 monographs and treatises, including *Stress Without Distress*, *The Stress of Life*, and *Stress in Health and Disease*. Selye received more than 80 medals and prizes and 17 honorary degrees (Malmo, 1986; Selye, 1964, 1976).

---

somatic weakness hypothesis The idea that vulnerability to illness depends on the weakest organ system.

Genetics and Somatic Weakness. The **somatic weakness hyothesis** states that people carry a vulnerability to certain physical disorders, depending on which organ system is weakest. For example, we know that people with hypertension show an exaggerated cardiac reaction to stress when compared to people with normal blood pressure. Several studies also indicate that children

CLOSE-UP
Stress and Infection

Have you ever wondered whether stress can lower your resistance to infection? Does it seem that you are more likely to get a cold after a period of emotional turmoil? Some answers to these questions have come from a new interdisciplinary field called *psychoneuroimmunology*, which studies the complex interactions among mental states, nervous system functioning, and immunity (D. L. Felton et al., 1987; S. Y. Felton & Olschowka, 1987; R. Glaser et al., 1990; Kiecolt-Glaser & R. Glaser, 1984). Although this field emerged only in the late 1970s, provocative information has already been gathered about the relationships between stress and infectious diseases caused by viruses, bacteria, and other microorganisms.

It is well-known that susceptibility to infection is governed by the immune system, which produces defensive cells (lymphocytes) and proteins (antibodies). Connections between the brain and immune system have been identified, and we know that hormones secreted under stress can impair immune function (Jemmott & Locke, 1984; A. Stein, Schleifer, & Keller, 1985). Moreover, it is possible to classically condition suppression of immunity in rats (Ader & Cohen, 1985). These findings suggest that mental events could alter immune function, modify susceptibility to infections, and perhaps even increase the risk of certain types of cancer.

Many studies show a relationship between stress and infection by respiratory viruses, herpes virus, and bacteria, as well as tumors induced by viruses. For example, one study showed that West Point cadets under stress because they were highly motivated but were getting poor grades were more likely to develop mononucleosis than cadets under less stress. In another study, distressed subjects were more likely to develop signs of a cold infection than were subjects under less stress (Cohen & Williamson, 1991). Other studies have shown that increased risk of cancer is found in those who feel more helpless, have less social support, are unable to express their negative emotions, and have weaker emotional defenses (Justice, 1985).

Preliminary research suggests that psychological factors also play a role in acquired immune deficiency syndrome (AIDS), a viral disease that destroys the immune system (O'Leary, 1990). Once a person is infected, impaired immunity is correlated with depression, dejection, anger, and hostility. Unfortunately, attempts to improve the immunity of AIDS patients by improving their mental state have failed.

Psychoneuroimmunology promises to help us understand how stress and infection are related and may lead to new treatments for infectious diseases.

and adolescents with a family history of hypertension show elevated heart rate and blood pressure responses to stress, even if their resting blood pressure is normal. Moreover, cardiac reactivity is more similar in identical twins than in fraternal twins (R. J. Rose & Chesney, 1986). These observations suggest that hypertension predisposes to CHD and that the predisposition may have a hereditary component.

Psychosocial Causes of Stress-Related Disorders

Psychological explanations for stress-related disorders have focused on the causal role of predisposing personality characteristics, poor coping mechanisms, and weak social supports.

Personality and Illness. Years of research have failed to find distinct personality types at risk for particular stress-related illnesses. We now recognize that the relationship between personality and illness is far more complex than was previously thought. Psychologists Howard Friedman and Stephanie Booth-Kewley (1987) suggest four ways in which personality and illness may be related:

1. Personality may be related to disease by leading the person toward unhealthy habits such as smoking and drug abuse.
2. Personality may have a direct effect upon illness. For example, Type A characteristics may directly damage coronary arteries.
3. Personality may be a consequence rather than a cause of illness. Being ill may cause attitudes and behavior to change, and we may misconstrue these effects as causes. (Most studies try to relate personality and illness after the fact.)
4. Personality may be related to illness through a biological third variable. For example, a hyperresponsive nervous system may cause both anxious personality and heart disease.

In order to help clarify the relationship between personality and illness, researchers have analyzed studies relating specific personality variables to stress-related illnesses. Associations between personality characteristics and illnesses are weak at best, with the possible exception of the Type A personality and CHD. Instead of finding ulcer-prone, asthma-prone, or migraine-prone personalities, researchers have found stronger evidence for a generic **disease-prone personality** that consists of traits of anger and hostility, anxiety, and depression. In support of Selye's GAS model, studies suggest that stress produces a generalized disruption of bodily processes rather than discrete diseases (H. S. Friedman & Booth-Kewley, 1987).

disease-prone personality Traits associated with increased likelihood of disease.

A number of studies support the concept of the disease-prone personality. In one study, college women scoring high on Type A features were found to be more prone to migraine and tension headaches than women with few Type A characteristics (Woods, Morgan, Day, Jefferson, & Harris, 1984). In another study, subjects scoring high on Type A characteristics reported more GI and respiratory symptoms, assorted pains, and sleep disorders than subjects with fewer Type A features (Woods & Burns, 1984). Finally, a study of 457 men and women revealed that early childhood anxiety symptoms were significant predictors of migraine headaches later in life (Merikangas, Angst, & Isler, 1990).

In conclusion, it appears that the relationship between personality and illness is not folklore, but there is insufficient evidence to prove that specific traits cause specific illnesses.

Coping Mechanisms. We have emphasized that stress cannot be defined on the basis of the stimulus alone because stimuli are stressful only if we believe we cannot cope with them. The impact of stressors can be moderated by the way we appraise situations and cope with them (see Figure 6-1). *Appraisal* is a complex process by which we judge whether a particular circumstance is important to our well-being, and if so, how. **Coping** is defined as attempts we make to manage stimuli or situations that we appraise as threatening (Thoits, 1986). Physical vulnerabilities, along with thoughts, feelings, and other psychological factors, can increase our chances of developing an illness, but the effects

coping Attempts to manage stimuli viewed as threatening.

Figure 6-1 Stress, coping, and illness. *Greater stress and physical illness result when stimuli are appraised as negative and when our coping resources are inadequate.*

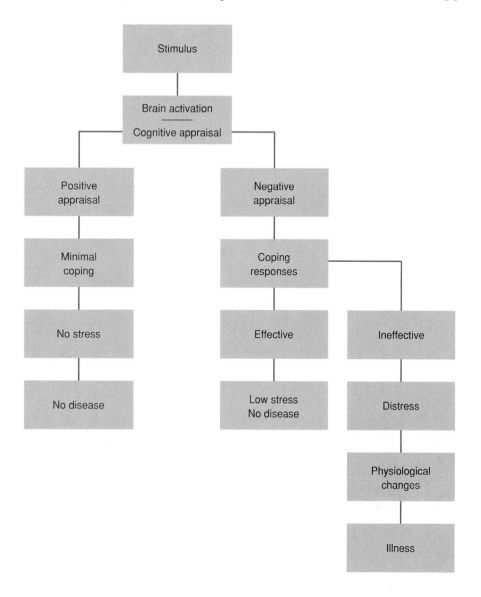

of these factors must be weighed against our coping abilities. Presumably, having stronger coping abilities makes us more resistant to stress (Folkman, R. S. Lazarus, Gruen, & DeLongis, 1986).

Three ways of coping with stress have been identified. *Problem-focused coping* involves direct attempts to change a situation by altering, removing, or avoiding it. *Emotion-focused coping* consists of reducing unpleasant feelings associated with stress. *Perception-focused coping* uses cognitive methods to reinterpret the meaning of stressful situations (Thoits, 1986).

Let's illustrate the use of the three coping strategies. Imagine that you are distressed because someone you find attractive is not interested in you. You could cope by avoiding the person (problem-solving coping) or by trying to "relax away" your distress (emotion-focused coping). If these methods do not work, you could tell yourself that sometimes people just are not made for each other (perception-focused coping).

Social Support. Many people find their coping abilities are bolstered through social support. *Social support* is defined as "functions performed for a distressed individual by significant others such as family members, friends, relatives, co-workers, and neighbors" (Thoits, 1986, p. 417). Social support is inversely related to illness—that is, higher levels of social support are correlated with a decreased incidence of physical illness.

Several hypotheses have been offered to explain the beneficial role of social support. The *buffering hypothesis* states that social support helps individuals cope by reducing the impact of stressful life events. The *main effect model* contends that social support provides individuals with stable social roles and a greater chance of having positive experiences. This model considers social support beneficial even when stress is minimal. Both models recognize that people who are embedded in social networks receive empathic understanding that enhances their self-esteem (Cohen & Wells, 1985).

In general, social support has the greatest effect when supporters are perceived as being similar to oneself in their experiences and cultural background, even when the supporter offers no real solution to the problem. Conversely, people perceived as dissimilar are often viewed as controlling and demanding (Cohen, Mermerstein, Kamarck, & Haberman, 1985; Cohen & Wells, 1985; Gottlieb, 1985; Rodin & Salovey, 1989; Steinglas, Westab, Kaplan, & DeNour, 1988; Thoits, 1986).

Marriage, Family, and Social Support. Happily married couples are better off socially and physically than unhappily married couples (Coyne & De-Longis, 1986). People in unhappy marriages are often more isolated and depressed, and they report more physical illnesses and alcohol problems. One study revealed that women who had been separated from their spouses for a year or less had weaker immune function and were more depressed than their married counterparts (Kiecolt-Glaser et al., 1987).

Spouses and family members can create problems by being overinvolved in each other's lives. They may be worried, overprotective, or overindulgent, and they may intrude in each other's affairs, thereby diminishing the other's sense of control and mastery.

Personal Factors and Coping. Although social support influences health and illness, each individual's reaction to stress is ultimately a personal matter. We are constantly trying to explain the situations in which we find ourselves, especially with regard to our state of health or illness. We tend to attribute responsibility for our condition to either external or internal factors. For example, someone may attribute a cold to an irresistible cold virus (external) or to personal negligence (internal). Over time, people develop attributional styles that influence how they cope. If we consistently see ourselves as inadequate and view things pessimistically, we are likely to develop feelings of helplessness and hopelessness. The attitude that we are not in control of our lives can determine whether we attempt to cope. And when we make the try, our attributions will affect the type and intensity of our coping (Peterson & Seligman, 1987; Rodin, 1986).

Animal studies show that a lack of control over noxious stimuli has adverse physical and behavioral consequences like those found in the stress response. Several clinical studies in humans have shown similar results. In one study, healthy people were exposed to loud noises. On one day subjects could terminate the noise by pressing the correct buttons, but on the "uncontrollable" day they failed to shut off the noise even when they pressed the same buttons. Subjects in the "uncontrollable" condition reported greater feelings of helplessness, tension, lack of control, stress, unhappiness, anxiety, and depression. They also had higher levels of stress hormones and higher ANS activity (Peterson & Seligman, 1987).

Additional support for the role of coping ability in reducing stress comes from Albert Bandura's self-efficacy research, which indicated that increased self-efficacy can diminish the negative effects of stressors on body physiology. In short, the stronger a person's belief in his or her coping ability, the weaker the stress response (Bandura, Taylor, Williams, Mefford, & Barchas, 1985).

6-4 ▨ TREATMENTS FOR STRESS-RELATED DISORDERS

Therapy for stress-related disorders entails medical as well as psychological treatments. In this section we discuss these treatments and how they are integrated.

▨ Medical Treatments

Individuals with stress-related disorders need medical attention, especially if there are serious physical complications. Depending on the illness, medication, dietary changes, or surgery may be indicated. For example, antihypertensive drugs may be prescribed for individuals with high blood pressure, antiinflammatory drugs can help reduce the discomfort of arthritis, and coronary bypass surgery may be necessary to counter the immediate risk of death from CHD. In our opening case illustration, Leonard was given medication to treat his ulcer and was told to make dietary changes. Many individuals with stress-related disorders suffer from symptoms of anxiety, and tranquilizers can provide them with some relief.

Medical therapy may relieve physical distress and reduce the immediate risk of complications, but it cannot modify the underlying psychological factors that contribute to stress-related disorders. For this reason, the soundest approach to treatment combines medical and psychological therapies.

▨ Psychological Treatments

Psychological treatments are designed to modify the cognitive and behavioral factors believed to contribute to illness. Individual, family, and marital therapy can help change faulty thinking patterns, enhance personal insight, and reduce the impact of interpersonal stressors. The ultimate goal is to encourage lifestyle changes that are more conducive to physical health. For example, there is preliminary evidence that Type A behavior can be altered by helping the individual modify the belief that hard-driving ambition is necessary for success. Type A behavior can also be modified by showing the person how to avoid potentially stressful situations (Haaga, 1987).

Leonard's therapist convinced him to learn to manage his time better, to leave some time for fun, and to alter his lifestyle in order to relieve some of the pressure. His style of living was deeply ingrained and difficult to modify. Leonard had poor insight into how his attitudes about his work and accomplishments contributed to his ulcer, and he also reported marital discord. Therefore, these issues were addressed in therapy (Spitzer et al., 1983).

Stress Management Techniques

stress management
Techniques for reducing
bodily arousal.

Health professionals employ a number of **stress management** techniques designed to reduce bodily arousal. These techniques, which include muscle relaxation, guided imagery, hypnosis, meditation, and biofeedback, are grounded in learning theory and behavioral medicine and are frequently part of a broader therapeutic program.

**progressive muscle
relaxation** An arousal-
reducing technique
involving contraction and
relaxation of muscles.

Muscle Relaxation. The procedure for **progressive muscle relaxation** has subjects alternately contract and relax major muscle groups. This technique, developed by physician Edmund Jacobsen in 1938, was originally a rigorous form of deep muscle relaxation that was taught over 50 or more sessions and required daily practice (Jacobsen, 1938). Over the years, abbreviated methods have been developed. In a typical sequence, the patient sits or reclines comfortably and alternately tenses and relaxes major muscle groups while concentrating on the difference between tension and relaxation. The patient practices this routine at home 15 to 20 minutes per day (Bernstein & Given, 1984; McGuigan, 1984).

guided imagery An
arousal-reducing technique
in which the patient
imagines pleasant
experiences.

Guided Imagery. **Guided imagery** techniques reduce bodily arousal by utilizing the individual's ability to imagine pleasurable experiences. Guided visual imagery is used most often, but sound, smell, taste, touch, and temperature imagery can be used as well. A guided imagery session lasts approximately half an hour. The following procedure was abbreviated for illustrative purposes:

> Close your eyes and begin to breathe slowly and naturally . . . and every time you exhale, just allow yourself to release the tension in your body. . . . Now I'd like you to imagine that you are at the beach . . . feel the warm sand beneath your feet. . . . Hear the sound of the surf rushing in and out. . . . Can you feel the sun caressing your body? . . . Smell the salt air . . . and taste the salt collected on your lips.

Hypnosis. In *hypnosis*, a method for achieving a trance state, the individual focuses on the inner sensations of calmness and reduced tension. Once the subject is in trance, the hypnotist makes suggestions that induce deep relaxation. The following illustrates an abbreviated trance induction (Barber, 1984; D. S. Weiss & Billings, 1988):

> Imagine that you are standing at the top of a beautiful staircase. I will count backward from 10 to 1 and as I do, imagine yourself walking down one step at a time. With each step feel yourself growing more relaxed—10 . . . 9 . . . more relaxed . . . 8 . . . 7 . . . deeper down . . . 6 . . . 5 . . . 4 . . . feeling heavy . . . 3 . . . 2 . . . 1. Now that you are at the bottom, take a deep breath. As you exhale slowly, feel yourself drifting into a state of deep relaxation. (Hadley & Studacher, 1989)

meditation A stress-
reducing technique
involving attention to a
repetitive stimulus.

Meditation. In **meditation** procedures, individuals reduce stress by directing their attention to a single repetitive stimulus. Meditation has been practiced in the Far East for centuries, and many ''Westernized'' forms of meditation have been developed. *Transcendental meditation* is the best-known and is the most widely practiced in the general population, but it is not commonly used in

Stress management techniques such as meditation and biofeedback are effective in reducing the state of overall bodily arousal that is part of the stress response.

TABLE 6-3   **BIOFEEDBACK PROCEDURES**

Modality	Measures	Clinical Uses
Electromyogram (EMG)	Muscle tension	Tension headaches, bruxism (tooth grinding), neuromuscular problems
Thermograph	Skin temperature	Migraines
Electrodermal response (EDR)	Sweat gland activity	ANS arousal, tension headaches, hypertension
Blood pressure (BP)	Resistance to blood flow in arteries	Hypertension
Electrocardiogram (ECG)	Heart rate	Cardiac rhythm problems

clinical practice. Standardized clinical techniques have been developed. For example, a subject can think of the same sound or word, such as the number 1, each time he or she exhales. Arousal is reduced as the body and mind enter a state of rest (Benson, 1975; Carrington, 1984).

biofeedback A technique that feeds back information about the body that is usually unnoticeable.

Biofeedback. Biofeedback is a therapeutic procedure that "feeds back" information to the patient about aspects of bodily functioning that people usually do not notice. Tones or colored lights signal changes in ANS arousal and muscle tension so that the person can learn how to control adverse stress reactions. The biofeedback machine or procedure itself does not produce the therapeutic effect. Rather, biofeedback is used in a package of stress management techniques as a tool to assist the person in self-regulation (J. A. Green & Shellenberger, 1985; McGovern, 1985; P. Norris, 1985; R. P. Olson, 1987; White & Tursky, 1985).

The modern practice of biofeedback dates back to research in the 1960s that indicated autonomic bodily processes could be conditioned, or controlled. In a classic paper, psychologist Neal Miller (1969) reported that rats could learn to control their heart rate and blood pressure if they were given a feedback signal. Subsequent research showed that other physiological responses could also be voluntarily controlled, including salivation, muscle tension, and sweat gland activity (R. P. Olson & M. S. Schwartz, 1987). Table 6-3 details biofeedback techniques used in stress management.

Evaluation of Stress Management Techniques. Stress management techniques are effective in the treatment of stress-related illness because they lower ANS arousal. Any measure that reduces arousal and makes the subject more calm will be effective against stress-related disorders.

There is controversy over whether some stress management techniques are better than others. Many studies show certain treatments to be superior to others in cases of specific stress-related illnesses (Lehrer & Woolfolk, 1984). In one study, 87 hypertensive patients were given either temperature biofeedback training or progressive relaxation treatment. At one month and again at one year after treatment, patients who had received temperature training had improved more than patients who had been taught muscle relaxation (Blanchard et al.,

1986). By contrast, other research shows that in treating migraines there is no difference between temperature biofeedback and assorted relaxation therapies. Likewise, most reviews have reported that differences between blood pressure biofeedback and various relaxation therapies are negligible (Achmon, Granek, Golomb, & Hart, 1989; Blanchard et al., 1985, 1986; Lehrer & Woolfolk, 1984; A. H. Roberts, 1985; M. S. Schwartz, 1987). However, the observation that biofeedback does not seem to offer an advantage over relaxation therapies should not be surprising. Biofeedback is not a distinct type of therapy but rather one of many tools that can be used to achieve relaxation (P. Norris, 1985; A. H. Roberts, 1985).

We are left with some unresolved issues, but the overwhelming consensus is that stress management techniques work—they are certainly better than no treatment at all. Considering the problems caused by stress and the fact that many individuals, including chidlren, cannot tolerate more aggressive medical treatments, psychologically based stress management techniques hold great promise.

SUMMARY

6-1 There are many ways of defining stress. We have defined it as a reaction to perceived threats against which coping resources are inadequate. Self-report questionnaires, behavioral observations, and physiological recordings can be used to measure stress. Stress and physical illness have long been thought to be related, but only since the early 1900s have their interconnections been investigated scientifically. The interdisciplinary fields of health psychology and behavioral medicine exemplify modern approaches to the mind-body relationship in health and illness.

6-2 Many physical disorders are influenced by psychological factors, including coronary heart disease, peptic ulcers, rheumatoid arthritis, headaches, and bronchial asthma. Although specific personality types have been thought to be associated with these conditions, only the association between Type A personality/hostility and coronary heart disease has received scientific support.

6-3 The diathesis-stress hypothesis states that psychological factors interact with organ system weakness in the development and maintenance of psychosomatic disorders. Stress alters brain and body physiology, rendering people more susceptible to organ breakdown and possibly to infectious disease. These effects are most prominent in people whose coping abilities are inadequate.

6-4 Treatment for stress-related disorders involves a combination of medical therapy and psychological treatments, including recommendations for attitude and lifestyle change, family and marital counseling, and stress management. Stress management techniques are part of a package of therapeutic procedures designed to reduce bodily arousal. They include muscle relaxation, guided imagery, hypnosis, and biofeedback.

TERMS TO REMEMBER

behavioral medicine (p. 142)
biofeedback (p. 160)
bronchial asthma (p. 149)
cardiovascular disorders (p. 143)
coping (p. 154)
coronary heart disease (p. 143)
diathesis-stress hypothesis (p. 150)
disease-prone personality (p. 154)
emergency theory (p. 150)
essential hypertension (p. 146)
general adaptation syndrome
    (p. 150)
guided imagery (p. 158)
health psychology (p. 143)
hostility complex (p. 145)
hypertension (p. 146)
meditation (p. 158)

migraines (p. 148)
peptic ulcer (p. 146)
progressive muscle relaxation
    (p. 158)
psychological factors affecting
    physical condition (p. 143)
psychosomatic hypothesis (p. 150)
psychosomatic medicine (p. 142)
rheumatoid arthritis (p. 148)
somatic weakness hypothesis
    (p. 152)
stress (p. 140)
stress management (p. 158)
stressor (p. 140)
stress-related disorders (p. 143)
tension headaches (p. 149)
Type A behavior pattern (p. 144)

SUGGESTED READINGS

Benson, H. (1975). *The relaxation response.* New York: Morrow.

Friedman, M., & Rosenman, R. (1974). *Type A behavior and your heart.* New York: Knopf.

Selye, H. (1974). *Stress without distress.* Philadelphia: Lippincott.

Selye, H. (1976). *The stress of life.* New York: McGraw-Hill.

Rodin, J., & Salovey, P. (1989). Health psychology. *Annual Review of Psychology, 40,* 533–579.

LEGAL AND ETHICAL ISSUES: STRESS AND LIE DETECTION

Since 1917, "lie detector" tests have been used in law enforcement to determine the innocence or guilt of suspects. Recently they have been used by banks and corporations in screening job applicants. In 1983, President Reagan required that lie detector tests be used to deter federal employees from disclosing classified information to the press or other parties. By the mid-1980s, lie detection was used 2 million times a year in the United States in screening prospective employees and in attempts to minimize thefts by employees (Holden, 1986).

Considering the widespread application of lie detector tests—which carry the risk of embarrassment, possible loss of a job, and criminal penalties to innocent people—we must ask if the tests are accurate. Before answering the question, let us look at the nature and technique of lie detection.

The lie detector, or polygraph, is designed to measure changes in the autonomic nervous system (ANS). Polygraph testing is based on the assumption that if someone feels guilty or is lying, he or she will feel stressed under questioning and the stress will be expressed as activation of the ANS. A typical polygraph machine monitors a person's heart rate, blood pressure, breathing, and skin resistance. This individual is asked a series of questions, some irrelevant and others relevant to the purpose of the investigation. For example, during investigation of a theft, the suspect might be asked, "What is your name?" (irrelevant), then "Did you steal the money?" (relevant). It is assumed that the pattern of autonomic responses to interrogation will be different for guilty and innocent people (Lykken, 1981; Saxe, Dougherty, & Cross, 1985).

Research shows that polygraph tests often find innocent people to be guilty and sometimes judge guilty people to be innocent. Moreover, polygraph tests can be beaten. Factors that can skew test results include the skill and experience of the tester, tensing of muscles, use of tranquilizing drugs, and prior exposure to polygraph testing. Some people just do not react autonomically when questioned (Lykken, 1981; Saxe, Dougherty, & Cross, 1985).

In 1983, the U.S. Congress conducted hearings on the scientific validity of polygraphs and found that they are inaccurate enough to limit their application. Certainly, different questions lead to different patterns of ANS response, but there is no unique physiological response that reveals deception. In 1988, Congress passed the Employee Protection Act, which prohibits the use of polygraphs for random examinations as part of a preemployment screening process. Polygraph testing can be used only in screening security guards and people who have access to controlled substances. In civil court cases, polygraph evidence is inadmissible in half of the states (Bales, 1988).

*C*hapter

S E V E N

*S*exual Disorders

OBJECTIVES

1. Explain the concept of sexuality.
2. Outline the four stages of the sexual response cycle and explain their relation to sexual dysfunctions.
3. Distinguish among sexual desire disorders, sexual arousal disorders, orgasm disorders, and sexual pain disorders.
4. Discuss the main causes of sexual dysfunctions.
5. Outline the basic principles of sex therapy and detail specific sex therapy techniques.
6. Differentiate among the types of paraphilias.
7. Explain how sexual arousal in the paraphilias deviates from normal patterns of sexual arousal.
8. Discuss the nature and causes of gender identity disorders.
9. Describe the treatment of gender identity disorders.

*P*aul was a 39-year-old man who was unable to maintain an erection for a length of time sufficient to reach orgasm. Ironically, Paul's worry often produced the very failure he feared. After many years of satisfying sex he had suddenly become unable to perform, and this had created difficulties in his relationship with his fiancée. Paul could keep his erection while masturbating, but he experienced very little pleasure from orgasm. He reported that it felt mechanical and the process took so much time he would become exhausted.

Fear of failure, difficulties with sexual arousal, and delayed orgasm are common sexual problems found in both men and women. In this chapter we explore the reasons for these and other sexual problems and look at how they can be treated.

7-1 ▨ SEXUAL DYSFUNCTIONS

sexuality The totality of one's sexual identity and experiences.

Sexuality is the totality of our sexual identity and experiences. It consists of our identity as male or female and our sexual orientation, which may be heterosexual, homosexual, bisexual, or asexual. Sexuality also consists of our sexual experiences and their relation to love, pleasure, and the meaning of life. Our sexual behavior is complex, influenced by interacting psychosocial experiences, environmental factors, and biological variables. In some cases, we do not function well sexually and our overall well-being is jeopardized. Sexual dysfunctions represent a departure from what is considered normal sexual functioning (American Psychiatric Association, 1987).

Sexuality in Historical Perspective

The current understanding of sexual dysfunctions reflects the influence of many historical figures, including pioneers such as Freud and psychiatrists Richard Krafft-Ebing (1840–1903) and Havelock Ellis (1859–1939). Freud and Krafft-Ebing viewed sexual problems as diseases, but Ellis more closely anticipated contemporary views. Ellis stressed the psychological basis of many sexual problems and disputed the moral prohibitions placed on sexual practices such as masturbation (Masters, Johnson, & Kolodny, 1985; Sadock, 1985).

In 1948, zoologist Alfred Kinsey published *Sexual Behavior in the Human Male*, and five years later he published *Sexual Behavior in the Human Female* (Kinsey, 1953; Kinsey, Pomeroy, & C. E. Martin, 1948). These reports were based on detailed interviews about sexual practices and behaviors with 12,000 individuals from a cross-section of society. Statistics regarding men's homosexual experiences and masturbation in women brought heated criticism.

The 1960s marked the beginning of a "sexual revolution" during which the open expression of sexuality was considered normal and natural. During this time, William Masters, a physician, and Virginia Johnson, a behavioral scientist, published results of their sex studies (1966, 1970). Since the mid-1950s, they had observed more than 10,000 instances of sexual behavior involving more than 700 men and women participating in a treatment program. Unlike the survey methods of Kinsey, Masters and Johnson's approach was based on *direct* observation and measurement of sexual behavior in their clinic.

sexual dysfunctions Inhibitions of desire or physiological responses necessary for sex.

The Nature and Assessment of Sexual Dysfunctions

Sexual dysfunctions are sexual disorders characterized by an inhibition of desire or of the physiological changes that make up the complete sexual re-

Current conceptions of sexual disorders reflect the ideas of pioneer researchers like Havelock Ellis, who stressed the psychological basis of many sexual problems.

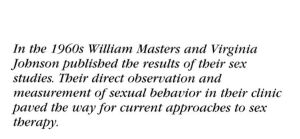

In the 1960s William Masters and Virginia Johnson published the results of their sex studies. Their direct observation and measurement of sexual behavior in their clinic paved the way for current approaches to sex therapy.

sexual response cycle
The four-stage cycle of sexual response.

sponse cycle (American Psychiatric Association, 1987). There are four stages in the **sexual response cycle**:

1. *Appetitive.* This stage is marked by an increase in sexual desire, achieved through fantasy or sex-related sensory stimulation.
2. *Excitement.* During this phase there is mounting sexual arousal, pleasure, and muscle tension. Physiological changes in males include erection of the penis. In females there is swelling of the breasts, an increase in blood supply in the vaginal area, vaginal swelling, and vaginal lubrication.
3. *Orgasm.* The peak of excitement induces the release of muscle tension and rhythmic thrusting movements of the pelvis. In males there is a reflexive ejaculation of semen; in females, muscular contractions of the vagina.
4. *Resolution.* This stage is marked by a return to preexcitement levels of arousal and muscle tension. There may be a sense of euphoria, relaxation, and fulfillment. Men are temporarily incapable of further orgasm, but women may have multiple orgasms (American Psychiatric Association, 1987).

Information about the sexual response is obtained by combining data from interviews, self-reports, and biomedical sources. In making a diagnosis of a sexual dysfunction, the clinician must find evidence that the problem is significantly affected by psychological factors and is not caused primarily by organic factors or by another mental disorder.

Interviews. Interviews regarding sexual dysfunctions focus on details about sexual desire, patterns of foreplay and arousal, and orgasm, viewed in the context of the person's past sexual experiences and problems. The interviewer needs to understand the patient's attitudes about self and sexual conduct; this information is critical in gaining perspective on the person's functioning. Negative attitudes about sex or self, in addition to anger, guilt, and shame, can have devastating effects on sexuality.

Self-Report Methods. Interview data is often complemented by information from self-report inventories, such as the *Sexual Interaction Inventory* (SII), the *Derogatis Sexual Function Inventory* (DSFI), and the *Sexual Arousal Inventory* (SAI) (Derogatis, 1978; Hoon, Hoon, & Wincze, 1976; J. LoPiccolo & Steger, 1978). The SII evaluates a couple's relationship in terms of sexual function and satisfaction by asking the man and woman to evaluate certain behaviors. For example, the couple may be asked to rate the satisfaction they feel when the man caresses the woman's breasts with his mouth. The DSFI estimates the frequency and quality of sexual behavior, and the SAI measures sexual arousal in women on the basis of how they say they might feel in 28 erotic scenarios.

Biomedical Testing. There is growing awareness among professionals that sexual dysfunctions may be partially rooted in vascular, neurological, and hormonal abnormalities. Great strides have been made in the biomedical evaluation of sexual dysfunction. However, most monitoring techniques are not commonly used in diagnosis because they are not accurate enough to warrant their expense and the discomfort they can create. The *nocturnal penile tumescence test* (NPT), the most reliable biomedical test, is used to assess erection problems. The NPT requires three nights in a sleep laboratory, during which erection size in dream sleep is measured. Erections are part of the normal physiological arousal of dream sleep, and it is believed if a man has erections at this time but not during sexual encounters, there is a psychological basis for his problem. The NPT is not 100 percent effective in distinguishing organic from psychologically based erection problems, but it can provide an important piece of diagnostic data (Conte, 1986).

Types of Sexual Dysfunctions

Psychosexual dysfunctions are classified according to inhibitions at one or more stages of the sexual response cycle. Table 7-1 lists the types of sexual dysfunction according to the DSM-III-R (American Psychiatric Association, 1987).

sexual desire disorders
Inhibitions of sexual desire.

hypoactive sexual desire disorder Lack of fantasy and desire to have sex.

Sexual Desire Disorders. **Sexual desire disorders** involve diminished desire during the appetitive stage of the sexual response cycle. **Hypoactive sexual desire disorder** is characterized by a persistent lack of sexual fantasy

PROFILE
Alfred C. Kinsey
(1894–1956)

Alfred C. Kinsey was one of the most controversial figures in the United States in the early 1950s. His books on male and female sexual behavior clashed with social taboos against the discussion of sex, and his research prompted shock and indignation among journalists, the clergy, educators, members of Congress, and fellow scientists. Yet his legacy is an important one for sexology (the study of sexual behavior). Kinsey's work meant that sex could now be studied openly and objectively.

Kinsey, who was descended from Pennsylvania Quakers, was raised in New Jersey in a deeply religious family. A neighbor remembers that on Sundays the Kinseys were allowed only to go to church and to eat. Alfred Kinsey was shy around girls and did not feel they were attracted to him. His father disapproved of dating. It may seem odd that a man with such a background could have been a pioneer in sex research, but in many ways sexology was an obvious choice for him.

Kinsey received his bachelor's degree in biology, magna cum laude, from Bowdoin College in Maine in 1916 and his doctorate from Harvard University in 1920. After graduation he accepted a teaching position at Indiana University's de-partment of zoology. His strength as a taxonomist, collector, and classifier was the very skill that led him into the study of sexual behavior. In the late 1930s he became aware of a relatively untouched field, sexology, that was ideal for taxonomic study. He began to interview people about their sexual ideas and practices and became completely absorbed in the subject. In 1941, Kinsey received a $1600 grant that marked the beginning of the Institute for Sex Research, which still exists at Indiana University.

Alfred Kinsey was a nature lover, camper, and camp counselor and was a devoted boy scout during his adolescent and teenage years. Moreover, he was an accomplished classical pianist and an expert gardener. He combed 2500 miles of the United States on foot, collecting wasps, and he and his wife spent their honeymoon exploring the White Mountains of New Hampshire. He designed a special lightweight backpack advertised in the 1928 Sears catalog as the "Kinsey Pack."

Kinsey's most famous books were *Sexual Behavior in the Human Male* (1948) and *Sexual Behavior in the Human Female* (1953) (Christenson, 1971).

sexual aversion disorder Distaste for sexual contact.

and desire that is noticeably different from the person's usual levels. **Sexual aversion disorder** involves an extreme distaste for sexual contact with another person. The mere thought of having sex is repugnant and often causes phobic anxiety. Engaging in sex causes extreme disgust (American Psychiatric Association, 1987).

TABLE 7-1   PSYCHOSEXUAL DYSFUNCTIONS

Sexual Desire Disorders	Sexual Arousal Disorders
• Hypoactive sexual desire disorder	• Female sexual arousal disorder
• Sexual aversion disorder	• Male erectile disorder
Orgasm Disorders	**Sexual Pain Disorders**
• Inhibited female orgasm	• Dyspareunia
• Inhibited male orgasm	• Vaginismus
• Premature ejaculation	

Marla said that her husband was a "great guy" who was kind and considerate. However, she couldn't bear having him touch her in a sensual way. In therapy Marla revealed that she came from a dysfunctional family in which both parents were alcoholic. She had no recollection of sexual abuse, but she did remember a lot of yelling and screaming. She recalls always being "on edge," and she later had drinking problems herself. When she entered treatment, she was alcohol-free.

After her mother died, Marla was left with the responsibility of taking care of her nearly invalid father. She strongly resented having to "clean up his garbage" and especially hated the way he demanded her support and time. During this time she had no desire for sex, which infuriated her husband. Afraid that he would leave her, she reluctantly submitted to his sexual requests, but she found sex disgusting and often felt the need to shower afterward because she felt "dirty."

sexual arousal disorders Decrease or loss of arousal during sex.

female sexual arousal disorder Inhibition of the lubrication-swelling response.

male erectile disorder Inability to develop or maintain an erection.

orgasm disorders Inhibition or delay of orgasm.

inhibited female orgasm Inhibition of orgasm in women.

Sexual Arousal Disorders. People with **sexual arousal disorders** have normal sexual desire but experience a persistent decrease or loss of arousal during sex. **Female sexual arousal disorder** is marked by an inhibition of the lubrication-swelling response during the excitement stage of the sexual response cycle. The condition was formerly called *frigidity*, but that term was abandoned by sex experts because its meaning was derogatory and too nonspecific.

Male erectile disorder is characterized by difficulty in developing or maintaining an erection sufficient to complete intercourse. Male arousal disorder, formerly called impotence, comprises more than 50 percent of men's sexual complaints and affects nearly 10 million men in the United States. Some men are never able to maintain an erection, but more common is the man in whom erectile functioning was previously normal. Some individuals may be able to maintain an erection only during masturbation. You may have already deduced that Paul, from our opening case, suffered from male erectile disorder (American Psychiatric Association, 1987; Masters et al., 1985; Sadock, 1985).

Orgasm Disorders. **Orgasm disorders** are characterized by normal sexual desire and arousal, but with delayed or inhibited orgasm. **Inhibited female orgasm**, sometimes called *anorgasmia*, is a delay or inhibition of orgasm, most commonly in a woman previously capable of orgasm (American Psychiatric As-

Sexual disorders often betray interpersonal problems. Many sexual problems are rooted in faulty communication and the alienation that results.

sociation, 1987). The diagnosis of inhibited female orgasm requires careful assessment, since 30 percent of women do not consistently reach orgasm, and many women report sexual satisfaction without orgasm (J. LoPiccolo & Stock, 1986). Thus, we must be careful not to confuse a normal sexual variation with a disorder. **Inhibited male orgasm** is apparently rare and has received little research attention. The large discrepancies between the frequencies of diagnosed cases of male and female orgasmic dysfunction have led to the charge of sex bias in diagnosis (Wakefield, 1987).

Premature ejaculation is a male disorder defined as consistent ejaculation just before or after penetration, and before the person wishes it. Since many men mistakenly believe that they should be able to withhold ejaculation for a long time, the clinician must be sure that the man's expectations are not unrealistic. For example, if a man is involved in 40 minutes of intense foreplay and then ejaculates on penetration, the diagnosis of premature ejaculation is not made, because it is reasonable to expect ejaculation at that point (American Psychiatric Association, 1987).

Premature ejaculation can be a chronic, lifelong problem, but it usually surfaces in situations where there is reason to hurry. For example, many men experience premature ejaculation when they have sex in the back seat of a car or when they are worried about being caught. Other men simply become overly excited during sex. It is difficult to calculate prevalence rates for premature

inhibited male orgasm
Inhibition of orgasm in men.

premature ejaculation
Ejaculation before the person wishes it.

ejaculation, since many men are ashamed and do not report the problem. The best estimate is that it affects 30 percent of the male population (American Psychiatric Association, 1987).

Raymond had his first sexual encounter at age 17. When he found out that his parents were going out to dinner and a movie, he invited a young woman to his house for "some fun." As soon as they started foreplay, Raymond began to worry that his parents would return early and catch them naked. He could hardly wait to "get it over with," although he wasn't fully conscious of this. Ten minutes into foreplay and before penetration, Raymond had an orgasm. This problem recurred several more times over the next few months.

Thereafter, Raymond always seemed to worry about getting caught. Each time he had sex he told himself that he would last longer, but he ejaculated prematurely at least three-fourths of the time. Raymond's premature ejaculation persisted well into adulthood, especially with new partners.

dyspareunia (*dis*-pah-*roo-ne*-ah) Genital pain before, during, or after sex.

vaginismus Spasm of the vagina during sex.

Sexual Pain Disorders. Dyspareunia consists of persistent genital pain experienced before, during, or after sexual intercourse. The diagnosis is made in the absence of physical findings and is rarely diagnosed in men. **Vaginismus** is an involuntary spasm of the outer third of the vagina that makes penetration by the penis difficult. Continued attempts to penetrate cause considerable pain, dread of sexual intercourse, and more tightness of the vagina. Dyspareunia has been estimated to affect 1 to 2 percent of the female population, and vaginismus apparently affects 2 to 3 percent (American Psychiatric Association, 1987; Masters et al., 1985).

Causes of Sexual Dysfunctions

There are many biological and psychosocial causes of sexual dysfunctions. In some cases the causes date back to early sexual experiences, but usually they relate to the person's immediate circumstances. It is difficult to specify causes for each sexual dysfunction, since many of the same factors are associated with different problems. In this section we look at some of the more important factors known to influence the development of sexual problems (Gendel & Bonner, 1988).

Biological Causes. Many organic factors are known to play a role in sexual problems, but organic factors do not play a major role in sexual dysfunctions. Some sexual problems result from the use of prescription or nonprescription drugs. For example, antihistamines, antihypertensive drugs, and alcohol can cause male erectile disorder. There is also research suggesting that male erectile disorder is caused by subtle chemical abnormalities. It is known that nitric oxide relaxes blood vessels, thereby facilitating erection. Some cases of erectile disorder may be caused by defects in the pathways over which nitric oxide exerts its relaxing effects (Rajer, Aronson, Bush, Dorey, & Ignarro, 1992). Circulatory problems that reduce blood flow can impair the physiological mechanisms necessary for sexual excitement in men and women. Structural abnormalities and infections are the cause of some pain disorders. The vaginal opening may be too small or too constricted for the woman to engage comfortably in intercourse (Masters et al., 1985; Sadock, 1985).

Psychosocial Causes. Psychological factors, including sociocultural, personal, and interpersonal matters, play a role in 60 to 80 percent of sexual problems (Gendel & Bonner, 1988a).

Attitudes and beliefs derived from custom and tradition play a major role in our sexual conduct. Society imposes restrictions on sexual behavior through parental influence, school, religion, and laws. Prohibitions against premarital sex, masturbation, and oral sex can inhibit sexual freedom, and in extreme cases, sex of any kind may be equated with dirtiness.

Society can also foster ignorance and myths about standards of sexual performance and ability. Many sexually dysfunctional people are simply ignorant about sexual anatomy and physiology and harbor erroneous beliefs about what constitutes satisfactory sexual functioning. For example, masculinity is often mistakenly associated with penis size; some people believe that women need large breasts to satisfy men; and some individuals believe that masturbation is a sign of sexual perversion. Such beliefs can lead to performance fears and problems in sexual arousal. In a 1990 survey of nearly 2000 Americans, 55 percent could not correctly answer 10 of 18 questions designed to test general sexual knowledge (Angier, 1990).

Sexual functioning can be disturbed by the acceptance of certain traditional sex-role expectations. For example, men are often expected to be aggressive and women are often expected to be passive and submissive. Following this thinking, some men selfishly seek their own satisfaction, and some women believe they should satisfy men even at the expense of their own enjoyment. Acceptance of these roles can lead to unsatisfying, mechanical sex without much intimacy.

Personal factors are important as well. People who feel inadequate or believe that sex is immoral can feel guilt, shame, and anxiety about their sexuality. **Performance anxiety**, the fear of sexual failure, increases general bodily arousal and inhibits sexual arousal, thereby adversely affecting sexual performance. Eventually, sexual failures create the anticipation of future failure, which creates more anxiety, more sexual failure, and so on.

performance anxiety
Fear of sexual failure.

Paul frequently worried during intercourse that he would lose his erection, and when it happened, it made him worry more the next time he engaged in sex. Eventually he tried to "will" an erection, which made matters even worse. He began to question his masculinity. At first his fiancée was patient, but she soon grew frustrated and began to make snide comments. This troubled Paul even more, and he found himself in a cycle of worry and failure he could not easily break.

A person whose sexual behavior is dominated by performance anxiety does not pay attention to the partner or to inner sensations, and sex becomes strained and mechanical. Masters and Johnson (1970) refer to the monitoring of one's own performance as **spectatoring**.

spectatoring
Monitoring of one's sexual performance.

Research suggests that the relationship between anxiety and sexual dysfunction is more complicated than was previously thought. Some studies show that increased anxiety is associated with *heightened* sexual arousal. One report stated that men had successfully engaged in sexual intercourse despite having been threatened with weapons if they failed. In fact, one man reported that he had had intercourse with one woman while another held a scalpel near his penis. These reports suggest that anxiety, per se, does not lead to sexual problems (Sarrell & Masters, 1982).

Some research suggests that anxiety leads to problems when the person is distracted from the pleasures of sex. Psychologist David Barlow and his associates (1986) conducted a series of experiments that showed men with arousal problems suffer a type of cognitive interference that impairs performance. Unlike sexually functional men, dysfunctional men are distracted from erotic cues by sexual performance demands. The men concentrate on their fear of failure or criticism or ridicule instead of concentrating on the sensations and pleasures of sex. Consequently, their sexual arousal is reduced.

Sexually dysfunctional men also experience more unpleasant feelings in sexual situations than do functional men. One line of research suggests that a tendency toward negative reactions to sex may be part of a personality trait called *erotophilia-erotophobia* (Byrne, 1983). Erotophilia reflects an attraction to erotic stimuli, and erotophobia is experienced as a distaste for sexual stimulation. Dysfunctional men are probably more erotophobic and may actively avoid erotic cues because they experience such stimulation as unpleasant.

Sexual satisfaction depends on more than the performance of particular actions. Often, sexual problems are a symptom of other problems in interpersonal relationships. People often use sex as "leverage" to equalize power in a bad relationship. Anger, resentment, and mistrust can alienate partners and damage the communication necessary for satisfying sex. When couples complain about a lack of communication, they are telling of their inability to express clearly their needs, desires, attitudes, likes, and dislikes. Disputes over careers, money, in-laws, child rearing, and leisure time can all impair communication and render the partners sexually unattractive to each other. As we will see shortly, most sex therapy programs emphasize improving relationships as an integral part of the therapy process.

Most sexual problems are not the result of traumatic experiences in childhood. Most people with sexual dysfunctions have never been sexually victimized, and many people who have been victimized lead normal sex lives. However, the trauma of rape, incest, or molestation can lead to later sexual disturbance and must be considered in any causal explanation of sexual dysfunction (Masters et al., 1985; Mrazek, 1984).

Treatment of Sexual Dysfunctions

Prior to 1970, the dominant treatment for sexual dysfunction was individual psychodynamic therapy, which presumed that sexual dysfunctions were manifestations of a more general character disturbance. Since the early 1970s, sex therapy has become an independent discipline that does not rely on any particular theory. The pioneering treatment approaches of Masters and Johnson became the foundation upon which others built. Modern sex therapy reflects their ideas (J. M. Friedman & Chernin, 1987; H. Kaplan, 1974; Masters et al., 1985; Masters & Johnson, 1966).

Principles and Techniques of Sex Therapy. Sex therapy follows certain general guidelines:

1. It focuses on the present dysfunction.
2. It is short-term and action-oriented.
3. It emphasizes education, communication, attitude change, and reduction of performance anxiety.

4. It assumes both partners are responsible and need to modify maladaptive lifestyles.
5. It combines behavioral, psychodynamic, cognitive, and family therapy treatments.

Within this framework, specialized techniques are used to enhance the therapeutic progress. Communication is improved by having couples share sexual fantasies, read erotic material, or view erotic films that demonstrate relevant sexual techniques. Communication is also enhanced by having the partners show each other how to effectively stimulate and caress. In sex therapy, couples are encouraged to provide constructive feedback about likes and dislikes (J. M. Friedman & Chernin, 1987; Gendel & Bonner, 1988a; J. LoPiccolo, 1978).

Sensate focus, an important sex therapy technique, is useful in communication training and anxiety reduction. **Sensate focus** consists of structured exercises in which partners explore each other's bodies without the demand to have intercourse and reach orgasm. To reduce performance anxiety, many sex therapists invoke the so-called *no coitus rule*, which prohibits the couple from having sexual intercourse during this stage of therapy.

sensate focus A couple's exploration of each other's bodies.

Modern sex therapy takes an action-oriented approach that assumes mutual responsibility between sexual partners. When basic principles are followed diligently sex therapy can be effective, enhancing a couple's overall well-being.

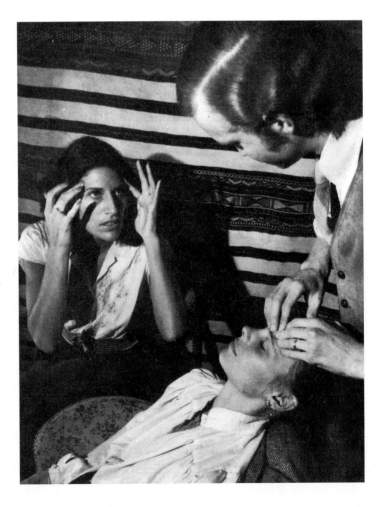

Sensate focus procedures last up to an hour and are practiced three or four times per week. The couple is instructed first to stimulate and explore each other's bodies through touch, sight, sound, and smell. Genital stimulation is initially discouraged. The goal is sensual pleasure, not sex. Later the partners are encouraged to stimulate each other's genitals until they can communicate without excessive performance anxiety. Many couples find sensate focus very clinical at first, but eventually they find that it is fun and it enhances intimacy. Sensate focus is especially useful in treating arousal disorders and premature ejaculation (J. LoPiccolo, 1978; Masters & Johnson, 1970; Masters et al., 1985).

Rather than end the relationship with his fiancée, Paul was encouraged to bring her into therapy to help with his arousal disorder. The rationale and technique of sensate focus was explained, and the two were instructed to pick a time when they could practice. They were encouraged to lie in bed naked and gently touch each other, until gradually they were able to touch each other's genitals without having intercourse or expecting orgasm. They repeated the procedure using moisturizing lotions.

In the next phase of sensate focus, they washed each other in the shower, again without intercourse. Paul gradually became able to maintain an erection for longer periods of time, and after several weeks the couple got carried away and Paul reached orgasm while erect.

Systematic desensitization using sex hierarchies, in which the person imagines increasingly more arousing sexual experiences and learns to "relax away" the anxiety, can further reduce performance anxiety. Attitude restructuring can be helpful for men who equate masculinity with erectile prowess and for women who have destructive attitudes about sexual submissiveness and their "duty" to satisfy their partners. Men and women often benefit from assertiveness training because it helps them communicate better and thereby balance the power structures in their relationships (Gendel & Bonner, 1988a; J. LoPiccolo, 1978; J. LoPiccolo & Stock, 1986).

A program of directed masturbation is helpful in treating inhibited female orgasm. The woman is gradually taught to explore her body and become aware of satisfying self-stimulation. Enhanced body feedback, sexual pleasure, and increased blood supply to the vaginal region increase the chances of orgasm. Using directed masturbation, 95 percent of women reach orgasm on their own and 85 percent reach orgasm with a partner. Ultimately, 40 percent of these women reach orgasm through penile-vaginal intercourse. In addition, *women's orgasm groups* have proved effective for women who are not seriously disturbed or locked in severe marital discord (Heiman, L. LoPiccolo, & J. LoPiccolo, 1976; J. LoPiccolo & Lobitz, 1978; J. LoPiccolo & Stock, 1986).

squeeze technique
A technique for treating premature ejaculation by squeezing the penis before orgasm.

start-stop method
A technique for treating premature ejaculation by pausing before orgasm.

Two related techniques are used to treat premature ejaculation. In the **squeeze technique**, the partner of the man being treated is instructed to stroke the man's penis until he is near orgasm. Then, when the man signals, the partner applies firm pressure to the head of the penis with the thumb and forefinger. This reduces the urge to ejaculate. In the **start-stop method**, the partner strokes the penis, then pauses until the man's urge to ejaculate diminishes. Stroking is resumed thereafter. Both methods can be applied during intercourse. Success rates above 90 percent have been reported for these methods (J. M. Friedman & Chernin, 1987; J. LoPiccolo & Stock, 1986).

Dyspareunia is best treated with a combination of relaxation, sensate focus, enhanced communication, and changing negative attitudes about sex. Vaginismus is treated by using plastic dilators to accustom the women to penile intercourse. The dilators which vary in size from the size of a finger to the size of an erect penis, are lubricated and inserted into the vagina for 15 minutes at a time. The largest dilator can usually be inserted after a week. If personal and relationship issues are in the process of being resolved, intercourse should proceed with less discomfort (Masters et al., 1985).

7-2   PARAPHILIAS

paraphilias (para-*fil*-ee-ahs) Sex directed toward objects, people, or activities normally not considered sexually attractive.

The **paraphilias** are sexual disorders in which intense sexual fantasies or activities are directed toward either nonhuman objects, suffering and humiliation, or children or any nonconsenting adult. The fantasies or activities deviate from those to which people are normally attracted. Affected individuals typically have three or four paraphilias at a time (American Psychiatric Association, 1987).

In diagnosing paraphilias it is important to distinguish between deviation and normal sexual variation. Many "normal" individuals are occasionally aroused by "deviant" fantasies or activities. Paraphilias are distinguished by their consistency and by their exclusion of mutual affection and sexual activity between consenting partners. More important, the paraphilic's fantasies or activities are *necessary* for sexual arousal and orgasm. For example, a man would be considered paraphilic if he were excited *only* when his lover dressed as a little girl during sex (American Psychiatric Association, 1987; Gendel & Bonner, 1988b).

Most of what we know about paraphilias comes from clinical case reports, so precise prevalence data is unavailable. Paraphilias are apparently uncommon in the general population and are rarely diagnosed in women. There is a flourishing pornography market involving paraphilias, so the actual prevalence of these disorders may be higher than we know. In general, individuals with paraphilias are secretive. Roughly half of known paraphilics are married, and they are motivated to conceal their fantasies and behaviors. Much of what we know about paraphilias comes from the study of paraphilic individuals whose behavior brings them in conflict with the law, especially when the paraphilia is acted out on children or nonconsenting adults (American Psychiatric Association, 1987).

Types of Paraphilias

Paraphilias are classified according to the type of fantasy or activity necessary for sexual arousal. Table 7-2 lists the different types of paraphilias by category (American Psychiatric Association, 1987).

transvestic fetishism
Urges to cross-dress.

Paraphilias Involving Nonhuman Objects. A paraphilic with **transvestic fetishism** has persistent, intense sexual urges and fantasies directed toward dressing in clothes considered appropriate only for people of the opposite sex. The transvestite is usually a heterosexual male who is aroused by wearing an article of women's clothing, such as underpants, a bra, or women's hosiery, under man's clothing. Some men will wear an entire woman's outfit, complete with makeup, jewelry, and other accessories. While cross-dressed, the transvestite masturbates or fantasizes that other men are attracted to him. Most trans-

TABLE 7.2 ▭ **TYPES OF PARAPHILIAS**

Nonhuman Objects	**Suffering and Humiliation**
• Transvestic fetishism	• Sexual masochism
• Fetishism	• Sexual sadism
Children and Nonconsenting Adults	
• Exhibitionism	
• Frotteurism	
• Voyeurism	
• Pedophilia	

vestites are not homosexual, but few have had extensive sexual contact with women (American Psychiatric Association, 1987).

Clinical case studies indicate that cross-dressing usually begins in early adolescence or even in childhood as early as 18 months. It involves dressing in the mother's shoes and wearing her jewelry and makeup. Certainly many toddlers dress in their mother's clothes yet do not become transvestites. It is difficult to accurately predict which children will develop transvestic fetishism. Follow-up studies indicate that many childhood cross-dressers become transvestites while others become homosexual, heterosexual, or asexual, but precise statistics are not available (American Psychiatric Association, 1987; Gendel & Bonner, 1988b; J. LoPiccolo & Lobitz, 1978).

Transvestites are usually heterosexual men who are sexually aroused by wearing an article of women's clothing. Some men, such as those in a cross-dresser's support group pictured here, will wear an entire woman's outfit.

CLOSE-UP
Paraphilias, Rape,
and Sexual Murders

Rape is alarmingly common. It is estimated that 1 in 6 women will be threatened by an attempted rape and that 1 in 24 will actually be raped in her lifetime. The frequency of rape is increasing four times faster than crime in general, and in the United States there is a rape every six minutes. Experts disagree whether rape is a crime of sex or a crime of aggression, but most agree that for some rapists one motive is to satisfy a sadistic drive. In *sadism rape*, actions are motivated by the paraphilic need to rape in order to attain sexual arousal. In such cases, the man can feel sexually potent only during rape (Gelman et al., 1990).

Some sadistic rapists can be sexually satisfied only if the victim is slain. In one study researchers analyzed the legal and psychiatric records of 25 serial sex murderers and found that 21 were motivated by violent sex fantasies (Prentky et al., 1989). The researchers speculated that the rapist commits crimes when he loses the inhibition that usually prevents him from acting out the violent fantasy. The sexual murders function as "trial runs" in which the rapist attempts to perform the

murders as imagined. Since the enactment of the murder can never precisely follow the fantasy, the rapist-murderer repeats the crime. Acting out the fantasies may provide new experiences for the paraphilic to fantasize about later, thereby motivating further acting out. Thus, the paraphilic's behavior is governed by fantasy that motivates action and more fantasy. The following table presents the different types of paraphilias identified in serial sex murderers (Prentky et al., 1989).

Paraphilia	No. of Subjects	Percent
Exhibitionism	5	25
Voyeurism	15	75
Fetishism	15	71
Cross-dressing	5	25

Source: Prentky, R. A., Burgess, A. W., Rokous, F., Lee, A., Hartman C., Ressler, R., and Douglas, J. (1989). "The presumptive role of fantasy in serial sexual homocide." *American Journal of Psychiatry, 146,* 887–891.

Frank was a 35-year-old car salesman who came to therapy after his wife discovered him masturbating while wearing her bra. Although their sex life was barely satisfying, she had had no idea of his paraphilia. Frank originally denied having a history of cross-dressing, but when his wife threatened to leave him unless he told the truth, he admitted cross-dressing as far back as he could remember. He recalled wanting to dress as a girl on Halloween, and by age 13 he was masturbating regularly while wearing his mother's underwear. He reported being sexually attracted to girls, but he did not date much because he was afraid his paraphilia would be discovered. He also reported having had several homosexual encounters at age 14, but he did not find men sexually attractive.

fetishism Sexual attraction to nonhuman objects.

Fetishism is characterized by strong urges and fantasies directed toward nonhuman objects. Shoes, boots, corsets, bras, or underpants are most often the objects of attraction. The man with a fetish will hold or fondle the object during masturbation or will request that his sex partner wear the object during intercourse. The fetishist has no desire to cross-dress. The absence or withdrawal of the fetish object can result in erectile failure (American Psychiatric Association, 1987; Gendel & Bonner, 1988b; J. K. Meyer, 1985).

Paraphilias Involving Suffering or Humiliation. Sexual sadism and sexual masochism are the opposite ends of a dimension involving the desire to punish and the desire to be punished. In **sexual sadism**, arousal is derived from imagining or actually injuring, humiliating, or dominating someone. Whipping, pinching, cutting, or spanking, making the person crawl, or walking the person on a leash like a dog are common. In extreme cases, only rape or murder can fully satisfy the sadist. The relationship of rape and sexual murders to paraphilias is discussed in "Close-up: Paraphilias, Rape, and Sexual Murders" (p. 179) (American Psychiatric Association, 1987).

sexual sadism Arousal from injuring, humiliating, or dominating someone.

In **sexual masochism**, arousal is derived from imagining or actually being victimized. One unusual example of masochistic behavior involves sexual arousal through oxygen deprivation to the brain. The masochist applies pressure to arteries leading to the brain. As the oxygen supply drops and the masochist is about to pass out, the pressure is released. Equipment failure and other mistakes occasionally result in death (American Psychiatric Association, 1987).

sexual masochism Arousal from being injured, humiliated, or dominated.

Vanessa was a 47-year-old business executive who told her therapist that she often fantasized about being abducted by aliens from another planet. In a typical fantasy, four or five aliens would carry her off in their spacecraft and force her to perform oral sex. Once on the alien planet, she was kept in a cage where alien men would use her as a sex object. She preferred that they slap her and pull her hair (but not hurt her) during sex. In her real life, she liked sexual domination by her husband, but he usually refused. Their conflict in this matter added to their ongoing marital problems.

Paraphilias Involving Children or Nonconsenting Persons. **Pedophilia** involves sexual urges and fantasies directed toward children younger than the age of puberty. Although many pedophiles are men attracted to boys, the most common are men attracted to young girls. The diagnosis of pedophilia can be made just on the basis of fantasy, but many pedophiles act out their fantasies and force children to perform oral sex or have intercourse. Some pedophiles even insert foreign objects into a child's anus, mouth, or vagina. Other pedophiles masturbate while watching, touching, or fondling a child. The pedophile is often a close friend or relative, and the victim may even be the pedophile's own child. Approximately 15 percent of cases involve incest; the most common type is father-daughter incest (American Psychiatric Association, 1987; Gendel & Bonner, 1988b).

pedophilia Sexual urges toward children under the age of puberty.

Lois had been molested by her grandfather since she was 7 years old. While babysitting, he would watch TV and read her stories on the sofa. During this time, he would place his hand over her genital area and rub gently. Eventually, he reached into her pants and fondled her clitoris while masturbating himself. At first she resisted, but he threatened that if she told anyone, her parents would abandon her forever. Once she reached puberty, he apparently lost interest in her. She later found out that her grandfather had also molested her younger brother.

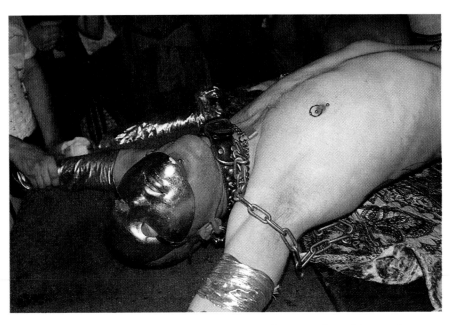

Some paraphilics are sexually aroused by suffering or humiliation. In many cases, such as the one shown here, whipping and total domination are typical scenarios.

exhibitionism
Excitement from exposing the genitals to a stranger.

voyeurism Arousal from viewing a naked stranger.

frotteurism (fro-*tour*-ism) Arousal from rubbing against strangers.

Exhibitionism is characterized by sexual excitement derived from fantasizing about or actually exposing one's genitals to a stranger. The exhibitionist male will often masturbate while exposed, especially if the victim reacts with shock or disgust. Fortunately, exhibitionists rarely pursue their victims sexually, because sexual arousal comes from their exposure rather than sexual contact.

In **voyeurism**, sexual arousal is derived from viewing a stranger who is naked or undressing. The voyeur does not desire sexual activity with the victim. (Note that viewing pornographic material is not considered voyeurism.) In **frotteurism**, arousal is obtained through fantasies or actions that involve rubbing against a nonconsenting person. In the most common situation, a fully clothed man rubs his penis against a woman's backside in a crowded bus or train (American Psychiatric Association, 1987).

Other paraphilias include telephone scatologia (obscene phone calls); necrophilia (sex with corpses); coprophilia (sexual interest in feces); urophilia (sexual interest in urine); zoophilia (sex with animals); klismaphilia (arousal from enemas); and partialism (sexual fixation on particular parts of the body) (American Psychiatric Association, 1987).

Causes of Paraphilias

The causes of paraphilias are poorly understood. Previous editions of the DSM regarded paraphilias as variants of personality disorders, reflecting prevailing beliefs that they evolved from abnormal childhood experiences. For example, psychoanalysis held that in paraphilias, sexual energy becomes attached to an object or activity that is not ordinarily arousing. But why this happens and why it persists has never been adequately explained.

Some paraphilias are believed to result from severe family disturbance. For example, pedophilia is strongly associated with childhood sexual abuse by family members. However, these explanations fall short, since most people from dysfunctional families do not become paraphilic (Gendel & Bonner, 1988; J. K. Meyer, 1985).

The most common behavioral explanation for paraphilias is based on classical conditioning. In this view, sexual arousal is conditioned to a previously natural stimulus. For example, a young boy may associate sexual pleasure with a stimulus, such as a shoe or a bra, which is present while he is masturbating. Subsequently, the association is reinforced each time he experiences pleasure by masturbating in the presence of the stimulus.

Treatments for Paraphilias

The treatment of paraphilias is difficult, and few good treatment outcome studies are available. The long list of treatments include psychodynamic, behavioral, group, and marital therapy. Special medications are used for some patients. Overall, these treatments have yielded only modest success.

Psychological Treatments. Psychological treatments for paraphilias attempt to modify the paraphilic's thinking and behavior. Sometimes therapists attempt to accomplish this by resolving the problems that give rise to the symptoms. For example, pedophiles usually begin to molest children while in the midst of severe marital dissatisfaction. Feeling unfulfilled and inadequate, the pedophile turns to helpless children in order to boost his self-esteem. Marital therapy has been used in these situations, but there is little evidence that it is effective (Gendel & Bonner, 1988b).

Behavioral techniques like *guided imagery* and *aversive conditioning* have been somewhat successful in treating pedophilia, exhibitionism, transvestic fetishism, and fetishism. Using guided imagery, the clinician has the person relax and imagine succeeding in sexually appropriate behaviors. Aversive conditioning pairs paraphilic fantasies with unpleasant stimuli such as electrical shocks. The goal is that the fantasy alone will trigger unpleasant feelings after it has been paired repeatedly with the aversive stimulus (Marks, Gelder, & Bancroft, 1970).

Rick was a 33-year-old man whose father deserted his family early in childhood. At age 12, Rick began masturbating while wearing women's panties that he stole from the clothesline. When panties were unavailable, he masturbated while viewing pictures of women in panties. To cope with his feelings of being unmasculine, he boxed, lifted weights, and joined the marines. He was arrested for stealing luggage from a hotel room after he had been drinking heavily, and he spent time in prison, where he received behavioral treatment.

In each treatment session, Rick viewed pictures of women wearing panties and was asked to hold panties in his hand. Each time a sexual stimulus was presented, a shock was delivered through finger electrodes. After 41 sessions of 12 stimulus presentations each, Rick reported he was no longer disturbed by the fetish. Booster sessions were required, but the spontaneous return of the fetish was very mild. Months later, he reported a normal sex life (Kushner, 1965).

Behavioral measures such as aversive conditioning employ noxious stimuli to reduce sexual arousal from paraphilic fantasies.

An alternative to aversive conditioning with electric shock is covert sensitization. In this approach, the patient is asked to imagine the arousal-producing stimulus and then imagine an aversive consequence, such as nausea (Cautela, 1966).

Biological Treatments. It has been hypothesized that paraphilics have an unusually high sex drive. Some have therefore been treated with medications that reduce levels of male hormones known as androgens. One drug that has been used successfully is medroxyprogesterone acetate, or MPA (Depo-Provera), which inhibits the release of male hormones known to increase sexual arousal. Most studies show that administration of MPA does reduce inappropriate sexual behavior (Berlin & Meinecke, 1981; Wincze, Bansal, & Malamud, 1986).

7-3   GENDER IDENTITY DISORDERS

gender identity
Awareness of being male or female.

gender identity disorders A mismatch between assigned sex and gender identity.

Gender identity refers to a person's awareness of being male or female, and *assigned sex* is the gender recorded on one's birth certificate. Gender identity usually matches assigned sex, but in some cases there is an inconsistency—most often, a physical male has a female gender identity. Conditions in which there is a perceived mismatch between gender identity and assigned sex are known as **gender identity disorders**. In the DSM-III-R, gender identity disorders are listed with *disorders first evident in infancy, childhood, or adolescence*, but because of their clear implications for sexuality and sexual functioning, we present them here with the sexual disorders.

Types of Gender Identity Disorders

gender identity disorder of childhood Distress about one's sex and a desire to be of the opposite sex.

The prominent feature of **gender identity disorder of childhood** is a persistent, severe distress about one's sex and a desire to be of the opposite sex. Girls have an aversion to feminine clothing and insist on wearing typical boy's clothing, and they prefer rough-and-tumble play. These girls are often perceived as tomboys. Boys are preoccupied with traditionally female activities, such as playing house; they prefer female companions and are frequently thought to be "sissies." Although most children with gender identity disorders are perceived by others as tomboys or sissies, not all children who engage in activities most typical of the opposite sex have a gender identity problem. Also, many males with gender identity problems cross-dress, but unlike transvestites, these people do not find cross-dressing sexually arousing (American Psychiatric Association, 1987).

transsexualism
Discomfort with one's assigned sex and desire to change it.

The hallmark of **transsexualism** is extreme and persistent discomfort with one's assigned sex, and a powerful desire to change it. Transsexualism is diagnosed only in people beyond the age of puberty. The transsexual is usually a man who has felt like a female trapped in a male body since early childhood. He has always felt more comfortable with traditional female activities and dress, and he has always wished to be a girl. Later in life, he finds his genitals and secondary sex characteristics foreign and disgusting and wants them removed (American Psychiatric Association, 1987; Stoller, 1985).

The psychological and emotional experiences of transsexuals are well stated in the following passages by Jan Morris, a writer who was formerly James Morris:

Transsexuals are usually males who have always felt like females trapped in a male body. James Morris underwent sex change surgery to become Jan Morris, a woman.

I was three or perhaps four years old when I realized that I had been born into the wrong body, and should really be a girl. I remember the moment well, and it is the earliest memory of my life. . . . What triggered so bizarre a thought I have long forgotten but the conviction was unfaltering from the start. . . .

By my mid-thirties my self-repugnance was more specific and more bitter, and I began to detest the body that had served me so loyally. After the conception of Virginia [his daughter] I began another tentative experiment with hormones, thinking that some degree of feminization might weaken the intensity of my distress, and allow me to stagger on through life. (J. Morris, 1974, pp. 1, 97)

Transsexualism is apparently rare, with a prevalence of 1 in 30,000 males and 1 in 100,000 females. Some transsexuals are able to deal with the problems of feeling trapped in the "wrong" body. Others suffer adverse psychological consequences: personality disturbance, anxiety, depression, and substance abuse are common, as are problems in occupational and interpersonal functioning (Gendel & Bonner, 1988; Stoller, 1985).

Causes of Gender Identity Disorders

The causes of gender identity disorders are unknown. Some investigators have argued that the causes are rooted in a disturbance in parent-child relationships. One hypothesis is that some parents will encourage a child to assume the role of the opposite sex. For example, the parent who wanted a girl may encourage a son to act in a stereotypically female way. Despite the attractiveness of this hypothesis, there is no compelling evidence for such disturbances in sex-role socialization (Gendel & Bonner, 1988b; Stoller, 1985).

Other investigators have proposed that gender identity disorders result from hormonal abnormalities during fetal development. It is well-known that hormones affect developing brain tissue and that experimental manipulation of hormones during fetal development in animals can produce offspring that exhibit behavior more appropriate to the opposite sex. Since this kind of research cannot be conducted in humans, it is difficult to decide whether similar mechanisms are at work in individuals who have gender identity problems (Gendel & Bonner, 1988b; Stoller, 1985).

Treatment of Gender Identity Disorders

sex reassignment surgery A sex change operation.

Individuals with these disorders find their gender identity irresistible. Psychotherapy cannot help these individuals accept their assigned sex. Many transsexuals are insistent about changing their physical sex. Some of these individuals undergo sex change operations, or **sex reassignment surgery**, to make their assigned sex match their gender identity. Most of these operations are male-to-female. Surgery is undertaken only after a two-year trial period during which the person gradually adjusts to living the role of the opposite sex.

The male-to-female surgical procedure involves removing the penis and creating a vagina. Female hormones are used to reduce facial hair and change the voice. Of course, the person is now sterile and cannot conceive a child, even though sexual intercourse is possible. Follow-up studies indicate that some transsexuals are happier after the sex reassignment, but others feel no better.

CLOSE-UP
The Issue of Homosexuality

Homosexuality is characterized by sexual attraction to, and sexual activity with, a member of the same sex. Historically, views of homosexuality have been beset with impassioned arguments about whether it is a preference, a sexual orientation, a deviation, or a sign of immorality. Since heterosexuality was considered the norm, the challenge for researchers and clinicians has been to uncover the abnormalities that caused homosexuality (Money, 1987).

Early attempts to explain homosexuality as a deviation focused on faulty childhood experiences and abnormal hormone functioning (J. K. Meyer, 1985). However, these studies were not compelling. Recent research has focused on the possibility that sexual orientation is determined by chemical influences on developing brain tissue during the prenatal period (L. Ellis & Ames, 1987). Some scientists have investigated structural differences between the brains of homosexual and heterosexual men. For example, one study found that a segment of the hypothalamus was smaller in homosexual than in heterosexual men (LeVay, 1991). A hereditary basis for homosexuality has also been indicated. In a study of homosexual men and their siblings, 52 percent of monozygotic twins were also homosexual compared to 22 percent of dizygotic twins and 11 percent of adoptive brothers (Bailey & Pillard, 1991). Although the significance of this finding is unclear, it does point to biological differences between homosexual and heterosexual men.

Today, the consensus among experts is that sexual orientation is probably determined biologically before birth, then reinforced by early childhood and adolescent experiences (L. Ellis & Ames, 1987; Holden, 1988). However, the influence of cultural norms cannot be ignored. The famous sexologist John Money noted that in some cultures, males are required to be homosexual until puberty but must live heterosexually thereafter (Holden, 1988).

Although most homosexuals are comfortable with their sexual orientation, others find that their homosexuality conflicts with their religious beliefs and with social attitudes that consider heterosexuality the norm. Troubled by this conflict, some homosexuals find it difficult to act out their sexual desires and experience extreme guilt when they do.

In the DSM-III-R, homosexuality is not classified as a mental disorder. However, "persistent and marked distress about one's sexual orientation" is subsumed under the category of "sexual disorders not otherwise specified." In these cases it is not homosexuality that is considered a disorder, but rather the distress of being homosexual while preferring not to be (American Psychiatric Association, 1987; J. K. Meyer, 1985). While most homosexuals do not wish to change their sexual orientation, it may be that society exerts pressures that some homosexuals cannot cope with. Whatever the case, it is clear that sexual orientation is fundamental to who we are.

Female-to-male sex change operations lead to greater emotional satisfaction than the more common male-to-female type (R. Green & Money, 1969; Masters et al., 1985; J. Morris, 1974; Stoller, 1985).

SUMMARY

7-1 Sexual dysfunctions are characterized by an inhibition in completing the four stages of the sexual response cycle (appetitive, excitement, orgasm, and resolution). Sexual desire disorders are characterized by a lack of fantasy and desire to engage in sexual activity, or by an aversion to sex. Sexual arousal disorders involve an inhibition in the physiological responses necessary to complete the sexual cycle. Orgasm disorders involve inhibited or delayed orgasm, and sexual pain disorders are marked by pain or muscular spasm during intercourse. Biological and psychological factors interact to cause sexual dysfunctions. Performance anxiety and spectatoring often distract individuals from attending to erotic cues. Sex therapy is short-term and action-oriented; it is geared toward anxiety reduction, enhanced communication, attitude change, education; and it assumes the partners share responsibility.

7-2 Paraphilias are sexual disorders consisting of intense sexual fantasies or actions directed toward nonhuman objects, toward suffering or humiliation, or toward nonconsenting persons. Paraphilias deviate from normal patterns of sexual arousal. The causes of paraphilias are poorly understood, but the more prominent views are psychodynamic and behavioral. Treatment for the paraphilias is difficult, and few controlled clinical outcome studies are available. The goal of treatment is either to modify paraphilic thinking and behavior by resolving problems that give rise to the symptoms, or to eliminate the behavior through aversive conditioning.

7-3 Gender identity disorders involve a mismatch between assigned sex and gender identity. Individuals with gender identity disorder of childhood have an aversion to clothing and activities typical of their gender and identify with the other sex. Transsexual men find their gender repugnant and wish to be a female. Some individuals unable to resolve their gender identity conflict undergo sex reassignment surgery to make their bodies match their gender identity.

TERMS TO REMEMBER

dyspareunia (p. 172)
exhibitionism (p. 181)
female sexual arousal disorder (p. 170)
fetishism (p. 179)
frotteurism (p. 181)
gender identity (p. 183)
gender identity disorder of childhood (p. 184)
gender identity disorders (p. 183)
hypoactive sexual desire disorder (p. 168)

inhibited female orgasm (p. 170)
inhibited male orgasm (p. 171)
male erectile disorder (p. 170)
orgasm disorders (p. 170)
paraphilias (p. 177)
pedophilia (p. 180)
performance anxiety (p. 173)
premature ejaculation (p. 171)
sensate focus (p. 175)
sex reassignment surgery (p. 185)
sexual arousal disorders (p. 170)
sexual aversion disorder (p. 169)

SUGGESTED READINGS

Kaplan, H. S. (1987). *The illustrated manual of sex therapy* (2nd ed.). New York: Brunner/Mazel.

Masters, W. H., & Johnson, V. E. (1966). *Human sexual response.* Boston: Little, Brown.

Masters, W. H., & Johnson, V. E. (1970). *Human sexual inadequacy.* Boston: Little, Brown.

Masters, W. H., Johnson, V. E., & Kolodny, R. C. (1985). *Human sexuality* (2nd ed.). Boston: Little, Brown.

Morris, J. (1974). *Conundrum.* New York: Signet.

LEGAL AND ETHICAL ISSUES: DATE RAPE

On February 10, 1992, former heavyweight boxing champion Mike Tyson was convicted of raping a Miss Black America beauty pageant contestant. During the trial, the victim testified that Tyson had raped her in his hotel room without any encouragement on her part. Tyson contended that he had previously made his sexual desires clear and that since the woman had accepted his invitation to come to his room, she was a willing participant in their sexual activities. This is a highly publicized example of date rape.

The term *date rape* was coined in the late 1980s to describe cases in which the victim is raped by an acquaintance or boyfriend while on a date. Men can also be victimized by date rape, but this is less common. A 1987 study of nearly 3000 college women estimated that nearly 5 percent of college women are victims of rape or attempted rape each year, and another study showed that roughly half of sexual assaults occurred at parties. Rapists are often under the influence of alcohol or drugs.

College judicial systems are poorly equipped to handle issues of date rape, and sadly, many colleges categorize date rape incidents as simple sexual harassment. Worse yet is that people involved in college judicial hearings are insensitive to the trauma involved. At issue is whether it is appropriate or even legitimate to deal with a legal charge in an extralegal setting. Even more problematic is that many rape victims do not even classify the misdeed as rape.

Many colleges and universities have begun to take remedial steps to counter ignorance about date rape. Mental health professionals, campus police, administrators, and students are developing rape prevention programs. These programs are designed to increase awareness that being forced, in any way, to have sex constitutes rape. Most experts agree that the participation of men is necessary to a successful rape prevention program. Thus far, gaining male involvement has been difficult, and most of the men who are peer educators have been victimized themselves.

Another critical factor in a successful rape prevention program is the firm support of the college administration. There are charges that support has been difficult to obtain because administrators fear that publicizing rape and rape prevention will frighten away prospective students and hurt enrollment. However, by the end of this decade, all colleges and universities that receive federal funding will probably be required to make records of campus crime available to students, prospective students, and staff. The statistics would include information about rape, including date rape (Moses, 1991a, b).

Chapter EIGHT

Substance Use Disorders

OBJECTIVES

1. Distinguish among substance use, substance abuse, and substance dependence.
2. Define the two primary characteristics of drug addiction.
3. Identify the intoxication effects of the six major types of psychoactive drugs.
4. Explain the role of biological factors in substance abuse and dependence.
5. Outline the four major psychosocial factors that contribute to substance abuse and dependence.
6. Discuss the medical treatments used for drug and alcohol addictions.
7. Discuss the psychological therapies used for substance use disorders.
8. Describe the important features of successful drug and alcohol rehabilitation.
9. Discuss the use of support groups in the treatment of drug and alcohol addictions.

J eff started drinking while he was in high school, and by his senior year he was getting drunk three or four times a week. He drank heavily in college and also began snorting cocaine. By the time he graduated from college, Jeff had developed a regular alcohol and cocaine habit. After graduation, Jeff got married and took a job as an assistant manager at a club where the trendy crowd was seriously drug-involved.

His drinking and drug use escalated. At his peak he was using about $2000 worth of cocaine every week. Jeff began stealing cash from his boss. At first he found it easy to hide his theft with some creative bookkeeping, but as his drug problem grew, his methods became careless, his job performance fell off, and his boss became suspicious. At age 24 Jeff was arrested for embezzling nearly $100,000 from his employer. Mandated into drug treatment by a judge, Jeff began rehabilitation depressed, unemployed, and separated from his wife.

Many of Jeff's behaviors are common among people with substance use disorders. In this chapter we will consider the nature of drug abuse problems like Jeff's and look at their causes and treatment.

8-1 ■ PSYCHOACTIVE SUBSTANCE USE DISORDERS

Drug use is common in modern American society. A recent nationwide survey found that the majority of Americans over the age of 12 admit to some nonmedical drug use during their lifetimes (see Table 8-1) (*National Household Survey on Drug Abuse*, 1988). Nonmedical drug use typically involves **psychoactive substances**, drugs that influence our emotions, thoughts, motivation, and behavior. Psychoactive drug use is usually legal and socially acceptable—it includes the caffeine in your morning coffee and the alcohol in your "happy hour" cocktail.

When regular drug use causes maladaptive behaviors and psychological changes in a person, it is considered a **psychoactive substance use disorder**. Two types of substance use disorders listed in the DSM-III-R are psychoactive substance abuse and psychoactive substance dependence. The National Institute of Mental Health estimates that 19 percent of the U.S. population has a substance use disorder and that two-thirds of these cases involve alcohol (W. Smith, 1989).

Psychoactive Substance Abuse

Psychoactive substance abuse is a maladaptive pattern of drug taking that lasts at least a month or occurs repeatedly over a longer time period. Drug use is maladaptive when characterized by one or both of the following features:

1. Drug use continues despite negative consequences, such as physical disease or occupational problems.
2. Drug use occurs in hazardous situations, such as driving while intoxicated. (American Psychiatric Association, 1987)

Two or three times a month Sarah meets her friends in the city for some drinks. She has several glasses of wine and, if it's available, a few "lines" of cocaine. She is usually pretty high when she drives home to the suburbs, and recently she was arrested for driving under the influence of alcohol. Except when she socializes with her friends, Sarah rarely drinks and never uses other drugs. She meets the criteria for a diagnosis of psychoactive substance abuse.

psychoactive substances Drugs that influence emotions, thoughts, motivation, and behavior.

psychoactive substance use disorder Maladaptive behaviors and psychological changes caused by regular drug use.

psychoactive substance abuse A maladaptive pattern of drug taking lasting at least a month.

TABLE 8-1   NATIONAL HOUSEHOLD SURVEY ON DRUG USE, 1988[a]

Drug	Lifetime Use		Used in Past Month	
	Number	% Pop.	Number	% Pop.
Alcohol	168,498,000	85.0	105,845,000	53
Cigarettes	149,005,000	75.0	57,121,000	29
Any illicit drug	72,496,000	37.0	14,479,000	7
Marijuana	65,748,000	33.0	11,616,000	6
Nonmedical use of psychotherapeutics	23,526,000	12.0	3,393,000	2
Cocaine	21,171,000	11.0	2,923,000	1.5
Hallucinogens	14,607,000	7.0	776,000	0.5
Inhalants	11,262,000	5.5	1,223,000	0.7
Crack cocaine	2,483,000	1.2	484,000	0.2
Heroin	1,907,000	1.0	——[b]	

[a]Based on an estimated 198.3 million members of the U.S. household population age 12 and older. These figures do not distinguish among experimental, recreational, and chronic drug use.
[b]Not available.

Source: Adapted from *National Household Survey on Drug Abuse*, 1988, Rockville, MD: NIDA.

Psychoactive Substance Dependence

psychoactive substance dependence A maladaptive pattern of drug use, with loss of control and possible physical addiction.

addiction Physical need for a drug.

tolerance Increasing need for higher drug doses, due to adaptation to the drug.

withdrawal Unpleasant physical and psychological reactions from reduction of drug use.

polysubstance dependence A pattern of dependence involving at least three drugs.

Some people's drug abuse escalates to a more serious level of psychological and physical dependence. **Psychoactive substance dependence** is a maladaptive pattern of drug use in which the person loses control over drug taking and may exhibit signs of a physical addiction. The DSM-III-R criteria for psychoactive substance dependence are listed in Table 8-2.

Addiction usually means that the person has developed a physical need for or dependence on a drug, manifested by tolerance and withdrawal symptoms. As the user's body adapts to the drug, he or she develops **tolerance**—the person needs increasingly higher drug doses in order to become intoxicated. Unpleasant physical and psychological reactions following reduction of drug use indicate **withdrawal**, or an *abstinence syndrome*. Although substance dependence often involves a physical addiction, not all people with substance dependence experience tolerance and withdrawal. The diagnosis can be assigned without those classic features of addiction. When a pattern of dependence involving at least three psychoactive drugs is present, the diagnosis is **polysubstance dependence**.

Jeff began his typical day at work by snorting some cocaine and chasing it with a few beers to take off the edge. Through the course of an average day he would consume at least a gram of cocaine and a dozen or more beers. After eight years of heavy drinking, Jeff could drink most of a case of beer before feeling really drunk. His weekend binges usually lasted from Friday after work to Sunday morning. On many occasions Jeff swore he was going to stop, but a day or two later he would feel so lousy he'd slip back. Over time Jeff began to make mistakes at work, losing track of the schemes he made to conceal his theft. His complicated

TABLE 8-2 ▦ **CRITERIA FOR PSYCHOACTIVE SUBSTANCE DEPENDENCE**

Criteria include at least three of the following, some of which have persisted for at least one month or have occurred repeatedly over a longer period:

1. Substance is often taken in larger amounts or over a longer period than intended.
2. Subject has a persistent desire to, or has made unsuccessful efforts to, cut down or control substance use.
3. Subject spends a great deal of time in substance-related activities (e.g., getting the drug).
4. Subject is frequently intoxicated or suffers withdrawal symptoms that interfere with major role obligations (e.g., work and school).
5. Important social, occupational, or recreational activities are given up or reduced owing to substance use.
6. Subject continues substance use despite social, physical, or psychological problems caused by substance use.
7. Subject has developed marked tolerance for the substance.
8. Subject shows withdrawal symptoms.
9. Subject relies on substance use to relieve or avoid withdrawal.

Source: Adapted from *Diagnostic and Statistical Manual of Mental Disorders* (3rd ed., rev.), 1987, Washington, DC: American Psychiatric Association.

lies trapped him, and as the truth caught up with him, his drinking and drug use escalated. By the time of his arrest Jeff had both severe alcohol and cocaine dependence.

8-2 ▦ TYPES OF PSYCHOACTIVE SUBSTANCE USE DISORDERS

Substance use disorders are classified according to which drug is involved. In this section we examine the features of substance abuse and dependence involving several major types of drugs, including alcohol, stimulants, opioids, sedatives, hallucinogens, and marijuana.

Alcohol Abuse and Dependence

Each year Americans drink some 500 million gallons of alcoholic beverages. About half of that is consumed by a minority of heavy drinkers who make up approximately 10 percent of the population. Alcohol abuse or dependence affects nearly 13 percent of the adult population in this country. These problems are three to five times more common in men then women, and they most often affect young adults, 20 to 35 years old. In 1990, the cost of alcohol problems to our society, including medical costs, legal costs, and lost job productivity, was estimated at $136 billion (*Alcohol and Health*, 1990).

The Effects of Alcohol. Ethyl alcohol is a potent neural depressant. Its short-term effects depend on the individual's *blood alcohol level*, the percent of the blood that is alcohol (see Figure 8-1).

Long-term alcohol abuse damages most body organs. With prolonged drinking the liver begins to metabolize alcohol more efficiently. A deadly complica-

Alcohol, the most widely used psychoactive substance in the United States, is a normal part of socializing for many people.

Figure 8-1 Effects of blood alcohol level.

Source: From *Principles of Behavioral Pharmacology* by L. W. Hamilton and C. R. Timmons, 1990, Englewood Cliffs, NJ: Prentice Hall.

Drinks	Behavioral Symptoms of Alcohol Ingestion (based on 150-lb person)	Blood Alcohol
	Decreased eye-hand coordination on complex tasks.	.01
	Decreased visual acuity; slower reaction times; swaying.	
	Loss of coordination; legally drunk in some states.	.10
	Legally drunk in most states.	
	Severe loss of coordination; blurred vision; nausea.	
	Confusion; slurred speech; ataxia.	.20
	Severe intoxication; sleepy; inattentive.	.30
	Comatose.	.40
	Death can occur.	.50

tion of chronic alcohol use is cirrhosis, a liver disease, which is the ninth leading cause of death in the United States, killing about 25,000 people each year. Excessive alcohol use also increases the risk of diabetes, hypertension, and stomach cancer. In addition to the medical complications, alcohol is responsible for approximately 50 percent of auto fatalities and other accidental deaths, including drownings, each year (Goodwin, 1985).

Because of its depressant effects on the brain, alcohol interferes with most complex mental processes, including attention, learning, memory, perception, language, and judgment. The behavioral and emotional effects of alcohol are often due to its interruption of these normal cognitive processes, a condition called *alcohol myopia* (Steele & Josephs, 1990).

During one summer vacation in high school, Jeff and his friends were drinking heavily and stopped at a gas station to use the bathroom. The attendant refused to give them the key and told them to leave, whereupon Jeff grew enraged and threatened him. When the attendant locked himself in the station, Jeff lost control and started throwing beer bottles through the front window. When his friends tried to get him to stop, he wouldn't, so they left. Jeff was picked up shortly afterward by the police.

A problematic relationship exists between alcohol and aggression. Alcohol increases aggressiveness by reducing inhibitions and impairing judgment, and it figures prominently in many violent crimes such as homicide, rape, and child abuse. It is not certain that alcohol alone is responsible for aggression, but the combination of alcohol problems with other personality and emotional disorders can lead to violent behavior (Bushman & H. M. Cooper, 1990; U.S. Department of Health and Human Services, 1987).

Patterns of Alcohol Abuse and Dependence. There are many variations of alcohol abuse and dependence. Over time, alcohol abusers become increasingly preoccupied with their drinking and are frequently intoxicated, sometimes in inappropriate settings, such as at work. Many alcohol abusers grow secretive and defensive about their drinking, often lying about the extent of their alcohol use. Although alcohol abusers try to excuse and justify their drinking, they typically continue to drink. The familiar term *alcoholism* is generally used to describe a condition of chronic alcohol dependence. In this chapter, **alcoholism** means alcohol dependence with physical addiction, and an *alcoholic* is a person with alcoholism.

alcoholism Alcohol dependence with physical addiction.

Researchers have distinguished two types of alcoholism. *Type I alcoholism* usually begins after age 25 and is characterized by frequent loss of control over drinking, guilt about drinking, and an anxious personality profile. *Type 2 alcoholism* begins before age 25, the drinking is more severe, and the person demonstrates frequent alcohol-related fighting and an antisocial personality (Cloninger, 1988).

The Course of Alcoholism. The development of alcoholism depends on both individual and environmental factors. In the 1950s, Elvin Jellinek, a physician, promoted the *disease model* of alcoholism. He thought alcoholism was a progressive illness with specific symptoms and a predictable course of development. Jellinek's (1960) model proved very influential and led to the identification of alcoholism as a disease by the American Medical Association. However, many questions have been raised about the validity of Jellinek's disease model.

On the basis of a 40-year study, psychiatrist George Vaillant (1983) concluded that alcoholism is not necessarily a chronic deteriorating disease. Vaillant emphasizes that drinking patterns are influenced by features of the person and the environment and that rather than having a single course of development, alcoholism has many—some chronic, some episodic, and some transient.

For many alcoholics drinking takes place throughout the day, including the morning, and is a solitary activity.

Other studies also support the idea that alcohol abuse does not necessarily lead to chronic alcoholism and that alcohol abuse and dependence are distinctive conditions. One recent investigation found that after four years, about a third of men initially diagnosed with alcohol abuse had alcohol dependence, but nearly half no longer even met the criteria for abuse. Furthermore, over half of those initially diagnosed with alcohol dependence did not show dependence at follow-up (Hasin, Grant, & Endicott, 1990).

Most alcoholism studies have examined the development of drinking patterns in men. Other studies indicate that the course of alcoholism is different in women. Alcoholic women usually begin their problem drinking later than men, and they are more likely to do so because of severe emotional disturbances such as depression (R. W. Wilsnack, S. C. Wilsnack, & Klassen, 1987).

The Consequences of Alcoholism. Despite variations in their drinking patterns, most alcoholics share in the unfortunate consequences of drinking. Alcoholics have above-average rates of social and psychological problems, including family distress, unemployment, antisocial behavior, suicide, and psychiatric disorders. Not surprisingly, the average life span of alcoholics is shorter than that of nonalcoholics.

When an alcoholic stops drinking, withdrawal may begin within a few hours, with symptoms such as body tremors, nausea, weakness, rapid heart rate, sweating, and mood changes. Severe withdrawal provokes a state of **delirium tremens** (D.T.'s), characterized by confusion, agitation, disorientation, and sometimes hallucinations (Korsten & Lieber, 1985).

Alcoholism is a leading cause of organic mental disorders, second only to Alzheimer's disease. One of the most serious, **Wernicke-Korsakoff syndrome**, is a condition of disorientation, confusion, memory loss, and confabu-

delirium tremens Severe alcohol withdrawal; a state of confusion, agitation, and disorientation.

Wernicke-Korsakoff (*wer*-nick-uh-*kor*-suh-kof) *syndrome* An alcohol-related organic mental disorder.

In this painting by a recovering alcoholic, the three doors represent paths to a destroyed world (left), an abyss (right), and a hopeful landscape (middle).

lation (inventing false stories): it results from the effects of alcohol and related vitamin deficiencies on the brain. If the alcoholic stops drinking altogether, however, there can be some recovery of cognitive functions (Bowden, 1990; Grant, 1987).

Stimulant Abuse and Dependence

stimulants Drugs that increase neural activity and arousal.

Stimulants are drugs that increase activity and arousal of the nervous system. This class includes cocaine and the amphetamines.

cocaine A stimulant drug derived from the coca plant.

Cocaine. For centuries some inhabitants of Peru and Bolivia have used the leaves of coca shrubs for their energizing effect. The active ingredient of these leaves is the stimulant **cocaine**. It was chemically isolated in 1864, and its medical application as an anesthetic was tested in the late 1800s. Until 1906 cocaine use was legal in the United States, and the drug was widely used in various remedies and tonics, including the original formula of Coca-Cola (Rosecan & Spitz, 1987).

Today cocaine is most often taken intranasally, or "snorted," in powder form, but it can also be injected intravenously. Two types of smokable cocaine, *freebase* and *crack*, are more potent because the drug is in a purer form (its free alkaloid base). In any form, cocaine is one of the most reinforcing psychoactive drugs. Research animals prefer cocaine over food and water, and they will work hard for a miniscule dose of the drug. When given unlimited access to cocaine, laboratory monkeys use so much that nearly all die within a few weeks (Geary, 1987; Nunes & Rosecan, 1987).

Cocaine can cause serious physical damage. Medical problems include seizures, heart failure, and stroke. The potential for psychological impairment from cocaine is also enormous. Chronic cocaine abusers experience depression, paranoia, and memory problems because of the long-term effects of the drug on the nervous system (Karan, Haller, & Schnoll, 1991).

The Course of Cocaine Abuse and Dependence. Cocaine abuse and dependence develop in three stages. In the *early stage*, frequent cocaine use leads to addictive thought patterns along with compulsive cocaine cravings, and the person's lifestyle is impaired. In the *middle stage*, the cocaine abuser loses control over drug use, and binges may last several days. In addition, the individual finds that the positive emotional effects of cocaine are diminished while the negative effects, such as jitteriness, increase. In the *late stage*, the person exhibits physical addiction, fails in efforts to stop, and manifests severe disruptions of behavior and psychological functioning (Washton, 1986).

Some cocaine addicts experience *cocaine paranoia*, an extreme and irrational fear of being threatened or endangered, which can provoke violent behavior (Karan et al., 1990). Crack smokers seem most prone to outbursts of violence, and there has been a dramatic rise in crack-related crime during the past several years (Greenberg, 1990). In addition, cocaine abusers commonly use other drugs, especially alcohol and tranquilizers. In a recent study, 84 percent of cocaine abusers were found to also abuse alcohol or have alcohol dependence (Regier et al., 1990).

When Jeff discovered cocaine in college, he couldn't believe how great it was. Not only did it help him party with more stamina and energy, it also gave him a feeling of power and intelligence. Most important, he was not depressed when he used cocaine because it took his mind off his problems with school and his

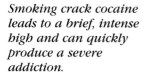

Smoking crack cocaine leads to a brief, intense high and can quickly produce a severe addiction.

parents. His cocaine use was somewhat controlled because he could not afford too much during college. But when Jeff started working and had more money, he found the drug increasingly irresistible. Eventually his excessive cocaine use was able to keep him alert, but he wasn't really getting high anymore. This is a sure sign of cocaine tolerance.

The *cocaine abstinence syndrome* is an extended process with three phases. During the *crash phase*, which lasts up to four days, drug cravings, depression, and agitation appear first, followed by exhaustion. During the *withdrawal phase*, which lasts up to ten weeks, anxiety and drug cravings invite relapse. During the *extinction phase*, which is an indefinitely long return to normal mood, occasional urges to take the drug still surface (Gawin & Kleber, 1986). Although there is evidence that cocaine abusers suffer withdrawal symptoms, no mechanism of tolerance has been found. Despite this uncertainty, most experts consider cocaine an addictive drug (Gawin, 1991).

Amphetamines. **Amphetamines** are stimulants that arouse the central and autonomic nervous systems, producing increased energy, alertness, activity, and euphoria. In addition to their psychoactive effects, amphetamines also increase blood pressure, heart rate, and respiration. Some prescription diet pills include amphetamines for their appetite-suppressing ability (Gold, Geyer, & Koob, 1989).

The "pep pill" Benzedrine first appeared in the 1920s. It was soon followed by other amphetamines, including dextroamphetamine (Dexedrine) and methamphetamine (Methedrine). In the past few years, so-called designer drugs like methylenedioxymethamphetamine (MDMA, or "ecstasy") have been derived from the older stimulants.

Prolonged amphetamine use leads to dependence, fear, panic, and violence, and it sometimes even produces an *amphetamine psychosis*, a state of extreme irrationality and confusion. The physical consequences of amphetamine use include convulsions, cardiac arrest, and, in some cases, malnutrition due to appetite loss. Withdrawal from amphetamine addiction may last for a few weeks, and it usually involves depression, energy loss, agitation, and a craving for sleep (Blum, 1984).

amphetamines
Stimulants that arouse the central and autonomic nervous systems.

Opioid Abuse and Dependence

The **opioids** are narcotic drugs derived from opium, an ingredient of poppy plants, and related synthetic drugs with similar effects. The opioid class includes morphine, codeine, and heroin. Several synthetic opioid drugs, including meperidine (Demerol) and methadone, have similar effects. **Heroin**, the most widely abused opioid, is a semisynthetic drug derived from morphine. In fact, heroin was introduced in the 1890s as a supposedly nonaddictive substitute for morphine. Today there are an estimated half-million heroin addicts in the United States. Within the past few years there has been a decline in intravenous use and a sharp increase in snorting and smoking heroin, especially among urban teenagers and young adults—probably because high-potency heroin has become readily available and because users fear exposure to HIV (AIDS) infection from shared syringes (Way, 1982).

Opioids influence the brain's pain regulation and pleasure mechanisms, but

opioids Narcotic drugs derived from opium and related synthetic drugs with similar effects.

heroin A semisynthetic opiate derived from morphine.

Heroin addicts like this man typically engage in intravenous drug injection, an activity that increases their risk of contracting hepatitis, HIV infection, and other diseases.

the effects of specific opioids vary. For example, injected heroin creates an intense euphoria (''rush''), followed in turn by loss of coordination, relaxation, and sleepiness (''nodding''). Codeine taken orally produces relaxation and feelings of well-being, but not the intense rush of heroin (Snyder, 1985; Thomason & Dilts, 1991).

The Course of Opioid Abuse and Dependence. Although many individual types of opioid abuse and dependence are possible, the most common involve heroin. Heroin use generally begins in the late teens or early twenties and develops into a chronic pattern of dependence, with many periods of relapse and remission. The average duration of heroin dependence is about nine years, but 20 to 25 percent of heroin users endure a lifelong addiction (Robertson, Bucknall, Skidmore, J. J. K. Roberts, & J. H. Smith, 1989; D. D. Simpson, Joe, W. E. K. Lehman, & Sells, 1986).

Heroin dependence carries a high risk for many physical problems, especially for intravenous drug users. Hepatitis, AIDS, skin abscesses, and liver disease are just a few of the adverse consequences of intravenous heroin use. Beyond the direct effects of the drug itself, the lifestyles of heroin addicts create a risk for premature death by overdose, suicide, accident, and violence. Heroin addicts have a mortality rate 20 times greater than nonaddicts of the same age (Thomason & Dilts, 1991).

The *opioid abstinence syndrome* begins within a few hours after the last use and reaches its peak in two or three days. The severity of withdrawal depends on the level of addiction, but even a mild case is painful. Drug cravings, runny nose, sweating, anxiety, hot and cold flashes, nausea, and body aches are typical symptoms. The gooseflesh bumps that arise on the skin prompted the slang expression "cold turkey" for opioid withdrawal (Jaffe, 1985).

Sedative Abuse and Dependence

sedatives Drugs with a calming or depressant effect.

Drugs with a calming or depressant effect on the nervous system are called **sedatives**. They include the barbiturates, benzodiazepines, and inhalants.

barbiturates CNS depressants derived from barbituric acid.

Barbiturates. **Barbiturates** are powerful central nervous system depressants derived from barbituric acid. Pentobarbital, secobarbital, and phenobarbital are common types of barbiturates. These drugs have been used medically for their tranquilizing or sedating effects and for controlling epileptic seizures. At low doses the barbiturates have effects like those of alcohol. When taken with alcohol their depressant effects are greatly magnified, sometimes to a lethal degree. Taken in high doses or in combination with other depressants, barbiturates can cause coma or even death by respiratory failure. Barbiturate withdrawal is one of the longest and most painful of all drug withdrawals, with symptoms of extreme anxiety, seizures, and even transient psychotic reactions lasting for as long as two weeks (Blum, 1984).

Benzodiazepines. The most commonly used sedatives are minor tranquilizers or antianxiety drugs of the *benzodiazepine* group, such as diazepam (Valium), lorazepam (Ativan), and alprazolam (Xanax) (see Chapter 5). Benzodiazepine intoxication is similar to the effect of barbiturates but much milder, and the withdrawal symptoms are likewise a milder version of barbiturate withdrawal.

Since benzodiazepines do not produce a significant "high," their potential for recreational abuse is not great. In fact, most individuals who develop benzodiazepine dependence are taking these drugs for medical or therapeutic purposes. The typical victim of benzodiazepine addiction is a woman who has been using the drugs for an anxiety disorder. The prevalence of benzodiazepine abuse and dependence has declined sharply from its peak in the 1970s. However, some people abuse benzodiazepines alone or in combination with other drugs, especially alcohol and cocaine (DuPont & Saylor, 1991).

inhalants Volatile chemicals inhaled through the nose or mouth.

Inhalants. Volatile chemicals that are inhaled through the nose and mouth are called **inhalants**. Inhalants are usually cheap and are available in common products like glue, paint thinner, and nail polish remover. The most widely abused inhalants have significant depressant effects on the nervous system. However, because various chemicals are used, there are many possible effects. Inhalant intoxication typically begins with a period of arousal and is followed by coordination loss, belligerence, apathy, impaired judgment, and dizziness. Irrational beliefs (delusions) and bizarre behavior may occur, and some users experience memory loss. The physical addictiveness of inhalants is questionable.

Inhalant abusers are generally younger, poorer, and more socially maladjusted than other drug abusers. Adolescents who abuse inhalants often have additional substance abuse problems, especially with alcohol. Chronic inhalant dependence is rare because these drugs are usually dropped in favor of others by late adolescence (Kerner, 1988; C. J. Weiss & Millman, 1991).

The use of inhalants is an increasingly serious problem with children and younger adolescents. The boy in this photo is sniffing glue.

Hallucinogen Abuse and Dependence

hallucinogens Drugs that produce hallucinations and psychedelic effects.

Hallucinogens are drugs that produce hallucinations and psychedelic (mind-altering) effects, such as vivid fantasies and intense emotions. Natural hallucinogenic drugs have long been used in medicinal and religious practices in some traditional cultures. For example, some American Indians of the Southwest employ mescaline, from the peyote cactus, in religious ceremonies.

The hallucinogen *lysergic acid diethylamide* (LSD) was first synthesized in the late 1930s by a research chemist who noted its unusual effects on his own perceptions and thoughts. Some LSD users report enhanced spiritual insights and creativity when they use the drug, but most researchers dispute such claims. The well-documented adverse consequences of a "bad trip" include anxiety, paranoia, confusion, and feelings of unreality. Even after the LSD high, some users have terrifying flashbacks to the drug experience (Blum, 1984; C. J. Weiss & Millman, 1991).

Phencyclidine (PCP, usually sold as "angel dust"), which was first marketed as an animal anesthetic, has potent hallucinogenic and euphoric effects. PCP also produces agitation, aggressiveness, confusion, and delirium. Excessive and chronic PCP abuse can cause convulsions, heart failure, and strokes, and it sometimes causes permanent cognitive and sensory impairments (C. J. Weiss & Millman, 1991).

Dependence on hallucinogens is extremely uncommon. Their interference with functioning is so severe that prolonged daily use is nearly impossible. Furthermore, tolerance is acquired so rapidly that regular intoxication is inhibited. Hallucinogen users rarely limit themselves to just these drugs: they typically use others, including alcohol, marijuana, and amphetamines (Blum, 1984; C. J. Weiss & Millman, 1991).

Marijuana Abuse and Dependence

marijuana   A drug
derived from the cannabis
plant, containing THC.

The hemp plant *Cannabis sativa* is the source of **marijuana**, a drug whose psychoactive ingredient is a chemical known as tetrahydrocannabinol (THC). Marijuana, hashish, and other THC products are *cannabinoid* drugs. Marijuana was used for thousands of years in Asian medicine for its mild sedative effects, and today it is the most widely used illegal drug in the United States. Although its popularity has declined since the late 1970s, surveys indicate that over 50 percent of the population aged 18 to 25 has used marijuana at least once (Kozel & Adams, 1986; *National Household Survey on Drug Abuse*, 1988).

Marijuana is usually smoked in a pipe or in cigarette form as a ''joint,'' but it can also be eaten. Its common effects are feelings of well-being, intensified sensory experiences, time distortions, and temporary impairment of memory and attention. Extremely potent marijuana sometimes produces hallucinations. Excessive marijuana use suppresses sex hormones and sex drive, especially in males. Chronic marijuana abusers may exhibit an *amotivational syndrome* of apathy and indifference, but the exact relation of this syndrome to marijuana use is unclear (Grinspoon & Bakalav, 1985; C. J. Weiss & Millman, 1991).

Most researchers agree that marijuana is not physically addictive because it does not produce tolerance. In fact, marijuana users sometimes show *reverse tolerance,* meaning that over time they need lower doses to achieve the same high. However, some heavy marijuana abusers exhibit an abstinence syndrome of irritability, appetite loss, insomnia, and drug cravings (Rohr, Skowland, & T. E. Martin, 1989).

8-3   CAUSES OF SUBSTANCE USE DISORDERS

Substance use disorders result from complex physical, psychological, and social influences. In this section we explore the main biological and psychosocial

Marijuana is the most widely used illegal drug in the United States. Despite some decline in use, it is still a popular social drug among adolescents and young adults.

causes of these disorders. Most research and theories in this field emphasize alcoholism, so more information is available about that problem.

Biological Causes

Numerous studies of hereditary and neurophysiological factors have demonstrated the importance of biological causes in substance use disorders.

Hereditary Factors. With the exception of alcoholism, substance use disorders have no strong genetic basis. However, family studies indicate that some people have a hereditary vulnerability to alcoholism because the relatives of alcoholics have above-average rates of alcoholism. In **familial alcoholism**, there is a family history of drinking problems, an early onset of abusive drinking in the late teens to early twenties, and usually a more severe pattern of dependence (Goodwin & Warnock, 1991).

familial alcoholism
A type of alcoholism characterized by family history, early onset, and severe drinking.

Twin studies have often yielded inconsistent data regarding hereditary contributions to alcoholism. Some studies find a higher concordance rate for drinking in monozygotic twins, but others do not (R. M. Murray, Clifford, & Gurlin, 1983). However, a major twin study at the University of Minnesota found evidence of significant genetic influence on male alcoholism (but little heritability of female alcoholism) (McGue, Pickens, & Svikis, 1992). Adoption studies provide the most persuasive evidence for the heritability of alcoholism. Children of alcoholic parents have been found to have above-average rates of alcoholism, even when raised by nonalcoholic adoptive parents (Cadoret & Gath, 1978; Goodwin, 1985b; Goodwin, Schulsinger, Hermansen, Guze, & Winokur, 1973). Some studies suggest the existence of two hereditary patterns, a *male-limited* (father-to-son) type and a *matrilineal* (mother-to-daughter) type (Bohman, Sigvardsson, & Cloninger, 1981; Cloninger, 1988; Cloninger, Bohman, & Sigvardsson, 1981).

Despite evidence of hereditary involvement, no genetic mechanism for alcoholism has yet been found. A recent study identified a specific gene in two-thirds of a sample of alcoholics and in only one-fifth of nonalcoholics, but this finding has been seriously questioned (Blum et al., 1990). In all likelihood there are several different genetic bases for predisposition toward alcoholism (Pickens et al., 1991).

The relationship between genes and alcoholism is not a simple one, and there are important environmental influences as well. In weighing the genetic hypothesis, keep in mind that although roughly a third of alcoholics have alcoholic parents, most do not. Furthermore, many people with a family history of alcoholism are not alcoholics. These facts indicate that hereditary factors alone do not fully explain alcoholism (Goodwin & Warnock, 1991; Searles, 1988).

During his treatment, Jeff admitted that both his father and his paternal grandfather had been heavy drinkers. He never considered them alcoholics because they always worked and were successful businessmen. Jeff's case is typical of male-limited familial alcoholism in which the father-son drinking pattern goes back a few generations in the family.

Neurophysiological Factors. Neurophysiological mechanisms in the brain may support the development of substance use disorders. The brains of some children of alcoholics exhibit abnormal electrical responses to stimuli. These abnormal responses are possible biological markers for alcoholism, suggesting impairments in the brain's information-processing mechanisms (Begleiter, Porjesz, Bihari, & Kissen, 1984). Sons of alcoholics are also less sensitive to alcohol's intoxicating effects, in terms of coordination and body sway (Lester & Carpenter, 1985). Such neurophysiological characteristics may not directly cause alcoholism, but they might contribute to a person's inability to recognize signs of intoxication, and this in turn could lead to excessive drinking (Hill, Steinhauer, & Zubin, 1987; Schuckit, 1987; Tarter & Alterman, 1988).

All psychoactive drugs interact with the brain's neurotransmitter systems. Some drugs influence the neurotransmitters in a highly precise fashion. For example, opioids, cocaine, and benzodiazepines clearly influence the brain's endorphin, dopamine, and GABA systems, respectively. Other drugs, such as alcohol, influence various neurotransmitters. Although it is doubtful that a single neurotransmitter controls all drug addictions, the dopamine systems have been implicated in the effects of several drugs, including amphetamines, cocaine, heroin, and alcohol. Dopamine has a role in the brain's pleasure and reward systems, and it is an important key to understanding drug addictions (Barnes, 1988; Matuschka, 1985; Wise, 1988).

Psychosocial Causes

Many characteristics of the individual and the environment affect the development of substance use disorders. In this section we discuss the role of personality, motivation, and sociocultural and family factors in these disorders.

Personality. Traditional psychoanalytic theory proposes that personality dynamics predispose certain individuals to alcohol and drug problems. Various hypotheses attribute these problems to unconscious dependency needs, oral fixations, or underlying aggressive impulses. Modern psychodynamic views, however, emphasize ego impairments, especially in need satisfaction, self-control, and social maturity (Khantzian, 1980; Wurmser, 1974).

Substance use can subdue the emotional discomfort engendered by unconscious conflicts and ego deficiencies, and drugs can serve as artificial defenses against emotional distress. For example, alcohol can chemically repress threatening impulses, and cocaine can energize someone who is depressed. The **self-medication hypothesis** proposes that substance abuse is prompted by the need to avoid or subdue emotional problems and to artificially create desirable emotional states (Khantzian, 1985). That is, people may use drugs as a form of medication to combat other problems. In support of the self-medication hypothesis, studies show that drug disorders and other mental disorders often coexist (see Figure 8-2) (Kushner, Sher, & Beitman, 1990; Regier et al., 1990).

The search for a specific *addictive or alcoholic personality* has been frustrated by methodological problems. Studies of addicts and alcoholics always produce a chicken-or-egg dilemma: Which came first, the personality traits or the substance use disorder? To resolve this dilemma, researchers look for traits that precede the onset of substance use. Evidence from prospective studies suggests that substance use disorders are predicted by childhood variables such

self-medication hypothesis A view that people abuse drugs in order to avoid or subdue emotional problems.

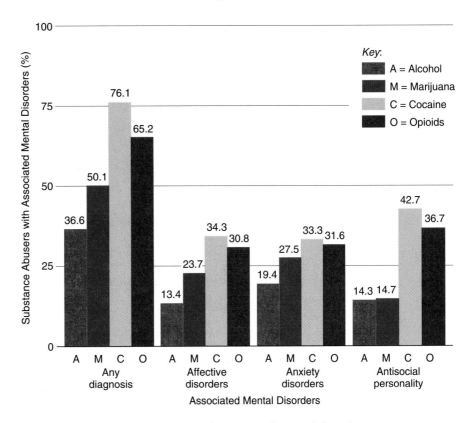

Figure 8-2 Substance abuse and associated mental disorders.

Source: Adapted from "Comorbidity of Mental Disorders with Alcohol and Other Drug Abuse" by D. A. Regier et al., 1990, *Journal of the American Medical Association, 264*, pp. 2511–2518.

as aggressiveness, antisocial behavior, poor impulse control, and rebelliousness. However, no distinct profile of traits defines a common core of addictions. In fact, personality traits alone do not predict substance use well in comparison to factors like peer drug abuse (Donovan, 1986; Lang, 1983; Shedler & Block, 1990).

Motivation. Learning theories have traditionally focused on motivational processes in the development of drug and alcohol habits. The **tension reduction theory** states that drug use is reinforced because drugs can reduce or relieve unpleasant states of tension, such as anxiety. This theory was initially proposed to explain alcohol use, but it extends to other tension-reducing drugs, such as opioids and sedatives. However, alcohol and other drugs do not always reduce tension; sometimes they even increase unpleasant feelings, like anger and guilt. The tension reduction theory is not accepted as a valid explanation of all substance use (Cappell & Greeley, 1987; Conger, 1956).

In addition to reducing tension, drug use can be reinforced by other physiological, emotional, and social consequences. For example, drinking often starts as part of social activity and is strengthened by the social reinforcement of peer acceptance. When drug use is reinforced, environmental cues act as

tension reduction theory
A view that drug use is reinforced because drugs lessen feelings of tension.

Alcohol use disorders generally begin in adolescence with excessive recreational drinking that escalates into more regular and habitual abuse.

conditioned stimuli that elicit drug urges and drug-taking behavior. Seeing a beer ad, for example, or talking with a drinking buddy can trigger the urge for alcohol (Ludwig, Cain, Wikler, Taylor, & Bendfieldt, 1977).

Cognitive and social learning theories emphasize the subjective motives for alcohol use, in particular, beliefs that people hold about drug effects and themselves. Someone who believes that alcohol has beneficial effects and who expects to function more competently when intoxicated will be motivated to drink. In studies of this *think-drink effect*, alcoholics express more positive beliefs about alcohol's influence than nonalcoholics (M. L. Cooper, Russell, & George, 1988; Critchlow, 1986; M. S. Goldman, S. A. Brown, & Christiansen, 1987; G. A. Marlatt & Rohsenow, 1981). The cognitive effects of alcohol can also encourage drinking. In some people drinking diminishes unpleasant states of self-consciousness (Hull, 1987), while for others it provides an excuse for personal failures and inadequacies (Berglas, 1987).

As a child, Jeff was anxious and reserved. When he started drinking and smoking marijuana in his teens, he believed he could overcome his inhibitions and become popular. Under the influence of drugs Jeff became happy-go-lucky, and he liked himself better drunk than sober, especially since he was able to talk to girls more easily. Jeff's attitudes about himself and his substance use illustrate the role of self-perception processes in motivating drug use.

Sociocultural Factors. The sociocultural context of substance use includes factors such as gender, relations with peers, socioeconomic status, and ethnic group.

At all ages, males have significantly higher rates of substance use disorders than females. Gender differences in drug use might reflect greater genetic vulnerability in men, but sociocultural factors are also important. American society is generally more tolerant of drug use by men than by women, and alcohol use in particular is perceived as more normal for men. However, drug use is commonly part of the teenage rites of passage into adulthood for both sexes.

Certainly most adolescents who experiment with alcohol and other drugs do not develop substance use disorders. Those who do are generally more socially deviant in terms of their attitudes and behaviors. Particularly among males, drug abuse often accompanies other forms of social maladjustment, such as delinquency, crime, and antisocial behavior (U.S. Department of Justice, 1988; Zucker & Lisansky Gomberg, 1986).

Drug use by peers is a powerful influence on the development of substance use problems. Adolescents are especially swayed by their peers, and the level of drug use by close friends strongly predicts a teenager's drug use. However, peer influence is not just a matter of chance or circumstances, since deviance-prone adolescents tend to seek out others with similar behavior and attitudes (Donovan, Jessor, & Jessor, 1983; Kandel & Yamaguchi, 1985; L. N. Robins & E. M. Smith, 1980).

Substance use disorders occur at all levels of socioeconomic status (SES), but they are more prevalent at the lower levels. Poverty, unemployment, and other social stressors relate directly to the risk of alcohol and drug dependence. In the United States, higher rates of alcoholism are found in members of racial minorities, including African-Americans, Hispanic-Americans, and American Indians. The lower SES of minority groups in the United States places them at greater risk for substance abuse problems as well as other mental health problems (Ley, 1985).

Ethnic and racial differences in substance use may reflect cultural traditions, genetic variables, or both. Substance use disorders are rare among Arabs, for example, because of strict prohibitions in the Moslem religion. The generally low rates of alcoholism among Asians may be due to a genetic intolerance for alcohol or to discouragement of intoxication in their cultures. Countries with winemaking traditions, such as France, have higher alcohol consumption and alcoholism rates. In the United States, alcoholism rates are high among people of Irish and Scandinavian descent and low among those of Jewish and Italian ancestry (de Lint, 1978; Helzer, 1987).

Family Factors. Besides their hereditary contributions, families also provide the primary social environment in which children learn many behaviors, including drug use and abuse. The presence of a substance-abusing parent is a major predictor of a child's drug abuse. Other family factors also increase the risk of drug problems among children. People with drug problems are more likely to come from families in which physical punishment, violence, conflict, and poor parent-child relationships prevailed. Parents of individuals with substance use disorders have above-average rates of various mental disorders, such as depression, antisocial personality, and anxiety disorders (Collins & Marlatt, 1981; T. Jacob, 1987; Rounsaville et al., 1991; Steinglass, Bennett, Wolin, & Reiss, 1987).

8-4   TREATMENT FOR SUBSTANCE USE DISORDERS

We have seen that there is no simple explanation for substance use disorders. This poses a serious challenge for their treatment. In this section we examine medical treatment, psychological therapy, rehabilitation, and support groups for these disorders.

Medical Treatments

Medical treatment of substance use disorders addresses the physical dimensions of the drug problem, primarily through detoxification and drug therapy.

detoxification Total elimination of drugs from the body by abstinence.

Detoxification. The initial goal of medical treatment is **detoxification**, the total elimination of the drug from the person's body. Detoxification requires a period of abstinence so the body becomes "clean." The length of time required depends on the drug or drugs used and the person's level of addiction. Alcohol detoxification, for example, is usually complete in about five days. Withdrawal symptoms are especially prominent during detoxification. The detoxification period can be made less painful with use of therapeutic drugs, such as tranquilizers for alcoholics, clonidine for heroin addicts, and antidepressants for cocaine addicts (Jaffe & Ciraulo, 1985; Rosecan & Nunes, 1987; Thomason & Dilts, 1991).

Drug Therapy. Another medical strategy employs therapeutic drugs to discourage further substance abuse. For example, disulfiram (Antabuse) disrupts the body's breakdown of alcohol: if alcohol is consumed, nausea, cold sweats, panic, and heart acceleration will follow. Other drugs block the intoxicating effects of psychoactive substances and thereby discourage their use. For example, the drug naloxone suppresses the intoxication effects of heroin.

Many problems arise in drug therapy, especially in regard to patients' compliance to treatment. A recent study found that fewer than 25 percent of treated alcoholics actually complied with disulfiram treatment (Fuller, 1989). Heroin addicts have similarly low compliance rates for naloxone treatment. Even with compliance, these strategies have limited long-term influence on recovery if they are used alone (Alterman, O'Brien, & McClellan, 1991).

methadone maintenance therapy A treatment for heroin addicts, using methadone, a synthetic opioid.

Methadone maintenance therapy employs the synthetic opioid methadone to help addicts gradually wean themselves from heroin. Methadone stimulates the same brain regions as heroin without producing the same intoxication. Methadone therapy was originally intended to help addicts detoxify more easily, but it has yielded mixed results. Many addicts have benefited from the proper use of methadone, but others have switched their addiction to methadone or combined heroin and methadone dependencies. Furthermore, many addicts sell their methadone and then purchase heroin and other drugs. The success of methadone programs is modest at best. Fewer than half of treated addicts remain clean for an extended time (Bratter, Pennacchia, & Ganya, 1985; D. D. Simpson, Joe, & Bracy, 1982).

At a methadone clinic such as the one shown here, heroin addicts can receive regulated doses of methadone to gradually wean themselves from heroin.

Psychological Therapies

Psychological treatments for substance disorders include psychotherapy, behavior therapy, and family therapy.

Psychotherapy. Traditional psychoanalysis has not been very successful with most addicts because it overemphasizes unconscious causes and downplays patients' drug use and physical addiction. In recent years, modified psychodynamic therapy has offered more useful and structured treatment that is focused directly on the patient's drug-related ego deficits, emotional disturbances, and defense mechanisms (Dodes & Khantzian, 1991; Forrest, 1985).

There has been little controlled research on psychotherapy with substance abusers, but a few projects show promising results. Researchers at the University of Pennsylvania demonstrated clear benefits of psychotherapy for heroin addicts. At a 12-month follow-up, treated addicts showed reduced drug use and improved social adjustment (Woody, McClellan, Luborsky, & O'Brien, 1987). The Harvard Cocaine Recovery Project demonstrated the value of psychodynamic group therapy for cocaine addicts (Khantzian, Halliday, & McAuliffe, 1990).

Successful psychotherapy for drug addicts depends on many individual variables, such as the patient's drug history, family pathology, associated psychological disorders, and social circumstances. The chances are better for patients with briefer, less severe addictions, previously good social adjustment, and

CLOSE-UP
Kicking the Nicotine Habit

Like most people, you probably don't consider cigarette smokers to be drug addicts. However, nicotine is an addictive drug, and a deadly one. Each year in the United States over 300,000 people die of smoking-related causes, exceeding by far the combined deaths from all other drugs. In fact, cigarette smoking is the major preventable cause of death in America. Most smokers know that withdrawal from nicotine involves unpleasant nicotine cravings, irritability, and anxiety. Nicotine addiction and withdrawal are so severe that millions of smokers knowingly risk their lives because they cannot quit (U.S. Department of Health and Human Services, 1986).

Unfortunately, the overall success of smoking treatments is poor. Fifty percent or more of quitters resume smoking within one year, and some experts even question whether treatment programs work at all (Schachter, 1982; J. L. Schwartz, 1985). Smokers who quit on their own with no formal treatment (self-quitters) are sometimes more successful than smokers undergoing treatment. One recent study of self-quitters found that they have no advantage over treated smokers, and about 80 percent of both groups were smoking again within a year (Cohen et al., 1989).

A few treatment techniques for smokers have been helpful in promoting quitting. Nicotine chewing gum and nicotine patches suppress the craving for a smoke and work especially well for heavy smokers. However, nicotine gum alone is rarely effective and it may even increase relapse potential (Grabowski, 1985). The antihypertensive drug clonidine inhibits nicotine withdrawal and aids in the early stages of quitting (Glassman et al., 1988). The *rapid smoking method*, a behavioral aversion therapy, temporarily inhibits smoking by requiring that the person chain-smoke to the point of physical distress. However, broad-spectrum programs seem to work best, combining behavioral techniques, support groups, stress control, and nicotine gum (Hymowitz, 1991; Lando, 1977).

Despite the modest success of formal smoking treatment programs, many people do quit. The U.S. Department of Health and Human Services estimates that half to two-thirds of smokers who try to quit will eventually succeed. Some studies even suggest that several failed attempts at quitting can actually promote long-term success. With smoking, the old saying seems to apply: "If at first you don't succeed, try, try again" (T. Baker & Brandon, 1988).

strong support from family members (Alterman et al., 1991; Kleber & Gawin, 1984; Kosten, Rounsaville, & Kleber, 1987; Saxe, Dougherty, & Esty, 1985).

Behavior Therapy. Behavior therapy for alcoholism has employed aversive conditioning with electric shock and has used nausea-producing drugs called *emetics* to inhibit alcohol cravings and drinking. For example, in a classical conditioning procedure, patients drink a small amount of alcohol along with the emetic drug, and the nausea that follows establishes a learned aversion to alcohol. Aversion therapy alone, however, has had limited success with alcoholics, since the conditioned aversion to alcohol fades quickly after treatment (Lawson, 1983; Wiens & Menustik, 1983).

An innovative and effective behavioral approach to drug treatment is **cue exposure therapy**, which promotes the extinction of drug cravings by repeatedly exposing the addict to drug-relevant cues or stimuli. For example, cocaine addicts watch videotapes of cocaine users and their paraphernalia, and alcoholics are exposed to the sight and smell of alcoholic beverages. Preliminary studies indicate that cue exposure does help addicts overcome urges that arise in real-life situations where drugs are present (Barnes, 1988; Monti, Abrams, Kadden, & Cooney, 1989).

In the 1970s, a heated controversy emerged over behavior therapy programs that tried to teach *controlled drinking* to alcoholics by reinforcing appropriate social drinking. Critics of controlled drinking, mostly supporters of the disease model of alcoholism, argued that total abstinence is the only sensible treatment for alcoholics. Today, controlled drinking is considered a reasonable therapy only for nonaddicted alcohol abusers and perhaps for younger, less dependent alcoholics. Controlled drinking is not feasible for older chronic alcoholics, and it can be dangerous because it harms their physical condition and undermines their resolve to avoid drinking (Marlatt, 1983; Nathan & Skinstad, 1987).

Contemporary behavioral programs take a broad-spectrum approach to substance use disorders, in which several therapeutic strategies are utilized. Reinforced abstinence, social skills training, self-management, and stress control are all components of effective treatment for addicts and alcoholics (Monti et al., 1989; Nathan & Niaura, 1985).

Family Therapy. Family therapy is fast becoming an integral part of treatment for substance use disorders. Since dysfunctional family relationships often promote addictions and relapse, the addict and other family members often need to change their interactions. Reviews of family therapy demonstrate its value in aiding recovery from alcoholism and drug problems (Heath & Stanton, 1991; O'Farrell, 1989).

Although many issues arise in family therapy for addictions, special attention has been given to the problem of codependence. **Codependence** is a relationship in which family members become dependent on the addict's behavior and respond to him or her in ways that contribute to the addiction. Codependent family members sometimes unwittingly "enable," or support, the addict's behavior. For example, someone who calls to report that a hung-over alcoholic spouse is sick and unable to work is enabling the spouse's alcoholism. Family therapy helps people to identify, challenge, and correct such codependent behavior patterns (Beattie, 1987; Heath & Stanton, 1991).

Rehabilitation

Rehabilitation is an extended program that usually includes medical treatment, psychotherapy, and group and family therapy. Its duration varies from several weeks to a year or more, and it can involve inpatient or outpatient treatment.

Therapeutic communities (TCs) are long-term residential rehabilitation programs for drug addicts. Beginning in the 1950s with Synanon, a program for

---

cue exposure therapy
Behavior therapy that exposes addicts to drug cues in order to extinguish drug cravings.

codependence A relationship in which family members are dependent on an addict's behavior.

rehabilitation Extended treatment for addictions, involving medical, psychological, group, and family therapies.

therapeutic communities
Long-term residential rehabilitation programs for addicts.

heroin addicts in California, TCs have proliferated in the past 30 years. These programs are highly structured, drug-free environments that emphasize group work and peer pressure. Through group encounters, TC clients learn to confront and support one another in recovery.

The success of TCs and other rehabilitation programs is hard to evaluate because of variability in the programs, inadequate follow-up, and high dropout rates. A major nationwide study of alcoholism rehabilitation in the United States found that after 18 months, about two-thirds of patients who completed treatment were improved, but only about a fourth were abstinent. After 4 years, over half were drinking again and only 7 percent were alcohol-free (Armor, Polich, & Stambul, 1978; Polich, Armor, & Braiker, 1981).

Successful rehabilitation depends on many factors besides formal treatment. All too often success is short-lived because patients return to an environment with drinking and drug-using friends, and they soon relapse. Family problems, social pressure, and emotional distress are all major contributors to relapse. Programs that teach patients how to recognize and cope with these relapse triggers promote more durable recovery from drug and alcohol dependencies (G. A. Marlatt, 1985).

Support Groups

support group A self-help group for people with a common interest in recovery from addictions.

One of the most widespread treatments for substance use disorders is the **support group**, a self-help program organized and run by people who share a common addiction and an interest in helping one another in recovery. The best-known support group is *Alcoholics Anonymous* (AA), which was begun in the 1930s. Following AA's lead, support groups for other addictions have appeared, including *Narcotics Anonymous*, *Cocaine Anonymous*, and *Smokers Anonymous*.

The impact of support groups, especially AA, is evidenced by their popularity. For example, AA today is a worldwide organization with over a million members. The AA perspective is that alcoholism is a lifelong disease that can be controlled only through complete abstinence. The program of recovery advocated by AA emphasizes the need for a spiritual reawakening and a firm commitment to change. This simple philosophy was clearly expressed by AA's founders:

> Most emphatically we wish to say that any alcoholic capable of honestly facing his problems in the light of our experience can recover. . . . Willingness, honesty, and open-mindedness are the essentials of recovery. (*Alcoholics Anonymous*, 1976)

Does AA work? Thousands of alcoholics attest to AA's success, but research on this question is scant. From the available data, we can conclude that AA works, but not for everyone. Those most likely to benefit from AA are men over 30 who have strong affiliation needs and who have had a severe loss of control over their drinking (Alford, 1980; Osborne & F. B. Glaser, 1985).

After completing a four-week inpatient rehabilitation program, Jeff began outpatient treatment at a community mental health clinic. Over the next 18 months Jeff

*Members of Alcoholics Anonymous use the support of the group to help
them recover from alcoholism.*

participated in individual, group, and marital therapy and became a regular at AA
meetings. Unlike most recovering addicts, he was able to maintain complete
abstinence from alcohol and cocaine, and at last check Jeff had been clean and
sober for nearly two years.

Evaluation of Treatments. All types of treatment for substance use disorders have been successful to some degree. However, about 50 percent of patients never complete treatment, and half of those who do will relapse within
a few years. Consequently, we need to be modest in discussing the meaning of
success for these treatments. Studies comparing different treatments find little
difference in their outcomes when other factors, especially patient characteristics, are controlled. Employed middle-class patients with family support and a
history of adequate functioning generally improve the most in any type of treatment. In addition, many people improve without any formal treatment. Apparently, the patient's characteristics and environment are as important in enabling
recovery as the treatment the patient obtained (Alterman et al., 1991; Emrick,
1982).

The best treatment programs combine several approaches in a *three-stage
model* of detoxification, rehabilitation, and aftercare with psychotherapy and
support groups. However, few substance abusers and addicts actually enroll in
such programs; in fact, most receive little or no formal treatment. For example,
an estimated 85 percent of alcoholics in the United States never seek treatment.
Nevertheless, about a third of alcoholics recover on their own—some perma-
nently, but most only temporarily (Holden, 1987).

PROFILE
William Griffith Wilson (1896–1971)

William Griffith Wilson, better known as Bill W., was a cofounder of Alcoholics Anonymous (AA), chief author of its main works, and a tireless organizer for AA.

Wilson was born in 1896 in rural Dorset, Vermont—ironically, in a room behind a bar. In 1909 his father abruptly deserted the family, and soon Bill and his younger sister were abandoned by their mother as well when she left them with her parents. While growing up, Bill was a determined boy who compulsively pursued his objectives. He was also prone to feelings of loneliness, helplessness, and guilt.

Bill's drinking began in the army during training for duty in World War I. After the war he and his wife moved to New York, where Bill became a successful Wall Street stockbroker—and a severe alcoholic. The 1929 market crash wiped him out, and over the next few years his drinking led to several hospitalizations, the last of which prompted his spiritual awakening and recovery.

In 1935, Bill and Dr. Robert Smith ("Dr. Bob") founded Alcoholics Anonymous, and from that first meeting AA has grown to an association of nearly 75,000 groups in over 100 countries, with more than a million members worldwide. Bill devoted the rest of his life to the organization

and worked to ensure that it stayed independent, democratic, decentralized, and nonprofessional. Bill's vision of AA was as a fellowship in which the only membership requirement was a desire to stop drinking.

Along the way, controversies and conflicts emerged over AA and its mission. Despite the objections of many AA members, Bill avoided the disease model of alcoholism, believing that alcoholism was a malady with physical, mental, and spiritual features. He was convinced that alcoholics need a profound spiritual awakening in order to recover, and in the 1960s he even experimented with LSD as a means to produce the desired spiritual change.

Bill was the primary author of the group's basic texts: *Alcoholics Anonymous* (the "Big Book"), *Twelve Steps*, and *Twelve Traditions*. Bill was described by admirers as devoted, shrewd, energetic, and intelligent, and he also possessed enormous curiosity and humor. He referred to himself as the "number one drunk in America," and he proposed adoption of an AA Rule No. 62: Don't take yourself so damn seriously. In 1971, Bill Wilson died of emphysema caused by the one addiction he couldn't beat—cigarettes (Kurtz, 1979; Thomsen, 1975).

SUMMARY

8-1 Psychoactive substances alter a person's emotions, thoughts, motivation, and behavior. Psychoactive substance abuse is maladaptive drug use that has adverse consequences. Psychoactive substance dependence is maladaptive drug use involving a loss of control and, often, physical addiction indicated by tolerance and withdrawal symptoms.

8-2 Features of substance use disorders depend on individual factors and the drug(s) of choice. Alcohol suppresses neurological and psychological functioning. Alcoholism, a physical addiction to alcohol, is responsible for many adverse economic, medical, and personal consequences. Cocaine and amphetamines are addictive stimulants. Opioids are narcotics, including morphine, codeine, and heroin, which induce euphoria and relaxation. Sedatives are depressants, such as barbiturates, benzodiazepines, and inhalants. Hallucinogenic drugs cause hallucinations and psychedelic effects. Marijuana is a cannabinoid with mild sedative and euphoric effects.

8-3 Substance use disorders have complex biological and psychosocial causes. Hereditary and physiological factors increase the risk for alcoholism. Many psychoactive drugs influence the brain's dopamine systems. No specific personality type is linked with drug problems. Drug use is motivated by self-medication needs, reinforcing effects of drugs, expectations about drug effects, and self-perception processes. Gender, social class, ethnicity, and culture influence the risk of drug problems. Drug abuse is predicted by social deviance, peer and parental drug use, parental psychopathology, and family discord.

8-4 Many treatments for substance use disorders are available. Detoxification and drug therapy are common medical treatments. Psychotherapy, behavior therapy, and family therapy are also used. Rehabilitation programs and therapeutic communities are long-term residential treatment approaches. Self-help support groups like AA are used for many types of drug problems. All treatments meet with modest success.

TERMS TO REMEMBER

addiction (p. 193)
alcoholism (p. 196)
amphetamines (p. 200)
barbiturates (p. 202)
cocaine (p. 198)
codependence (p. 213)
cue exposure therapy (p. 213)
delirium tremens (p. 197)
detoxification (p. 210)
familial alcoholism (p. 205)
hallucinogens (p. 203)
heroin (p. 200)

inhalants (p. 202)
marijuana (p. 204)
methadone maintenance therapy (p. 210)
opioids (p. 200)
polysubstance dependence (p. 193)
psychoactive substances (p. 192)
psychoactive substance abuse (p. 192)
psychoactive substance dependence (p. 193)

psychoactive substance use disorder
  (p. 192)
rehabilitation (p. 213)
sedatives (p. 202)
self-medication hypothesis (p. 206)
stimulants (p. 198)
support group (p. 214)

tension reduction theory (p. 207)
therapeutic communities (p. 213)
tolerance (p. 193)
Wernicke-Korsakoff syndrome
  (p. 197)
withdrawal (p. 193)

SUGGESTED READINGS

Blane, H. T., & Leonard, K. E. (Eds.). (1987). *Psychological theories of drinking and alcoholism.* New York: Guilford.

Blum, K. (1984). *The handbook of abusable drugs.* New York: Gardner.

Frances, R. J., & Miller, S. I. (Eds.). (1991). *Clinical textbook of addictive disorders.* New York: Guilford.

LEGAL AND ETHICAL ISSUES: COMPULSORY DRUG TESTING AND TREATMENT

Every year thousands of people in the United States are tested for drug use and mandated into treatment because the tests are positive. During the past decade, American society has grown enormously apprehensive about drugs, and this mood has led to some controversial laws and practices. Mental health professionals are especially concerned about the practical and ethical implications of compulsory drug testing and treatment.

In the 1980s, the Reagan administration promoted compulsory drug testing of federal employees and encouraged testing in the private sector. In 1989 the U.S. Supreme Court ruled in favor of compulsory drug testing for employees of the Federal Railway Administration, even when there is no evidence or suspicion of drug use. Today compulsory drug testing is routine in many major organizations, including Fortune 500 companies, school systems, state government agencies, and college and professional sports teams.

The public perception that drug testing is necessary was fueled by incidents such as the 1989 Exxon Valdez disaster, in which an intoxicated tanker captain ran his ship aground and spilled millions of gallons of oil, causing massive environmental damage. However, serious questions have been raised about compulsory drug testing, because of the uncertain reliability of the tests and because many worry that a "witch hunt" attitude may erode our basic civil rights. The 1989 Supreme Court ruling concluded that the "special needs" of a government agency outweighed individuals' Fourth Amendment rights against unlawful search and seizure (Mallory, 1990).

As a consequence of drug testing and drug-related arrests, many people are ordered into treatment programs. In recent years, most referrals to drug and alcohol programs have been involuntary patients sent by courts, schools, and employers. Despite its good intentions, the practice of mandating drug treatment is ethically problematic. Many mandated clients do not have genuine substance use disorders in need of treatment. There are also ethical questions about coercing those with real drug dependencies into treatment (Peele, 1989). In addition, problems of confidentiality arise when referring agencies, such as probation departments, insist on receiving treatment records.

In addition to the ethical problems, there are practical problems in compulsory treatment. Success in drug treatment depends largely on the patient's motivation, and mandated patients have at best mixed motives. How serious can someone be about treatment that is perceived as a punishment for drug use?

Whether compulsory drug testing and treatment actually deter substance use is unknown, but they are increasingly common features of the legal and mental health practices in this country. In the future, these programs must be carefully evaluated to determine whether they are in the best interest of society and individuals (Leukefeld & Tims, 1988).

Chapter NINE

Mood Disorders and Suicide

OUTLINE

9-1 Mood Disorders
Manic Episode • Major Depressive Episode • Types of Mood Disorders

9-2 Causes of Mood Disorders
Biological Causes • Psychosocial Causes

9-3 Treatments for Mood Disorders
Biological Treatments • Psychological Treatments

9-4 Suicide
Characteristics of Suicide Victims • Teenage Suicide • Suicide Prevention

OBJECTIVES

1. Distinguish between mood disorders and normal mood variations.
2. Outline the diagnostic criteria for manic and major depressive episodes.
3. Describe the symptoms of bipolar and depressive disorders.
4. Discuss the genetic and biochemical bases of mood disorders.
5. Compare psychodynamic, behavioral, cognitive, interpersonal, and family explanations for depression.
6. Describe drug and electroconvulsive treatments for mood disorders.
7. Detail psychological treatments for depression.
8. Discuss suicide prediction.
9. Outline and explain risk factors in teenage suicide.
10. Discuss the practice of suicide prevention.

*J*ason, a depressed 32-year-old factory worker, was brought to the psychologist's office by his wife. Throughout the evaluation he appeared frail and lifeless and spoke in a soft monotone, responding only when asked a question. Since being fired at work for taking too many sick days, Jason had slept 14 to 16 hours a day. He had no appetite and did not participate in family affairs. He had even considered suicide.

Further evaluation revealed that Jason had been unusually energetic and euphoric about a year before his depression. During this time he had slept only one or two hours a night, and he had started two businesses that had ultimately failed.

Jason's symptoms are common in individuals with mood disorders. In this chapter we look at the types of mood disorders and explore the causes of and treatments for these conditions.

9-1 ▨ MOOD DISORDERS

mood Emotional state.

Mood is a term we use to describe our emotional state. It refers to the way we feel at a given point in time. Most of us feel happy when we reach a desired goal, such as earning a good grade or gaining the approval of friends and family. We often feel sad when we lose a good friend or fail to reach our goals. Much of the time we are neither happy nor sad. These are normal mood variations, and they are characteristic of mental health.

mood disorders
Episodes of mania,
depression, or both.

Individuals like Jason display disturbances in emotional expression that interfere with their everyday functioning. Their moods become excessively high or low for an extended duration, and the return to a "normal" mood state is impaired. In the DSM-III-R, these disturbances are classified as **mood disorders**, defined by episodes of depression or mania, or an alternation of the two. Table 9-1 outlines the primary symptoms of manic and major depressive episodes (American Psychiatric Association, 1987).

▨ Manic Episode

manic episode A period
of elevated or irritable
mood.

A **manic episode**, also known as *mania*, is a distinct period during which an elevated or irritable mood dominates the individual. During the manic episode at least three of the symptoms listed in Table 9-1 are present.

Symptoms of Manic Episode. The mood of a person in a manic episode is *elevated or euphoric*, indicating a feeling of extreme well-being. During this time the individual experiences *inflated self-esteem*, and self-confidence may overflow all reasonable bounds. In severe cases, psychotic *delusions* or false beliefs may occur. For example, the manic person might stand near the United Nations building and confidently offer unsolicited, inexpert solutions to the Mideast crisis. Although he was not delusional, Jason admitted that his confidence was boundless during his manic episode. He felt great and thought he could accomplish anything.

Along with euphoria, manic individuals have a *decreased need for sleep*. Many sleep only a few hours a night, like Jason, or not at all for several days.

TABLE 9-1   SYMPTOMS OF MANIC AND MAJOR DEPRESSIVE EPISODES

Manic Episode	Major Depressive Episode
• Elevated or irritable mood	• Depressed mood
• Inflated self-esteem	• Loss of interest or pleasure
• Decreased need for sleep	• Significant weight loss or weight gain
• Excessive talkativeness	• Insomnia or hypersomnia
• Flight of ideas	• Psychomotor agitation or retardation
• Distractibility	• Fatigue
• Increased goal-directed activity	• Feelings of worthlessness or guilt
• Excessive pleasure seeking	• Concentration difficulties
	• Recurrent thoughts of death

Source: From *Diagnostic and Statistical Manual of Mental Disorders* (3rd ed., rev.), 1987, Washington, DC: American Psychiatric Association.

Mania is also manifested in *excessive talkativeness*. The individual talks more than usual and is often loud, complaining, and hostile. Frequently, speech is full of nonsensical jokes and puns, and it has a "pressured" quality—it seems that the person talks just for the sake of talking.

Cognitive disruptions are reflected in the individual's experience of racing and disorganized thoughts. Manic thinking, called the *flight of ideas*, is quite accelerated and often incoherent. In addition, concentration and attention are impaired, as indicated by the person's easy *distractibility*.

In most cases manic episodes are accompanied by an *increase in goal-directed activity*. These individuals often get involved in a variety of political, social, or occupational activities, in a domineering or intrusive way. They undertake new business ventures foolishly and impulsively, without sufficient planning, foresight, or preparation. Such ventures usually fail. *Excessive pleasure-seeking* is common in mania. The manic person is prone to substance abuse and reckless activities, such as high-speed driving, gambling, or unaffordable vacations (American Psychiatric Association, 1987).

Jason impulsively started a taxi service and an auto repair business in his garage while trying to hold his factory job. Both businesses failed within three months, and he eventually lost his full-time job. During his manic episode, Jason also drank heavily because he felt he was "speeding too much."

Types and Course of Manic Episode. Manic episodes most often strike people for the first time in their early twenties. The symptoms peak within several days and may last for days, weeks, or, in some cases, months, creating significant problems in social and occupational functioning. Some individuals may be so out of control and dangerous that involuntary hospitalization is required (American Psychiatric Association, 1987; H. H. Lehman, 1985; Reus, 1988).

A milder, related problem is sometimes found. The *hypomanic episode*, or *hypomania*, is also a mood disturbance with elevated mood and other symptoms seen in mania. However, hypomania lacks the intensity of a full-blown manic episode, and it is not as debilitating (American Psychiatric Association, 1987).

Major Depressive Episode

major depressive episode A period of depressed mood and loss of pleasure.

The most common mood disturbance is the **major depressive episode** (MDE), which is marked by depressed mood or a loss of pleasure, along with at least five of the symptoms shown in Table 9-1. The symptoms persist more or less continuously for at least two weeks (American Psychiatric Association, 1987).

Symptoms of Major Depressive Episode. Individuals experiencing an MDE feel significant emotional pain that affects virtually every aspect of their lives. In addition to their *depressed mood*, depressed people suffer a *loss of pleasure*. They seem to be incapable of experiencing positive feelings, and they lack motivation to pursue formerly enjoyable activities. Jason, for example, was an avid sports fan, but during his depressive episode he rarely watched televised sports and he lost interest in his favorite baseball team.

Physical disturbances are also part of MDE. Many depressed individuals experience diminished appetite and dramatic *weight loss*, while others overeat and end up with a *weight gain*. Sleep disturbance is also common. *Insomnia* is the most common difficulty, usually manifest by trouble falling asleep, repeated awakenings, or early morning awakening. In some cases, such as Jason's, there is excessive sleeping, called *hypersomnia*.

Perhaps the most common physical sign of an MDE is *fatigue*. Depressed individuals commonly complain of feeling exhausted and just cannot seem to get going. The energy crisis may also show up as a general slowing of mental and behavioral functioning, known as *psychomotor retardation*. The depressed person may feel lethargic and listless and may speak with a soft, dull, monotonic voice, as Jason did. Sometimes the person exhibits restless and fidgety behavior called *psychomotor agitation*.

Depression, in its various forms, affects nearly 20 percent of the adult population. Many depressed people, such as the man pictured here, are despondent and feel powerless to change their lives.

Feelings of worthlessness or guilt are quite often present in an MDE. Depressed people may feel inadequate, incompetent, unintelligent, or unattractive, and they may condemn themselves as guilty for their failures. Psychotically depressed individuals may even have delusions of guilt, believing that they have a serious disease as punishment for their sins.

Cognitively, depression appears in disruptions of thinking. In particular, *concentration difficulties* abound. Thinking is slowed, and the person may also complain of being unable to remember simple things like whether the electric bill was paid or the time of a scheduled dental appointment.

Many depressed individuals have *recurrent thoughts of death*. Frequently there is no serious suicidal intent, but suicidal thinking may lead to an actual attempt. Jason, for example, thought of committing suicide but vowed that he would not do it because it would devastate his family (American Psychiatric Association, 1987).

Types and Course of Major Depressive Episode. There are two subtypes of major depressive episode. Individuals suffering from the *melancholic type* are especially unable to experience pleasure. Their depression is worse in the morning, and it is accompanied by significant weight loss and by early morning awakening (American Psychiatric Association, 1987; H. H. Lehman, 1985; Reus, 1988).

Another type of MDE has a *seasonal pattern*, meaning that depressive episodes typically occur during the fall or winter and improve in the spring or summer of each year. This is sometimes called **seasonal affective disorder**. The clinical picture is one of an atypical depression dominated by physical symptoms that include fatigue, overeating, weight gain, carbohydrate cravings, and hypersomnia. This type of MDE is four times more prevalent in women than in men (American Psychiatric Association, 1987; Blehar & Rosenthal, 1989).

The first onset of major depression is usually in the early twenties, but it can occur at almost any age. Episodes usually worsen over a period of days or weeks and can last more than six months. Eighty percent of individuals recover within one to two years, but the remainder follow a chronic course, with symptoms lasting beyond two years. Depressive symptoms recur in more than 50 percent of patients. Onset before age 20 and a history of other mood disorders are the best predictors of recurrence (American Psychiatric Association, 1987; Belsher & Costello, 1988; Giles, Jarret, Biggs, Guzick, & Rush, 1989; Klerman, 1990).

Brenda suffered her first MDE at age 17 and relapsed twice by the time she was 25. During each episode her symptoms were so debilitating that she was hospitalized for several weeks. Subsequently she remained somewhat depressed for years, but the symptoms were much milder than they were during her MDEs. At age 42 Brenda had another episode, which was triggered by an auto accident that left her injured and unable to work for two months. Even after she had recovered from her injuries, she reported that everything was bleak and she thought of suicide.

Types of Mood Disorders

The DSM-III-R divides mood disorders into two main types, bipolar and depressive disorders. **Bipolar disorders** are marked by periods of mania or hypo-

seasonal affective disorder A mood disturbance in which a person is depressed in winter and fall.

bipolar disorders Disorders involving periods of mania, hypomania, and depression.

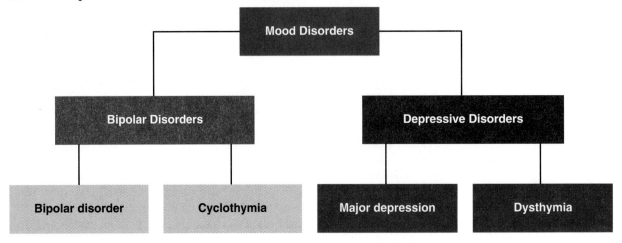

Figure 9-1 Classification of mood disorders.

depressive disorders
Disorders involving depression without mania.

mania and depressive episodes—hence the term *bipolar*. **Depressive disorders** involve depression in the absence of manic or hypomanic symptoms. Since there are no manic or hypomanic episodes in the depressive disorders, they are often called *unipolar depressions*. Figure 9-1 outlines the types of mood disorders according to the DSM-III-R.

bipolar disorder
A mood disorder marked by alternation of mania and depression.

Bipolar Disorders. **Bipolar disorder**, formerly called *manic depression*, is characterized by at least one full manic and one full depressive episode. The manic episode typically occurs first, with the depressive episode following either immediately or after a period of normal mood lasting months or years. Some patients are "rapid cyclers"—they have two or more cycles involving mania and depression within the same year. Bipolar disorder is further subclassified as *mixed*, *manic*, or *depressed*, depending on the features of the current or most recent episode.

Jason was in the midst of an MDE at the time of his interview. Since he had suffered a full manic episode in the previous year, his diagnosis was *bipolar disorder, depressed*. Historical evaluation also revealed that he had experienced similar mood swings at the age of 28, but they were not severe enough to debilitate him.

Bipolar disorder is found in nearly 1 percent of the adult population, affecting men and women with equal frequency (American Psychiatric Association, 1987; Regier et al., 1988). Even with treatment, 30 percent relapse within one to two years (Harrow, Goldberg, Grossman, & Meltzer, 1990).

cyclothymia   A mood disturbance with hypomanic and depressive episodes.

Cyclothymia is a chronic mood disorder consisting of recurrent hypomanic and depressive periods that are less severe than those seen in bipolar disorder. Once considered a personality disorder, cyclothymia is now viewed as a milder but more chronic form of bipolar disorder. Cyclothymic individuals are "sensation seekers" who live a high-risk lifestyle involving daredevil activities, substance abuse, and sexual excesses. Nearly 4 percent of psychiatric outpatients are diagnosed as cyclothymic (American Psychiatric Association, 1987; Reus, 1988).

Paula, age 36, entered therapy after hospitalization for a failed suicide attempt. She had a long history of hypomanic and depressive episodes. Paula reported that prior to being hospitalized, she had been juggling relationships with three men. On several occasions, she had invited one man to sleep at her home and then left under the pretext that she had "something to do" and would be back shortly. During her absence Paula had met one of the other men for sex at a motel; then she came back home and had sex with the first man. Her suicide attempt followed a situation in which one of her boyfriends discovered her scheme and threatened to kill both her and the other man.

major depression
A mood disorder with major depressive episodes.

Depressive Disorders. Depression, which is often called "the common cold of psychiatric disturbance," affects as much as 20 percent of the adult population in its various forms (Regier et al., 1988). **Major depression** is marked by one or more major depressive episodes without a history of mania (American Psychiatric Association, 1987). The chances of suffering major depression in a lifetime is nearly 6 percent, and it is twice as common in women as in men (Blazer et al., 1988; Boyd & M. M. Weissman, 1981; Nolen-Hoeksema, 1987; M. M. Weissman & Boyd, 1983, 1985).

There are sex differences in the kinds of symptoms reported. Women are more likely than men to experience appetite problems and weight gain, physical complaints, expressed anger and hostility, and a slower response to treatment (E. Frank, Carpenter, & Kupfer, 1988). Table 9-2 shows some of these differences in a sample of 230 patients.

In 1987, an American Psychological Association task force, made up largely of women psychologists, sought to ascertain why women are at greater risk for depression than men. The task force concluded that the higher prevalence of depression in women may be due to such gender-related factors as a background of physical and sexual abuse, menstruation, pregnancy, childbirth, menopause, abortions, birth control, and being unhappily married with children (McGrath, Puryear Keita, Strickland, & Felipe Russo, 1990).

dysthymia A chronic depressed mood.

Dysthymia, also called *depressive neurosis*, is characterized by a chronic depressed mood with symptoms that are milder than those of major depression (American Psychiatric Association, 1987). Dysthymic people overreact to ordi-

TABLE 9-2   MALE-FEMALE DIFFERENCES IN DEPRESSION SYMPTOMS

Symptom	Women Number	%	Men Number	%
Increased appetite	81	49	13	28
Weight gain	71	43	12	26
Expressed anger	125	70	24	48
Hypochondriasis	42	24	4	8

Source: Adapted from "Sex Differences in Recurrent Depression: Are There Any That Are Significant?" by E. Frank, L. L. Carpenter, and D. J. Kupfer, 1988, *American Journal of Psychiatry, 145*, 41–45.

CLOSE-UP
Premenstrual Syndrome— A Proposed Mood Disorder

Many women experience mood disturbances just before menstruation. The symptoms of *premenstrual syndrome* (PMS) include marked emotional changes, crying, sadness, irritability, anger, and tension. In addition, women with PMS may experience breast tenderness, headaches, weight gain, muscle or joint pain, bloating, and cravings for specific foods (Gitlin & Pasnau, 1989). In the DSM-III-R, PMS is called *late luteal phase dysphoric disorder* and is listed as a proposed or tentative category needing further study (American Psychiatric Association, 1987).

Methodological flaws have hampered research on PMS. Currently there is no consensus on how to rate symptoms, so it is impossible to determine prevalence accurately. Estimates are that 40 percent of women experience mild premenstrual symptoms and 2 to 10 percent have more serious symptoms and have some difficulty in everyday functioning (Logue & Moos, 1986).

The precise nature of the relationship between PMS and mood disorder is unclear. Women with mood disorders have a higher rate of PMS, and women with PMS have a higher risk of mood disorders. This suggests that PMS and mood disorders are related, but it does not tell us how (McMillan & Pihl, 1987). Attempts to define PMS as a distinct diagnostic category by looking at possible biological and psychosocial causes have not clarified the picture. Most biological explanations have focused on the causal role of hormones, but the findings are inconsistent. One popular explanation for PMS is that the physiological changes which take place just before menstruation make mood symptoms more likely in women who are either extremely sensitive to those physiological effects or poorly adjusted psychologically (Gitlin & Pasnau, 1989).

There is little doubt that many women experience symptoms referred to as PMS. The diagnostic issue is whether PMS is a distinct condition or simply another type of depression. This is not a trivial matter, since, as we learned in Chapter 4, accurate diagnosis leads to the most effective treatments. Clearly, more research will be needed to settle the issue.

nary stressors and exhibit low self-esteem, self-blame, feelings of inadequacy, gloominess, skepticism, and passivity. Moreover, they are viewed by others as being manipulative, demanding, and complaining. Since the depressive symptoms appear to be part of the person's usual functioning, dysthymia has been considered by many since Freud and Kraepelin to be a personality disorder (Phillips, Gunderson, Hirschfeld, & L. E. Smith, 1990). In fact, *depressive personality* may be a distinct diagnostic category in the DSM-IV (D. N. Klein, 1990). Dysthymia affects 3 percent of the adult population (M. M. Weissman, Leaf, Bruce, & Florio, 1988).

Depression in Children and Adolescents. The diagnostic criteria for depressive disorders are primarily based on adults' symptoms. There are lower prevalence rates in children and adolescents. Identifying depression in these groups is more challenging because symptoms are not always expressed the way they are in adults.

Childhood depression is often marked by somatic complaints, psychomotor

Children and adolescents also suffer from depression. Teenagers like the girl shown here often experience a negative body image and low self-esteem and withdraw from social relationships.

agitation, separation anxiety, phobias, and hallucinations (Ryan et al., 1987). Adolescent girls are likely to be preoccupied with a negative body image and a consequent impairment in self-esteem. Dissatisfied with the way she looks, an adolescent girl may be self-critical and may withdraw from social relationships. This diminishes self-esteem–building experiences and sets off a chain of events that leaves the young woman more isolated and more depressed (Allgood-Merten & Lewinsohn, 1990). Adolescent and teenage boys often act out their depression by being physically aggressive (Gjerde, J. Block, & J. H. Block, 1988).

9-2 CAUSES OF MOOD DISORDERS

It is generally accepted that mood disorders are rooted in biological abnormalities and psychosocial experiences. In this section we explore some of the more prominent biological and psychosocial explanations.

Biological Causes

Since the early 1960s, researchers have focused their attention on the possible causal role of hereditary and biochemical abnormalities.

Hereditary Causes. It has long been observed that mood disorders run in families, suggesting a hereditary predisposition to these conditions. The findings from many twin, family, and adoption studies indicate that the more genes an individual shares with an affected person, the greater the risk of that individual developing a mood disorder. Of all the mood disorders, bipolar disorder has the strongest hereditary component, with concordance rates as high as 70 percent for monozygotic twins. This is triple the rate for dizygotic twins (Gershon, Nurnberger, Berrettini, & L. R. Golden, 1985).

In general, relatives of the affected person bear a greater risk of having bipolar disorder than individuals from the general population (Faraone, Kremen, & Tsuang, 1990). One family study conducted at five university medical centers showed that the risk of bipolar disorder in relatives was 5.7 percent. This rate is nearly six times higher than in the general population (Rice et al., 1987). Finally, the risk of bipolar disorder in adoptees is best predicted by the presence of the disorder in biological rather than adoptive parents (Mendlewicz & Rainer, 1977; Wender et al., 1986).

Behavioral genetics studies of major depression are also consistent with a hereditary explanation of mood disorders. Concordance rates for monozygotic and dizygotic twins are 40 and 11 percent, respectively (Faraone et al., 1990). Moreover, the risk of major depression among relatives of an affected person is two to three times higher than in the general population. For some mood disorders, such as dysthymia, hereditary factors are apparently insignificant (Blehar, M. M. Weissman, Gershon, & Hirschfeld, 1988; Goodwin & Guze, 1984).

Attempts to pinpoint the genes responsible for mood disorders have been promising, but not definitive. Thus far, researchers have not been able to determine whether these disorders involve a single gene or a combination of genes (Faraone et al., 1990; Merikangas, Spence, & Kupfer, 1989). Previous studies linking bipolar disorder to chromosome 11 have not been replicated (Egeland et al., 1987).

Biochemical Causes. Explaining the biochemical basis of mood disorders has proved no easy task. One problem was the assumption that depression is a single disorder. Actually, depression is probably a group of disorders with different underlying biochemical causes. Research has pointed to causal roles for several neurotransmitters, including serotonin, acetylcholine, and the endorphins (McNeal & Cimbolic, 1986). The most influential biochemical explanation is based on evidence that some depressed individuals have abnormalities in the metabolism of norepinephrine (NE), a neurotransmitter belonging to the catecholamine group. The **catecholamine hypothesis** states that depression is the result of NE deficiency while an excess of NE produces mania. Although much research has supported this idea, it is evident that the catecholamine hypothesis is not a complete explanation for mood disorders (Board on Mental Health and Behavioral Medicine, Institute of Medicine, 1985; Schildkraut, 1965; Schildkraut, A. I. Green, & Mooney, 1985).

Recently, researchers have begun to see the biochemical basis of depression as a failure in chemical regulation rather than as a simple matter of too much or too little of a substance. One well-supported explanation is the **dysregulation hypothesis,** which holds that depression results from a chronic impairment of mechanisms that normally control the action of NE and other neurotransmitters within neurons or at the synapse. Such impairment leads to unstable neural activity and increases vulnerability to depression (Siever & Davis, 1985).

There is mounting evidence that mood disorders involve impaired biochemistry outside as well as inside the brain. The **dexamethasone suppression test** (DST) is a laboratory test used extensively to detect biochemical abnormalities in the H-P-A axis, which consists of the hypothalamus and the pituitary and adrenal glands (The American Psychiatric Task Force on Laboratory Tests in Psychiatry, 1987). H-P-A abnormalities are detected by the DST in 40 to 50 percent of individuals with major depression but in only 10 percent of normal

catecholamine hypothesis The idea that depression is caused by deficiency of NE, mania by an excess of NE.

dysregulation hypothesis The idea that depression is caused by impairment of neurotransmitter control mechanisms.

dexamethasone suppression test A lab test used to detect endogenous depression.

endogenous depression
Depression caused by
physiological problems.

reactive depression
Depression caused by
adverse life experiences.

continuity hypothesis
The idea that biological
problems make people
vulnerable and life events
trigger depression.

control subjects. Thus, individuals who test positive on the DST are presumed to be suffering from **endogenous depression,** that is, depression caused by internal physiological problems. **Reactive depression** is caused by adverse life experiences.

The distinction between endogenous and reactive depression has not proved reliable, and researchers generally agree that there is a continuum of causes in which biological factors play more or less of a role. According to the **continuity hypothesis,** biological abnormalities confer a vulnerability to depression, and life events trigger and maintain depressive episodes. If the DST were a reliable measure of endogenous depression, we would expect a strong correlation between test results and response to medications known to influence body and brain chemistry. In fact, DST results do not accurately predict a person's response to medication (The American Psychiatric Task Force on Laboratory Tests in Psychiatry, 1987; Kathol, Jaeckle, Lopez, & Meller, 1989; Kraus, Grof, & G. M. Brown, 1988; Reus, 1988). It is hoped that more clinically useful information can be obtained by combining DST results with other measures of H-P-A activity (Flam, 1991).

Psychosocial Causes

Psychosocial explanations for mood disorder are usually derived from prominent theories of abnormal behavior, including psychodynamic, behavioral, cognitive, interpersonal, and family and marital perspectives.

Psychodynamic Views. In his book *Mourning and Melancholia* (1917), Freud wrote that depression is an emotional reaction to the real or imagined loss of a parent in childhood. The child loves yet hates the parent for leaving. According to the psychodynamic **anger-in hypothesis,** guilt over feelings of hatred causes the person to turn the anger inward in the form of self-criticism, self-hatred, and possibly self-destructive behavior. Thus, early loss sensitizes the individual to feelings of abandonment, interpersonal problems, and depression later in life (Meissner, 1985). Revised psychoanalytic theories of depression state that loss damages the ego and thereby impairs self-esteem, so the person feels inferior, lonely, isolated, and helpless (Hirschfeld & Shea, 1985).

anger-in hypothesis
The idea that guilt over
hatred forces people to
turn anger inward.

Behavioral Views. Behavioral views of depression were derived originally from operant conditioning theories. Psychologist Charles Ferster proposed that depression was the result of a reduction of positive reinforcement stemming from the loss of a parent, a separation, or some other drastic life change. Ferster hypothesized that such a loss can reduce access to reinforcers, and some individuals may lack the social skills necessary to secure reinforcers.

According to social learning theories, relating to others has consequences that we appraise as positive (satisfying), negative (unsatisfying), or neutral. Positive outcomes make us feel good about ourselves, and negative outcomes diminish positive feelings. Psychologist Peter Lewinsohn claims that we feel depressed if we have few positive experiences or many negative ones. This creates a vicious cycle in which being depressed stifles our motivation to get involved in pleasurable interactions, and we become even more depressed (Lewinsohn, Munoz, Youngren, & Zeiss, 1978).

Modern psychodynamic theories claim that the loss of a loved one predisposes a person to depression later in life.

Psychologist Martin Seligman has proposed the learned helplessness model, which suggests that people become depressed when they believe they are incapable of controlling unpleasant events in their lives.

negative cognitive triad
A "blueprint" of distorted thoughts that leads to depression.

learned helplessness model The idea that people become depressed when they feel unable to control unpleasant events.

attributional reformulation The idea that depression comes from ways in which people explain unpleasant events.

Cognitive Views. Cognitive theorists such as psychiatrist Aaron Beck say that depression is related to faulty thinking. According to Beck, real or imagined failure sets us up for the expectation of failure. When faced with situations in which we expect to fail, we privately and automatically engage in negative self-talk. We automatically tell ourselves, "Since I've failed before, I'll probably fail again." We unknowingly form the expectation of failure into a "mental blue-print" that shapes our outlook (A. T. Beck, Rush, Shaw, & Emery, 1979).

This blueprint, the **negative cognitive triad**, consists of distorted thoughts and attitudes about the self, the world, and the future (see Table 9-3). Depressed individuals see themselves as inadequate, unworthy, unintelligent, unattractive, and helpless. They see the world as a cold and insensitive place, and they view their future as unpromising. The depressed person may make a *self-fulfilling prophesy:* the person expects the worst and gets it (A. T. Beck et al., 1979; Burns, 1980).

Another popular cognitive view of depression, proposed by psychologist Martin Seligman, is the **learned helplessness model**, which suggests that individuals become depressed when they believe they are unable to control unpleasant events (Maier & Seligman, 1976). This model was based on experiments in the 1960s which showed that dogs initiated few attempts to terminate electrical shock if they had made many previous attempts that failed. In subsequent studies, human subjects also displayed helplessness after failing to shut off a loud noise. (Overmeier & Seligman, 1967).

The original learned helplessness model has been expanded into two cognitive explanations for depression. The idea of **attributional reformulation** states that depression is a consequence of the ways in which we try to explain unpleasant events (Abramson, Seligman, & Teasdale, 1978). There are three dimensions to our attributions:

1. *The internal-external dimension.* We can explain unpleasant events as the result of our own internal deficiencies or ascribe them to external factors.

TABLE 9-3 ▬ **COGNITIVE DISTORTIONS IN DEPRESSION**

1. ALL-OR-NOTHING THINKING: You see things in black-and-white categories. If your performance falls short of perfect, you see yourself as a total failure.

2. OVERGENERALIZATION: You see a single negative event as a never-ending pattern of defeat.

3. MENTAL FILTER: You pick out a single negative detail and dwell on it exclusively so that your vision of all reality becomes darkened, like the drop of ink that discolors the entire beaker of water.

4. DISQUALIFYING THE POSITIVE: You reject positive experiences by insisting they "don't count" for some reason or other. In this way you can maintain a negative belief that is contradicted by your everyday experiences.

5. JUMPING TO CONCLUSIONS: You make a negative interpretation even though there are no definite facts that convincingly support your conclusion.
    a. *Mind Reading.* You arbitrarily conclude that someone is reacting negatively to you, and you don't bother to check this out.
    b. *The Fortune Teller Error.* You anticipate that things will turn out badly, and you feel convinced that your prediction is an already established fact.

6. MAGNIFICATION (CATASTROPHIZING) OR MINIMIZATION: You exaggerate the importance of things (such as your goof-up or someone else's achievement), or you inappropriately shrink things until they appear tiny (your own desirable qualities or the other fellow's imperfections). This is also called the "binocular trick."

7. EMOTIONAL REASONING: You assume that your negative emotions necessarily reflect the way things really are: "I feel it, therefore it must be true."

8. SHOULD STATEMENTS: You try to motivate yourself with shoulds and shouldn'ts, as if you had to be whipped and punished before you could be expected to do anything. "Musts" and "oughts" are also offenders. The emotional consequence is guilt. When you direct should statements toward others, you feel anger, frustration, and resentment.

9. LABELING AND MISLABELING: This is an extreme form of overgeneralization. Instead of describing your error, you attach a negative label to yourself: "I'm a *loser.*" When someone else's behavior rubs you the wrong way, you attach a negative label to him: "He's a goddam louse." Mislabeling involves describing an event with language that is highly colored and emotionally loaded.

10. PERSONALIZATION: You see yourself as the cause of some negative external event which in fact you were not primarily responsible for.

Source: "Definitions of Cognitive Distortions" from *Feeling Good: The New Mood Therapy* by David D. Burns, M.D. Copyright © 1980 by David D. Burns, M.D. Reprinted by permission of William Morrow & Company, Inc.

2. *The stable-unstable dimension.* We can believe that bad outcomes result either from stable, persistent causes or from unstable, temporary factors.

3. *The global-specific dimension.* We can believe that unpleasant events occur

PROFILE
Aaron T. Beck
(b. 1921)

In a 1982 survey of clinical and counseling psychologists, Aaron Beck was voted one of the ten most influential psychotherapists. He has advanced our understanding and treatment of mental disorders, especially depression.

Beck was born in Providence, Rhode Island. He received his bachelor's degree from Brown University in 1942 and his M.D. from Yale University in 1946. Later, he held hospital positions in neurology and psychiatry. Beck has been on the faculty of the Department of Psychiatry of the University of Pennsylvania Medical School since 1954 and is the director of its Center for Cognitive Therapy.

Beck developed his cognitive theory as a practicing psychoanalyst. He observed that while his patients were free-associating, certain thoughts on the fringes of their consciousness would arise suddenly and automatically. Curiously, such thoughts were usually followed by an unpleasant mood. Beck asked his patients to focus on these automatic thoughts, and he noticed negative themes about present, past, and future experiences. When working with more severely de-

pressed patients, Beck observed that negative automatic thoughts occupied a more central position in their minds. Beck wove these early observations into his cognitive theory of depression, and they formed the theoretical basis for his cognitive therapy (A. T. Beck, 1991).

One of the most important themes in Beck's childhood was his love of nature and curiosity about everything. A highlight of his childhood was the microscope his father bought him when he was 10 years old.

Aaron Beck has authored or coauthored over 250 articles and eight books, including *Depression: Clinical, Experimental, and Theoretical Aspects* (1967); *Cognitive Therapy and the Emotional Disorders* (1976); *Anxiety Disorders and Phobias* (1985); and *Cognitive Therapy of Personality Disorders* (1990). He is also the author of one of the most widely used depression scales, the Beck Depression Inventory, and he has received many awards and honors, including the American Psychological Association's Distinguished Scientific Award for the Applications of Psychology (1989).

because of general or global factors that will affect many different situations, or we can believe there are specific causes that apply only in some circumstances.

The *attributional style* of depressed people is characterized by *internal, stable,* and *global* attributions. Depressed individuals believe that they lack what it takes to control events (internal) and that their personal inadequacy is chronic (stable). Making matters worse, they believe their inadequacies will affect many different situations (global) (Abramson et al., 1978). For example, John has trouble attracting women. He becomes depressed when he believes that he is stupid (internal), that he will always be stupid (stable), and that all women will find him to be stupid (global).

hopelessness depression
An expectation that one cannot do anything about unpleasant outcomes.

The second extension of the learned helplessness model proposes that some individuals experience **hopelessness depression**, the expectation that one is powerless to do anything about unpleasant outcomes (Abramson, Metalsky, & Alloy, 1989; Needles & Abramson, 1990). The attributional model considers depression to be due to *internal* factors; in contrast, hopelessness depression occurs in response to uncontrollable global and stable events, whether or not the person assumes personal responsibility for them. For example, Jack cannot seem to attract eligible women. Even though he feels confident about his looks and intelligence, he experiences hopelessness depression because he does not believe his situation will change.

interpersonal theory of depression The idea that depression is caused by disrupted interpersonal relationships.

Interpersonal Views. The **interpersonal theory of depression** proposes that mental problems are caused by disrupted interpersonal relationships (Klerman, M. M. Weissman, Rounsaville, & Chevron, 1984). It focuses on problems involving intimacy, marital strife, poor social support, and other difficulties. Interpersonal theory is derived from the clinical impressions of psychiatrists Adolph Meyer and Harry Stack Sullivan and the *attachment theory* of psychoanalyst John Bowlby. Bowlby proposed that we have an inborn tendency to attach or bond to other people because attachment serves a survival function by providing warmth, support, and protection. If we do not develop strong bonds early in childhood, we become vulnerable to disturbed interpersonal relations later in life.

Family and Marital Views. There is growing evidence that depression can be caused by disrupted family and marital functioning. Overall, families of depressed individuals do not function as well as families of nondepressed people or families of individuals with other psychological problems (Coyne, Kahn, & Gotlib, 1987; Keitner & I. W. Miller, 1990).

Depressed individuals report more marital problems, poorer communication with spouses, less sexual satisfaction, and more of a desire to change their marital relationship than nondepressed individuals. This is especially true of depressed women who find little intimacy and support from their husbands. A review of the family and marital research suggests that interpersonal problems are not only a consequence of depression—they can also cause depression and impair one's recovery from it (Gotlib & Whiffen, 1989; Schmaling & Jacobsen, 1990).

9-3   TREATMENTS FOR MOOD DISORDERS

A full range of biological and psychological therapies are used in the treatment of mood disorders. Despite the wide array of available therapies, only one in three individuals with mood disorders is treated. Apparently, many do not seek help while others go untreated because their mood disorder is misdiagnosed (Giles et al., 1989; Reus, 1988).

TABLE 9-4   ANTIDEPRESSANT DRUGS

Generic Name	Trade Name
TRICYCLIC ANTIDEPRESSANTS	
Amitriptyline	Elavil
Desipramine	Norpramin
Doxepin	Sinequan, Adapin
Imipramine	Tofranil
Nortriptyline	Aventyl, Pamelor
MONOAMINE OXIDASE INHIBITORS	
Phenelzine	Nardil
Isocarboxazid	Parnate

Biological Treatments

The most common biological treatments for mood disorders involve antidepressant or antimanic drugs and electroconvulsive therapy (ECT). Each treatment may be used alone or in combination.

Drug Therapy. The effectiveness of specific drugs in the treatment of mood disorders is well documented. When used appropriately, they relieve symptoms and make the person more amenable to psychological therapies (Consensus Development Panel, NIMH/NIH, 1985).

antidepressants Drugs used in treating depression.

Antidepressants are drugs that increase energy levels and elevate mood. *Tricyclic antidepressants* and *monoamine oxidase inhibitors* (MAOIs) have been the most commonly prescribed antidepressants for years (see Table 9-4) (Hollister, 1988). However, newer drugs, such as amoxapine (Asendin), trazodone (Desyrel), and bupropion (Wellbutrin), are as just as effective and work faster in many patients.

The precise mechanism of action of antidepressant drugs is unknown, but they are believed to work by increasing the availability of norepinephrine and serotonin in brain synapses. Tricyclics are most effective in patients with physical symptoms like sleep and appetite disturbance, loss of sex drive, and psychomotor slowing; they help in approximately 70 to 80 percent of cases. By contrast, the MAOIs work best for depressed individuals with atypical features such as phobias, hypochondriasis, and anxiety. Antidepressant drugs are also useful in preventing recurrences of major depressive episodes (E. Frank et al., 1990). Since 1988, fluoxetine (Prozac) has become the top-selling medicine in the United States for severe cases of major depression.

Antidepressant drugs produce some troublesome side effects as well. Most side effects are minor and diminish over time. However, even minor side effects can affect whether the person continues taking the prescribed medication. Tricyclics can produce fatigue, dry mouth, constipation, tremors, and blurred vision. MAOIs can elevate blood pressure dangerously, especially when they are taken along with certain cheeses, liver, herring, beans, or other foods that contain aged proteins. Prozac has been blamed for violent and suicidal behavior in

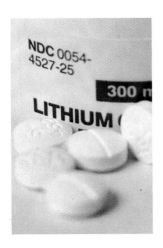

Antidepressants and mood-stabilizing drugs such as lithium help reduce the symptoms of mood disorders in 60 to 80 percent of cases but produce troublesome side effects for some people.

some patients, but despite sensational media accounts and dramatic testimonials of its dangerousness, controlled studies have not proved that Prozac is responsible for such behaviors ("Scientologists Fail," 1991).

Lithium carbonate has proved valuable in controlling acute manic episodes, and it aids in the prevention of both manic and major depressive episodes (Hollister, 1988). The success rate is 60 to 80 percent. There are apparently many mechanisms whereby lithium produces its mood-stabilizing effects. Overall, lithium corrects the overactivity of catecholamine neurotransmitters believed to be responsible for mania.

Jason's psychiatrist prescribed lithium for his bipolar disorder, and within two weeks there was a noticeable reduction of his manic symptoms. Jason was eventually stabilized on a maintenance dosage and showed no recurrences of his mood disorder at a six-month follow-up.

Although lithium is generally the first choice for the treatment of mania, other drugs can be prescribed if lithium fails. These alternatives include carbamazepine (Tegretol), valproic acid (Depakene), and clonazepam (Klonopin) (Pope, McElroy, Keck, & Hudson, 1991; Prien & Gelenberg, 1989).

Electroconvulsive Therapy. In *electroconvulsive therapy* (ECT), electrical current delivered to the head produces a central nervous system convulsion. ECT was originally used in the late 1930s to treat schizophrenia but is now used primarily to treat otherwise untreatable cases of depression.

The use of ECT has always been controversial in medical circles and in the view of the public because of its potential side effects and the prevailing view that it is barbaric. These considerations and the advent of new psychotropic drugs in the 1950s led to a decline in the use of ECT. Over the years, however, equipment and procedures have improved considerably, making ECT safer. Today, serious complications occur in fewer than one in a thousand cases.

The modern application of ECT uses less electrical current. Severe memory loss followed older ECT procedures, but this has been minimized by placing both electrodes over the right side of the head. There are no firm statistics on the frequency of application, but apparently ECT is being used more often in psychiatry (H. H. Goldman, 1988; National Institutes of Health Consensus Development Conference Statement, 1985; R. D. Weiner, 1985).

Research shows ECT to be as safe and effective as antidepressants, helping 70 percent of patients. It is clearly superior to antidepressants for patients who are delusional or suicidal, or for people who do not respond to antidepressants (Janicak et al., 1985).

Lynnette was a 53-year-old woman with a 20-year history of recurrent major depressive episodes and two suicide attempts. Over the years she was given several tricyclics, but she could not tolerate their side effects. Nardil elevated her mood and allowed her to function fairly well for periods of time. Unfortunately, after several months Nardil would make her manic.

When Lynnete was under extreme family pressures she would consider suicide. She reported that while driving she wondered what it would be like to have a head-on collision with an oncoming car. The thoughts were so intense that she struggled to prevent herself from acting on the impulse. After five ECT treatments, she was still somewhat depressed but no longer suicidal.

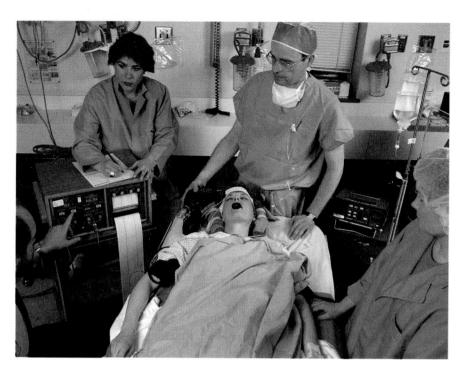

The use of ECT for depression has always been controversial because of its potentially serious side effects. Improvement in equipment and procedures, making it safer and more effective, account for its increased use in modern psychiatry.

Psychological Treatments

For some individuals with mood disorders, psychotherapy is the sole treatment, and for others it is combined with biological treatments. Psychotherapy can assist people in dealing with the consequences of destructive lifestyles, such as relationship problems, loss of jobs, or substance abuse. Family and spouse involvement can be helpful when therapy focuses on education about the disorder, emotional support, and consideration of interpersonal issues.

Psychodynamic Therapy. Psychodynamic therapy focuses on the individual's emotional response to the therapist, who challenges the patient's unrealistic fears of abandonment, reactions to criticism, and feelings of being devalued. The goal is to help the individual to understand the unrealistic nature of these feelings, to express anger, and to cope with relationships without fear of loss. In contrast to traditional psychodynamic treatment, short-term dynamic therapy for depression involves more active participation on the part of the therapist, downplays free association and regression, and stresses current problems viewed in the context of past losses and disappointments (Hirschfeld & Shea, 1985; Meissner, 1985).

Behavior Therapy. Behavior therapy for mood disorders is designed to help the person increase the frequency of positively reinforcing interactions and decrease the frequency of negative experiences. In behavioral programs, depressed individuals are taught to monitor their mood and activities so they can experience more pleasure and avoid unpleasant outcomes. For example, the person may be instructed to keep a daily mood diary in which he or she numerically rates mood in response to activities engaged in that day. Through role playing, the individual learns the social skills necessary to resolve conflicts and gain satisfaction in interpersonal situations. Behavior therapy encourages people to stay active and helps them to better manage their time by constructing daily activities schedules (Lewinsohn et al., 1978).

Cognitive Therapy. Cognitive therapy helps depressed individuals restructure the distorted thinking that gives rise to depression (A. T. Beck, 1985). Using Beck's model, the first step teaches patients about the connection between dysfunctional thoughts and mood. Patients use a diary to help them learn to identify specific dysfunctional thoughts that arise in mood-relevant situations. Once these thought patterns are identified, the therapist challenges them and shows the patient more rational and productive ways of interpreting circumstances.

The patient eventually learns to replace depression-causing thoughts with more positive ways of thinking (Karasu, 1990a, b). For example, a depressed mother complains to her therapist that her son's failure in school is her fault. She says, "I should have helped him more with his homework. I'm not a good mother." Another, more rational way to look at this is to say, "Homework is his responsibility. I can only help so much. I try as best I can, considering my other responsibilities."

interpersonal therapy for depression
Treatment for depression, designed to correct faulty relationship patterns.

Interpersonal and Family Therapy. **Interpersonal therapy for depression** (IPT) is a short-term treatment designed to correct faulty relationship patterns. The process of IPT initially involves identifying these problems by examining past and present interactions with significant others. As specific depressive symptoms are identified, the individual is shown how they relate to social disturbances. In IPT, there is little attempt to change personality; instead, the goal is to help the person change his or her destructive style of relating to others. Where appropriate, IPT also utilizes specific behavioral and cognitive techniques to modify interpersonal behavior (Klerman et al., 1984).

Family therapy is not usually considered a primary treatment for mood disorders, but it is indicated when problems in family relationships contribute to the individual's emotional disturbance. In these cases, the goal is to improve interactions among family members and thereby alleviate feelings of depression in the individual (Coyne et al., 1987; Gotlib & Whiffen, 1989).

Effectiveness of Psychotherapy for Mood Disorders. Clinical outcome studies consistently show that psychotherapy for depression is effective, but no one treatment is significantly better than others.

One major study conducted by the National Institute of Mental Health involved 250 depressed patients at three research centers (Elkin et al., 1989). Patients were divided into four treatment groups in order to compare cognitive-behavior therapy (CBT), IPT, antidepressant medication, and a placebo (inactive medication). Both CBT and IPT were as effective as antidepressant medication, and IPT was slightly more effective than CBT. As expected, all treatments were more effective than the placebo.

Another major study compared cognitive therapy, CBT, behavioral techniques, and nonspecific verbal therapies to each other and to antidepressants. All forms of treatment were equally effective, and the therapeutic gains were retained at follow-up. All treatments reduced depressive symptoms but did not entirely eliminate them (Robinson, Berman, and Neimeyer, 1990).

Though therapy for depression is effective, much more research is still needed in this area. Greater effort must be made to match specific symptoms and depression types to particular treatments (Elkin, Pilkonis, Docherty, & Stotsky, 1988a, b).

9-4 SUICIDE

There is a strong association between depression and suicide. Although most depressed individuals do not take their own lives, being depressed increases the risk dramatically. Suicide is the eighth leading cause of death in the United States, estimated conservatively at more than 20,000 per year. This figure does not include deaths from self-destructive or reckless behavior, such as substance abuse, which may not be officially recorded as suicide. Thus, the actual number of completed suicides may be as high as 25,000 to 30,000 each year. The number of attempted suicides is probably ten times as high (L. Eisenberg, 1986; L. Levy, 1988; Wekstein, 1979).

Characteristics of Suicide Victims

People from all walks of life commit suicide, but certain individuals are more likely to take their own lives. Age, gender, race, and culture are demographic variables associated with suicide risk. Interpersonal and economic problems, physical illnesses, mental disorders, and family influences are also important factors in predicting suicide.

More than 20,000 people kill themselves each year in the United States. Most people who commit suicide see their situations as hopeless and believe that suicide is the only way out.

Age. In general, the distribution of suicide shows two peaks, in adolescence and in people over the age of 45. Although age itself is not responsible for suicide, it increases the risk of suicide when combined with other factors, such as having an incurable illness.

Gender. Men are two to four times more likely to actually commit suicide, but women are twice as likely to attempt it. One popular hypothesis holds that men are more likely to commit suicide because they are more serious about it and therefore select more lethal methods.

In one study, 143 male and 61 female suicides were carefully evaluated (Rich, Ricketts, Fowler, & Young, 1988). The results indicated that men were more likely to use firearms as their method of suicide, whereas women were more likely to use less immediately fatal methods, such as drugs or poisons. Substance abuse and depression were the most frequent diagnoses. Men were more likely to be substance abusers and to have experienced serious economic problems. However, women were more likely to be depressed.

Race and Culture. White males are twice as likely as African-American males to commit suicide in the United States. The suicide rates of African-American women and older African-American men are generally lower than those of whites (E. Robins, 1985).

Suicide is most prevalent in industrialized nations. Hungary, Austria, Finland, and Denmark have the highest suicide rates, while Ireland has a low rate; the rate of suicide in the United States falls in the middle (Department of Economic and International Affairs, 1985).

Interpersonal and Economic Problems. Some individuals see suicide as the only way out of unbearable interpersonal problems. Suicide risk is especially associated with the loss of a loved one, divorce, separation, and rejection. One study found that nearly a quarter of the people who committed suicide had lost a close relationship in the previous year (E. Robins, 1985).

Loss of a job, heavy debt, or job demotion can also increase suicide risk. Ironically, some studies have found a positive correlation between suicide and increased income. Apparently, doctors, lawyers, and others with a high income more often fear financial ruin (E. Robins, 1985).

David, a 56-year-old real estate broker, told his therapist that he was considering suicide because he believed his annual income would drop from $250,000 to $100,000. He feared that this would not permit him to maintain his lifestyle. He would be humiliated and would have to shoot himself. As it turned out, psychotherapy helped him overcome his suicidal tendencies.

Physical Illness and Mental Disorders. Many people who commit suicide are beset by physical illness. People who are in excruciating pain, or who are disabled and see no way out, may view suicide as an end to their misery. Suicide risk also increases in people with mental disorders, especially depression, substance use disorders, and schizophrenia (Black, Winokur, & Nasrallah, 1987, 1988).

The relationship between depression and suicide is strengthened by observations of biochemical abnormalities. At autopsy, the brains of depressed individuals who committed suicide have abnormally low levels of serotonin and signs of increased H-P-A activity, findings that are consistent with biochemical explanations of depression (Arora & Meltzer, 1989; Nemeroff, Owens, Bissette, Andorn, & Stanley, 1988).

Interpersonal, economic, physical, and mental problems may increase suicide potential in adults by causing hopelessness depression. According to Aaron Beck, the depressed person consistently misinterprets experiences in a negative way and therefore expects negative outcomes. More important, the person feels powerless to do anything about it (A. T. Beck, G. Brown, Berchick, Stewart, & Steer, 1990; Cole, 1989).

Family Influences. Family members of suicide victims have an above-average rate of suicide. One explanation for this is that genetic factors may elevate suicide risk through a predisposition to a mood disorder. Evidence for a genetic predisposition comes from studies showing that concordance rates for suicide are higher in identical twins who are also concordant for mental disorder (H. Roy, Segal, Cantewell, & Robinette, 1991).

Heredity notwithstanding, friends and relatives may act as models for suicide. The impact of suicide is most potent in individuals who are easily influenced, especially teenagers (Berman, 1988).

Behavioral Signs of Intent. Fifty to eighty percent of the people who commit suicide have previously verbalized their intentions. "I wish I were dead," "I wish I had the guts to kill myself," or "I wonder what people will think when I'm gone" are communications of suicide intent that should be taken seriously. As a rule, suicide risk increases if the individual has verbalized a desire to be dead and has already considered methods.

In addition to verbalizing their intent, many people make suicidal gestures, such as swallowing a dozen aspirins, drinking a bottle of cough medicine, or superficially cutting their wrists. These behaviors are not necessarily lethal in themselves, but they need to be viewed as danger signs.

Teenage Suicide

The incidence of suicide among teenagers has increased steadily since the early 1950s, and it is now the second leading cause of death in this age group. Most studies attempting to define the characteristics of teenage suicide attempters and victims have been based on retrospective reviews of records, without control groups. Media coverage of teen suicide has complicated the picture by providing dramatic anecdotal reports rather than scientific analyses of suicide victims, their families, and friends. These limitations notwithstanding, an image of the teenager at risk is beginning to emerge.

The typical teenager who commits suicide is a white male with high suicidal intent as evidenced by prior talk of suicide, suicide threats or attempts, or a long-standing desire to be dead. Contrary to popular myth, teens who talk about killing themselves frequently follow through. The risk of suicide increases with a diagnosis of major depression, bipolar disorder, or substance abuse. The combination of mood disorder and substance abuse is a particularly lethal combination (J. C. Levy & Deykin, 1989; Shaffi, Carigan, Whittinghill, & Derrick, 1985).

The teenager at risk is not likely to have received prior psychological treatment, and there is often a strong family history of mood disorder and suicide.

CLOSE-UP
Teenage Suicide and Imitation

Steven, a 17-year-old high school student, committed suicide by carbon monoxide poisoning after seeing a film in which two teens killed themselves using the same method. Steven's diary documented suicidal thinking for at least two years prior to the film, several suicidal gestures, and a failed suicide attempt by carbon monoxide poisoning. The diary also revealed anger at his parent's divorce and conflict over his homosexuality. Steven's diary also indicated that he identified with the movie's victims. (Berman, 1988)

The idea that suggestion can increase suicide risk is not new. In 1774, Johann Wolfgang von Goethe wrote a romantic novel called *The Sorrows of Young Werther.* In his novel Goethe described the plight of a young artist who, torn by fantastic dreams and hopeless passions, shot himself in the head. The book was read by many in Europe and was blamed for instigating impressionable teenagers to commit suicide.

In recent years, it has been noted that teenage suicides sometimes occur in clusters, often following television and newspaper accounts of another suicide. Such observations have led to the hypothesis that some impressionable teenagers imitate suicide. A variation of the imitation hypothesis states that media coverage of suicide triggers suicide in teenagers already at risk, who probably would have attempted suicide at a later date.

Studies attempting to confirm the imitation hypothesis have not been compelling. One study conducted in the New York area found there were 22 teenage suicides in the two weeks following TV movies about suicide, compared to 14 suicides in the two weeks before the movies (Gould & Shaffer, 1986). Another study in California and Pennsylvania found no increase in teen suicide in the two weeks following TV movies about teenage suicide (Philips & Carstensen, 1986). However, these and other studies could not determine whether the suicide victims had ever seen the movies (Philips & Paight, 1987). In conclusion, it does not appear that there is any simple relationship between teenage suicide and media presentations. Accounts of suicide in the media probably present a model for suicide methods in teens who are already predisposed.

Recent conflict with parents, boyfriends, or girlfriends is common in the immediate background of suicidal teens. Suicide risk increases with the availability of firearms in the home, and keeping guns locked away or unloaded does not seem to lower the risk (Brent et al., 1988).

Suicide Prevention

Suicide prevention depends on a solid understanding of the risk profiles of suicide attempters and victims. Prevention involves several strategies, depending on characteristics of the individual and the setting in which evaluation occurs. *Crisis intervention* is a direct approach to reducing suicide risk as quickly as possible. It can involve addressing the immediate problems of someone al-

Interpersonal conflicts, depression, and substance abuse contribute to suicide in teenagers. As the second leading cause of death among teenagers, suicide leaves families and friends devastated.

ready in therapy who has characteristics consistent with the risk profile. It may involve encouraging an individual making suicidal gestures to visit a hospital emergency room or suicide prevention center or to call a suicide hot line.

If suicide potential is high, the person may be involuntarily admitted to a hospital for observation. On suicide watch, the hospital staff makes sure the potential victim does not have access to open windows, sharp objects, drugs, or other means of acting out suicidal desires. Intervention is intensive and is designed to deal with the immediate stress factors that are precipitating the suicidal behavior. Broader therapeutic issues can be addressed once suicidal tendencies have subsided.

Another important factor in suicide prevention is education. Hospital and suicide prevention center staff are trained to judge suicide risk and to immediately intervene when necessary. Education has also extended to school staff as well as to students themselves. Many schools have suicide prevention programs designed to raise awareness of teenage suicide and channel "at risk" teens into counseling.

Suicide hot lines try to help desperate people cope with their problems rather than resort to suicide as the only solution.

SUMMARY

9-1 Mood disorders, which involve disturbances in the regulation of mood, include episodes of mania, depression, or an alternation of the two. Mania is characterized by symptoms of elevated or irritable mood, and depression involves depressed mood or loss of interest in usual activities. Bipolar disorder and cyclothymia consist of periods of mania followed by periods of depression. Depressive disorders, which include major depression and dysthymia, are characterized by depression without a history of mania.

9-2 Mood disorders are caused by biological problems and/or psychosocial experiences. Biological hypotheses focus on heredity and biochemical abnormalities. Twin, family, and adoption studies show that mood disorders run in families, which suggests a hereditary basis. Biochemical studies show that regulation of amine neurotransmitters and hormones is abnormal in many depressed people. Psychological explanations for mood disorders follow traditional theoretical arguments. Psychodynamic theories view depression as the result of early childhood loss and consequent damage to the ego or self-esteem. Behavioral theories see depression as the consequence of reinforcer scarcity or the inability to secure reinforcers. Cognitive explanations focus on faulty thinking. Interpersonal and family theories claim that depression results from disturbances in interpersonal relationships and family functioning.

9-3 Biological treatments for mood disorders include antidepressant medications, lithium, and ECT. They are most often used in conjunction with psychotherapy. Drug treatments reduce symptoms in as many as 80 percent of affected patients. ECT works best in patients who do not respond to antidepressants and who are psychotic and/or suicidal. Psychotherapy works as well as drugs, and the different psychotherapies are nearly equally effective.

9-4 Suicide is a serious social problem, and suicide rates are increasing, especially in teenagers. Risk factors include age, gender, race, economic and interpersonal problems, physical illness, mental disorder, and substance abuse. Individuals who see their situation as hopeless are at greatest risk. Substance abuse, family suicide models, recent interpersonal conflict, and availability of firearms in the home are associated with elevated risk of suicide in teens. In order to prevent suicide, researchers compile risk profiles and design crisis intervention treatments.

TERMS TO REMEMBER

anger-in hypothesis (p. 231)
antidepressants (p. 236)
attributional reformulation (p. 232)
bipolar disorder (p. 226)
bipolar disorders (p. 225)
catecholamine hypothesis (p. 230)
continuity hypothesis (p. 231)
cyclothymia (p. 226)
depressive disorders (p. 226)
dexamethasone suppression test (p. 230)
dysregulation hypothesis (p. 230)
dysthymia (p. 227)
endogenous depression (p. 231)

hopelessness depression (p. 235)
interpersonal theory of depression (p. 235)
interpersonal therapy for depression (p. 239)
learned helplessness model (p. 232)
major depression (p. 227)
major depressive episode (p. 224)
manic episode (p. 222)
mood (p. 222)
mood disorders (p. 222)
negative cognitive triad (p. 232)
reactive depression (p. 231)
seasonal affective disorder (p. 225)

SUGGESTED READINGS

Beck, A. T. (1976). *Cognitive therapy and the emotional disorders.* New York: Signet.

Burns, D. D. (1980). *Feeling good: The new mood therapy.* New York: Signet.

Lewinsohn, P. M., Munoz, R. F., Youngren, M. A., & Zeiss, A. M. (1978). *Control your depression.* Englewood Cliffs, NJ: Prentice-Hall.

LEGAL AND ETHICAL ISSUES:
SUICIDE PREVENTION—A DISSENTING VIEW

Marie, age 69, was dying of incurable emphysema and inoperable lung cancer. After her doctor recommended that she be hooked up to life-sustaining equipment, Marie asked her daughter Rose what she thought. Rose said no. Although the doctor told Marie's family that he would agree to life-sustaining equipment if Marie were his own mother, the family stood firm in their decision, and Marie died the next day. After her mother's death, Rose purchased a controversial guide to suicide by Derek Humphrey, president of the Hemlock Society, called *Final Exit*. Rose stated that she did not want her children to suffer the way she had suffered or to have a doctor be in control (Ames, Wilson, Sawhill, Glick, & King, 1991).

It is generally accepted by both mental health professionals and the general public that suicide should be prevented because individuals who commit suicide are mentally ill and therefore not responsible for their actions. Since suicide is believed to be a consequence of mental illness, most psychologists and psychiatrists assume ethical and legal responsibility for preventing it.

Psychiatrist Thomas Szasz argues against suicide prevention. He views suicide as a basic human right. Preventing people from doing what they wish with their lives deprives them of their freedom and dignity, especially when there is great suffering, as with Marie and Rose. Empowering psychologists, psychiatrists, and the state with coercive prevention brings great prestige and power but does not rectify the infringement of individual civil rights.

Szasz believes that there are cases in which suicide prevention is not only recommended but legally required, such as when an individual requests help in preventing his or her suicide. He also contends that suicide should be prevented when society is infringed on. For example, society should not allow a person to jump from a roof in sight of a crowd of people or to use an illegal gun to commit suicide.

In order to protect individuals from being deprived of their free will, Szasz recommends a "psychiatric will" in which the person specifies whether suicide is permissible, and under what circumstances. He insists that mental health professionals should not assume the duty to protect people from their deadly intentions, since a determined person will probably succeed. Families might sue the professional for malpractice when the patient succeeds in committing suicide (Szasz, 1986).

Chapter TEN

Schizophrenia

OBJECTIVES

1. Identify the major symptoms of schizophrenia.
2. Distinguish among the DSM-III-R types of schizophrenia.
3. Outline the course of development of schizophrenia.
4. Discuss the significance of genetic studies of schizophrenia.
5. Describe the brain abnormalities associated with schizophrenia.
6. Explain the contributions of psychosocial factors to schizophrenia.
7. Summarize the features of an integrated theory of schizophrenia.
8. Discuss the advantages and disadvantages of drug therapy for schizophrenia.
9. Describe the role of psychotherapy, behavior therapy, and family therapy in the treatment of schizophrenia.

I n the 1950s, four genetically identical sisters in their early twenties were admitted for treatment at the National Institute of Mental Health (NIMH) in Washington, D.C. To ensure their privacy, they were called the Genains, from Greek words meaning "dreadful gene," and were given fictional first names using the initials NIMH: Nora, Iris, Myra, and Hester. Throughout childhood all four had exhibited emotional and behavioral disturbances, and on admission to NIMH, the sisters were each diagnosed as schizophrenic. During their stay they were tested and treated with state-of-the-art techniques, and after three years they were released.

In 1981, NIMH arranged for the Genain sisters to return to Washington for testing with modern technology that was unavailable during their first stay. Assessment of their behavior over the previous 25 years, as well as neuropsychological testing, brain imaging, and biochemical evaluations of these remarkable sisters, provided significant evidence for several hypotheses about schizophrenia. As we examine the nature of schizophrenia in this chapter, we will consider the relevance of the Genains to our understanding of this puzzling mental disorder (Mirsky & Quinn, 1988; Rosenthal, 1963).

10-1 ▪ SCHIZOPHRENIC DISORDERS

schizophrenia A psychotic disorder with severe symptoms affecting judgment, emotions, perception, and behavior.

psychosis A mental state of impaired reality testing.

Schizophrenia, the most severe mental disorder, is a problem that has been described through history as madness, insanity, and lunacy. Today, **schizophrenia** is considered a psychotic disorder characterized by severe symptoms in the realm of judgment, emotions, perceptions, and behavior. The schizophrenic person suffers from a **psychosis**, a mental state in which there is an extreme impairment in reality testing and sometimes the creation of a new reality. Approximately 1 percent of the U.S. population is schizophrenic. Schizophrenia is a chronic disorder, and its cost to society is enormous.

Modern schizophrenia research began in the late 1800s with psychiatrist Emil Kraepelin, who identified a psychosis that began in adolescence and progressed for many years. He labeled this disorder *dementia praecox*, meaning a premature mental deterioration.

The term *schizophrenia* was introduced in the early 1900s by the Swiss psychiatrist Eugen Bleuler, who derived the term from two Greek words meaning "split mind." The mental splitting in schizophrenia refers to a disorganization of emotions, behavior, and mental processes, not a split personality, as is commonly thought. Unlike Kraepelin, Bleuler believed that schizophrenia did not always begin early in life and lead to long-term deterioration. Bleuler distinguished four important features of schizophrenia, known as the four A's: disturbances of *affect*, or emotion; *ambivalence* in feelings and attitudes; irrational mental *associations*; and *autism*, a self-absorbed withdrawal (Cancro, 1985).

Since Kraepelin and Bleuler, many investigators have contributed to our understanding of schizophrenia. Today it is recognized as a disorder in which the symptoms may vary greatly from person to person.

Symptoms of Schizophrenia

The symptoms of schizophrenia affect all areas of mental life. Although no two schizophrenics have exactly the same symptoms, most exhibit problems in thought, perception, emotion, motivation, sense of self, and behavior.

Thought Disorders. Disturbed judgment and reasoning have long been considered core symptoms of schizophrenia. Thought disorders are divided into disorders of *form* (how the person thinks) and *content* (what the person thinks).

Several abnormalities in the form of schizophrenic thinking are called *formal thought disorder. Loose associations* are disorganized or confused ideas that, when verbalized, seem incoherent. Such verbalizations are called *word salad.* The following comments were made by a young schizophrenic woman:

> I'm going to marry Geraldo Rivera. . . . I think we're going to get married in Madison Square Garden, just like Sly Stone did. Mick Jagger wants to marry me. If I have Mick Jagger, I don't have to covet Geraldo Rivera. Mick Jagger is St. Nicholas and the Maharishi is Santa Claus. I want to form a gospel rock group called the Thorn Oil, but Geraldo wants me to be the music critic on Eyewitness News, so what can I do? (Sheehy, 1983, p. 104)

Other peculiarities in schizophrenic thought and speech are *clanging,* in which the person speaks in rhymes, and *neologisms,* which are invented words that express some idiosyncratic thought. Schizophrenic thinking often seems very irrational and defies the rules of logic, as in the statement "Jesus was a Jew; I'm a Jew; therefore, I'm Jesus" (H. E. Lehman & Cancro, 1985). Impairment of abstract thought is also common among schizophrenics. For example, when asked to explain the saying "Strike while the iron is hot," the schizophrenic may respond with a literal and concrete reply: "You have to hit something because you shouldn't need to iron so many clothes."

delusions False beliefs held despite a lack of evidence.

Delusions are disorders of thought content, defined as false beliefs that are strongly held by the person despite a lack of evidence for them (see Table 10-1). In response to their delusions, schizophrenics may engage in bizarre or even aggressive behavior. For example, John Hinckley, who attempted to assassinate President Ronald Reagan in 1981, was driven by a delusion that the actress Jodie Foster would be attracted to him if he killed the president. Although delusions can prompt violent behavior, as in the case of John Hinckley, most schizophrenics are not dangerous or violent toward others and are more likely to avoid than provoke confrontations.

John Hinckley, a young man diagnosed as schizophrenic, responded to the delusion that he could win the attentions of actress Jodie Foster by attempting to assassinate President Ronald Reagan.

TABLE 10-1   **TYPES OF DELUSIONAL BELIEFS**

- *Grandeur:* The belief that one has some magical or extraordinary abilities or characteristics. *Example: Margaret is convinced that God has appointed her to save the world from nuclear war.*
- *Identification:* The belief that one is some famous, celebrated, or powerful figure. *Example: Sidney wears a Nazi uniform and claims to be the reincarnation of Adolf Hitler.*
- *Persecution:* The belief that others want to harm, threaten, or manipulate one. *Example: George thinks that his landlord is poisoning him by putting chemicals in the water.*
- *Reference:* The belief that events in the world and others' behavior refer or relate to oneself. *Example: When a stranger on the bus laughs, Sheila is sure that she is being mocked.*
- *Sin or guilt:* The belief that one is responsible for some tragedy or misfortune that has taken place. *Example: On hearing of a train collision in another city, Marcos is tormented by a feeling that it is his fault.*
- *Thought broadcasting:* The belief that one can telepathically send thoughts into others' minds. *Example: While driving, Annie thinks she controls other drivers by transmitting mental commands to them.*
- *Thought insertion:* The belief that others are inserting thoughts into one's own mind. *Example: Lee imagines that a terrorist group is sending violent fantasies into his mind by radio signals.*

Perceptual Disturbances. Normal perceptual activity is disrupted in schizophrenia. **Hallucinations**, for example, are false perceptions that have no basis in reality. The most common hallucinations are auditory experiences, such as hearing voices, but the senses of touch, smell, and sight may be affected as well. Hallucinations can provoke extreme emotions and behavior, as reflected in the poetry of the shoemaker Joseph Kallinger, the schizophrenic who was driven to murder by *command hallucinations* from a phantom named Charlie:

hallucinations False perceptions with no basis in reality.

> (i cannot free myself from charlie)
> bodiless rider, he rides thunderbolts in Hell
> with the Devil sings doom songs
> through his mouthless face
> then comes to me with bloody instructions
> (his favorite word is kill)
> (Schreiber, 1983, pp. 380–381)

Schizophrenic perceptions are often distorted. Sights, sounds, and odors may seem peculiar or lack reality. In addition, many schizophrenics exhibit *attentional disturbances*. They have difficulty in voluntarily controlling attention, and their minds wander or go blank. They are unable to filter out distracting stimulation, and they experience sensory overload and confusion. These remarks describe sensory disruptions experienced by a young schizophrenic girl:

> I heard people talking but I did not grasp the meaning of the words. The voices were metallic, without warmth or color. From time to time a word detached itself from the rest. It repeated itself over and over in my head, absurd as though cut off by a knife. (Sechehaye, 1951, p. 7)

People with schizophrenia are often plagued by irrational delusions and hallucinations. Joseph Kallinger, flanked by police in this photo, committed murder in response to commands from a hallucinated phantom.

Emotional and Motivational Disturbances. Many schizophrenics demonstrate *flat* or *blunted affect*, a lack of normal emotional responsiveness even when warranted by circumstances. For example, when informed of his grandmother's death, one patient replied nonchalantly, "Okay, can I have some cigarettes?" At other times, schizophrenics exhibit powerful emotions, sometimes without explanation or apparent provocation. Such sudden and unpredictable changes in feelings indicate *emotional lability*. Perceptual and thought disorders sometimes provoke these emotional reactions, as described by one schizophrenic:

> Something threatening was coming up. I had the feeling I wasn't alone in the room any more. Then I heard a monotonous sound in my ears that didn't come from myself and which I couldn't explain. . . . It was like an emotion, but deeper. I had the feeling something was looking for me. (Romme & Escher, 1989, p. 211)

Attitudes of disinterest and *apathy* are also typical of most schizophrenics. For example, the disheveled appearance of the schizophrenic may reflect an indifference to dress and grooming. Such attitudes undermine the schizophrenic's attempts at productive, goal-directed behavior. As a result, they are unable to engage in ordinary activities like socializing and work.

Altered Sense of Self. Not only are sensory perceptions distorted in schizophrenia, but self-perceptions are impaired as well. *Inadequate ego boundaries*—lessening of perceived distinctions between the self, other people, and objects—are associated with the schizophrenic's altered sense of self. The result is confused identity and episodes of *depersonalization*, feelings of unreality about the self, as described by a young schizophrenic man:

> It struck me that if I stared long enough at the environment that I would blend with it and disappear just as if the place was empty and I had disappeared. It is as if you get yourself to feel you don't know who you are or where you are. (Laing, 1965, p. 110)

The Genain quadruplets, shown as babies and at age 51, were studied at the National Institute of Mental Health. They provided significant evidence of the genetic and environmental factors contributing to schizophrenia.

Behavioral Disturbances. With such severe psychological symptoms, it is not surprising that the behavior of schizophrenics is also disturbed. Social isolation and withdrawal are common in schizophrenics. To others, the behavior of a schizophrenic appears eccentric, disorganized, and purposeless. The behavioral disturbances of schizophrenics range from minimal activity or movement to bizarre, excessive, and compulsive behaviors. Alex, for example, was a schizophrenic who spent his waking hours pacing in a circle, muttering and cursing to himself, claiming he could not stop or else the planet would explode.

On their first admission to NIMH, the Genain sisters exhibited a variety of symptoms. Nora, the first to be admitted, was described as withdrawn, hallucinating, delusional, and slow of speech. Iris complained of numerous physical symptoms, insomnia, a belief that she was being watched, and auditory hallucinations. Myra was the least impaired, but she exhibited psychomotor slowness, overly dramatic behavior, anxiety, and depression. Hester had the most severe problems; she was fearful, confused, withdrawn, and hallucinating (Mirsky & Quinn, 1988).

Types of Schizophrenia

Defining the core of schizophrenia has challenged researchers and clinicians for over a century. No one symptom is found in all cases, and the variations in symptoms are countless. Today, schizophrenia is recognized as a group of several related disorders rather than a single disorder.

The DSM-III-R diagnosis of schizophrenia is made when other psychotic disorders have been ruled out and when the following symptoms have been present for at least six months:

> **A.** One of the following for at least one week:
> 1. Two of these: Delusions, prominent hallucinations, incoherence or loose associations, catatonic behavior, flat or grossly inappropriate affect.
> 2. Bizarre delusions (e.g., thought broadcasting).
> 3. Hallucinations of a voice, such as a voice keeping up a running commentary on the person's behavior or thoughts, or two or more voices conversing with each other.
>
> **B.** The person's functioning, as in work, social relations or self-care, is markedly below the level shown before the disturbance. (American Psychiatric Association, 1987)

The DSM-III-R lists the major types of schizophrenia as paranoid, catatonic, disorganized, and undifferentiated types. The first three resemble the forms of dementia praecox proposed by Kraepelin a century ago (paranoia, catatonia, and hebephrenia); the last combines features of the others.

paranoid schizophrenia
A schizophrenic type with delusions of persecution, reference, or grandeur and associated hallucinations.

Paranoid Schizophrenia. Paranoid schizophrenia is characterized by delusions of persecution, reference, or grandeur and by hallucinations associated with delusional themes. The classic paranoid schizophrenic is plagued by fears of being harmed or controlled by others. Auditory hallucinations are common, especially hearing voices that relate to the delusional thoughts and fears:

> I would go into stores, the subway, on the street, or any public place and people would be able to talk directly into my mind and hearing, insulting and saying anything they felt about me, reading my inner thoughts and saying them back at me with their criticism. (Spitzer, Skodol, Gibbon, & Williams, 1983, p. 145)

catatonic schizophrenia
Schizophrenia with severe psychomotor disturbances such as stupor, negativism, and excitement.

Catatonic Schizophrenia. The most prominent symptoms of **catatonic schizophrenia** are psychomotor disturbances, such as stupor, negativism, and excitement. The *catatonic stupor* is a state in which movement and responsiveness to the environment are greatly diminished. The person may sit or stand motionless for many hours. *Negativism* is exhibited when the person resists movement or refuses to follow instructions. A catatonic schizophrenic emerging from a stupor may exhibit dramatic excitement, characterized by emotional agitation and apparently purposeless activity.

Zack was a catatonic schizophrenic who had been hospitalized continuously for over ten years. Usually he slumped quietly in his chair, not speaking or taking note of events around him. However, every few weeks, with no outside provocation, he would hop up, strip naked, and soak his clothes in the bathroom sink. Afterward, dressed and dripping wet, he would charge around the ward shouting about the lady from the water company.

Disorganized Schizophrenia. Incoherent speech, loose associations, irrationality, and disorganized behavior characterize **disorganized schizophrenia**. The person with this disorder exhibits emotional responses that are inappropriate, unpredictable, or even grossly exaggerated. He or she may experience delusions and hallucinations, but they tend to be inconsistent and lack the distinctive theme of the paranoid type. Behavior is very eccentric or bizarre, and the individual often exhibits peculiar mannerisms and facial expressions. The following passage describes the appearance of a schizophrenic woman, given the pseudonym Sylvia Frumkin, whose story is poignantly told in the book *Is There No Place on Earth for Me?*

> She had tied another pair of blue jeans around her neck. She also wore around her neck a chain with a pop top from a soda can on it. . . . On her head was a bandanna. Knotted into the bandanna was a spoon. "The spoon looks a little stupid, but it keeps my posture good." (Sheehy, 1983, p. 104)

Undifferentiated Schizophrenia. Mixed symptoms that do not conform to the paranoid, catatonic, or disorganized types characterize **undifferentiated schizophrenia**. Many schizophrenics have symptoms that change from one type to another over time, and this pattern is also labeled undifferentiated schizophrenia.

disorganized schizophrenia
Schizophrenia with incoherent speech, loose associations, irrationality, and disorganized behavior.

undifferentiated schizophrenia
Schizophrenia with mixed symptoms that do not conform to the paranoid, catatonic, or disorganized types.

Because of their extreme fears, paranoid schizophrenics such as the man below may suspect others and accuse them of harboring ill intentions. People with catatonic schizophrenia, such as the woman at right, often remain immobilized for long periods in unusual positions.

TABLE 10-2 ▦ **TYPE I AND TYPE II SCHIZOPHRENIA**

Type I	Type II
Sudden onset	Slower onset
Normal intellect	Intellectual deterioration
No brain damage	Brain abnormality
No negative symptoms	Prominent negative symptoms
Good drug response	Poor drug response

All four Genain quadruplets were assigned the diagnosis of schizophrenic reaction, catatonic type on their initial admission to NIMH. In the years before their second stay at NIMH, Nora, Iris, and Hester were admitted several times to state mental hospitals, and at various times they were also given diagnoses of hebephrenic schizophrenia (now called disorganized schizophrenia) and chronic undifferentiated schizophrenia.

Instead of the DSM-III-R subtypes, some experts classify schizophrenia according to its domination by positive or negative symptoms. **Positive symptoms** include delusions, hallucinations, loose associations, and disorganized behavior. **Negative symptoms**, which are deficits in normal behavior, include flat affect, apathy, social withdrawal, and poor attention. *Type I* and *Type II* schizophrenia are defined by the absence and presence of negative symptoms, respectively, as well as by their courses and causes and the patient's response to treatment, as shown in Table 10-2 (Andreasen, 1985; Carpenter, Heinrichs, & Wagman, 1988; Crow, 1985).

positive symptoms
Delusions, hallucinations, loose associations, and disorganized behavior.

negative symptoms
Deficits such as flat affect, apathy, social withdrawal, and poor attention.

▦ The Course of Schizophrenia

For most of its victims, schizophrenia is a chronic disorder that begins in adolescence or young adulthood and persists for many years. The majority of schizophrenics experience more than one episode during their lifetimes. Generally, schizophrenia develops in three phases, the prodromal, active, and residual phases.

In the *prodromal phase*, the individual shows signs of deterioration marked by thinking disturbances, neglect of personal hygiene, personality and mood changes, and social withdrawal. In the *active phase*, schizophrenic symptoms are clearly present. This phase can persist indefinitely. In the *residual phase*, which resembles the prodromal phase, the schizophrenic exhibits diminished emotional expression and thinking disturbances without frank delusions or hallucinations; people with these features are diagnosed with **schizophrenia, residual type**.

When the deterioration is slow and insidious, the condition is known as **process schizophrenia**, which is associated with a history of poor adjustment and a poor prognosis. **Reactive schizophrenia** refers to a sudden onset of symptoms as a reaction to some stressful event, and is associated with relatively good adjustment history and prognosis (Herron, 1987).

What is the fate of the schizophrenic over time? In general, ten years after the first episode, approximately a quarter of schizophrenics are recovered, half

schizophrenia, residual type A diagnosis for schizophrenics in the residual phase.

process schizophrenia Schizophrenia with slow onset, poor premorbid adjustment, and poor prognosis.

reactive schizophrenia Schizophrenia with sudden onset, better premorbid adjustment, and better prognosis.

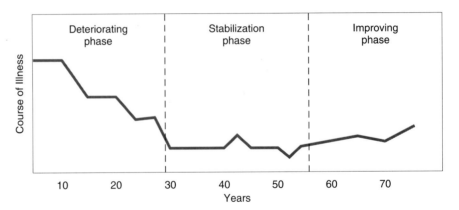

Figure 10-1 The course of chronic schizophrenia. The most severe deterioration occurs within the first five to ten years, followed by less dramatic symptoms for several years until stabilization begins. After a long period of stabilization, many schizophrenics actually show improvement later in life.

Source: From "National Institute of Mental Health Longitudinal Study of Chronic Schizophrenia: Prognosis and Predictors of Outcome" by A. Breier, J. L. Schreiber, J. Dyer, and D. Picker, 1991, *Archives of General Psychiatry, 48,* pp. 239–246.

have improved, and the rest either have died or have been hospitalized without improvement. Significant health hazards are associated with schizophrenia, including a high risk of circulatory and respiratory diseases, a high rate of alcoholism and drug abuse, and high suicide rates. Curiously, many chronic schizophrenics actually improve later in life (see Figure 10-1). However, numerous factors determine the long-term outcome for a schizophrenic individual (see Table 10-3) (Allebeck, 1989; M. Bleuler, 1978; Breier, Schrieber, Dyer, & Pickar, 1991; Caldwell & Gottesman, 1990; J. M. Goldstein, 1988; Harding, Brooks, Ashikaga, Strauss, & Breier, 1987; McGlashan, 1988; Regier et al., 1990).

TABLE 10-3   OUTCOME PREDICTORS FOR SCHIZOPHRENIA

Predictor Variables	
Good Outcome	**Poor Outcome**
Good premorbid adjustment	Poor premorbid adjustment
No family history of schizophrenia	Family history of schizophrenia
Sudden onset	Slow onset
Precipitating stress	No precipitating stress
Good response to medication	Poor response to medication
Positive symptoms	Negative symptoms
Later age of onset	Early age of onset
Female gender	Male gender

Source: Adapted from "A Selective Review of Recent North American Long-term Followup Studies of Schizophrenia" by T. H. McGlashan, 1988, *Schizophrenia Bulletin, 14,* pp. 515–542.

At NIMH in 1981, Nora and Iris were diagnosed as chronic undifferentiated schizophrenics and Myra and Hester were diagnosed with schizophrenia, residual type. Since their first NIMH stay, Nora and Iris had been admitted for psychiatric treatment six times, had tried and failed at several jobs, and had spent much of their time in group or foster care homes. Hester had the most chronic and unremitting disturbance and had been admitted for treatment on twelve occasions after her first discharge from NIMH. The healthiest of the sisters was Myra, who had had no other admissions and had married, raised two children, and worked in the intervening years (Mirsky & Quinn, 1988).

10-2 ▦ THE CAUSES OF SCHIZOPHRENIA

Given the complexity of schizophrenic disorders, it is not surprising that they have no single cause. In this section we discuss the diverse biological and psychosocial causes of schizophrenia as well as an integrated view of this disorder.

The Biological Causes of Schizophrenia

Potent hereditary and neurophysiological influences on schizophrenia have been demonstrated by studies on schizophrenics and their relatives.

Hereditary Causes. Family, twin, and adoption studies all support the idea that schizophrenia has a hereditary basis. Biological relatives of schizophrenics have an increased risk of schizophrenic disorders. The degree of genetic closeness to a schizophrenic is a strong predictor of a person's risk for schizophrenia (see Figure 10-2) (Gottesman, McGuffin, & Farmer, 1987; Karlsson, 1982; Kendler, Gruenberg, & Tsuang, 1985; Kessler, 1980). The concordance rate for schizophrenia is two to four times greater for monozygotic twins than for dizygotic twins (Gottesman et al., 1987; Kendler, 1983). Some evidence shows higher concordance among monozygotic twins with negative symptoms but not with positive symptoms, suggesting a more potent genetic basis for negative symptoms of schizophrenia (Dworkin & Lenzenweger, 1984).

Adoption studies provide the most persuasive evidence for hereditary factors in schizophrenia. The biological children of schizophrenic parents have rates of schizophrenia ten times above average, even when raised by nonschizophrenic adoptive parents (Kety, 1988). However, adoption studies do not prove that heredity is solely responsible for schizophrenia (Marcus et al., 1987). For example, researchers in Finland found that mental problems in the adoptive family raise the risk of schizophrenia in biological children of schizophrenic parents, whereas a healthy adoptive family environment reduces the risk for the child (Tienari et al., 1987).

The relatives of schizophrenics are more vulnerable to a group of **schizophrenic spectrum disorders** that include schizophrenia and *schizoaffective disorder*, a psychosis combining schizophrenic and mood disorder symptoms, as well as paranoid and schizotypal personality disorders (see Chapter 13). Some other psychotic disorders may also be part of this hereditary spectrum of disorders (see Table 10-4) (Baron et al., 1985; Coryell & Zimmerman, 1989; Kendler et al., 1986; Wender, 1977).

Research has not yet found a specific genetic mechanism for schizophrenia. The **multifactorial polygenic model** proposes that many genes contribute to

schizophrenic spectrum disorders A group of related disorders, including schizophrenia, schizoaffective disorder, and paranoid and schizotypal personality disorders.

multifactorial polygenic model The theory that many genes contribute to vulnerability to schizophrenia.

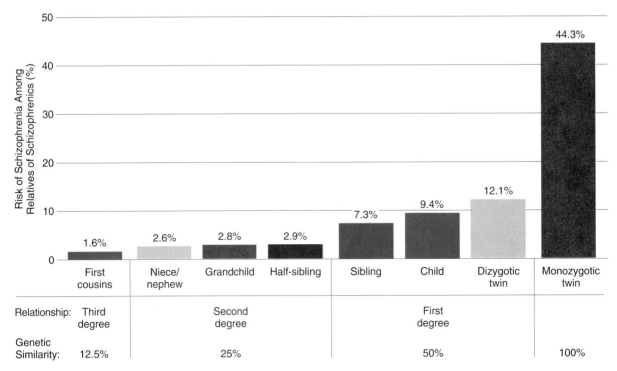

Figure 10-2 Risk of schizophrenia among relatives of schizophrenics (data from pooled European family and twin studies, 1920–1978).

Source: Adapted from "Clinical Genetics as Clues to the 'Real' Genetics of Schizophrenia (A Decade of Modest Gains While Playing for Time)" by I. I. Gottesman, P. McGuffin, and A. E. Farmer, 1987, *Schizophrenia Bulletin, 13*, pp. 23–47.

schizophrenia, so vulnerability depends on the number of those genes a person carries (Faraone & Tsuang, 1985). In fact, there may be several different genetic predispositions for schizophrenia (Garver, Reich, Isenberg, & Cloninger, 1989). The hunt for the "*schizogenes*" seeks hereditary biological markers, such as eye

TABLE 10.4 MAJOR PSYCHOTIC DISORDERS

Disorder	Features
Brief reactive psychosis	Stress-related schizophrenic symptoms lasting less than a month
Schizophreniform disorder	Schizophrenic symptoms lasting one to six months
Schizoaffective disorder	Combined schizophrenic and mood disorder symptoms
Delusional (paranoid) disorder	Delusional beliefs in the absence of other perceptual or thought disorders

CLOSE-UP
High-Risk Children

Children of schizophrenic parents have a very high risk of schizophrenia. A child with one schizophrenic parent has a 10 percent risk of developing the disorder, and a child with two schizophrenic parents has a 35 percent risk. Studies of high-risk children can provide valuable insights into both the hereditary and developmental factors acting to produce schizophrenia.

One objective of these high-risk studies is to identify early characteristics that predict the development of schizophrenia. Pinpointing reliable predictors may simplify the evaluation of a child's need for interventions that might prevent schizophrenia from occurring. Many developmental characteristics have been identified in high-risk children at different ages:

- *Infancy:* Low birth weight, abnormal sensory and motor activity, and short attention span
- *Early childhood:* Poor coordination, cognitive impairment, abnormal emotions, withdrawal, and passivity
- *Middle childhood:* Neurological, perceptual, and attentional deficits; poor emotion control; and poor interpersonal relations

- *Adolescence:* Neurological and intellectual impairment, poor emotion control, poor social behavior, and school maladjustment

Even though they are significantly more likely to develop schizophrenia than others, the majority of high-risk children do not actually become schizophrenic. One potential benefit of high-risk studies is that they may inform us about aspects of the child's personality, environment, and biological status that diminish the risk of schizophrenia.

Researchers have identified a few important *protective factors,* including the mental health of the caretaking parent, higher socioeconomic status, parents' emotional support for the child, and the overall quality of stimulation provided for the child. Awareness of these protective factors will not by itself prevent schizophrenia, but it can be a basis for preventive measures that may reduce some children's risk for this serious disorder (Asarnow, 1988; Fish, 1987; Sameroff, Seifer, Zax, & Barocas, 1987).

---

movement irregularities, brain activity, and blood factors, that accompany schizophrenia and may reveal the locations of critical genes (Crowe et al., 1991; Erlenmeyer-Kimling, 1987; Kennedy et al., 1988; McGue & Gottesman, 1989; Sherrington et al., 1988).

Mr. Genain appears to have been the source of his daughters' presumed genetic predispositions to schizophrenia. His behavior indicated paranoid thinking and severe emotional disturbances. He was erratic, suspicious, domineering, and prone to excessive drinking. His mother had once been hospitalized for a "nervous breakdown," and other relatives on his side of the family also showed signs of psychological problems.

Neurophysiological Causes. Schizophrenia has been associated with abnormalities in several brain neurotransmitter systems. However, abnormalities

dopamine hypothesis of schizophrenia A view that the biochemical cause of schizophrenia is an abnormality in the brain's dopamine neurotransmitter system.

in the dopamine neurotransmitter system have received the most attention. The **dopamine hypothesis of schizophrenia** initially stated that too much dopamine was present in the schizophrenic's brain, but later research showed that idea to be too simplistic (Snyder, 1976). The sensitivity and density of dopamine receptors in some brain regions were found to be more important than the amount of dopamine. Recent studies point to deficient release and breakdown of dopamine as well as high receptor sensitivity in the schizophrenic's brain (Heritch, 1990; Weinberger, 1987; Wong et al., 1986). One new theory argues that schizophrenia is due to dopamine overactivity in the pathways linking the midbrain to the limbic system and underactivity in the pathways linking the midbrain and cortex (Weinberger, 1987).

The dopamine hypothesis does not completely explain schizophrenia, since research also implicates other neurotransmitters, including serotonin and norepinephrine. Moreover, dopamine abnormalities are not present in all schizophrenics but are especially common in those with positive symptoms. The diversity of types and symptoms in schizophrenia is more consistent with the idea that several neurotransmitter systems may be involved (Davis, Kahn, Grant, & Davidson, 1991).

Modern advances in brain research, using imaging techniques like CT and PET scans (see Chapter 4), have provided dramatic evidence that there are differences between normal and schizophrenic brains (see Figure 10-3). Abnormalities in several major brain structures have been found, strongly suggesting that schizophrenia is a brain disease (Andreasen, 1988). These brain abnormalities may be due to genetic influences, prenatal factors disrupting brain development, viral infections, or some combination of events (Barr, Mednick, & Munk-Jorgensen, 1990; T. D. Cannon, Mednick, & Parnas, 1989; Torrey, 1988).

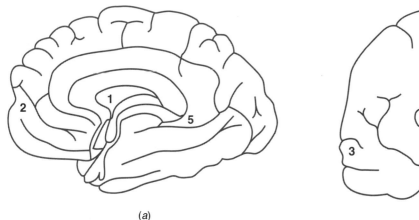

(a)

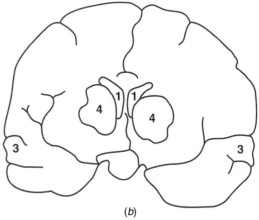

(b)

Figure 10-3 Brain abnormalities in schizophrenia. (*a*) A cross section produced by cutting the brain lengthwise along a midline (left–right) axis; (*b*) a cross section produced by cutting the brain along a plane parallel to the facial plane. Locations of brain abnormalities are numbered: (1) enlarged cerebral ventricles; (2) atrophy and low metabolic rate in frontal lobes; (3) asymmetry and low metabolic rate in temporal lobes; (4) high-density dopamine receptors in basal ganglia; (5) atrophy and neural disorganization in limbic system.

Ventricular enlargement, excess size of the fluid-filled chambers (ventricles) in the brain, is present in 25 to 50 percent of schizophrenics (see Figure 10-4) (Kleinman, Casanova, & Jaskiw, 1988; McCarley et al., 1989; Pearlson et al., 1989; S. Raz & N. Raz, 1990). Research suggests that ventricular enlargement and the corresponding brain damage may result from both genetic and environmental factors (DeLisi et al., 1986; Suddath, Christinson, Torrey, Casanova, & Weinberger, 1990). Many schizophrenics also exhibit defects in the frontal and temporal lobes of the cortex, including brain atrophy (degeneration) and low metabolic activity (Andreasen et al., 1990; Buchsbaum, 1990; Shelton et al., 1988; Suddath et al., 1990). In addition, there are structural differences called *asymmetries* in the left and right temporal lobes (Buchanan, Kirkpatrick, Heinrichs, & Carpenter, 1990; Crow, 1990; Crow et al., 1989).

Subcortical damage is also sometimes present in the limbic system, a structure involved in memory, arousal, and emotion. Tissue atrophy, abnormal neural growths, and cellular disorganization have all been noted (Conrad, Abebe, Austin, Forsythe, & Scheibel, 1991). The basal ganglia, a subcortical area that influences movement, sensation, and attention, may also be damaged (Buchs-

Figure 10-4 Genain PET scans. Figures (*a*) to (*d*) are PET (positron emission tomography) images of the brains of the Genain quadruplets showing various degrees of abnormal frontal lobe activity as compared with the image of a normal control subject (*e*). Blue and green areas represent regions of lower metabolic activity, while yellow, orange, and red areas indicate greater activity.

Source: M. S. Buchsbaum.

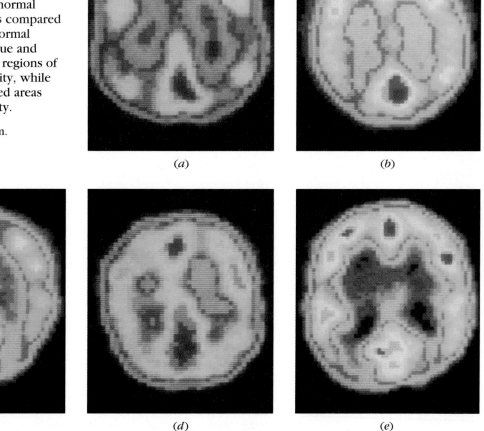

(*a*) (*b*)

(*c*) (*d*) (*e*)

PROFILE
E. Fuller Torrey
(b. 1937)

Psychiatrist E. Fuller Torrey, has conducted important research on the biology of schizophrenia and has long been an outspoken advocate for schizophrenics and their families.

Torrey was born in Utica, New York. He decided as a child to become a doctor, and his interest in psychiatry was stimulated when one of his sisters developed schizophrenia at age 17. Torrey graduated from Princeton University and earned his medical degree at McGill University in 1963. He also received a master's degree in anthropology from Stanford University. He served as a Peace Corps physician for two years in Ethiopia and as a medical officer in the Indian Health Service in Alaska. From 1977 to 1985 Dr. Torrey worked as a psychiatrist at St. Elizabeth's Hospital in Washington, D.C., and at present he is with the Twin Study Unit of NIMH.

Dr. Torrey's work on schizophrenia has covered a wide spectrum of activities, including clinical psychiatry, neurological and genetics research, and field studies in Ireland and New Guinea. He believes that schizophrenia is due to brain impairment caused by hereditary, neurodevelopmental, and viral influences. Currently, Dr. Torrey is conducting research on identical twins with schizophrenia or bipolar disorder and on possible viral causes of schizophrenia.

On many occasions Dr. Torrey has been harshly critical of psychological theories and treatments for schizophrenia, and he has also criticized psychiatry's medical model, which he has likened to a platypus, a dead-end in evolution. He has recommended that psychiatry be allowed to die out so that its functions can be redistributed between neurology and the behavioral sciences.

In addition to other professional activities, Dr. Torrey has been a strong supporter of rights for the mentally ill and their families, and in 1984 he received the Special Friends Award from the National Alliance for the Mentally Ill. His views on mental illness reflect a unique combination of expert knowledge and compassion.

Dr. Torrey is the author of 11 books and over 100 professional publications. He also wrote a book about the poet Ezra Pound, which was nominated by the National Book Critics Circle as one of the five best biographies of 1983. His major works include *Surviving Schizophrenia: A Family Manual* (1988), *The Death of Psychiatry* (1974); and *Schizophrenia and Civilization* (1980).

baum, 1990). In general, signs of brain damage in the cortex and subcortical regions are more common in schizophrenics with the negative symptom/Type II pattern.

Schizophrenics often show neurological "*soft signs*" that suggest disruptions of brain activity. These soft signs include slow electrical activity of the frontal lobes, impaired stimulus processing, and irregular eye movements while tracking a moving stimulus. Further disturbances are also indicated by problems in coordination, sensory integration, attention, and memory. Although no single pattern is invariably present, the evidence points to multiple neurophysiological dysfunctions in the schizophrenic brain (Clementz & Sweeney, 1990; Holzman, 1987; Levin, Yurgelun-Todd, & Craft, 1989).

None of the Genain sisters had clear structural abnormalities, such as enlarged ventricles, but all four had some deficits in frontal lobe electrical and chemical activity. In addition, the visual regions of their brains showed some unusual activity that might have indicated perceptual disturbances or hallucinations. Overall, Nora and Hester had more signs of brain dysfunction than did Myra and Iris (Buchsbaum et al., 1984; Mirsky & Quinn, 1988).

The Psychosocial Causes of Schizophrenia

For the past century, psychiatrists and psychologists have debated the influence of psychosocial factors on schizophrenia. In this section we examine what is known about the contributions of personality, family, stress, and sociocultural variables.

Personality. Freud set a precedent for later psychodynamic views of schizophrenia by interpreting paranoia as a defensive projection of homosexual impulses. In his famous analysis of the psychotic Dr. Schreber, Freud stated,

> We should be inclined to say that what was characteristically paranoic about the illness was the fact that the patient, as a means of warding off a homosexual wish-phantasy, reacted precisely with delusions of persecution of this kind. (1963, p. 161)

Post-Freudians stress that a failure in ego defenses is largely responsible for schizophrenic symptoms. Hallucinations and delusions are thought to be expressions of irrational unconscious activity overwhelming weak ego defenses (Bellack, Hurvich, & Gediman, 1973; Federn, 1952). For example, one patient hallucinated a terrible odor from his body as an unconscious expression of self-hatred, symbolizing the attitude ''I'm rotten'' (Arieti, 1974).

Family Factors. Psychoanalytic theory was the initial impetus for family studies of schizophrenia. The **schizophrenogenic mother hypothesis** was an early view that blamed schizophrenia on the harmful influence of a cold and domineering mother. Although some case reports support this hypothesis, it is not considered a valid explanation for most cases of schizophrenia (Fromm-Reichmann, 1948; Sullivan, 1952).

The **double-bind hypothesis** (mentioned in Chapter 3) claims that schizophrenics are victims of inconsistent or contradictory messages from family members (Bateson, Jackson, Haley, & Weakland, 1956). Such double-bind messages cannot be refuted and leave the person in a ''damned if you do, damned if you don't'' situation:

> A young schizophrenic man impulsively put his arm around his mother during her visit and she stiffened up, causing him to withdraw his arm. His

schizophrenogenic mother hypothesis
The view that a cold, domineering mother causes schizophrenia.

double-bind hypothesis
The view that schizophrenics are victims of inconsistent and contradictory messages from family members.

mother then asked, "Don't you love me anymore?" and when he blushed, she said, "Dear, you must not be so easily embarrassed and afraid of your feelings." (Bateson et al., 1956)

Research concludes that double-bind communications have little causal effect on schizophrenia, and when they exist, they are most likely the result of mental disorders among family members (Helmersen, 1983).

Some studies show that communication problems in families are associated with schizophrenia. Two areas of family interaction in particular are relevant:

• *Communication deviance:* Deficits in the clarity and accuracy of communications by family members (Doane, 1978; Wynne, Singer, Bartko, & Toohey, 1977)
• *Expressed emotion:* The level of hostility, criticism, and emotional involvement among family members (Koenigsberg & Handley, 1986; Leff & Vaughn, 1985)

Communication deviance is related to an increased risk for episodes of schizophrenia in high-risk adolescents (Goldstein & Strachan, 1987), and high expressed emotion in families increases the likelihood of relapse for schizophrenics (Vaughn, Snyder, Jones, Freeman, & Falloon, 1984). These family factors alone do not necessarily cause schizophrenia. Keep in mind that the deviant behaviors of a schizophrenic's relatives may reflect a family-based genetic disturbance, and the stress of living with a schizophrenic can promote abnormal interactions among family members. Further research is needed to determine whether these family factors are causes, correlates, or consequences of schizophrenia (McFarlane & Beels, 1983).

During their childhood the Genain sisters were exposed to many damaging family influences. Their father was very suspicious and intrusive, and he often exhibited frenzied rages in the presence of the girls. In addition, Mr. Genain was emotionally and perhaps even sexually abusive toward them. Mrs. Genain was an overprotec-

Expressed emotion in families has been associated with schizophrenia. The family in this photo manifests the negative affect and angry confrontations that typify high expressed emotion.

tive and restrictive mother. The girls were not allowed to play with other children, and later they were prevented from dating. Both parents actively promoted jealousy and competition among the girls and even assigned them ranks in the family, playing them off against one another. (Mirsky & Quinn, 1988)

Stressful Events. Questions about the role of stressful events in schizophrenia have puzzled theorists and researchers for many years. Studies indicate three types of relationship between schizophrenia and stressful life events.

First, stressful events, especially extreme or catastrophic ones, can precipitate episodes of schizophrenia. For example, the victim of a brutal assault may be so overwhelmed by the experience that he or she begins to exhibit psychotic symptoms, such as paranoid delusions. Second, stressful life events often arise as a result of the schizophrenic's severe psychological disturbances. For example, a schizophrenic who is agitated by hallucinated voices may harass people on the street and be arrested. Third, stressful life events may contribute in a general way to the risk for numerous mental disorders, including schizophrenia.

To what extent stressful life events are responsible for schizophrenia is unknown. It is unlikely that stressful events alone account for many instances of schizophrenia. However, for the schizophrenic person, the experience of stressful events often accompanies other contributing factors, such as family problems and socioeconomic distress (Dohrenwend & Egri, 1981; Gruen & Biron, 1984; Lukoff, Snyder, Ventura, & Neuchterlein, 1984; Rabkin, 1980; Tennant, 1985).

Sociocultural Causes. The prevalence rates of schizophrenia are generally highest among the poorest segments of society, especially in densely populated urban centers. Among schizophrenics, low socioeconomic status (SES) corresponds to a more severe disorder, as measured by the number of hospitalizations, relapse rates, and the duration of the disorder (Torrey & Bowler, 1990).

downward social drift hypothesis The view that poverty is a consequence of disabilities caused by schizophrenia.

The *social stress hypothesis* (see Chapter 3) suggests that stressful conditions of poverty, such as alienation, unemployment, poor housing, and unsafe neighborhoods, promote the development of schizophrenia. In contrast, the **downward social drift hypothesis** proposes that low SES is a consequence of the schizophrenic's mental disabilities, which prevent effective social and occupational functioning (Eaton, 1980). In support of this idea, investigators found that most schizophrenic men have lower levels of occupational achievement than their nonschizophrenic fathers, indicating a downward socioeconomic drift from the previous generation (Silverton & Mednick, 1984).

No simple causal relationship between SES and schizophrenia exists. Rather, there seems to be a reciprocal give-and-take between mental disabilities and social distress that culminates in the disadvantaged positions of most schizophrenics.

An Integrated View of Schizophrenia

Numerous biological and psychosocial influences all contribute pieces to the puzzle of schizophrenia, but the way the pieces fit together is not well understood. Two related views that seek to integrate our understanding of the causes of schizophrenia are the diathesis-stress and vulnerability models.

diatesis-stress model of schizophrenia The theory that schizophrenia is due to interactions of genetic factors and environmental stress.

The Diatesis-Stress Model. In the **diatesis-stress model of schizophrenia**, the disorder is thought to result from a combination of genetic factors and environmental stress. *Diatesis* refers to the hereditary predisposition that is assumed to be a necessary condition for schizophrenia. However, the diatesis alone is not sufficient; it must interact with environmental stress in order for the disorder to develop. The meaning of *stress* in this model is open-ended; it may include sociocultural conditions, family processes, and other life events (Rosenthal, 1970).

vulnerability model The theory that genetic, physiological, brain, and developmental abnormalities establish vulnerability to schizophrenia.

The Vulnerability Model. According to the **vulnerability model**, genetic factors, physiological dysfunctions, brain abnormalities, and developmental problems all contribute to the risk of schizophrenia. The vulnerability model, which is similar to the diatesis-stress model, attributes schizophrenia to an interaction between individual characteristics and environmental stress (Mirsky & Duncan, 1986; Zubin & Spring, 1977). This interaction is depicted graphically in Figure 10-5 in the case of the Genain quadruplets.

The high level of social stress associated with poverty creates an increased risk for many mental health problems, including schizophrenia.

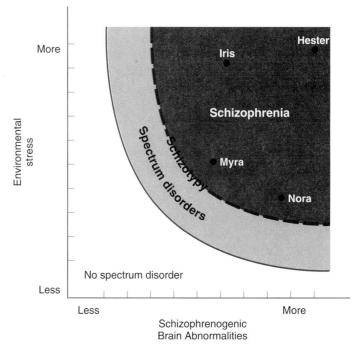

Figure 10-5 A vulnerability model of schizophrenia. The positions of the Genain sisters are based on evidence from neurological tests and family history. Hester and Nora had high levels of neurological impairment, but greater life stress (e.g., more difficult birth) resulted in Hester's more severe illness. Roughly equal in brain disturbances, Iris and Myra had many symptomatic differences, with Iris the more severely impaired.

Source: "The Genain Quadruplets" by A. F. Mirsky and O. W. Quinn, 1988, *Schizophrenia Bulletin, 14*, pp. 595–612.

10-3 ▨ THE TREATMENT OF SCHIZOPHRENIA

The complex symptoms of schizophrenia require a multifaceted treatment. To this end, several strategies have been used with varying degrees of success, including drug therapy, psychotherapy, behavior therapy, family therapy, and group and milieu therapies. Rehabilitation methods such as these address the many disabilities linked with schizophrenia.

▨ Drug Therapy

antipsychotic drugs
Drugs that control the symptoms of schizophrenia by reducing dopamine activity.

The modern era of drug therapy for schizophrenia began in the 1950s with the introduction of chlorpromazine (Thorazine) and other antipsychotic medications called phenothiazines. These **antipsychotic drugs** control the symptoms of schizophrenia by reducing the brain's dopamine activity. They are more effective against positive symptoms than negative symptoms. However, about 10 percent of schizophrenics derive little or no benefit from antipsychotic medications. Aside from their direct impact on schizophrenic symptoms, these drugs sometimes improve attention, abstract thinking, and information-processing abilities (Cassens, Inglis, Appelbaum, & Gutheil, 1990; Silverman et al., 1987; G. M. Simpson & P. R. A. May, 1985; Spohn & Strauss, 1989).

Clozapine (Clozaril), which was recently introduced for use in the United States, has been successful in patients who do not respond well to other antipsychotic drugs. Unlike other antipsychotic drugs, clozapine blocks the action of serotonin and norepinephrine rather than dopamine. Despite some questions about its high cost and its side effects, clozapine is a promising medication for many treatment-resistant schizophrenics (Kane, Honigfeld, Singer, Meltzer, & the Clozaril Collaborative Study Group, 1988).

tardive dyskinesia
Involuntary movement disorder as a side effect of antipsychotic drugs.

Antipsychotic drugs almost always produce some side effects, depending on dosage, potency, and duration of use. Ironically, the dopamine-blocking ability of these medications is responsible for both their therapeutic results and many of their side effects. Common movement side effects resemble the symptoms of Parkinson's disease and include muscle tremors, spasms, and an inability to sit or stand still. **Tardive dyskinesia** is an antipsychotic drug–induced movement disorder characterized by involuntary facial movements, like grimacing and chewing, as well as disruptions in breathing, affecting 10 to 20 percent of medicated patients (American Psychiatric Association Task Force on the Late Neurological Effects of Antipsychotic Drugs, 1980; Yassa, Nair, Iskander, & Schwartz, 1990). A rare but potentially fatal side effect of unknown origin is *neuroleptic malignant syndrome*. Its symptoms include muscle rigidity, fever, cardiovascular distress, and changes in consciousness (Levenson, 1985).

Table 10-5 lists the major antipsychotic drugs and their relative potencies.

At various times since the mid-1950s, all of the Genain sisters received antipsychotic medications. The drugs dramatically reduced the severity of symptoms for Nora and Hester, but they were much less effective for Iris. Myra enjoyed more periods without medication than her sisters, and when she stopped taking her drugs for the follow-up testing in 1981 she showed the least mental deterioration (Mirsky & Quinn, 1988).

TABLE 10-5   ANTIPSYCHOTIC DRUGS FOR SCHIZOPHRENIA

Generic Drug	Trade Name	Potency[a]
Chlorpromazine	Thorazine	1.0
Thioridazine	Mellaril	1.0
Loxapine	Loxitane	7.5
Molindone	Moban	10.0
Perphenazine	Trilafon	12.5
Trifluoperazine	Stelazine	25.0
Thiothixene	Navane	25.0
Fluphenazine	Prolixin	50.0
Haloperidol	Haldol	50.0

[a]Based on equivalent dosage of chlorpromazine; for example, haloperidol (Haldol) is 50 times more potent than chlorpromazine (Thorazine).

Source: Adapted from "Schizophrenia: Somatic Treatment" by G. M. Simpson and P. R. A. May, 1985, in H. I. Kaplan & B. J. Sadock (Eds.), *Comprehensive Textbook of Psychiatry* (vol. 1, 4th ed.), Baltimore: Williams & Wilkins.

Psychotherapy

Psychodynamic therapy has been the main psychological treatment for schizophrenics, but in recent years *supportive psychotherapy* has also been employed.

Psychodynamic Therapy. Psychodynamic therapy seeks to bolster ego functioning by supporting the schizophrenic's reality testing, impulse control, and sense of identity. Therapists take a more involved and active stance with schizophrenic patients than with nonpsychotic patients and usually deemphasize interpretation in favor of empathic support (Arieti, 1974; Schulz, 1985).

Even Freud doubted that psychoanalysis was appropriate for psychotic patients, and researchers tend to confirm his doubts. Insight-oriented psychotherapy alone has had little value in treating schizophrenia and may sometimes be harmful, because probing interpretations may overstimulate and distress the patient (Drake & Sederer, 1986; Keith & Matthews, 1984; P. R. A. May, Tuma, Dixon, 1984; M. H. Stone, 1986). As stated by E. Fuller Torrey, insight therapy with schizophrenics is "analogous to directing a flood into a town already ravaged by a tornado" (Torrey, 1988a, p. 222).

Supportive Psychotherapy. Supportive psychotherapy for schizophrenics involves empathic understanding, practical advice, and concrete problem solving. A recent study comparing insight-oriented therapy and reality-oriented supportive psychotherapy found modest benefits from both, though supportive therapy was more effective at preventing relapse. Psychotherapy helps schizophrenic patients best in conjunction with antipsychotic drugs and when treatment addresses the patient's social withdrawal, maladaptive behav-

supportive psychotherapy Therapy using empathy, practical advice, and problem solving.

iors, and practical, everyday problems in living (Coursey, 1989; Glass et al., 1989; J. G. Gunderson et al., 1984).

Behavior Therapy

token economy A structured contigency management program in an inpatient setting.

Despite the lack of a compelling behavioral explanation for schizophrenia, behavior therapy has been successfully adapted for its treatment. One of the first behavioral strategies for schizophrenics was the **token economy**, a structured contingency management program employed in inpatient settings such as mental hospitals. In token economies, patients earn rewards for exhibiting desirable behaviors, such as good personal hygiene, and punishment for unacceptable behaviors, such as refusing medication. Token programs have little direct influence on the primary symptoms of schizophrenia, but they can encourage improvements in the patient's interpersonal behavior and self-help skills (Ayllon & Azrin, 1968; G. L. Paul & Lentz, 1977).

Comprehensive behavior change programs that emphasize the development of specific skills hold promise for the rehabilitation of schizophrenic patients. The Social and Independent Living Skills (SILS) program at the Veterans Administration hospital in Brentwood, California, illustrates this approach. The SILS program applies behavior therapy techniques in ten skill areas relevant to community living, relapse prevention, and problem solving. For example, a conversation skills module teaches patients the following behaviors: verbal and nonverbal active listening, self-disclosure, identification of emotions, open- and closed-ended questions, and topic identification (Wallace et al., 1980; Wallace, Boone, Donahue, & Foy, 1985).

The Social and Independent Living Skills (SILS) program in Brentwood, California, uses social skills training to help schizophrenics cope with the problems of everyday living.

Family Therapy

The impetus for family therapy with schizophrenics was initially the double-bind hypothesis, whose authors promoted treatment not just for the patient but also the patient's family. Soon many others were exploring the use of family therapy to correct problems in the relationships and communications among relatives of schizophrenics.

According to psychiatrist Theodore Lidz, two types of families give rise to schizophrenia. In the *skewed family* there is an extreme power imbalance, with one dominant and one passive parent, and in the *schismatic family* the parents actively compete for power or control over the children. Lidz's family therapy sought to reduce the destructive emotional bondage of the schizophrenic to other family members, especially the parents (1973). Like Lidz, psychiatrist Murray Bowen used family therapy to lessen emotional overinvolvements and foster differentiation among members of the schizophrenic's family (1985).

Although controlled studies on family therapy with schizophrenics are lacking, some research shows promising results. For example, family therapy that reduces the level of expressed emotion among family members lessens the risk of relapse for schizophrenics (Leff & Vaughn, 1985). Programs that combine family therapy, social skills training, and educational workshops for family members successfully reduce relapse rates (Falloon & Liberman, 1983; Hogarty et al., 1986; Hogarty et al., 1991; Strachan, 1986). A two-year follow-up study showed that relapse rates were over twice as high when patients received only antipsychotic drugs instead of receiving drugs and integrated psychoeducational and family treatment (Leff, Kuipers, Berkowitz, & Sturgeon, 1985).

Group and Milieu Therapies

Although group therapy has often been used with schizophrenics, studies indicate that it adds very little to drug treatment and by itself may even be damaging. Some evidence suggests that schizophrenic patients in group therapy had even poorer outcomes than comparable patients who were untreated (Kanas, 1986; Keith & Matthews, 1984; P. R. A. May et al., 1984; Mosher & Keith, 1980).

milieu therapy A residential treatment program for schizophrenics, stressing group involvement, patient responsibility, and social interaction.

Residential treatment programs that emphasize group involvement, patient responsibility, and social interactions are called **milieu therapy**. Milieu therapy typically focuses on helping schizophrenics acquire practical, everyday problem-solving skills, and it can be beneficial in their aftercare or posthospital treatment (Liberman, 1985; Mosher & Menn, 1978).

Rehabilitation

The rehabilitation of the schizophrenic patient is a difficult task that must address three related goals. First, the primary symptoms or impairments of the patient must be addressed with antipsychotic drug therapy. Second, schizophrenics need help with the secondary disabilities due to their disorder, including deficits in social skills and problem-solving abilities. Third, patients need concrete assistance with the persistent social handicaps that are typically linked with schizophrenia, such as unemployment and poverty. Comprehensive rehabilitation for the victims of schizophrenia requires integration of biological, family, and individual therapies, as well as vocational and environmental interventions (Anthony & Liberman, 1986).

Homeless people, like the man in this photo, have extremely high rates of severe mental illness that often goes unnoticed and untreated.

The drug therapy revolution improved the lives of millions of schizophrenics, enabling them to leave mental institutions and return to their communities. In part because of the success of antipsychotic drugs, the number of chronically hospitalized schizophrenics in the United States dropped from 550,000 to about 110,000 between 1955 and 1985. Deinstitutionalization of the mentally ill has further reduced the inpatient population, and most of the 1 million–plus schizophrenics in the United States today are treated mainly as outpatients (Rosenstein, Milazzo-Sayre, & Manderscheid, 1989). The need for quality aftercare and rehabilitation among schizophrenics is great, but often unmet. Ultimately, successful rehabilitation for schizophrenics will require the integration of both scientific therapies and sound social policy.

SUMMARY

10-1 The schizophrenic disorders are psychotic conditions in which reality contact is severely impaired. Symptoms arise in the form and content of thought, perception and attention, emotional responses, motivation, the sense of self, and behavior. There are four main types of schizophrenia: paranoid, catatonic, disorganized, and undifferentiated. Alternative classifications emphasize positive or negative symptom patterns and the reactive or process type of premorbid adjustment. Schizophrenia has three phases—*prodromal*, *active*, and *residual*—and it usually persists for many years. The outcome of schizophrenia is variable and is determined by both individual and environmental factors.

10-2 Some people have a hereditary predisposition toward schizophrenia and schizophrenic spectrum disorders, but no genetic mechanism has been isolated. Schizophrenics exhibit abnormalities in the brain's dopamine system, the brain's electrical activity; and brain structures, including the frontal and temporal lobes, the limbic system, the basal ganglia, and the cerebral ventricles. Psychosocial factors involved in schizophrenia include inadequate ego defenses, disturbed family relationships and communication, stressful life events, and low SES. Diathesis-stress and vulnerability models consider the interactions of individual predispositions and stress to be the cause of schizophrenia.

10-3 Antipsychotic drug therapy reduces brain dopamine activity, controls positive symptoms, and may cause some serious side effects. Psychotherapy alone has little value in treating schizophrenia, but it can be of benefit in conjunction with drug therapy. Behavioral approaches such as token economies and skills training programs teach adaptive coping behaviors to schizophrenics. Family therapy corrects damaging relationships among members of the schizophrenic's family. Group therapies have been largely ineffective for schizophrenics. Milieu therapy emphasizes practical problem solving and social interactions in aftercare for schizophrenics. Rehabilitation for schizophrenics addresses the symptoms as well as associated psychological disabilities and social handicaps of the patient.

TERMS TO REMEMBER

antipsychotic drugs (p. 269)
catatonic schizophrenia (p. 255)
delusions (p. 251)
diathesis-stress model of
    schizophrenia (p. 268)
disorganized schizophrenia (p. 256)
dopamine hypothesis of
    schizophrenia (p. 262)
double-bind hypothesis (p. 265)
downward social drift hypothesis
    (p. 267)
hallucination (p. 252)
milieu therapy (p. 272)
multifactorial polygenic model
    (p. 259)
negative symptoms (p. 257)
paranoid schizophrenia (p. 255)

positive symptoms (p. 257)
process schizophrenia (p. 257)
psychosis (p. 250)
reactive schizophrenia (p. 257)
schizophrenia (p. 250)
schizophrenia, residual type
    (p. 257)
schizophrenic spectrum disorders
    (p. 259)
schizophrenogenic mother
    hypothesis (p. 265)
supportive psychotherapy (p. 270)
tardive dyskinesia (p. 269)
token economy (p. 271)
undifferentiated schizophrenia
    (p. 256)
vulnerability model (p. 268)

SUGGESTED READINGS

Andreasen, N. (1984). *The broken brain.* New York: Harper & Row.
Sheehan, S. (1983). *Is there no place on earth for me?* New York: Vintage Books.
Torrey, E. F. (1988). *Surviving schizophrenia: A family manual.* New York: Harper & Row.

LEGAL AND ETHICAL ISSUES: THE HOMELESS MENTALLY ILL

Psychological problems are especially prevalent among the three-quarters of a million homeless people in the United States today. Approximately half of the homeless population exhibits either alcoholism (30 to 40 percent) or drug abuse (10 to 20 percent), and one-third suffers from severe mental illness, particularly mood disorders (21 to 29 percent) and schizophrenia (10 to 13 percent) (Fischer & Breakey, 1991; P. H. Rossi, 1990). In fact, the United States has more homeless than hospitalized schizophrenics (Torrey, 1988b). A survey in New York City found that 80 percent of homeless mentally ill adults are schizophrenic (Susser, Struening, & Conover, 1989).

Many blame the problem on the deinstitutionalization of hundreds of thousands of patients from mental hospitals since the 1960s. This practice, although well-intentioned, was not supported by adequate aftercare, housing, or monitoring for those released, and consequently many fell through the cracks in the mental health system and landed on the streets. However, deinstitutionalization alone is not to blame, since broader social, political, and economic forces have also played a role (Shadish, Lurigio, & D. A. Lewis, 1989; Torrey, 1988b).

Complex ethical and legal questions arise in regard to the homeless mentally ill. Joyce Brown, a homeless New York City woman with paranoid schizophrenia, became a celebrity in 1987 because of her legal fight against involuntary commitment to a mental hospital. A judge ruled in her favor and she was released to return to life on the streets. Joyce Brown's case raises important questions. Do mentally ill people have the right to refuse treatment? Should society force homeless people into treatment? In most states, mentally ill people can refuse treatment, but this is a limited right that a court can revoke (Appelbaum, 1988).

For the homeless mentally ill who need and want treatment, few mental health services exist. However, changes are under way as a result of the Stewart B. McKinney Homeless Assistance Act of 1987, which authorized federal funds for mental health services for the homeless (Levine & Rog, 1990). At the local level, many communities are starting special programs, such as Project HELP in New York City, which offers evaluation and, if necessary, hospitalization for the homeless mentally ill (Marcos, Cohen, Nardacci, & Brittain, 1990).

No simple solution for the problem of the homeless mentally ill has been offered. Some advocate a return to the old system of involuntary institutionalization while others favor letting the mentally ill choose for themselves, even if they choose the streets. Ultimately, the solution will be determined by political and legal changes as society struggles to come to terms with the moral and economic dimensions of homelessness (Lamb, 1990).

Chapter ELEVEN

*D*isorders of Childhood

OBJECTIVES

1. Describe the four anxiety disorders of childhood.
2. Outline the causes of childhood anxiety disorders.
3. Identify the symptoms of attention deficit hyperactivity disorder.
4. Discuss the causes of and treatments for attention deficit hyperactivity disorder.
5. Discuss the major types of conduct disorder and juvenile delinquency.
6. Assess the contributions of family, social, and genetic causes to conduct disorders.
7. Characterize the four levels of mental retardation.
8. Describe the causes of organic and cultural-familial types of mental retardation.
9. Outline the symptoms and causes of autistic disorder.
10. Distinguish among the major types of specific developmental disabilities and their causes.

*I*ncreasingly frightened by his temper outbursts and moodiness, Byron's mother brought him to a psychologist for evaluation. Although he was well over 6 feet tall, Byron seemed much younger than his 16 years because of his childlike mannerisms and speech.

Over the previous three years Byron's emotional condition had worsened considerably. When he lost his temper he would break household objects, and he had even pushed his mother down on a few occasions. Socially, Byron was very anxious and immature. Although he longed for friends and a social life, he rarely initiated interactions and spent most of his free time watching TV. His only social activity was occasional contact with some neighborhood children a few years younger than himself. Tense, isolated, and lonely at school, he was often the butt of jokes and cruel pranks. Byron's fear of his classmates was so intense that he often became nauseated while preparing for school.

Byron's emotional difficulties and social maladjustment are illustrative of some common anxiety and conduct disorders in children and adolescents. In this chapter we will examine how these and other psychological disorders of childhood develop and how they are treated.

Psychological disorders in the *developmental period* from birth to age 18 affect 15 to 19 percent of children in the United States. Childhood disorders are often transient reactions to developmental and environmental stressors, but in some cases they foreshadow continued maladustment through adulthood. Three of the disorders discussed in this chapter are DSM-III-R *Axis I clinical syndromes*, and three are *Axis II developmental disorders*:

- *Axis I:* Anxiety disorders, attention deficit hyperactivity disorder, conduct disorder
- *Axis II:* Mental retardation, autistic disorder, specific developmental disorders (American Psychiatric Association, 1987)

11-1 ANXIETY DISORDERS OF CHILDHOOD

Anxiety disorders are among the most common mental disorders in children as well as adults (see Chapter 5). Anxiety disorders during childhood are considered to be problems of *overcontrol*, in which the child's emotional disturbances are expressed mainly as internal or subjective symptoms like apprehension and fear.

Types of Childhood Anxiety Disorders

Much like their counterparts in adults, anxiety disorders of childhood are characterized by fear, tension, worry, apprehension, and somatic complaints. Three anxiety disorders are diagnosed exclusively in children and adolescents: separation anxiety disorder, overanxious disorder, and avoidant disorder. A fourth type, phobia disorder, is found in people of all ages, but it has some unique features in children. About 10 percent of school-age children suffer from anxiety disorders (Andersen, Williams, McGee, & Silva, 1987).

Separation Anxiety Disorder. **Separation anxiety disorder** is defined by excessive anxiety over separation from parents and family members that lasts

separation anxiety disorder Excessive anxiety over separation from parents and family members.

278

Children with separation anxiety are afraid to be separated from their parents, fearing that something bad will happen to them.

at least two weeks. Some children worry that harm will come to family members and are distressed if they are apart from them. Fears of travel and going to school are common, as are separation nightmares and physical symptoms, such as headaches. Children with separation anxiety disorder seem to be at greater risk for anxiety disorders in adulthood, especially agoraphobia (Crowell & Waters, 1990).

avoidant disorder
Shrinking from contact with strangers because of fear.

Avoidant Disorder. **Avoidant disorder** is manifested as a shrinking from contact with strangers because of fear. The avoidant child desires social involvement but is inhibited, easily embarrassed, and self-doubting. Children with avoidant disorder are shy, timid, and withdrawn in the company of unfamiliar people, but they can function normally with family and friends. Avoidant disorder in childhood is associated with a greater risk of developing social phobias in adolescence and adulthood (R. G. Klein & Last, 1989).

overanxious disorder
Excessive and unrealistic anxiety not focused on a specific object or situation.

Overanxious Disorder. Excessive and unrealistic anxiety that is not focused on a specific object or situation characterizes the **overanxious disorder**. The overanxious child is a worrier who is typically very self-conscious, self-critical, and perfectionistic, often exhibiting nervous habits like nail biting and lip chewing (R. G. Klein & Last, 1989).

Phobia Disorder. *Phobia disorder* in childhood is similar to adult phobias. The phobic child displays an extreme fear and avoidance behavior. Common *simple phobias* in childhood involve fears of darkness, animals, insects, and bodily injury. Children with *social phobias* are afraid of situations in which

Overanxious children are chronic worriers who often exhibit nervous habits like nail biting.

school phobia Extreme fear and avoidance of school.

others may evaluate or criticize them, and they avoid social activity that is potentially embarrassing, such as parties or dances (Wenar, 1990).

At different times in his life Byron exhibited the features of a few anxiety disorders. He described himself as a "nervous wreck," particularly at school, because of problems in relating to his classmates. He was frightened of having to socialize with the kids on his bus and in school, so he would avoid them as much as possible by taking an early bus and eating lunch alone. Byron's symptoms included several elements of avoidant disorder, overanxious disorder, and social phobia.

School phobia is an extreme fear and avoidance of school, often accompanied by a resistance against attending school, or *school refusal*. School phobia can be an expression of separation anxiety disorder, but it can also arise from real or imagined school-related fears, such as fear of tests, bullies, and harsh teachers. Between 1 and 2 percent of school-age children develop school phobia, most commonly in the first few grades (Trueman, 1984; Wenar, 1990).

After her mother's recovery from a severe illness, 12-year-old Teri was unable to leave for school without suffering severe bouts of anxiety. During the illness Teri had been haunted by thoughts that her mother would die, and even after her mother came home from the hospital the child's fears did not subside. When she had to go to school, the expectation that her mother might die made her panic and refuse to leave the house. Extreme separation anxiety fueled Teri's school phobia.

Causes of Childhood Anxiety Disorders

Like adult anxiety disorders, childhood anxiety disorders have been shown to have multiple biological and psychosocial causes.

Biological Causes of Childhood Anxiety Disorders. Genetic predispositions toward anxiety disorders are suspected because anxiety symptoms are 2 to 3 times more prevalent among children whose parents have anxiety disorders (Carey & Gottesman, 1981). In addition, first-degree relatives of children with anxiety disorders have twice the normal rate of anxiety disorders (Turner, Beidel, & Costello, 1987; M. N. Weissman, 1985). One study found that 83 percent of the mothers of children treated for anxiety disorders had a history of anxiety disorders (Last, Hersen, Kazdin, Francis, & Grubb, 1987).

Innate temperament factors have been implicated in childhood anxiety disorders. For example, anxiety symptoms and shyness are more likely to develop in infants who have an *inhibited temperament*, shown by overexcitability of the autonomic nervous system and a lower threshold for emotional responses like fear. However, the evidence cited in support of these biological causes can also be interpreted to mean that environmental or family factors produce anxiety disorders in children (Kagan, Reznick, & Snidman, 1990).

Psychosocial Causes of Childhood Anxiety Disorders. Psychodynamic explanations of anxiety disorders assign a crucial role to the child's emotional conflicts and defense mechanisms. In Freud's classic "Little Hans" case (discussed in Chapter 2), 5-year-old Hans had a horse phobia that was interpreted as a defensive expression of his Oedipal fear of his father. In children, as in adults, the symptoms of anxiety disorders are thought to reflect defenses against unconscious conflicts (Werkman, 1985).

Dennis had never known his father and had never had to share his mother with anyone else. When he was 7 years old, however, his mother became pregnant and made plans to marry her boyfriend. At this time Dennis became overanxious and school phobic, and he feared that his teacher didn't like him anymore. Dennis's symptoms pointed to a projection of fear based on an anticipated "loss" of his mother.

Cognitive and behavioral hypotheses emphasize that anxiety and fear in children are learned responses. For example, phobic avoidance is reinforced by a reduction of tension when the child escapes from distressing situations (R. G. Klein & Last, 1989). The social learning view holds that children imitate the anxiety symptoms of others, especially family members. In so doing, they also acquire negative self-efficacy beliefs that maintain the anxiety and associated avoidance behavior (Bandura, 1981).

Other aspects of the family environment can affect the child's development of anxiety disorders. Parental depression, marital discord, and family stresses such as a death, are correlated with children's risk of anxiety disorders (Hetherington & B. Martin, 1986). However, these factors have no specific or exclusive relationship with these disorders. Similarly, children's social problems with peers, teachers, and others are associated with anxiety, but their role in causing anxiety disorders is open to question (Wenar, 1990).

Treatment of Childhood Anxiety Disorders

Childhood anxiety disorders have been treated with strategies similar to therapies used in adults for anxiety, including drug therapy, psychotherapy, and behavioral therapy.

Drug Therapy. Drug therapy has had limited success with childhood anxiety disorders. Antianxiety drugs, such as benzodiazepines, are sometimes helpful for separation anxiety and overanxious disorder, and the antidepressant Tofranil has been used for separation anxiety and school phobia. However, drug therapy is not often employed for childhood anxiety disorders because of its limited success and the potentially serious side effects (Gittelman & Kanner, 1986; Rapoport & Kruesi, 1985).

Psychological Therapies. Psychological treatments for childhood anxiety disorders have generally proved helpful. Insight-oriented therapy employs techniques adapted to the developmental needs and capabilities of children. For example, *play and art therapies* use expressive approaches more suitable for young children than the conversational ("talking therapy") techniques used with adults (Casey & Berman, 1985; Kovacs & Paulauskas, 1986; M. Lewis, 1986).

Many treatment studies suggest that behavioral and social learning therapies are best for specific anxiety and phobia symptoms. Desensitization and modeling therapies work well for childhood phobias, and contingency management programs have been successful in treating separation anxiety disorders and school phobias (C. L. Carlson, Figueroa, Lahey, 1986; Kazdin, 1990; Weisz, B. Weiss, Alicke, & Klotze, 1987).

In play therapy children are given opportunities to understand and cope with emotional issues through expressive activities such as playing with puppets.

Kenny was a 10-year-old boy with severe separation anxiety disorder. He would not leave his parents, attend school, or even play alone outside. His treatment involved a behavioral exposure procedure in which he was given control over his own progress. He began with simple separation tasks, and after six weeks he was attending half-days at school. After three months of treatment he no longer showed signs of separation anxiety (R. G. Klein & Last, 1989).

11-2 ■ DISRUPTIVE BEHAVIOR DISORDERS

disruptive behavior disorders Problems of undercontrol expressed in socially disruptive behaviors.

The **disruptive behavior disorders** are problems of undercontrol in which symptoms are expressed in socially disruptive activity. This group includes attention deficit hyperactivity disorder, conduct disorders, and oppositional defiant disorder.

Attention Deficit Hyperactivity Disorder

attention deficit hyperactivity disorder A disorder characterized by inattention, impulsiveness, and overactivity.

Attention deficit hyperactivity disorder (ADHD) is a disruptive behavior disorder characterized by inattentiveness, impulsiveness, and overactivity. In the past this condition was called *hyperkinesis*, *minimal brain dysfunction*, *hyperactive child syndrome*, and *attention deficit disorder*. ADHD is one of the major behavioral problems of childhood, affecting up to 5 percent of the school-age population. It is three to six times more common in boys than girls (Barkley, 1990).

Children with ADHD have difficulty sustaining their attention and are easily distracted. They are impulsive, they lack emotional control, and they engage in thoughtless behavior. For example, hyperactive children will yell in class and jump out of their seats without regard for the consequences of their behavior.

Restless, fidgety, and driven behavior are signs of hyperactivity. The ADHD child seems unable to sit still or relax and is always "on the go." Deficiencies in rule-governed behavior are also prominent features of ADHD; the child has difficulty in planning and regulating behavior, for example, in playing games and following instructions (American Psychiatric Association, 1987; Barkley, 1990; S. B. Campbell & Werry, 1986).

Along with their primary symptoms, many ADHD children exhibit impairments in learning, intelligence, problem solving and memory. The academic achievement of ADHD children is usually below average, and they have high rates of grade repetition and dropping out of school. Social maladjustment is also common among ADHD children. Because they have difficulty getting along with others, ADHD children are often unpopular and are perceived as socially immature by their peers (Grenell, Glass, & Katz, 1987; Tarnowski, Prinz, & Nay, 1986; Whalen & Henker, 1985).

From the time he started school, Michael was in trouble almost every day. He was uncooperative in class and rarely concentrated on assignments, preferring instead to wander around annoying the other children. His behavior made him a social outcast at school. Classmates did not want to play with him and actively avoided him. At home he also had problems getting along with his parents and older brother. Michael's academic and social maladjustment are typical of children with ADHD.

Developmental Features of ADHD. According to the DSM-III-R, ADHD begins before age 7, and in many children its signs appear in the earliest years of life. Common problems during infancy include eating and sleeping difficulties, emotional irritability, and delayed language and motor development. Between the ages of 3 and 6, ADHD children exhibit a medley of disruptive behaviors and self-control problems, such as tantrums, noncompliance, recklessness, and excessive motor activity (S. B. Campbell, 1985).

In elementary school the ADHD child faces many new frustrations because of demands to perform classroom tasks and comply with rules. The demands of school often precipitate unpleasant emotional and behavioral reactions that contribute to academic and social difficulties. Up to 80 percent of ADHD children continue to show some symptoms in adolescence, and serious maladjustment is present in about half. During the teenage years hyperactive behavior diminishes, but inattention and poor impulse control persist (Barkley, 1985; S. B. Campbell, 1990).

Follow-up research demonstrates that ADHD children are at increased risk for antisocial behavior, crime, drug and alcohol use, emotional disturbances, and personality disorders (see Table 11-1). Poor prognosis is associated with aggressive and antisocial behaviors, below-average intelligence, and family discord, especially for ADHD boys (Gittelman, Mannuzza, Shenker, & Bonagura, 1985; Lambert, 1988; Mannuzza et al., 1991; Mannuzza, Gittelman-Klein, Honig, & Giampino, 1989; Mannuzza, R. G. Klein, Bonagura, Konig, & Shenker, 1988; Thorley, 1984; Wallander & Hubert, 1985; G. Weiss & Hechtman, 1986).

When he was in second grade, Louis was diagnosed as a hyperactive child. Although his IQ was well above average, he had persistent difficulty with his schoolwork. He had been a serious discipline problem from an early age. When

TABLE 11-1 ▒ CRIMINAL ACTIVITY AND ADHD IN YOUNG MEN[a]

Arrest History	Arrested at Least Once		Arrested More Than Once	
	ADHD	Control	ADHD	Control
Any offense	39%	20%	26%	8%
Aggressive offense	18%	7%	3%	2%
Felony offense	25%	7%	12%	3%

[a]The initial diagnosis used DSM-III criteria for attention deficit disorder with hyperactivity (ADDH).

Source: Adapted from "Hyperactive Boys Almost Grown Up: IV. Criminality and Its Relationship to Psychiatric Status" by S. Mannuzza, R. Gittelman-Klein, P. H. Konig, and T. L. Giampino, 1989, *Archives of General Psychiatry, 46,* pp. 1073–1079.

Louis entered high school he began to use alcohol, cocaine, and hallucinogenic drugs, and he got into fights regularly. He dropped out of school in tenth grade, and by age 20 he had been arrested several times on assault and drug charges.

Causes of ADHD. Research on ADHD supports a hereditary hypothesis. Identical twins and close relatives of affected children have an elevated risk of ADHD. Though no specific genetic mechanism has yet been found, some data hint at a dominant gene (Biederman et al., 1986; Cantwell, 1975; Deutsch & Kinsbourne, 1990; Deutsch & Swanson, 1985; McMahon, 1980; Willerman, 1973).

Besides the genetic evidence, there are other indicators that ADHD is a biological disorder. Prenatal problems, birth complications, illness in infancy, allergies, lead poisoning, and brain injury are some of the physical factors that have appeared in ADHD cases. However, none of these factors is invariably present, and none is specifically associated with ADHD (David, Hoffman, Sverd, & Clark, 1977; Hartsough & Lambert, 1985; Marshall, 1989).

Minor brain disturbances have been implicated in hyperactivity, inattentiveness, and impulse control problems. In the past these symptoms were attributed to **minimal brain dysfunction** (MBD), a concept that refers to a nonspecific set of neurological "soft signs" (for example, EEG abnormalities, coordination problems, and developmental delays). Because it has proved to be an ambiguous concept, MBD is no longer used to explain ADHD (Rie, 1980; D. M. Ross & S. A. Ross, 1976).

Nevertheless, many studies show diverse aspects of neurological disturbance in ADHD. Most ADHD children do not have distinctive brain damage, though electrical activity levels in their frontal lobes are abnormally low. In addition, abnormalities are present in the catecholamine, serotonin, and acetylcholine neurotransmitter systems, which are essential for attention, inhibition of behavior, regulation of arousal, and emotion (Deutsch & Kinsbourne, 1990; Lou, Henriksen, & Bruhn, 1984; Zametkin & Rapoport, 1986).

The development of ADHD and its associated emotional and social maladjustments is also affected by the child's social environment. Interactions between the disruptive ADHD child and frustrated parents can evolve into a system

minimal brain dysfunction A concept referring to nonspecific neurological "soft signs."

of chronic family distress. Trouble between ADHD children and their parents often begins in infancy because of the child's difficult temperament and the parent's inability to manage the child. The reciprocal pattern of antagonism can emerge with other people as well, and the child can develop mutually punishing relationships with peers and teachers (Hetherington & B. Martin, 1986; C. L. Lee & Bates, 1985; Thomas & Chess, 1984).

Treatment of ADHD. The standard medical treatment for ADHD is stimulant drugs, such as methylphenidate (Ritalin), pemoline (Cylert), and dextroamphetamine (Dexedrine). Although less commonly used, antidepressant drugs and antihypertensive drugs sometimes benefit ADHD children as well. Drugs improve attention and reduce impulsive, hyperactive behavior in most cases. Children maintained on these drugs usually exhibit better social skills and self-control and are perceived more positively by adults and peers (Pliszka, 1987; Solanto, 1984; Whalen, 1982).

However, drugs do not cure ADHD, and when they are stopped the symptoms usually return. Despite some behavioral improvements, stimulants have little effect on academic achievement or on the long-term prognosis for the ADHD child. In addition, these drugs have side effects, including sleep problems, diminished appetite, and a slowing of physical growth (Vincent, Varley, & Leger, 1990; Whalen, 1982).

In the 1970s, considerable attention was given to the role of diet in causing hyperactivity. Pediatrician Ben Feingold proposed that food additives like dyes and preservatives were responsible for hyperactivity, and he promoted a diet free of those substances as a treatment (1975). Controlled studies question the efficacy of the *Feingold diet* for ADHD, but some children definitely benefit from it (Connors, 1980; Varley, 1984). Evidence of food allergies in a subgroup of ADHD children suggests that dietary intervention can be a reasonable treatment in some cases (Marshall, 1989).

Learning-based treatments control the disruptive behavior of the ADHD child and motivate the acquisition of self-control by the child. Parental involvement is critical to the success of behavioral programs, since parents are primarily responsible for structuring the child's activity and providing rewards and punishments (Barkley, 1983; R. J. Morris & McReynolds, 1986). Cognitive approaches can also help the child develop better self-regulation of impulses and behavior (Whalen, Henker, & Hinshaw, 1985). For example, the strategy of *self-instructional training* teaches ADHD children to talk to themselves to improve their problem-solving and self-monitoring skills (Meichenbaum, 1974).

Despite their short-term benefits, neither drug therapy nor learning-based treatments have been proved to establish reliable long-term benefits for ADHD children. Comparative evaluation of treatments for this disorder is complicated by the fact that only a minority of ADHD children actually receive formal treatment. However, comprehensive treatment for ADHD usually involves stimulant medications, behavior management, and self-control training for the child (Whalen & Henker, 1991).

Conduct Disorders

conduct disorder
Behavior disturbance characterized by persistent violations of age-appropriate rules or norms.

A **conduct disorder** (CD) is a behavioral disturbance characterized in most circumstances by persistent violations of age-appropriate rules or norms. Conduct disorders are found in 4 to 8 percent of children and are reportedly more prevalent in boys. The range of behaviors in CD is quite broad and includes antisocial behavior, fighting, stealing, lying, cruelty, aggression, destructiveness, truancy, and running away.

The DSM-III-R identifies three types of conduct disorder: group, solitary aggressive, and undifferentiated types. In the *group type*, the child's unacceptable behavior occurs mainly with peers, as in gang-related activity. Aggressive behavior is sometimes present, but it is not necessarily part of this type. In the *solitary aggressive type*, the child exhibits aggression as an individual. The problem is usually more severe than the group type. In the *undifferentiated type*, the child shows a mixture of symptoms of the group and solitary aggressive types of CD (American Psychiatric Association, 1987).

Children with conduct disorders display many problems in normal socialization. They have less empathy and concern for others, and they exhibit more deviations in moral development. In extreme cases, the CD child demonstrates little or no conscience and acts out of a selfish, need-dominated sense of right and wrong. CD children often have legal, social, and family difficulties, and many also have other psychological disorders, including ADHD, emotional disturbances, and learning disabilities (Kazdin, 1987; B. Martin & Hoffman, 1990; Quay, 1986).

juvenile delinquency
Violation of the law by a minor.

A problem intertwined with conduct disorders is **juvenile delinquency**, a legal term that indicates a violation of some law by a minor. Psychologist Herbert Quay has identified three types of delinquency that conform closely to the types of CD already described. *Unsocialized/psychopathic* delinquents are the most antisocial type. Their social attachments are minimal, and they usually commit their aggressive crimes alone. *Socialized/subcultural* delinquency refers to crime in the context of group activity by a juvenile who demonstrates some capacity for social relationships. *Neurotic/disturbed* delinquency involves criminal activity that is motivated by emotional disturbances (Quay, 1986).

Gangs, which can provide socially deviant support networks for youths, may promote the socialized/subcultural type of juvenile delinquency, which manifests itself in criminal activity.

At age 15, Ronnie was arrested for auto theft, along with three friends, after a minor accident while they were joyriding in a stolen car. Starting at age 11, he had been involved in many similar incidents as well as other criminal activity, including burglaries, shoplifting, vandalism, and extorting money from illegal aliens. He did not like violence, however, and tended to stay away from it when at all possible. Ronnie's behavior illustrates both the group type of conduct disorder and socialized/subcultural delinquency.

Developmental Features of Conduct Disorders. As in ADHD, early signs of conduct disorder are sometimes expressed in infancy as a difficult temperament pattern that is stable over time. One of the most stable traits of childhood is aggressiveness, extending from the preschool years through adolescence. Childhood aggression is associated with later conduct disorders and delinquency. The amount and severity of aggressive antisocial behavior in childhood predicts aggression in adulthood, especially for boys (Eron & Huesman, 1990; Loeber, 1982; Olweus, 1979; L. N. Robins, 1966; Rutter, 1987).

oppositional defiant disorder A disorder defined by negativistic, hostile, and defiant behavior.

A significant developmental predictor of CD is **oppositional defiant disorder**, a disruptive behavior disorder defined by negativistic, hostile, and defiant behavior not accompanied by serious antisocial or aggressive behavior. Although oppositional defiant disorder and CD have some common features—in particular, lying and mild aggression—they are distinct disorders. Most CD children exhibit the symptoms of oppositional defiant disorder in their early years (Loeber, Lahey, & Thomas, 1991).

Byron exhibited many features of oppositional defiant disorder in early childhood. He was argumentative and uncooperative with his mother, and when he did not get what he wanted, he would sulk and be very rude for days. On the few occasions when he was punished, he would bait, curse, and annoy his mother without mercy. Usually his behavior would wear down his mother and she would give in to his demands in order to have some peace.

Causes of Conduct Disorders. Conduct disorders are diverse behavior problems influenced by genetic, physiological, family, and sociocultural factors. Genetic studies have not directly addressed the heritability of CDs, but they have examined many related behaviors. Aggressiveness is a moderately heritable trait, as evidenced by above-average rates of aggressive and antisocial behavior in the parents of CD children (Plomin, Nitz, & Rave, 1990). A Danish study of over 14,000 adopted boys found elevated crime rates among biological sons of criminals even though they were raised by noncriminal adoptive parents (Mednick, Gabrielli, & Hutchings, 1984).

To date, no compelling physiological explanation for conduct disorders has been found, though some evidence points to overactivity in the brain's dopamine system and underactivity in the serotonin system (Quay, 1986). The impact of hormones on behavior is disputed, but studies suggest hormone-related brain differences may affect aggression. The most consistent male-female behavior difference is the male's greater propensity for aggression, and male sex hormones are associated with aggression in both sexes (Eagly & Steffer, 1986; Plomin et al., 1990).

Family life is an extremely influential variable in the development of conduct disorders and delinquency. When the family environment includes parental

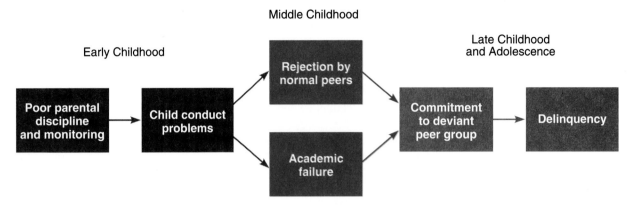

Figure 11-1 Development of antisocial behavior.

Source: From "Developmental Perspective on Antisocial Behavior" by G. R. Patterson, B. D. DeBaryshe, and E. Ramsey, 1989, *American Psychologist, 44,* pp. 329–335.

aggression and antisocial behavior, similar behavior often appears in the children. Many chronically violent children have been the victims of physical abuse by their parents. Children with extreme conduct disorders all too often come from homes where parental emotional disorders, substance dependence, and violence are a "normal" part of family life (Lahey et al., 1988; Loeber & Dishon, 1984; D. G. Perry, L. C. Perry, & Boldizar, 1990).

Parental styles of discipline are also associated with the development of conduct disorders. Detachment, extreme permissiveness, and lack of supervision by parents are related to self-control problems in children. In addition, erratic, harsh, or inconsistent discipline can provoke rebellious, defiant reactions in children. According to the **coercion hypothesis**, many CD children and their parents develop a cycle of reciprocal exchanges in which they demonstrate a give-and-take of punishment and negative reinforcement. Such mutual coercion took place between Byron and his mother; his antagonistic behavior was reinforced when she yielded to his demands, but his behavior also provoked her to be demanding toward him (Patterson, 1982, 1986).

Influences outside the family also shape the behavior of CD and delinquent children. Peer groups that reinforce antisocial and aggressive behavior can provide a deviant social support system for a child. In fact, children from troubled homes tend to seek supports outside the home. For example, urban youth gangs can provide a strong, albeit antisocial, support system for members. Psychologist Gerald Patterson, the author of the coercion hypothesis, proposes a scheme that integrates family and extrafamilial influences in antisocial behavior, as shown in Figure 11-1 (Patterson, DeBaryshe, & Ramsey, 1989).

Socioeconomic distress further increases a child's vulnerability to aggressive antisocial behavior. In recent years, gang-related violence among impoverished urban youths has become an enormous social problem. Between 1984 and 1989, homicide arrests among youths doubled in the United States. The increase was particularly striking for urban minority youths, nearly half of whom live in poverty (Binder, 1988; Ewing, 1990).

Debate continues about the relationship of media violence to actual aggres-

coercion hypothesis
The view that CD children and their parents develop patterns of reciprocal coercive interactions.

sion. Recent incidents of violence in theaters screening violent films suggest a connection. However, research reviews indicate that the association between media violence and real-life aggression is complex and is moderated by many factors. Generally, studies find two related results—aggressive youths prefer to watch violent films and programs, *and* exposure to media violence enhances aggressiveness in some children (Friedrich-Cofer & Huston, 1986; Wood, Wong, & Chachere, 1991).

Treatment of Conduct Disorders. Although various forms of psychotherapy have been employed with CD children, the most encouraging results come from programs using social learning strategies with children and their families. Training parents in effective child management skills can break the cycle of mutual parent-child coercion (Miller & Prinz, 1990; Patterson, 1982). Other cognitive-behavioral methods, such as anger control training, have also been successful in reducing aggressiveness. Improvements in CD and delinquent children are often short-lived, however, and the evidence for lasting change is disappointing (Kazdin, 1987; Redner, Snellman, & Davidson, 1983).

juvenile diversion programs Community-based efforts to intervene with delinquent youths.

Juvenile diversion programs are community-based efforts to intervene with delinquent youths before their behavior leads to incarceration. Diversion programs usually integrate juvenile offenders with nondelinquents from their community in counseling, group activity, and recreational affairs (Davidson, Redner, Blakely, Mitchell, & Emshoff, 1987). One program, the St. Louis Experiment, successfully reduced antisocial behavior for at least one year in many of the participants (Feldman, Caphinger, & Wodarski, 1983).

The best-known approach to residential treatment is the *Achievement Place* model. Delinquent youths live in a group home environment and are involved in a token economy that encourages the development of prosocial behavior (Kirigin, Brankmann, Atwater, & Wolf, 1982). Achievement Place and other residential programs report good results while the delinquents are in the program, but there is little evidence of lasting change after the youths return to their communities (Quay, 1986).

11-3 DEVELOPMENTAL DISORDERS

developmental disorders Disturbances in acquisition of cognitive, language, motor, or social skills.

Developmental disorders are disturbances in the acquisition of cognitive, language, motor, or social skills that appear before age 18 and often last into adulthood. Three types of developmental disorders are mental retardation, autistic disorder, and specific developmental disorders.

Mental Retardation

mental retardation Significantly subaverage intellectual functioning and deficits in adaptive behavior.

Mental retardation (MR) is a condition defined by significantly subaverage intellectual functioning and deficits in adaptive behavior appearing in the developmental period. Subaverage intelligence means a score of 70 or less on a standardized IQ test (American Association on Mental Deficiency, 1977; American Psychiatric Association, 1987). *Adaptive behavior* is assessed by rating several areas of the individual's functioning, such as personal self-sufficiency, community self-sufficiency, and responsibility (Nihira, 1978). Although the exact prevalence of MR is unknown, 1 to 3 percent of the population is thought to be retarded.

Mentally retarded people represent a diverse population. Many function self-sufficiently, working and raising families, but others are seriously handicapped and require constant supervision and care. Four levels of retardation have been distinguished: mild, moderate, severe, and profound (see Table 11-2).

Developmental Features of Mental Retardation. The course of MR is not uniform in all cases. Nearly three-fourths of retarded people are under age 18, but two-thirds of this group lose their diagnosis in adulthood. The decline in diagnosed prevalence of MR in adulthood may reflect both improved skills in the individual and changing adaptive demands. The developmental course of retarded people is not conditioned solely by their intelligence; it reflects their medical conditions, personalities, and social circumstances as well. In most MR people development progresses through the normal stages, but it proceeds more slowly than in the average person. However, other MR individuals show major deviations from normal development because of brain damage (B. Weiss, Weisz, & Bromfield, 1986; Wenar, 1990).

Beyond their intellectual deficits, mentally retarded people often experience other adjustment problems. Between 25 and 40 percent of MR people also suffer from other mental disorders, in particular anxiety, mood, and personality disorders (Menolascino, 1990). Most MR people are mildly retarded and are fully aware of their limitations. This commonly generates frustration, low self-esteem, and emotional distress (Reiss, 1985). Rejection and discrimination by non-retarded people further impair the social adjustment of the retarded individual. In addition, many retarded people have neurological and physical handicaps such as seizures, paralysis, and sensory impairments (Guralnick, 1986).

TABLE 11-2   FEATURES OF MENTAL RETARDATION

Level of Retardation	Percent of MR Cases	Characteristics
Mild (IQ 50/55–70; mental age to 11–12)	85%	• Educable up to sixth-grade level • Many independent living skills • Unskilled or semiskilled work • Needs assistance in many areas
Moderate (IQ 35/40–50/55; mental age to 8–9)	10%	• Educable up to second-grade level • Semi-independent living skills • Trainable for unskilled work • Needs supervision in many areas
Severe (IQ 20/25–35/40; mental age to 5–6)	3–4%	• Educable up to kindergarten level • Trainable for simple self-care • Suitable for group home • Needs close supervision and care
Profound (IQ below 20/25; mental age to 3–4)	1–2%	• Educable up to preschool level • Minimal self-care and language • Physical handicaps often present • Custodial care required

The actor Chris Burke has proven that people with Down syndrome can successfully develop their talents and skills despite their mental retardation.

Despite considerable obstacles, many retarded people are capable of functioning adequately within the limits set by their handicap. With society's increasing recognition of the potentials and rights of MR people, they are finding more options available than ever before. Job and housing opportunities have improved, as have legal rights for the retarded. Nevertheless, the MR person today remains at high risk for serious psychological and social distress.

Biological Causes of Mental Retardation. Genetic, neurological, and environmental processes that impair brain functioning can produce mental retardation. **Organic retardation**, which accounts for 25 percent of MR cases, refers to MR with clear biological causes. It is most prevalent in people with profound, severe, and moderate levels of retardation. Hereditary predispositions influence mental retardation as well as normal intelligence (Akesson, 1986; Vandenberg & Vogler, 1985).

organic retardation MR with clear biological causes.

The most common type of organic retardation is **Down syndrome**, which is usually caused by having an extra chromosome 21 (*trisomy 21*). Down syndrome is most often due to an error in formation of the mother's egg, but sometimes the father's sperm is defective. The risk of bearing a Down syndrome infant increases from 1 in 3000 for women under age 30 to 1 in 100 for women over 40, but most affected infants are born to women under 35. Down syndrome usually causes moderate MR, but lower or higher levels are also possible. People with Down syndrome were formerly mislabeled *mongoloids* because an extra fold of skin gave an "oriental look" to their eyes. They tend to be shorter than average and often have congenital heart defects (Szymanski & Crocker, 1985).

Down syndrome A form of organic retardation caused by an extra chromosome 21.

Mental retardation is associated with dozens of other, rarer genetic defects. Many of these specific hereditary problems interfere with metabolic processes and thereby lead to brain damage. For example, children with *phenylketonuria* (PKU) are unable to metabolize the amino acid phenylalanine, and the buildup of this chemical causes mental retardation. When given a diet that is free of phenylalanine, the PKU child develops normally (Matthews, Barabas, Cusak, & Ferrari, 1986; Szymanski & Crocker, 1985).

Environmental influences, too, can cause retardation by damaging the brain of the unborn child. Organic retardation can be caused by prenatal maternal illness, such as German measles (rubella) and encephalitis, and by maternal drug use. MR is common in children with *fetal alcohol syndrome* (FAS), whose mothers severely abused alcohol during pregnancy (Abel & Sokol, 1987). Worldwide, a leading cause of MR is malnutrition, prenatally and in the first few years of life. Malnutrition inhibits brain maturation and severely disrupts associated intellectual development. In some poor countries, epidemic malnutrition is a catastrophic social and political problem (Baumeister, 1987).

By age 14, Billy had spent about half his life in various institutions because of mild retardation, hyperactivity, and aggressiveness. Billy's mother had been addicted to alcohol and narcotics during her pregnancy with him, and although he had no distinct physical defects, he exhibited some neurological quirks, such as vision and coordination problems. Billy's symptoms suggest that he sustained some brain damage before birth due to drug exposure.

Psychosocial Causes of Mental Retardation. In addition to biological processes, the social and psychological environments influence intellectual development. When psychosocial causes are prominent in MR and no distinct biological causes exist, the condition is called **cultural-familial retardation**. About 75 percent of MR individuals, most of whom are mildly retarded, have cultural-familial retardation (Zigler, 1967).

cultural-familial retardation An MR type with psychosocial causes.

The two psychosocial factors most strongly related to cultural-familial retardation are parental retardation and low socioeconomic status. Beyond their genetic contributions to a child's intelligence, parents also establish the child's primary learning environment. Retarded and intellectually impaired parents do not provide adequate intellectual stimulation for their children, who are thus deprived of critical learning experiences (T. J. Bouchard & Segal, 1985).

Rates of MR are consistently highest for economically disadvantaged children. Poverty implies many things that establish higher risks for retardation, including poor health care, poor education, inadequate family resources, and emotional distress. Given the limited occupational skills and earning potential of MR parents, retardation can be both a cause and consequence of economic distress (Scott & Carran, 1987).

Extreme emotional deprivation is another psychosocial risk factor for mental retardation. Children whose emotional needs are not met sometimes show inhibited intellectual development. Studies of abused, neglected, and institutionalized children find that lasting cognitive and emotional problems result from deprivation (Baroff, 1983).

Treatment and Prevention of Mental Retardation. Interventions for MR have had mixed success. Because there is such diversity among the mentally retarded, no one approach is considered best. However, the most common approach involves educating the retarded client in specific skills areas.

mainstreaming An educational strategy that places MR children in regular classes.

segregation An educational strategy that places MR children in classes with other MR children.

Two educational strategies for retarded children are mainstreaming and segregated education. **Mainstreaming** places retarded children in a regular class with nonretarded children. **Segregation** places retarded children in classes with other MR children. Mainstreaming is best for mildly retarded children, who can benefit academically by exposure to nonretarded peers. Since many main-

Educational strategies for mentally retarded children typically combine mainstreaming in regular classes (top) and segregation in special classes (below).

streamed MR children are not comfortable with or accepted by nonretarded classmates, their education may combine mainstreamed and segregated classes (N. M. Robinson & H. B. Robinson, 1976).

Educational programs for retarded children typically incorporate some elements of behavior modification. These techniques have been used to good advantage in teaching language, speech, self-help, and problem-solving skills. The behavioral principles of reward and punishment are easily adapted to special education settings, and today structured contingency management programs are standard features of classroom procedures for mentally retarded clients (Matson, 1983).

The prevention of mental retardation is a topic with social, moral, and political implications. A few types of MR, including Down syndrome, can be detected before birth by *amniocentesis,* a technique that identifies some chromosomal and genetic defects. In those cases, prevention can mean abortion of affected fetuses. Another prevention measure is genetic counseling for prospective parents who have family histories of retardation. This enables them to make more informed decisions about having children.

Early childhood education can prevent or reduce the rates of MR in high-risk children who have a history of familial retardation and poverty. Studies demonstrate that a stimulating preschool environment for high-risk children leads to modest IQ gains. Although enriched preschool programs like *Head Start* can improve the intellectual ability of a child, the long-term duration of such improvement depends on many factors, especially the home and educational environments (Bricker, 1986; Consortium for Longitudinal Studies, 1983).

Mentally retarded people were formerly doomed to life in institutions, but since the 1960s the number of retarded persons in public institutions has been reduced by about half. Today, the law requires that retarded people be provided with the "least restrictive environment" possible, and retarded people live in a variety of settings, including community residences and group homes. Efforts at *normalization* of the environment for mentally retarded people are intended to maximize their integration into the local community and, hopefully, to enhance their quality of life (Landesman & Butterfield, 1987).

Autistic Disorder

autistic disorder
A severe developmental disorder with impaired social, communication, and imaginative activity, beginning before age 3.

Autistic disorder is a severe developmental disorder that is primarily distinguished by four features:

• Qualitative impairment in social interaction
• Impairment in communication and imagination
• Restricted repertoire of activity and interests
• Onset before age 3 (American Psychiatric Association, 1987)

Infantile autism was first distinguished in 1943 as a disorder separate from childhood psychosis and mental retardation. It was considered mainly a disorder of social development (Kanner, 1943). Today, the DSM-III-R classifies autistic disorder as a **pervasive developmental disorder**, a condition with severe deviations from normal development in all areas of functioning. Autistic disorder, or *autism*, is a rare disorder that occurs in about 4 out of 10,000 people, more commonly in males (M. Campbell & W. H. Green, 1985).

pervasive developmental disorder   A condition of severe deviations from normal development.

The autistic child is withdrawn and socially isolated, exhibiting little interest in other people. Play, imitation, friendship, and most social activities are alien to autistic children, who care little for the company or comfort of others. Even when they are hurt or distressed, some autistic children react negatively to the nurturing attempts of others.

Cognitive impairments are apparent in the autistic person's language, communication, and imaginative activity. About 50 percent of autistic people exhibit *mutism*, a severe deficit or absence of spontaneous speech. Those who do speak often use idiosyncratic or deviant language forms, such as referring to themselves in the third person (*he* or *she*) rather than first person (*I*). *Echolalia* is an autistic speech pattern in which the person senselessly repeats what someone else has said. Autistic speech rhythms often sound flat and monotonic or have a singsong quality. Autistics have problems in nonverbal communication as well, including making eye contact and understanding facial expressions.

Autistic behaviors sometimes include bizarre and self-injurious activities.

Autistic children typically prefer solitary activities and will spend hours repetitiously manipulating toys or other objects.

Stereotyped behaviors are repetitive actions without clear purpose, such as hand flapping or spinning objects. Some kinds of autistic self-stimulation can be damaging; children may hit or scratch themselves repeatedly. Autistic people may exhibit a *compulsive sameness* in their behavior and become terribly disturbed when their routines or environment are altered (M. Campbell & W. H. Green, 1985).

As an infant Audrey was unresponsive to her mother's cuddling and often felt stiff and rigid when held. She also did not respond to her mother's voice and would avoid making eye contact with anyone. She shrank from contact with most people and was content to play alone in her room for hours, constantly rearranging her toys, staring at her hand, gesturing to herself, and whirling around in circles (R. G. Meyer & Osborne, 1987).

Developmental Features of Autism. Autism is generally a chronic disorder with a poor prognosis. Perhaps 10 to 15 percent of autistic children have a good prognosis, meaning their symptoms will lessen and they can lead a semi-independent life. However, only 1 to 2 percent ever improve to a state free of symptoms and residual effects. The long-term outcome for autistic people depends on several factors, such as intelligence, language ability, and degree of neurological impairment. The generally poor prognosis for autistic people is shaped by the fact that nearly 75 percent of them are mentally retarded and about 25 percent have seizure disorders (R. Paul, 1987).

Three types of autism with different developmental courses can be identified. Autistics of the *aloof type* exhibit extreme social withdrawal, language deficiency, and severe or profound retardation, and they have the worst prognosis. The *passive type* have better language ability, more social involvement, better manageability, and a better prognosis. The *active-but-odd type* have the best prognosis. Their social activity, speech, and intelligence are most developed, but they often have other mental disorders (Wing & Attwood, 1987).

Causes of Autism. Traditional psychological theories attributed autism to the influence of rejecting and critical parents (Bettelheim, 1967), but evidence from controlled studies consistently fails to support this view. The parents of autistic children do have problems, but they are more likely the result of the stress of raising an autistic child than the cause of autism (McAdoo & DeMyer, 1978). Abnormal personality traits such as emotional detachment are found in parents of autistic children, but they do not necessarily cause the autism (Narayan, Moyes, & Wolff, 1990).

Today, biological explanations of autism are dominant. Hereditary influences are indicated by twin studies showing monozygotic twins have a higher concordance rate for autism than dizygotic twins (Folstein & Rutter, 1977; Ritvo, B. J. Freeman, Mason-Brothers, Mo, & Ritvo, 1985). About 2 percent of nontwin siblings of autistic children also have the disorder; this rate is over 100 times that of the general population (B. J. Freeman et al., 1989). Some genetic disorders are related to both autism and mental retardation. The most common genetic abnormality in autism is the **fragile X syndrome**, a hereditary condition usually seen in males, in which part of the X chromosome is broken (see Figure 11-2). Fragile X accounts for about 10 percent of cases of autism and is also associated with cases of mental retardation, ADHD, and anxiety disorders (Bregman, Leckman, & Ort, 1988; W. T. Brown et al., 1986).

fragile X syndrome A hereditary abnormality in which part of the X chromosome is broken.

Brain damage and dysfunctions are present in most autistic people. Among these problems are seizures and abnormal electrical activity in the brain as well as structural problems in the temporal lobes, left hemisphere, thalamus, cerebellum, and limbic regions of the brain (Ballotin et al., 1989; Courchesne, 1987; McBride et al., 1988; Piven et al., 1990). Neurotransmitters, particularly the brain's dopamine and serotonin systems, are sometimes affected. However, no specific pattern of brain damage or disturbance has been identified in all cases of autism (G. S. Golden, 1987; Piven et al., 1991).

The determinants of the neurological problems in autism are not certain, but most likely there are multiple sources. In addition to possible genetic contributions, many biological factors have been implicated, including prenatal injury and disease, birth complications, and postnatal illnesses (Hertzig & Shapiro, 1990). A recent study discovered that 11 percent of autistic people had been exposed to unusual viral, bacterial, and metabolic diseases affecting the brain. This suggests a connection between neurological infections and vulnerability to autism (Ritvo et al., 1990).

Treatment of Autism. The success of treatments for autism has been modest at best. A controversial psychodynamic approach is practiced at the Orthogenic

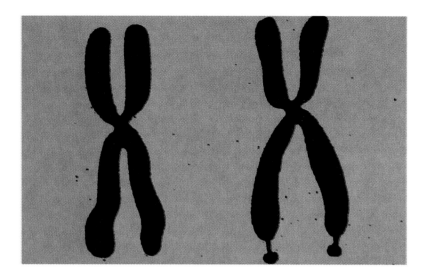

Figure 11-2 Fragile X syndrome. *Fragile X syndrome, caused by defects on the X chromosome, has been associated with autism and mental retardation, especially in boys. In this photo, the defective X chromosome is on the right; a normal X is on the left.*

Source: Science Vu/Visuals Unlimited.

School of the University of Chicago. Psychoanalyst Bruno Bettelheim, the late director of the school, recommended removing autistic children from their homes and immersing them in a total therapeutic milieu in which they could safely emerge from their withdrawn state (Bettelheim, 1967). Although Bettelheim reported great success in curing autism, controlled research is lacking and some evidence suggests that such programs may even be harmful for autistic children (Riddle, 1987; Schreibman, Charlop, & Britten, 1983).

Antipsychotic drugs have benefited some autistic people and are most helpful in controlling agitated behavior, hyperactivity, and aggressiveness. These medications do not directly improve social or language skills, however, and because of their powerful side effects they are not widely used with autistic children (M. Campbell, Anderson, W. H. Green, & Deutsch, 1987). Promising results have recently been noted with fenfluramine, a stimulant, but questions remain about its reliability (M. Campbell, 1988).

Treatment programs based on behavioral and learning principles have consistently positive results. Autistic children and adults benefit from education when it is highly structured and tied to reinforcement. Psychologist Ivar Lovaas of the University of California, Los Angeles, has generated an enormous amount of data supporting this approach. His language and behavior training program provides intensive individual training for 40 or more hours per week, and he reports that nearly half of his autistic students eventually have age-appropriate academic placements (Lovaas, 1987; Lovaas et al., 1980).

Treatment of autism is most successful in a structured, goal-oriented learning environment. A comprehensive strategy for treating autism addresses the following areas: (1) training in cognitive skills, language, and social behavior; (2) acquiring specific learning skills; (3) reducing rigid and stereotyped behavior; (4) eliminating maladaptive behavior; and (5) alleviating family distress (Rutter, 1985).

Specific Developmental Disorders

When inadequate development of academic, language, speech, or motor skills significantly interferes with academic achievement or daily life, a **specific de-**

CLOSE-UP
The Savant Syndrome

- A 30-year-old sculptor creates animals in clay and bronze that are acclaimed in national art circles.
- A 7-year-old boy with no formal training plays classical piano flawlessly and reproduces complex pieces after hearing them only once.
- Identical twins can identify the day of the week for any date within 2000 years and can calculate 20-digit prime numbers.

What do all these examples have in common? They are behaviors of developmentally disabled people who have single, highly developed talents called *splinter skills.* These people were formerly called *idiots savants.* Today they are said to have *savant syndrome,* a condition found in as many as 1 in 10 autistic people and in about 1 in 2000 mentally retarded people.

In the 1988 film *Rain Man,* Dustin Hoffman portrayed Raymond Babbit, an autistic man with phenomenal recall and calculation abilities. As shown by that character, the core of the savant syndrome is an amazingly accurate memory that is narrowly focused and performs with little feeling or conscious effort. In addition to their prodigious memory skills, some savants have demonstrated striking artistic, musical, and mathematical talents.

The exact causes of savant syndrome are not known despite a century of study. Ironically, the syndrome seems to depend on a pattern of brain damage that interferes with the conscious cognitive memory system that most ordinary people employ. Furthermore, low intelligence and deficient abstract thinking seem to be necessary ingredients. Researchers suspect that the savant syndrome involves damage to the normal memory pathways connecting the cortex and the limbic system. Savant syndrome might represent a unique compensation by the brain for congenitally damaged memory circuits. Oddly enough, the brain mechanisms responsible for savants' remarkable splinter skills may also be responsible for their intellectual deficits.

Whatever the cause, research on savant syndrome has shed light on the enormous complexity of human memory and behavior and has illustrated how poorly the brain's memory systems are understood. George, an autistic savant with fantastic computational skills, offers an explanation of his talent as true as it is mysterious: "I've got a good brain, that's how I do it" (Treffert, 1988; 1989).

specific developmental disorder Inadequate development of academic, language, speech, or motor skills.

velopmental disorder** is present. This DSM-III-R classification overlaps considerably with those problems commonly known as *learning disabilities* (LD). These disorders are found in 10 to 15 percent of school-age children, more commonly in boys than girls (Ceci, 1987; Kavanaugh & Truss, 1988). Table 11-3 summarizes the features of major learning disabilities associated with four specific developmental disorders.

Causes of Specific Developmental Disorders. Brain dysfunction and damage are implicated in some learning disabilities. Structural problems in the cortex and thalamus are associated with dyslexia and with speech and language disorders. Some evidence indicates that dyslexia is based on deficient visual

TABLE 11-3 ▦ SPECIFIC DEVELOPMENTAL DISORDERS (SDD)
AND FEATURES OF LEARNING DISABILITIES (LD)

Specific Developmental Disorder (DSM-III-R)	Learning Disability Features
Developmental reading disorder (dyslexia)	• Letter and word confusion • Visual perceptual deficits • Poor reading comprehension
Developmental expressive language disorder	• Speech production problems • Grammar and vocabulary deficits • Inadequate sentence structure
Developmental receptive language disorder	• Speech comprehension problems • Impaired communication • Poor language learning
Developmental articulation disorder	• Mispronounced speech sounds • Incorrectly used speech sounds • Lisps and nonspeech sounds

processing mechanisms in the thalamus. Language and reading disorders are often explained as disturbances of the left hemisphere, and dysfunctions of the right hemisphere are suspected in nonverbal learning disabilities, such as math, spatial, and social perception deficits (L. Baker & Cantwell, 1985a, b; Hynd & Semrud-Clikeman, 1989; Jansky, 1985; Naylor, 1980; Semrud-Clikeman & Hynd, 1990).

developmental lag hypothesis The view that learning disabilities are due to slow maturation of the brain.

The **developmental lag hypothesis** proposes that learning disabilities are due to abnormally slow maturation of the brain mechanisms involved in acquiring skills like reading and speech. Atypical brain development in LD can be influenced by heredity, prenatal factors, low birth weight, and birth complications (Hynd & Semrud-Clikeman, 1989; Pennington & S. D. Smith, 1988). Specific developmental disorders can also be the result of psychosocial factors, such as inadequate language modeling by parents, poor education, and deprivation of language, reading, and communication experiences. Primary emotional and motivational problems can impair learning in some children to such an extent that SDD develops (Bruck, 1987; Licht & Kistner, 1986; Perlmutter, 1987).

During infancy and early childhood Byron had exhibited developmental delays in several areas. His physical coordination was poor, and he did not speak at all until he was nearly 2 years old. On entering kindergarten at age 6, he was thought to be mentally retarded, but he was subsequently diagnosed as learning-disabled. Both of Byron's parents had a history of learning problems, and his father was severely dyslexic. Throughout his school career Byron had been in special education classes.

educational remediation A treatment for LD in which structured training in specific skills is provided.

Treatment for Learning Disabilities. The preferred modern approach to treating learning-disabled children is **educational remediation**, with structured training in specific reading, speech, writing, listening, problem solving, and other

PROFILE
Bruno Bettelheim
(1903–1990)

Bruno Bettelheim was an advocate of the psychodynamic perspective. His interests ranged across psychology to include such diverse topics as social prejudice, reading, parenting, child development, and child psychopathology.

Viennese by birth, Bettelheim became interested in Freudian psychology during his adolescence. He later studied psychoanalysis with Freud and graduated from the University of Vienna with a Ph.D. in psychology in 1938. Soon afterward he was interred in the Dachau and Buchenwald concentration camps for nearly two years. After he was released he emigrated to the United States. He began teaching at the University of Chicago, where he remained until his retirement. For 34 years he was director of the university's Orthogenic School, a residential treatment school for emotionally disturbed children. Bettelheim based his approach on the belief that children's emotional disturbances are caused by poor parenting. His approach to treatment required placing children in a loving, supportive environment in which they could develop without fear.

Bettelheim's theories were often attacked as unproven speculations that were potentially damaging because they unjustly blamed parents for their children's mental problems. In his later works Bettleheim modified some of his harsher judgments of parents, concluding that most are innately "good enough." Recently, startling accusations have been made against him by some former staff and students at the Orthogenic School: they claim Bettelheim was an abusive, bullying megalomaniac who intimidated and physically punished students. Bettelheim's defenders maintain that although he was often blunt and stern, he was also caring and committed to his patients.

Bettelheim was a prolific author. His work encompassed many areas of psychology, including autism (*The Empty Fortress*, 1967), parenting (*A Good Enough Parent*, 1987), fairy tales (*The Uses of Enchantment*, 1976), and survival in concentration camps (*The Informed Heart*, 1960).

Disabled by a stroke in 1987 and despondent over the death of his wife a few years earlier, Bettelheim found the last years of his life increasingly unpleasant, and in March 1990 he committed suicide by asphyxiation, leaving behind a legacy both remarkable and controversial.

basic skills. This approach generally integrates educational strategies with behavior modification techniques like shaping, positive reinforcement, and modeling. Special education for the LD child requires careful assessment of the child's abilities and individualized training that capitalizes on the child's strengths to maximize learning (Lyon & Moats, 1988; D. D. Smith & S. Robinson, 1986).

SUMMARY

11-1 The anxiety disorders of childhood include separation anxiety and over-anxious, avoidant, and phobia disorders. Their diverse causes include hereditary predispositions, temperament, emotional conflicts, learning processes, and family distress. Drug therapy has limited success in these disorders, and psychological and behavioral treatments are the preferred approaches.

11-2 Disruptive behavior disorders involve disruptive social activity. Attention deficit hyperactivity disorder is defined by inattention impulsiveness, and hyperactivity and is associated with social and academic adjustment problems. There is no single cause for ADHD, but genetic factors, brain disturbances, and disruptions in family behavior all contribute. Treatment for ADHD involves stimulant drugs and behavior modification. Conduct disorders are aggressive, antisocial, and disruptive behaviors that are related to juvenile delinquency. Aggressive antisocial behaviors are influenced by heredity, hormonal factors, family aggression, and the sociocultural environment. Social learning therapy and juvenile diversion programs have some beneficial effects on conduct-disordered and delinquent youths.

11-3 Mental retardation (MR) is characterized by significantly subaverage intelligence and inadequate adaptive behavior. MR occurs in mild, moderate, severe, and profound levels. Organic retardation has biological causes, including chromosomal, genetic, and prenatal problems. Cultural-familial retardation is mainly due to psychosocial deprivation. Educational programs, behavior modification, and early intervention are all used to treat retarded people. Autistic disorder involves severe deficits in social interaction, language, and behavior. Psychological factors have little role in autism, but biological causes, such as heredity, brain damage, and brain dysfunctions, abound. Most treatments have limited success with autism, though drugs and behavior modification have been helpful in some cases. Specific developmental disorders and learning disabilities (LDs) involve deficits in skills for reading, language, and speech. These problems are based on neurological factors and delayed development. Educational remediation is the main treatment for learning-disabled children.

TERMS TO REMEMBER

attention deficit hyperactivity
   disorder (p. 282)
autistic disorder (p. 294)
avoidant disorder (p. 279)
coercion hypothesis (p. 288)
conduct disorder (p. 285)
cultural-familial retardation (p. 292)

developmental disorders (p. 289)
developmental lag hypothesis
   (p. 299)
disruptive behavior disorders
   (p. 282)
Down syndrome (p. 291)
educational remediation (p. 299)

fragile X syndrome (p. 296)
juvenile delinquency (p. 286)
juvenile diversion programs
   (p. 289)
mainstreaming (p. 292)
mental retardation (p. 289)
minimal brain dysfunction (p. 284)
oppositional defiant disorder
   (p. 287)

organic retardation (p. 291)
overanxious disorder (p. 279)
pervasive developmental disorder
   (p. 294)
school phobia (p. 280)
segregation (p. 292)
separation anxiety disorder (p. 278)
specific developmental disorder
   (p. 298)

SUGGESTED READINGS

Kazdin, A. E. (1987). *Conduct disorders in childhood and adolescence.* Newbury Park, CA: Sage.

Klein, R. G., & Last, C. G. (1989). *Anxiety disorders in children.* Newbury Park, CA: Sage.

Matson, J. L., & Mulick, J. A. (eds.) (1991). *Handbook of mental retardation* (2nd ed.). New York: Pergamon.

Treffert, D. A. (1989). *Extraordinary people: Understanding savant syndrome.* New York: Ballantine.

Wenar, C. (1990). *Developmental psychopathology: From infancy through adolescence.* New York: McGraw-Hill.

LEGAL AND ETHICAL ISSUES:
MENTAL HEALTH SERVICES FOR CHILDREN

Children have been a neglected group as far as mental health services are concerned. Of the approximately 63 million children under age 18 in the United States, 15 to 19 percent have mental health problems. In addition to the 6 to 8 million children with mental disorders, millions more are at risk for psychological and developmental disorders. Among these at-risk children are 14 million who live in poverty, 7 million who have alcoholic parents, and 1 million who are neglected and abused (Dougherty, 1988).

Between 20 and 30 percent of children with mental health problems receive some formal treatment; the majority do not. The availability of mental health services for children does not come close to meeting the need. In 1989 only 30 publicly funded state and county mental hospitals in the United States had separate units for children. Per capita spending by the states for treatment of mentally disturbed children is one-fifth of the amount allocated for disturbed adults. In addition to the lack of funding, there is a lack of mental health providers for children. Relatively few psychologists (1 percent) and psychiatrists (10 percent) are trained as specialists in childhood disorders (Tuma, 1989).

Recent attempts have been made to fill the gap between needs and services. In 1984 the Federal Child and Adolescent Service Program authorized funds for the states to develop more integrated mental health programs for children. The 1986 Amendment to the Education of the Handicapped Act authorized services for preschoolers who are at risk for developmental delays in cognitive, language, or psychosocial skills (Gallagher, 1989).

A promising intervention that emerged from this legislation is "home visiting" as a family support service for at-risk children, especially for children in impoverished and single-parent families. Home visitors provide counseling, problem solving, and casework services, and to date over 4000 of these programs have been implemented (R. N. Roberts, Wasik, Costo, & Ramey, 1991).

Despite recent strides in upgrading the delivery of mental health services for children, much improvement is needed. Although the effectiveness of various therapies for children has been demonstrated, too few children have access to such treatment, and thus, their long-term development is compromised (Saxe, Cross, & Silverman, 1988).

Chapter TWELVE

Eating and Impulse Control Disorders

OBJECTIVES

1. Describe the symptoms of anorexia nervosa and bulimia nervosa.
2. Define obesity and explain why it might be considered an eating disorder.
3. Discuss the hereditary and neurochemical bases of eating disorders.
4. Explain four psychosocial theories about eating disorders.
5. Outline medical and psychological treatment strategies for eating disorders.
6. Describe the nature of impulse control disorders.
7. Detail the main symptoms of kleptomania, pathological gambling, pyromania, and trichotillomania.
8. Explain the causes of impulse control disorders.
9. Differentiate among the treatment approaches for impulse control disorders.

S tephanie awakens and plans her breakfast, but before she eats, she decides to exercise. Although she is already thinner than she should be, she thinks she is too fat and doesn't like herself because of it.

After exercising, Stephanie plans her busy college day, and as the tension starts to build, she is getting the urge to eat. She quickly gobbles down a pound of bacon and three eggs with five pieces of toast, a quart of orange juice, and some coffee. Then she walks to the bakery, buys and devours six doughnuts and four brownies, and caps off her eating binge with several soft drinks and two candy bars. Throughout the binge Stephanie tells herself that she should stop, but she just can't control herself.

Bloated and nauseated, Stephanie thinks how much she hates herself, and when she gets back home, she forces herself to vomit by sticking her fingers down her throat. She is constantly preoccupied with her shape, but she is not able to resist the eating binges. Stephanie has gone through a similar routine almost every day for the last several weeks, but she has also gone through periods of fasting and significant weight loss (Norman, 1988).

As odd as Stephanie's behavior may appear, such behavior is not unusual in people suffering from eating disorders. In this chapter we try to understand the nature of eating disorders and see what can be done to treat them.

12-1 ■ EATING DISORDERS

eating disorders Gross disturbances in eating behavior.

Eating disorders are characterized by gross disturbances in eating behavior. In the DSM-III-R, eating disorders are classified along with *disorders first evident in infancy, childhood, or adolescence* because their onset is usually during those ages (American Psychiatric Association, 1987). However, eating disorders often persist well into adulthood. The study of eating disorders, including anorexia nervosa, bulimia nervosa, and obesity, has become an independent specialty area.

Anorexia Nervosa

anorexia nervosa Refusal to maintain normal body weight.

Anorexia means a loss of appetite, but complete loss of appetite is uncommon in anorexia nervosa. Instead, **anorexia nervosa** consists of a refusal to maintain a normal body weight, fear of becoming fat, distorted body image, and amenorrhea (cessation of menstruation) in females (American Psychiatric Association, 1987).

Symptoms of Anorexia Nervosa. Individuals with anorexia nervosa refuse to maintain normal body weight and are at least 15 percent below what is considered normal weight for their height and age. They fear becoming fat and are preoccupied with being thin even though they are already underweight. Anorexic individuals also exhibit a distorted body image. Although they may be emaciated, they overestimate their body size, feel fat, or think that some part of their body is fat. However, distorted body image is not unique to anorexia nervosa. Many adolescent girls of normal weight and people with other eating disorders also report feeling fat (Horne, VanVactor, & Emerson, 1991; Hsu, 1982; Penner, L. Thompson, & Coovert, 1991).

Anorexic individuals go to great lengths to lose weight. They avoid high-calorie foods, become exercise fanatics, and compulsively engage in all sorts of aerobic activities, including jogging, cycling, and dancing. They are also ob-

Anorexia nervosa can result in life-threatening complications. Anorexics refuse to maintain a normal body weight and believe they are fat when they are not. Many become emaciated, like the young woman at right. Some—such as the singer Karen Carpenter, above—even die as a result of this eating disorder.

bulimarexia (boo-leem-uh-*reck*-see-uh) Binge-purge symptoms in anorexia.

sessed with food and its preparation (Norman, 1988). An anorexic person may go to great lengths to prepare an elaborate feast for guests, then not eat any of it. Anorexics often hoard and hide food in secret places in order to conceal their behavior.

An intriguing twist in the clinical picture of anorexic individuals is that 30 to 50 percent go through periods of fasting followed by binges on high-calorie junk foods (Russell, 1979). Binges end with self-induced vomiting or the taking of laxatives or diet pills to lose weight. This binge-purge eating pattern is called **bulimarexia**. Binge-purge symptoms usually begin within a year and a half of the onset of anorexia (Kassett, Gwirtsman, Kaye, Brandt, & Jimerson, 1988).

It is estimated that anorexia nervosa affects nearly 1 percent of the population (Mitchell & Eckert, 1987; Norman, 1988). Ninety-five percent of anorexics are female (American Psychiatric Association, 1987). Most victims are young women between the ages of 12 and 18, but some women are first affected in their early thirties.

Fasting, binge eating, and purging create a host of potentially serious physical problems, such as anemia, dehydration, and heart failure. Mortality rates in anorexia nervosa are between 5 and 18 percent (American Psychiatric Association, 1987; Andreasen & Black, 1991). Individuals with anorexia nervosa also have an increased risk of mood and anxiety disorders and alcoholism (Halmi et al., 1991).

Bulimia Nervosa

Newsweek magazine declared 1981 as the year of the binge-purge syndrome, underscoring the widely held belief that bulimia nervosa is a modern disorder (*Newsweek,* January 4, 1981, p. 26). Although scattered accounts of the condition date back more than 250 years, it was not until the 1980s that bulimia nervosa was classified as a distinct disorder rather than a variant of anorexia nervosa or obesity.

Symptoms of Bulimia Nervosa. The word *bulimia* means "great hunger." It was derived from two Greek words, *bous* ("head of cattle") and *limos* ("hunger"). Of course, bulimic individuals do not eat entire cows. **Bulimia nervosa** is characterized by binge eating, lack of control over eating, purging, and concern about body shape, usually in individuals of normal weight (American Psychiatric Association, 1987).

bulimia nervosa Binge eating and purging.

Bulimic people go through recurrent episodes of *binge eating* during which they eat large quantities of high-calorie junk foods in a short time. During binges, bulimics can consume many times the normal amount of food, quitting when they suffer abdominal pain or vomiting or when they fall asleep. After a binge the bulimic usually feels guilty, self-critical, and depressed. A common confession is, "I hate myself after I do it, but I do it anyway" (American Psychiatric Association, 1987).

Some experts consider the loss of control over eating to be the primary feature of bulimia nervosa. Bulimic individuals cannot resist an eating binge. After a binge, bulimics experience a powerful desire to purge themselves of the food and do so by vomiting, spitting out food, or taking enemas, laxatives, or diuretics (American Psychiatric Association, 1987; Norman, 1988; Walsh, Kisseleff, Cassidy, & Dantzic, 1989). Table 12-1 lists the purging methods used by a sample of 275 bulimics (Mitchell, Hatsukami, Eckert, & Pyle, 1985). Binge eating and purging lead to serious medical complications, including cardiac abnormalities, hair loss, dental erosion, throat damage, and numerous metabolic disturbances (Devlin et al., 1990; Fava, Copeland, Schweiger, & Herzog, 1989; Halmi, 1985).

It is clear that Stephanie had many of the features found in anorexia nervosa and bulimia nervosa. Her fasting, preoccupation with thinness, and distorted body image are indicative of anorexia nervosa. Her binges and purging indicate that she had the bulimarexia type of anorexia nervosa (Norman, 1988).

TABLE 12-1 ▦ PURGING METHODS USED BY 275 BULIMIC PATIENTS

Purging Method	Number of Subjects	Percentage
Vomiting	238	88.1
Spitting out food	177	64.5
Laxatives	163	60.6
Diet pills	134	50.2
Diuretics	90	33.9

Source: From "Characteristics of 275 Patients with Bulimia" by J. E. Mitchell, D. Hatsukami, E. D. Eckert, and R. L. Pyle, 1985, *American Journal of Psychiatry, 142,* pp. 482–485.

Bulimics can consume large quantities of high-calorie junk foods during a binge. Afterward they feel guilty and purge the food they have eaten.

Bulimia nervosa usually begins in adolescence or early adulthood. It has a chronic course and is associated with increased risk of substance abuse and depression (Bulik, 1987; Hing & Williamson, 1987; A. B. Levy, Dixon, & Stern, 1989; Schleisser-Carter, S. A. Hamilton, O'Neill, Lydiard, & Malcolm, 1989; Swift, Andrews, & Barklage, 1986). Typically, binges are followed by periods of normal eating, then a return to binge eating. Many bulimic women find that their symptoms worsen premenstrually (Gladis & Walsh, 1987). The onset of the symptoms often follows an important life change, such as leaving home, starting a new job or school, or a change in a romantic relationship. For example, a 21-year-old woman began binge eating and vomiting after her fiancé broke off their engagement five days before the wedding.

The prevalence of bulimia nervosa varies with age and gender. It affects nearly 5 percent of women in their late teens and early twenties and 1 percent of all adolescent girls and young adult women. In contrast, bulimia affects less than 0.5 percent of the male population (Fairburn, Phil, & Beglin, 1990; King, 1986, 1989; Mitchell & Eckert, 1987). Males usually have a later age of onset and a history of obesity, and they are more likely than female bulimics to be homosexual or asexual (Carlat & Camargo, 1991). Bulimia nervosa is more common in whites, but its prevalence is increasing in minority populations (Hsu, 1987; Mumford & Whitehouse, 1988; Nasser, 1986).

Obesity

obesity Body weight more than 20 percent above normal for height and age.

Obesity is a condition of excess of body fat. It is usually defined as body weight exceeding the recommended upper limit for height and age by 20 percent or more. Unfortunately, this method of defining obesity makes prevalence estimates difficult since height-weight standards come from life insurance charts, which may not represent the general population. Depending on how obesity is determined, 15 to 50 percent of the American population is considered obese (Bray, 1986; Norman, 1988).

Obesity is not classified as an eating disorder in the DSM-III-R because it is not associated with *distinctive* psychological or behavioral characteristics (American Psychiatric Association, 1987). However, researchers are beginning to identify specific characteristics of obese people. A multisite study of nearly 2000 individuals seeking treatment indicates that 46 percent of obese people binge-eat without the purging seen in bulimia and bulimarexia. In addition, obese bingers have high rates of depression, substance abuse, anxiety, and somatization (Youngstrom, 1991).

Obesity is a serious health problem. It increases the risk of cardiovascular disease; diabetes; respiratory problems; digestive, joint, bone, and kidney abnormalities; and mortality, especially in men. Obese individuals are also socially, occupationally, and educationally disadvantaged. They are socially stigmatized and discriminated against in forming interpersonal relationships because they are often viewed by others as unattractive, lazy, and responsible for their condition (Bray, 1986; Foreyt, 1987).

12-2 CAUSES OF EATING DISORDERS

Eating disorders arise from a complex interplay of hereditary, physiological, psychological, and sociocultural factors. In this section we explore some of the more important causal explanations for these conditions.

Biological Causes of Eating Disorders

Factors known or suspected to cause eating disorders include heredity and neurotransmitter activity. Moreover, eating disorders persist partly because of the metabolic consequences of fasting, binge eating, purging, and dieting.

Hereditary Causes of Eating Disorders. Research suggests a hereditary basis for anorexia nervosa and bulimia nervosa (Andreasen & Black, 1991). Some studies demonstrate an increased risk of anorexia nervosa in family members of anorexics, and a greater risk of bulimia in families of bulimics, when compared to the general population. For example, 6 to 10 percent of the first-degree female relatives of anorexics are also anorexic (Kassett et al., 1989). Twin studies also suggest a hereditary basis for anorexia nervosa and bulimia nervosa. Monozygotic twins have higher concordance rates for these disorders than dizygotic twins (Crisp, A. Hall, & Holland, 1985; Holland, A. Hall, R. Murray, Russell, & Crisp, 1984; Kendler et al., 1991).

There is considerable evidence for a hereditary predisposition to obesity. In a study of more than 4000 twins, concordance rates for obesity were twice as high for monozygotic twins as for dizygotic twins (Stunkard, Foch, & Hrubek, 1986). In another study comparing children reared in adoptive families, the best predictor of obesity in adoptees was obesity in the biological parents. This study found an especially strong correlation between obesity in mothers and obesity in their adult offspring (Price, Cadoret, Stunkard, & Croughton, 1987).

Other studies have tried to uncover a hereditary basis for obesity by looking at similarities in weight change in twins who are overfed. In one study, twins were overfed for 84 days while changes in body weight, body fat, and fat mass were measured. "Co-twins" were more similar in these measures of obesity than twins from different pairs, suggesting that genetic mechanisms may regulate the tendency to store energy as fat or lean tissue (C. Bouchard et al., 1990). Finally, there is evidence that metabolism (the rate at which the body burns calories) is governed by hereditary factors (S. B. Roberts, Savage, Coward, Chew, & Lucas, 1988).

In conclusion, heredity seems to play a role in the development and maintenance of eating disorders by conferring a predisposition to excess weight and anorexia and bulimia nervosa.

Neurochemical Causes of Eating Disorders. Hereditary predispositions to eating disorders may be expressed in physiological processes. Several neurotransmitters and other body chemicals are known to regulate eating behavior in animals and are suspected to play similar roles in humans. Thus far, the role of these chemicals has not been ascertained, because of difficulties in taking direct measurements in humans. Also, weight loss and weight gain produce metabolic changes that confound our ability to determine cause-and-effect relationships between these events (Fava et al., 1989).

Norepinephrine and dopamine stimulate eating, and serotonin inhibits eating by activating hypothalamic neurons (see Figure 12-1). Lower-than-average norepinephrine levels in anorexic individuals may partially explain why they do not maintain normal body weight. Some studies show that bulimics have lower-than-average serotonin levels, which may account for their inability to control appetite during a binge. However, research on the role of dopamine in anorexia nervosa and bulimia nervosa has yielded inconsistent findings (A. S. Kaplan & Woodside, 1987).

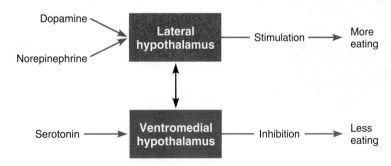

Figure 12-1 Hypothalamic regions control eating in animals. Stimulation of the lateral hypothalamus facilitates eating, and activation of the ventromedial hypothalamus inhibits eating.

Impairment in neurotransmitter regulation is also suspected in obesity. Further evidence for the causal role of specific neurotransmitters in eating disorders comes from drug treatment studies. Antidepressant drugs known to influence neurotransmitter levels have been shown to reduce binge-purge behavior in bulimic individuals (Hughs, Wells, & Cunningham, 1985; H. G. Pope, Hudson, & Jonas, 1983).

energy balance   The ratio of calories consumed to calories burned.

Metabolic Causes of Eating Disorders. Body weight depends on **energy balance**, the ratio of calories consumed to calories burned. A *positive energy balance* means you consume more calories than you burn, and a *negative energy balance* means you expend more calories than you consume. Caloric intake depends exclusively on food consumption, and energy expenditure depends largely on metabolism and physical activity.

Most individuals attempt to lose weight primarily through dieting, but ironically, dieting contributes to obesity by lowering metabolism. When challenged by reduced food intake, your body tries to conserve energy by burning calories more efficiently, thereby making weight loss more difficult. Food deprivation also increases craving for high-calorie foods and increases the likelihood of a food binge and weight gain. Such effects are more pronounced in women because they typically have lower metabolic rates than men. With each successive attempt to diet, metabolic efficiency increases, making weight loss more and more difficult.

Reduced metabolic rate is a causal factor not only in obesity but in bulimia nervosa as well. It has been hypothesized that bulimic individuals gain weight easily. Binge eating, purging, and exercising all increase the bulimic's metabolic rate and may thereby provide a means of keeping weight down (Striegel-Moore, Silberstein, & Rodin, 1986).

Lowered metabolism during food restriction probably provided a survival advantage for early humans during times of food scarcity. Unfortunately, lowered metabolism works to the disadvantage of many modern people not faced with famine (Altemus et al., 1991; Brownell, Greenwood, Stellar, & Shrager, 1986; Obarzanek, Lessem, D. S. Goldstein, & Jimerson, 1991;).

set-point model   The idea that control mechanisms maintain body weight within a limited range.

Another way of conceptualizing the role of metabolic factors in eating disorders, especially obesity, is the **set-point model**, which proposes that control mechanisms, located in the lateral hypothalamus of the brain, strive to maintain body weight within a limited range (Keesey, 1986) (see Figure 12-1). The model is based on observations that changes in the amount or type of food consumed do not fully account for changes in body weight. For example, laboratory rats do not lose as much weight as expected when their food intake is restricted, nor do they gain as much as expected when more food is available. Humans show similar effects, suggesting that body weight is under the control of genetically determined physiological variables that govern how food is metabolized.

When a person is dieting, set-point mechanisms are triggered to reduce calorie expenditure, making further weight loss more difficult. This could explain why many dieters find it harder to lose weight the longer they diet, and why the lost weight is often regained. Moreover, when we overeat, we burn calories more easily. This may explain why most overweight individuals do not gain weight indefinitely.

Psychosocial Causes of Eating Disorders

For many years, psychological and social factors have been proposed as causes of eating disorders. Recent research has tried to confirm these hypotheses, with mixed success. Most of the research has focused on personality, family, cognitive, and sociocultural variables.

Personality Factors. Classical psychoanalysts once proposed that anorexia nervosa was an attempt to avoid oral impregnation, with food refusal symbolically allowing the person to subdue sexual tensions during puberty. On the basis of case studies, various psychoanalytic theories have described the obese person as passive-dependent, emotionally frustrated, and love-starved. According to these views, food serves to fulfill the need for love and to reduce feelings of anxiety and depression.

Scientific attempts to explain obesity have focused on personality trait differences between obese and normal-weight individuals, but large-scale studies with adults and children have not been able to uncover such differences. Apparently there is no distinct *obese personality*, nor are there any traits that consistently correlate with obesity.

In the 1970s, psychologist Stanley Schachter showed that obese individuals are unable to distinguish among internal sensations and often mistake arousal states, such as anxiety, for hunger. Schachter's **internality-externality hypothesis** states that normal-weight individuals are influenced more by internal hunger cues, whereas obese individuals are motivated to eat in response to external stimuli. Compared to nonobese people, obese individuals are *stimulus-bound* and *reactive*. Schachter showed that obese people ate more food when the food tasted better, looked more attractive, or was easier to consume. For example, an obese person will eat more peanuts when they are already shelled and will eat less Chinese food if he or she has chopsticks (Schachter, L. Friedman, & Handler, 1974; Schachter & Rodin, 1974; Striegel-Moore & Rodin, 1986).

Subsequent research has failed to consistently confirm Schachter's hypothesis. Obese people are not necessarily any more stimulus-bound and reactive than people of normal weight. Responsiveness to external stimuli can be identified at birth and probably interacts with many other factors to produce obesity in some people (Striegel-Moore & Rodin, 1986).

internality-externality hypothesis The idea that normal-weight individuals are influenced by internal cues, obese individuals by external cues.

Psychologist Stanley Schachter hypothesizes that obese individuals are influenced to eat more by the attractiveness of food than by internal hunger cues.

Family Factors. Psychiatrist Hilde Bruch disagreed with sexual interpretations of anorexia nervosa. She proposed that the condition was primarily related to developmental problems. Bruch held that anorexics have *autonomy disturbances* due to being raised by overprotective and intrusive parents. The anorexic girl struggles for control, identity, competence, and effectiveness, but she fails. The consequences are distortions of body image, failure to recognize internal hunger cues, and, most important, a paralyzing sense of ineffectiveness (1986, 1982, 1973). More recent studies indicate that anorexics who restrict food intake have more significant autonomy disturbances than bulimarexics (Strauss & Ryan, 1987).

In some ways Stephanie admired her mother, but she also hated her because she felt her mother never allowed her to grow up, to be independent, or to experiment with life. Paradoxically, for Stephanie, being independent also meant being isolated, so she always gave in to her mother's desire for her to be well-behaved and studious. Her refusal to maintain her weight was a rebellion against her parent's control (Norman, 1988).

Family systems theories view anorexia nervosa as a product of enmeshed, overprotective, and rigid families. These families resolve problems poorly and the parents often involve the child in their conflicts (Andreasen & Black, 1991). Families of bulimic individuals exhibit some of these features, and the parents also expect perfection in their children (Minuchin, Rosman, & L. Baker, 1978). In support of this idea, one study found that mothers of bulimic daughters reported dissatisfaction with overall family functioning and also thought their daughters were unattractive and should lose more weight (Pike & Rodin, 1991).

Cathy Rigby was a famous American gymnast who was expected to win the gold medal in the 1972 Olympics. When she finished tenth, she believed she had failed everyone. She had been a sickly child and was overprotected by her alcoholic father, by her mother, and later by her overbearing gymnastics coach. She did not go to her high school prom because she was totally absorbed in gymnastics and perfection.

Cathy thought she should be thin, and when her weight rose from 95 to 105 pounds at age 16, she felt that her "identity was threatened." She began purging, and her weight plummeted to 79 pounds. She was hospitalized twice and nearly died from an electrolyte imbalance. Years later, she had to take fertility pills in order to get pregnant because her physiology had been so harmed by her bout with this eating disorder.

Cathy Rigby eventually recovered from her anorexic and bulimic symptoms and developed a new career on the stage. Today she is married and has two daughters (M. Goodman & Kahn, 1991).

Cognitive Factors. Cognitive factors also play a role in eating disorders. Anorexic and bulimic individuals exhibit cognitive distortions like those seen in depressed people. Their attitudes about themselves and their body shape strongly influence their eating behavior. The typical young woman affected by one of these disorders might say, "I'm not thin, therefore I must be fat," or "To be thin is to be successful, attractive, and happy" (Agras & Kirkley, 1986; Fairburn, Z. Cooper, & P. J. Cooper, 1986; Fernandez, 1984; Powers, Schulman, Gleghorn, & Prange, 1987).

Olympic gymnast Cathy Rigby nearly died as a consequence of anorexia and bulimia. Her perfectionism and her overprotective family may have set the stage for her problems.

We have seen that dieting can contribute to weight gain by lowering metabolism and increasing the risk of binge eating. Although dietary restraint may work for some people, it can lead to overeating in others. Disinhibited eating, or loss of control over eating, is especially common in response to anxiety, depression, alcohol consumption, or breaking a diet (Herman & Polivy, 1975; Ruderman, 1985, 1986). It is quite problematic for obese and bulimic individuals with low self-esteem. Once a diet is broken, cognitive factors often take over, and the person may say "What's the use? I broke my diet. I failed, so I might as well go all the way."

escape theory The idea that disinhibited eating provides an escape from self-awareness.

In an attempt to integrate data on binge eaters, researchers have advanced the **escape theory,** which proposes that disinhibited eating provides dieters and bulimics with an escape from unpleasant feelings engendered by their awareness of not meeting the high standards and expectations of others (Heatherton, 1991). Such individuals are able to avoid these feelings by distracting themselves from unpleasant states of self-awareness. Paradoxically, narrowing of attention has the self-defeating effect of triggering more of the binge episodes that created the problem in the first place. In the long run, periods of overeating negate the weight loss effects of dieting (Heatherton, Polivy, & Herman, 1991; Kirschenbaum & Dykman, 1991; Polivy, Heatherton, & Herman, 1988; Striegel-Moore & Rodin, 1986; Wardle & Beales, 1988).

PROFILE
Hilde Bruch
(1904–1984)

Hilde Bruch was one of the most prominent figures in the study and treatment of eating disorders because she recognized the role of emotional factors in these disorders. Researcher Albert Stunkard said that "she created the field" of eating disorders. Bruch was born in Germany, and she received her medical degree from the University of Freiburg in 1929. She left Germany in 1933, after Hitler rose to power. Bruch practiced pediatrics in London for a year, then came to the United States, where she received an appointment at the Babies' Hospital of Columbia University, College of Physicians and Surgeons (Lidz, 1985; Stunkard, 1986).

Bruch's initial claim to fame came in 1939, when she disputed the prevailing view of *Froehlich's syndrome,* a condition in boys that was believed to be caused by some unknown pituitary abnormality. These children were sluggish and obese and had small genitals. Bruch cogently demonstrated that the boys were fat because they ate too much and that their genitals appeared small only because they were obscured by folds of fat. Shortly thereafter, Bruch argued that children became obese because their mothers did not want them and used food as a substitute for parental love (Lidz, 1985).

After receiving psychiatric and psychoanalytic training, Bruch moved to Houston and became professor of psychiatry at Baylor University. In striking contrast to her usual modest style, she went to Houston in a Rolls Royce because she refused to "kowtow to Texas Cadillacs." In Texas, she developed a great reputation as an authority on anorexia nervosa, and she received patients and letters requesting expert advice from all over the world (Lidz, 1985).

Bruch was a skilled lecturer and psychiatrist, but she was not well liked by everyone. She was a "searcher of the truth": she refused to conform to generally accepted principles of psychiatry if they did not conform to her own clinical experience (Lidz, 1985).

Hilde Bruch authored more than 200 publications, including 7 books. Her most famous are *Don't Be Afraid of Your Child, The Importance of Overweight, The Golden Cage,* and *Eating Disorders: Obesity, Anorexia Nervosa, and the Person Within.* She also received many awards and honors, including the prestigious Joseph B. Goldberger Award in Clinical Nutrition in 1981, which had never before been given to a psychiatrist (Lidz, 1985).

Sociocultural Factors. In American culture, a preference for thinness, especially in women, molds individuals' attitudes about body shape. The sociocultural point of view holds that eating disorders are caused by an abnormal, culturally determined desire for thinness. We need only look at the figures of fashion models to understand the implicit pressures for women to be thin. The

The preference for thinness in American culture, as exemplified by fashion models, can create implicit pressure on women to strive to be thin.

desire to be thin leads to dietary restraint, food deprivation, fasting, and possibly binge eating. In women whose body weight tends to be above average, the guilt, shame, and anxiety of such "imperfection" may provoke overeating and weight gain and thereby maintain the problem (Agras & Kirkley, 1986).

12-3 ▨ TREATMENT OF EATING DISORDERS

The main goals in the treatment of eating disorders are the restoration of good health and the development of healthier eating habits. Toward these ends, medical treatment, psychotherapy, behavior therapy, and family therapy are employed. In cases of obesity, exercise and proper dieting are emphasized (Andreasen & Black, 1991; Norman, 1988).

▨ Medical Treatment

Individuals with eating disorders often suffer serious medical complications. This is especially true of many anorexic patients, who are emaciated and in overall poor health. In treating these individuals, the primary goals are to encourage a slow, steady weight gain and to establish normal eating habits. If the

CLOSE-UP
Obesity and Socioeconomic Status

The possibility that body weight and socioeconomic status (SES) are related was suggested more than a century ago. Many studies since the 1950s have confirmed the relationship, and differences between developed and developing societies have been discovered. SES is usually defined on the basis of income or educational level. Developed societies are identified on the basis of their level of modernization, and developing societies are defined as non-Western, traditional, and agricultural.

In developed societies, obesity is six times more common in women of lower SES, and in general, higher SES is associated with thinness. The inverse relationship between SES and obesity is remarkably constant across the United States and European countries, but it is not as strong for men or for children of either sex. In developed societies, obesity is more common among people of "manual-class" homes than in "nonmanual-class" homes, and it is apparent by age 23.

For men, women, boys, and girls in developing societies, the relationship between obesity and SES is strong but in the opposite direction. For example, in developing countries in Africa, Asia, and North and South America, *higher* SES is associated with being overweight.

Although these relationships between obesity and SES are impressive, such correlations do not tell us about cause and effect. However, we can speculate about causal factors. In developing societies, the low rate of obesity in people of lower SES may be due to scarcity of food and the possibility these people are likely to expend more energy through physical labor. Obesity in people of higher SES may be due to their greater social influence, greater access to food, and cultural values favoring fatter bodies. In many cultures, fatness is a symbol of social prestige and sexual attractiveness. For example, in Nigeria, daughters of the rich are sent to "fattening huts" before they are married.

In developed societies obesity is unacceptable, especially for women, in whom being thin is related to higher self-esteem. Women of higher SES diet more often than women of lower SES. Moreover, higher-status women may know more about the benefits of exercise, and they can better afford to join expensive health clubs. Clearly, SES is a factor that must be seriously considered in understanding obesity (Sobal & Stunkard, 1989).

patient weighs less than 70 percent of the ideal for age and height, these goals are best realized through hospitalization. During the hospital stay, tube-feeding may be necessary if the patient does not gain weight by conforming to the treatment program. Individuals with bulimia nervosa may also require hospitalization because of the medical consequences of binge eating and purging (Andreasen & Black, 1991; Hsu, 1986; Norman, 1988).

Stephanie was hospitalized after losing 25 percent of her ideal body weight. She refused to conform to the treatment program and lost 5 more pounds within two weeks. On several occasions, she vomited after eating. Stephanie began to gain weight when she realized that she would not be released from the hospital unless she regained a healthy body weight. The prospect of having to be tube-fed also increased her motivation to conform to the program (Norman, 1988).

Antipsychotic and antidepressant drugs and lithium have been used successfully for brief periods in the treatment of anorexia nervosa, but their long-term usefulness has not been established. Approximately 50 percent of anorexics relapse after hospital treatment, and there is no compelling evidence that any therapy is particularly effective in preventing relapse (Andreasen & Black, 1991; Hsu, 1986; Norman, 1988). Since bulimia nervosa often coexists with depression, antidepressants, particularly monoamine oxidase inhibitors, can be helpful in minimizing bulimic symptoms as well as the symptoms of depression (Walsh et al., 1988).

Surgical procedures like *intestinal bypass surgery* and *stomach stapling* are helpful for massively obese individuals who do not respond to conservative weight management techniques. These techniques minimize the absorption of food and may also alter set-point. Appetite suppressants, such as amphetamines, are widely used but are not recommended for the treatment of obesity because of the risk of abuse and the tolerance that develops (Norman, 1988).

Psychotherapy

Many forms of psychotherapy have been used in the treatment of eating disorders. Although psychoanalysis has not proved effective, psychodynamically oriented approaches that focus on underlying conflicts and moods have been generally successful. For example, anorexic patients tend to deny their illness and are generally uncooperative. Therefore, the therapist begins by explaining that the person's abnormal eating behavior and body weight are a cover-up for underlying problems and self-doubt. The patient is encouraged to express feelings about the need to be perfect and about ineffectiveness. As these issues are worked through, a new personality emerges (Bruch, 1962, 1973, 1977, 1982, 1986; Hsu, 1986).

Cognitive therapy has been widely used in the treatment of eating disorders. For example, cognitive therapy helps bulimics correct dysfunctional attitudes about being perfect and needing approval from others (Wilson, 1986). One study compared cognitive therapy, behavior therapy, and interpersonal therapy in the treatment of bulimia nervosa (Fairburn et al., 1991). All three approaches were effective in reducing the frequency of overeating and general psychiatric disturbance. However, cognitive therapy was more effective than the other two treatments in changing disturbed attitudes about shape and body weight. Other research shows that psychotherapy combined with the use of antidepressants reduces bulimic symptoms (Craighead & Agras, 1991; Mitchell et al., 1990).

Cognitive therapy also helps obese individuals modify dysfunctional attitudes by helping them set realistic goals, cope with mistakes, and increase motivation. Restructured attitudes facilitate adherence to lifestyle change, exercise, and proper nutrition and help in improving relationships (Andreasen & Black, 1991; Norman, 1988).

Behavior Therapy

Behavior therapy has become an important component of treatment programs for eating disorders. In applying behavior therapy techniques, the therapist directly addresses the maladaptive behaviors of individuals with eating disorders through reinforcement. For example, nearly 80 percent of anorexic patients improve when hospital staff positively reinforces weight gain by allowing increased physical and social activity and more visits from family and friends. Bed rest and bedroom isolation are used to discourage noncompliant behavior. It is important that weight gain happen slowly so the patient does not feel a loss of control and autonomy (Hsu, 1986).

Behavior therapy is also an important facet of weight control programs for obese individuals, especially those who have a hard time with exercise and diet routines. The obese individual is taught to monitor and modify eating patterns, to control stimuli that trigger eating, and to increase physical activity. The person learns to eat slowly, to prepare meals, and to substitute alternative activities for eating. By learning to control the factors that contribute to overweight, the person gains motivation (Brownell & Wadden, 1986; Kirschenbaum, 1988).

A good comprehensive behavioral treatment for weight control is the *LEARN program* designed by psychologist Kelly Brownell (1987). Each letter of *LEARN* stands for one aspect of the program—*l*ifestyle, *e*xercise, *a*ttitudes, *r*elationships, and *n*utrition—reflecting the multidimensional nature of obesity and weight management. The individual is educated as to how to achieve goals for each aspect of LEARN. Table 12-2 describes some LEARN techniques.

Family Therapy

The intent of family therapy is to modify the dysfunctional family structures believed to contribute to eating disorders. For example, anorexic individuals often come from families in which the parents are overprotective and intrusive. Research shows that family therapy is especially suited for teenage patients who are not chronically disturbed by other psychiatric problems (Russell, Zmuckler, Dare, & Eisler, 1987).

In family therapy, Stephanie admitted her anger toward her mother, whom she both loved and hated. Although she felt "suffocated" by her mother, Stephanie also felt "empty" when she thought of living on her own. Stephanie improved as she began to accept that her anorexia nervosa represented a pathological attempt to resolve her autonomy conflict.

TABLE 12-2   *LEARN* WEIGHT CONTROL PROGRAM TECHNIQUES

Lifestyle • Prevent automatic eating. • Shop on a full stomach. • Prepare in advance for special events. **Exercise** • Increase lifestyle activities. • Use stairs whenever possible. • Increase walking. **Attitude** • Set realistic goals.	• Outlast urges to eat. • Cope positively with slips and lapses. **Relationships** • Identify and select a weight loss partner. • Exercise with a partner. • Tell your partner how to help. **Nutrition** • Eat a balanced diet. • Make low-calorie foods appetizing. • Be aware of caloric values of foods.

Source: Adapted from *The LEARN Program for Weight Control* by K. D. Brownell, 1987, Philadelphia, University of Pennsylvania School of Medicine.

Stephanie's parents also talked about their marital problems, and in the context of family therapy, they felt supported. They grew to recognize their overinvolvement in Stephanie's life as well, and she began to perceive them as being happier and stronger. Six months after being released from the hospital, Stephanie was still concerned about food and eating but was near her ideal weight (Norman, 1988).

The family structure of individuals with bulimia nervosa is characterized by abnormally close ties, emotional enmeshment, and minimal autonomy for family members. Therefore, family therapy helps the patient separate from the family without losing all connections. This is accomplished by encouraging the person to express needs and feelings as an individual and to relinquish his or her role as the mediator of family conflicts (Wooley & Kearney-Cooke, 1986).

Exercise and Dieting

The treatment of obesity requires changing the person's energy balance to produce weight loss. This is achieved through restriction of caloric intake, initiation of regular exercise, or, preferably, a combination of both. Although most people attempt to lose weight primarily through dieting, abundant evidence indicates that exercise works best.

Individuals who exercise regularly weigh less, have less body fat, have a higher resting metabolic rate, and can eat more without gaining weight than people who do not exercise. Regular exercise can also improve our mood, enhance our self-concept, and aid in keeping weight off. Although any type of exercise is better than none, aerobic exercise such as walking, jogging, cycling, and swimming yields the best weight loss results. Despite the proven positive

People who exercise regularly weigh less, have less body fat, tend to be happier, and have more positive self-images than people who do not exercise.

effects of exercise, 50 percent of individuals who begin an exercise program drop out within six months (Stern & Lowney, 1986).

The numerous weight loss diets make up a multimillion-dollar industry. However, not only are most of the popular diets ineffective in the long term, but many are nutritionally unsound and potentially dangerous because of physiological complications that might result. Diet books and programs overseen by "authorities" are often no better. From a psychological perspective, any restrictive diet increases the risk of binge eating. The best diets are nutritionally sound and set a goal of slow, steady weight loss. Support groups like Weight Watchers and Overeaters Anonymous can help motivate adherence to exercise and proper eating behavior (T. Hall, 1990; Norman, 1988; Stern & Lowney, 1986).

12-4 IMPULSE CONTROL DISORDERS

impulse control disorders Failure to resist impulses, drives, or temptations to perform harmful acts.

Impulse control disorders are characterized by a failure to resist impulses, drives, or temptations to perform an act that is harmful. People with impulse control disorders feel mounting tension before performing the act, intense satisfaction once the act is completed, and guilt and shame afterward. While the person performs the act, it "feels right" (American Psychiatric Association, 1987).

Types of Impulse Control Disorders

We have already discussed substance use disorders, paraphilias, and eating disorders, which are mental disorders characterized by nearly irresistible impulses. Kleptomania, pathological gambling, pyromania, and trichotillomania represent a category of impulse control disorders not otherwise classified (American Psychiatric Association, 1987).

kleptomania Irresistible impulses to steal.

Kleptomania. The main feature of **kleptomania**, a Greek word for "stealing madness," is an irresistible impulse to steal. Unlike drug addicts or individuals with antisocial personalities, kleptomaniacs do not steal for the object's monetary value or for personal use. In most cases, the person has the money to purchase the object, which is often discarded, secretly returned, or given away. In a typical scenario, the person goes shopping and suddenly feels an unpremeditated "pressure" to take an object. These features differentiate kleptomania from ordinary shoplifting. Fewer than 5 percent of apprehended shoplifters are true kleptomaniacs (American Psychiatric Association, 1987; Booth, 1988).

True kleptomania is apparently uncommon, but when it does occur, females are affected more often than males. Although kleptomania is as yet poorly understood, the typical kleptomaniac is a woman in her thirties who had started stealing by age 20. Although she has probably never sought treatment, she suffers from her self-destructive acts with guilt and shame. She may have a history of sexual dysfunction; she is likely to be unhappily married to an emotionally uncaring husband; and she probably experienced an extremely stressful childhood. She has probably been depressed for many years. She probably has a coexisting personality disorder and may experience dissociative states (M. J. Goldman, 1991).

Kleptomania typically coexists with other mental disturbances, especially mood disorders. These observations raise the possibility that kleptomania is an expression of some other psychiatric disturbance. In one study of 20 klepto-maniacs, all had a history of major mood disorders, especially bipolar disorder; 16 had a past diagnosis of anxiety disorders; 12 had eating disorders; and 10 had a history of substance abuse or dependence (McElroy, H. G. Pope, Hudson, Kreck, & White, 1991). Curiously, the onset of a mood disorder preceded the onset of kleptomania by no more than a year, suggesting that these mood prob-lems trigger stealing. Many individuals reported an increased frequency of steal-ing when they were depressed or manic, and they admitted that stealing relieved their distress. Moreover, patients taking lithium or antidepressants reported par-tial or complete elimination of the urge to steal. These findings suggest that kleptomania may actually be a variant of a mood disorder.

pathological gambling
Inability to resist the urge to gamble.

Pathological Gambling. **Pathological gambling** is marked by a chronic inability to resist the urge to gamble, despite the adverse consequences of losing (American Psychiatric Association, 1987). Pathological gamblers are preoccu-pied with gambling, and the problem intensifies under stress. These individuals usually gamble alone and try to conceal their actions from family and friends. Pathological gamblers differ from social gamblers in that the latter gamble mainly for diversion, with friends or at resort casinos, and are willing to lose only a fixed amount of money (Booth, 1988).

The pathological gambler inevitably incurs great debt, borrows money that cannot be paid back, then gambles more. The person may pawn personal items, engage in tax evasion, forge checks, and sometimes embezzle money to feed the problem. The pathological gambler often ends up destitute (Booth, 1988; Norman, 1988).

Pathological gamblers are unable to resist the urge to gamble, despite the adverse consequences of losing. Even at resort casinos they prefer to gamble alone, thus concealing their gambling from friends and relatives.

According to the DSM-III-R, 2 to 3 percent of the adults in the United States are pathological gamblers, a figure that is consistent with more recent estimates from New York, New Jersey, and Maryland. These figures, however, may be gross underestimates, since they are derived primarily from gamblers in self-help groups and inpatient treatment settings. Moreover, data from New York, New Jersey, and Maryland indicate that another 1.5 percent of the population are probable pathological gamblers (American Psychiatric Association, 1987; Volberg & Steadman, 1988, 1989).

pyromania Deliberate fire-setting.

Pyromania. Pyromania involves deliberately setting fires on more than one occasion (American Psychiatric Association, 1987). Pyromaniacs are fascinated by fire, fire equipment, watching fires, sounding alarms, and watching fire fighters in action. Unlike arsonists, pyromaniacs are looking for pleasure, not revenge or money (Booth, 1988).

Ben had been fascinated by fires since age 7, and he was twice suspended from school for setting fires in wastepaper baskets. At home he set fires to draperies, dish towels, and scrap wood. As an adult, Ben was frequently present at major blazes and was entranced by them. After being arrested for starting a fire in a warehouse, Ben admitted to setting other fires in the area. Although he agreed with the arresting officer that setting fires was wrong, Ben told him, "It's just as good as sex."

Pyromania is a rare disorder that is more common in men and is associated with lower intelligence, learning disabilities, attention deficit hyperactivity disorder, bed-wetting in childhood, temper outbursts, and recklessness. Pyromania in women is associated with sexual promiscuity (American Psychiatric Association, 1987; Booth, 1988).

trichotillomania (*trich*-oh-*till*-oh-*mania*) Inability to resist impulses to pull out one's hair.

Trichotillomania. Trichotillomania involves an inability to resist the impulse to pull out one's hair (American Psychiatric Association, 1987).

Barbara was a 35-year-old woman who sought treatment for a lifelong relationship problem with her father. While describing her situation, she reported an irresistible urge to pull out her eyebrows. In recent months she had been plucking her hair daily, leaving the underlying skin irritated and bleeding. In order to conceal her condition, she wore heavy layers of eyebrow pencil. After she had plucked her eyebrows, she started pulling out her scalp hair, leaving ugly bald patches.

In one study of 60 chronic trichotillomaniacs, the typical sufferer was a 34-year-old woman who had been pulling out her hair for 21 years (Christenson, MacKenzie, & Mitchell, 1991). These individuals usually pull out hair from more than one site (see Table 12-3). The study also revealed that trichotillomaniacs use many methods to resist hair pulling, including putting barriers on their heads, wearing mittens, sitting on their hands, hiding tweezers, and putting petroleum jelly on their hands or hair. Chronic hair pullers have a higher lifetime prevalence of anxiety, mood and eating disorders, as well as substance use disorders. This fact has prompted questions about whether trichotillomania is a distinct disorder or a symptom of other conditions.

Several researchers believe that trichotillomania is a variant of obsessive-

TABLE 12-3   SITES FROM WHICH 60 TRICHOTILLOMANIACS
PULLED OUT HAIR

Site	Number of Subjects	Percentage
Scalp	45	75
Eyelashes	32	53
Eyebrows	25	42
Pubic area	10	17
Beard/face	6	10
Mustache	4	7
Arm	6	10
Leg	4	7
Chest	2	3
Abdomen	1	2

Source: From "Characteristics of 60 Adult Chronic Hair Pullers" by
G. A. Christenson, T. B. MacKenzie, and J. E. Mitchell, 1991, *American
Journal of Psychiatry, 148*, pp. 365–370.

compulsive disorder. Although this clinical issue awaits resolution, it is interesting to note that Barbara's hair pulling completely disappeared when she was treated with Prozac, a drug commonly used for obsessive-compulsive disorder (Christenson et al., 1991).

Causes of Impulse Control Disorders

The causes of impulse control disorders are poorly understood. Psychosocial explanations have been primarily psychodynamic in nature, and in recent years some studies have suggested a biological basis for these conditions.

Psychosocial Causes. In the psychodynamic view, impulse control disorders are believed to be behavioral expressions of underlying conflicts (Booth, 1988). Psychodynamic theory holds that kleptomaniacs feel unloved and neglected and have sexual disturbances. Feeling depressed, kleptomaniacs steal as a substitute for the love and esteem they sorely miss. Since the objects are not stolen for their monetary profit, stealing represents an "intrapsychic profit" (M. J. Goldman, 1991).

Pathological gambling is considered a kind of masturbation and a source of self-esteem in people whose childhood sexual impulses have been frustrated. Some analysts argue that pathological gamblers have an unconscious wish to be punished by castration for masturbating. Bearing on the idea that pathological gamblers wish to be punished is a statement by the winner of the 1981 World Series of Poker. When asked what he would do with the money, he promptly replied, "Lose it" (Booth, 1988; Ginsburg, 1985).

Pyromania is believed to be a means of sexual gratification or a way of combating feelings of inferiority. In support of this idea, it has been noted that some pyromaniacs masturbate while watching fires. One psychodynamic explanation of trichotillomania focuses on the mother's attempt to foster extreme dependency (Booth, 1988; Ginsburg, 1985).

Biological Causes. Modern studies of pathological gamblers suggest brain dysfunction as a causal agent (Roy et al., 1988). Pathological gamblers exhibit abnormal norepinephrine transmission, which may underlie the personality trait of *sensation seeking*. This trait, which involves pleasure seeking and impulsivity, is common in people who enjoy taking risks (Zuckerman, 1979, 1984; Zuckerman, Ballenger, Jimerson, Murphy, & Post, 1983).

Brain abnormalities have also been suggested as causes of trichotillomania. A study of ten women with trichotillomania showed higher-than-normal glucose metabolism in the cerebellum and the parietal lobe of the cerebral cortex, brain regions known to regulate motor behavior and tactile recognition. Although these findings are based on a small sample, they suggest that trichotillomania may be part of a spectrum of *grooming disorders* that include the compulsive handwashing of obsessive-compulsive disorder, the hair pulling of trichotillomania, and the severe nail biting that characterizes a condition called *onychophagia* (Swedo et al., 1991).

Treatment of Impulse Control Disorders

Insight-oriented therapy is the treatment used most often for impulse control disorders. In recent years, behavior therapy, self-help groups, and psychotropic medication have been used with increasing frequency.

Psychological Treatments. Treatment usually involves insight-oriented therapy designed to resolve underlying conflicts. For example, the therapist will attempt to discover the personal significance of stealing to a kleptomaniac, thereby helping the patient cope with the guilt and shame of his or her actions. Aversive conditioning has also been used for this condition by following stealing with a punishment (M. J. Goldman, 1991).

One of the greatest problems in treating pathological gamblers is that they do not consider their behavior abnormal. They tend to seek help only under pressure from family. Since there are similarities between gambling and alcoholism, Gamblers Anonymous, modeled after Alcoholics Anonymous, was founded in 1957. Gamblers Anonymous is based on peer pressure, confession, and help through the guidance of reformed gamblers. Support groups for families and children of pathological gamblers are available as well (Booth, 1988; Kellner, 1982).

Highly structured, comprehensive inpatient programs similar to those used for alcoholics and drug addicts are also becoming more popular in the treatment of pathological gambling. Few outcome studies have investigated the effectiveness of these programs. However, one study showed that 56 percent of treated gamblers had abstained from gambling after hospital discharge (Taber, McCormick, Russo, Adkins, & Ramirez, 1987).

The most successful treatment for trichotillomania appears to be behavior therapy consisting of self-monitoring, disruption of the behavior through mild punishment, and token reinforcement for not pulling out hair. There are also a few case reports of successful treatment using hypnosis. By and large, however, the effectiveness of psychological treatments for impulse control disorders is modest (Friman, Finney, & Christopherson, 1984; Friman & O'Connor, 1984).

Biological Treatments. Little research exists to verify the effectiveness of psychoactive medications for impulse control disorders. Several studies indicate that antidepressants help kleptomaniacs control their compulsion, and drugs used in treating obsessive-compulsive disorder help trichotillomaniacs reduce hair pulling. Much more research is needed in order to prove the value of these treatments (Christenson et al., 1991; Fishbain, 1988; McElroy & Kreck, 1989).

SUMMARY

12-1 Eating disorders are characterized by disturbances in eating behavior. Anorexia nervosa involves a refusal to maintain normal weight. Bulimia nervosa involves binge eating and purging. Obesity is not classified as an eating disorder in the DSM-III-R, but it is a pattern of disturbed eating that can lead to serious medical and social consequences.

12-2 Eating disorders are caused by an interaction of hereditary, physiological, and psychosocial variables. There is evidence of a strong hereditary predisposition toward obesity, and there is less compelling evidence for a hereditary component to anorexia nervosa and bulimia nervosa. Neurotransmitter dysfunctions involving norepinephrine, serotonin, and dopamine are suspected to play a role in eating disorders. Psychodynamic explanations have focused on disturbed eating as an expression of underlying childhood conflicts. Family systems theories view eating disorders as consequences of dysfunctional family interactions. Cognitive theories blame disturbed eating on faulty attitudes equating body shape with self-image. Behavioral theories explain eating disorders as a matter of faulty self-control and hyperresponsiveness to external stimuli.

12-3 Treatment of eating disorders is designed to restore normal weight and encourage sound eating habits. Psychodynamic, behavioral, cognitive, and family therapies have been applied successfully. Hospitalization is necessary for patients who are emaciated or ill from fasting, binge eating, and purging. Surgical procedures are sometimes used for massively obese individuals who do not respond to more conventional treatments.

12-4 Impulse control disorders consist of failure to resist acting on an impulse that can be harmful. Kleptomania involves impulsive stealing; pathological gambling consists of a failure to resist gambling despite the prospect of major loss; pyromania is marked by impulsive setting of fires; and trichotillomania is characterized by pulling out hair. Little is known about the causes of impulse control disorders, though they are considered to be behavioral expressions of underlying conflicts. There is some evidence for neurotransmitter abnormalities in pathological gamblers and abnormal brain metabolism in trichotillomania. Treatment of impulse control disorders usually involves insight-oriented therapy or behavior therapy. Antidepressants are effective in selected patients.

TERMS TO REMEMBER

anorexia nervosa (p. 306)
bulimarexia (p. 307)
bulimia nervosa (p. 308)
eating disorders (p. 306)
energy balance (p. 312)
escape theory (p. 315)
impulse control disorders
(p. 322)

internality-externality hypothesis
(p. 313)
kleptomania (p. 322)
obesity (p. 310)
pathological gambling (p. 323)
pyromania (p. 324)
set-point model (p. 312)
trichotillomania (p. 324)

SUGGESTED READINGS

Brownell, K. D. (1987). *The LEARN program for weight control.* Philadelphia: University of Pennsylvania School of Medicine.

Bruch, H. (1973). *Eating disorders: Obesity, anorexia, and the person within.* New York: Basic Books.

Bruch, H. (1978). *The golden cage.* Cambridge, Mass.: Harvard University Press.

LEGAL AND ETHICAL ISSUES: DISCRIMINATION AGAINST THE OBESE

It is well-known that obesity is a serious health hazard. Obesity carries social, educational, and employment disadvantages as well. Obese individuals, especially women, are often viewed by others as lazy and lacking in self-respect and therefore responsible for their condition. This view has led to prejudicial treatment of obese individuals in social situations and possibly to discrimination in gaining educational and employment opportunities.

Several studies indicate that obese individuals are educationally disadvantaged. For example, obese individuals are less likely to be ranked in the top third of their high school class even when their IQ and Scholastic Aptitude Test scores are similar to those of normal-weight students. Obese individuals may also be at a disadvantage in gaining college admission. A study of obese and nonobese women of equal IQ and high school standing revealed that there were fewer obese females in Ivy League colleges. These data raise the suspicion of prejudicial college admission policies.

Since obese individuals are stigmatized, it is not surprising that they generally attain a lower socioeconomic status than individuals of normal weight. Obese people may be less likely to secure higher-paying jobs because they are often seen by employers as less competent, less productive, and indecisive. Some research indicates that they earn less money. In a study of 1660 Manhattan residents, overweight women were less likely to achieve a higher SES than their parents.

Of course, it is possible that the diminished success of obese individuals has nothing to do with discrimination. Their failure to achieve may be a reflection of the low self-esteem with which they approach educational and employment opportunities. Although it is difficult to sort out the reasons, we are sometimes made aware of discriminatory practices when we read newspaper and magazine articles. We see documented cases of airline flight attendants, civil service workers, and others who are dismissed because they are overweight. Although federal laws now formally protect obese people against discrimination on the grounds of their obesity alone, they still face subtle forms of discrimination on many fronts (Bray, 1986; Wooley & Wooley, 1979).

Chapter THIRTEEN

Personality Disorders

OBJECTIVES

1. Name and identify the symptoms of the 11 major personality disorders.
2. Describe the DSM-III-R classification of personality disorder clusters.
3. Outline the major biological causes of personality disorders.
4. Identify the psychosocial factors that contribute to personality disorders.
5. Discuss the biological approach to treating personality disorders.
6. Summarize the psychodynamic theory of personality disorders and their treatment.
7. Explain the rationale and methods of behavioral and cognitive therapies for personality disorders.

*M*aria entered therapy at age 34 because she was feeling depressed about her chronic marital problems and her inability to choose a career. In her marriage she was extremely dependent on her husband, a successful businessman, and she strongly resented her financial dependency. She felt that she did not deserve such a successful husband and was terrified that he might divorce her. At the same time, she hated him for doing so well in his career, and she often taunted him to leave her. In the preceding ten years Maria had received training for several jobs, but upon completion of her training she either did not work in that field or worked only briefly before quitting.

Since her mid-teens Maria had experienced recurring bouts of depression and suicidal impulses. Aside from her husband, she had almost no social relationships; her unpredictable moods, erratic behavior, and stormy temper alienated practically everyone. Maria's case illustrates several aspects of personality disorders, whose nature, causes, and treatment are discussed in this chapter.

personality disorder
A pattern of maladaptive, inflexible, and distressing personality traits.

Personality consists of general, stable traits of behavior, emotion, and thought. When these traits are maladaptive, inflexible, and distressing, the person is said to have a **personality disorder** (PD). Although they may have many different symptoms, most individuals with personality disorders have the following features in common:

- Inflexible and maladaptive responses to stress
- Disabilities in work and social relationships
- Lack of insight into their condition (Vaillant & Perry, 1985)

People with personality disorders generally experience impairments in their capacity to respond to stressful situations, and they typically fall into "vicious cycles" in which their rigid, habitual attempts to cope worsen the problem. Difficulty in relating to other people is a hallmark of personality disorders, and their symptoms are especially prominent in social interaction. The symptoms of personality disorders are usually *ego-syntonic*, meaning that the person perceives the symptomatic behavior, thought, or feeling as "the way I am" rather than as a problem needing correction (American Psychiatric Association, 1987; Millon, 1981; Vaillant & J. C. Perry, 1985).

Personality disorders are relatively common, with an estimated prevalence of 6 to 10 percent of the population. They are found in nearly 50 percent of patients seeking help at psychiatric clinics (Merikangas & M. Weissman, 1986). There are strong associations between personality disorders and other major mental disorders. Researchers at the Cornell Medical Center in New York found that patients with one or more personality disorders also had high rates of substance abuse (53 percent), anxiety disorders (50 percent), depression (23 percent), and psychosis (16 percent) (Koenigsberg, R. D. Kaplan, Gilmore, & A. M. Cooper, 1985). Individuals with personality disorders are likely to experience many types of psychological and interpersonal problems during their lives. Social maladjustment, emotional disturbances, occupational impairment, family distress, and marital discord are commonly associated with personality disorders.

According to the DSM-III-R, personality disorders are diagnosed as *Axis II disorders* and are distinct from the major clinical syndromes of Axis I (see Chapter 4). However, personality disorders and Axis I disorders often coexist in the same individual. Because of their prevalence and because they coexist with so many other mental health problems, personality disorders are being looked at more seriously than ever before by researchers and clinicians.

13-1 TYPES OF PERSONALITY DISORDERS

The DSM-III-R recognizes 11 distinctive personality disorders that are assumed to originate in childhood or adolescence and are considered to be chronic impairments. Personality disorders are grouped into three clusters, labeled A, B, and C, according to similarities in their symptoms (see Table 13-1). In addition to the 11 main PDs, the DSM-III-R also offers a diagnosis for people with mixed PD symptoms, called *personality disorder not otherwise specified*. Figure 13-1 depicts the prevalence rates and Figure 13-2 the sex ratios of personality disorders among a sample of psychiatric patients.

The DSM-III-R classification of personality disorders has been questioned on several grounds. Some of the personality disorders have similar and overlapping diagnostic criteria and thus do not seem to be distinctive problems. Also, the symptoms are sometimes described in the DSM-III-R in subjective or inferential terms, which reduce their reliability. Furthermore, studies do not provide consistent support for the idea that personality disorders are naturally grouped into three coherent clusters (Livelsey, 1987; Morey, 1988; Widiger, Frances, Spitzer, & Williams, 1988; Widiger, Truci, Hurt, Clarkin, & Frances, 1987).

Despite some valid criticisms, the DSM-III-R classification of personality disorders is the most widely used system. For that reason, we rely on the DSM-III-R definitions of personality disorders throughout this chapter.

Cluster A: The Eccentric Disorders

Cluster A Eccentric, odd, or withdrawn types; paranoid, schizoid, and schizotypal personality disorders.

Cluster A personality disorders are characterized as eccentric, odd, or withdrawn types. They include the paranoid, schizoid, and schizotypal personality disorders.

paranoid personality disorder A personality disorder characterized by distrust, suspiciousness, fear, and jealousy.

Paranoid Personality Disorder. Traits of distrust, suspiciousness, fear, and jealousy are central features of the **paranoid personality disorder**. People with this disorder perceive others as threatening or demeaning and often expect to be misused or maltreated. The individual with a paranoid personality is guarded in relating to others, suspecting that people have hidden motives for their actions. They experience considerable distress in social relationships, and they are often perceived as cold, humorless, and sullen.

Despite some similarities to more severe conditions, paranoid PD is not

TABLE 13-1 PERSONALITY DISORDER CLUSTERS

Cluster A	Cluster B	Cluster C
• Paranoid	• Antisocial	• Avoidant
• Schizoid	• Borderline	• Dependent
• Schizotypal	• Narcissistic	• Obsessive-compulsive
	• Histrionic	• Passive-aggressive

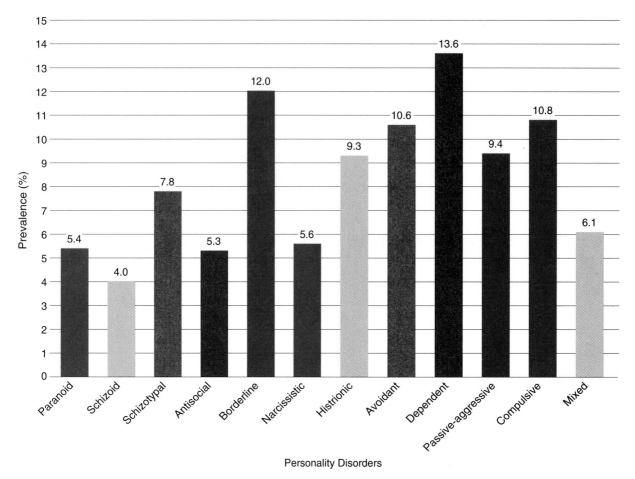

Figure 13-1 Prevalence of personality disorders among adult psychiatric patients.

Source: Adapted from ''The Avoidant Personality'' by T. Millon, 1986, in A. M. Cooper, A. J. Francis, and M. H. Sacks (Eds.), *The Personality Disorders and Neuroses.* New York: Basic Books.

necessarily related to paranoid schizophrenia or delusional (paranoid) disorder. In general, the person with paranoid PD retains good reality contact and does not exhibit the psychotic features of those other disorders. However, paranoid PD is considered part of the schizophrenic spectrum, and for some patients it is the premorbid personality for those psychotic disorders (Kety, Rosenthal, Wender, Schulsinger, & Jacobson, 1978).

Jimmy agreed to attend marriage counseling at the request of his wife, Beth, after several fights prompted by his groundless suspicions that she was having an affair. His two previous marriages had ended because of similar jealousies and accusations. Jimmy had worked as a salesman in the same company for over ten years, but he had no close friends there. He was superficial in his interactions with co-workers because he believed that if people knew too much about him they might be able to hurt him.

schizoid personality disorder A personality disorder characterized by restricted emotional reactions and social indifference.

Schizoid Personality Disorder. The **schizoid personality disorder** is characterized by restricted emotional reactions and a pattern of social indifference. The schizoid person is aloof and disconnected from others. This interpersonal detachment is motivated not by fear but by a basic disinterest in other people and their lives. These individuals are often perceived as loners or extreme introverts whose interests are mainly in solitary activities. The person with schizoid PD is emotionally restricted and unexpressive, exhibiting few positive or negative feelings toward events or people (Siever & Kendler, 1986).

Tim was a computer technician in his mid-forties who worked nights monitoring the equipment for a large company. He lived alone and had never married. Tim rarely dated, had no friends, and spent most of his leisure time at home playing computer games or just "hacking."

schizotypal personality disorder A personality disorder characterized by interpersonal deficits and peculiarities in thinking.

Schizotypal Personality Disorder. Interpersonal deficits and peculiarities in thinking are the main signs of the **schizotypal personality disorder**. This disorder sometimes resembles schizophrenia, but the individual has no psychotic hallucinations or delusions. People with schizotypal PD often exhibit superstitious or magical thoughts that are not as bizarre as delusions but are usually perceived as idiosyncratic, odd, or irrational. The emotional life of the schizotypal individual is dominated by social anxiety, feelings of alienation, and suspiciousness. The person's behavior is often eccentric, and deficient social skills lead to unsatisfying relationships.

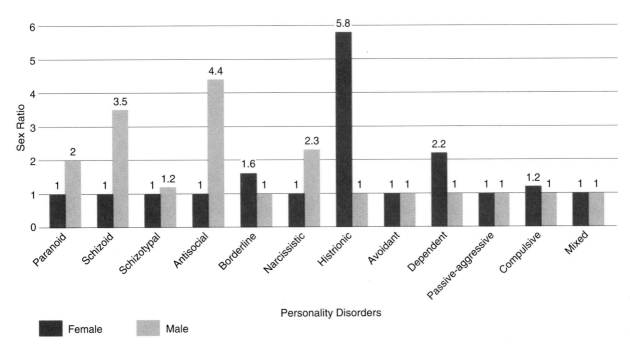

Figure 13-2 Sex ratios of personality disorders among adult psychiatric patients.

Source: Adapted from "The Avoidant Personality" by T. Millon, 1986, in A. M. Cooper, A. J. Francis, and M. H. Sacks (Eds.), *The Personality Disorders and Neuroses.* New York: Basic Books.

After numerous confrontations with her supervisors, Arlene was referred for psychological evaluation by the company personnel officer. She explained that she had always been "a kook." Starting in high school, Arlene had been involved with numerous healing fads. She had problems at work because she insisted on extravagantly decorating her cubicle with hundreds of objects and pictures with "healing powers," including pyramids, quartz crystals, herbs, plants, and religious articles.

The schizotypal PD has a prevalence of about 3 percent in the general population. Although some of its symptoms overlap with those of other personality disorders (notably, schizoid, paranoid, and avoidant disorders), oddities in thinking, speech, and perception set schizotypal PD apart. The schizotypal PD sometimes resembles the prodromal and residual stages of schizophrenia, and some authorities even suggest that it is a variant of schizophrenia as much as a personality disorder. Like paranoid PD, schizotypal PD belongs to the schizophrenic spectrum of disorders and is considered one of the most severe personality disorders (Kety, 1985; Kety et al., 1978; Lenzenweger & Loranger, 1989; Siever & Kendler, 1986).

Cluster B: The Dramatic Disorders

Cluster B Dramatic, emotional, or erratic types: antisocial, borderline, narcissistic, and histrionic personality disorders.

Cluster B personality disorders are dominated by dramatic, emotional, or erratic features and include the antisocial, borderline, narcissistic, and histrionic types.

antisocial personality disorder A personality disorder characterized by antisocial behavior, such as fighting, lying, stealing, and cruelty.

Antisocial Personality Disorder. As its name suggests, the **antisocial personality disorder** is defined by a history of antisocial behavior, including fighting, lying, stealing, cruelty, and delinquency. The rights, feelings, and property of others are of little concern to individuals with antisocial PD. Even after harming others, the antisocial person experiences little remorse for his or her actions. This personality disorder is common in people with a history of criminal activity, violence, and drug abuse. Antisocial PD is found in about 3 percent of men and 1 percent of women in the general population, and it is present in about half of incarcerated male criminals (Andreasen & Black, 1991; Reid, 1986).

Because of its connections with many types of social deviance, the antisocial PD is the most widely studied of all personality disorders. Early signs of antisocial personality are found in aggressive and destructive conduct disorders of childhood and adolescence. Chronic antisocial behavior is widely recognized as being indicative of psychological disturbance, and the individual with antisocial PD is also likely to exhibit social and occupational maladjustment.

psychopathy An extreme antisocial personality disorder characterized by callous, aggressive behavior and a lack of empathy and conscience.

Antisocial personality disorder has been given other labels, such as moral insanity, sociopathy, and psychopathy. Some researchers consider **psychopathy** to be an extreme case of antisocial PD. The *psychopath*, usually a man, has a long history of callous and aggressive behavior and is lacking in conscience, fear, and empathy (Cleckley, 1976). A frightening aspect of the psychopath's behavior is that his crimes against others are not necessarily motivated by hatred: he may simply be indifferent to their rights. Gary Gilmore, who was executed in 1977 for murder, expressed a characteristically psychopathic attitude toward violence.

> I pulled up near a gas station. I told the service station guy to give me all of his money. I then took him to the bathroom and told him to kneel down

Gary Gilmore was executed for murder in Utah in 1977. Like most psychopaths he expressed no remorse for his actions.

and then I shot him in the head twice. The guy didn't give me any trouble but I just felt like I had to do it. (Spitzer, Skodol, Gibbon, & Williams, 1983, p. 67)

borderline personality disorder A personality disorder characterized by instability in mood, self-image, and relationships and by impulsive, self-defeating relationships

Borderline Personality Disorder. The **borderline personality disorder** is marked by instability in mood, self-image, and relationships and by impulsive, self-defeating behavior. Borderline individuals alternate between extremes of emotion, especially depression, anxiety, and anger. Their lack of impulse control frequently leads to self-damaging behavior like drug use, self-mutilation, sexual promiscuity, and suicide attempts.

Borderline individuals feel uncertain about their personal identities and self-concepts. Their goals, attitudes, and values are unclear, and they have no certain answers to basic questions like "Who am I?" and "What do I like?" People with this disorder have higher-than-average rates of substance abuse and depression.

In their relationships, borderlines run hot and cold, swinging between intense attachment to and rejection of others, whom they alternately view as ideal and evil. These features of the borderline PD are easily perceived as fickleness and unpredictability by those with whom they interact. Afraid of both abandonment and being overwhelmed by others, the borderline person vacillates between extreme intimacy and distancing in relationships (M. H. Stone, 1986).

In the years since graduating from college, Maria had been unable to discover what kind of work she was cut out for. She changed her mind repeatedly, but she never found her niche. In fact, Maria saw herself as unfit for almost any job. Her feelings about her husband's career success shifted between loving admiration and hateful rage. She fantasized about killing herself in order to "get back at

Serial killers such as Albert DeSalvo, the Boston Strangler (top), Jeffrey Dahmer (center), and Ted Bundy (bottom) often live anonymously, wearing a mask of normality between their murderous sprees.

CLOSE-UP
Serial Killers

- The Boston Strangler
- The Hillside Stranglers
- The Nightstalker
- Son of Sam
- Ted Bundy
- Jeffrey Dahmer

These infamous names are associated with some of the most heinous crimes of modern times. In contrast to most murderers, serial killers commit many homicides, often over many years. Otherwise they live in obscurity. Some wear a mask of normality, like John Wayne Gacy, a successful businessman and "model citizen" who was convicted of 33 sex killings of young boys in the Midwest. Others live on the fringe of society, alienated and anonymous, like Jeffrey Dahmer, an apparently innocuous and mild-mannered recluse who confessed to the murder and mutilation of 15 young men over a period of 12 years.

Unlike most homicides, serial murder is a coldly premeditated act that is an end in itself. Serial murders, sometimes called recreational or lust killing, can be motivated by the thrill of killing: the Hillside Stranglers claimed they killed 10 young women "for fun." However, most serial killers are acting out violent fantasies with deep and painful personal meanings. For example, Jeffrey Dahmer's seduction and brutal murders of

young men were apparently linked to his struggle with his own homosexual impulses.

What compels someone to such horrifying acts? Serial killers have usually been portrayed as extreme psychopaths, individuals with no conscience who are motivated by their urges and have neither fear of punishment nor remorse for their deeds. Many were physically and sexually abused as children and have been otherwise victimized by family and society. However, many serial killers are not typical psychopaths; they often lead law-abiding lives between frenzies of murder. Ted Bundy, for example, was working on a prelaw degree during the period in which he coldly murdered 35 women. Other aberrations prevalent in serial killers include sexual sadism, necrophilia, cannibalism, psychosis, and drug addiction. In addition, neurological impairments are common, perhaps the result of head injury or drug and alcohol abuse, all of which are common in serial killers.

Whether insane, neurologically impaired, or simply evil, serial killers seem to be more common today than ever, and unfortunately for them, their victims, and society, their acts are not predictable or preventable (J. Levin & Fox, 1985; J. Norris, 1988).

him," and at one point she schemed to have a child with birth defects in order to embarrass him socially and force him to divorce her.

Originally, "borderline" meant a disorder on the border between neurosis and psychosis. Today, borderline PD is recognized as a separate problem, although it is often associated with neurotic and psychotic symptoms. Borderline PD appears to be most strongly associated with mood disorders, such as depression and cyclothymia. Among people with borderline PD, the lifetime prevalence of depression is approximately 50 percent (Perry, 1985). One major study of psychiatric inpatients with borderline PD found that 67 percent had a substance use disorder, most commonly involving alcohol and tranquilizers (Dulit, Fyer, Haas, T. Sullivan, & Frances, 1990). Psychotic symptoms, especially of a paranoid type, are also sometimes associated with borderline PD, as are other severe personality disorders, such as schizotypal PD and paranoid PD (Fyer, Frances, T. Sullivan, Hart, & Clarkin, 1988).

narcissistic personality disorder A personality disorder characterized by self-love, self-admiration, and attitudes of superiority.

Narcissistic Personality Disorder. In Greek mythology, Narcissus was a youth so enchanted by his beautiful reflection in a pond that he could not stop admiring it. Eventually he fell into the pond and drowned. The **narcissistic personality disorder** is expressed by extreme self-love, self-admiration, and attitudes of superiority. Narcissists assume that they are entitled to special attention and consideration from others, but they are often exploitative and unsympathetic in return. Interpersonal relations are inevitably disrupted because of the self-centered and demanding style of the narcissist.

The narcissist usually has serious difficulties with self-esteem and related emotions. Despite a surface attitude of competence and self-satisfaction, narcissistic individuals are inclined to feel an inner emptiness, and they commonly complain of depression, boredom, interpersonal difficulties, and jealousy (Kernberg, 1986).

Charles was mandated into treatment at a drug clinic after his arrest for cocaine possession. He was astonished that he had been caught, since he prided himself on being smarter than the police and other drug users. He was powerfully muscled after years of working out, and he had spent much of his time pursuing sexual conquest of women. By his late twenties, Charles had been fired from or quit

The mythological youth Narcissus, pictured in this seventeenth-century engraving, was so taken with his own beauty that he could not stop admiring his reflection. Like him, narcissistic personalities have exaggerated perceptions of their own attributes.

countless jobs because of fights with bosses, whom he derided as stupid. Charles was an only child who, by his own reckoning, had been spoiled by parents he disdained as weak and ineffectual.

histrionic (hiss-tree-*on*-ik) *personality disorder* A personality disorder characterized by excessive emotionality and attention seeking.

Histrionic Personality Disorder. **Histrionic personality disorder** is a pattern involving excessive emotionality and dramatic attention-seeking behavior. This PD was formerly labeled the *hysterical personality*. The histrionic individual craves approval, praise, and recognition from others and is self-centered and demanding. Extreme and exaggerated displays of emotion are distinctive features of this disorder. The person uses crying, temper fits, seductive behavior, and flirtation in attempts to elicit attention and sympathy.

The histrionic PD is the least severe of the Cluster B disorders. It is nearly six times as common among women than men. This personality type may accompany some Axis I conditions, such as somatoform disorders, in which the symptoms serve the attention-seeking motives of the patient. For example, hypochondriacal patients often display histrionic features in their exaggerated complaints about minor ailments. In addition, anxiety problems, such as separation anxiety, are common correlates of histrionic personality disorder (Vaillant & J. C. Perry, 1985).

Sally sought counseling for "bad nerves." Her clothes, makeup, and accessories were more suitable for a teenager than a 53-year-old woman. In her first interview, she remarked several times that younger men were always attracted to her and that no one could guess her real age. Her anxiety was caused by the impending breakup of her third marriage. Her husband had threatened her with a divorce after an incident in a restaurant. She had humiliated him by cursing him loudly after he commented how much weight a female neighbor had lost. Sally had taken his remark as a personal insult and had thrown a tantrum.

Cluster C: The Anxious Disorders

Cluster C Anxious, fearful, or inhibited types: avoidant, dependent, obsessive-compulsive, and passive-aggressive personality disorders.

The personality disorders of **Cluster C** are defined by anxious, fearful, or inhibited behavior. This group encompasses four diagnoses: the avoidant, dependent, obsessive-compulsive, and passive-aggressive personality disorders.

avoidant personality disorder A personality disorder characterized by shyness, social anxiety, fear of criticism, and inhibited social behavior.

Avoidant Personality Disorder. Extreme shyness, social anxiety, fear of criticism, and inhibited social behavior are the key features of **avoidant personality disorder**. Individuals with avoidant PD usually have no close friends, and over time they grow increasingly isolated from other people. Avoidant PD in adults is regularly preceded by avoidant disorder and social anxiety in childhood.

Avoidant PD is easily confused with social phobia, but research shows that the avoidant person feels more emotional distress, is more socially sensitive, and is less socially competent than the phobic person. In social phobia the fears are more situation-specific, such as speaking in public, whereas in avoidant PD there is more generalized interpersonal anxiety (Millon, 1986).

A high school guidance counselor referred Robert for evaluation. At age 17 he had never dated and was completely without friends. In fact, he remembered having had only one friend, briefly, during elementary school. Robert was painfully shy and insecure, and he described himself as a weird kid who did not fit in with other people. Although he wanted to develop friendships, he believed that no one would accept him, and he was unable to initiate social contacts.

dependent personality disorder A personality disorder characterized by excessive dependency and difficulty making decisions.

Dependent Personality Disorder. Dependent personality disorder is defined by excessive dependency on others and extreme difficulty in making decisions or taking initiative for oneself. The dependent person relies on others to take charge and is frequently submissive and compliant to demands by others. Additional features of dependent PD include passivity, sensitivity to criticism, and lack of self-confidence.

Dependent PD is sometimes preceded by separation anxiety disorder of childhood or adolescence. As might be expected, children who find independent action difficult are more inclined to develop this personality disorder. In adults with dependent PD, symptoms of agoraphobia and depression are not uncommon, although it is not clear whether the dependent personality is a cause or a consequence of these emotional problems (Esman, 1986).

Despite having a college degree, high intelligence, and considerable artistic ability, Mark was employed in an unskilled, low-paying clerical position. He was completely dominated by his wife and was incapable of asserting himself with her or anyone else. For example, he was only permitted to watch TV programs she chose. Mark had had severe school phobia as a child, and in college he had received barely passing grades because of overwhelming test anxiety. His pursuit of a career was hampered by his anxiety and by his subordination to his wife. Mark ultimately terminated his therapy when his wife insisted that he change to a new therapist of her choice.

obsessive-compulsive personality disorder A personality disorder characterized by inflexible attitudes, perfectionism, and preoccupation with rules and details.

Obsessive-Compulsive Personality Disorder. Obsessive-compulsive personality disorder is defined by inflexible attitudes, perfectionism, a rigid sense of morality, and preoccupation with rules and details. The features of this disorder are closely related to the symptoms of obsessive-compulsive disorder and are often present in people prior to the onset of that anxiety disorder (see Chapter 5).

People with obsessive-compulsive PD are perceived as exceptionally moralistic and conscientious. They exhibit a strict, black-and-white view of the world, according to which things are either right or wrong. Their perfectionism produces emotional distress because they rarely feel they are good enough. In dealing with others, they tend to be emotionally restricted and are often critical of others' faults. Usually such a person is more interested in work and performance than in other people (Oldham & Frosch, 1986).

Mr. Lewis was a remarkably neat and well-organized man who regarded others as an interference to the perfect progression of his life. For years he kept an almost inflexible schedule. On weekdays he arose at 6:47, ate two eggs (soft-boiled for 2 minutes and 45 seconds), and was at his desk at 8:15. Lunch was at 12:00, dinner at 6:00, bedtime at 11:00. Any change in schedule caused him to feel anxiety, annoyance, and a sense that he was doing something wrong and wasting time. (Spitzer et al., 1983)

passive-aggressive personality disorder A personality disorder characterized by resentment of and resistance to demands, using passive means.

Passive-Aggressive Personality Disorder. Individuals with **passive-aggressive personality disorder** are resentful of demands placed on them by others, and they resist those demands by passive means, such as forgetting their obligations, procrastinating, being stubborn, and dawdling. A passive-aggressive strategy for shirking responsibility is to work so slowly or ineffectively that someone else finishes the job.

The passive-aggressive person seems to use these strategies as an indirect way to express aggressive or hostile feelings. These individuals seem to be unable to vent anger in a straightforward manner, yet they deny any hostile intent behind their behavior. Some passive-aggressive adults have a history of defiant or oppositional behavior in childhood (Esman, 1986).

Stan was pushed into marriage counseling when his wife threatened to divorce him. In their 15 years of marriage, she had become increasingly responsible for managing most aspects of their lives, including the children, the bills, and domestic chores. He repeatedly sabotaged her attempts to balance the household budget, making unnecessary purchases and forgetting to pay bills. Stan rarely contributed to the upkeep of the house and claimed that his few small duties, like taking out the garbage, often just slipped his mind. When his wife complained about his laziness, he would walk away quietly.

Other Personality Disorders

In addition to the 11 specific personality disorders in Clusters A, B, and C, the DSM-III-R provides a diagnosis for people with unusual or mixed features: *personality disorder not otherwise specified*. Such individuals have a combination of symptoms from various PDs, but they do not fit exactly the criteria of any one PD.

Hank was a recovering alcoholic and narcotics addict who had not used drugs or alcohol for over 15 years. He sought therapy under duress from his wife, who was threatening divorce unless he changed. Hank was a charmer, especially of women, whom he had used throughout his life. Despite his superficial "macho" attitude, he was a deeply insecure man who felt powerless to control his life and sought out women to take care of him. Once he had "won" a woman, he would resort to arrogantly irresponsible behavior and would soon be reliant on her to support him. Hank's behavior reflected elements of narcissistic, dependent, and passive-aggressive personality disorders.

The DSM-III-R proposed two other diagnoses—sadistic personality disorder and self-defeating personality disorder—that are still being studied. At present, little evidence supports the reliability and validity of these diagnoses.

sadistic personality disorder A personality disorder characterized by cruel, aggressive, manipulative, and demeaning behavior.

The **sadistic personality disorder** is characterized by cruel, aggressive, manipulative, and demeaning behavior directed toward others. Abusiveness and violence are common in the sadist's social relationships, because the sadist lacks concern for people and derives pleasure from harming or humiliating others. There are similarities between sadistic personality disorder and the more aggressive antisocial personality disorder. However, the antisocial person does not generally hurt others just for pleasure. There may also be an association between this personality disorder and sexual sadism, in which the person derives sexual arousal and satisfaction from sadistic acts like beating and humiliating someone.

self-defeating personality disorder A personality disorder characterized by chronic masochistic or self-defeating behavior.

A pattern of chronic masochistic or self-defeating behavior is characteristic of the **self-defeating personality disorder**. Although sexual masochism may be present, it has no necessary connection with this disorder. People with self-defeating personalities are drawn to situations and relationships in which they

The writings of the Marquis de Sade (1740–1814) detail the erotic pleasures of inflicting suffering on others, giving rise to the term sadism. *This nineteenth-century engraving shows him consorting with demons.*

are subject to failure, humiliation, suffering, and distress. For example, someone who repeatedly gets involved with physically or verbally abusive partners may have a self-defeating personality.

13-2   CAUSES OF PERSONALITY DISORDERS

Historically, psychodynamic theories have been the dominant explanations of personality disorders. In recent years, however, biological, behavioral, and cognitive hypotheses have been offered as well.

Biological Causes of Personality Disorders

There is no single compelling biological explanation for all personality disorders. Nonetheless, some evidence points to the role of hereditary and neurophysiological processes in several of these disorders.

Hereditary Factors. Hereditary predispositions are suspected to contribute to some personality disorders, particularly the paranoid, schizotypal, antisocial, and borderline PDs. Paranoid and schizotypal PDs are part of the schizophrenic spectrum, a hereditary group of disorders that also includes schizophrenia (Baron, Gruen, Asnis, & Lord, 1985; Kety et al., 1978;). Adoption and twin studies suggest that antisocial PD is partly due to genetic factors (Christiansen, 1977; Grove, 1974). Family studies of the borderline PD indicate an association with a hereditary *affective spectrum* of disorders, including depression and bipolar disorder (Baron et al., 1985; J. R. Gunderson & Elliot, 1985; Soloff & Millward, 1983).

During the 1960s, researchers proposed a link between violence and a rare chromosomal abnormality, the *XYY syndrome*. Affected men have an extra Y chromosome; they are usually taller than average and have subaverage intelligence. Public attention was drawn to this condition because violent crimes were committed by some XYY men, such as Richard Speck, who murdered eight student nurses in Chicago in 1966. Some studies seemed to support a link between XYY syndrome and criminal behavior because there are above-average rates of the condition in male prison inmates. However, most researchers today conclude that the crimes of XYY men are not likely to be more violent than those of other men, and the disproportionately high number of XYY men in prison may reflect a greater likelihood of arrest, perhaps due to poorer judgment (Witkin et al., 1976).

In 1966 Richard Speck, who had the XYY syndrome, murdered eight student nurses in Chicago. His case raised questions about the link between that chromosomal pattern and violent antisocial behavior.

Neurophysiological Factors. Although no distinctive neurophysiological causes of personality disorders have been found, some data suggests associations between nervous system activity and these disorders. Various neurotransmitter abnormalities have been linked with personality disorders. Schizotypal PD and borderline PD are associated with increased activity in the dopamine and norepinephrine systems, respectively. Diminished serotonin activity may play a role in the impulsive aggressive behavior of the antisocial personality (Siever & Davis, 1991).

Temperament is an innate foundation for emotional and behavioral traits and may be the basis of some personality disorders. For example, an irritable or anxious temperament can predispose a child to develop an avoidant PD. In addition, the difficult temperament pattern predicts a higher risk of childhood conduct disorders and antisocial personality (Thomas & Chess, 1977). A neurophysiological hypothesis about the cause of borderline PD attributes its symptoms to a built-in defect in the body's ability to control emotions and regulate behavioral responses to emotional states (D. Klein, 1977).

Cortical immaturity in the brains of adults with antisocial PD is evidenced by the fact that their EEG patterns show slow brain wave activity more typical of children. Neurological impairment is further suggested because antisocial individuals have abnormally low levels of anxiety or fear and have deficient responses to painful and punishing stimuli. However, these abnormalities may be the result of the antisocial person's lifestyle, which often includes fighting, head trauma, and drug use (Elliot, 1988; Hare, 1970, 1978, 1984; Shader, Scharfman, & Dreyfuss, 1986).

The *psychobiological model* proposes that the basic dimensions of personality have biological roots and are related to both personality disorders and Axis I syndromes. For example, the *affective instability dimension* of personality is associated with both borderline PD and mood disorders, perhaps because of a common abnormality of norepinephrine regulation. Although this model emphasizes the genetic and physiological bases of personality disorders, it recognizes that interactions between biological vulnerability and environmental influences affect personality development (Siever & Davis, 1991).

Psychosocial Causes of Personality Disorders

Psychosocial explanations of personality disorders focus on personality, learning, and family processes that contribute to pathological development.

Personality Factors. Traditional Freudian theory described several *character types* in terms of personality structures, developmental fixations, and ego defenses. For example, the *anal-retentive character* is epitomized by rigidity and stinginess, stemming from problems in the anal stage, during which toilet training was distressing for the young child (Freud, 1916; Reich, 1933/1972). Since Freud's time, numerous psychodynamic hypotheses for the personality disorders have been promoted by various authors. Case material supporting these views has been provided, but controlled research is generally lacking. Table 13-2 presents the major psychodynamic factors that have been proposed to affect personality disorders.

In contrast to Freud's view, modern psychodynamic theory attributes personality disorders to early interpersonal experiences that disturb personality and social development. Object relations theory emphasizes the importance of parent-child relationships in the development of basic personality structures and defenses. For example, in the case of borderline personality, inconsistent parental behavior and affection may lead the child to internalize incompatible (good versus bad) images of the parent. To cope with these inconsistent images, the child employs the defense mechanism of **splitting**, by which the two opposing aspects of the parental image are mentally separated. The child internalizes and identifies with inconsistent parental images, thereby engendering inconsistencies in his or her self-concept. In addition, the child projects the "split" images onto others; this process results in the borderline's vacillating perceptions of and unpredictable behavior toward others (Kernberg, 1976, 1984).

As a child, Maria had been abandoned by her mother on several occasions and had been left for long periods with relatives. She idolized her mother and praised her excessively, but she was terrified of her mother's criticism and deeply resented

splitting   A defense mechanism that separates opposing aspects of an image.

TABLE 13-2   **PSYCHODYNAMIC FACTORS IN PERSONALITY DISORDERS**

Personality Disorder	Psychodynamic Factors
Paranoid	• Parental hostility and rejection • Projection of homosexual impulses
Schizoid	• Deficient mother-child bond • Defensive withdrawal from others
Antisocial	• Inadequate superego controls • Acting out aggressive impulses
Borderline	• Early parent-child disturbances • Splitting and projection defenses
Narcissistic	• Lack of maternal empathy • Defensively overidealized self
Dependent	• Maternal overprotection • Inadequate ego individuation

PROFILE
Otto Kernberg
(b. 1928)

Psychiatrist Otto Kernberg is a leading figure in modern psychodynamic psychology, best known for his work on object relations theory and personality disorders.

Austrian by birth, Kernberg was educated in Chile, obtaining his bachelor's degree in 1947 and his M.D. degree in 1953 from the University of Chile, Santiago. After receiving his medical degree he pursued psychoanalytic training, and from 1961 until 1973 he was affiliated with the Menninger Foundation in Topeka, Kansas. He is now medical director of the New York Hospital–Cornell Medical Center and is on the faculty of the Columbia University Center for Psychoanalytic Training and Research.

Kernberg's theories integrate ideas from classical psychoanalysis, ego psychology, and object relations theory. His most influential ideas are found in his model of personality disorders and their treatment. Kernberg's view of personality disorders is at odds with the DSM-III-R classification, which, he argues, artificially divorces personality disorders from other neurotic and psychotic disorders to which they are psychologically related.

Kernberg's *psychostructural model* classifies PDs according to levels of psychic organization, indicated by ego, superego, object relations, and instinctual drives. The higher-level *neurotic organization* has a relatively well integrated personality with a harsh superego, a stable self-concept, adequate object relations, and advanced ego defenses. The lowest-level *borderline organization* is characterized by poor ego and superego integration as well as primitive defenses like splitting, denial, and projection. The most severe personality disorders are at this level, including the borderline, narcissistic, paranoid, and schizotypal types.

Kernberg's clinical work, like his theoretical contributions, has had a great impact on the treatment of personality disorders. One of his contributions was an innovative residential treatment program for patients with severe personality disorders.

A prolific author, Kernberg has written numerous papers and books on psychoanalytic theory and therapy, including *Borderline Conditions and Pathological Narcissism* (1975), *Object Relations Theory and Clinical Psychoanalysis* (1976), *Internal World and External Reality* (1980), and *Severe Personality Disorders: Psychotherapeutic Strategies* (1984).

having been abandoned by her as a child. Maria was overwhelmed with anxiety whenever her mother visited, and prior to the visits she became agitated and hostile. Her alternating between idealizing her mother and being angry toward her illustrates borderline splitting.

Learning Factors. In the past, behavioral theorists neglected the study of personality, and, in fact, they avoided the use of personality concepts as explanations for behavior. In recent years, however, behaviorists have been adapting their theories to the personality disorders, analyzing PDs in terms of the learned behavior patterns of individuals. For example, a behavioral analysis of avoidant PD focuses on the ways in which specific people or situations come to elicit avoidant behavior patterns (Barlow, 1981; Turkat & Maisto, 1985; Turner & Hersen, 1981).

Personality traits, including maladaptive ones, can be acquired through learning in interactions with the environment and can reflect attempts to cope with environmental forces. For example, people with antisocial PD sometimes imitate parents who exhibit violent, criminal, and antisocial behaviors. Psychologist Theodore Millon proposes that personality disorders are *learned styles* of feeling, thought, and action. For example, the avoidant person exhibits an "active-detached style" in which he or she takes individual initiative in withdrawing from relationships or interactions with others (Millon, 1981).

According to cognitive theory, the disturbances that constitute personality disorders are attributable to learned *schemata*, or belief systems. Inadequate or irrational judgments, attitudes, and assumptions are considered to be the cognitive basis of personality disorders. We might find the following schemata in someone with a paranoid personality: "People will eventually try to hurt me," "People cannot be trusted, because they will always take advantage of me," "People will try to bother or annoy me," and "Don't get mad, get even" (A. Freeman & Leaf, 1989).

Although behavioral and cognitive theories have begun to address some of the features of personality disorders, they have not offered coherent explanations for how these complex problems develop.

Family Factors. As we have seen in previous chapters, disturbances in family life are common in virtually all mental disorders. This is also true for personality disorders. A number of family risk factors predict the likelihood of some PDs.

The most compelling evidence for family involvement is found in antisocial PD. Parental psychopathology, parental alcoholism and drug abuse, and family violence are especially strong predictors of this disorder. To what extent these family factors reflect genetic predispositions is unknown. Heredity notwithstanding, exposure to these disruptive influences can promote antisocial behavior and attitudes, since the child identifies with and imitates the parents and other family members.

Exposure to abuse appears to be an important factor in some severe personality disorders. In a study of over 900 U.S. military personnel, 57 percent of patients with a childhood history of physical and sexual abuse had personality disorders (G. R. Brown & Anderson, 1991). Adults with antisocial PD are likely to have been children who were subjected to harsh physical punishment or abusive treatment by their parents (Reid, 1986). Individuals with borderline PD are also unusually likely to have been victimized by physical and sexual abuse during childhood (J. L. Herman, J. C. Perry, & van der Kolk, 1989). One study of female and male borderline patients found that 71 percent had been sexually abused, 42 percent had been physically abused, and 65 percent had a history of multiple abuses (Ogata et al., 1990).

During childhood Maria had been sexually molested by her alcoholic father, and in early adolescence she was raped by her stepfather, who was also an alcoholic. Her mother did not believe her when she reported what had happened, and Maria was made out by members of her family to be a vicious liar.

13-3 ▪ TREATMENT OF PERSONALITY DISORDERS

Personality disorders have traditionally been considered difficult if not impossible to correct. Individuals with these disorders do not usually recognize that they have a problem and are consequently reluctant to seek treatment. When they do seek help, it is often because of the adverse interpersonal, legal, and occupational consequences of their disorders rather than their discomfort with the symptoms. In this section we examine the biological and psychological treatment strategies used today for these disorders.

Biological Treatment of Personality Disorders

Biological treatment for personality disorders primarily involves drug therapy to alleviate associated emotional symptoms, such as anxiety, fears, and depression. For some patients with borderline PD, antidepressant medication has been useful in easing the mood problems that are so prevalent (Cowdry & Gardner, 1988). Short-term use of antianxiety medication can also be helpful for some PD patients, such as the avoidant person, but is not recommended as long-term treatment because of its potential for drug dependence (Kocsis & Mann, 1986).

In the absence of clear evidence about underlying biochemical defects in personality disorders, drug therapies remain secondary treatments that are used with caution, usually in conjunction with psychological therapies.

For over ten years Maria had been taking different prescription medications for her emotional distress. At various times she used antidepressants, lithium, and antianxiety drugs. In her late twenties she had developed a psychological and physical dependency on lorazepam, an antianxiety drug, but she was eventually weaned from that medication.

Psychological Treatment of Personality Disorders

The treatment of personality disorders has been dominated by psychoanalysis since Freud's time. Recently, however, behavioral and cognitive treatments have been adapted to these problems.

Psychodynamic Therapy. Although psychodynamic therapy has been used for the whole domain of personality disorders, it has focused mainly on the more severe types, such as the borderline and narcissistic conditions. Otto Kernberg views the most severe personality disorders as forms of the borderline personality organization. Kernberg's *expressive psychotherapy* is a psychodynamic approach to borderline patients that focuses on the patient's immediate expressions of transference and interprets them as "here and now" concerns rather than as manifestations of childhood problems. Therapy addresses the borderline patient's emotional and behavioral inconsistencies through instructive confrontations (Kernberg, 1984).

Miss L., a patient in her late twenties, had a severe borderline personality dominated by schizoid and masochistic features. She was extremely inhibited sexually and had sadomasochistic sexual fantasies involving mutilation of her own and her partner's genitals. Her transference reaction was also highly sexualized, and she wished her therapist would rape and murder her. By openly expressing and exploring her distressing fantasies in therapy she was able to tolerate and integrate the erotic and sadistic feelings that she had defensively split. Eventually, she was able to become romantically and sexually involved with a man for the first time. (Kernberg, 1984)

Psychoanalyst Heinz Kohut, a major figure in *self psychology*, developed an important theory of and treatment for the narcissistic personality. In Kohut's view, narcissistic PD is an extreme defensive reaction to powerful feelings of inadequacy and low self-esteem. Pathological narcissism is assumed to result from a lack of parental empathy in the early years of life, which disrupts the child's self-concept formation. Kohut's therapy provides an empathic relationship in which the patient is able to develop a healthier self-image (Kohut, 1971).

Behavior Therapy. Techniques of behavior therapy can be applied to some symptoms of personality disorders. Despite a lack of systematic research on the effectiveness of behavioral treatments for personality disorders, case reports are encouraging about their potential. Some behavioral techniques are being explored for treating various personality disorder symptoms:

• Desensitization for anxiety in avoidant PD
• Assertiveness training for dependent PD
• Impulse control training for borderline PD (Turner & Hersen, 1981)

Cognitive Therapy. Cognitive therapy is also being used more widely for patients with personality disorders. Many dysfunctional thinking patterns in these patients are accessible to conscious reflection and can be addressed through methods of cognitive therapy, such as confrontation, persuasion, and cognitive restructuring. In individuals with personality disorders, cognitive therapy corrects the pathological schemata and cognitive errors that are responsible for emotional and behavioral disturbances (A. T. Beck & A. Freeman, 1989).

Psychiatrist Heinz Kohut (1913–1981) developed an explanation of narcissistic personality from the perspective of self psychology.

In conjunction with antidepressant medication, a combination of behavioral and cognitive strategies proved helpful for Maria. She was able to modify her anxiety by learning to use muscle relaxation techniques and meditation exercises. In addition, her depression and impulsiveness were addressed through cognitive restructuring, and she learned to regulate some of her self-defeating thoughts by rationally evaluating them.

Evaluating the effectiveness of treatment for personality disorders is especially difficult. Despite strides in diagnosis and assessment, there is disagreement about the symptoms and causes of these disorders. In addition, patients with personality disorders usually seek treatment to alleviate the social and emotional consequences of their personality disorders rather than for the symptoms themselves. The best we can say is that many therapies may help, but their long-term benefits for the patient's personality disorder are uncertain.

SUMMARY

13-1 Personality disorders (PDs) consist of maladaptive personality traits that the DSM-III-R classifies into 11 main types in 3 clusters. Cluster A consists of the paranoid, schizoid, and schizotypal PDs, whose main symptoms are, respectively, suspiciousness and distrust, emotional indifference and detachment, and eccentric behavior and thinking. Cluster B comprises the antisocial, borderline, narcissistic, and histrionic PDs. Antisocial behavior and a disregard for others are the core of the antisocial PD. Unstable emotions and self-image as well as poor impulse control define the borderline PD. Extreme self-love and a sense of entitlement are features of the narcissistic PD. Dramatic attention-seeking behavior defines histrionic PD. Cluster C comprises the avoidant, dependent, obsessive-compulsive, and passive-aggressive PDs. Social interaction is avoided because of fear in avoidant PD. Excessive dependency and submissiveness are symptoms of the dependent PD. Rigid behavior and perfectionism characterize the obsessive-compulsive PD. Indirect expression of hostility is found in the passive-aggressive PD.

13-2 Few biological causes for personality disorders have been clearly identified. Genetic factors are suspected in the antisocial, borderline, and schizotypal PDs. There is nonspecific physiological impairment in people with antisocial PD and perhaps borderline PD. Problems in early object relations are psychodynamic causes of severe personality disorders. Learning experiences and family disturbances also contribute to some PDs. Physical and sexual abuse are often critical contributing factors in antisocial and borderline PDs.

13-3 Drug therapy for PDs relieves emotional disturbances associated with the symptoms. Psychodynamic therapy helps patients to change by allowing free expression and by providing an empathic, supportive relationship. Behavior therapy techniques, such as desensitization and assertiveness training, have been adapted for use with PDs. Cognitive therapy corrects the inadequate and irrational schemata, or beliefs, that impair the patient with a personality disorder.

TERMS TO REMEMBER

antisocial personality disorder
 (p. 336)
avoidant personality disorder
 (p. 339)
borderline personality disorder
 (p. 337)
Cluster A (p. 333)
Cluster B (p. 336)
Cluster C (p. 339)
dependent personality disorder
 (p. 342)
histrionic personality disorder
 (p. 339)
narcissistic personality disorder
 (p. 338)
obsessive-compulsive personality
 disorder (p. 342)

paranoid personality disorder
 (p. 333)
passive-aggressive personality
 disorder (p. 342)
personality disorder (p. 332)
psychopathy (p. 336)
sadistic personality disorder
 (p. 343)
schizoid personality disorder
 (p. 335)
schizotypal personality disorder
 (p. 335)
self-defeating personality disorder
 (p. 343)
splitting (p. 346)

SUGGESTED READINGS

Cleckley, H. (1976). *The mask of sanity.* St. Louis: Mosby.

Kernberg, O. (1984). *Severe personality disorders: Psychotherapeutic strategies.* New Haven, CT: Yale University Press.

Millon, T. (1981). *Disorders of personality: DSM-III Axis II.* New York: Wiley.

Norris, J. (1988). *Serial killers: The growing menace.* New York: Doubleday.

LEGAL AND ETHICAL ISSUES:
IS ANTISOCIAL PERSONALITY DISORDER PREVENTABLE?

Given its prevalence, stability, and associations with severe social maladjustment, antisocial personality disorder is a major mental health problem. Fifty percent or more of repeat felons, especially violent criminals, have antisocial personality disorder, and they constitute a large proportion of the U.S. prison population. There is little doubt that antisocial personality disorder is a problem worth preventing, but whether it can be prevented is hard to ascertain.

Tertiary prevention means direct treatment of an already existing disorder and its consequences. In the case of antisocial personality disorder, attempts at therapy and rehabilitation have largely been failures. The most usual corrective measure is incarceration, which is widely recognized as useless for rehabilitating criminals with antisocial personality disorder, as shown by their high criminal recidivism rates (Quay, 1986).

Secondary prevention involves attempts to cut short the course of a problem after it appears. Efforts at secondary prevention of problems associated with antisocial personality disorder encompass programs for conduct-disordered and delinquent youths, who have already shown signs of antisocial behavior. For example, one community-based program designed as an alternative to incarceration for delinquents is the California Treatment Project, which integrates counseling, social activity, and recreation in residential settings. Such secondary prevention efforts have short-term benefits, although their long-term success is questionable (Reid, 1986).

Primary prevention seeks to prevent a problem before it appears. The greatest promise for prevention lies in programs that address the most prominent risk factors, such as family violence, poverty, and inadequate parenting. No primary prevention programs have yet been devised specifically for antisocial personality disorder, but interventions that seek to decrease antisocial behavior in children are potentially useful. In addition, prenatal health care, preschool enrichment programs, and child management training for parents can relieve stress in high-risk families and possibly obviate some of the family conditions that propagate antisocial behavior (R. N. Roberts, Wasik, Costo, & Ramey, 1991).

Antisocial personality disorder is a complex problem that reflects not only pathology within the individual, but also broader family and societal disturbances. Although the efficacy of most prevention services has not been clearly demonstrated, the attempts are strongly justified by the serious ramifications of ASPD for society.

Chapter

FOURTEEN

Organic Mental Syndromes and Disorders

OBJECTIVES

1. Outline the fundamentals of neurological and mental status examinations.
2. Briefly describe the main features of delirium; dementia; amnestic syndrome; hallucinosis; and delusional, mood, anxiety, and personality syndromes.
3. Identify the major causes of organic mental syndromes.
4. Describe the symptoms and causes of Alzheimer's disease and multi-infarct dementia.
5. Describe the symptoms of seizure disorders, AIDS dementia complex, Parkinson's disease, Pick's disease, Huntington's chorea, and neurosyphilis.
6. Identify brain pathologies associated with seizure disorders, AIDS dementia complex, Parkinson's disease, Pick's disease, Huntington's chorea, and neurosyphilis.
7. Discuss medical treatments for organic mental syndromes and disorders.
8. Explain the role of psychological treatments for organic mental syndromes and disorders.

*A*bbot was a 56-year-old bank officer who had become increasingly forgetful. He often went to work without his briefcase; he misplaced his eyeglasses; he did not follow through on assignments and prepared incomplete reports. He lost interest in his usual activities and hobbies and was forced to retire.

Abbot became withdrawn and often got lost when he went for his morning walk. He remained pleasant and quiet most of the time, but he had occasional boisterous periods. He could not be trusted to turn off the gas jets when he cooked, he had to be constantly reminded of the time of day, and he shaved with the wrong side of the razor. Despite a strong background in economics and banking, he now retained little of his grasp of relevant economic statistics. His speech was vague and he often misused words. Abbot finally consulted a neurologist, but he disappeared from the waiting room and was found three hours later in a local shopping mall. (Spitzer, Skodol, Gibbon, & Williams, 1983)

Deterioration of mental functioning is a common result of brain disease. In this chapter we explore relationships among abnormal brain functioning, mental activity, and behavior.

In previous chapters we discussed mental disorders whose development is believed to be a product of interacting biological and psychosocial factors. In organic mental syndromes and disorders, psychological, emotional, and behavioral abnormalities are directly caused by brain dysfunction. As we will see, these syndromes and disorders are distinguished by their causes. *Organic mental disorders* are conditions caused by identifiable brain impairments; the term *organic mental syndrome* is used to describe a mental problem without reference to a specific cause. In order to understand neurological disorders, we need some basic information about brain-behavior relationships and about how neurological problems are evaluated (American Psychiatric Association, 1987).

14-1 ASSESSMENT OF BRAIN DYSFUNCTION

Our knowledge of how brain structure and function relate to mental activity and behavior has expanded dramatically since the 1960s. This is especially true of the relationships between brain functioning and mental disorders. Despite important advances in our knowledge, however, there are countless unanswered questions. In this section we present some basic information about the brain and describe how understanding its functioning helps us evaluate the presence of organic mental syndromes and disorders.

Overview of Brain Functioning

Thoughts, emotions, and behaviors are related to brain activity. In order for us to function normally, the brain structures that underlie our psychological experiences must be intact and working properly. When the brain is damaged, brain activity goes awry and may result in a mental problem.

The Electrochemical Basis of Neuronal Functioning. The human brain contains approximately 100 billion neurons, or nerve cells, which form the fundamental biological basis of our psychological experiences. Neurons transmit information to one another via electrochemical signals. When a neuron is sufficiently stimulated, its electrical activity is altered. Depending on the nature of the stimulation, the neuron may either increase or decrease its firing rate. Whether the neuron is excited or inhibited, the message is communicated to a neighboring neuron through a change in the activity of chemical neurotransmitters at the synapse (a tiny gap between neurons). Neuronal activity is integrated into a meaningful psychological event.

Neuronal Organization. Neurons are organized into anatomical and functional circuits called *systems*, which perform particular functions. Neuronal systems also interact, so activity in one system ultimately exerts widespread influences over other systems (Andreasen & Black, 1991; Carlson, 1986; Nauta & Feirtag, 1990).

Some neuronal systems have special relevance to our understanding of organic mental disorders. The **prefrontal system** (prefrontal cortex) plays a major role in attention, abstract thought, creative problem solving, social behavior, and movement. The prefrontal cortex is the foremost portion of the frontal lobes and comprises nearly 29 percent of the cerebral cortex (see Figure 14-1) (Andreasen & Black, 1991).

prefrontal system Brain circuitry that plays a role in attention, perception, thought, problem solving, social behavior, and movement.

The case of Phineas Gage provides a dramatic example of how prefrontal damage can affect us. In 1848, Gage was accidentally injured when a gunpowder explosion propelled a metal bar through the left frontal lobe of his brain. Although he survived, he experienced remarkable personality changes, becoming childish and irresponsible and exhibiting socially inappropriate behavior (Rozensweig & Leiman, 1989).

limbic system Brain circuitry that governs emotions, integration of sensory experiences, and memory.

The **limbic system** is an evolutionarily primitive collection of brain structures involved in emotional expression, integration of our sensory experiences, and the formation of memories. Many limbic structures are buried in the temporal lobes (see Figure 14-2). An often-cited example of memory deficits that follow limbic system damage is the classic case of H. M. (Andreasen & Black, 1991):

H.M. had both temporal lobes removed in an attempt to control his convulsions. After surgery, his IQ remained above average, but he could not form new memories.

Figure 14-1 Language systems in the brain.

Source: Adapted from *Physiology and Behavior,* 3rd ed., by N. R. Carlson, 1986, Boston: Allyn and Bacon.

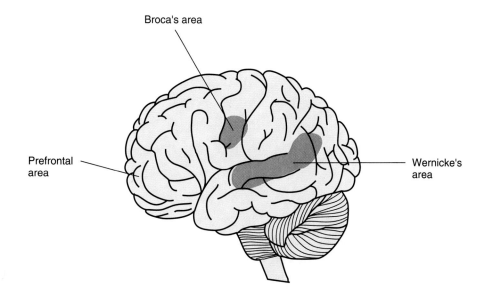

Broca's area

Prefrontal area

Wernicke's area

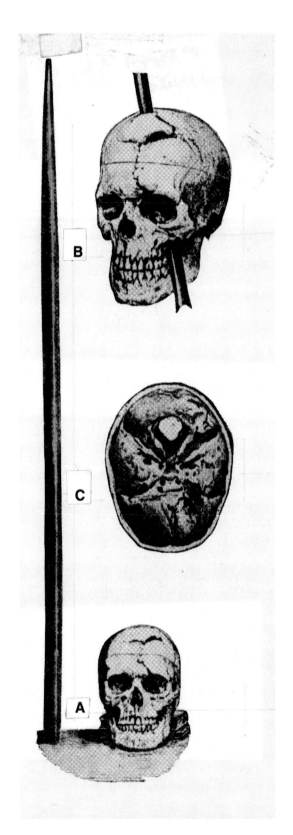

Phineas Gage, whose skull is pictured here, suffered profound personality changes after a metal bar was accidentally propelled through his left frontal lobe.

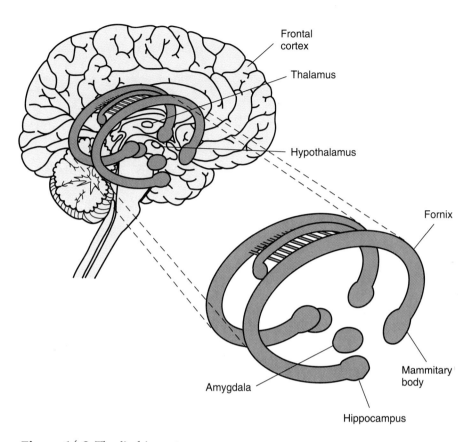

Figure 14-2 The limbic system.

Source: Adapted from *An Introduction to Physiological Psychology,* 3rd ed., by A. M. Schneider and B. Tarshis, 1986, New York: Random House.

His family had moved to a new house after the surgery, and when H.M. went out, he could not remember the address of the new house. He would return to his old house. He did the same jigsaw puzzles over and over again without showing any learning effect, and he read the same magazines repeatedly without finding their contents familiar. H.M. was able to recognize people he had known before the operation, but he could not recognize people he had met for the first time after the surgery, no matter how many times he saw them. (Milner, 1970)

Language systems consist of neuronal circuits that account for our ability to produce and comprehend spoken and written words. They are usually located in the left neocortex, the outer layer of the cerebral cortex. Two major language areas are Broca's area and Wernicke's area (see Figure 14-1). **Broca's area**, in the left frontal lobe, controls the production of speech. Damage to this brain region results in halting, stuttering speech with poor grammatical structure. **Wernicke's area**, in the left temporal lobe, is involved in our ability to understand and integrate speech. Damage to Wernicke's area results in an inability to comprehend speech (Andreasen & Black, 1991; Carlson, 1986; Rozensweig & Leiman, 1989).

The **extrapyramidal motor system** helps control movement (see Figure 14-3). Damage to a major segment of this system, the *basal ganglia*, can pro-

language systems Neuronal circuitry that governs production and comprehension of words.

Broca's area Brain region that controls production of speech.

Wernicke's (ver-nick-uhz) **area** Brain region that controls understanding and integration of speech.

extrapyramidal (extra-puh-*ram*-ih-dull) **motor system** Brain circuitry that controls movement.

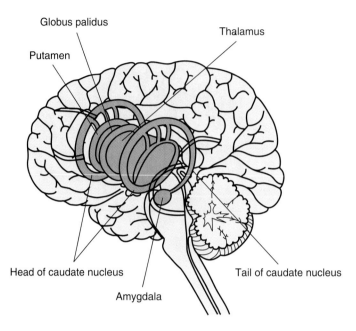

Figure 14-3 The basal ganglia.

Source: Adapted from *Physiology and Behavior,* 3rd ed., by N. R. Carlson, 1986, Boston: Allyn and Bacon.

duce stiff muscles, tremors, muscle restlessness, and difficulties in initiating movements. Of special interest for this chapter is the observation that some basal ganglia diseases also lead to gross cognitive disturbances and emotional changes (Mueller & Fields, 1988).

Neurological and Mental Status Examination

Suspicion of brain dysfunction should prompt a clinician to refer the patient to a neurologist for further evaluation. In a comprehensive evaluation, the neurologist takes the patient's history and performs a general medical examination and a neurological and mental status examination. In many cases, the brain is examined directly, using brain imaging techniques.

neurological examination Tests to detect dysfunction of the nervous system.

Neurological Examination. A **neurological examination** consists of a series of tests used to detect dysfunction of the nervous system. A comprehensive examination is a sequence with three parts. First, the neurologist gathers historical information regarding the onset and development of symptoms. Information about family problems, financial difficulties, sexual behavior, lawsuits, and addictions can shed light on the scope of the person's disabilities and aid in making a diagnosis.

Next, the neurologist conducts a general medical examination. Abnormalities of the skin and the joints, heart, lungs, and other internal organs can affect nervous system functioning and thus account for an organic mental disorder. For example, in a child who walks unsteadily and has erratic eye movements, an abdominal lump suggests a brain tumor (Lechtenberg, 1982).

Finally, the neurologist conducts a series of tests designed to evaluate sensation, muscle strength, coordination, and reflexes. Abnormalities in any of these areas can indicate dysfunction in brain regions known to govern these functions, and this information will point to the type and location of damage. For example, during the neurological examination the patient is asked to touch his or her nose with the eyes closed and to reach for a point in space. Knowledge of which parts of the brain control such functions can help pinpoint the region of brain damage (Lechtenberg, 1982; S. Solomon, 1985).

mental status examination Assessment of cognitive, behavioral, and emotional functions.

Mental Status Examination. A **mental status examination** is a systematic assessment of cognitive, behavioral, and emotional functions (Ginsberg, 1985; Mueller, Kiernan, & Langston, 1988; Strub & Black, 1983). By asking questions and observing the person's behavior, the neurologist evaluates the following:

- *Appearance.* How is the person dressed? Does the person pay attention to personal hygiene?
- *Attitude.* Is the person cooperative, evasive, or apathetic?
- *Behavior.* Is the individual fidgety, relaxed, or clumsy?
- *Thought processes and content.* Does the person hallucinate or have delusions or illusions? Is the person preoccupied, and is abstract thinking intact?
- *Mood, affect, and emotional regulation.* Is the individual depressed, somber, irritable, cheerful, euphoric, guilty, or angry?
- *Alertness.* Is the individual sleepy, lethargic, or alert?
- *Orientation.* Can the person give his or her own name, present location, and time of day?
- *Memory.* Can the person remember recent and remote events?
- *Impulse control and frustration tolerance.* Can the individual control anger, hostility, fear, guilt, and sexual feelings when it would be inappropriate or maladaptive to exhibit these feelings?
- *Judgment.* Is the person capable of making social decisions and anticipating outcomes?
- *Insight.* Does the person have self-awareness?

Symptoms uncovered during a mental status examination may suggest mental problems resulting from brain dysfunction. Table 14-1 lists some of these symptoms.

Christine, a 59-year-old married woman, was taken to the hospital by her husband because of changes in her personality over the last three months. Christine also had problems sleeping and was neglecting family responsibilities. She repeatedly called the police and fire departments for no apparent reason and bought several expensive items. She did not have any psychiatric history; there were no psychiatric problems in her family; and her current behavior was quite uncharacteristic of her usual personality functioning. Her collection of symptoms suggested an organic condition consistent with syphilis.

During the initial questioning she denied any history of syphilis, but after laboratory results came back positive she admitted having been treated for syphilis in 1941. The patient received appropriate antibiotic treatment and returned to her normal functioning within two months after discharge from the hospital. (R. Binder, 1988)

TABLE 14-1   SYMPTOMS OF AN ORGANIC MENTAL DISORDER

1. Fluctuating performance on a series of mental status exams.
2. Memory problems and other signs of cognitive impairment, including a reduced fund of knowledge and trouble with calculations.
3. Disorientation with respect to time and/or place.
4. Visual hallucinations.
5. Sensations of bugs crawling under the skin.
6. Picking at nightclothes or covers.
7. Prior physical illness or current abnormal physical condition.
8. Autonomic signs such as rapid and irregular heartbeat, fever, sweating, and hypertension.
9. Recent drug or medication use.
10. Any sudden unexplained personality or emotional changes.

Source: From ''Organic Mental Disorders'' by R. Binder, 1988, in H. H. Goldman (Ed.), *Review of General Psychiatry* (2nd ed.). Norwalk, CT: Appleton and Lange.

Direct Evaluation of the Brain

In Chapter 4 we described sophisticated techniques used to look inside the brain and study its structure and physiology. These techniques include EEGs, CT scans, PET scans, MRI, and regional cerebral blood flow. They are used to detect seizures, tumors, lesions, brain atrophy, and chemical and circulatory dysfunctions. The results of these tests can help describe and explain the underlying pathology responsible for the symptoms and can suggest appropriate treatment.

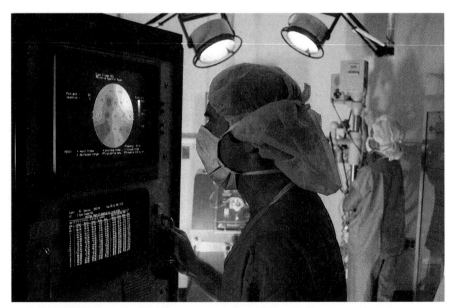

Brain imaging techniques are used to detect brain abnormalities that require surgery. The neurosurgeon shown here is monitoring cerebral blood flow during surgery.

Abbot was referred for several laboratory studies, including an EEG and a CT scan, which indicated some cerebral atrophy of unknown cause. Although testing could not specify the nature or cause of his disease, it did help in ruling out other potential sources of his cognitive impairment. (Spitzer et al., 1983)

14-2 ▓ ORGANIC MENTAL SYNDROMES

organic mental syndrome Symptoms and signs of mental disorder, without reference to cause.

An **organic mental syndrome** is a collection of symptoms and behavior signs due to dysfunction of the brain, but without reference to cause. In most cases, the cause is unknown but is presumed to relate to brain impairment. Even when the cause is known, the term *syndrome* may be used as a descriptor. Thus, an organic mental syndrome is not a diagnosis, but rather a description of symptoms and observed signs (see Table 14-2).

▓ Delirium

delirium Difficulties in maintaining attention.

Delirium is characterized by difficulties in maintaining attention. Individuals suffering from delirium find it difficult to answer questions because they either forget the question or are easily distracted and never process the question. Maintaining a coherent stream of thought is virtually impossible; consequently, thinking is disorganized, fragmented, and lacking in goal direction. In delirium, visual hallucinations are common. Sleep disturbances and disorientation as to time and place are also common. Time disorientation often appears as the first symptom. Typically, delirium fluctuates over the course of a week, and the episode rarely lasts more than a month (American Psychiatric Association, 1987; R. Binder, 1988).

Josephine, a 45-year-old woman, was brought to the hospital by family members who were concerned that she was becoming increasingly frightened and suspicious. She believed that she was being threatened by the upstairs neighbors and that it was unsafe to be at home. Josephine also claimed that she saw babies being lowered from the window of the upstairs apartment, a claim her family said was untrue.

A mental status examination revealed that Josephine was agitated and frightened, with pressured speech and delusions of persecution. Although she was

TABLE 14-2 ▓ **ORGANIC MENTAL SYNDROMES**

Syndrome	Main Features
Delirium	Problems of attention; disorientation.
Dementia	Impairment of verbal, arithmetic, and memory functions.
Amnestic syndrome	Memory deficit.
Hallucinosis	Hallucinations.
Delusional, mood, and anxiety syndromes	Resemble psychotic, mood, and anxiety disorders.
Personality syndrome	Marked personality disturbance.

Source: From *Diagnostic and Statistical Manual of Mental Disorders* (3rd ed., rev.), 1987, Washington, DC: American Psychiatric Association.

oriented as to time and place and her memory functions were intact, her condition worsened over the next few days. As her heartbeat became irregular and her blood pressure increased, she became totally disoriented and hallucinated that her mother was in the room.

Urine and blood tests revealed high barbiturate levels in Josephine's body. Her condition was diagnosed as delirium caused by barbiturate withdrawal. (R. Binder, 1988)

Causes of Delirium. Although the diagnosis of an organic mental syndrome is made exclusively on the basis of symptoms and signs, in many cases the causes are known. The most common causes of delirium are metabolic imbalances, which can be caused by kidney, liver, or thyroid disease; hypoglycemia (low blood sugar); or fever. Any such condition can affect the brain. For unknown reasons, nearly a third of patients recovering from open-heart surgery experience delirium (L. W. Smith & Dimsdale, 1989). Withdrawal from alcohol produces the classic delirium tremens, and a number of other psychoactive drugs, such as antipsychotics and barbiturates, can also induce delirium. Less commonly, delirium is produced by head injury, brain lesions, infections, and seizures (Andreasen & Black, 1991; R. Binder, 1988).

Dementia

dementia (dih-*men*-chuh) Deterioration of mental abilities.

Dementia is marked by a deterioration of intellectual abilities, including memory, comprehension, calculation, and knowledge. An individual suffering from dementia forgets easily, especially when retrieval involves recent memories. For example, the person may be unable to recall the names of three objects five minutes after hearing them but may be able to recall childhood experiences with great accuracy. Personality change is often conspicuous. For example, a usually neat person may become sloppy, or a normally active person may become indifferent and withdrawn. Depression and dementia often coexist, with dementia sometimes complicated by delirium (American Psychiatric Association, 1987; R. Binder, 1988).

During his neurological examination, Abbot was given the name and location of the hospital he was in and was then told the time. Ten minutes later he had forgotten all the information. He was also confused about recent and remote events. He believed his father had died recently when, in fact, he had died years earlier. Abbot's forgetfulness, language difficulties, and decreased fund of knowledge indicated that he was suffering from dementia. (Spitzer et al., 1983)

Causes of Dementia. Dementia is found primarily in elderly people and is most commonly caused by Alzheimer's disease and brain infarcts (strokes) in which brain tissue is destroyed. Alcoholism, head trauma, metabolic disturbances, and infections may also be causal factors. Dementia has also been reported as a neurological consequence of infection by the HIV virus, which causes AIDS (Tross & Hirsch, 1988).

The course of dementia is variable and depends on the cause. It may become progressively worse when caused by brain disease; it may be more or less stable, as in the case of head injury. Five to 15 percent of all dementias, often those caused by drugs or infections, are reversible (R. Binder, 1988).

Dementia is a frequent consequence of head trauma. This man, injured in a car accident, is using a computer as part of his therapy.

Amnestic Syndrome

amnestic syndrome
Memory deficit.

The main symptom of **amnestic syndrome** is a memory deficit, or amnesia. In *anterograde amnesia* the individual has difficulty recalling events that have occurred since the brain trauma. In *retrograde amnesia* the person cannot recall experiences that occurred shortly before the injury. The memory deficit is worse for recent and intermediate memory and is somewhat less for immediate and remote memory. For example, the person cannot remember something that was said just a few minutes ago (recent) or may forget a famous event that occurred several years ago (intermediate). However, if not distracted, the person can repeat a sequence of digits (immediate) or can remember events from childhood (remote). Otherwise, the amnestic does not exhibit a general intellectual impairment, as seen in delirium and dementia. The course of the amnestic syndrome depends on its cause (American Psychiatric Association, 1987; R. Binder, 1988).

Causes of Amnestic Syndrome. Causes of amnestic syndrome include limbic system disease, infection, hemorrhage, epilepsy, surgical trauma, electroconvulsive therapy (ECT, or shock treatment), and carbon monoxide poisoning. Depressant drug intoxication and head trauma can also produce varying degrees of amnesia (American Psychiatric Association, 1987; R. Binder, 1988; Wells, 1985).

Hallucinosis

hallucinosis syndrome
Hallucinations.

The **hallucinosis syndrome** involves hallucinations without other prominent psychological symptoms. The type of hallucination depends upon the underlying organic process. For example, alcohol and hallucinogens may produce auditory hallucinations. Hallucinogenic drugs also produce visual hallucinations, as will diseases that produce a toxic state, such as liver failure (American Psychiatric Association, 1987; R. Binder, 1988; Wells, 1985).

Delusional, Mood, Anxiety, and Personality Syndromes

delusional syndrome
Paranoid delusions.

There are several organic syndromes that closely resemble mental disorders described in previous chapters. The patient with **delusional syndrome** exhibits paranoid delusions of persecution, grandeur, reference, and/or jealousy. However, unlike schizophrenic patients, individuals suffering from organic delusional syndrome are likely to exhibit poor insight, intellectual impairment, social withdrawal, and hallucinations of smell, taste, and touch.

Delusional syndrome is associated with abuse of amphetamines (speed), LSD (acid), PCP (angel dust), and alcohol. Sometimes, delusional syndrome results from epilepsy, head trauma, brain tumor, or cardiovascular disease (American Psychiatric Association, 1987; Cornelius et al., 1991).

organic mood syndrome
Depressive or manic episodes.

Organic mood syndrome is characterized by depressive or manic episodes, and **organic anxiety syndrome** involves generalized anxiety or panic attacks. Neither condition is well understood. Brain infections, cancer, drugs, endocrine diseases, and head trauma are the most common causes of mood and anxiety syndromes (American Psychiatric Association, 1987; R. Binder, 1988; Lechtenberg, 1982; Wells, 1985).

organic anxiety syndrome Generalized anxiety or panic attacks.

organic personality syndrome Disturbance in personality functioning.

Patients with **organic personality syndrome** exhibit either a lifelong personality disturbance or a significant change in personality functioning. The afflicted individual exhibits conspicuous mood variations, unprovoked aggression, poor social judgment, inappropriate sexual behavior, apathy, and paranoia. These patients often have frontal lobe lesions or are presumed to have brain damage that affects the frontal lobes (American Psychiatric Association, 1987; R. Binder, 1988; Lechtenberg, 1982; Wells, 1985).

14-3   ORGANIC MENTAL DISORDERS

organic mental disorder
Psychological or behavioral abnormality caused by known brain impairment.

An **organic mental disorder** is a psychological or behavioral abnormality caused by an identifiable brain impairment. The DSM-III-R specifies three types of organic mental disorders: *presenile and senile dementias, organic mental disorders caused by psychoactive substance use,* and *organic mental disorders caused by physical disorders coded on Axis III* (American Psychiatric Association, 1987).

Dementias

Presenile dementia appears before age 65, and senile dementia appears after that age. Most dementias are due to Alzheimer's disease; a smaller percentage are caused by multiple strokes (American Psychiatric Association, 1987; Lechtenberg, 1982).

Alzheimer's disease
Dementia caused by irreversible neuronal damage.

Alzheimer's Disease. Alzheimer's disease is an irreversible dementia marked by a specific and progressive degeneration of brain neurons. Alzheimer's disease accounts for nearly 60 percent of the dementias in patients over age 65. The total number of Alzheimer's patients in the United States has been estimated at more than 1.5 million, a figure amounting to far less than 1 percent of the general population. Within the next 50 years, the number is expected to rise fivefold as our population becomes more elderly (American Psychiatric Association Task Force on Alzheimer's Disease, 1988; Carlson, 1986).

Alzheimer's disease usually presents as a form of presenile dementia. Eighty

Alzheimer's disease, an irreversible condition that accounts for nearly 60 percent of dementias in patients above the age of 65, leaves the afflicted person helpless, with profound intellectual impairment.

percent of patients show symptoms between the ages 45 and 65. There is a progressive deterioration of intellectual abilities, including memory, abstract thought, language, and other higher mental functions.

Personality characteristics eventually change for the worse as the initially withdrawn patient becomes more boisterous and assaultive (R. Binder, 1988; Lechtenberg, 1982). Depressive and psychotic symptoms occur in 30 to 40 percent of patients. Isolated depressed mood and paranoid symptoms are more common than full-blown mood syndromes or psychotic disorders. The depressive symptoms are worst early in the disease and most often involve depressed mood, anxiety, and feelings of helplessness, hopelessness, and worthlessness. Physical symptoms of depression, such as insomnia and weight loss, are less common. Whether these symptoms are psychological reactions to the patient's awareness of the disease or manifestations of the underlying neuropathology cannot yet be determined (American Psychiatric Association Task Force on Alzheimer's Disease, 1988; Fischer, Simayani, & Danielczyk, 1990; Lazarus, Newton, Cohler, Lesser, & Schweon, 1987; Wragg & Jeste, 1989).

Alzheimer's disease is ultimately fatal. Since deterioration of mental functions is progressive and irreversible, the victim grows more and more helpless and eventually requires custodial care, either at home or in a nursing facility. Once the diagnosis is made, the life expectancy is usually six to ten years (Carlson, 1986; Lechtenberg, 1982).

Causes of Alzheimer's Disease. Upon autopsy, microscopic examination of brain tissue reveals tangled neuronal processes called *neurofibrillary tangles* and abnormal chemical deposits known as *senile plaques*. These abnormalities are associated with degenerating acetylcholine neurons in the forebrain (Andreasen & Black, 1991; R. Binder, 1988; Lechtenberg, 1982).

Although a definitive diagnosis of Alzheimer's disease can be determined only by microscopic examination of brain tissue during autopsy, the symptoms are fairly consistent. Abbot was checked for other possible causes of his dementia, but every other factor was ruled out. His symptoms indicated a diagnosis of Alzheimer's disease. (Spitzer et al., 1983)

Although it is easy to describe Alzheimer's disease in neurological and psychological terms, experts cannot explain the reasons for the degeneration of neurons. The strongest risk factors are age, Down syndrome, a history of head injury, female gender, and having a first-degree relative with the disease. Several studies have found that over several generations, 50 percent of relatives of patients with presenile Alzheimer's disease were affected, suggesting a hereditary cause. Evidence of a hereditary basis for later-onset Alzheimer's is less compelling, since only 14 to 24 percent of first-degree relatives of these patients develop the disease. The genetic contribution may be much stronger than we know, however, since many of the patient's first-degree relatives die of other causes before the age at which they would show symptoms of Alzheimer's disease (N. R. Carlson, 1986; Mohs, Breitner, Silverman, & Davis, 1987).

In 1986, researchers discovered a neuronal protein believed to be responsible for the brain damage typical of Alzheimer's disease. Subsequently, the protein, called *beta-amyloid*, was mapped to chromosome 21, the same chromosome involved in Down syndrome. Virtually all Down syndrome patients who live past age 40 develop senile plaques like those seen in Alzheimer's patients.

By the end of 1987, researchers knew that although the amyloid protein was significant in the production of Alzheimer's disease, it was probably not the primary cause. These amyloid deposits are probably a normal part of aging, but they appear to be naturally removed in normal brains. In Alzheimer's patients, beta-amyloid is apparently not removed. One team of researchers has provided evidence that a fragment of the amyloid protein is toxic to neurons in tissue culture and may be the toxic agent in the brains of Alzheimer's patients (F. E. Bloom & Lazerson, 1988; Goldgaber, Lerman, McBride, Saffiotti, & Gadjusek, 1987; J. L. Marx, 1989a; St. George-Hyslop et al., 1987; Selkoe, Bell, Podlisny, Price, & Cork, 1987; Tanzi et al., 1987; Tariot, Newhouse, Mueller, Mellow, & Cohen, 1988; Wolozin, Pruchinicki, Dickson, & Davies, 1986; Yankner et al., 1989).

multi-infarct dementia Intellectual impairment due to strokes.

Multi-Infarct Dementia. In **multi-infarct dementia**, there is an impairment of intellectual functioning due to disease of the brain's circulatory system (American Psychiatric Association, 1987). *Cerebral infarctions*, or strokes, are areas affected by obstructed blood vessels. Oxygen supply is cut off, and surrounding brain tissue is destroyed as a result. Infarcts account for as many as 10 percent of all cases of dementia (Lechtenberg, 1982).

Symptoms of multi-infarct dementia appear abruptly, and the deterioration is "patchy," meaning that some but not all intellectual functions are disrupted. After each infarct there is partial recovery of function, which diminishes with further strokes. The person exhibits other neurological symptoms and depression in addition to the dementia. Current hypertension or a history of hypertension is the medical factor most commonly found in multi-infarct patients (R. Binder, 1988; Fischer et al., 1990).

psychoactive substance–induced organic mental disorders Mental disorders caused by drug use.

Psychoactive Substance–Induced Organic Mental Disorders

Psychoactive substance–induced organic mental disorders are conditions derived from drug use and are marked by psychological, emotional, or behavior symptoms. Psychoactive drug use produces organic mental disorders by altering neurotransmitter action and blood flow within the brain. The specific type of mental disorder depends largely on the drug used. For example, alcohol is known to reduce cerebral blood flow and produce dementia, delirium, hallucinations, and amnestic syndrome. Cocaine and other stimulants can produce delusions and delirium. Marijuana and hallucinogenic drugs may cause organic delusional and mood syndromes (American Psychiatric Association, 1987; R. J. Mathew & Wilson, 1991). Other organic effects of drug use are discussed in Chapter 8.

Stephen, a 22-year-old medical student, abused cocaine, PCP, and amphetamines. One night he dreamed he was a dog living in a world of heightened smells, a world in which all other sensations paled next to his olfactory sense. In his dream, he went into the clinic and sniffed like a dog, recognizing 20 patients by their unique odors rather than by their faces. Like a dog, Stephen could smell all their emotions. After three weeks, his senses returned to normal. (Sacks, 1985)

Other Organic Mental Disorders

There are many other physical conditions, coded on Axis III of the DSM-III-R, that result in organic mental disorders. Some of the more prominent are seizure disorders, AIDS, Parkinson's disease, Huntington's chorea, Pick's disease, and neurosyphilis.

seizure disorders Brain abnormalities involving disorganized electrical activity.

Seizure Disorders. Seizure disorders, often called *epilepsies*, are a diverse group of brain abnormalities characterized by disorganized electrical activity in the brain. Seizures are associated with disturbances in cognitive functioning, altered perceptions and consciousness, and stereotyped movements called seizures or epileptic activity. These movements may range from slight shaking to uncontrolled jerking and thrashing. People with seizure disorders have an increased risk of personality disorders, psychosis, depression, and suicide attempts. The specific psychological effect of a seizure depends mainly upon the type of seizure and the personality of the patient. Seizure disorders affect 1 in 200 people in the general population and are responsible for 3 to 10 percent of mental hospital admissions each year (Lechtenberg, 1982).

Generalized seizures involve abnormal electrical discharge in both cerebral hemispheres. *Grand mal seizures* induce loss of consciousness, followed by a period of muscle rigidity and generalized convulsions in which the person thrashes about, bites the tongue, and loses bladder control. *Petit mal epilepsy* induces an altered state of consciousness in which the person is unresponsive, is in a daze for a few seconds, and has little or no movement (Lechtenberg, 1982).

The most common type of seizure, and the one of greatest interest to psychologists is the *complex partial seizure* (this disorder is also known as psychomotor, temporal lobe, and Jacksonian epilepsy—named after the British neurologist John Hughlings Jackson, who studied this condition extensively). Twenty to thirty percent of all epileptics suffer from complex partial seizures.

Complex partial seizures are so named because the seizure starts in one brain region and gradually spreads to other regions in a "Jacksonian march," never involving the entire brain and body. During phases of the seizure, individuals may perform compulsive rituals, such as turning the head to the left or

PROFILE
John Hughlings Jackson (1835–1911)

John Hughlings Jackson is considered the founder of the science of neurology, and to him we owe the development of concepts central to our understanding of brain functioning (Sacks, 1985). Jackson, born in England, was one of five children of a farmer. Despite only having had a grade school education, he became a physician, and in 1862 he became a staff member of the National Hospital, Queen Square, London, where he worked for the next 45 years. He died of pneumonia at age 76.

Jackson is most famous for his work on epilepsy. Some say his interest was piqued because his wife suffered from a form of seizure disorder now called Jacksonian epilepsy. His conclusions about the nature of epilepsy were based on a careful study of a few patients and on gross examination of the brain, without the benefit of animal experimentation or the microscopic study of brain tissue common today. The currently accepted concept that all movement involves a balancing of excitatory and inhibitory influences comes from Jackson's research on epilepsy.

Jackson was shy, restless, and easily fatigued. He had no hobbies and hated all forms of exercise. He rarely sat through a whole dinner, habit-

ually left the theater after the first act, and rarely went to a medical meeting until it was nearly over. Although poorly educated, Jackson read voraciously. He claimed that books were not for adornment: he would go to a bookstore, buy a book, rip off the cover, tear the book in half, stuff the halves of the book into two pockets, and then leave the store.

Jackson suffered from both vertigo and migraines. When a colleague approached him on a street corner one day to tell him of an important scientific observation, Jackson interrupted to say, "Don't bother me now, I'm making some observations on my own migraine." He had no children and lived alone for 45 years after the premature death of his wife, who died of a cerebral blood clot.

John Hughlings Jackson published nearly 300 articles, mostly in obscure scientific journals. He rarely used illustrations, diagrams, or statistical data. He did not write books, saying that if he did, "my enemies would find me out." Jackson carried on an active medical practice, though his writings showed little interest in the patient as a person (Lennox, 1970).

right or drinking or pouring water. Auditory hallucinations of music, bizarre sounds, or threatening voices are common, as are delusions of reference. Between epileptic seizures, there may be schizophrenic symptoms with obsessive and paranoid traits. Some patients have even reported religious conversions and mystical experiences (Berg, Franzen, & Wedding, 1987; Lechtenberg, 1982; McKenna, Kane, & Parrish, 1985; Wells, 1985).

Causes of Seizure Disorders. In most cases, the disorganized electrical activity in seizures is *idiopathic*, that is, of unknown origin. However, some factors have been identified as causal agents. Seizures can result from head trauma, tumors, brain surgery, infection, vascular disease, and many metabolic disturbances. The age of the patient at the onset of seizures is important. In general, the later the onset, the greater the likelihood that the seizure is due to brain disease. Seizures that first occur after the age of 30 are likely to be the consequence of a brain tumor (Berg et al., 1987; Lechtenberg, 1982; Wells, 1985).

AIDS Dementia Complex. *Acquired immune deficiency syndrome* (AIDS) is a disease caused by the human immunodeficiency virus (HIV). The virus destroys the body's immune system and also produces neuropsychological dysfunctions. The **AIDS dementia complex** (ADC) involves a progressive deterioration of intellectual abilities. The first symptom is impairment of memory and concentration, which progresses rapidly and eventually affects most cognitive functions. The most common form of cognitive deficit involves mental slowing and problems with recent memory and attention. Impairment in concentration and visuospatial problem solving is also evident. However, vocabulary, the general fund of knowledge, and abstract thinking are preserved. Apathy, withdrawal, muteness, and various movement problems are eventually apparent in a majority of patients (Faulstich, 1987; N. R. S. Hall, 1988; Lunn et al., 1991; Navia, Jordan, & Price, 1986; Tross & Hirsch, 1988).

Psychological symptoms appear in 25 percent of HIV-infected individuals, and 40 percent of AIDS patients show signs of cognitive impairment long before other symptoms appear. In such cases, signs of mental slowing, delirium, amnesia, depression, and psychotic symptoms are often mistaken for something else. Upon autopsy, two-thirds of individuals who die of AIDS show evidence of neuronal damage. Brain imaging studies reveal neuronal degeneration in cortical as well as subcortical brain regions (Lunn et al., 1991; Navia et al., 1986; S. W. Perry, 1990).

Parkinson's Disease. Another organic mental disorder is **Parkinson's disease**, a progressive movement disorder evidenced by rhythmic tremors of the limbs at rest, unemotional facial expression, muscle stiffness, and difficulties initiating movement. Parkinson's disease results from destruction of a motor nucleus in the brain, the *substantia nigra*. More than half of Parkinson's patients experience dementia and impairment in orientation and short-term memory. Unlike Alzheimer's patients, the Parkinson's patient generally retains long-term memory, object recognition, language ability, and normal social behavior. The famous boxer Muhammad Ali suffers from Parkinson's-like tremors, slowed speech, and unemotional facial expression due to repeated blows to the head. Unlike Parkinson's disease, however, Ali's condition is not progressive (Dakof & Mendelsohn, 1986; Lechtenberg, 1982; Mueller & Fields, 1988).

Most individuals with Parkinson's disease are depressed, anxious, apathetic, and socially isolated, and they experience feelings of helplessness. It is unclear whether such symptoms are a direct result of brain pathology or a consequence of knowing one has a devastating illness (Dakof & Mendelsohn, 1986; Lechtenberg, 1982).

Huntington's Chorea. **Huntington's chorea** (*chorea* means "dance") involves purposeless, fluid movements of the limbs and trunk, or jerking and writhing movements. All patients with this disease eventually develop a pro-

AIDS dementia complex
Intellectual impairment due to HIV infection.

Parkinson's disease
A movement disorder with dementia.

Huntington's chorea
(core-*e*-uh) A movement disorder with profound dementia.

Former heavyweight boxing champion Muhammed Ali, shown in peak condition fighting Joe Frazier, now suffers from Parkinson's-like symptoms as a result of repeated punches to the head.

Folk singer Woody Guthrie suffered from Huntington's chorea, a hereditary condition that leaves its victims with a severe movement disorder and profound dementia.

found dementia with impairment in memory, calculation, and comprehension. Severe personality disturbances, paranoia, depression, hallucinations, delusions, and assaultiveness are also common. Huntington's chorea is a hereditary disorder that affects the basal ganglia (Lechtenberg, 1982).

Pick's disease Dementia similar to Alzheimer's disease.

Pick's Disease. **Pick's disease**, a type of dementia often confused with Alzheimer's disease, involves a progressive and irreversible deterioration of mental functioning. People with Pick's disease have poor insight, language deficits, memory problems, dramatic mood changes, and personality disorganization more profound than in Alzheimer's disease. The causes of Pick's disease are unknown, but there is evidence of cerebral atrophy and various neuronal abnormalities (Lechtenberg, 1982).

neurosyphilis Neurological consequences of syphilis.

Neurosyphilis. Syphilis is a sexually transmitted infectious disease. **Neurosyphilis** is the neurological consequence of syphilis microorganisms invading the brain. Symptoms include insomnia, apathy, poor impulse control, unprovoked rage, and social skills deficits. All patients with neurosyphilis eventually experience dementia. They are forgetful and have trouble with attention span, calculations, writing, use of language, and abstract thought. Delusions and delirium are commonly reported (Lechtenberg, 1982).

14-4 ▬ TREATMENT OF ORGANIC MENTAL SYNDROMES AND DISORDERS

Some organic mental syndromes and disorders are amenable to medical treatment. When psychological treatments are used, they are designed mainly to support patients and families in coping with the illness.

▬ Medical Treatments

The treatment of organic mental syndromes and disorders presents a special challenge for health professionals. Unlike disorders of psychosocial origin, organic conditions absolutely require appropriate medical attention as the primary treatment. The type of treatment will depend on the underlying abnormality, the setting in which the person is being treated (for example, hospital inpatient or outpatient status), and the age and overall health of the individual. For irreversible conditions such as Alzheimer's disease and AIDS, the goal is to provide the patient with as much comfort as possible while the disease progresses. As a rule, any medical care designed to manage the person's overall health can be beneficial.

Detailed descriptions of medical procedures are far beyond the scope of this text, but certain general considerations can be noted. The soundest treatment approach is to correct the underlying pathology when it is known and treatable. In cases of organic mental disorder produced by infection, antibiotics can be prescribed. For example, organic mood syndrome produced by neurosyphilis may be successfully treated with penicillin. Currently, AIDS is incurable, though clinical trials indicate that the drugs zidovudine (Retrovir, formerly called azidothymidine or AZT) and didanosine (DDI) may delay the progression of the disease in people who have been infected with HIV but are not yet symptomatic. There is also evidence that zidovudine may alleviate some of the cognitive impairment in AIDS patients (Faulstich, 1987; N. R. S. Hall, 1988; J. L. Marx, 1989b; Navia et al., 1986; Tross & Hirsch, 1988).

A new experimental drug, *Peptide T*, has been proved to reduce cognitive impairment seen in AIDS dementia complex. Moreover, improvements in cognitive ability are correlated with improved brain imaging test results, suggesting that Peptide T may halt the progression of neuronal damage.

Organic mental disorders can result from brain abnormalities for which surgery may be necessary. This surgeon is removing a tumor with the aid of a three-dimensional reconstruction of a CT scan, which helps to pinpoint the location of the growth.

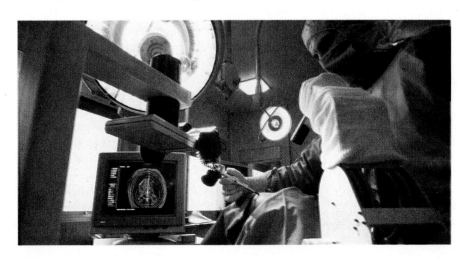

CLOSE-UP
Head Injury and Homicide

Organic impairment does not lead to violent or homicidal behavior in most individuals. However, there is mounting suspicion, and some evidence, that some people who commit homicide are brain-damaged. In the United States, there are more than 20,000 arrests each year for murder and manslaughter. Only 1 percent of those convicted are sentenced to death, and only a tiny fraction are executed. In states that have a death penalty, the murderer can be spared execution if there are mitigating circumstances, such as evidence of brain impairment. However, convicted murderers are rarely evaluated for brain impairment.

One study, conducted by a team of neurologists and psychiatrists, evaluated 13 male and 2 female death row inmates, using a complete battery of neurological, laboratory, psychiatric, and psychological tests. The data was analyzed in the context of family interviews and examination of legal records.

All 15 subjects had a history of head injury, and most had been injured several times. The head injuries were the result of various traumas, such as being thrown into the sink by the father; being hit in the head with a baseball bat, a club, or a heavy metal pipe; falling from a roof; or jumping from a moving car and landing on the head. In all cases, the injuries could be verified by scars, skull indentations, CT scans, or other objective indicators. Depending on the location and type of head injury, subjects suffered seizures, facial paralysis, cortical atrophy, blackouts, dizziness, amnesia, episodic rages, hallucinations, and other neurological signs. Nine of the fifteen subjects had exhibited psychiatric symptoms during childhood; six were chronically psychotic, with bizarre sadistic delusions; and four had attempted suicide during childhood or adolescence.

Remarkably, none of the obvious indicators of brain damage were considered during trials and sentencing or in subsequent appeals, probably because they were not suspected and therefore not looked for. Although the sample was small, this study raises a question: As a group, are murderers simply psychopathic or neuropsychiatrically impaired individuals? If these preliminary findings are replicated, they are certain to fuel the controversy over capital punishment (D. O. Lewis, Pincus, Feldman, Jackson, & Bard, 1986).

Tumors and other structural problems may require surgery. Brain tumors are one of the most common causes of organic personality syndrome and are responsible for many cases of epilepsy.

Many drug-induced mental disorders prove to be completely reversible once the person ceases drug use. For example, treatment of organic hallucinosis can involve having the person withdraw from the abused drug. Administration of antianxiety, antidepressant, or antipsychotic drugs can provide relief from psychological and emotional symptoms.

The most common treatment for seizure disorders is anticonvulsant medication. Although the precise mechanism of action is not well understood, it is believed that effective drugs lower the excitability of neurons and thereby raise the seizure threshold (Groves & Rebec, 1988). For complex partial seizures, carbamazepine (Tegretol) or phenytoin (Dilantin) have proved effective. Some research, however, indicates that Dilantin may worsen cognitive problems in people whose seizures are due to severe head injuries (T. Adler, 1991).

For patients with incurable brain diseases such as AIDS dementia complex and Alzheimer's disease, therapy can help the patient and the patient's family cope with the devastating effects of the illness.

Psychological Treatments

Recognition of a neurological basis for psychological symptoms does not preclude psychological assistance as part of the treatment. A neurological disorder can have a devastating psychological and emotional impact on the patient and concerned family. Understandably, the afflicted person may experience fear, anger, guilt, and depression. For example, many AIDS patients have feelings of guilt, depression, hopelessness, anxiety, and anger associated with recognition of having a deadly disease. Therapy helps the person and family cope with the consequences of the disorder (N. R. S. Hall, 1988; Navia et al., 1986; S. W. Perry, 1990; Tross & Hirsch, 1988).

In many cases, the affected person is no longer capable of performing usual daily tasks and activities. Job responsibilities and family and social obligations usually prove difficult if not impossible to meet. In these cases, psychological therapy may address reorganizing the immediate environment in order to minimize the impact of the person's deficit. Another component of therapy may consist of helping the family understand the nature and course of the disease so they can assist in the patient's management.

Not to be overlooked are the potentially devastating financial burden and legal implications that often come with diseases that require long-term care. The staggering costs of long-term treatment cannot be considered separately from the disease itself. Thus, a necessary component of therapy is to direct the individual and the family in securing financial and legal counseling (Overman & Stoudemire, 1988).

SUMMARY

14-1 Organic mental syndromes and disorders are conditions caused by dysfunction of the brain. Assessment of these conditions requires an understanding of neuronal systems and how abnormalities in their structure and function relate to mental disorders. Neurological examination tests sensation, muscle strength, reflexes, and coordination. Mental status examination assesses cognitive, emotional, and behavioral functions. Brain imaging techniques permit direct observation of the brain.

14-2 An organic mental syndrome is a collection of symptoms due to brain dysfunction without reference to cause. Delirium involves problems in maintaining attention. Dementia involves a deterioration of intellectual abilities. Amnestic syndrome is characterized by memory deficits. Hallucinosis involves visual and auditory hallucinations. Organic mood, anxiety, and personality syndromes are conditions whose symptoms resemble mood, anxiety, and personality disorders.

14-3 Organic mental disorders are mental abnormalities caused by identifiable brain disease. Alzheimer's disease and multi-infarct dementia are forms of dementia. Alzheimer's disease is caused by degeneration of acetylcholine neurons, and multi-infarct dementia is caused by strokes. Drug abuse leads to many organic mental syndromes, the precise nature of which depends upon the drug used. Organic mental disorders are part of the symptom picture of epilepsy, Parkinsons' and Pick's diseases, and neurosyphilis. Dementia is also a common neurological complication of HIV infection.

14-4 Treatment of organic mental syndromes and disorders is primarily medical. The method chosen depends on the underlying physical cause and can involve surgery, medication, or antibiotics. Psychological treatment focuses on supporting the patient and family in order to help them cope with the disability. Depression, anxiety, and other psychiatric consequences of being disabled are addressed with psychotherapy and medication. The patient may need help with the legal and financial consequences of a progressive disorder.

TERMS TO REMEMBER

AIDS dementia complex (p. 371)
Alzheimer's disease (p. 366)
amnestic syndrome (p. 365)
Broca's area (p. 359)
delirium (p. 363)
delusional syndrome (p. 366)
dementia (p. 364)
extrapyramidal motor system
  (p. 359)
hallucinosis syndrome (p. 365)
Huntington's chorea (p. 371)
language systems (p. 359)
limbic system (p. 357)
mental status examination (p. 361)
multi-infarct dementia (p. 368)

neurological examination (p. 360)
neurosyphilis (p. 372)
organic anxiety syndrome (p. 366)
organic mental disorder (p. 366)
organic mental syndrome (p. 363)
organic mood syndrome (p. 366)
organic personality syndrome
  (p. 366)
Parkinson's disease (p. 371)
Pick's disease (p. 372)
prefrontal system (p. 357)
psychoactive substance–induced
  organic mental disorder (p. 368)
seizure disorders (p. 369)
Wernicke's area (p. 359)

SUGGESTED READINGS

Perry, S. W. (1990). Organic mental disorders caused by HIV: Update on early diagnosis and treatment. *American Journal of Psychiatry, 147*, 696–710.

Sacks, O. (1985). *The man who mistook his wife for a hat.* New York: Harper & Row.

Strub, R. L., & Black, F. W. (1983). *The mental status examination in neurology.* Philadelphia: Davis.

Thompson, R. F. (1985). *The brain. An introduction to neuroscience.* New York: Freeman.

LEGAL AND ETHICAL ISSUES: FINANCIAL AND LEGAL COUNSELING

Organic mental disorders often lead to permanent mental and physical disability and great financial burden. In the case of irreversible conditions such as Alzheimer's disease, long-term nursing care is inevitable—and the annual cost can easily exceed $20,000. Approximately half of this cost is borne by the family (Overman & Stoudemire, 1988). As the disease progresses, financial and legal counseling becomes necessary.

The prospect of expensive long-term care for Alzheimer's patients raises some questions: Will the patient accept or refuse medical care? If it is accepted, what type of care will the patient consent to? Patients can accept (or legally refuse) all medical care as long as they give *informed consent*. Legally, consent is considered informed if the patient is told about the diagnosis and prognosis, the details of treatment, and the risks of refusing treatment. Informed consent also means that the person is not coerced into making a decision and is competent to render a decision.

Competence is a legal matter determined by the courts. A person is considered competent if he or she has the mental capacity to make a reasonable choice if given adequate information. In emergency situations, the physician is permitted to assess and treat the condition against the apparent will of the patient as long as the physician attempts to contact the patient's family or guardian.

Determination of competence also applies to financial and related legal matters. Ultimately, the Alzheimer's patient will not be competent to manage and protect financial assets. Once the person becomes senile, who will make important decisions? Physicians who treat Alzheimer's patients recommend that as soon as the diagnosis seems certain, the patient should designate *power of attorney*. This allows a legally appointed person to make important decisions about extended health care and the patient's estate. Many states also have provisions for *living wills*. These legal documents permit individuals, while still mentally competent, to specify their wishes about how they should be treated if they are rendered incompetent.

Making plans for the later stages of dementia is certainly an unpleasant task, but if appropriately addressed, preparation will spare both the patient and the family further hardship (Overman & Stoudemire, 1988).

Chapter FIFTEEN

Family Violence and Divorce

OUTLINE

15-1 Family Violence
Marital Violence • Child Abuse • Causes of Family Violence • Treatment of Family Violence

15-2 Divorce
Causes of Divorce • Consequences of Divorce • Treatment of Divorce

OBJECTIVES

1. Distinguish among the types of family violence.
2. Discuss the causes and consequences of marital violence.
3. Define child sexual abuse, physical abuse, and neglect.
4. Identify the short-term and long-term effects of child abuse.
5. Outline the primary causes of child abuse.
6. Describe the treatment strategies for family violence.
7. Explain the causes of divorce.
8. Identify the effects of divorce on children and adults.
9. Discuss divorce therapy and divorce mediation.

*V*ince was ordered into treatment for alcohol abuse by family court. He had been accused of physically abusing his 9-year-old son by beating him with a belt because he did not like the boy's grades. His son's teacher notified the authorities when the boy came to school with large bruises, made by the belt buckle, on his cheek and arms. Although he admitted losing control on that occasion, Vince was hostile and resentful about being brought up on such charges. He claimed that he often used physical punishment with his children and believed it was his right to do so.

Vince had a history of violent behavior with other family members as well. He and his wife were accustomed to physical confrontations, and the police had been involved a number of times. His first marriage had ended after less than two years because of his violent temper and physical abuse. Now his second marriage was falling apart; his wife had an order of protection against him and was seeking legal separation.

Vince was an alcoholic and former heroin addict who had had numerous run-ins with the police since early adolescence. As a child he had been the victim of sexual and physical abuse by his narcotics-addicted father. Vince's life exhibits many of the features characteristic of violent families. In this chapter we look at the nature and causes of severe family problems and explore ways in which they can be treated.

Throughout this text we have focused on individuals' psychological disorders. When we have discussed family problems, they have usually been considered as causes or effects of individual disorders. The approach we have taken reflects the DSM-III-R, which emphasizes individual mental disorders and gives limited attention to family problems. In the DSM-III-R, family problems are listed as *V codes*, or conditions not attributable to a mental disorder (American Psychiatric Association, 1987). Because of their prevalence, severity, and social implications, family violence and divorce are major mental health concerns deserving of separate discussion. In this chapter we examine their causes, consequences, and treatment.

15-1 ▪ FAMILY VIOLENCE

You have undoubtedly read or heard many stories of family violence, and in all likelihood you have known families in which violence has occurred. Television, magazines, and newspapers constantly report cases of child abuse, homicide, and brutality within families.

Surprisingly, there is no real consensus on the definition of family violence. The definitions used in legal matters, psychological theories, and research are not consistent. For the purposes of this chapter, we define **family violence** as behavior that involves acts or threats of physical or psychological harm between members of a family. The essence of family violence is that someone's physical or mental well-being is violated by a family member.

By any definition, family violence is a widespread phenomenon that is not confined to American society. Historical records are replete with accounts of family violence, and in the past, violent practices have been part of many cultural traditions. For example, *infanticide*, the killing of infants, was practiced for centuries in many countries in order to limit population and to eliminate

family violence Behavior involving acts or threats of physical or psychological harm against family members.

undesired children, such as those with birth defects (Emery, 1989; J. Hamilton, 1988; Hutchings, 1988).

In fact, family violence is still widespread in many cultures. A study of 90 traditional non-Western societies found wife beating in 84 percent and physical punishment of children in 74 percent (Levinson, 1988). A sign of the influence of gender on family violence is that husband beating was present in only 27 percent of those societies. Surveys reveal that in the United States approximately half of all families exhibit some form of family violence. What we know about the prevalence of family violence is based primarily on reported cases, and most experts agree that they represent only the tip of the iceberg (Steinmetz, 1990; Straus, Gelles, & Steinmetz, 1980).

Family violence takes many forms, including child abuse, marital violence, sibling violence, parent abuse, and elder abuse. Although we can distinguish among different types of family violence, they often occur together, in the same families, and do not necessarily represent separate problems. Research on family violence is a relatively new field, and the greatest amount of attention has been devoted to marital violence and child abuse. Consequently, we will direct our discussion to these better-understood problems.

Marital Violence

Violence between spouses appears to be the most common form of family violence. Studies report marital violence in 15 to 75 percent of couples in the United States. Such a wide range probably reflects differences in how these cases are defined and reported. A reasonable estimate is that about one-third of wives and one-fifth of husbands are the victims of significant marital violence at some point during their marriage. In about half of marriages with violent episodes, both husband and wife exhibit violent behavior. Although severe and chronic marital violence is more often directed against wives, the rates of spousal homicide are nearly equal for wives and husbands (Margolin, Sibner, & Gleberman, 1988; Steinmetz & Lucca, 1988; Thaxton, 1985).

Wife Abuse. In this country, nearly a million women seek medical treatment annually as a result of being beaten by their husbands. Additionally, more than 1000 women are murdered by their husbands each year. Wife beating was formerly considered a legitimate right of husbands; even today many men think that the use of physical force against their wives is acceptable. In 1871 Massachusetts was the first state to outlaw wife beating. Nevertheless, the practice has continued, and until recently the legal system minimized its significance (Browne, 1988; M. Martin, 1988).

Psychologist Lenore Walker describes three phases in *wife battering*. The *tension-building phase* includes discrete incidents, usually of "minor" aggressions like pushing, that do not escalate into major episodes of violence. The *acute battering phase* involves an episode of severe violence that may be prompted by an insignificant event. After the battering comes a *phase of calm and contrition*, in which the batterer becomes apologetic and seeks to placate his victim. The cycle begins again when the batterer's tension increases and his self-control decreases (Walker, 1990).

Fights between Vince and his wife, Joan, were a regular occurrence. The fights were mostly about his drinking, their financial problems, and her sexual disinterest

The tragedy of battered women was dramatically illustrated in the case of Hedda Nussbaum, arrested with her husband, Joel Steinberg, in New York in 1987 for the death of their adopted daughter, Lisa. The trial revealed that Nussbaum had long been victimized by her husband's violence.

in him. They could ignore each other for a few weeks, but inevitably their arguing led to slapping and pushing matches. The battering generally occurred when Joan "got in Vince's face" while he was drunk. His pattern was to punch and choke her until she stopped fighting back. Afterward he would binge-drink for a few days, and eventually he would beg her forgiveness and promise to change.

battered woman syndrome Helplessness, submissiveness, depression, and low self-esteem in battered women.

The cycle of violence that Walker describes may persist for many years, usually escalating over time. The victimized wife often develops the **battered woman syndrome**, a condition characterized by feelings of helplessness, submissiveness, depression, and low self-esteem. A chronically battered woman may have a powerful love/hate bond with her husband, and despite the brutal treatment she receives, she may act in a protective manner toward him, blaming herself for the violence (Walker, 1984, 1990).

The most obvious cases of wife abuse are those in which physical violence is present. Many other forms of abuse exist, including threats of violence, sexual violence, mental degradation, and forcible restraint. In recent years, attention has been drawn to the problem of *marital rape*, which often goes along with physical abuse. Most physically battered wives report at least one instance of marital rape (Pagelow, 1988). In fact, marital rape is the most common type of rape in the United States, affecting nearly one in seven women. The courts are just beginning to deal with the legal issues, and in some states marital rape is not yet considered a crime.

Husband Abuse. Husband abuse is not as widespread as wife abuse, but it is not as rare as many people assume. About 30 percent of American husbands are victims of abuse by their wives, though fewer than 1 percent are severely abused. As we have already mentioned, husbands are victims of spousal homicide nearly as often as wives. However, the wife who murders her husband is usually responding to the husband's abusiveness (Petrie & Garner, 1990).

Statistics on husband abuse are scant. In all probability, husband abuse is seriously underreported, perhaps because men are reluctant to admit they are maltreated. Where husband abuse is present, there is generally mutual abuse by both spouses (Steinmetz & Lucca, 1988).

Child Abuse

child abuse Physical, sexual, or psychological maltreatment of children.

Child abuse refers to physical, sexual, or psychological maltreatment of a child under 18 years of age. Included in this definition are *acts of commission*, such as beating or raping a child, and *acts of omission*, like leaving a child unattended or neglecting a child's medical needs (Hart, Germain, & Brassard, 1987).

Today child abuse is a major social concern. That has not always been true, however. The first child protective agency in the world, the New York Society for the Prevention of Cruelty to Children, was founded in 1875 and set the standard for advocating children's rights. Ironically, the society's early efforts to shape child protection laws were based on animal protection laws. Nearly a century passed before all states had laws mandating the reporting of child abuse (Cicchetti & K. Olsen, 1990).

Inconsistent definitions produce great variation in the statistics on child abuse. Compounding the uncertainty, it is believed that only a minority of child abuse cases are actually reported. A survey by the National Committee for Prevention of Child Abuse found that over 2.5 million reports of child abuse were made in the United States during 1990. This figure is over half a million more than that reported five years earlier. Physical abuse accounted for 27 percent of cases: sexual abuse, 15 percent; neglect, 46 percent; and other maltreatment, including emotional abuse, 13 percent. Of the reported cases in 1990, over 1200 resulted in fatalities (The National Committee on the Prevention of Child Abuse, 1990).

battered child syndrome Physical and behavioral symptoms of abused children.

Types of Child Abuse. In 1962, pediatrician C. Henry Kempe and his colleagues introduced the **battered child syndrome**, a medical description of the physical symptoms of severely abused children (Kempe, Silverman, Steele, Droegemueller, & Silver, 1962). Since that time, physicians, courts, psychologists, and researchers have struggled to identify the many signs and forms of child abuse. Today, four types of child abuse are recognized: physical abuse, sexual abuse, emotional abuse, and neglect. A common denominator of all child abuse is *psychological maltreatment*, a denial or frustration of the child's needs (Hart et al., 1987).

physical abuse Infliction of a nonaccidental physical injury.

Physical abuse is the infliction of a nonaccidental physical injury on a child. Most physical abuse involves minor injuries given in the course of punishing children. Children are physically abused throughout the developmental period, but most cases occur before age 9. There are some questions about the reliability of reported data, but it appears that the perpetrator of physical abuse is as likely to be the mother of the child as the father. However, mothers more often abuse very young children, and fathers are more likely to abuse adolescents.

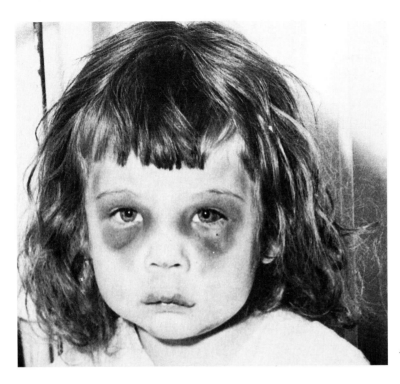

The face of this 3-year-old girl shows the clear physical signs of violent maltreatment by her stepfather. As with most battered children, her physical injuries will soon heal, but the emotional trauma will linger.

Identification of physical abuse may be simply a matter of noting obvious physical trauma, such as burns, scabs, welts, and bruises; however, in many children the signs of physical abuse are hidden. Typically, abusers view the abuse as punishment, and many abusers inflict injuries in the course of what they perceive as justified discipline. Indeed, our society has yet to define the boundary between acceptable corporal punishment and physical abuse. Today, most American parents use physical punishment with their children, and in many states the law permits school authorities to employ corporal punishments (Cicchetti & K. Olsen, 1990; D. A. Wolfe, 1987).

Vince regularly imposed physical punishment on his three children. One of his favorite methods was to hoist the children up by their hair. He also forced them to hold heavy objects, such as bricks, until their arms and backs ached. If they dropped the objects before he let them, Vince would whip them with a belt.

child sexual abuse
Sexual interaction between an adult and a minor child.

Child sexual abuse refers to sexual interaction between an adult and a child of minority age as defined by state law. Child sexual abuse includes sexual touching or fondling, molestation without intercourse, sexual intercourse, and coercing a child to perform sexual acts. Unlike physical abuse, sexual abuse may leave no external identifiable mark, and in the majority of cases physical abuse does not accompany sexual abuse. Ninety percent of the perpetrators of child sexual abuse are male, and eighty percent of victims are female (Koss, 1990).

Estimates of the prevalence of child sexual abuse vary enormously, with studies reporting figures of 6 to 62 percent in girls and 3 to 30 percent in boys. The true extent is unknown, since only a minority of incidents are ever reported, but about 25 percent of girls and 10 percent of boys are probably affected.

PROFILE
C. Henry Kempe
(1922–1984)

C. Henry Kempe, a pediatrician and devoted advocate for children, was best known for his landmark paper on the battered child syndrome. His work provided an impetus for research on child abuse and its treatment.

Kempe was born in Breslau, Germany (now Wrocław, Poland), in 1922. His family emigrated to England when he was 15 years old. In 1938 he and his family were brought to California through the efforts of a refugee organization. After graduating from the University of California, Berkeley, Kempe attended medical school at the University of California, San Francisco, taking his M.D. in 1945. After two years of army service and further training in pediatrics at the Yale University School of Medicine, he returned to San Francisco as an instructor. In 1956, Dr. Kempe became chairman of the Department of Pediatrics at the University of Colorado School of Medicine.

Kempe's 1962 paper on the battered child syndrome ushered in the modern era of child abuse study, stimulated research on its causes and consequences, and provoked changes in laws mandating the reporting of child abuse. Dr.

Kempe was a dedicated supporter of children's rights and welfare. He established the National Center for Child Abuse and Neglect in Denver in 1974, and the following year he founded the International Society for the Prevention of Child Abuse and Neglect. His interest in children's health needs also took him to India to take part in a World Health Organization smallpox program.

In addition to working as a pediatrician, Dr. Kempe was an energetic teacher, organizer, and lobbyist for the cause of child abuse prevention. At a time when few people recognized the extent and seriousness of the problem, he helped to raise public and professional consciousness of child abuse. In 1984, at age 62, Dr. Kempe died of a heart attack.

During his career, Dr. Kempe lectured and wrote extensively on various aspects of child abuse and its treatment. His books include *Helping the Battered Child and His Family* (with R. E. Helfer, 1972); *The Abused Child: A Multidisciplinary Approach to Developmental Issues and Treatment* (with H. P. Martin, 1976); and *Child Abuse* (with R. Kempe, 1978).

Family members perpetrate about half of the acts of sexual abuse against children in the United States. Close male relatives—usually uncles, brothers, and grandfathers—account for about 75 percent of child sexual abuse by family members, and fathers or stepfathers for most of the remaining cases (Peters, 1988; Wyatt & Powell, 1988).

Between the ages of 7 and 10, Eileen was forced to perform oral and manual sex on her older brother and male cousin. In addition, they repeatedly molested her,

In recent years many celebrities, such as actress and talk-show host Oprah Winfrey, have revealed that they suffered sexual abuse as children.

but they did not have intercourse with her. Because they threatened to kill her if she told anyone, she never revealed the abuse to her parents.

child neglect Failure to provide minimum care for a child's well-being.

Child neglect is the failure of a parent or guardian to provide a minimum degree of care for a child's physical well-being. Neglect covers many types of behavior, from the total abandonment of a child to the lack of adequate supervision. Neglect is the most prevalent form of child abuse, often accompanying other types, especially physical abuse (Hart et al., 1987; New York State Society for the Prevention of Cruelty to Children, 1990).

Linda was charged with child neglect after police found her 2-year-old son wandering in the street near their home. Linda had fallen asleep after drinking and smoking marijuana, and the baby had walked out the door. Luckily for the boy, some neighbors spotted the child and called the police.

emotional abuse
Psychological maltreatment that impairs a child's emotional well-being.

Emotional abuse involves psychological maltreatment that impairs the child's emotional well-being. Of all types of child abuse, emotional abuse is most difficult to identify and verify. Certainly, emotional abuse is a component of physical abuse, sexual abuse, and neglect, but it also occurs without the other forms of abuse. Many different types of child emotional abuse exist, including mental cruelty; rejection; degradation; emotional deprivation; and terrorizing, corrupting, or isolating the child (Garbarino, Guttmann, & Seeley, 1986; Hart et al., 1987).

When she was very young, Jeanine was informed by her mother that she was "a mistake." Throughout her childhood, Jeanine was told how horrible she was and how much trouble she caused her mother. She was blamed for all the problems her mother encountered, from difficulty on her job to fights with her numerous boyfriends.

Consequences of Child Abuse. The diversity of reported effects of child abuse is astounding. Physical and emotional abuse are associated with many behavioral and emotional disorders of childhood and adolescence. Aggressive antisocial behavior, academic and social maladjustment, substance use disorders, and depression are more common in abused children. The effects of neglect are not as clear as the effects of physical and sexual abuse. However, children subjected to neglect exhibit diverse developmental delays. They may experience delayed language acquisition, physical health problems, and emotional disturbances such as depression. An extreme but rare condition in neglected infants is *failure to thrive*, in which the child exhibits a general deficiency in physical, social, and emotional development (Cicchetti & K. Olsen, 1990; Fontana, 1985; Hart et al., 1987).

The greatest attention has been devoted to the effects of child sexual abuse. In many respects this is the most serious type of abuse; its effects can be both devastating and permanent. The immediate short-term effects include such emotional disturbances as fear, anxiety, anger, and guilt. The symptoms of many victims are similar to those seen in other types of posttraumatic stress disorder, including excessive anxiety and flashbacks to the abuse. Two common reactions to child sexual abuse are *inappropriate sexual acting out*, such as public masturbation or sexual seductiveness, and *dissociation*, a splitting of conscious

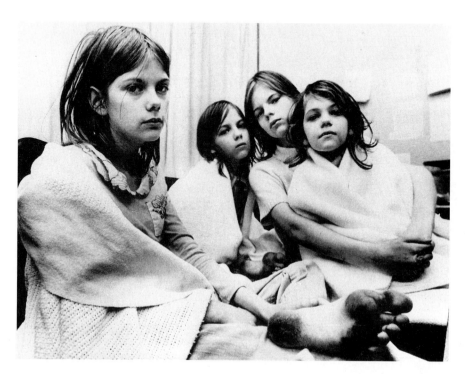

Neglected children are deprived of their right to emotional and physical well-being. These four orphans were found by police wandering barefoot in subfreezing weather after their uncle put them out of his house.

experiences. The following statements by victims describe their experiences of dissociation (Finkelhor, 1986, 1988; Wyatt & Powell, 1988):

> It's like I rise up out of my body. I could feel myself sitting in a chair, and I could feel myself floating up out of my body. (Bass & Davis, 1988, p. 43)

> The actual rape memories for me are like from the end of a tunnel. That's because I literally left my body at the scene. (Bass & Davis, 1988, p. 72)

sexually abused child's disorder A disturbance characterized by increased sexual awareness, sexual acting out, dissociation, and unexplained fears.

Some experts are promoting a new diagnostic category, the **sexually abused child's disorder**. Victims show increased awareness of sexual behavior, an ability to describe or demonstrate specific sexual activities, inappropriate preoccupation with or acting out of sexual activity, dissociation, and unexplained fears and avoidance of specific people or settings. This diagnosis has not yet been adequately tested, but it is consistent with previous studies on the effects of child sexual abuse (Corwin, 1988).

In addition to its immediate effects on the victim, child sexual abuse has many long-term consequences, which may not appear for years (see Figure 15-1). Numerous long-term psychological problems have been identified in relation to child sexual abuse (J. C. Beck & van der Kolk, 1987; Becker, 1988; Becker & Coleman, 1988; Briere & Runtz, 1988; G. R. Brown & Anderson, 1991; Browne & Finkelhor, 1986; Chu & Dill, 1990; Cicchetti & K. Olsen, 1990; Finkelhor, 1990; Goldston, Turnquist, & Knutson, 1989; J. Kaufman & Zigler, 1987; Peters, 1988; Sanders & Giolas, 1991; J. A. Stein, Golding, Siegel, Burnam, & Sorensen, 1988; Wyatt & Powell, 1988):

- Depression
- Suicide
- Dissociative disorders
- Personality disorders
- Schizophrenia
- Cognitive deficits
- Anxiety disorders
- Substance use disorders
- Sexual deviations
- Antisocial behavior
- Prostitution
- Family violence

The long-term effects of child sexual abuse rarely occur as individual symptoms. They often appear as complex patterns of disturbance, as expressed in the remarks of a 28-year-old survivor of child sexual abuse who is now a high school guidance counselor:

> My father not only molested me, he molested all my cousins and all the girls in the neighborhood. . . . The peak of it all was at about eight. That's when he first raped me. It was pretty regular after that, at least three times a week. . . . I was very self-destructive in terms of drugs and fighting. I started taking drugs at nine. I started hustling. I did just about everything. . . . Between what was happening to me at home with him and having to fight and live on the streets too, I always thought the only freedom would be to go

Not only do characteristics of the abuser contribute to family violence, but in many cases the victim's traits and behavior unintentionally increase the risk of being abused. Children who are physically, intellectually, or emotionally handicapped are more likely to be physically abused than the average child. In some cases, the child's handicap may so anger or frustrate the parent that he or she becomes abusive. In other instances, the handicapped child is simply an easier target for an abusive parent (Iverson & Segal, 1990; Starr, 1988).

Abused wives' feelings of entrapment and helplessness can actually perpetuate their condition of victimization. For example, a depressed woman who has resigned herself to being battered provides the battering husband with a passive and defenseless victim for further violence. The battered woman syndrome is a consequence of abuse, but at the same time it can also be a factor in preserving the dysfunctional marriage in which violence exists. Although the victims' behaviors may be associated with greater risk of abuse, it is important to recognize that the ultimate responsibility for family violence rests with the abuser, not the victim (Strube, 1988; Walker, 1984).

relational pathology
Severely dysfunctional interactions and relationships among family members.

Family Factors. In general, family violence reflects **relational pathology**, a severe dysfunction of the interactions and relationships among family members (Cicchetti & K. Olsen, 1990). Individual pathology can contribute to violent behavior, but broader features of the family system are also at work. Commonly found in violent families are marital discord, social isolation, and family stress, such as unemployment and financial problems. These factors can prompt violence, result from violence, and maintain violence (Leonard & T. Jacob, 1988; Starr, 1988; Steinmetz, 1990; Straus et al., 1980; Strube, 1988; Widom, 1989).

Neither Vince nor his wife had much involvement with people outside their immediate family. Vince had no contact with his parents or older brother, and what friendships he had were bar buddies whom he saw only when drinking. Since marrying Vince, Joan had grown alienated from her family and friends. At first she had lied to them about his abusiveness, trying to rationalize it, but eventually she just avoided her parents, siblings, and friends. Vince and Joan's social isolation enhanced their conflicts and intensified their mutual anger.

Spouse abuse is more likely to occur when both spouses hold rigid traditional sex roles—that is, dominant male and subordinate female. Many wife batterers perceive themselves to be justified and believe they have the right to physically abuse their wives. Battered wives may hold complementary views about their subordinate position. Some husbands become abusive when real or imagined threats to their status in the family provoke their violent reactions (Thaxton, 1985; Walker, 1990).

In families where physical abuse of children exists, there is usually a history of coercive interactions between parents and children, and the parents have inadequate child-rearing skills. Physical abuse and neglect of children cut across all lines of socioeconomic status, race, and religion. However, they are more common in families living under stressful circumstances, including large family size and poverty (Biller & R. S. Solomon, 1986; Cicchetti & K. Olsen, 1990; Starr, 1988).

Other dysfunctional relationships are also prevalent in families where sexual abuse of children is present. An especially damaging form of sexual abuse is *incest*, which involves an inappropriate sexual relationship between parent and child. Incest is often associated with severe disturbances in the parents' marital relationship. The nonabusive parent, usually the mother, has sometimes been depicted as a silent conspirator in the incest. In some cases the nonabusive parent knows about or suspects the incest and does nothing because of denial or because of fear of the abuser's reaction. However, many nonabusive parents are completely oblivious to the sexual abuse, which is a closely guarded secret between the abuser and the victim (Madonna, Van Scoyk, & Jones, 1991; D. A. Wolfe, V. V. Wolfe, & Best, 1988).

Sociocultural Factors. Family violence is most common in societies where other forms of violence also flourish. In the United States—an exceptionally violent society—and throughout the world, the aggressors are usually male and the victims are usually women and children. The historical devaluation of women and children has fostered attitudes conducive to family violence. The secondary status of women and children in many cultures is congruent with their victimization by male family members. Family violence is not simply an expression of individual problems but is a manifestation of socially defined power relationships, as prescribed by traditional male and female sex roles (Bersani & Chen, 1988; D. Glaser, 1990).

Although family violence cuts across socioeconomic lines, there is a greater incidence among families at the lower SES levels. The relationship between SES and family violence may to some extent reflect a greater likelihood that incidents among poorer segments of society will be reported, but it is unlikely that reporting bias entirely explains the association. A link between poverty and violent behavior applies not only within the family but also to aggression outside the family. Social and personal stress associated with poverty is well documented, and poverty can easily foster conditions that promote anger, frustration, and aggression (Biller & R. S. Solomon, 1986; Starr, 1988; Steinmetz, 1990).

Treatment of Family Violence

Diverse approaches to treating family violence have emerged in recent years, but since this is a relatively new field many questions remain unanswered. Today, treatments for family violence involve four strategies: abuser-oriented, victim-oriented, family-oriented, and social interventions.

Abuser-oriented Interventions. Based on the assumption that abusive parents and spouses are responsible for their behavior, the abuser-oriented intervention focuses on curtailing their violent behavior and on changing their attitudes about the use of aggression. In many cases abusers are treated for associated mental disorders, such as depression and alcoholism.

Individual and group therapy for child abusers seeks to improve their parenting skills, impulse control, and stress management abilities. Programs for child abusers have produced modest benefits, but reports of further abuse are common (Cicchetti & K. Olsen, 1990). Treatment for spouse abusers has also had limited success, and programs for wife batterers have high dropout and recurrence rates (Sonkin et al., 1985).

Abusive behavior can be treated indirectly by addressing issues in the abuser's life that are associated with violence. Since many abusers are socially isolated, one way to alter the conditions that foster abuse is to improve the abusers'

CLOSE-UP
Children of Alcoholics

In the United States today there are approximately 27 million children of alcoholics, of whom 7 million are under 18 years of age. As a group, they have high rates of psychological disturbances, including substance use disorders, conduct disorders, antisocial behavior, juvenile delinquency, criminal behavior, academic underachievement, psychosomatic symptoms, anxiety disorders, and depression (Freiberg, 1991; U.S. Department of Health and Human Services, 1990).

Children of alcoholics are more likely to be the victims of physical abuse and neglect. A major study by the American Humane Association found that in a sample of over 32,000 cases of child abuse and neglect, the rate of parental alcoholism was twice that of the United States as a whole (American Humane Society, 1980). The link between parental alcoholism and sexual abuse is less certain, but studies show that alcohol use is often a factor in child sexual abuse (U.S. Department of Health and Human Services, 1990).

Beyond the direct effects of physical and sexual abuse, children of alcoholics are subjected to greater familial stress and emotional maltreatment. They are more likely to be exposed to violence between their parents and to bear the brunt of the coercive and threatening behavior of the alcoholic parent. The emotional needs of children often go unmet because the family's energy and resources are devoted to coping with the alcoholic parent. Many are forced to grow up too fast and are expected to assume adult responsibilities beyond their years.

Psychologist Janet Woititz has written extensively about adult children of alcholics. She believes they share certain traits. Because of their experience with alcoholic parents, they have trouble in several areas, including judging what is normal, completing projects, telling the truth, having fun, controlling impulses, and developing intimate relationships. In addition, adult children of alcoholics experience great difficulty in the domain of personal responsibility; they are often either very irresponsible or superresponsible (1990).

Despite the clinical relevance of Woititz's ideas, researchers have not found distinctive traits in adult children of alcoholics, except for higher rates of alcohol abuse and alcohol-related health problems (Fulton & Yates, 1990). Nevertheless, personal accounts and self-help groups like Al-Anon have raised awareness of problems experienced by adult children of alcoholics. As more controlled studies are completed, a clearer picture of this high-risk group will emerge.

Abuser-oriented intervention concentrates on changing attitudes about the use of aggression. One of the ways to combat child abuse is to increase public awareness of the problem.

social support systems and enhance their social skills in order to support more prosocial behavior. Training in assertiveness and problem-solving skills can help abusers overcome the feelings of helplessness and low self-esteem that feed their abusive behavior (Edleson, 1990; Sedlak, 1988).

Vince's therapy emphasized his recovery from alcoholism, as well as the development of anger control skills. He began participation in an early recovery alcoholism group and also was required to attend AA meetings regularly. In his individual therapy, he worked on acquiring anger control skills in self-instructional training. Cognitive therapy helped Vince interpret anger situations more clearly so he would not blow events out of proportion. After four months of treatment, Vince had maintained his sobriety, lost his temper less often, and had not exhibited abusive behavior toward his children.

Victim-oriented Interventions. As we have seen, family violence has severe and far-reaching psychological effects on many victims. Many people are treated for psychological problems without ever being identified as victims of family violence. For example, survivors of child sexual abuse often have no conscious recollection of their victimization, although they may be in therapy for problems stemming from it.

Child victims of physical and sexual abuse have been treated successfully with many child therapy techniques. Play therapy is a useful part of treatment, especially for younger children. Sexually abused children who are unable or reluctant to verbalize their experience are often able to express themselves through playing with anatomically correct dolls (Wheeler & Berliner, 1988).

A recent phenomenon in the treatment of battered wives is the *woman's shelter*. The first shelter for battered women in the United States opened in 1972 in St. Paul, Minnesota. Today there are over 800 nationwide. In a typical shelter, women and their children are given short-term accommodations, group counseling, and legal assistance. Shelters fill an important need. However, their long-term benefit is open to question, especially since many battered women return to their abusive spouses (Traicoff, 1982).

Another popular victim-oriented intervention is the support group (for example, *Al-Anon* and *Incest Survivors Anonymous*). These groups offer victims of abuse a social support network that can help them overcome their sense of isolation and helplessness.

Family-oriented Interventions. The use of family therapy in cases of family violence seems quite feasible. In fact, systems theorists consider family therapy the correct approach because they take violence as an indication of severe dysfunction in the relationships among family members. Case reports of successful treatment with family therapy have been published, but there has been little controlled research on this issue (Bedrosian, 1982).

Many experts discourage family therapy in cases of spouse abuse and child sexual abuse. Some see family therapy as an opportunity for abusers to vindicate themselves while continuing to assert control over their victims. An important question in family therapy is whether victims are willing to be honest when the abuser is present in the therapy session. Many victims are understandably cautious about revealing the true extent of violence in the family, out of fear of revenge (Edleson, 1990; Nadelson & Sauzier, 1990).

Anatomically correct dolls are often used in assessing and treating victims of child sexual abuse.

Social Interventions. During the past twenty years, social policies have become more attuned to the problem of family violence. As a result, important political and legal actions have been taken to safeguard family members from one another. All states have mandatory reporting laws for child abuse, which require health professionals, educators, and others to file reports of suspected abuse.

In 1984, the Attorney General's Task Force on Domestic Violence recommended that more vigorous action be taken by police departments in investigating and dealing with incidents of family violence. The task force suggested that serious incidents be considered criminal offenses and treated accordingly. Arresting the perpetrators of family violence seems to reduce repeat abuse, but whether it has a long-term deterrent effect is still in question (Sherman & Berk, 1984).

Social policies on child abuse have produced mixed results. Few question the value of mandatory reporting of child abuse, but the consequences of such reporting for the child and the family are not necessarily always positive. Many abused children have been automatically removed from parental custody and placed in children's shelters or foster care. Although the intention of protecting the child is noble, the reality is that the child can be traumatized by the sudden loss of the family and exposure to inadequate foster care (Finkelhor, 1990; Newberger, 1985; Repucci & Haugaard, 1989).

Many treatment interventions for family violence have proved helpful for victims, abusers, and the family as a whole. At present, the effective components of treatment for the complex problem of family violence are unknown. It is certain, however, that the success or failure of treatment depends on many factors associated with violence, including individual psychopathology, social stressors, and family conditions.

15-2 ▨ DIVORCE

The breakup of families through divorce is one of the most stressful transitions in the lives of adults and children. However, divorce is not necessarily a problem or a reflection of individual disturbances in the divorcing spouses. In fact, divorce is most often an attempt at solving family problems. Given its high incidence in our society today, divorce is being reconsidered as a normal phase in the development of many families.

Figure 15-2 shows that the rate of divorce in the United States gradually rose to a peak in the late 1970s, with brief "minipeaks" corresponding to times of social distress, notably World Wars I and II. Today, nearly half of the new marriages in the United States are expected to end in divorce. Sixty percent of divorced families have children, and about forty percent of American children born in the 1970s will eventually become *children of divorce* (Emery, 1988).

▨ Causes of Divorce

> "All happy families are alike, but an unhappy family is unhappy after its own fashion."

As Tolstoy's observation implies, the causes of family unhappiness are numerous and are specific to each family. Divorce is surely a reflection of family unhappiness. Here we discuss the major sociocultural and psychological causes of divorce.

Sociocultural Causes. Sociologists perceive marriage and divorce in the context of evolving habits and attitudes in society at large. Between 1960 and 1980 the divorce rate in the United States more than doubled, and during that period there were also dramatic social changes. In particular, a liberalization of American society was under way, as evidenced by the civil rights and women's movements. In addition, there were broad economic changes, including the greater involvement of married women in the workplace.

Along with these other significant social changes, divorce became a more "normal" phenomenon, and the stigma long associated with divorce began to erode. In a sense, divorce became easier from a social perspective. Not only was divorce perceived as an ordinary event, but changes in the divorce laws made divorce more accessible to people at all levels of society (J. K. Rice & D. G. Rice, 1986; White, 1990).

Psychological Causes. Divorcing couples cite many reasons for the dissolution of their marriages. Unsurprisingly, the most common reason given is

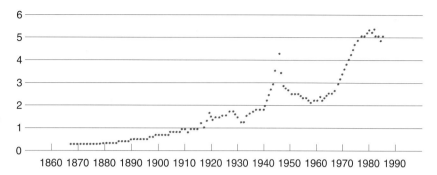

Figure 15-2 Annual U.S divorce rates per 1000 population, 1867–1985.

Source: From *Marriage, Divorce, and Children's Adjustment* by R. E. Emery, 1988, Newbury Park, CA: Sage. Based on data from Plateris (1974), monthly vital statistics reports, and Glick & Lin (1986).

long-standing mutual dissatisfaction. The sources of marital dissatisfaction are sometimes clear-cut, like the discovery of a spouse's infidelity, and sometimes quite vague, like incompatibility. For many divorcing couples, the failure of a marriage is determined by failed hopes and unmet personal expectations (White, 1990).

Historically in this country, and at present in many other cultures, marriage has been a union based primarily on economic and social considerations rather than romance or personal needs. Romantic, "happily ever after" myths that pervade modern notions of marriage do not adequately prepare couples for many ordinary marital difficulties. The roots of a divorce may lie in beliefs or fantasies that spouses brought with them into the marriage. The fantasy of marrying a "Prince Charming" or "Good Mommy" can set the stage for marital distress when the fantasy remains unfulfilled (Kaslow, 1981).

Monica and Tony sought marital counseling at the urging of their pastor. Monica had been raised in a struggling working-class family, and her dream was to marry someone rich who would "save her" from the fate suffered by her mother. At first Tony seemed like the ideal husband. He and Monica came from similar backgrounds, but through hard work and determination Tony had become a successful stockbroker. After four years of marriage, however, Tony had suffered a financial disaster resulting in the loss of his job, all their savings, and their home. Although he was confident he would eventually recoup these losses, Monica wanted a divorce because she felt betrayed by his failure.

The risk of divorce is further increased for individuals with specific psychological problems like alcoholism and depression. However, these individual problems may not be simply causes of divorce—they may be the result of marital difficulties preceding the actual divorce. In addition, the likelihood of divorce is influenced by forces originating outside the couple, including job stress, unemployment, problems with in-laws, and legal difficulties.

Consequences of Divorce

Divorce is a major transition that affects most aspects of the lives of family members. Despite its greater acceptance as a social phenomenon, divorce is still perceived as an unfortunate event. Research on the consequences of divorce supports this perception; divorce has many adverse effects on the adults as well as the children.

Consequences of Divorce for Adults. Divorced adults have higher rates of mental health problems than nondivorced and never-married adults. Substance use disorders, emotional disorders, psychosomatic disorders, suicide rates, and admissions to mental health care facilities are significantly elevated among divorced people. The most serious adverse effects of divorce appear to dissipate over time, and after several years most divorced people will have adjusted (B. L. Bloom, White, & Asher, 1979; Hodges, 1986; Kitson & Morgan, 1990).

The transition from married to single status brings social stresses and problems for the adult. Many aspects of social life are conditioned by the roles played as a couple. Relationships with children, in-laws and other relatives, and friends, especially married couples, undergo change when people divorce. The longer the marriage has lasted, the more disruptive the transition to divorced status will usually be (Kirkpatrick, 1988; R. S. Weiss, 1979).

The most severe social disruption for divorced couples is often in their relationships with their children. The noncustodial parent, usually the father, has only limited contact with and involvement in the lives of the children, and this can cause significant emotional distress for the parent. Ninety percent of the time the custodial parent is the mother, and the responsibility of raising children unassisted can be a tremendous burden. Moreover, custodial mothers often bear the brunt of their children's anger and resentment over the divorce (Hetherington, Hagan, & Anderson, 1989; Wallerstein, 1986).

The economic consequences of divorce are not equally divided. The majority of divorced women experience a significant loss of income following divorce. Their financial hardship is compounded by lower earning potential, child-related expenses, and inadequate or nonexistent child support payments from ex-husbands. Divorce throws many mothers into the ranks of the impoverished. Men, however, may enjoy a relative improvement in financial status after divorce, particularly if they do not meet their child support obligations (Hetherington et al., 1989).

Consequences of Divorce for Children. The majority of divorces involve children, who are unfortunate bystanders in the drama. Children are even more likely than adults to experience difficulties adjusting to divorce. They have less adequate coping skills and less control over circumstances. Boys are inclined to exhibit various externalizing or acting-out symptoms, including conduct disorders, delinquency, aggressive behavior, and temper tantrums. By contrast, girls are more likely than boys to show internalizing symptoms, such as depression and anxiety (Emery, 1988).

For most children, the first few years after the divorce are the most difficult. As time passes, however, they typically adapt to the new living conditions. Not

The way children adjust to divorce depends on many factors, especially the quality of their relationship with their custodial parent.

all children adjust well, though, and in some the effects persist into adulthood (Frost & Pakiz, 1990). Some research suggests that emotional consequences of divorce may be delayed for several years, especially in girls. This *sleeper effect* can engender adjustment problems in adolescents and young adults, who are struggling with their feelings about romantic relationships (Wallerstein, & Blakeslee, 1989).

Children's adjustment to divorce depends on a number of variables. A particularly important role is played by the quality of the child's relationship with the noncustodial parent. Children who lose contact with the noncustodial parent may feel abandoned and rejected. The relationship between the parents after the divorce is also important in shaping the adjustment of the child. Children whose parents continue their conflict even after the marriage ends are more likely to have emotional and behavioral problems (Hodges, 1986).

Children's living conditions after divorce influence their general mental status. Not only does the typical custodial mother suffer financially from divorce, but so do her children. Postdivorce economic deprivation is associated with children's problems in social, educational, and personal well-being (Hetherington et al., 1989).

Pat initiated family therapy because of her inability to manage her older son. Since she had divorced her husband 15 months previously, 9-year-old Sam had been out of control. He was verbally and physically abusive toward his mother and younger brother and was getting into trouble in school because of his noncompliance. Sam claimed he hated his mother because she made his father leave.

In concluding our discussion of the consequences of divorce, we want to emphasize that most adjustment difficulties resulting from divorce are transient and can eventually be overcome. In addition, there are positive consequences of divorce. Obviously, most couples divorce because their marriage is no longer tolerable and they perceive divorce as a solution to their problems. In fact, after divorce many adults experience emotional relief and improved feelings of confidence and competence. For children, too, it may be better to endure a divorce than to undergo the chronic stress of a conflict-filled family (J. K. Rice & D. G. Rice, 1986).

Treatment of Divorce

The treatment of divorce involves a mix of family, marital, and individual therapy. Two interventions that show promise with divorcing families are divorce therapy and divorce mediation.

divorce therapy
Treatment to diminish the negative consequences of divorce.

Divorce Therapy. A relatively new phenomenon, **divorce therapy**, seeks to diminish and resolve the negative consequences of the transition from marriage to divorce. The goal is to aid the adjustment of all concerned (J. K. Rice & D. G. Rice, 1986). Divorce therapy generally assumes that the process of divorcing follows distinctive stages. One model of divorce proposes three stages through which families move: the predivorce, during divorce, and postdivorce periods (Kaslow, 1981).

The *predivorce period* is a time of deliberation or decision making. Couples undergo extended soul-searching prior to divorce and often enter therapy before actually committing themselves to divorce. In this period spouses confront their disillusionment with the marriage and their ambivalence about remaining together or splitting up. Therapy helps clarify their feelings and examines the benefits and costs of staying married or divorcing.

In the *during divorce period*, the decision to divorce is final and the legal process has begun. Therapeutic issues revolve around the emotional distress spouses are experiencing, such as anxiety, anger, resentment, guilt, and anticipated loss. In this period, one priority is preparing the children for the separation and eventual dissolution of the family. To this end, children are usually included in family sessions.

Therapy in the *postdivorce period* facilitates the family members' attempts to regain their emotional balance. In addition, problem-solving work is done on issues of custody, child discipline, visitation, and child support. In this period it is important to help ex-spouses contend with their new independence and loneliness and to help the children cope with life in a divorced family. Some divorce therapists employ ceremonial rituals to symbolically free family members from the past, such as the *"unwedding"* ceremony:

They pledge to liberate each other and promise to relinquish the dreams they had for the marriage. They vow to free themselves from bitterness, not to harbor anger or to contaminate future relationships with residual enmity against their former spouse. After the "I do's" are said, the minister concludes with: "In the presence of your understanding and compassionate friends, seeing that you are indeed earnest in your intention to liberate one another, I pronounce you unmarried." (Kaslow, 1981, p. 690)

divorce mediation
A nonadversarial strategy for helping couples separate.

Divorce Mediation. Although not strictly a form of treatment or therapy, **divorce mediation** helps divorcing couples arrange the terms of their separation in a nonadversarial fashion. Divorce mediation is an alternative to the traditional process of divorce, which pits spouses in a legal battle against one another.

Divorce mediators rely on family and marital therapy techniques. Their main objective, however, is to construct a divorce agreement that is best suited to the needs of both spouses. To a large degree, successful mediation is a matter of helping divorcing spouses to identify what is important to them and how to compromise.

From economic and emotional perspectives, divorce mediation is a beneficial approach. A mediated divorce usually costs less than a traditional divorce, and spouses whose divorces are mediated have fewer adjustment problems afterward. Keep in mind that the willingness to use divorce mediation reflects the quality of the relationship between the spouses. In severely antagonistic marriages, neither spouse is likely to want a mediated settlement or to be capable of cooperating in achieving one (Emery, 1988; Lemmon, 1985).

SUMMARY

15-1 Family violence includes several types of spouse and child abuse. Marital violence involves both wife and husband abuse. The consequences of marital violence encompass physical and emotional injury, battered woman syndrome, and even homicide. Child abuse refers to the physical, sexual, and emotional abuse of children, as well as to child neglect. Psychological and medical effects of child abuse range from minor injuries to devastating physical and mental disorders. The diverse causes of family violence include neurological disturbances in the abusers, dysfunctional family relationships, and sociocultural variables. Numerous treatments for family violence have been used, including abuser-oriented, victim-oriented, family-oriented, and social interventions.

15-2 Divorce has increased dramatically during the past 30 years because of changes in society's and individuals' attitudes toward marriage and divorce. Adverse effects of divorce for adults and children have been identified. Psychological health is affected by divorce, but the effects are mediated by individual, economic, and social factors. Divorce therapy helps divorcing families adjust to their new status. Divorce mediation is a strategy for facilitating a nonadversarial separation agreement.

TERMS TO REMEMBER

battered child syndrome (p. 383)
battered woman syndrome (p. 382)
child abuse (p. 383)
child neglect (p. 386)
child sexual abuse (p. 384)
divorce mediation (p. 401)
divorce therapy (p. 400)
emotional abuse (p. 386)

episodic dyscontrol syndrome (p. 390)
family violence (p. 380)
physical abuse (p. 383)
relational pathology (p. 391)
sexually abused child's disorder (p. 388)

SUGGESTED READINGS

Bass, E. & Davis, L. (1988). *The courage to heal: A guide for women survivors of child sexual abuse.* New York: Harper & Row.

Gold, J. (Ed.). (1988). *Divorce as a developmental process.* Washington, DC: American Psychiatric Press.

van Hasselt, V. B., Morrison, R. L., Bellack, A. S., & Hersen, M. (1988). *Handbook of family violence.* New York: Plenum.

Woititz, J. G. (1990). *Adult children of alcoholics* (expanded ed.). Deerfield Beach, FL: Health Communications.

LEGAL AND ETHICAL ISSUES: BATTERED WOMAN SYNDROME AS A DEFENSE IN HOMICIDE CASES

In 1985 Madelyn Diaz shot her sleeping husband to death and was indicted on second-degree murder charges. Testimony revealed that Madelyn had been repeatedly and brutally abused by her husband, a police officer. The day before she shot him he had held his gun to their baby's head and threatened to shoot if Madelyn didn't have sex with him. She was acquitted by a jury after pleading self-defense on the basis of the battered woman syndrome. (Blackman, 1989)

Since 1983, when the battered woman syndrome was first used successfully as a self-defense plea in a homicide case, many jurisdictions in the United States have recognized its legitimacy. Prior to 1983, battered woman syndrome had been entered in homicide cases as grounds for insanity or diminished capacity defenses. However, those defenses often led to undesirable consequences for the defendant, such as the stigma of being labeled mentally ill. Some women who pleaded insanity due to battered woman syndrome were even required to enter mental hospitals.

Self-defense pleas have historically required a demonstration that the defendant had a reasonable belief of imminent danger and was motivated by that belief. Unlike traditional examples of self-defense, in cases of battered woman syndrome there is often no immediate danger; for example, Madelyn Diaz's husband was asleep when she shot him.

Despite the absence of an immediate threat, battered women believe themselves endangered and fear future harm, and their belief is critical to the defense. The history of victimization and the expectation of further violence are the crux of the battered woman's plea. Several important features of battered woman syndrome support its admissibility:

- Learned helplessness. The woman believes that she can do nothing to stop the violence against her.
- Diminished perceptions of alternatives to killing. The woman believes that there is no other choice.
- The woman believes that the abusive husband has exceeded the ordinary level of "tolerable" abuse.

The battered woman's self-defense plea recognizes that women with this condition are not mentally ill. In fact, battered woman syndrome is an expectable reaction to extreme victimization. The fundamental issue at stake is that battered women who have killed their mates have acted as a matter of personal survival (Blackman, 1989; Browne, 1988; Micklow, 1988).

*A*ppendix:
A Preview of the DSM-IV

The DSM-IV is scheduled to be published in late 1993. The DSM-IV task force is exploring research relevant to the diagnostic criteria for individual disorders, the subtyping of disorders, and the organization of disorders in categories. The following section summarizes issues being considered by the task force and tentative changes that have been proposed to date (American Psychiatric Association).

1. Anxiety Disorders

a. The relationship between generalized anxiety disorder and mood disorders is being explored, and the evidence for a diagnostic category called *mixed anxiety-depression* is being considered.

b. Social phobia may be split into subtypes to distinguish generalized social phobia from social phobia related to specific performance fears, such as public speaking.

c. Simple phobias may be subtyped to reflect the feared stimulus.

d. Symptom thresholds for diagnosing panic attacks and panic disorder should be determined.

e. Both obsessions *and* compulsions will be required in the diagnosis of obsessive-compulsive disorder; cognitive compulsions will be added to the list of possible compulsive behaviors.

f. Types of stressors in posttraumatic stress disorder may be broadened to include highly traumatic events even if they are not beyond the realm of ordinary experience; a new category of trauma-related conditions may be created that will include posttraumatic stress disorder and dissociative disorders.

2. Stress-Related Disorders

The category *psychological factors affecting physical condition* may be subclassified on the basis of the types of psychological factors involved, including psychological state (anxiety, sadness); personality traits; behavioral patterns; and interpersonal dysfunctions.

405

3. Sexual Disorders

The task force is reviewing the current diagnostic criteria for all sexual disorders and is considering two new diagnoses: hypersexual desire disorder and low-intensity orgasm disorder.

4. Substance Use Disorders

a. More precise definition of distinctions between abuse and dependence reflects research showing that many substance abusers do not become dependent.
b. More scientific support is needed for nicotine and caffeine abuse categories.
c. An anabolic steroid subgroup may be added.
d. Substance-induced organic mental disorders may be placed in categories described by phenomenology. For example, cocaine-induced delusions would warrant a diagnosis of cocaine delusional disorder and would be categorized with other delusional disorders regardless of cause.

5. Mood Disorders

a. Boundaries between dysthymia and major depression will be distinguished; "pure" dysthymia may be included along with dysthymia with subsequent major depressive episodes.
b. The addition of depressive personality disorder is being considered.
c. The melancholic subtype of major depressive episode needs to be validated.
d. Distinctions will be drawn between bipolar disorder and cyclothymia.
e. Postpartum depression may be classified as a subtype of major depressive episode.
f. The task force will review the validity of seasonal affective disorder and late luteal phase dysphoric disorder (premenstrual syndrome, or PMS).

6. Schizophrenia and Other Psychotic Disorders

a. The major focus of the task force is to determine whether current criteria for schizophrenia are too narrow, resulting in underdiagnosis of schizophrenia.
b. A minimum duration of symptoms will be necessary to make the diagnosis of schizophrenia.
c. Negative symptoms will be emphasized in diagnostic criteria.
d. The relationship between schizophrenia and schizoaffective disorder and mood disorders with psychotic features will be examined.

7. Childhood Disorders

a. The naming of these disorders may be changed to read "disorders usually first *diagnosed* in childhood or adolescence" rather than the current "disorders usually first *evident* in childhood or adolescence" in order to reflect observations that many childhood disorders, such as attention deficit hyperactivity disorder, often persist into adulthood.
b. Relationships among childhood disorders, eating disorders, and personality disorders will be described.
c. The category *attention deficit disorder without hyperactivity* will be reintroduced.
d. The definition of conduct disorder may be narrowed.
e. Criteria for childhood anxiety and mood problems will be more consistent with criteria for adult disorders.

8. Eating Disorders

a. The diagnostic criteria for anorexia and bulimia nervosa will be revised.
b. Anorexia nervosa will be split to include bulimic and nonbulimic subtypes.
c. Diagnostic criteria for bulimia nervosa may be broadened to include individuals who do *not* purge.
d. A new diagnosis called *binge eating disorder* is being considered for individuals who binge-eat but who do not meet the criteria for bulimia nervosa.

9. Personality Disorders

a. Symptom boundaries between Axis II personality disorders and Axis I mental disorders need to be clarified, as illustrated by the problem of where to place schizotypal and cyclothymic disorders.
b. Criteria for antisocial personality disorder will emphasize more traditional symptoms of psychopathy—that is, inability to experience guilt, to learn from experience, and to bond to others.

10. Organic Mental Syndromes and Disorders

a. Organic syndromes will probably be placed within categories in which they share phenomenology; for example, organic mood disorder would be classified as a type of secondary mood disorder.
b. Dementia, delirium, and amnestic syndromes will be reclassified as cognitive impairment disorders.

Glossary

A-B-C model Behavioral analysis that assesses behavior and its antecedents and consequences.

abnormal psychology The scientific study of abnormal behavior and mental disorders.

addiction A physical need for or dependence on a drug, as shown by tolerance and withdrawal symptoms.

adoption study A behavior genetics method of studying people raised by adoptive rather than biological parents.

agoraphobia An anxiety disorder marked by intense fear of being in places or situations in which the person believes escape would be difficult.

AIDS dementia complex An AIDS-related neurological impairment involving progressive loss of intellectual abilities.

alcoholism A condition of alcohol dependence with physical addiction to alcohol.

alienation A state of meaninglessness resulting from a lack of goals, values, or purpose in life.

Alzheimer's disease Irreversible dementia characterized by specific and progressive degeneration of brain neurons.

amnestic syndrome An organic mental syndrome involving a memory deficit, or amnesia.

amphetamines A group of stimulant drugs, including benzedrine, dextroamphetamine, methamphetamine, and MDMA.

analytical psychology Jung's psychodynamic theory, which emphasizes the origins of personality and behavior in the collective unconscious.

analytic attitude The psychodynamic approach to therapy comprised of neutrality, openness, a desire to help, and the use of interpretations.

anger-in hypothesis A psychodynamic explanation stating that guilt over feelings of hatred toward a lost loved one predisposes the person to depression later in life.

anorexia nervosa An eating disorder that involves refusal to maintain normal body weight, fear of becoming fat, distorted body image, and amenorrhea.

antidepressants Drugs that increase energy levels and elevate mood; they are used in the treatment of depression.

antipsychotic drugs Drugs that control the symptoms of schizophrenia by reducing the brain's dopamine activity.

antisocial personality disorder A personality disorder defined by a history of antisocial behavior and disregard for the rights and feelings of others.

anxiety A complex negative emotional state comprised of fear, apprehension, worry, tension, and physiological arousal.

anxiety disorder A mental disorder involving symptoms of anxiety and a persistent set of thoughts, feelings, and behaviors that affect normal functioning.

assertiveness training A behavioral strategy designed to help people express positive and negative feelings in socially acceptable ways.

409

attention deficit hyperactivity disorder   A disruptive behavior disorder defined by inattentiveness, impulsiveness, and overactivity.

attributional reformulation   A revision of the learned helplessness model, stating that depression is the result of internal, stable, and global attributions of unpleasant outcomes.

authenticity   A way of living in which individuals assume responsibility for their own existence.

autistic disorder   A severe developmental disorder with onset before age 3, distinguished by impairments in social interaction, communication, and imagination and a restricted repertoire of activity and interests.

aversion therapy   A behavior therapy technique that eliminates undesired behaviors by associating them with aversive stimuli.

avoidant disorder   A childhood anxiety disorder manifested by shrinking from contact with strangers because of fear.

avoidant personality disorder   A personality disorder defined by extreme shyness, social anxiety, fear of criticism, and inhibited social behavior.

barbiturates   Sedative drugs that depress neural activity, including phenobarbital, pentobarbital, and secobarbital.

battered child syndrome   A medical description of the physical symptoms of severely abused children.

battered woman syndrome   A condition in abused women, characterized by feelings of helplessness, submissiveness, depression, and low self-esteem.

behavioral assessment   Analysis and classification of behavior.

behavioral medicine   A discipline that integrates knowledge from medical and behavioral sciences and behavior therapy in order to understand and treat physical illnesses.

behavior genetics   The study of the hereditary basis of behavior.

behaviorism   A school of psychology that stresses the objective study of behavior.

behavior therapy   A therapy based on the principles of classical and operant conditioning.

benzodiazepines   The most commonly used antianxiety drugs, which raise levels of the neurotransmitter GABA.

biofeedback   A stress management technique that feeds back information about bodily functioning that is usually unnoticeable.

biogenic view   A belief that abnormal behavior is due to biological causes.

biological perspective   The viewpoint that attributes mental disorders to biological causes.

biological therapy   A medical treatment approach that attempts to correct the physical disturbances that underlie abnormal behavior.

bipolar disorder   A mood disorder characterized by one full manic and one full depressive episode.

bipolar disorders   Mood disorders that involve periods of mania or hypomania and depressive episodes.

body dysmorphic disorder   A somatoform disorder involving the strong belief, in the absence of evidence, that one's body is deformed or defective.

borderline personality disorder   A personality disorder characterized by instability in mood, self-image, and relationships and by impulsive, self-defeating behavior.

boundaries   Family roles and rules that govern relationships among family members.

brain imaging   Procedures used to derive images of structural and chemical characteristics of the brain.

Broca's area   An area in the left frontal lobe of the brain that controls production of speech.

bronchial asthma   A respiratory disorder involving constriction of bronchial airways, wheezing, and breathing difficulties.

bulimarexia   The binge-purge pattern of anorexia nervosa.

bulimia nervosa   An eating disorder characterized by binge eating, lack of control over eating, purging, and concern about body shape.

cardiovascular disorders   Disorders characterized by abnormalities in heart and blood vessel function.

case study   In-depth examination of one person's life and development.

catatonic schizophrenia   A type of schizophrenia characterized by prominent psychomotor disturbances, including stupor, negativism, and excitement.

catecholamine hypothesis   A biochemical explanation for mood disorders, stating that depression involves a deficiency and mania an excess of norepinephrine.

child abuse   Physical, sexual, or psychological maltreatment of a child under age 18.

child neglect   The failure of a parent of guardian to provide a minimum degree of care for a child's physical well-being.

child sexual abuse   Sexual interaction between an adult and a minor child, including touching, molestation, sexual exploitation, and intercourse.

classical conditioning   A type of learning in which new associations between environmental stimuli and reflexive responses are acquired.

client-centered therapy   A humanistic therapy characterized by the therapist's unconditional positive regard, empathy, and honesty.

Clinical Analysis Questionnaire (CAQ)   A self-report inventory used to measure normal and pathological personality factors.

clinical psychology   The specialization in psychology

that studies the causes and treatment of abnormal behavior.

Cluster A   Personality disorders characterized as odd, eccentric, or withdrawn types, including paranoid, schizoid, and schizotypal personality disorders.

Cluster B   Personality disorders dominated by dramatic, emotional, or erratic features, including antisocial, borderline, narcissistic, and histrionic personality disorders.

Cluster C   Personality disorders defined by anxious, fearful, or inhibited behavior, including avoidant, dependent, obsessive-compulsive, and passive-aggressive personality disorders.

cocaine   A stimulant drug derived from the coca plant.

codependence   A relationship in which family members are dependent on and contribute to the addict's behavior.

coercion hypothesis   The belief that conduct-disordered children and their parents develop a cycle of reciprocal exchanges of punishment and negative reinforcement.

cognitive-behavior therapy   A therapy that alters maladaptive thoughts and behaviors, using techniques from social learning theory and behaviorism.

cognitive theory   A theory that emphasizes the role of learned thinking patterns in psychological disturbances.

cognitive therapy   A treatment approach that seeks to change faulty beliefs and assumptions that maintain abnormal behavior and emotional distress.

community mental health movement   An approach to treating and preventing mental health problems by addressing the social context in which they occur.

compulsions   Seemingly purposeful behaviors or rituals performed repeatedly according to certain rules and in the same stereotyped way.

concordance rate   The percentage of twin pairs in which both twins have the same disorder.

conduct disorder   A behavioral disturbance characterized by persistent violations of age-appropriate rules or norms.

contingency management   A behavior therapy strategy that modifies behavior by manipulating its reinforcing and punishing consequences.

continuity hypothesis   A causal explanation for depression, which says that biochemical abnormalities predispose people to depression and life stresses trigger and maintain depressive episodes.

conversion disorder   A somatoform disorder involving loss or alteration of physical functioning, without organic basis.

coping   Attempts to manage stimuli or situations appraised as threatening.

coronary heart disease   Narrowing of coronary arteries because of a buildup of fats.

correlational research   A method for estimating the strength of associations between variables.

countertransference   In psychoanalysis, the analyst's feelings and attitudes toward the patient.

covert sensitization   A cognitive-behavioral aversion therapy that inhibits behavior by associating it with imagined unpleasant consequences.

cue exposure therapy   A behavior treatment for drug addiction that promotes extinction of drug cravings by repeated exposure to drug-relevant cues.

cultural-familial retardation   A type of mental retardation with prominent psychosocial causes and no distinct biological causes.

cyclothymia   A chronic mood disorder involving hypomanic and depressive episodes less severe than those in bipolar disorder.

defense mechanisms   Ego strategies that attempt to cope with psychic conflicts and emotional distress.

delirium   An organic mental syndrome characterized by difficulties in maintaining attention.

delirium tremens   Symptoms of severe alcohol withdrawal, including agitation, confusion, disorientation, and hallucinations.

delusional syndrome   An organic mental syndrome in which the person exhibits paranoid delusions of persecution, grandeur, reference, and jealousy.

delusions   Disorders of thought content, defined as false beliefs strongly held despite a lack of evidence.

dementia   An organic mental syndrome marked by a deterioration of intellectual abilities, including memory, comprehension, calculation, and knowledge.

dependent personality disorder   A personality disorder defined by excessive dependency and extreme difficulty in making decisions or taking initiative.

depersonalization disorder   A dissociative disorder characterized by feelings of being "unreal" or other alterations of the normal sense of self.

depressive disorders   Mood disorders involving depression in the absence of manic or hypomanic symptoms.

determinism   The idea that events obey laws of cause and effect.

detoxification   A medical treatment designed to eliminate drugs from the body through total abstinence.

developmental disorders   Disturbances in the acquisition of cognitive, language, motor, or social skills that appear before age 18.

developmental lag hypothesis   The belief that learning disabilities are due to abnormally slow maturation of brain mechanisms for acquiriing skills like reading and speech.

dexamethasone suppression test   A laboratory test used to detect biochemical abnormalities in the H-P-A axis; used to evaluate endogenous depression.

diathesis-stress hypothesis   A model for psychosomatic disorders stating that physical illness results from the interaction of physical weakness and psychological stress.

diathesis-stress model of schizophrenia The theory that schizophrenia is caused by a combination of genetic factors and environmental stress.

direct observation A behavioral assessment strategy in which trained observers code and classify behavior.

disease-prone personality A complex of traits associated with illness, including depression, anger, hostility, and anxiety.

disorganized schizophrenia A type of schizophrenia characterized by incoherent speech, loose associations, irrationality, and disorganized behavior.

disruptive behavior disorders Childhood problems of undercontrol in which symptoms are expressed in socially disruptive activity.

dissociative disorders Mental disorders involving alterations in consciousness, identity, or memory.

divorce mediation A strategy for helping divorcing couples arrange separation terms in a nonadversarial fashion.

divorce therapy Treatment designed to diminish and resolve the negative consequences of the transition from marriage to divorce.

dopamine hypothesis of schizophrenia The belief that schizophrenia is caused by abnormalities in the brain's dopamine neurotransmitter system.

double-bind hypothesis The belief that inconsistent and contradictory messages from family members cause schizophrenia.

Down syndrome A type of organic mental retardation usually caused by an extra chromosome 21.

downward social drift hypothesis The belief that low socioeconomic status is a consequence of schizophrenics' mental disabilities, which prevent effective functioning.

DSM-III-R A descriptive multiaxial diagnostic system used to categorize mental disorders.

DSM-IV A research-based diagnostic system intended to succeed the DSM-III-R.

dyspareunia A sexual dysfunction in which the person experiences genital pain before, during, or after sexual intercourse.

dysregulation hypothesis The idea that depression is caused by an impairment in the regulation of neurotransmitter activity at brain synapses.

dysthymia A mood disorder involving chronic depressed mood; milder than major depression.

eating disorders Disorders characterized by gross disturbances in eating behavior.

educational remediation An approach to treating learning-disabled children through structured training in specific skills like reading and speech.

ego The part of personality that mediates between the individual and the external world, according to the reality principle.

ego analysis A psychodynamic therapy that uses ego support and ego-building strategies.

ego psychology A psychodynamic theory that views the ego as the central integrating force in personality.

electroconvulsive therapy A treatment for depression in which controlled electrical current is used to produce brain seizures.

electrophysiological recording Procedures used to measure activity of the brain and autonomic nervous system.

emergency theory A model that states when stress disrupts homeostasis, the ANS is activated to prepare us for fight or flight.

emotional abuse Psychological maltreatment that impairs emotional well-being.

empiricism A philosophy that emphasizes the role of sensory experience in the development of ideas.

endogenous depression Depression caused by internal physiological problems.

energy balance The ratio of calories consumed to calories burned.

enmeshment A state of intense involvement among and unclear boundaries between family members.

environmental determinism The belief that behavior is caused by environmental forces.

epidemiology The study of the distribution of disorders in the general population.

episodic dyscontrol syndrome A neurologically based pattern of uncontrolled outbursts of rage and aggression due to nonspecific brain defects.

escape theory The belief that disinhibited eating provides dieters and bulimics with an escape from unpleasant feelings of self-awareness.

essential hypertension High blood pressure of unknown origin, presumed to be related to psychological factors.

exhibitionism A paraphilia involving sexual arousal through actual or imagined exposure of one's genitals to a stranger.

existential anxiety The apprehensiveness that comes from awareness of personal freedom and responsibility.

existentialism A philosophy that explores the facts of subjective human existence.

existential therapy A treatment approach that helps individuals understand, confront, and cope with the problems of human existence.

experimental research A method of controlled manipulation designed to assess the cause-and-effect relationships among variables.

exposure therapy A behavioral treatment in which the patient is exposed to feared stimuli.

extrapyramidal motor system Brain circuitry that helps control movement.

familial alcoholism A hereditary type of alcoholism characterized by a family history, early onset, and a severe pattern of drinking.

Family Interaction Coding System   A 29-category coding system used to evaluate effectiveness of treatment programs for children.

family life cycle   Stages of family development, in which family structures and functioning change through adaptation to life events.

family study   A behavior genetics method for assessing the prevalence of a behavior or disorder among members of a family.

family systems perspective   The view that abnormal behavior is an expression of dysfunctional interactions and relationships among family members.

family systems therapy   A treatment approach that seeks to improve the family's adaptation to stress by reducing emotional overinvolvement between family members.

family violence   Behavior that involves acts or threats of physical or psychological harm between family members.

female sexual arousal disorder   A sexual dysfunction marked by inhibition of the lubrication-swelling response during the excitement stage necessary for intercourse.

fetishism   A paraphilia in which the person has strong sexual urges or fantasies directed toward nonhuman objects.

flooding   A behavior therapy technique involving prolonged exposure of the patient to a frightening stimulus.

fragile X syndrome   A hereditary condition, usually affecting males, in which part of the X chromosome is broken, causing autism and mental retardation.

free association   A psychoanalytic technique in which the patient reports any thoughts, feelings, impulses, or memories that come to mind.

frotteurism   A paraphilia in which an individual becomes sexually aroused by rubbing against a nonconsenting person.

gender identity   One's awareness of being male or female.

gender identity disorder of childhood   A disorder in which the child feels distress about his or her sex and wants to be of the opposite sex.

gender identity disorders   Disorders that involve a perceived mismatch between gender identity and assigned sex.

general adaptation syndrome   A three-stage model that describes the body's reaction to stressors.

generalized anxiety disorder   Persistent fear and chronic worry about two or more life circumstances.

Gestalt therapy   A humanistic therapy that emphasizes awareness of immediate experience, self-understanding, and personal responsibility.

guided imagery   A stress management technique that utilizes the patient's ability to imagine pleasurable experiences.

hallucinations   False perceptions that have no basis in reality.

hallucinogens   Drugs that produce hallucinations and psychedelic effects, such as mescaline, LSD, and PCP.

hallucinosis syndrome   An organic mental syndrome involving hallucinations without other prominent psychological symptoms.

health psychology   Application of psychological knowledge and principles in the understanding of health, illness, and prevention of illness.

heroin   A semisynthetic opioid drug derived from morphine.

histrionic personality disorder   A personality disorder involving excessive emotionality and dramatic attention-seeking behavior.

homeostasis   The tendency for a system to maintain a state of balance.

hopelessness depression   Depression resulting from the expectation that one is powerless to do anything about unpleasant events.

hostility complex   The active component of the Type A behavior pattern, involving anger, competitiveness, and irritability.

humanism   A philosophical movement that stresses the value and uniqueness of individuals and explains behavior in human terms.

humanistic and existential perspectives   Phenomenological viewpoints based on the assumptions of freedom, responsibility, and personal growth that examine subjective individual experiences.

humoral theory   Hippocrates' view that mental and physical abnormalities are caused by imbalances of bodily fluids, or humors.

Huntington's chorea   An inherited movement disorder involving purposeless, fluid movements; jerking and writhing movements; and dementia.

hypertension   High blood pressure.

hypoactive sexual desire disorder   A sexual dysfunction in which there is a persistent lack of sexual fantasy and desire.

hypochondriasis   A somatoform disorder marked by preoccupation with a minor symptom and misinterpretation of that symptom as sign of serious disease.

id   The primitive unconscious part of personality that is dominated by life and death instincts.

implosion   A behavior therapy technique involving prolonged exposure to an imagined frightening stimulus.

impulse control disorders   Disorders characterized by a failure to resist impulses, drives, or temptations to perform an act that is harmful.

inhalants   Volatile chemicals inhaled through the nose and mouth, usually with depressant effects.

inhibited female orgasm   A sexual dysfunction in women involving delay or absence of orgasm.

inhibited male orgasm A sexual dysfunction in men involving delay or absence of orgasm.

integrationism The view that merges biogenic and psychogenic explanations of abnormal behavior into a comprehensive perspective.

intelligence testing Tests of an individual's intellectual or cognitive ability.

internality-externality hypothesis The view that individuals of normal weight are influenced more by internal hunger cues while obese individuals are motivated to eat in response to external stimuli.

interpersonal theory A psychodynamic theory that views personality, development, and mental disorders in the context of social relationships.

interpersonal theory of depression The idea that depression is caused by disrupted interpersonal relationships.

interpersonal therapy for depression Short-term therapy for depression, designed to correct faulty relationship patterns.

interview A method of investigating mental, emotional, and behavioral functioning by asking questions and evaluating the patient's responses.

juvenile delinquency A legal term that indicates a violation of some law by a minor.

juvenile diversion programs Community-based efforts to intervene with delinquent youths before their behavior leads to incarceration.

kleptomania An impulse control disorder involving an irresistible impulse to steal.

labeling theory The view that interprets mental disorders in terms of society's labeling of people who exhibit deviant behavior.

language systems Neuronal circuits, including Broca's and Wernicke's areas, that account for our ability to produce and comprehend spoken and written words.

law of effect A learning principle that states behaviors are strengthened by satisfying effects and weakened by dissatisfying effects.

learned helplessness model A causal explanation for depression, based on the idea that people become depressed when they believe they cannot control unpleasant events.

learning perspective The view that abnormal behavior results from faulty or maladaptive learning experiences.

libido The energy of the sexual instinct, according to Freud's psychoanalytic theory.

limbic system The brain circuitry involved in emotional expression, integration of sensory experiences, and memory formation.

logotherapy An existential treatment approach concerned with activating the patient's will to meaning.

mainstreaming An educational strategy of placing retarded children in regular classes with nonretarded children.

major depression A mood disorder characterized by one or more major depressive episodes without a history of mania.

major depressive episode A mood disturbance characterized by depressed mood or loss of pleasure.

maladaptive behavior Behavior that interferes with the ability to cope with everyday responsibilities and demands.

male erectile disorder A sexual dysfunction characterized by inability to develop or maintain an erection sufficient to complete intercourse.

manic episode An emotional state characterized by elevated or irritable mood.

marijuana A drug derived from the cannabis plant, which has mild sedative and euphoric effects.

medical model The view that abnormal behavior reflects an underlying disease or bodily disturbance.

meditation Procedures through which individuals reduce stress by directing attention to a single repetitive stimulus.

mental retardation A condition defined by significantly subaverage intellectual functioning and deficits in adaptive behavior, appearing in the developmental period.

mental status examination Systematic assessment of cognitive, behavioral, and emotional functions.

methadone maintenance therapy A treatment that employs the synthetic opioid methadone to help addicts wean themselves from heroin.

migraines Vascular headaches marked by throbbing, stabbing sensations confined to one side of the head.

milieu therapy A residential treatment program for schizophrenics, emphasizing group involvement, patient responsibility, and social interaction.

minimal brain dysfunction A concept defined by nonspecific neurological "soft signs," such as EEG abnormalities, coordination problems, and developmental delays.

Minnesota Multiphasic Personality Inventory (MMPI, MMPI-2) A self-report inventory used to measure abnormal personality characteristics.

modeling therapy A treatment technique that utilizes the principles of observational learning in order to change behavior.

mood An emotional state.

mood disorders Mental disorders characterized by episodes of mania, depression, or an alternation of the two.

moral treatment An eighteenth-century reform movement advocating humane living conditions for the mentally ill.

multifactorial polygenic model The theory that many genes contribute to vulnerability to schizophrenia.

multi-infarct dementia Deterioration of mental functions due to disease of brain's cardiovascular system.

multiple personality disorder A dissociative disorder in which the person has two or more distinct personalities.

narcissistic personality disorder A personality disorder expressed by extreme self-love, self-admiration, and attitudes of superiority.

naturalism The belief that disorders of the mind and body have natural physical causes.

nature-nurture debate A debate about whether behavior is caused by innate factors ("nature") or experiences ("nurture").

need hierarchy In Maslow's theory, a sequence of needs, organized from lower to higher levels, whose satisfaction produces self-actualization.

negative cognitive triad A mental blueprint characteristic of depressed people, consisting of distorted thoughts about the self, the world, and the future.

negative symptoms Schizophrenic deficits in normal behavior including flat affect, apathy, social withdrawal, and poor attention.

neurological examination A series of tests designed to detect dysfunction in the nervous system.

neurophysiological assessment Studies designed to find structural and functional abnormalities in the nervous system.

neuropsychological testing Testing used to detect and measure brain damage and cognitive disability.

neuroses A group of distressing symptoms that the person recognizes as unacceptable.

neurosyphilis Neurological consequences of syphilis, involving insomnia, apathy, poor impulse control, unprovoked rage, social skills deficits, and dementia.

neuroticism Traits of self-consciousness, fear of impulses, vulnerability to stress, anger, hostility, and depression.

neurotransmitters The chemicals that neurons use to communicate with one another.

normative group The comparison or reference group used in test standardization.

obesity A condition of excess body fat, usually defined as more than 20 percent above normal for height and age.

object relations theory A psychodynamic theory that focuses on the importance of early relationships in the development of personality.

observational learning A type of learning that requires the observation and imitation of modeled behavior.

obsessions Recurrent, distressing, and intrusive ideas, images or impulses that the person recognizes as unacceptable.

obsessive-compulsive disorder An anxiety disorder characterized by obsessions, compulsions, or both.

obsessive-compulsive personality disorder A personality disorder defined by inflexible attitudes, perfection-ism, a rigid sense of morality, and preoccupation with rules and details.

operant conditioning A type of learning in which instrumental behaviors (operants) are strengthened by reinforcement and weakened by punishment.

opioids Narcotic drugs derived from opium, including codeine, morphine, and heroin; also, related synthetic drugs with similar effects.

oppositional defiant disorder A disruptive behavior disorder defined by negativistic, hostile, and defiant behavior without serious antisocial or aggressive behavior.

organic anxiety syndrome An organic mental syndrome characterized by generalized anxiety or panic attacks.

organic mental disorder Psychological or behavioral abnormality caused by identifiable brain impairment.

organic mental syndrome A group of symptoms due to brain dysfunction, without reference to cause.

organic mood syndrome An organic mental syndrome characterized by depressive or manic episodes.

organic personality syndrome An organic mental syndrome marked by lifelong personality disturbance or by significant change in personality functioning.

organic retardation Mental retardation with clear biological causes.

orgasm disorders Sexual dysfunctions involving delayed or inhibited orgasm.

overanxious disorder A childhood anxiety disorder characterized by excessive and unrealistic anxiety that is not focused on a specific object or situation.

panic disorders Anxiety disorders characterized by recurrent panic attacks, anticipatory anxiety, and phobic avoidance.

paranoid personality disorder A personality disorder defined by distrust, suspiciousness, fear, and jealousy.

paranoid schizophrenia A type of schizophrenia characterized by delusions of persecution, reference, or grandeur and by hallucinations associated with delusional themes.

paraphilias Sexual disorders involving sexual fantasies or activities directed toward nonhuman objects, suffering or humiliation, or children or nonconsenting adults.

Parkinson's disease A progressive movement disorder marked by tremors, unemotional facial expression, muscle stiffness, difficulties in initiating movement, and dementia.

passive-aggressive personality disorder A personality disorder involving resentment of and passive resistance to demands, through forgetting, procrastinating, and dawdling.

pathological gambling An impulse control disorder marked by a chronic inability to resist the urge to gamble despite the adverse consequences of losing.

pedophilia   A paraphilia characterized by sexual fantasies or activities directed toward children younger than the age of puberty.

peptic ulcer   An open sore in the gastrointestinal tract.

performance anxiety   Fear of sexual failure.

personal distress cirterion   A definition of abnormal behavior in terms of an individual's unpleasant emotional experiences.

personality disorder   A pattern of maladaptive, inflexible, and distressing personality traits.

pervasive developmental disorder   A condition involving severe deviations from normal development in all areas of functioning.

phenomenology   The study of individual subjective consciousness and experience.

phobia disorders   Types of anxiety disorder involving an intense fear of an object, situation, or activity and the urge to avoid feared stimuli.

physical abuse   The infliction of a nonaccidental physical injury.

Pick's disease   A dementia in which there is a progressive and irreversible deterioration of mental functioning.

polysubstance dependence   A patter of drug dependence involving at least three psychoactive drugs.

positive symptoms   Schizophrenic symptoms such as delusions, hallucinations, loose associations, and disorganized behavior.

posttraumatic stress disorder   An anxiety disorder involving a severe reaction to some catastrophic event beyond the realm of ordinary human experience.

prefrontal system   The brain circuitry involved in attention, perception, abstract thought, creative problem solving, social ability and responsibility, and movement.

premature ejaculation   A sexual disorder in which the man ejaculates semen just before or after penetration and before either person wishes it.

preparedness theory   An explanation of phobias stating that we have evolved biological tendencies toward certain fears because of their survival value to our species.

process schizophrenia   A type of schizophrenia with slow onset and poor premorbid adjustment and prognosis.

progressive muscle relaxation   A stress management technique based on alternately contracting and relaxing major muscle groups.

projective tests   Tests like the Rorschach inkblot test, in which person is asked to interpret an ambiguous stimulus.

prospective study   A study of a group of subjects over an extended period of time.

psychiatry   The branch of medicine that specializes in the diagnosis and treatment of mental disorders.

psychoactive substance abuse   A maladaptive pattern of drug taking lasting at least one month or occurring repeatedly over a longer period of time.

psychoactive substance dependence   A maladaptive pattern of drug use, involving loss of control and, often, physical addiction.

psychoactive substance–induced organic mental disorders   Mental disorders caused by drug use and marked by psychological, emotional, or behavioral symptoms.

psychoactive substances   Drugs that influence emotions, thoughts, motivation, and behavior.

psychoactive substance use disorder   A pattern of psychoactive substance use that causes maladaptive behaviors and psychological changes.

psychoanalysis   Freud's treatment approach, which attempts to uncover and resolve the unconscious conflicts behind abnormal behavior.

psychodynamic perspective   The view that attributes abnormal behavior to internal psychic conflicts.

psychogenic amnesia   A dissociative disorder characterized by inability to recall important personal information.

psychogenic fugue   A dissociative disorder involving sudden and unexpected travel away from home and the assumption of a new identity.

psychogenic view   A perspective that attributes abnormal behavior to psychological causes.

psychological factors affecting physical condition   A DSM-III-R category for stress-related disorders.

psychopathy   An extreme antisocial personality disorder characterized by aggressive antisocial behavior and a lack of conscience, fear, and empathy.

psychosexual development   Freud's psychoanalytic theory of development, which proposes that libido is focused on different bodily functions through the oral, anal, phallic, latency, and genital stages.

psychosis   A mental state involving extreme impairment in reality testing, and sometimes the creation of a new reality.

psychosomatic hypothesis   The idea that psychological factors play a role in the causation and maintenance of physical disorders.

psychosomatic medicine   A medical discipline focused on relationships between emotional conflicts and physical disease.

psychosurgery   A biological therapy involving brain surgery to correct the symptoms of mental disorders.

psychotherapy   A treatment approach that uses psychological methods, like patient-therapist dialogue, to overcome mental disturbances.

psychotropic drugs   Drugs that are used to change thinking, emotions, and behavior for therapeutic purposes.

pyromania   An impulse control disorder involving deliberate setting of fires on more than one occasion.

rational-emotive therapy   A cognitive therapy that uses logical persuasion, argumentation, and reasoning to eliminate irrational thoughts.

rationalism A philosophy that states knowledge is due to innate capabilities of thought and sensory experience.

reactive depression Depression that results from adverse life experiences.

reactive schizophrenia A type of schizophrenia with sudden onset and good premorbid adjustment and prognosis.

reciprocal determinism The assumption that there are mutual causal influences among environmental variables, person variables, and behavior.

rehabilitation Extended treatment for substance use disorders, including medical treatment, psychotherapy, and group and family therapy.

relational pathology A severe dysfunction of interactions and relationships among family members.

reliability Consistency of test scores.

resistance The patient's struggle against self-awareness and improvement in psychoanalysis.

retrospective study A method that collects information "after the fact" in order to assess the relationship of earlier and later variables.

rheumatoid arthritis A chronic joint disease involving stiffness, pain, swelling, and tenderness.

Rorschach test A projective test that discovers hidden aspects of personality and psychological functioning by having subjects interpret meaningless inkblots.

sadistic personality disorder A personality disorder characterized by cruel, aggressive, manipulative, and demeaning behavior toward others.

schizoid personality disorder A personality disorder characterized by restricted emotional reactions and a pattern of social indifference.

schizophrenia A psychotic disorder characterized by severe symptoms in judgment, emotions, perceptions, and behavior.

schizophrenia, residual type A disorder in the residual phase of schizophrenia, characterized by diminished emotional expression and thinking disturbances without delusions or hallucinations.

schizophrenic spectrum disorders A group of related disorders, including schizophrenia, schizoaffective disorder, and paranoid and schizotypal personality disorders.

schizophrenogenic mother hypothesis A view that blames schizophrenia on the influence of a cold and domineering mother.

schizotypal personality disorder A personality disorder characterized by interpersonal deficits and peculiarities in thinking.

school phobia An extreme fear and avoidance of school, often accompanied by school refusal.

seasonal affective disorder A proposed diagnostic category for people who become depressed during fall and winter and improve during spring and summer.

sedatives A class of drugs with calming or depressant effects, such as barbiturates, benzodiazepines, and inhalants.

segregation Educational placement of a retarded child in classes with other retarded children.

seizure disorders Organic mental disorders characterized by disorganized electrical activity in the brain; also called epilepsies.

self-actualization An inherent drive to fulfill individual potential.

self-concept A sense of identity, composed of self-perceptions and associated values.

self-defeating personality disorder A personality disorder characterized by a pattern of chronic masochistic or self-defeating behavior.

self-efficacy expectations Beliefs people hold about their ability to perform specific behaviors.

self-instructional training A cognitive-behavior therapy that modifies a person's private self-talk to improve behavior and emotional states.

self-medication hypothesis A view that substance abuse is prompted by the need to avoid or subdue emotional problems and create desirable emotional states.

self-report inventories Paper-and-pencil questionnaires in which subjects are asked to report about aspects of psychological functioning.

self theory Rogers's humanistic theory, which proposes that psychological well-being depends on a healthy self-concept.

sensate focus A sex therapy technique that involves nondemanding sensual exploration of the partner's body.

separation anxiety disorder A childhood anxiety disorder defined by excessive anxiety over separation from parents and family members.

set-point model A theory of obesity that proposes that control mechanisms located in the lateral hypothalamus of the brain strive to maintain body weight within a specific range.

sex reassignment surgery Surgery for transsexuals, to make assigned sex match gender identity.

sexual arousal disorders Sexual dysfunctions in which arousal is lacking or decreased.

sexual aversion disorder A sexual desire disorder marked by extreme distaste for sexual contact with another person.

sexual desire disorders Disorders in which there is diminished sexual desire during the appetitive stage of the sexual response cycle.

sexual dysfunctions Sexual disorders characterized by inhibition of desire or of the physiological changes that make up the complete sexual response cycle.

sexuality The totality of one's sexual identity and experiences.

sexually abused child's disorder A pattern found in

victims of child sexual abuse, marked by increased sexual awareness, acting out, dissociation, unexplained fears, and avoidance of specific people and situations.

sexual masochism   A paraphilia in which the person is aroused by imagining or actually being injured, humiliated, or dominated by the sex partner.

sexual pain disorders   Sexual dysfunctions characterized by pain before, during, or after intercourse.

sexual response cycle   The four-stage cycle of sexual response, consisting of the appetitive, arousal, orgasm, and resolution stages.

sexual sadism   A paraphilia in which the person is aroused by imagining or actually injuring, humiliating, or dominating someone.

shaping   A systematic use of reinforcement to encourage gradual acquisition of responses; also called the method of successive approximations.

short-term dynamic psychotherapy   A time-limited psychodynamic treatment designed to help patients quickly recognize their conflicts by confronting defenses.

simple phobias   Irrational fears of specific objects or situations.

single-case research   Experimental study of a single individual who serves as his or her own control group.

social learning theory   A cognitive-behavioral theory that emphasizes the interaction of cognition and environmental variables in behavior.

social norm   A conventional rule of conduct for a society.

social phobia   Morbid fear of evaluation in social situations.

social stress hypothesis   The belief that people who experience high levels of social stress have a greater risk of abnormal behavior.

sociocultural perspective   A viewpoint that explains abnormal behavior in terms of the impact of sociocultural forces on the individual.

somatic weakness hypothesis   The view that individuals carry a vulnerability to certain physical disorders, depending on which organ system is weakest.

somatization disorder   Multiple persistent physical complaints for which no medical cause can be found.

somatoform disorder   A mental disorder involving physical symptoms suggestive of a physical disorder, for which no organic cause can be found.

somatoform pain disorder   A somatoform disorder involving pain in the absence of physical findings.

spectatoring   Monitoring of one's sexual performance.

specific developmental disorder   Inadequate development of academic, language, speech, or motor skills that significantly interferes with academic achievement or daily life.

splitting   A defense mechanism by which opposing aspects of parental images are mentally separated.

squeeze technique   A sex therapy procedure used to treat premature ejaculation by having the partner of the man being treated gently squeeze the man's penis just before he reaches orgasm and then resume sexual interaction after the urge to ejaculate has diminished.

standardization   The process of determining consistent rules for administering and scoring a psychological test.

Stanford-Binet Intelligence Scale   A test of cognitive abilities for ages 2 to adult.

start-stop method   A sex therapy procedure for treating premature ejaculation by having the partner stop stroking the penis just before orgasm and then resume after the urge to ejaculate diminishes.

statistical deviation   A rare or uncommon event, such as abnormal behavior.

stimulants   A class of drugs that increase the arousal of the nervous system, such as cocaine and amphetamines.

strategic family therapy   Therapy that attempts to change the dysfunctional family homeostasis that is responsible for abnormal behavior.

stress   A relationship between a person and the environment that is appraised as exceeding coping resources and endangering well-being.

stress management   Arousal-reducing treatment procedures, which include muscle relaxation, guided imagery, hypnosis, meditation, and biofeedback.

stressor   A stimulus that causes stress.

stress-related disorders   Physical symptoms or ailments to which thoughts, emotions, and behaviors contribute.

structural family therapy   Therapy that corrects the dysfunctional structural problems in family systems, including family roles, rules, and power balance.

structured interview schedules   An interview method using predetermined topics, questions, and scoring system.

superego   The moral part of personality, which evaluates good and bad according to conscience and the ego ideal.

supernaturalism   The belief that behavior can be influenced by gods, demons, spirits, and magic.

support group   A self-help group organized and run by people interested in recovery from their common addiction.

supportive psychotherapy   A treatment for schizophrenia that involves empathic understanding, practical advice, and concrete problem solving.

systematic desensitization   A behavior therapy technique for reducing fear and anxiety responses by pairing relaxation with gradual exposure to fear-producing stimuli.

tardive dyskinesia   An antipsychotic drug–induced movement disorder characterized by involuntary facial movements and breathing disruptions.

tension headaches   Dull generalized headaches caused by tension in neck and head muscles.

tension reduction theory A theory that drug use is reinforced by reduction or relief of unpleasant states of tension.

Thematic Apperception Test (TAT) A projective test of psychological functioning, in which the subject interprets black-and-white sketches.

therapeutic communities Long-term residential rehabilitation programs for drug addicts.

thought stopping A behavioral technique used to reduce the impact of anxiety-producing thoughts by having the person reproduce the thought, then dismiss it by shouting "stop."

token economy A behavior therapy that uses structured contingency management programs in inpatient settings such as mental hospitals.

tolerance The drug user's increased need for higher doses of a substance over time in order to become intoxicated, due to the body's adaptation to the drug.

transference In psychoanalysis, the patient redirects feelings held for parents, family members, or authority figures toward the therapist.

transsexualism A gender identity disorder in which there is persistent discomfort with assigned sex and a desire to change it.

transvestic fetishism A paraphilia involving the persistent desire to dress in clothes considered appropriate for the opposite sex.

triangle A three-way relationship among individual family members or subsystems.

trichotillomania An impulse control disorder characterized by an inability to resist the impulse to pull out one's hair.

twin study Behavior genetics method that examines the occurrence of abnormal behavior or mental disorders among twins.

Type A behavior pattern A cluster of behaviors and personality characteristics involving competitive striving for achievement, hostility, aggressiveness, and time urgency; associated with coronary heart disease.

unconscious determinism The psychodynamic assumption that behavior is controlled by unconscious processes.

undifferentiated schizophrenia A type of schizophrenia with mixed symptoms that do not conform to the paranoid, catatonic, or disorganized types.

unstructured interview A form of interview in which covered topics depend on the clinician's judgment and the patient's immediate needs.

vaginismus A sexual pain disorder involving involuntary spasms of the vagina that make penetration by the penis difficult.

validity The degree to which a test measures what it claims to measure; its accuracy.

voyeurism Sexual arousal derived from observing a stranger who is naked or undressing.

vulnerability model The theory that genetic factors, physiological dysfunctions, brain abnormalities, and developmental problems contribute to vulnerability to schizophrenia.

Wechsler Adult Intelligence Scale An intelligence test that provides measures of verbal and nonverbal abilities.

Wernicke's area An area in the left temporal lobe of the brain that controls our ability to understand and integrate speech.

Wernicke-Korsakoff syndrome An organic mental disorder caused by alcoholism-related vitamin deficiency, with symptoms of disorientation, confusion, memory loss, and confabulation.

withdrawal Unpleasant physical and psychological reactions following reduction of drug use; also called abstinence syndrome.

References

Abel, E. L., & Sokol, R. J. (1987). Incidence of fetal alcohol syndrome and economic impact of FAS-related anomalies. *Drug and Alcohol Dependency, 19*, 51–70.

Abramson, L. Y., Metalsky, G. I., & Alloy, L. B. (1989). Hopelessness and depression: A theory-based subtype of depression. *Psychological Review, 96*, 358–372.

Abramson, L. Y., Seligman, M. E. P., & Teasdale, J. D. (1978). Learned helplessness in humans: Critique and reformulation. *Journal of Abnormal Psychology, 87*, 49–74.

Achmon, J., Granek, M., Golomb, M., & Hart, J. (1989). Behavioral treatment of essential hypertension: A comparison between cognitive therapy and biofeedback of heart rate. *Psychosomatic Medicine, 51*, 152–164.

Adams, H. E., Feuerstein, M., & Fowles, J. L. (1980). Migraine headache: Review of parameters, etiology, and intervention. *Psychological Bulletin, 87*, 217–237.

Adams, H. E., Tollison, C. D., & Carson, T. P. (1981). Behavior therapy with sexual deviations. In S. Turner, K. S. Calhoun, & H. E. Adams (Eds.), *Handbook of clinical behavior therapy*. New York: Wiley.

Ader, R., & Cohen, N. (1985). CNS-immune system interactions: Conditioning phenomena. *The Behavioral and Brain Sciences, 8*, 379–394.

Adler, A. (1927). *Understanding human nature*. New York: Greenberg.

Adler, T. (1991, July). Efficacy of seizure drug in head injuries debated. *Psychological Monitor*, p. 17.

Adler, T. (1991, August). AIDS drug might help neurological problems. *Psychological Monitor*, p. 9.

Agras, W. S., & Kirkley, B. G. (1986). Bulimia: Theories of etiology. In K. D. Brownell & P. J. Foreyt (Eds.), *Handbook of eating disorders*. New York: Basic Books.

Akesson, H. O. (1986). The biological origin of mild mental retardation. *Acta Psychiatrica Scandinavica, 74*, 3–7.

Alcoholics Anonymous (3rd ed.). (1976). New York: Alcoholics Anonymous World Services.

Allebeck, P. (1989). Schizophrenia: A life-threatening disease. *Schizophrenia Bulletin*, *15*, 81–89.

Alexander, F. (1946). The principle of flexibility. In F. Alexander & T. M. French (Eds.), *Psychoanalytic therapy*. New York: Ronald Press.

Alford, G. S. (1980). Alcoholics Anonymous: An empirical outcome study. In W. R. Miller (Ed.), *Addictive behaviors* (Vol. 5). Oxford: Pergamon Press.

Allgood-Merten, B., & Lewinsohn, P. M. (1990). Sex differences and adolescent depression. *Journal of Abnormal Psychology*, *99*, 55–63.

Altemus, M., Hetherington, M. M., Phil, D., Flood, M., Licinio, J., Nelson, M. L., Bernitz, A. S., & Gold, P. W. (1991). Decrease in resting metabolic rate during abstinence from bulimia nervosa. *American Journal of Psychiatry*, *148*, 1071–1072.

Alterman, A. I., O'Brien, C. P., & McClellan, A. T. (1991). Differential therapeutics for substance abuse. In R. J. Frances & S. I. Miller (Eds.), *Clinical textbook of addictive disorders*. New York: Guilford Press.

American Association on Mental Deficiency. (1977). *Manual on terminology and classification in mental retardation*. Washington, DC: Author.

American Humane Society. (1980). *National analysis of official child neglect and abuse reporting 1978*. Englewood, CA: Author.

American Psychiatric Association. (1952). *Diagnostic and statistical manual of mental disorders* (1st ed.). Washington, DC: Author.

American Psychiatric Association. (1968). *Diagnostic and statistical manual of mental disorders* (2nd ed.). Washington, DC: Author.

American Psychiatric Association. (1980). *Diagnostic and statistical manual of mental disorders* (3rd ed.). Washington, DC: Author.

American Psychiatric Association. (1987). *Diagnostic and statistical manual of mental disorders* (3rd ed., rev.). Washington, DC: Author.

American Psychiatric Association Task Force on Alzheimer's Disease. (1988). The Alzheimer's disease imperative: The challenge for psychiatry. *American Journal of Psychiatry*, *145*, 1550–1551.

American Psychiatric Association Task Force on DSM-IV. (1991). *DSM-IV options book: Work in progress*. Washington, DC: Author.

American Psychiatric Association Task Force on Laboratory Tests in Psychiatry. (1987). The dexamethasone suppression test: An overview of its current status in psychiatry. *American Journal of Psychiatry*, *144*, 1253–1262.

American Psychiatric Association Task Force on the Late Neurological Effects of Antipsychotic Drugs. (1980). Tardive dyskinesia: Summary of a Task Force Report of the American Psychiatric Association. *American Journal of Psychiatry*, *137*, 1163–1172.

American Psychological Association. (1987). *Casebook on ethical principles of psychologists*. Washington, DC: Author.

American Psychological Association. (1990). Ethical principles of psychologists. *American Psychologist*, *45*, 390–395.

Ames, K., Wilson, L., Sawhill, R., Glick, D., & King, P. (1991, August 26). Last rights. *Newsweek*, pp. 40–41.

Anastasi, A. (1988). *Psychological testing* (6th ed.). New York: Macmillan.

Andersen, J. C., Williams, S., McGee, R., & Silva, P. A. (1987). DSM-III disorders in preadolescent children. *Archives of General Psychiatry*, *44*, 69–76.

Anderson, K. O., Bradley, L. A., Young, L. D., McDaniel, L. K., & Wise, C. M. (1985). Rheumatoid arthritis: A review of psychological factors related to etiology, effects and treatment. *Psychological Bulletin*, *98*, 358–387.

Andreasen, N. (1984). *The broken brain: The biological revolution in psychiatry*. New York: Harper & Row.

Andreasen, N. (1985). Positive vs. negative schizophrenia: A critical evaluation. *Schizophrenia Bulletin*, *11*, 380–389.

Andreasen, N. C. (1988). Brain imaging: Applications in psychiatry. *Science*, *239*, 1381–1388.

Andreasen, N. C., & Black, D. W. (1991). *Introductory textbook of psychiatry.* Washington, DC: American Psychiatric Press.

Andreasen, N. C., Ehrhardt, J. C., Swayze, V. W., Alliger, R. J., Yuh, W. T. C., Cohen, G., & Ziebell, S. (1990). Magnetic resonance imaging of the brain in schizophrenia: The pathophysiologic significance of structural abnormalities. *Archives of General Psychiatry, 47,* 35–44.

Angell, M. (1985). Disease as a reflection of the psyche. *New England Journal of Medicine, 312,* 1570–1572.

Angier, N. (1990, September 6). Americans' sex knowledge is lacking, poll says. *The New York Times.*

Anthony, W. A., & Liberman, R. P. (1986). The practice of psychiatric rehabilitation: Historical, conceptual, and research base. *Schizophrenia Bulletin, 12,* 522–559.

Appelbaum, P. S. (1986). Tarasoff and the clinician. *American Journal of Psychiatry, 142,* 425–429.

Appelbaum, P. S. (1988). The right to refuse treatment with antipsychotic indicators: Retrospect and prospect. *American Journal of Psychiatry, 145,* 413–419.

Arieti, S. (1974a). Individual psychotherapy of schizophrenia. In S. Arieti (Ed.), *American handbook of psychiatry* (2nd ed.). New York; Basic Books.

Arieti, S. (1974b). *Interpretation of schizophrenia* (2nd ed.). New York: Basic Books.

Armor, D. J., Polich, J. M., & Stambul, H. B. (1978). *Alcoholism and treatment.* New York: Wiley.

Arora, R., & Meltzer, H. Y. (1989). Serotonergic measures in the brains of suicide victims: 5-HT2 binding sites in the frontal cortex of suicide victims and control subjects. *American Journal of Psychiatry, 146,* 730–736.

Asarnow, J. R. (1988). Children at risk for schizophrenia: Converging lines of evidence. *Schizophrenia Bulletin, 14,* 613–631.

Axelrod, J., & Reisine, T. D. (1984). Stress hormones: Their interaction and regulation. *Science, 224,* 452–459.

Ayllon, T., & Azrin, N. H. (1968). *The token economy: A motivational system for therapy and rehabilitation.* New York: Appleton.

Bailey, J. M., & Pillard, R. C. (1991). A genetic study of male sexual orientation. *Archives of General Psychiatry, 48,* 1089–1096.

Baker, L., & Cantwell, D. P. (1985). Developmental language disorder. In H. I. Kaplan & B. J. Sadock (Eds.), *Comprehensive textbook of psychiatry, IV* (Vol. 2). Baltimore: Williams & Wilkins.

Baker, L., & Cantwell, D. P. (1985). Developmental articulation disorder. In H. I. Kaplan & B. J. Sadock (Eds.), *Comprehensive textbook of psychiatry, IV* (Vol. 2). Baltimore: Williams & Wilkins.

Baker, T., & Brandon, T. H. (1988). Behavioral treatment strategies. In *A report of the Surgeon General: The health consequences of smoking: Nicotine addiction.* Rockville, MD: U.S. Department of Health and Human Services.

Bales, J. (1988). Bill reigning in polygraphs takes legislative fast track. *American Psychological Association Monitor,* 17.

Ballotin, U., Bejor, M., Cecchini, A., Martelli, A., Palazzi, S., & Lanzi, G. (1989). Infantile autism and computerized tomography brain-scan findings: Specific versus nonspecific abnormalities. *Journal of Autism and Developmental Disorders, 19,* 109–116.

Bandura, A. (1969). *Principles of behavior modification.* New York: Holt.

Bandura, A. (1977a). Self-efficacy: Toward a unifying theory of behavior change. *Psychological Review, 84,* 191–215.

Bandura, A. (1977b). *Social learning theory.* Englewood Cliffs, NJ: Prentice-Hall.

Bandura, A. (1981). Self-referent thought: A developmental analysis of self-efficacy. In J. H. Flavell & L. Ross (Eds.), *Social cognitive development: Frontiers and possible futures.* Cambridge: Cambridge University Press.

Bandura, A. (1982). Self-efficacy mechanism in human agency. *American Psychologist, 37*, 122–147.

Bandura, A. (1984). Representing personal determinants in causal structures. *Psychological Review, 91*, 508–511.

Bandura, A., Taylor, C. B., Williams, S. L., Mefford, I. N., & Barches, J. D. (1985). Catecholamine secretion as a function of perceived coping self-efficacy. *Journal of Consulting and Clinical Psychology, 53*, 406–414.

Barber, T. X. (1984). Hypnosis, deep relaxation and active relaxation: Data, theory, and clinical applications. In R. L. Woolfolk and P. M. Lehrer (Eds.), *Principles and practice of stress management*. New York: Guilford Press.

Barkley, R. A. (1983). Hyperactivity. In R. J. Morris & T. R. Kratchowill (Eds.), *The practice of child therapy*. New York: Pergamon Press.

Barkley, R. A. (1985). The social interactions of hyperactive children: Developmental changes, drug effects, and situational variation. In J. Swanson & L. Bloomingdale (Eds.), *Research on attention deficit disorders*. New York: Pergamon Press.

Barkley, R. A. (1990). Attention deficit disorders: History, definition, and diagnosis. In M. Lewis & S. M. Miller (Eds.), *Handbook of developmental psychopathology*. New York: Plenum.

Barlow, D. H. (1981). *Behavioral assessment of adult disorders*. New York: Guilford Press.

Barlow, D. H. (1986). Causes of sexual dysfunction: The role of anxiety and cognitive interference. *Journal of Consulting and Clinical Psychology, 54*, 140–148.

Barlow, D. H. (1991). Introduction to special issue on diagnosis, dimensions, and the DSM-IV: The science of classification. *Journal of Abnormal Psychology, 100*, 243–244.

Barnes, D. B. (1988a). Breaking the cycle of addiction. *Science, 241*, 1029–1030.

Barnes, D. B. (1988b). The biological tangle of drug addiction. *Science, 241*, 415–417.

Baroff, G. S. (1983). *Mental retardation: Nature, cause, and management*. Washington, DC: Hemisphere.

Baron, M., Gruen, R., Asnis, L., & Lord, S. (1985). Familial transmission of schizotypal and borderline personality disorders. *American Journal of Psychiatry, 142*, 927–934.

Baron, M., Gruen, R., Rainer, J. D., Kane, J., Asnis, L., & Lord, S. (1985). A family study of schizophrenic and normal control probands: Implications for the spectrum concept of schizophrenia. *American Journal of Psychiatry, 142*, 447–455.

Barr, C. E., Mednick, S. A., & Munk-Jorgensen, P. (1990). Exposure to influenza epidemics during gestation and adult schizophrenia. *Archives of General Psychiatry, 47*, 869–874.

Barrios, B. A. (1988). On the changing nature of behavioral assessment. In A. S. Bellak & M. Herson (Eds.), *Behavioral assessment: A practical handbook* (3rd ed.). New York: Pergamon Press.

Bass, E., & Davis, L. (1988). *The courage to heal: A guide for women survivors of child sexual abuse*. New York: Harper & Row.

Bateson, G., Jackson, D., Haley, J., & Weakland, J. (1956). Toward a theory of schizophrenia. *Behavioral Science, 1*, 251–264.

Baumeister, A. A. (1987). Mental retardation: Some conceptions and dilemmas. *American Psychologist, 42*, 796–800.

Beattie, M. (1987). *Codependent no more*. Center City, MN: Hazelden.

Beck, A. T. (1976). *Cognitive therapy and the emotional disorders*. New York: Signet.

Beck. A. T. (1978). *Depression inventory*. Philadelphia: Center for Cognitive Therapy.

Beck, A. T. (1985). Cognitive therapy. In H. I. Kaplan and B. J. Sadock (Eds.), *Comprehensive textbook of psychiatry, IV*. Baltimore: Williams & Wilkins.

Beck, A. T. (1991a). Cognitive therapy: A 30-year perspective. *American Psychologist, 46*(4), 368–375.

Beck, A. T. (1991b). Personal communication.

Beck, A. T., Brown, G., Berchick, R. J., Stewart, B. L., & Steer, R. A. (1990). Relationship between hopelessness and ultimate suicide: A replication with psychiatric outpatients. *American Journal of Psychiatry, 147,* 190–195.

Beck, A. T., & Emery, G. (1985). *Anxiety and phobias: A cognitive approach.* New York: Basic Books.

Beck, A. T., & Emery, G., with Greenberg, R. L. (1985). *Anxiety disorders and phobias.* New York: Basic Books.

Beck, A. T., & Freeman, A. (1989). *Cognitive therapy of personality disorders.* New York: Guilford Press.

Beck, A. T., Rush, A. J., Shaw, B. F., & Emery, G. (1979). *Cognitive therapy of depression.* New York: Guilford Press.

Beck, J. C., & van der Kolk, B. (1987). Reports of childhood incest and current behavior of chronically hospitalized psychotic women. *American Journal of Psychiatry, 144,* 1474–1476.

Becker, J. V. (1988). The effects of child sexual abuse on adolescent sexual offenders. In G. E. Wyatt & G. J. Powell (Eds.), *Lasting effects of child sexual abuse.* Newbury Park, CA: Sage.

Becker, J. V., & Coleman, E. M. (1988). Incest. In V. B. van Hasselt, R. L., Morrison, A. S. Bellack, & M. Hersen (Eds.), *Handbook of family violence.* New York: Plenum.

Bedrosian, R. C. (1982). Using cognitive and systems interventions in the treatment of marital violence. In J. C. Hansen (Ed.), *Clinical approaches to family violence.* Rockville, MD: Aspen.

Begleiter, H., Porjesz, B., Bihari, B., & Kissen, B. (1984). Event-related brain potentials in boys at risk for alcoholism. *Science, 225,* 1493–1496.

Bellack, L., Hurvich, M., & Gediman, H. (1973). *Ego functioning in schizophrenics, neurotics and normals.* New York: Wiley.

Belle, D. (1990). Poverty and women's mental health. *American Psychologist, 45,* 385–389.

Belsher, G., & Costello, C. G. (1988). Relapse after recovery from unipolar depression: A critical review. *Psychological Bulletin, 104,* 84–96.

Bender, L. (1938). A visual motor test and its clinical use. *American Orthopsychiatric Journal, Research Monographs,* No. 3.

Benson, H. (1975). *The relaxation response.* New York: Morrow.

Berg, R., Franzen, M., & Wedding, D. (1987). *Screening for brain impairment. A manual for mental health practice.* New York: Springer.

Berglas, S. (1987). The self-handicapping model of alcohol abuse. In H. T. Blane & K. E. Leonard (Eds.), *Psychological theories of drinking and alcoholism.* New York: Guilford Press.

Berlin, F., & Meinecke, C. (1981). Treatment of sex offenders with antiandrogenic medication: A conceptualization, review of treatment modalities, and preliminary findings. *American Journal of Psychiatry, 138,* 601–607.

Berman, A. L. (1988). Fictional depiction of suicide in television films and imitation effects. *American Journal of Psychiatry, 145,* 982–986.

Bernstein, D. A., & Given, B. A. (1984). Progressive relaxation: Abbreviated methods. In R. L. Woolfolk & P. M. Lehrer (Eds.), *Principles and practice of stress management.* New York: Guilford Press.

Bersani, C. A., & Chen, H. T. (1988). Sociological perspectives in family violence. In V. B. van Hasselt, R. L. Morrison, A. S. Bellack, & M. Hersen (Eds.), *Handbook of family violence.* New York: Plenum.

Bettelheim, B. (1967). *The empty fortress.* New York: Free Press.

Beutler, L. E., & Kendall, P. C. (1991). Ethical dilemmas: A comment on Jacob, Krahn, and Leonard. *Journal of Consulting and Clinical Psychology, 59,* 245.

Biederman, J., Munir, K., Knee, D., Habelow, W., Armentano, M., Autor, S., Hoge, S. K., & Waterman, C. (1986). A family study of patients with attention deficit disorder and normal controls. *Journal of Psychiatric Research, 20,* 263–274.

Biller, H. B., & Solomon, R. S. (1986). *Child maltreatment and paternal deprivation: A manifesto for research, prevention and treatment.* Lexington, MA: Lexington Books.

Binder, A. (1988). Juvenile delinquency. *Annual Review of Psychology, 39,* 253–282.

Binder. R. (1988). Organic mental disorders. In H. H. Goldman (Ed.), *Review of general psychiatry* (2nd ed.). Norwalk, CT: Appleton and Lange.

Black, D. W., Winokur, G., & Nasrallah, A. (1987). Suicide in subtypes of major affective disorder. *Archives of General Psychiatry, 44,* 878–880.

Black, D. W., Winokur, G., & Nasrallah, A. (1988). Effect of psychosis on suicide risk in 1593 patients with unipolar and bipolar disorder. *American Journal of Psychiatry, 145,* 849–852.

Blackman, J. (1989). *Intimate violence: A study of injustice.* New York: Columbia University Press.

Blanchard, E. B., Andrasik, F., Evans, D. D., Neff, D. F., Appelbaum, K. A., & Rodichok, L. D. (1985). Behavioral treatment of 250 chronic headache patients: A clinical replication series. *Behavior Therapy, 16,* 308–327.

Blanchard, E. B., McCoy, G. C., Musso, A., Gerardi, M. A., Pallmeyer, T. P., Gerardi, R. J., Cotch, P. A., Siracusa, K., & Andrasik, F. (1986). A controlled comparison of thermal biofeedback and relaxation training in the treatment of essential hypertension: I. Short-term and long-term outcome. *Behavior Therapy, 17,* 563–579.

Blanck, G., & Blanck, R. (1974). *Ego psychology: Theory and practice.* New York: Columbia University Press.

Blazer, D., Swartz, M., Woodbury, M., Manton, K. G., Hughs, D., & George, L. K. (1988). Depressive symptoms and depressive diagnosis in a community population. *Archives of General Psychiatry, 45,* 1078–1084.

Blehar, M. C., & Rosenthal, N. E. (1989). Seasonal affective disorders and phototherapy: Report of a National Institute of Mental Health-sponsored workshop. *Archives of General Psychiatry, 46,* 469–475.

Blehar, M. C., Weissman, M. M., Gershon, E. S., & Hirschfeld, R. M. A. (1988). Family and genetic studies of affective disorders. *Archives of General Psychiatry, 45,* 289–292.

Bleuler, M. (1978). *The schizophrenic disorders: Long-term patient and family studies.* New Haven, CT: Yale University Press.

Bloom, B. L., White, S. W., & Asher, S. J. (1979). Marital disruption as a stressful life event. In G. Levinger & O. C. Moles (Eds.), *Divorce and separation: Context, causes, and consequences.* New York: Basic Books.

Bloom, F. E., & Lazerson, A. (1988). *Brain, mind, and behavior* (2nd ed.). New York: Freeman.

Blum, K. (1984). *Handbook of abusable drugs.* New York: Gardner.

Blum, K., Noble, E. P., Sheridan, P. J., Montgomery, A., Ritchie, T., Jagadeeswaran, P., Nogami, H., Briggs, A. H., & Cohn, J. B. (1990, April 18). Allelic association of human dopamine D2 receptor gene in alcoholism. *Journal of the American Medical Association, 263,* 2055–2060.

Board of Professional Affairs, Committee on Professional Standards. (1988). Casebook for providers of psychological services. *American Psychologist, 43,* 557–563.

Board on Mental Health and Behavioral Medicine, Institute of Medicine. (1985). Research on mental illness and addictive disorders: Progress and prospects. *American Journal of Psychiatry, 142* (Suppl.), 1–41.

Bohman, M., Sigvardsson, S., & Cloninger, C. R. (1981). Maternal inheritance of alcohol abuse. *Archives of General Psychiatry, 38,* 965–969.

Booth, G. K. (1988). Disorders of impulse control. In H. H. Goldman (Ed.), *Review of general psychiatry* (2nd ed.). Norwalk, CT: Appleton and Lange.

Boszormenyi-Nagy, I., & Spark, G. (1973). *Invisible loyalties: Reciprocity in intergenerational family therapy.* New York: Harper & Row.

Bouchard, C., Tremblay, A., Despres, J. P., Nadeau, A., Lupien, P. J., Theriault, G., Dussault, J., Moorjani, S., Pinault, S., & Fournier, G. (1990). The response to long-term overfeeding in identical twins. *New England Journal of Medicine, 322,* 1477–1482.

Bouchard, T. J., & Segal, N. L. (1985). Environment and IQ. In B. Wolman (Ed.), *Handbook of intelligence: Theories, measurements and applications.* New York: Wiley.

Bowden, S. C. (1990). Separating cognitive impairment in neurologically asymptomatic alcoholism from Wernicke-Korsakoff syndrome: Is the neuropsychological distinction justified? *Psychological Bulletin, 107,* 355–366.

Bowen, M. (1985). *Family therapy in clinical practice.* New York: Jason Aronson.

Bowers, T., & Clum, G. (1988). Relative contributions of specific and nonspecific treatment effects: Meta-analysis of placebo controlled behavior therapy research. *Psychological Bulletin, 103,* 315–323.

Boyd, J. H., & Weissman, M. M. (1981). Epidemiology of affective disorders. *Archives of General Psychiatry, 38,* 1039–1046.

Brady, J. P. (1958). Ulcers in "executive" monkeys. *Scientific American, 199,* 95–100.

Bratter, T. E., Pennacchia, M. C., & Ganya, D. C. (1985). From methadone maintenance to abstinence: The myth of metabolic disorder theory. In T. E. Bratter & G. G. Forrest (Eds.), *Alcoholism and substance abuse: Strategies for clinical intervention.* New York: Free Press.

Bray, G. A. (1986). Effects of obesity on health and happiness. In K. D. Brownell & P. J. Foreyt (Eds.), *Handbook of eating disorders.* New York: Basic Books.

Breggin, P. R. (1980). Brain-disabling therapies. In E. Valenstein (Ed.), *The psychosurgery debate: Scientific, legal and ethical perspectives.* San Francisco: Freeman.

Bregman, J. D., Leckman, J. F., & Ort, S. I. (1988). Fragile-X syndrome: Genetic predisposition to psychopathology. *Journal of Autism and Developmental Disorders, 18,* 343–354.

Breier, A., Schrieber, J. L., Dyer, J., & Picker, D. (1991). National Institute of Mental Health longitudinal study of chronic schizophrenia: Prognosis and predictors of outcome. *Archives of General Psychiatry, 48,* 239–246.

Brent, D. A., Peyser, J. A., Goldstein, C. E., Kolko, D. J., Allan, M. J., Allman, C. J., & Zelanak, J. P. (1988). Risk factors for adolescent suicide. *Archives of General Psychiatry, 45,* 581–588.

Breslau, N., Davis, G. C., Andreski, P., & Peterson, E. (1991). Traumatic events and post-traumatic stress disorder in an urban population of young adults. *Archives of General Psychiatry, 48,* 216–222.

Breuer, J. (1989). Anna O. In P. Gay (Ed.), *The Freud reader.* New York: Norton.

Bricker, D. D. (1986). An analysis of early intervention programs: Attendant issues and future directions. In R. J. Morris & B. Blatt (Eds.), *Special education: Research and trends.* New York: Pergamon Press.

Briere, J., & Runtz, M. (1988). Post sexual abuse trauma. In G. E. Wyatt & G. J. Powell (Eds.), *Lasting effects of child sexual abuse.* Newbury Park, CA: Sage.

Brown, G. R., & Anderson, B. (1991). Psychiatric morbidity in adult inpatients with childhood histories of sexual and physical abuse. *American Journal of Psychiatry, 148,* 55–61.

Brown, W. T., Jenkins, E. C., Cohen, I. L., Fisch, G. S., Wolf-Schein, E. G., Gross, A., Waterhouse, L., Fein, D., Mason-Brothers, A., Ritvo, E., Ruttenberg, B. A., Bentley, W., & Castells, S. (1986). Fragile X and autism: A multicenter survey. *American Journal of Medical Genetics, 23,* 341–352.

Browne, A. (1988). Family homicide: When victimized women kill. in V. B. van Hasselt, R. L. Morrison, A. S. Bellack, & M. Hersen (Eds.), *Handbook of family violence.* New York: Plenum.

Browne, A., & Finkelhor, D. (1986). Impact of child sexual abuse: A review of the research. *Psychological Bulletin, 99,* 66–77.

Brownell, K. D. (1987). *The LEARN program for weight control.* Philadelphia: University of Pennsylvania School of Medicine.

Brownell, K. D., Greenwood, M. R. C., Stellar, E., & Shrager, E. E. (1986). The effects of repeated cycles of weight loss and regain in rats. *Physiology and Behavior, 38,* 459–464.

Brownell, K. D., & Wadden, T. A. (1986). Behavior therapy for obesity: Modern approaches and better results. In K. D. Brownell & P. J. Foreyt (Eds.), *Handbook of eating disorders*. New York: Basic Books.

Bruce, M. L., Takeuchi, D. T., & Leaf, P. J. (1991). Poverty and psychiatric status: Longitudinal evidence from the New Haven Epidemiologic Catchment Area Study. *Archives of General Psychiatry, 48,* 470–474.

Bruch, H. (1962). Perceptual and cognitive disturbances in anorexia nervosa. *Psychosomatic Medicine, 24,* 187–194.

Bruch, H. (1973). *Eating disorders.* New York: Basic Books.

Bruch, H. (1977). Psychological antecedents of anorexia nervosa. In R. A. Vigersky (Ed.), *Anorexia nervosa.* New York: Raven Press.

Bruch, H. (1982). Anorexia nervosa: Theory and therapy. *American Journal of Psychiatry, 139,* 1531–1538.

Bruch, H. (1986). Anorexia nervosa: The therapeutic task. In K. D. Brownell and P. J. Foreyt (Eds.), *Handbook of eating disorders.* New York: Basic Books.

Bruck, M. (1987). Social and emotional adjustments of learning-disabled children: A review of the issues. In S. J. Ceci (Ed.), *Handbook of cognitive, social and neuropsychological aspects of learning disabilities* (Vol. 1). Hillsdale, NJ: Erlbaum.

Buchanan, R. W., Kirkpatrick, B., Heinrichs, D. W., & Carpenter, J. W., Jr. (1990). Clinical correlates of the deficit syndrome of schizophrenia. *American Journal of Psychiatry, 147,* 290–294.

Buchsbaum, M. (1990). The frontal lobes, basal ganglia, and temporal lobes as sites for schizophrenia. *Schizophrenia Bulletin, 16,* 379–389.

Buchsbaum, M. S., and Haier, R. J. (1987). Functional and anatomical brain imaging: Impact on schizophrenia research. *Schizophrenia Bulletin, 13,* 115–132.

Buchsbaum, M. S., Mirsky, A. F., DeLisi, L. E., Morihisa, J., Karson, C. N., Mendelson, W. B., King, A. C., Johnson, J., & Kessler, R. (1984). The Genain quadruplets: Electrophysiological, positron emission, and x-ray tomographic studies. *Psychiatry Research, 13,* 95–108.

Bukstein, O. G., Brent, D. A., & Kaminer, Y. (1989). Comorbidity of substance abuse and other psychiatric disorders in adolescents. *American Journal of Psychiatry, 146,* 1131–1141.

Bulik, C. A. (1987). Drug and alcohol abuse by bulimic women and their families. *American Journal of Psychiatry, 144,* 1604–1606.

Burns, D. D. (1980). *Feeling good: The new mood therapy.* New York: Signet.

Bushman, B. J., & Cooper, H. M. (1990). Effects of alcohol on human aggression: An integrative research review. *Psychological Bulletin, 107,* 341–354.

Butcher, J. N. (1987). Introduction to special series on cultural factors in understanding and assessing psychopathology. *Journal of Consulting and Clinical Psychology, 55,* 459–460.

Butcher, J. N. (1989). *MMPI-2, User's guide.* Minneapolis: National Computer Systems.

Butcher, J. N., & Bemis, K. M. (1984). Abnormal behavior in cultural context. In H. E. Adams & P. B. Sutker (Eds.), *Comprehensive handbook of psychopathology.* New York: Plenum.

Byrne, D. (1983). The antecedents, correlates, and consequences of erotophobia-erotophilia. In C. M. Davis (Ed.), *Challenges in sexual science.* Philadelphia: Society for the Scientific Study of Sex.

Cadoret, R. J., & Gath, A. (1978). Inheritance of alcoholism in adoptees. *British Journal of Psychiatry, 132,* 252–258.

Caldwell, C. B., & Gottesman, I. I. (1990). Schizophrenics kill themselves too: A review of risk factors for suicide. *Schizophrenia Bulletin, 16,* 571–589.

Campbell, M. (1988). Fenfluramine treatment of autism. *Journal of Child Psychology and Psychiatry, 29,* 1–10.

Campbell, M., Anderson, L. T., Green, W. H., & Deutsch, S. I. (1987). Psychopharmacology. In D. J. Cohen & A. M. Donnellan (Eds.), *Handbook of autism and pervasive developmental disorders.* New York: Wiley.

Campbell, M., & Green, W. H. (1985). Pervasive developmental disorders of childhood. In H. I. Kaplan & B. J. Sadock (Eds.), *Comprehensive textbook of psychiatry, IV* (Vol. 2). Baltimore: Williams & Wilkins.

Campbell, S. B. (1985). Hyperactivity in preschoolers: Correlates and prognostic implications. *Clinical Psychology Review, 5,* 405–428.

Campbell, S. B. (1990). The socialization and social development of hyperactive children. In M. Lewis & S. M. Miller (Eds.), *Handbook of developmental psychopathology.* New York: Plenum.

Campbell, S. B., & Werry, J. S. (1986). Attention deficit disorder (hyperactivity). In H. C. Quay & J. S. Werry (Eds.), *Psychopathological disorders of childhood* (3rd ed.). New York: Wiley.

Cancro, R. (1985). History and overview of schizophrenia. In H. I. Kaplan & B. J. Sadock (Eds.), *Comprehensive textbook of psychiatry* (Vol. 1, 4th ed.). Baltimore: Williams & Wilkins.

Cannon, T. D., Mednick, S. A., & Parnas, J. (1989). Genetic and perinatal determinants of structural brain deficits in schizophrenia. *Archives of General Psychiatry, 46,* 883–889.

Cannon, W. B. (1929). *Bodily changes in pain, hunger, fear and rage: An account of recent researches into the function of emotional excitement.* New York: Appleton.

Cantwell, D. P. (1975). Genetic studies of hyperactive children: Psychiatric illness in biological and adopting parents. In R. R. Fieve, D. Rosenthal, & H. Brill (Eds.), *Genetic research in psychiatry.* Baltimore: Johns Hopkins University Press.

Cappell, H., & Greeley, J. (1987). Alcohol and tension reduction: An update on research and theory. In H. T. Blane & K. E. Leonard (Eds.), *Psychological theories of drinking and alcoholism.* New York: Guilford Press.

Carey, G., & Gottesman, I. I. (1981). Twin and family studies of anxiety, phobic, and obsessive-compulsive disorders. In D. F. Klein & J. Rabkin (Eds.), *Anxiety: New research and changing concepts.* New York: Raven Press.

Carlat, D. J., & Camargo, C. A. (1991). Review of bulimia nervosa in males. *American Journal of Psychiatry, 148,* 831–843.

Carlson, C. L., Figueroa, R. G., & Lahey, B. B. (1986). Behavior therapy for childhood anxiety disorders. In R. Gittelman (Ed.), *Anxiety disorders of childhood.* New York: Guilford Press.

Carlson, N. R. (1986). *Physiology of behavior* (3rd ed.). Boston: Allyn and Bacon.

Carpenter, W. T., Heinrichs, D. W., & Wagman, A. M. I. (1988). Deficit and nondeficit forms of schizophrenia: The concept. *American Journal of Psychiatry, 145,* 578–583.

Carr, D. B., Sheehan, D. V., Surman, O. S., Coleman, J. H., Greenblatt, D. J., Heninger, G. R., Jones, K. J., Levine, P. H., & Watkins, W. D. (1986). Neuroendocrine correlates of lactate induced anxiety and their response to chronic alprazolam therapy. *American Journal of Psychiatry, 142,* 947–950.

Carrington, P. (1984). Modern forms of meditation. In R. L. Woolfolk & P. M. Lehrer (Eds.), *Principles and practice of stress management.* New York: Guilford Press.

Carter, E. A., & McGoldrick, M. (1980). The family life cycle and family therapy: An overview. In E. A. Carter & M. McGoldrick (Eds.), *The family life cycle: A framework for family therapy.* New York: Gardner.

Casey, R. J., & Berman, J. S. (1985). The outcome of psychotherapy with children. *Psychological Bulletin, 98,* 388–400.

Cassens, G., Inglis, A. K., Appelbaum, P. S., & Gutheil, T. G. (1990). Neuroleptics: Effects on neuropsychological function in chronic schizophrenic patients. *Schizophrenia Bulletin, 16,* 477–499.

Caton, C. L. M., Wyatt, R. J., Grunberg, J., & Felix, A. (1990). An evaluation of a mental health program for homeless men. *American Journal of Psychiatry, 147,* 286–289.

Cattell, R. B. (1973). A check on the 28 factor clinical analysis questionnaire structure on normal and pathological subjects. *Journal of Multivariate Experimental Personality and Clinical Psychology, 1,* 3–12.

Cattell, R. B., Eber, H. W., & Tatsuoka, M. M. (1970). *Handbook for the sixteen P.F. (16PF).* Champaign, IL: Institute for Personality and Ability Testing.

Cattell, R. B., & Johnson, R. C. (Eds.) (1986). *Functional psychological testing: Principles and instruments.* New York: Brunner/Mazel.

Cattell, R. B., & Scheier, I. H. (1963). *The IPAT anxiety scale questionnaire manual.* Champaign, IL: Institute for Personality and Ability Testing.

Cautela, J. R. (1966). Treatment of compulsive behavior by covert sensitization. *Psychological Record, 16,* 33–41.

Cautela, J. R. (1973). Covert processes and behavior modification. *Journal of Nervous and Mental Disease, 157,* 27–35.

Ceci, S. J. (Ed.). (1987). *Handbook of cognitive, social and neuropsychological aspects of learning disabilities* (Vol. 1). Hillsdale, NJ: Erlbaum.

Charney, D. S., Galloway, M. P., & Heninger, G. R. (1984). The effects of caffeine on plasma MHPG, subjective anxiety, autonomic symptoms and blood pressure in healthy humans. *Life Science, 35,* 135–144.

Charney, D. S., Heninger, G. R., & Jatlow, P. I. (1985). Increased anxiogenic effects of caffeine in panic disorders. *Archives of General Psychiatry, 42,* 233–243.

Christenson, C. V. (1971). *Kinsey: An autobiography.* Bloomington: Indiana University Press.

Christenson, G. A., MacKenzie, T. B., & Mitchell, J. E. (1991). Characteristics of 60 chronic hair pullers. *American Journal of Psychiatry, 148,* 365–370.

Christiansen, K. O. (1977). A review of studies of criminality in twins. In S. A. Mednick & K. O. Christiansen (Eds.), *Biosocial bases of criminal behavior.* New York: Gardner.

Chu, J. A., & Dill, D. L. (1990). Dissociative symptoms in relation to childhood physical and sexual abuse. *American Journal of Psychiatry, 147,* 887–892.

Cicchetti, D., & Olsen, K. (1990). The developmental psychopathology of child maltreatment. In M. Lewis & S. M. Miller (Eds.), *Handbook of developmental psychopathology.* New York: Plenum.

Clark, R. W. (1980). *Freud: The man and the cause, a biography.* New York: Random House.

Cleckley, H. (1976). *The mask of sanity* (5th ed.). St. Louis: Mosby.

Clementz, B. A., & Sweeney, J. A. (1990). Is eye movement dysfunction a biological marker for schizophrenia? A methodological review. *Psychological Bulletin, 108,* 77–92.

Clinard, M. B., & Meier, R. F. (1989). *Sociology of deviant behavior* (7th ed.). Fort Worth, TX: Holt, Rinehart and Winston.

Clomipramine Collaborative Study Group. (1991). Clomipramine in the treatment of patients with obsessive-compulsive disorder. *Archives of General Psychiatry, 48,* 730–738.

Cloninger, C. R. (1988). Etiologic factors in substance abuse: An adoption study perspective. In R. W. Pickens & D. S. Svikis (Eds.), *Biological vulnerability to drug abuse.* Rockville, MD: National Institute on Drug Abuse.

Cloninger, C. R., Bohman, M., & Sigvardsson, S. (1981). Inheritance of alcohol abuse: Cross fostering analysis of adopted men. *Archives of General Psychiatry, 38,* 861–868.

Cohen, S., Lichtenstein, E., Prochaska, J. O., Rossi, J. S., Gritz, E. R., Carr, C. R., Orleans, C. T., Schoenbach, V. J., Biener, L., Abrams, D., DiClemente, C., Curry, S., Marlatt, G. A., Cummings, K. M., Emont, S. L., Giovino, G., & Ossip-Klein, D. (1989). Debunking myths about self-quitting: Evidence from 10 prospective studies of persons who attempt to quit smoking by themselves. *American Psychologist, 44,* 1355–1365.

Cohen, S., Mermerstein, R. J., Kamarck, T., & Haberman, H. M. (1985). Measuring the functional components of social support. In I. G. Sarason & B. R. Sarason (Eds.), *Social support: Theory research and applications.* The Hague, The Netherlands: Martinus Nijhoff.

Cohen, S., & Wells, T. A. (1985). Stress, social support, and the buffering hypothesis. *Psychological Bulletin, 98,* 310-357.

Cohen, S., & Williamson, G. M. (1991). Stress and infectious disease in humans. *Psychological Bulletin, 109,* 5-24.

Cole, D. A. (1989). Psychopathology of adolescent suicide: Hopelessness, coping beliefs, and depression. *Journal of Abnormal Psychology, 98,* 248-255.

Collins, R. L., & Marlatt, G. A. (1981). Social modeling as a determinant of drinking behavior: Implications for prevention and treatment. *Addictive Behaviors, 6,* 233-240.

Combs, J. R., & Ludwig, A. M. (1982). Dissociative disorders. In J. H. Greist, J. W. Jefferson, & R. L. Spitzer (Eds.), *Treatment of mental disorders.* New York: Oxford University Press.

Conger, J. J. (1956). Reinforcement theory and the dynamics of alcoholism. *Quarterly Journal of Studies on Alcohol, 17,* 296-305.

Connors, C. K. (1980). Artificial colors and the diet of disruptive behavior: Current status of research. In R. M. Knight & D. J. Bakker (Eds.), *Treatment of hyperactive and learning disabled children.* Baltimore: University Park Press.

Conrad, A. J., Abebe, T., Austin, R., Forsythe, S., & Scheibel, A. B. (1991). Hippocampal pyramidal cell disarray in schizophrenia as a bilateral phenomenon. *Archives of General Psychiatry, 48,* 413-417.

Consensus Development Panel, NIMH/NIH. (1985). Mood disorders: Pharmacological prevention of recurrences. *American Journal of Psychiatry, 142,* 469-476.

Consortium for Longitudinal Studies. (1983). *As the twig is bent.* London: Erlbaum.

Conte, H. R. (1986). Multivariate assessment of sexual dysfunction. *Journal of Consulting and Clinical Psychology, 54,* 149-157.

Coons, P. M., Milstein, V., & Marley, C. (1982). EEG studies of multiple personalities and a control. *Archives of General Psychiatry, 39,* 823-825.

Cooper, A. M. (1985). Will neurobiology influence psychoanalysis? *American Journal of Psychiatry, 142,* 1395-1402.

Cooper, M. L., Russell, M., & George, W. H. (1988). Coping, expectancies and alcohol abuse: A test of social learning formulations. *Journal of Abnormal Psychology, 97,* 218-230.

Cornelius, J. R., Day, N. L., Fabrega, H., Jr., Mezzich, J., Cornelius, M. D., & Ulrich, R. F. (1991). Characterizing organic delusional syndrome. *Archives of General Psychiatry, 48,* 749-753.

Corwin, D. L. (1988). Early diagnosis of child sexual abuse. In G. E. Wyatt & G. J. Powell (Eds.), *Lasting effects of child sexual abuse.* Newbury Park, CA: Sage.

Coryell, W. H., & Zimmerman, M. (1989). Personality disorders in the families of depressed, schizophrenic, and never-ill probands. *American Journal of Psychiatry, 146,* 496-502.

Costantino, G. (1986). Cuento therapy: A culturally sensitive modality for Puerto Rican children. *Journal of Consulting and Clinical Psychology, 54,* 639-645.

Courchesne, E. (1987). A neurophysiological view of autism. In E. Schopler & G. B. Mesibov (Eds.), *Neurobiological issues in autism.* New York: Plenum.

Coursey, R. D. (1989). Psychotherapy with schizophrenia: The need for a new agenda. *Schizophrenia Bulletin, 15,* 349-353.

Cowdry, R. W., & Gardner, R. L. (1988). Pharmacotherapy of borderline personality disorder: Alprazolam, carbamazepine, trifluoperazine, and tranylcypromine. *Archives of General Psychiatry, 45,* 111-119.

Coyne, J. C., & DeLongis, A. (1986). Going beyond social relationships in adaptation. *Journal of Consulting and Clinical Psychology, 54,* 454-460.

Coyne, J. C., Kahn, J., & Gotlib, I. H. (1987). Depression. In T. Jacob (Ed.), *Family interaction and psychopathology.* New York: Plenum.

Craighead, L. W., & Agras, W. S. (1991). Mechanisms of action in cognitive-behavioral and pharmacological interventions for obesity and bulimia nervosa. *Journal of Consulting and Clinical Psychology, 59*, 115–125.

Crisp, A. H., Hall, A., & Holland, A. J. (1985). Nature and nurture in anorexia nervosa: A study of 34 pairs of twins, one pair of triplets, and an adoptive family. *International Journal of Eating Disorders, 4*, 5–27.

Critchlow, B. (1986). The powers of John Barleycorn: Beliefs about the effects of alcohol on social behavior. *American Psychologist, 41*, 751–764.

Crow, T. J. (1985). The two-syndrome concept: Origins and current status. *Schizophrenia Bulletin, 11*, 471–486.

Crow, T. J. (1990). Temporal lobe asymmetries as the key to the etiology of schizophrenia. *Schizophrenia Bulletin, 16*, 433–443.

Crow, T. J., Ball, J., Bloom, S. R., Brown, R., Bruton, C. J., Colter, N., Frith, C. D., Johnstone, E. C., Owens, D. G. C., & Roberts, G. W. (1989). Schizophrenia as an anomaly of development of cerebral asymmetry: A postmortem study and a proposal concerning the genetic basis of the disease. *Archives of General Psychiatry, 46*, 1145–1150.

Crowe, R. R. (1974). An adoption study of antisocial personality. *Archives of General Psychiatry, 31*, 785.

Crowe, R. R., Black, D. W., Wesner, R., Andreasen, N. C., Cookman, A., & Roby, J. (1991). Lack of linkage to chromosome 5q11-q13 markers in six schizophrenic pedigrees. *Archives of General Psychiatry, 48*, 357–361.

Crowell, J. A., & Waters, E. (1990). Separation anxiety. In M. Lewis & S. M. Miller (Eds.), *Handbook of developmental psychopathology*. New York: Plenum.

Dakof, G. A., & Mendelsohn, G. A. (1986). Parkinson's disease: The psychological aspects of a chronic illness. *Psychological Bulletin, 99*, 375–387.

Davanloo, H. (Ed.). (1980). *Short-term dynamic psychotherapy*. New York: Jason Aronson.

David, O. J., Hoffman, S. D., Sverd, J., & Clark, J. (1977). Lead and hyperactivity: Lead levels among hyperactive children. *Journal of Abnormal Child Psychology, 5*, 405–410.

Davidson, W. S., Redner, R., Blakely, C. H., Mitchell, C. M., & Emshoff, J. G. (1987). Diversion of juvenile offenders: An experimental comparison. *Journal of Consulting and Clinical Psychology, 55*, 68–75.

Davis, J. M., Barter, J. T., & Kane, J. M. (1989). Antipsychotic drugs. In H. I. Kaplan & B. J. Sadock (Eds.), *Comprehensive textbook of psychiatry* (Vol. 2, 5th ed.). Baltimore: Williams & Wilkins.

Davis, J. M., & Glassman, A. H. (1989). Antidepressant drugs. In H. I. Kaplan & B. J. Sadock (Eds.), *Comprehensive textbook of psychiatry* (Vol. 2, 5th ed.). Baltimore: Williams & Wilkins.

Davis, K. L., Kahn, R. S., Grant, K., & Davidson, M. (1991). Dopamine in schizophrenia: A review and reconceptualization. *American Journal of Psychiatry, 148*, 1474–1486.

Delaney, E., & Hopkins, T. (1987). *Stanford-Binet intelligence scale—Examiner's handbook: An expanded guide for fourth edition users*. Chicago: Riverside.

de Lint, J. (1978). Alcohol consumption and alcohol problems from an epidemiological perspective. *British Journal of Alcohol and Alcoholism, 13*, 75–85.

DeLisi, L. E., Goldin, L. R., Hamovit, J. R., Maxwell, M. E., Kurtz, D., & Gershon, E. S. (1986). A family study of the association of increased ventricular size with schizophrenia. *Archives of General Psychiatry, 43*, 148–153.

Department of Economic and International Affairs. (1985). *Demographic yearbook* (37th ed.). New York: United Nations.

Derogatis, L. R. (1978). *Derogatis sexual functioning inventory*. Baltimore: Clinical Psychometrics Research.

Descartes, R. (1968). *Discourse on method and other writings*. Baltimore: Penguin.

Deutsch, C. K., & Kinsbourne, M. (1990). Genetics and biochemistry in attention deficit disorder. In M. Lewis & S. M. Miller (Eds.), *Handbook of developmental psychopathology*. New York: Plenum.

Deutsch, C. K., & Swanson, J. M. (1985). An adoptive parents and siblings study of attention deficit disorder. *Behavior Genetics, 15,* 590–591.

Devlin, M. J., Walsh, T., Kral, J. G., Heymsfield, S. B., Pi-Sunyer, F. X., & Dantzic, S. (1990). Metabolic abnormalities in bulimia nervosa. *Archives of General Psychiatry, 47,* 144–148.

DeVos, G. A. (1974). Cross-cultural studies of mental disorder: An anthropological perspective. In S. Arieti (Ed.), *American handbook of psychiatry* (Vol. 2). New York: Basic Books.

Doane, J. (1978). Family interaction and communication deviance in disturbed and normal families: A review of research. *Family Process, 17,* 357–376.

Dodes, L. M., & Khantzian, E. J. (1991). Individual psychodynamic psychotherapy. In R. J. Frances & S. I. Miller (Eds.), *Clinical textbook of addictive disorders.* New York: Guilford Press.

Dohrenwend, B. P., Dohrenwend, B. S., Gould, M. S., Link, B., Neugebauer, R., & Wunsch-Hitzig, R. (1980). *Mental illness in the United States: Epidemiological estimates.* New York: Praeger.

Dohrenwend, B. P. & Egri, G. (1981). Recent stressful life events and episodes of schizophrenia. *Schizophrenia Bulletin, 7,* 12–23.

Donnelly, J. D. (1985). Psychosurgery. In H. I. Kaplan & B. J. Sadock (Eds.), *Comprehensive textbook of psychiatry* (Vol. 2). Baltimore: Williams & Wilkins.

Donovan, J. E., Jessor, R., & Jessor, L. (1983). Problem drinking in adolescence and young adulthood: A follow-up study. *Journal of Studies on Alcohol, 44,* 109–137.

Donovan, J. M. (1986). An etiologic model of alcoholism. *American Journal of Psychiatry, 143,* 1–11.

Dougherty, D. (1988). Children's mental health problems and services: Current federal efforts and policy implications. *American Psychologist, 43,* 808–812.

Dowd, E. T., & Healy, J. M. (Eds.). (1986). *Case studies in hypnotherapy.* New York: Guilford Press.

Drake, R. E., & Sederer, L. I. (1986). The adverse effects of intensive treatment of chronic schizophrenia. *Comprehensive Psychiatry, 27,* 313–326.

Dulit, R. A., Fyer, M. R., Haas, G. L., Sullivan, T., & Frances, A. J. (1990). Substance use in borderline personality disorder. *American Journal of Psychiatry, 147,* 1002–1007.

DuPont, R. L., & Saylor, K. E. (1991). Sedatives/hypnotics and benzodiazepines. In R. J. Frances & S. I. Miller (Eds.), *Clinical textbook of addictive disorders.* New York: Guilford Press.

Dworkin, R. H., & Lenzenweger, M. F. (1984). Symptoms and the genetics of schizophrenia: Implications for diagnosis. *American Journal of Psychiatry, 141,* 1541–1546.

Eagly, A. H., & Steffen, V. J. (1986). Gender and aggressive behavior: A meta-analytic review of the social psychological literature. *Psychological Bulletin, 100,* 309–330.

Eaton, W. W. (1980). A formal theory of selection for schizophrenia. *American Journal of Sociology, 86,* 149–158.

Edleson, J. L. (1990). Judging the success of interventions with men who batter. In D. J. Besharov (Ed.), *Family violence: Research and public policy issues.* Washington, DC: AEI Press.

Edwards, A. J. (1974). *Selected papers of David Wechsler.* New York: Academic Press.

Egeland, J. A., et al. (1987). Bipolar affective disorders linked to DNA markers on chromosome eleven. *Nature, 325,* 783–787.

Eisenberg, L. (1986). Does bad news about suicide beget bad news? *New England Journal of Medicine, 315,* 705–706.

Eisenberg, M. M. (1978). *Ulcers.* New York: Random House.

Elkin, I., Pilkonis, P. A., Docherty, J. P., & Stotsky, S. M. (1988a). Conceptual and methodological issues in comparative studies of psychotherapy and pharmacotherapy, I: Active ingredients and mechanisms of change. *American Journal of Psychiatry, 145,* 909–917.

Elkin, I., Pilkonis, P. A., Docherty, J. P., & Stotsky, S. M. (1988b). Conceptual and methodological issues in comparative studies of psychotherapy and pharmacotherapy, II: Nature and timing of treatment effects. *American Journal of Psychiatry, 145*, 1070–1076.

Elkin, I., Shea, M. T., Watkins, J. T., Imber, S. D., Stotsky, S. M., Collins, J. F., Glass, D. R., Pilkonis, P. A., Leber, W. R., Docherty, J. P., Fiester, S. J., & Parloff, M. B. (1989). National Institute of Mental Health Collaborative Research Program. *Archives of General Psychiatry, 46*, 971–982.

Ellenberger, H. (1974). Psychiatry from ancient to modern times. In S. Arieti (Ed.), *American handbook of psychiatry* (Vol. 1). New York: Basic Books.

Elliot, F. (1988). Neurological problems. In V. B. van Hasselt, R. L. Morrison, A. S. Bellack, & M. Hersen (Eds.), *Handbook of family violence*. New York: Plenum.

Ellis, A., & Dryden, W. (1987). *The practice of rational-emotive therapy*. New York: Springer.

Ellis, A., & Harper, R. A. (1975). *A new guide to rational living*. Englewood Cliffs, NJ: Prentice-Hall.

Ellis, A., & Whiteley, J. M. (1979). *Theoretical and empirical foundations of rational-emotive therapy*. Monterey, CA: Brooks/Cole.

Ellis, L., & Ames, M. A. (1987). Neurohormonal functioning and sexual orientation: A theory of homosexuality-heterosexuality. *Psychological Bulletin, 101*, 233–258.

Emery, R. E. (1988). *Marriage, divorce, and children's adjustment*. Newbury Park, CA: Sage.

Emery, R. E. (1989). Family violence. *American Psychologist, 44*, 321–328.

Emmelkamp, P. M. G. (1982). *Phobic and obsessive-compulsive disorders: Theory, research and practice*. New York: Plenum.

Emrick, C. D. (1982). Evaluation of alcoholism therapy methods. In E. M. Pattison & E. Kaufman (Eds.), *Encyclopedic handbook of alcoholism*. New York: Gardner.

Erikson, E. (1959). *Identity and the life cycle*. New York: Norton.

Erlenmeyer-Kimling, L. (1987). Biological markers for the liability to schizophrenia. In H. Helmchen & F. A. Henn (Eds.), *Biological perspectives of schizophrenia*. New York: Wiley.

Eron, L. D., & Huesman, L. R. (1990). The stability of aggressive behavior—even unto the third generation. In M. Lewis & S. M. Miller (Eds.), *Handbook of developmental psychopathology*. New York: Plenum.

Esman, A. H. (1986). Dependent and passive-aggressive personality disorders. In A. M. Cooper, A. J. Frances, & M. H. Sacks (Eds.), *The personality disorders and neuroses*. New York: Basic Books.

Ethics Committee of the American Psychological Association. (1988). Trends in ethics cases, common pitfalls, and published resources. *American Psychologist, 43*, 564–572.

Ewing, C. P. (1990). *Kids who kill*. New York: Lexington Books.

Eysenck, H. J., & Eysenck, S. G. G. (1969). *Eysenck personality inventory manual*. San Diego, CA: Educational and Industrial Testing Service.

Fairburn, C. G., Cooper, Z., & Cooper, P. J. (1986). The clinical features and maintenance of bulimia. In K. D. Brownell & P. J. Foreyt (Eds.), *Handbook of eating disorders*. New York: Basic Books.

Fairburn, C. G., Jones, R., Peveler, R. C., Carr, S. J., Solomon, R. A., O'Connor, M. E., Burton, J., & Hope, R. A. (1991). Three treatments for bulimia nervosa. *Archives of General Psychiatry, 48*, 463–469.

Fairburn, C. G., Phil, M., & Beglin, S. J. (1990). Studies of the epidemiology of bulimia nervosa. *American Journal of Psychiatry, 147*, 401–408.

Falloon, I. R. H., & Liberman, R. P. (1983). Behavioral family interventions in the management of chronic schizophrenia. In W. R. McFarlane (Ed.), *Family therapy in schizophrenia*. New York: Guilford Press.

Faraone, S. V., Kremen, W. S., & Tsuang, M. T. (1990). Genetic transmission of major affective disorder: Quantitative models and linkage analysis. *Psychological Bulletin*, *108*, 109-127.

Faraone, S. V., & Tsuang, M. T. (1985). Genetics of schizophrenia. *Psychological Bulletin*, *98*, 41-66.

Faravelli, C., Webb, T., Ambonetti, A., Fonnesu, F., & Sessarego, A. (1986). Prevalence of traumatic early life events in 31 agoraphobic patients with panic attacks. *American Journal of Psychiatry*, *142*, 1493-1494.

Faulstich, M. E. (1987). Psychiatric aspects of AIDS. *American Journal of Psychiatry*, *144*, 551-556.

Fava, M., Copeland, P. M., Schweiger, U., & Herzog, D. B. (1989). Neurochemical abnormalities of anorexia nervosa and bulimia nervosa. *American Journal of Psychiatry*, *146*, 963-971.

Federn, P. (1952). *Ego psychology and the psychoses.* New York: Basic Books.

Feingold, B. F. (1975). *Why your child is hyperactive.* New York: Random House.

Feldman, R. A., Caphinger, T. E., & Wodarski, J. S. (1983). *The St. Louis conundrum: The effective treatment of antisocial youths.* Englewood Cliffs, NJ: Prentice-Hall.

Felton, D. L., Felton, S. Y., Bellinger, D. L., Carlson, S. L., Ackerman, K. D., Madden, K. S., Olschowka, J. A., & Livnat, S. (1987). Noradrenergic sympathetic neural interactions with the immune system: Structure and function. *Immunology Review*, 225-260.

Felton, S. Y., & Olschowka, J. (1987). Noradrenergic sympathetic innervation of the spleen, II: Tyrosine hydroxylase (TH)-positive nerve terminals from sympathetic-like contacts on lymphocytes in the splenic white pulp. *Journal of Neurosciences Research*, 37-48.

Fernandez, R. C. (1984). Disturbances in cognition: Implications for treatment. In P. S. Powers & R. C. Fernandez (Eds.), *Current treatment of anorexia nervosa and bulimia.* New York: Krager.

Fine, R. (1979). *A history of psychoanalysis.* New York: Columbia University Press.

Finkelhor, D. (1986). *A sourcebook on child sexual abuse.* Beverly Hills, CA: Sage.

Finkelhor, D. (1988). The trauma of child sexual abuse: Two models. In G. E. Wyatt & G. J. Powell (Eds.), *Lasting effects of child sexual abuse.* Newbury Park, CA: Sage.

Finkelhor, D. (1990a). Early and long-term effects of child sexual abuse: An update. *Professional Psychology: Research and Practice, 21*, 325-330.

Finkelhor, D. (1990b). Prevention approaches to child sexual abuse. In M. Lystad (Ed.), *Violence in the home: Interdisciplinary perspectives.* New York: Brunner/Mazel.

Fish, B. (1987). Infant predictors of the longitudinal course of schizophrenic development. *Schizophrenia Bulletin, 13*, 395-409.

Fischer, P., Simayani, M., & Danielczyk, W. (1990). Depression in dementia of the Alzheimer's type and in multi-infarct dementia. *American Journal of Psychiatry, 147*, 1484-1487.

Fischer, P. J., & Breakey, W. R. (1991). The epidemiology of alcohol, drug, and mental disorders among homeless persons. *American Psychologist, 46*, 1115-1128.

Fishbain, D. A. (1988). Kleptomania behavior response to perphenazine-amitryptiline HCL combination. *Canadian Journal of Psychiatry, 33*, 241-242.

Flam, F. (1991). Better tests for the depressed. *Science, 253*, 621.

Folkman, S., Lazarus, R. S., Gruen, R. J., & DeLongis, A. (1986). Appraisal, coping, health status and psychological symptoms. *Journal of Personality and Social Psychology, 50*, 571-579.

Folstein, S., & Rutter, M. (1977). Infantile autism: A genetic study of 21 twin pairs. *Journal of Child Psychology and Psychiatry, 18*, 297-321.

Fontana, V. J. (1985). Child maltreatment and battered child syndromes. In H. I. Kaplan & B. J. Sadock (Eds.), *Comprehensive textbook of psychiatry, IV* (Vol. 2). Baltimore: Williams & Wilkins.

Foreyt, J. P. (1987). Issues in the assessment and treatment of obesity. *Journal of Consulting and Clinical Psychology, 55,* 677–684.

Forrest, G. G. (1985). Psychodynamically oriented treatment of alcoholism and substance abuse. In T. E. Bratter & G. G. Forrest (Eds.), *Alcoholism and substance abuse: Strategies for clinical intervention.* New York: Free Press.

Foster, S. L., Bell-Dolan, D. J., & Barge, D. A. (1988). Behavioral observation. In A. S. Bellak & M. Herson (Eds.), *Behavioral assessment: A practical handbook* (3rd ed.). New York: Pergamon Press.

Frances, A., Pincus, H. A., Widiger, T. A., Davis, W. W., & First, M. B. (1990). DSM-IV: Work in progress. *American Journal of Psychiatry, 147,* 1439–1448.

Frances, A. J., Widiger, T. A., & Pincus, H. A. (1989). The development of DSM-IV. *Archives of General Psychiatry, 46,* 373–375.

Frank, E., Carpenter, L. L., & Kupfer, D. J. (1988). Sex differences in recurrent depression: Are there any that are significant? *American Journal of Psychiatry, 145,* 41–45.

Frank, E., Kupfer, D. J., Perel, J. M., Cornes, C., Jarrett, D. B., Mallinger, A. G., Thase, M. E., McEarchran, A. B., & Groshoconski, V. J. (1990). Three year outcomes for maintenance therapies in recurrent depression. *Archives of General Psychiatry, 47,* 1093–1099.

Frank, J. D. (1974). *Persuasion and healing.* New York: Schocken.

Frankl, V. E. (1963). *Man's search for meaning: An introduction to logotherapy.* New York: Pocket Books.

Frankl, V. E. (1967). *Psychotherapy and existentialism.* New York: Simon & Schuster.

Frederiksen, N. (1986). Toward a broader conception of human intelligence. *American Psychologist, 41,* 445–452.

Freeman, A., & Leaf, R. C. (1989). Cognitive therapy applied to personality disorders. In A. Freeman, K. M. Simon, L. E. Beutler, & H. Arkowitz (Eds.), *Comprehensive handbook of cognitive therapy.* New York: Plenum.

Freeman, A., Simon, K. M., Bentler, L. E., & Arkowitz, H. (Eds.). (1989). *Comprehensive handbook of cognitive therapy.* New York: Plenum.

Freeman, B. J., Ritvo, E. R., Mason-Brothers, A., Pingree, C., Yokota, A., Jenson, W. R., McMahon, W. M., Peterson, B., Mo, A., & Schroth, P. (1989). Psychometric assessment of first-degree relatives of 62 autistic probands in Utah. *American Journal of Psychiatry, 146,* 361–364.

Freiberg, P. (1991, April). Panel hears of families victimized by alcoholism. *APA Monitor,* p. 30.

Freud, S. (1916). Some character-types met with in psychoanalytic work. In *Standard edition* (Vol. 14). London: Hogarth Press.

Freud, S. (1917). Mourning and melancholia. In J. Strachey & A. Freud (Eds.), *The standard edition of the complete works of Sigmund Freud* (Vol. 14). London: Hogarth Press.

Freud, S. (1933). *New introductory lectures on psychoanalysis.* New York: Norton.

Freud, S. (1936). *The problem of anxiety.* New York: Norton.

Freud, S. (1949). *An outline of psychoanalysis.* New York: Norton.

Freud, S. (1953). *Three essays on sexuality.* In *Standard edition* (Vol. 7). London: Hogarth Press. (First German edition, 1905)

Freud, S. (1959). Analysis of a phobia in a five year old boy. In *Collected papers* (Vol. 3). New York: Basic Books.

Freud, S. (1961). *The ego and the id.* In *Standard edition* (Vol. 19). London: Hogarth Press. (First German edition, 1923)

Freud, S. (1963a). *Theory and technique.* New York: Collier.

Freud, S. (1963b). *Three case histories.* New York: Macmillan.

Friedman, H. S., & Booth-Kewley, S. (1987). The disease-prone personality: A metanalytic view of the construct. *American Psychologist, 42,* 539–555.

Friedman, H. S., & Booth-Kewley, S. (1988). Validity of the type-A construct: A reprise. *Psychological Bulletin, 104,* 381–384.

Friedman, J. M., & Chernin, L. (1987). Sexual dysfunction. In L Michelson & L. M. Ascher (Eds.), *Anxiety and stress disorders.* New York: Guilford Press.

Friedman, M., & Rosenman, R. H. (1974). *Type-A behavior and your heart.* New York: Knopf.

Friedman, M. J. (1988). Toward rational pharmacotherapy for PTSD: An interim report. *American Journal of Psychiatry, 145,* 281–285.

Friedrich-Cofer, L., & Huston, A. C. (1986). Television violence and aggression: The debate continues. *Psychological Bulletin, 100,* 364–371.

Friman, P. C., Finney, J. W., & Christopherson, E. R. (1984). Behavioral treatment of trichotillomania: An evaluative review. *Behavior Therapist, 15,* 249–265.

Friman, P. C., & O'Connor, W. A. (1984). The integration of hypnotic and habit reversal techniques in the treatment of trichotillomania. *Behavior Therapist, 7,* 166–167.

Fromm-Reichmann, F. (1948). Notes on the development of treatment of schizophrenics by psychoanalytic psychotherapy. *Psychiatry, 11,* 263–273.

Frost, A. K., & Pakiz, B. (1990). The effects of marital disruption on adolescents: Time as a dynamic. *American Journal of Orthopsychiatry, 60,* 544–555.

Fuller, R. K. (1989). Current status of alcoholism treatment outcome research. In L. S. Harris (Ed.), *Problems of drug dependence 1989.* Rockville, MD: National Institute on Drug Abuse.

Fulton, A. I., & Yates, W. R. (1990). Adult children of alcoholics: A valid diagnostic group? *Journal of Nervous and Mental Disease, 178,* 505–509.

Fyer, A. J., Mannuzzo, S., Gallops, M. S., Martin, L. Y., Aaronson, C., Gorman, J. M., Liebowitz, M. R., & Klein, D. F. (1990). Familial transmission of simple phobias and fears. *Archives of General Psychiatry, 47,* 252–256.

Fyer, M. R., Frances, A. J., Sullivan, T., Hart, S. W., & Clarkin, J. (1988). Comorbidity of borderline personality disorder. *Archives of General Psychiatry, 45,* 348–352.

Gallagher, J. J. (1989). A new policy initiative: Infants and toddlers with handicapping conditions. *American Psychologist, 44,* 387–391.

Garbarino, J., Guttmann, E., & Seeley, J. W. (1986). *The psychologically battered child.* San Francisco: Jossey-Bass.

Garber, H. J., Weilberg, J. B., Buonanno, F. S., Manschreck, T. C., & New, P. F. J. (1988). Use of magnetic resonance imaging in psychiatry. *American Journal of Psychiatry, 145,* 164–171.

Gartrell, N., Herman, J., Olarte, S., Feldstein, M., & Localio, R. (1986). Psychiatrist–patient sexual contact: Results of a national survey, I: Prevalence. *American Journal of Psychiatry, 143,* 1126–1131.

Garver, D. L., Reich, T., Isenberg, K. E., & Cloninger, C. R. (1989). Schizophrenia and the question of genetic heterogeneity. *Schizophrenia Bulletin, 15,* 421–430.

Gawin, F. H. (1991). Cocaine addiction: Psychology and neurophysiology. *Science, 251,* 1580–1586.

Gawin, F. H., & Kleber, H. D. (1986). Abstinence symptomatology and psychiatric diagnosis in cocaine abusers: Clinical observations. *Archives of General Psychiatry, 43,* 107–113.

Geary, N. (1987). Cocaine: Animal research studies. In H. I. Spitz & J. S. Rosecan (Eds.), *Cocaine abuse: New directions in treatment and research.* New York: Brunner/Mazel.

Gelberg, L., Linn, L. S., & Leake, B. D. (1988). Mental health, alcohol and drug use, and criminal history among homeless adults. *American Journal of Psychiatry, 145,* 191–196.

Gelenberg, A. J. (1983). Anxiety. In E. L. Bassuk, S. C. Schoonover, & A. J. Gelenberg (Eds.), *The practitioner's guide to psychoactive drugs* (2nd ed., pp. 167–201). New York: Plenum.

Gelman, D., Springen, K., Elam, R., Joseph, N., Robins, K., & Hager, M. (1990, July 23). The mind of the rapist. *Newsweek,* pp. 46–53.

Gendel, E. S., & Bonner, E. J. (1988a). Sexual dysfunction. In H. H. Goldman (Ed.), *Review of general psychiatry* (2nd ed.). Norwalk, CT: Appleton and Lange.

Gendel, E. S., & Bonner, E. J. (1988b). Gender identity disorders and paraphilias. In H. H. Goldman (Ed.), *Review of general psychiatry* (2nd ed.). Norwalk, CT: Appleton and Lange.

Gershon, E. S., Nurnberger, J. I., Berrettini, W. H., & Golden, L. R. (1985). Affective disorders: Genetics. In H. I. Kaplan & B. J. Sadock (Eds.), *Comprehensive textbook of psychiatry IV*. Baltimore: Williams & Wilkins.

Giles, D. E., Jarret, R. B., Biggs, M. M., Guzick, D. S., & Rush, A. J. (1989). Clinical predictors of recurrence in depression. *American Journal of Psychiatry, 146*, 764–767.

Ginsberg, G. L. (1985b). Psychiatric history and mental status examination. In H. I. Kaplan & B. J. Sadock (Eds.), *Comprehensive textbook of psychiatry* (Vol. 1, 4th ed.). Baltimore: Williams & Wilkins.

Ginsburg, G. L. (1985a). Adjustment and impulse control disorders. In H. I. Kaplan & B. J. Sadock (Eds.), *Comprehensive textbook of psychiatry* (4th ed.). Baltimore: Williams & Wilkins.

Giorgi, A. (1970). *Psychology as a human science.* New York: Harper & Row.

Gitlin, M. J., & Pasnau, R. O. (1989). Psychiatric syndromes linked to reproductive function in women: A review of current knowledge. *American Journal of Psychiatry, 146*, 1413–1422.

Gittelman, R., & Kanner, A. (1986). Psychopharmacology. In H. C. Quay & J. S. Werry (Eds.), *Psychopathological disorders of childhood* (3rd ed.). New York: Wiley.

Gittelman, R., Mannuzza, S., Shenker, R., & Bonagura, N. (1985). Hyperactive boys almost grown up; I. Psychiatric status. *Archives of General Psychiatry 42*, 937–947.

Gjerde, P. F., Block, J., & Block, J. H. (1988). Depressive symptoms and personality during late adolescence: Gender differences in the externalization-internalization of symptom expression. *Journal of Abnormal Psychology, 97*, 475–486.

Gladis, M. M., & Walsh, T. (1987). Premenstrual exacerbation of binge eating in bulimia. *American Journal of Psychiatry, 144*, 1592–1595.

Glaser, D. (1990). Violence in the society. In M. Lystad (Ed.), *Violence in the home: Interdisciplinary perspectives.* New York: Brunner/Mazel.

Glaser, R., Kennedy, S., LaFuse, W. P., Bonneau, R. H., Speicher, C., Hillhouse, J., & Glaser, J. (1990). Psychological stress-induced modulation of interleukin 2 receptor gene expression and interleukin 2 production in peripheral blood leukocytes. *Archives of General Psychiatry, 47*, 707–712.

Glass, L. L., Katz, H. M., Schnitzer, R. D., Knapp, P. H., Frank, A. F., & Gunderson, J. G. (1989). Psychotherapy of schizophrenia: An empirical investigation of the relationship of process to outcome. *American Journal of Psychiatry, 146*, 603–608.

Glassman, A. H., Steiner, F., Walsh, T., Raizoram, P. S., Fleiss, J. L., Cooper, T. B., & Covey, L. S. (1988). Heavy smokers, smoking cessation, and clonidine. *Journal of the American Medical Association, 259*, 2853–2866.

Gold, L. H., Geyer, M. A., & Koob, G. F. (1989). Neurochemical mechanisms involved in behavioral effects of amphetamines and related designer drugs. In K. Asghar & E. DeSouza (Eds.), *Pharmacology and toxicology of amphetamines and related designer drugs* (NIDA Research Monograph 94). Rockville, MD: National Institute on Drug Abuse.

Goldblatt, M., & Munitz, H. (1976). Behavioral treatment of hysterical leg paralysis. *Journal of Behavior Therapy and Experimental Psychiatry, 7*, 259–263.

Golden, C. J., Purisch, A. D., & Hammeke, T. A. (1985). *Luria-Nebraska neuropsychological test battery: Forms I and II (manual).* Los Angeles: Western Psychological Services.

Golden, G. S. (1987). Neurological functioning. In D. J. Cohen & A. M. Donnellan (Eds.), *Handbook of autism and pervasive developmental disorders.* New York: Wiley.

Goldfried, M. R., & Davison, G. C. (1976). *Clinical behavior therapy.* New York: Holt, Rinehart and Winston.

Goldgaber, D., Lerman, M. I., McBride, O. W., Saffiotti, U., & Gadjusek, D. C. (1987). Characterization of chromosomal localization of cDNA encoding brain amyloid of Alzheimer's disease. *Science, 235,* 877–880.

Golding, J. M., Smith, R., & Kashner, M. (1991). Does somatization disorder occur in men? *Archives of General Psychiatry, 48,* 231–235.

Goldman, H. H. (1988a). Introduction to psychiatric treatment. In H. H. Goldman (Ed.), *General review of psychiatry* (2nd ed.). Norwalk, CT: Appleton and Lange.

Goldman, M. J. (1991). Kleptomania: Making sense of the nonsensical. *American Journal of Psychiatry, 148,* 986–996.

Goldman, M. S., Brown, S. A., & Christiansen, B. A. (1987). Expectancy theory: Thinking about drinking. In H. T. Blane & K. E. Leonard (Eds.), *Psychological theories of drinking and alcoholism.* New York: Guilford Press.

Goldstein, J. M. (1988). Gender differences in the course of schizophrenia. *American Journal of Psychiatry, 145,* 684–689.

Goldstein, M. J., & Strachan, A. M. (1987). The family and schizophrenia. In T. Jacob (Ed.), *Family interaction and psychopathology.* New York: Plenum.

Goldston, D. B., Turnquist, D. C., & Knutson, J. F. (1989). Presenting problems of sexually abused girls receiving psychiatric services. *Journal of Abnormal Psychology, 98,* 314–317.

Goodman, M., & Kahn, T. (1991, May 6). Cathy Rigby, flying high. *People,* pp. 107–109.

Goodwin, D. W. (1985a). Alcoholism and alcoholic psychoses. In H. I. Kaplan & B. S. Sadock (Eds.), *Comprehensive textbook of psychiatry* (Vol. 1, 4th ed.). Baltimore: Williams & Wilkins.

Goodwin, D. W. (1985b). Alcoholism and genetics. *Archives of General Psychiatry, 42,* 171–174.

Goodwin, D. W., & Guze, S. B. (1984). *Psychiatric diagnosis* (3rd ed.). New York: Oxford University Press.

Goodwin, D. W., Schulsinger, F., Hermansen, L., Guze, S. B., & Winokur, G. (1973). Alcohol problems in adoptees raised apart from alcoholic biological parents. *Archives of General Psychiatry, 28,* 238–243.

Goodwin, D. W., & Warnock, J. K. (1991). Alcoholism: A family disease. In R. J. Frances & S. I. Miller (Eds.), *Clinical textbook of addictive disorders.* New York Guilford Press.

Gorman, J. M., Batista, D., Goetz, R. R., Dillon, D. J., Liebowitz, M. R., Fyer, A. J., Kahn, J. P., Sandberg, D., & Klein, D. F. (1989). A comparison of sodium bicarbonate and sodium lactate infusion in the induction of panic attacks. *Archives of General Psychiatry, 46,* 145–150.

Gorman, J. M., & Davis, J. M. (1989). Antianxiety drugs. In H. I. Kaplan & B. J. Sadock (Eds.), *Comprehensive textbook of psychiatry* (Vol. 2, 5th ed.). Baltimore: Williams & Wilkins.

Gorman, J. M., Liebowitz, M. R., Fyer, A., & Stein, J. (1989). A neuroanatomical hypothesis for panic disorder. *American Journal of Psychiatry, 146,* 148–161.

Gotlib, I. H., & Whiffen, V. E. (1989). Depression and marital functioning: An examination of specificity and gender differences. *Journal of Abnormal Psychology, 98,* 23–30.

Gottesman, I. I., McGuffin, P., & Farmer, A. E. (1987). Clinical genetics as clues to the "real" genetics of schizophrenia (a decade of modest gains while playing for time). *Schizophrenia Bulletin, 13,* 23–47.

Gottlieb, B. H. (1985). Theory into practice: Issues that surface in planning interventions which mobilize support. In I. G. Sarason & B. R. Sarason (Eds.), *Social support: Theory research and applications.* The Hague, The Netherlands: Martinus Nijhoff.

Gould, M. S., & Shaffer, D. (1986). The impact of television suicide in television movies. *New England Journal of Medicine, 315,* 690–695.

Gove, W. R. (1982). The current status of the labeling theory of mental illness. In W. R. Gove (Ed.), *Deviance and mental illness.* Beverly Hills, CA: Sage.

Grabowski, J. (Ed.). (1985). *Pharmacological adjuncts in smoking cessation.* Rockville, MD: National Institute on Drug Abuse.

Graham, J. R., & Lilly, R. S. (1984). *Psychological testing.* Englewood Cliffs, NJ: Prentice-Hall.

Grant, I. (1987). Alcohol and the brain: Neuropsychological correlates. *Journal of Consulting and Clinical Psychology, 55,* 310–324.

Gray, J. A. (1985). Issues in the neuropsychology of anxiety. In A. H. Tuma & J. D. Maser (Eds.), *Anxiety and the anxiety disorders.* Hillsdale, NJ: Erlbaum.

Greden, J. F. (1974). Anxiety or caffeinism: A diagnostic dilemma. *American Journal of Psychiatry, 131,* 1089–1092.

Green, J. A., & Shellenberger, R. D. (1985). Biofeedback research and the ghost in the box: A reply to Roberts. *American Psychologist, 41,* 1003–1005.

Green, R. (1987). *The sissy boy syndrome.* New Haven, CT: Yale University Press.

Green, R., & Money, J. (1969). *Transsexualism and sex reassignment.* Baltimore: Johns Hopkins University Press.

Greenberg, J. (1990, September 3). All about crime. *New York,* pp. 20–32.

Greene, R. L. (1980). *The MMPI: An interpretive manual.* New York: Grune & Stratton.

Grenell, M. M., Glass, C. R., & Katz, K. S. (1987). Hyperactive children and peer interaction: Knowledge and performance of social skills. *Journal of Abnormal Psychology, 15,* 1–13.

Griest, J. H., & Jefferson, J. W. (1988). Anxiety disorders. In H. H. Goldman, (Ed.), *Review of general psychiatry* (2nd ed.). Norwalk, CT: Appleton and Lange.

Grinspoon, L., & Bakalav, J. B. (1985). Drug dependence: Nonnarcotic agents. In H. Kaplan & B. J. Sadock (Eds.), *Comprehensive textbooks of psychiatry, IV* (Vol. 1). Baltimore: Williams & Wilkins.

Groves, P. M., & Rebec, G. V. (1988). *Introduction to biological psychology* (3rd ed.). Dubuque, IA: Wm. C. Brown.

Gruen, R., & Biron, M. (1984). Stressful life events and schizophrenia. *Neuropsychobiology, 12,* 206–208.

Gunderson, J. G., & Elliot, G. R. (1985). The interface between borderline personality disorder and affective disorder. *American Journal of Psychiatry, 142,* 277–288.

Gunderson, J. G., Frank, A. F., Katz, H. M., Vanicelli, M. L., Frosch, J. P., & Knapp, P. H. (1984). Effects of psychotherapy in schizophrenia, II: Comparative outcomes of two forms of treatment. *Schizophrenia Bulletin, 10,* 564–598.

Guralnick, M. J. (1986). The peer relations of young handicapped and non-handicapped children. In P. S. Strain, M. J. Guralnick, & H. M. Walker (Eds.), *Children's social behavior: Development, assessment and modification.* New York: Academic Press.

Gurman, A. S., & Kniskern, D. P. (1981). Family therapy outcome research: Knowns and unknowns. In A. S. Gurman & D. P. Kniskern (Eds.), *Handbook of family therapy.* New York: Brunner/Mazel.

Haaga, D. A. (1987). Treatment of the Type-A behavior pattern. *Clinical Psychology Review, 7,* 557–574.

Hadley, J., & Studacher, C. (1989). *Hypnosis for change.* Oakland, CA: New Harbinger.

Hall, C. S., & Lindzey, G. (1985). *Theories of personality.* New York: Wiley.

Hall, N. R. S. (1988). The virology of AIDS. *American Psychologist, 43,* 907–913.

Hall, T. (1990, January 3). And now the last word on dieting: Don't bother. *The New York Times,* p. C1.

Halmi, K. A. (1985). Eating disorders. In H. I. Kaplan & B. J. Sadock (Eds.), *Comprehensive textbook of psychiatry* (4th ed.). Baltimore: Williams & Wilkins.

Halmi, K. A., Eckert, E., Marchi, P., Sampugnaro, V., Apple, R., & Cohen, J. (1991). Comorbidity of psychiatric diagnosis in anorexia nervosa. *Archives of General Psychiatry, 48,* 712–718.

Hamilton, J. (1988). Child abuse and family violence. In N. Hutchings (Ed.), *The violent family: Victimization of women, children and elders.* New York: Human Sciences Press.

Hamilton, L. W., & Timmons, C. R. (1990). *Principles of behavioral pharmacology.* Englewood Cliffs, NJ: Prentice-Hall.

Harding, C. M., Brooks, G. W., Ashikaga, T., Strauss, J. S., & Breier, A. (1987). The Vermont longitudinal study of persons with severe mental illness, II: Long-term outcome of subjects who retrospectively met DSM-III criteria for schizophrenia. *American Journal of Psychiatry, 144,* 727–735.

Hare, R. (1970). *Psychopathy: Theory and research.* New York: Wiley.

Hare, R. D. (1978). Electrodermal and cardiovascular correlates of sociopathy. In R. D. Hare & D. Schilling (Eds.), *Psychopathic behavior: Approaches to research.* New York: Wiley.

Hare, R. D. (1984). Performance of psychopaths on cognitive tasks related to frontal lobe function. *Journal of Abnormal Psychology, 93,* 133–140.

Harrow, M., Goldberg, J. F., Grossman, L. S., & Meltzer, H. Y. (1990). Outcome in manic disorders. *Archives of General Psychiatry, 47,* 665–671.

Hart, S. N., Germain, R. B., & Brassard, M. R. (1987). The challenge: To better understand and combat psychological maltreatment of children and youth. In M. R. Brassard, R. Germain, & S. N. Hart (Eds.), *Psychological maltreatment of children and youth.* New York: Pergamon Press.

Hartmann, H. (1958). *Ego psychology and the problem of adaptation.* New York: International Universities Press.

Hartsough, C. S., & Lambert, N. M. (1985). Medical factors in hyperactive and normal children: Prenatal, developmental, and health history findings. *American Journal of Orthopsychiatry, 55,* 190–201.

Harwood, A. (1977). *Rx: Spiritist as needed—A study of a Puerto Rican community mental health resource.* New York: Wiley.

Hasin, D. S., Grant, B., & Endicott, J. (1990). The natural history of alcohol abuse: Implications for definitions of alcohol use disorders. *American Journal of Psychiatry, 147,* 1537–1541.

Hathaway, S. R., & McKinley, J. C. (1940). A multiphasic personality schedule (Minnesota): I. Construction of the schedule. *Journal of Psychology, 10,* 249–254.

Hayward, C., Killen, J. D., & Taylor, C. B. (1989). Panic attacks in young adolescents. *Journal of Abnormal Psychology, 146,* 1061–1062.

Heath, A. W., & Stanton, M. D. (1991). Family therapy. In R. J. Frances & S. I. Miller (Eds.), *Clinical textbook of addictive disorders.* New York: Guilford Press.

Heatherton, T. F. (1991). Binge eating as an escape from self-awareness. *Psychological Bulletin, 110,* 86–108.

Heatherton, T. F., Polivy, J., & Herman, C. P. (1991). Restraint, weight loss, and variability of body weight. *Journal of Abnormal Psychology, 100,* 78–83.

Hetherington, E. M., Hagen, M. S., & Anderson, E. R. (1989). Marital transitions: A child's perspective. *American Psychologist, 44,* 303–312.

Hetherington, E. M., & Martin, B. (1986). Family factors and psychopathology in children. In H. C. Quay & J. S. Werry (Eds.), *Psychopathological disorders of childhood* (3rd ed.). New York: Wiley.

Heiman, J., LoPiccolo, L., and LoPiccolo, J. (1976). *Becoming orgasmic: A sexual growth program for women.* Englewood Cliffs, NJ: Prentice-Hall.

Heinrichs, D. W., & Buchanan, R. W. (1988). Significance and meaning of neurological signs in schizophrenia. *American Journal of Psychiatry, 145,* 11–18.

Heller, K., Price, R. H., Reinharz, S., Riger, S., Wandersman, A., & D'Aunno, T. A. (1984). *Psychology and community change: Challenges of the future* (2nd ed.). Pacific Grove, CA: Brooks/Cole.

Helmersen, P. (1983). *Family interaction and communication in psychopathology: An evaluation of recent perspectives.* London: Academic Press.

Helzer, J. E. (1987). Epidemiology of alcoholism. *Journal of Consulting and Clinical Psychology, 55,* 284–292.

Heritch, A. J. (1990). Evidence for reduced and dysregulated turnover of dopamine in schizophrenia. *Schizophrenia Bulletin, 16,* 605–615.

Herman, C. P., & Polivy, J. (1975). Anxiety, restraint, and eating behavior. *Journal of Abnormal Psychology, 84,* 666–672.

Herman, J. L., Perry, J. C., & van der Kolk, B. A. (1989). Childhood traumas in borderline personality disorder. *American Journal of Psychiatry, 146,* 490–495.

Herron, W. G. (1987). Evaluating the process-reactive dimension. *Schizophrenia Bulletin, 13,* 357–359.

Hertzig, M. E., & Shapiro, T. (1990). Autism and pervasive developmental disorders. In M. Lewis & S. M. Miller (Eds.), *Handbook of developmental psychopathology.* New York: Plenum.

Hilgard, E. R., & Bower, G. H. (1975). *Theories of learning* (4th ed.). Englewood Cliffs, NJ: Prentice-Hall.

Hilgard, E. R., Hilgard, J. R., & Kaufmann, W. (1983). *Hypnosis in the relief of pain* (2nd ed.). Los Altos, CA: Kaufmann.

Hill, S. Y., Steinhauer, S. R., & Zubin, J. (1987). Biological markers for alcoholism: A vulnerability model conceptualization. In P. C. Rivers (Ed.), *Alcohol and addictive behavior, Nebraska Symposium on Motivation 1986.* Lincoln: University of Nebraska Press.

Hing, L. D., & Williamson, D. A. (1987). Bulimia and depression: A review of the affective variant hypothesis. *Psychological Bulletin, 102,* 150–158.

Hippocrates (Vol. V). (P. Potter, Trans.). (1988). Cambridge, MA: Harvard University Press.

Hirschfeld, R. M. A., & Shea, M. T. (1985). Affective disorders. In H. I. Kaplan & B. J. Sadock (Eds.), *Comprehensive textbook of psychiatry, IV.* Baltimore: Williams & Wilkins.

Hodges, W. F. (1986). *Interventions for children of divorce: Custody, access, and psychotherapy.* New York: Wiley.

Hoffman, L. (1981). *Foundations of family therapy: A conceptual framework for systems change.* New York: Basic Books.

Hogarty, G. E., Anderson, C. M., Reiss, D. J., Kornblith, S. J., Greenwald, D. P., Javna, C. D., Madonia, M. J., & the EPICS Schizophrenia Research Group. (1986). Family psychoeducation, social skills training and maintenance chemotherapy in the aftercare treatment of schizophrenia: I. One year effects of a controlled study on relapse and expressed emotion. *Archives of General Psychiatry, 43,* 633–642.

Hogarty, G. E., Anderson, C. M., Reiss, D. J., Kornblith, S. J., Greenwald, D. P., Ulrich, R. F., Carter, M., & the Environmental-Personal Indicators in the Course of Schizophrenia (EPICS) Research Group. (1991). Family psychoeducation, social skills training, and maintenance chemotherapy in the aftercare treatment of schizophrenia. *Archives of General Psychiatry, 48,* 340–347.

Holden, C. (1986). Days may be numbered for polygraphs in the private sector. *Science, 232,* 279.

Holden, C. (1987). Is alcoholism treatment effective? *Science, 236,* 20–22.

Holden, C. (1988, May). Doctor of sexology. *Psychology Today,* pp. 45–48.

Holland, A. J., Hall, A., Murray, R., Russell, G. F. M., & Crisp, H. H. (1984). Anorexia nervosa: A study of 34 twin pairs and one set of triplets. *British Journal of Psychiatry, 145,* 414–419.

Hollander, E., Liebowitz, M. R., Gorman, J. M., Cohen, B., & Klein, D. F. (1989). Cortisol and sodium lactate induced panic. *Archives of General Psychiatry, 46,* 135–141.

Hollister, L. E. (1988a). Antipsychotics and mood stabilizers. In H. H. Goldman (Ed.), *Review of general psychiatry.* Norwalk, CT: Appleton and Lange.

Hollister, L. E. (1988b). Antidepressants. In H. H. Goldman (Ed.), *Review of general psychiatry.* Norwalk, CT: Appleton and Lange.

Holmes, T. H., & Rahe, R. H. (1967). Social readjustment rating scale. *Journal of Psychosomatic Research, 11*, 213-218.

Holzman, P. S. (1987). Recent studies of psychophysiology in schizophrenia. *Schizophrenia Bulletin, 13*, 49-76.

Hoon, E. E., Hoon, P. W., & Wincze, J. (1976). An inventory for the measurement of female sexual arousability: The SAI. *Archives of Sexual Behavior, 5*, 291-300.

Horne, R. L., VanVactor, J., & Emerson, S. (1991). Disturbed body image in patients with eating disorders. *American Journal of Psychiatry, 148*, 211-215.

Horney, K. (1937). *The neurotic personality of our time.* New York: Norton.

Hsu, L. K. G. (1986). The treatment of anorexia nervosa. *American Journal of Psychiatry, 143*, 573-581.

Hsu, L. K. G. (1987). Are eating disorders becoming more common in blacks? *International Journal of Eating Disorders, 6*, 113-124.

Hughs, P. L., Wells, L. A., & Cunningham, L. J. (1985). Treating bulimia with desipramine: A placebo controlled double-blind study. *Archives of General Psychiatry, 43*, 182-186.

Hull, J. G. (1987). Self-awareness model. In H. T. Blane & K. E. Leonard (Eds.), *Psychological theories of drinking and alcoholism.* New York: Guilford Press.

Hunter, R., & Macalpine, I. (1963). *Three hundred years of psychiatry 1535-1860.* London: Oxford University Press.

Hurst, M. W., Jenkins, C. D., & Rose, R. M. (1976). The relation of psychological stress to onset of medical illness. *Annual Review of Medicine, 27*, 1316-1319.

Hutchings, N. (Ed.). (1988). *The violent family: Victimization of women, children and elders.* New York: Human Sciences Press.

Hymowitz, N. (1991). Tobacco. In R. J. Frances & S. I. Miller (Eds.), *Clinical textbook of addictive disorders.* New York: Guilford Press.

Hynd, G. W., & Semrud-Clikeman, M. (1989a). Dyslexia and brain morphology. *Psychological Bulletin, 106*, 447-482.

Hynd, G. W., & Semrud-Clikeman, M. (1989b). Dyslexia and neurodevelopmental pathology: Relationships to cognition, intelligence, and reading skill acquisition. *Journal of Learning Disabilities, 22*, 204-216.

Inter-Society Commission for Heart Disease Resources. (1970). Atherosclerosis study group and epidemiology study groups: Primary prevention of the atherosclerotic diseases. *Circulation, 42*, A55-A95.

Isaacs, M. B., & Montalvo, B. (1989, November-December). The difficult divorce. *The Family Therapy Networker*, p. 49.

Iverson, T. J., & Segal, M. (1990). *Child abuse and neglect: An information and reference guide.* New York: Garland.

Jacob, R. B., Moller, M. B., Turner, S. M., & Wall, C., III. (1985). Otoneurological examination in panic disorder and agoraphobia with panic attacks. *American Journal of Psychiatry, 142*, 715-720.

Jacob, T. (1987). Alcoholism: A family interaction perspective. In P. C. Rivers (Ed.), *Alcohol and addictive behavior, Nebraska Symposium on Motivation 1986.* Lincoln: University of Nebraska Press.

Jacob, T., Krahn, G. L., & Leonard, K. (1991). Parent-child interactions in families with alcoholic fathers. *Journal of Consulting and Clinical Psychology, 59*, 176-181.

Jacob, T., & Leonard, K. (1991). Experimental drinking procedures in the study of alcoholics and their families: A consideration of ethical issues. *Journal of Consulting and Clinical Psychology, 59*, 249-255.

Jacobsen, E. (1938). *Progressive relaxation.* Chicago: University of Chicago Press.

Jaffe, J. H. (1985). Opioid dependence. In H. Kaplan & B. J. Sadock (Eds.), *Comprehensive textbook of psychiatry, IV* (Vol. 1). Baltimore: Williams & Wilkins.

Jaffe, J. H. & Ciraulo, D. A. (1985). Drugs used in the treatment of alcoholism. In J. H. Mendelson & N. K. Mello (Eds.), *The diagnosis and treatment of alcoholism* (2nd ed.). New York: McGraw-Hill.

Janicak, P. G., Davis, J. M., Gibbons, R. D., Ericksen, S., Chang, S., & Gallagher, P. (1985). Efficacy of ECT: A meta-analysis. *American Journal of Psychiatry, 142,* 297–302.

Jansky, J. J. (1985). Developmental reading disorder (alexia and dyslexia). In H. I. Kaplan & B. J. Sadock (Eds.), *Comprehensive textbook of psychiatry, IV* (Vol. 2). Baltimore: Williams & Wilkins.

Jemmott J. B., III, & Locke, S. E. (1984). Psychosocial factors, immunologic mediation and human susceptibility to infectious diseases: How much do we know? *Psychological Bulletin, 95,* 78–108.

Jellinek, E. M. (1960). *The disease concept of alcoholism.* Highland Park, NJ: Hillhouse Press.

Jones, E. (1955). *The standard edition of the complete psychological works of Sigmund Freud* (pp. 159–168). London: Hogarth Press.

Jones, E. (1981). *The life and work of Sigmund Freud* (Vol. 1). New York: Basic Books.

Jung, C. G. (1982). *Contributions to analytical psychology.* New York: Harcourt Brace Jovanovich.

Justice, A. (1985). Review of effects of stress on cancer in laboratory animals: Importance of time of stress application and type of tumor. *Psychological Bulletin, 98,* 108–138.

Kagan, J., Reznick, J. S., & Snidman, N. (1990). The temperamental qualities of inhibition and lack of inhibition. In M. Lewis & S. M. Miller (Eds.), *Handbook of developmental psychopathology.* New York: Plenum.

Kanas, N. (1986). Group therapy with schizophrenics: A review of controlled studies. *International Journal of Group Therapy, 36,* 339–351.

Kandel, D. B., & Yamaguchi, K. (1985). Developmental patterns of the use of legal, illegal, and medically prescribed psychotropic drugs from adolescence to young adulthood. In C. L. Jones & R. J. Battjes (Eds.), *Etiology of drug abuse: Implications for prevention* (NIDA Research Monograph 56). Rockville, MD: National Institute on Drug Abuse.

Kane, J., Honigfeld, G., Singer, J., Meltzer, H., & the Clozaril Collaborative Study Group. (1988). Clozapine for the treatment-resistant schizophrenic. *Archives of General Psychiatry, 45,* 789–796.

Kanner, L. (1943). Autistic disturbances of affective contact. *Nervous Child, 2,* 217–250.

Kaplan, A. S., & Woodside, D. B. (1987). Biological aspects of anorexia nervosa and bulimia nervosa. *Journal of Consulting and Clinical Psychology, 55,* 645–653.

Kaplan, H. (1974). *The new sex therapy.* New York: Plenum.

Kaplan, H. I. (1985). Psychological factors affecting physical conditions (psychosomatic disorders). In H. I. Kaplan & B. J. Sadock (Eds.), *Comprehensive textbook of psychiatry* (Vol. 2, 4th ed.). Baltimore: Williams & Wilkins.

Karan, L. D., Haller, D. L., & Schnoll, S. (1991). Cocaine. In R. J. Frances & S. I. Miller (Eds.), *Clinical textbook of addictive disorders.* New York: Guilford Press.

Karasu, T. B. (1990a). Toward a clinical model of psychotherapy for depression, I: Systematic comparison of three psychotherapies. *American Journal of Psychiatry, 147,* 133–147.

Karasu, T. B. (1990b). Toward a clinical model of psychotherapy for depression, II: An integrative and selective approach. *American Journal of Psychiatry, 147,* 269–278.

Karlsson, J. L. (1982). Family transmission of schizophrenia: A review and synthesis. *British Journal of Psychiatry, 140,* 600–606.

Karno, M., Golding, J. M., Sorenson, S. B., & Burman, M. A. (1988). The epidemiology of obsessive-compulsive disorder in five U.S. communities. *Archives of General Psychiatry, 45,* 1094–1099.

Karoly, P., & Kanfer, F. H. (Eds.). (1982). *Self-management and behavior change: From theory to practice.* New York: Pergamon Press.

Kaslow, F. W. (1981). Divorce and divorce therapy. In A. S. Gurman & D. P. Kniskern (Eds.), *Handbook of family therapy.* New York: Brunner/Mazel.

Kassett, J. A., Gershon, E. S., Maxwell, M. E., Guroff, J. J., Kazuba, D. M., Smith, A. L., Brandt, H. A., & Jimerson, D. C. (1989). Psychiatric disorders in first-degree relatives of probands with bulimia nervosa. *American Journal of Psychiatry, 146,* 1468–1471.

Kassett, J. A., Gwirtsman, H. E., Kaye, W. H., Brandt, H. A., & Jimerson, D. C. (1988). Pattern of onset of bulimic symptoms in anorexia. *American Journal of Psychiatry*, *145*, 1287–1288.

Kathol, R. G., Jaeckle, R. S., Lopez, J. F., & Meller, W. H. (1989). Pathophysiology of H-P-A axis abnormalities in patients with major depression: An update. *American Journal of Psychiatry*, *146*, 311–317.

Kaufman, J., & Zigler, E. (1987). Do abused children become abusive parents? *American Journal of Orthopsychiatry*, *57*, 186–192.

Kaufman, W. (19975). *Existentialism from Dostoevsky to Sartre.* New York: Meridian.

Kavanaugh, J. F., & Truss, T. J. (1988). *Learning disabilities: Proceedings of the national conference.* Parkton, MD: York Press.

Kazdin, A. E. (1986). Comparative outcome studies of psychotherapy: Methodological issues and strategies. *Journal of Consulting and Clinical Psychology*, *54*, 95–105.

Kazdin, A. E. (1987a). *Conduct disorder in childhood and adolescence.* Newbury Park, CA: Sage.

Kazdin, A. E. (1987b). Treatment of antisocial behavior in children: Current status and future directions. *Psychological Bulletin*, *102*, 187–203.

Kazdin, A. E. (1990). Psychotherapy for children and adolescents. *Annual Review of Psychology*, *41*, 21–54.

Kazdin, A. E., & Wilson, G. T. (1980). *Evaluation of behavior therapy: Issues, evidence, and research strategies.* Lincoln: University of Nebraska Press.

Keesey, R. E. (1986). A set-point theory of obesity. In K. D. Brownell & P. J. Foreyt (Eds.), *Handbook of eating disorders.* New York: Basic Books.

Keith, S. J., & Matthews, S. M. (1984). Schizophrenia: A review of psychosocial treatment strategies. In J. B. W. Williams & R. L. Spitzer (Eds.), *Psychotherapy research: Where are we and where should we go?* New York: Guilford Press.

Keitner, G. I., & Miller, I. W. (1990). Family functioning and major depression: An overview. *American Journal of Psychiatry*, *147*, 1128–1137.

Kellner, R. (1982). Disorders of impulse control. In J. H. Griest, J. W. Jefferson, & R. L. Spitzer (Eds.), *Treatment of mental disorders.* New York: Oxford University Press.

Kempe, C. H., Silverman, F. N., Steele, B. B., Droegemueller, W., & Silver, H. K. (1962). The battered child syndrome. *Journal of the American Medical Association*, *181*, 17–24.

Kendall, P. C., & Norton-Ford, J. D. (1982). *Clinical psychology: Scientific and professional dimensions.* New York: Wiley.

Kendler, K. S. (1983). Overview: A current perspective on twin studies of schizophrenia. *American Journal of Psychiatry*, *140*, 1413–1425.

Kendler, K. S., Gruenberg, A. M., & Tsuang, M. T. (1985). Psychiatric illness in first degree relatives of schizophrenic and surgical control patients: A family study using DSM-III criteria. *Archives of General Psychiatry*, *42*, 770–779.

Kendler, K. S., Gruenberg, A. M., & Tsuang, M. T. (1986). A DSM-III-R family study of the nonschizophrenic psychotic disorders. *American Journal of Psychiatry*, *143*, 1098–1105.

Kendler, K. S., MacLean, C., Neale, M., Kessler, R., Heath, A., & Eaves, L. (1991). The genetic epidemiology of bulimia nervosa. *American Journal of Psychiatry*, *148*, 1627–1637.

Kennedy, J. L., Giuffa, L. A., Moises, H. W., Cavalli-Sforza, L. L., Pakstis, A. J., Kidd, J. R., Castiglione, C. M., Sjogren, B., Wetterberg, L., & Kidd, K. K. (1988). Evidence against linkage of schizophrenia to markers on chromosome 5 in a northern Swedish pedigree. *Nature*, *336*, 167–170.

Kernberg, O. F. (1976). *Object relations theory and clinical psychoanalysis.* New York: Jason Aronson.

Kernberg, O. F. (1984). *Severe personality disorders: Psychotherapeutic strategies.* New Haven, CT: Yale University press.

Kernberg, O. F. (1986). Narcissistic personality disorder. In A. M. Cooper, A. J. Frances, & M. H. Sacks (Eds.), *The personality disorders and neuroses.* New York: Basic Books.

Kerner, K. (1988). Current topics in inhalant abuse. In R. A. Crider & B. A. Rouse (Eds.), *Epidemiology of inhalant abuse: An update* (NIDA Research Monograph). Rockville, MD: National Institute on Drug Abuse.

Kerr, M. E. (1981). Family systems theory and therapy. In A. S. Gurman & D. P. Kniskern (Eds.), *Handbook of family therapy*. New York: Brunner/Mazel.

Kessler, S. (1980). The genetics of schizophrenia: A review. *Schizophrenia Bulletin, 6*, 14–26.

Kettl, P. A., & Marx, I. M. (1986). Neurological factors in obsessive-compulsive disorder. *British Journal of Psychiatry, 149*, 315–319.

Kety, S. (1985). Schizotypal personality disorder: An operational definition of Bleuler's latent schizophrenia. *Schizophrenia Bulletin, 11*, 590–594.

Kety, S. S. (1988). Schizophrenic illness in the families of schizophrenic adoptees: Findings from the Danish national sample. *Schizophrenia Bulletin, 14*, 217–222.

Kety, S. S., Rosenthal, D., Wender, P. H., Schulsinger, F., & Jacobson, B. (1978). The biologic and adoptive families of adopted individuals who became schizophrenic: Prevalence of mental illness and other characteristics. In L. D. Wynne (Ed.), *The nature of schizophrenia*. New York: Wiley.

Keyes, D. (1982). *The minds of Billy Milligan*. New York: Bantam.

Khantzian, E. J. (1980). An ego/self theory of substance dependence: A contemporary psychoanalytic perspective. In D. J. Lettieri, M. Sayers, & H. W. Pearson (Eds.), *Theories on drug abuse: Selected contemporary perspective* (NIDA Research Monograph No. 30). Rockville, MD: National Institute of Alcohol Abuse and Alcoholism.

Khantzian, E. J. (1985). The self-medication hypothesis of addictive disorders: Focus on heroin and cocaine dependence. *American Journal of Psychiatry, 142*, 1259–1264.

Khantzian, E. J., Halliday, K. S., & McAuliffe, W. E. (1990). *Addiction and the vulnerable self: Modified dynamic group therapy for substance abusers*. New York: Guilford Press.

Kiecolt-Glaser, J. K., Fisher, L. D., Ogrocki, P., Stout, J. C., Speicher, C. E., & Glaser, R.. (1987). Marital quality, marital disruption and immune function. *Psychosomatic Medicine, 49*, 13–34.

Kiecolt-Glaser, J. K., & Glaser, R. (1984). Stress and transformation of lymphocytes to Epstein-Barr virus. *Journal of Behavioral Medicine, 7*, 1–12.

King, M. B. (1986). Eating disorders in general practice. *British Medical Journal, 293*, 1412–1414.

King, M. B. (1989). Eating disorders in a general practice population: Prevalence, characteristics, and follow-up at 12 and 18 months [Monograph supplement]. *Psychological Medicine, 14*, 1–34.

Kinsey, A. C. (1953). *Sexual behavior in the adult female*. Philadelphia: Saunders.

Kinsey, A. C., Pomeroy, W. B., & Martin, C. E. (1948). *Sexual behavior in the human male*. Philadelphia: Saunders.

Kirby, F. D., & Shields, F. (1972). Modification of arithmetic response rate and attending behavior in a seventh-grade student. *Journal of Applied Behavior Analysis*, 79–84.

Kirigin, K. A., Brankmann, C. J., Atwater, J. D., & Wolf, M. M. (1982). An evaluation of teaching-family (Achievement Place) group homes for juvenile offenders. *Journal of Applied Behavior Analysis, 15*, 1–16.

Kirkpatrick, M. (1988). Some clinical perceptions of middle-aged divorcing women. In J. Gold (Ed.), *Divorce as a developmental process*. Washington, DC: American Psychiatric Press.

Kirschenbaum, D. S. (1988). Treating adult obesity in 1988: Evolution of a modern program. *Behavior Therapist, 11*, 3–6.

Kirschenbaum, D. S., & Dykman, B. M. (1991). Disinhibited eating by resourceful, restrained eaters. *Journal of Abnormal Psychology, 100*, 227–230.

Kitson, G. C., & Morgan, L. A. (1990). The multiple consequences of divorce: A decade review. *Journal of Marriage and the Family, 52*, 913–924.

Kleber, H. D., & Gawin, F. H. (1984). *Cocaine abuse: A review of current and experi-*

mental treatments (NIDA Research Monograph Series 1984a, Monograph 50-111-129). Rockville, MD: National Institute on Drug Abuse.

Klein, D. (1977). Pharmacological treatment of borderline disorder. In P. Hartocollis (Ed.), *Borderline personality disorders: The concept, the syndrome, the patient.* New York: International University Press.

Klein, D. F., Rabkin, J. G., & Gorman, J. M. (1985). Etiological and pathophysiological inferences from the pharmacological treatment of anxiety. In A. H. Tuma & J. D. Maser (Eds.), *Anxiety and the anxiety disorders.* Hillsdale, NJ: Erlbaum.

Klein, D. N. (1990). Depressive personality: Reliability, validity, and relation to dysthymia. *Journal of Abnormal Psychology, 99,* 412–421.

Klein, R. G., & Last, C. G. (1989). *Anxiety disorders in children.* Newbury Park, CA: Sage.

Kleinman, J. E., Casanova, M. F., & Jaskiw, G. E. (1988). The neuropathology of schizophrenia. *Schizophrenia Bulletin, 14,* 209–216.

Klerman, G. L. (1990). Treatment of recurrent major depressive disorder. *Archives of General Psychiatry, 47,* 1158–1162.

Klerman, G. L., Weissman, M. M., Rounsaville, B. J., & Chevron, E. S. (1984). *Interpersonal psychotherapy of depression.* New York: Basic Books.

Kline, P. (1981). *Fact and fantasy in Freudian theory* (2nd ed.). London: Methuen.

Klorman, R., Brumaghim, J. T., Salzman, L. F., Strauss, J., Borgstedt, A. D., McBride, M. C., & Loeb, S. (1988). Effects of methylphenidate on attention-deficit hyperactivity disorder with and without aggressive/noncompliant features. *Journal of Abnormal Psychology, 97,* 413–422.

Kocsis, J. H., & Mann, J. J. (1986). Drug treatment of personality disorders and neuroses. In A. M. Cooper, A. J. Frances, & M. H. Sacks (Eds.), *The personality disorders and neuroses.* New York: Basic Books.

Koenigsberg, H. W., & Handley, R. (1986). Expressed emotion: From predictive index to clinical construct. *American Journal of Psychiatry, 143,* 1361–1373.

Koenigsberg, H. W., Kaplan, R. D., Gilmore, N. M., & Cooper, A. M. (1985). The relationship between syndrome and personality disorder in DSM-III: Experience with 2,462 patients. *American Journal of Psychiatry, 142,* 207–212.

Kohut, H. (1971). *The analysis of the self.* New York: International Universities Press.

Kolb, L. C. (1987). A neuropsychological hypothesis explaining posttraumatic stress disorders. *American Journal of Psychiatry, 144,* 989–995.

Koocher, G. P. (1991). Questionable methods in alcoholism research. *Journal of Consulting and Clinical Psychology, 59,* 246–248.

Korsten, M. A., & Lieber, C. S. (1985). Medical complications of alcoholism. In J. H. Mendelson & N. K. Mello (Eds.), *The diagnosis and treatment of alcoholism* (2nd ed.). New York: McGraw-Hill.

Koss, M. P. (1990). The women's mental health research agenda: Violence against women. *American Psychologist, 45,* 374–380.

Kosten, T. R., Rounsaville, B. J., & Kleber, H. D. (1987). Multidimensionality and prediction of treatment outcome in opioid addicts: 2.5 year follow-up. *Comprehensive Psychiatry, 28,* 3–13.

Kovacs, M., & Paulauskas, S. (1986). The traditional psychotherapies. In H. C. Quay & J. S. Werry (Eds.), *Psychopathological disorders of childhood* (3rd ed.). New York: Wiley.

Kozel, N. J., & Adams, E. H. (1986). Epidemiology of drug abuse: An overview. *Science, 234,* 970–974.

Kraepelin, E. (1923). *Textbook of psychiatry.* New York: Macmillan.

Krantz, D. S., & Manuck, S. B. (1984). Acute psychophysiological reactivity and risk of cardiovascular disease: A review and methodological critique. *Psychological Bulletin, 96,* 435–464.

Kraus, R. P., Grof, P., & Brown, G. M. (1988). Drugs and the DST: Need for reappraisal. *American Journal of Psychiatry, 145,* 666–674.

Krug, S. E. (1980). Clinical analysis questionnaire manual. Champaign, IL: Institute for Personality and Ability Testing.

Krug, S. E., & Laughlin, J. E. (1976). *Handbook for the IPAT depression scale.* Champaign, IL: Institute for Personality and Ability Testing.

Kurtz, E. (1979). Not-God: A history of Alcoholics Anonymous. Center City, MN: Hazelden.

Kushner, M. (1965). The reduction of a long-standing fetish by means of aversive conditioning. In L. P. Ullman & L. Krasner (Eds.), *Case studies in behavior modification.* New York: Holt, Rinehart and Winston.

Kushner, M. G., Sher, K. J., & Beitman, B. D. (1990). The relation between alcohol problems and the anxiety disorders. *American Journal of Psychiatry, 147,* 685–695.

Lahey, B. B., Hartdagen, S. E., Frick, P. J., McBurnett, K., Connor, R., & Hynd, G. W. (1988). Conduct disorder: Parsing the confounded relation to parental divorce and antisocial personality. *Journal of Abnormal Psychology, 97,* 334–337.

Laing, R. D. (1959). *The divided self.* London: Tavistock.

Lamb, H. R. (1990). Will we save the homeless mentally ill? *American Journal of Psychiatry, 147,* 649–651.

Lambert, N. (1988). Adolescent outcomes for hyperactive children: Perspectives on general and specific patterns of childhood risk for adolescent educational, social, and mental health problems. *American Psychologist, 43,* 786–799.

Landesman, S., & Butterfield, E. C. (1987). Normalization and deinstitutionalization of mentally retarded individuals: Controversy and facts. *American Psychologist, 42,* 809–816.

Lando, H. A. (1977). Successful treatment of smokers with a broad-spectrum behavioral approach. *Journal of Consulting and Clinical Psychology, 45,* 361–366.

Lang, A. R. (1983). Addictive personality: A viable construct? In P. K. Levison, D. R. Gerstein, & D. R. Maloff (Eds.), *Commonalities in substance abuse and habitual behavior.* Lexington, MA: Lexington Books.

Last, C. G., Hersen, M., Kazdin, A. E., Francis, G., & Grubb, H. (1987). Psychiatric illness in the mothers of anxious children. *American Journal of Psychiatry, 144,* 1580–1583.

Lawson, D. M. (1983). Alcoholism. In M. Hersen (Ed.), *Outpatient behavior therapy: A clinical guide.* New York: Grune & Stratton.

Lazarus, L. W., Newton, N., Cohler, B., Lesser, J., & Schweon, C. (1987). Frequency and presentation of depressive symptoms in patients with primary degenerative dementia. *American Journal of Psychiatry, 144,* 41–45.

Lazarus, R. S., & Folkman, S. (1984). *Stress, appraisal, and coping.* New York: Springer.

Lechtenberg, R. L. (1982). *The psychiatrist's guide to diseases of the nervous system.* New York: Wiley.

Lee, C. L., & Bates, J. E. (1985). Mother–child interaction at age two years and perceived difficult temperament. *Child Development, 56,* 1314–1323.

Lee, M. A., Flagel, P., Greden, J. F., & Cameron, D. G. (1988). Anxiogenic effects of caffeine on panic and depressed patients. *American Journal of Psychiatry, 145,* 632–635.

Leff, J., Kuipers, L., Berkowitz, R., & Sturgeon, D. (1985). A controlled trial of social intervention in the families of schizophrenic patients: Two year follow-up. *British Journal of Psychiatry, 146,* 594–600.

Leff, J., & Vaughn, C. (1985). *Expressed emotion in families.* New York: Guilford Press.

Lehman, H. E. (1985). Affective disorders: Clinical features. In H. I. Kaplan & B. J. Sadock (Eds.), *Comprehensive textbook of psychiatry* (4th ed.). Baltimore: Williams & Wilkins.

Lehman, H. E., & Cancro, R. (1985). Schizophrenia: Clinical features. In H. I. Kaplan & B. J. Sadock (Eds.), *Comprehensive textbook of psychiatry* (Vol. 1, 4th ed.). Baltimore: Williams & Wilkins.

Lehrer, P. M., & Woolfolk, R. L. (1984). Are stress reduction techniques interchangeable or do they have specific effects? A review of the comparative empirical literature. In

R. L. Woolfolk & P. M. Lehrer (Eds.), *Principles and practice of stress management.* New York: Guilford Press.

Lemmon, J. A. (1985). *Family mediation practice.* New York: Free Press.

Lennox, W. G. (1970). John Hughlings Jackson. In W. Haymaker & F. Schiller (Eds.), *The founders of neurology* (2nd ed.). Springfield, IL: Charles C. Thomas.

Lenzenweger, M. F., & Loranger, A. W. (1989). Psychosis proneness and clinical psychopathology. *Journal of Abnormal Psychology, 98,* 3–8.

Leonard, K. E., & Jacob, T. (1988). Alcohol, alcoholism, and family violence. In V. B. van Hasselt, R. L. Morrison, A. S. Bellack, & M. Hersen (Eds.), *Handbook of family violence.* New York: Plenum.

Lester, D., & Carpenter, J. A. (1985). Static ataxia in adolescents and their parentage. *Alcoholism: Clinical and Experimental Research, 9,* 212.

Leukefeld, C. G., & Tims, F. M. (1988). *Compulsory treatment of drug abuse: Research and clinical practice* (NIDA Research Monograph 86). Rockville, MD: National Institute on Drug Abuse.

LeVay, S. (1991). A difference in hypothalamic structure between heterosexual and homosexual men. *Science, 253,* 1034–1037.

Levenson, J. L. (1985). Neuroleptic malignant syndrome. *American Journal of Psychiatry, 142,* 1137–1145.

Levinthal, C. F. (1990). *Introduction to physiological psychology.* Englewood Cliffs, NJ: Prentice-Hall.

Levy, A. B., Dixon, K. N., & Stern, S. L. (1989). How are depression and bulimia related? *American Journal of Psychiatry, 146,* 162–169.

Levy, J. C., & Deykin, E. Y. (1989). Suicidality, depression, and substance abuse in adolescence. *American Journal of Psychiatry, 146,* 1462–1467.

Levy, L. (1988). Suicide, homicide and other psychiatric emergencies. In H. H. Goldman (Ed.), *General review of psychiatry* (2nd ed.). Norwalk, CT: Appleton and Lange.

Ley, B. W. (1985). Alcohol problems in special populations. In J. H. Mendelson & N. K. Mello (Eds.), *The diagnosis and treatment of alcoholism* (2nd ed.). New York: McGraw-Hill.

Lewinsohn, P. M., Duncan, E. M., Stanton, A. K., & Hautzinger, M. (1986). Age at first onset for nonbipolar depression. *Journal of Abnormal Psychology, 95,* 378–383.

Lewinsohn, P. M., Munoz, R. F., Youngren, M. A., & Zeiss, A. M. (1978). *Control your depression.* Englewood Cliffs, NJ: Prentice-Hall.

Lewis, D. O., Pincus, J. H., Feldman, M. F., Jackson, L., & Bard, B. (1986). Psychiatric, neurological, and psychoeducational characteristics of 15 death row inmates in the United States. *American Journal of Psychiatry, 143,* 838–845.

Lewis, M. (1986). Principles of intensive individual psychoanalytic psychotherapy with childhood anxiety disorders. In R. Gittelman (Ed.), *Anxiety disorders of childhood.* New York: Guilford Press.

Levin, J., & Fox, J. A. (1985). *Mass murder: America's growing menace.* New York: Plenum.

Levin, S., Yurgelun-Todd, D., & Craft, S. (1989). Contributions of clinical neuropsychology to the study of schizophrenia. *Journal of Abnormal Psychology, 98,* 341–356.

Levine, I. S., & Rog, D. J. (1990). Mental health services for homeless mentally ill persons. *American Psychologist, 45,* 963–968.

Levinson, D. (1988). Family violence in cross-cultural perspective. In V. B. van Hasselt, R. L. Morrison, A. S. Bellack, & M. Hersen (Eds.), *Handbook of family violence.* New York: Plenum.

Liberman, R. P. (1985). Schizophrenia: Psychosocial treatment. In H. I. Kaplan & B. J. Sadock (Eds.), *Comprehensive textbook of psychiatry* (Vol. 1, 4th ed.). Baltimore: Williams & Wilkins.

Liberthson, R., Sheehan, D. V., King, M. E., & Weyman, A. E. (1986). The prevalence of mitral valve prolapse in patients with panic disorders. *American Journal of Psychiatry, 143,* 511–515.

Licht, B. G., & Kistner, J. A. (1986). Motivational problems of learning-disabled children: Individual differences and their implications for treatment. In J. K. Torgesen & B. Y. L. Wong (Eds.), *Psychological and educational perspectives on learning disabilities.* New York: Academic Press.

Lidz, T. (1973). *The origin and treatment of schizophrenic disorders.* New York: Basic Books.

Lidz, T. (1985). In memorium: Hilde Bruch. *American Journal of Psychiatry, 142,* 869–870.

Liebowitz, M. R., Fyer, A. J., & Gorman, J. M. (1984). Lactate provocation of panic attacks, I: Clinical and behavioral findings. *Archives of General Psychiatry, 41,* 764–770.

Liebowitz, M. R., Gorman, J. M., Fyer, A., Dillon, D., Levitt, M., & Klein, D. F. (1986). Possible mechanisms for lactate's induction of panic. *American Journal of Psychiatry, 143,* 495–502.

Lipowski, Z. J. (1988). Somatization: The concept and its clinical application. *American Journal of Psychiatry, 145,* 1358–1368.

Livelsey, W. J. (1987). A systematic approach to the delineation of personality disorders. *American Journal of Psychiatry, 144,* 772–777.

Locke, J. (1963). *The works of John Locke* (Vol. 1). Darmstadt: Scientia Verlag Aalen. (reprint)

Loeber, R. (1982). The stability of antisocial and delinquent child behavior: A review. *Child Development, 53,* 1431–1446.

Loeber, R., & Dishon, T. J. (1984). Boys who fight: Familial and antisocial correlates. *Journal of Consulting and Clinical Psychology, 52,* 759–768.

Loeber, R., Lahey, B. B., & Thomas, C. (1991). Diagnostic conundrum of oppositional defiant disorder and conduct disorder. *Journal of Abnormal Psychology, 100,* 379–390.

Logue, C. M., & Moos, R. H. (1986). Premenstrual symptoms: Prevalence and risk factors. *Psychosomatic Medicine, 48,* 388–414.

LoPiccolo, J. (1978). Direct treatment of sexual dysfunctions. In J. LoPiccolo & L. LoPiccolo, (Eds.), *Handbook of sex therapy.* New York: Plenum.

LoPiccolo, J., & Lobitz, W. C. (1978). The role of masturbation in the treatment of orgasmic dysfunction. In J. LoPiccolo & L. LoPiccolo, (Eds.), *Handbook of sex therapy.* New York: Plenum.

LoPiccolo, J., & Steger, J. C. (1978). The new sexual interaction inventory: A new instrument for assessment of sexual dysfunction. In J. LoPiccolo & L. LoPiccolo (Eds.), *Handbook of sex therapy.* New York: Plenum.

LoPiccolo, J., & Stock, W. E. (1986). Treatment of sexual dysfunction. *Journal of Consulting and Clinical Psychology, 54,* 158–167.

Lou, H. C., Henriksen, L., & Bruhn, P. (1984). Focal cerebral hypoperfusion in children with dysphasia and/or attention deficit disorder. *Archives of Neurology, 41,* 825–829.

Lovaas, O. I. (1987). Behavioral treatment and normal education and intellectual functioning in young autistic children. *Journal of Consulting and Clinical Psychology, 55,* 3–9.

Lovaas, O. I., Ackerman, A. B., Alexander, D., Firestone, P., Perkins, J., & Young, D. (1980). *Teaching developmentally disabled children: The me book.* Austin, TX: Pro-Ed.

Lovaas, O. I., & Newsom, C. D. (1976). Behavior modification with psychotic children. In H. Leitenberg (Ed.), *Handbook of behavior modification and behavior therapy.* Englewood Cliffs, NJ: Prentice-Hall.

Ludwig, A. M., Cain, R. B., Wikler, A., Taylor, R. M., & Bendfeldt, F. (1977). Physiologic and situational determinants of drinking behavior. In M. A. Gross (Ed.), *Alcohol intoxication and withdrawal: Vol. 16. Studies in alcohol dependence.* New York: Plenum.

Lukoff, D., Snyder, K., Ventura, J., & Neuchterlein, K. H. (1984). Life events, familial stress, and coping in the developmental course of schizophrenia. *Schizophrenia Bulletin, 10,* 258–292.

Lunn, S., Skydsbjerg, M., Schulsinger, H., Parnas, J., Pederson, C., & Mathiesen, L. (1991). A preliminary report on the neuropsychologic sequelae of HIV. *Archives of General Psychiatry, 48,* 139–142.

Lykken, D. T. (1981). *A tremor in the blood: Uses and abuses of the lie detector.* New York: McGraw-Hill.

Lyon, G. R., & Moats, L. C. (1988). Critical issues in the instruction of the learning disabled. *Journal of Consulting and Clinical Psychology, 56,* 830–835.

McAdoo, W. G., & DeMyer, M. K. (1978). Research related to family factors in autism. *Journal of Pediatric Psychology, 2,* 162–166.

McBride, P. A., Anderson, G. M., Hertzig, M. E., Sweeney, J., Kream, J., Cohen, D. J., & Mann, J. J. (1988). Serotonergic function in male young adults with autistic disorder. *Archives of General Psychiatry, 46,* 213–221.

McCarley, R., Faux, S., Shenton, M., LeMay, M., Cane, M., Ballinger, R., & Duffy, F. (1989). CT abnormalities in schizophrenia. *Archives of General Psychiatry, 46,* 698–708.

McCullough, P. (1980). Launching children and moving on. In E. A. Carter & M. McGoldrick (Eds.), *The family life cycle: A framework for family therapy.* New York: Gardner.

McElroy, S. L., & Kreck, P. E., Jr. (1989). Pharmacological treatment of kleptomania and bulimia nervosa. *Journal of Clinical Psychopharmacology, 9,* 358–360.

McElroy, S. L., Pope, H. G., Hudson, J. I., Keck, P. E., & White, K. L. (1991). Kleptomania: A report of 20 cases. *American Journal of Psychiatry, 148,* 652–657.

McFarlane, W. R., & Beels, C. C. (1983). Family research in schizophrenia: A review and integration for clinicians. In W. R. McFarlane (Ed.), *Family therapy in schizophrenia.* New York: Guilford Press.

McGlashan, T. H. (1988). A selective review of recent North American long-term follow-up studies of schizophrenia. *Schizophrenia Bulletin, 14,* 515–542.

McGovern, H. (1985). Commentary on Roberts's criticism of biofeedback. *American Psychologist, 41,* 1007.

McGrath, E., Puryear Keita, G., Strickland, B. R., & Felipe Russo, N. (1990). Women and depression: Risk factors and treatment issues. Washington, DC: American Psychological Association.

McGue, M., & Gottesman, I. I. (1989). Genetic linkage in schizophrenia. *Schizophrenia Bulletin, 15,* 453–461.

McGue, M., Pickens, R. W., & Svikis, D. S. (1992). Sex and age effects on the inheritance of alcohol problems: A twin study. *Journal of Abnormal Psychology, 101,* 3–17.

McGuigan, F. J. (1984). Progressive relaxation: Origins, principles, and clinical application. In R. L. Woolfolk & P. M. Lehrer (Eds.), *Principles and practice of stress management.* New York: Guilford Press.

McKenna, P. J., Kane, J. M., & Parrish, K. (1985). Psychotic syndromes in epilepsy. *American Journal of Psychiatry, 142,* 895–904.

McKeon, J., McGuffin, P., & Robinson, P. (1984). Obsessive-compulsive neurosis following head injury: A report of 4 cases. *British Journal of Psychiatry, 144,* 190–192.

McMahon, R. C. (1980). Genetic etiology in the hyperactive child syndrome: A critical review. *American Journal of Orthopsychiatry, 50,* 145–149.

McMillan, M. J., & Pihl, R. O. (1987). Premenstrual depression: A distinct entity. *Journal of Abnormal Psychology, 96,* 149–154.

McNalley, R. J. (1987). Preparedness and phobias: A review. *Psychological Bulletin, 101,* 283–303.

McNalley, R. J. (1990). Psychological approaches to panic disorder: A review. *Psychological Bulletin, 108,* 403–419.

McNeal, E. T., & Cimbolic, P. (1986). Antidepressants and biochemical theories of depression. *Psychological Bulletin, 99,* 361–374.

Maddi, S. (1967). The existential neurosis. *Journal of Abnormal Psychology, 72,* 311–325.

Madonna, P. G., Van Scoyk, S., & Jones, D. P. H. (1991). Family interactions within incest and nonincest families. *American Journal of Psychiatry, 148,* 46–49.

Maher, W. B., & Maher, B. A. (1985). Psychopathology: I. From ancient times to the eighteenth century. In G. A. Kimble & K. Schlesinger (Eds.), *Topics in the history of psychology* (Vol. 2). Hillsdale, NJ: Erlbaum.

Mahler, M. (1975). *The psychological birth of the human infant.* New York: Basic Books.

Maier, S. F., & Seligman, M. E. P. (1976). Learned helplessness: Theory and evidence. *Journal of Experimental Psychology: General, 105,* 3–46.

Mallory, H. P. (1990). Fourth Amendment—The "reasonableness" of suspicionless drug testing of railroad employees. *The Journal of Criminal Law and Criminology, 80,* 1052–1085.

Malmo, R. B. (1986). Obituary: Hans Hugo Selye. *American Psychologist, 41,* 92–93.

Mannuzza, S., Gittelman-Klein, R., Konig, P. H., & Giampino, T. L. (1989). Hyperactive boys almost grown up: IV. Criminality and its relationship to psychiatric status. *Archives of General Psychiatry, 46,* 1073–1079.

Mannuzza, S., Klein, R. G., Bonagura, N., Konig, P. H., & Shenker, R. (1988). Hyperactive boys almost grown up: II. Status of subjects without a mental disorder. *Archives of General Psychiatry, 45,* 13–18.

Mannuzza, S., Klein, R. G., Bonagura, N., Malloy, P., Giampino, T. L., & Addalli, K. A. (1991). Hyperactive boys almost grown up: V. Replication of psychiatric status. *Archives of General Psychiatry, 48,* 77–83.

Marcos, L. R., Cohen, N. L., Nardacci, D., & Brittain, J. (1990). Psychiatry takes to the streets: The New York City initiative for the homeless mentally ill. *American Journal of Psychiatry, 147,* 1557–1561.

Marcus, J., Haus, S. L., Nagler, S., Auerbach, J. G., Mirsky, A. F., & Aubrey, A. (1987). Review of the NIMH Israeli kibbutz-city study and the Jerusalem infant developmental study. *Schizophrenia Bulletin, 13,* 425–437.

Margolin, G., Sibner, L. G., & Gleberman, L. (1988). Wife battering. in V. B. van Hasselt, R. L. Morrison, A. S. Bellack, & M. Hersen (Eds.), *Handbook of family violence.* New York: Plenum.

Marks, I. (1982). Anxiety disorders. In J. H. Greist, J. W. Jefferson, & R. L. Spitzer (Eds.), *Treatment of mental disorders* (pp. 234–265). New York: Oxford University Press.

Marks, I. M., Gelder, M. G., & Bancroft, J. (1970). Sexual deviants two years after electrical aversion. *British Journal of Psychiatry, 117,* 73–85.

Marlatt, G. A. (1983). The controlled drinking controversy: A commentary. *American Psychologist, 38,* 1097–1110.

Marlatt, G. A. (1985). Cognitive factors in the relapse process. In G. A. Marlatt & J. Gordon (Eds.), *Relapse prevention.* New York: Guilford Press.

Marlatt, G. A., & Rohsenow, D. J. (1981, December). The "think-drink" effect. *Psychology Today,* pp. 60–69.

Marshall, P. (1989). Attention deficit disorder and allergy: A neurochemical model of the relation between the illnesses. *Psychological Bulletin, 106,* 434–446.

Martin, B., & Hoffman, J. A. (1990). Conduct disorders. In M. Lewis & S. M. Miller (Eds.), *Handbook of developmental psychopathology.* New York: Plenum.

Martin, M. (1988). Battered women. In N. Hutchings (Ed.), *The violent family: Victimization of women, children and elders.* New York: Human Sciences Press.

Marx, I. (1988). Blood-injury phobia: A review. *American Journal of Psychiatry, 10,* 1207–1213.

Marx, J. L. (1989a). Brain protein yields clues to Alzheimer's disease. *Science, 243,* 1664–1666.

Marx, J. L. (1989b). Wider use of AIDS drug advocated. *Science, 245,* 811.

Masling, J. (Ed.). (1983). *Empirical studies of psychoanalytic theories* (Vol. 1). Hillsdale, NJ: Analytic Press.

Maslow, A. H. (1970). *Motivation and personality.* New York: Harper & Row.

Maslow, A. H. (1971). *The farther reaches of human nature.* New York: Viking.

Masters, W. H., & Johnson, V. E. (1966). *Human sexual response.* Boston: Little, Brown.

Masters, W. H., & Johnson, V. E. (1970). *Human sexual inadequacy.* Boston: Little, Brown.

Masters, W. H., Johnson, V. E., & Kolodny, R. C. (1985). *Human sexuality* (2nd ed.). Boston: Little, Brown.

Matarazzo, J. D. (1981). Obituary: David Wechsler. *American Psychologist, 36,* 1542–1543.

Mathew, R. J., & Wilson, W. D. (1991). Substance abuse and cerebral blood flow. *American Journal of Psychiatry, 148,* 292–305.

Mathews, A. M., Gelder, M. G., & Johnston, D. W. (1981). *Agoraphobia: Nature and treatment.* New York: Guilford Press.

Mathews, K. A. (1988). Coronary heart disease and Type-A behaviors: Update on and alternative to the Booth-Kewley and Friedman quantitative review. *Psychological Bulletin, 104,* 373–380.

Mathews, K. A. , & Haynes, S. G. (1986). Type-A behavior pattern and coronary risk: Update and critical evaluation. *American Journal of Epidemiology, 123,* 923–960.

Matson, J. L. (1983). Mentally retarded children. In R. J. Morris & T. R. Kratchowill (Eds.), *The practice of child therapy.* New York: Pergamon Press.

Matthews, W. S., Barabas, G., Cusak, E., & Ferrari, M. (1986). Social quotients of children with phenylketonuria before and after discontinuation of dietary therapy. *American Journal of Mental Deficiency, 91,* 92–94.

Matuschka, P. R. (1985). The psychopharmacology of addiction. In T. E. Bratter & G. G. Forrest (Eds.), *Alcoholism and substance abuse: Strategies for clinical intervention.* New York: Free Press.

May, P. R. A., Tuma, A. H., & Dixon, W. J. (1984). Schizophrenia: A follow-up study of the results of five forms of treatment. *Archives of General Psychiatry, 38,* 776–784.

May, R. (1983). *The discovery of being.* New York: Norton.

May, R., Angel, E., & Ellenberger, H. (1958). *Existence.* New York: Basic Books.

Mednick, S. A., Gabrielli, W. F., Jr., & Hutchings, B. (1984). Genetic influences in criminal convictions: Evidence from an adoption cohort. *Science, 224,* 891–894.

Meichenbaum, D. (1974). *Cognitive behavior modification.* Morristown, NJ: General Learning Press.

Meichenbaum, D. (1977). *Cognitive-behavior modification: An integrative approach.* New York: Plenum.

Meissner, S. J. (1985). Theories of personality and psychopathology: Classical psychoanalysis. In H. I. Kaplan & B. J. Sadock (Eds.), *Comprehensive textbook of psychiatry, IV.* Baltimore: Williams & Wilkins.

Melton, G. B. (1988). Ethical and legal issues in AIDS-related practice. *American Psychologist, 43,* 941–947.

Mendlewicz, J., & Rainer, J. D. (1977). Adoption study supporting genetic transmission in manic-depressive illness. *Nature, 268,* 327–329.

Menolascino, F. J. (1990). The nature and types of mental illness in the mentally retarded. In M. Lewis & S. M. Miller (Eds.), *Handbook of developmental psychopathology.* New York: Plenum.

Merikangas, K. R., Angst, J., & Isler, H. (1990). Migraine and psychopathology. *Archives of General Psychiatry, 47,* 849–853.

Merikangas, K. R., Spence, M. A., & Kupfer, D. J. (1989). Linkage studies of bipolar disorder: Methodological and analytic issues. *Archives of General Psychiatry, 46,* 1137–1144.

Merikangas, K. R., & Weissman, M. (1986). Epidemiology of DSM-III Axis II personality disorders. In A. J. Francis & R. E. Hales (Eds.), *American Psychiatric Association annual review* (Vol. 5). Washington, DC: American Psychiatric Association.

Meyer, J. K. (1985a). Ego-dystonic homosexuality. In H. I. Kaplan & B. J. Sadock (Eds.), *Comprehensive textbook of psychiatry* (Vol. 1, 4th ed.). Baltimore: Williams & Wilkins.

Meyer, J. K. (1985b). Paraphilias. In H. I. Kaplan & B. J. Sadock (Eds.), *Comprehensive textbook of psychiatry* (Vol. 1, 4th ed.). Baltimore: Williams & Wilkins.

Meyer, R. G., & Osborne, Y. H. (1987). *Case studies in abnormal behavior* (2nd ed.). Boston: Allyn and Bacon.

Micklow, P. L. (1988). Domestic abuse and the legal system. In V. B. van Hasselt, R. L. Morrison, A. S. Bellack, & M. Hersen (Eds.), *Handbook of family violence*. New York: Plenum.

Miller, G. E., & Prinz, R. J. (1990). Enhancement of social learning family interactions for childhood conduct disorder. *Psychological Bulletin, 108*, 291–307.

Miller, N. E. (1969). Learning of visceral and glandular responses. *Science, 163*, 434.

Millon, T. (1977). *Millon multiaxial inventory manual*. Minneapolis: NCS Interpretive Scoring Systems.

Millon, T. (1981). *Disorders of personality, DSM-III and Axis II*. New York: Wiley.

Millon, T. (1986). The avoidant personality. In A. M. Cooper, A. J. Frances, & M. H. Sacks (Eds.), *The personality disorders and neuroses*. New York: Basic Books.

Milner, B. (1970). Memory and the medial temporal regions of the brain. In D. H. Pribram & D. E. Broadbent (Eds.), *Biology of memory*. New York: Academic Press.

Minuchin, S. (1974). *Families and family therapy*. Cambridge, MA: Harvard University Press.

Minuchin, S., & Fishman, H. C. (1981). *Family therapy techniques*. Cambridge, MA: Harvard University Press.

Minuchin, S., Rosman, B., & Baker, L. (1978). *Psychosomatic families*. Cambridge, MA: Harvard University Press.

Mirsky, A. F., & Duncan, C. C. (1986). Etiology and expression of schizophrenia: Neurobiological and psychosocial factors. *Annual Review of Psychology, 37*, 291–319.

Mirsky, A. F., & Quinn, O. W. (1988). The Genain quadruplets. *Schizophrenia Bulletin, 14*, 595–612.

Mischel, W. (1973). Toward a social learning reconceptualization of personality. *Psychological Review, 80*, 252–283.

Mitchell, J. E., & Eckert, E. D. (1987). Scope and significance of eating disorders. *Journal of Consulting and Clinical Psychology, 55*, 628–634.

Mitchell, J. E., Hatsukami, D., Eckert, E. D., & Pyle, R. L. (1985). Characteristics of 275 patients with bulimia. *American Journal of Psychiatry, 142*, 482–485.

Mitchell, J. E., Pyle, R. L., Eckert, E. D., Hatsukami, D., Pomeroy, C., & Zimmerman, R. (1990). A comparison study of antidepressants and structured intensive group psychotherapy in the treatment of bulimia nervosa. *Archives of General Psychiatry, 47*, 149–157.

Modell, J. G., Mountz, J. M., Curtis, G. C., & Greden, J. F. (1989). Neurophysiologic dysfunction in basal ganglia/limbic striatal and thalamocortical circuits as pathogenic mechanisms of obsessive-compulsive disorder. *Journal of Neuropsychiatry, 1*, 27–36.

Mohs, R. C., Breitner, J. C. S., Silverman, J. M., & Davis, K. L. (1987). Alzheimer's disease: Morbid risk among first-degree relatives. *Archives of General Psychiatry, 44*, 405–408.

Monahan, J. (1981). *The clinical prediction of violent behavior*. Rockville, MD: National Institute of Mental Health.

Money, J. (1987). Sin, sickness, or status? Homosexual gender identity and psychoneuroimmunology. *American Psychologist, 42*, 384–399.

Monti, P. M., Abrams, D. B., Kadden, R. M., & Cooney, N. L. (1989). *Treating alcohol dependence: A coping skills training guide*. New York: Guilford Press.

Morey, L. (1988). The categorical representation of personality disorders: A cluster analysis of DSM-III-R personality features. *Journal of Abnormal Psychology, 97*, 314–321.

Morris, J. (1974). *Conundrum*. New York: Signet.

Morris, R. J., & McReynolds, R. A. (1986). Behavior modification with special needs children: A review. In R. J. Morris & B. Blatt (Eds.), *Special education: Research and trends*. New York: Pergamon Press.

Morrison, J. (1989). Childhood sexual histories of women with somatization disorder. *American Journal of Psychiatry, 146*, 249–243.

Moses, S. (1991a). Rape prevention must involve men. *American Psychological Association Monitor, 22*, 35–36.

Moses, S. (1991b). Campus crime common, survey shows. *American Psychological Association Monitor, 22*, 35.

Mosher, L., & Keith, S. J. (1980). Psychosocial treatment: Individual, group, family, and community support approaches. *Schizophrenia Bulletin, 6*, 10–41.

Mosher, L. R., & Menn, A. Z. (1978). Community residential treatment for schizophrenia: Two year follow-up. *Hospital and Community Psychiatry, 29*, 715–723.

Mrazek, F. J. (1984). Sexual abuse of children. In B. Lahey & A. E. Kazdin (Eds.), *Advances in child clinical psychology* (Vol. 6). New York: Plenum.

Mueller, J., & Fields, H. L. (1988). Brain and behavior. In H. H. Goldman (Ed.), *Review of general psychiatry* (2nd ed.). Norwalk, CT: Appleton and Lange.

Mueller, J., Kiernan, R. J., & Langston, J. W. (1988). The mental status examination. In H. H. Goldman (Ed.), *Review of general psychiatry* (2nd ed.). Norwalk, CT: Appleton and Lange.

Mumford, D. B., & Whitehouse, A. M. (1988). Increased prevalence of bulimia nervosa among Asian schoolgirls. *British Medical Journal, 297*, 718.

Murray, H. A. (1943). *Thematic apperception test manual.* Cambridge, MA: Harvard University Press.

Murray, R. M., Clifford, C., & Gurlin, H. M. (1983). Twin and adoption studies: How good is the evidence for a genetic role? In M. Galanter (Ed.), *Recent developments in alcoholism* (Vol. 1). New York: Gardner.

Myers, J. K., Lindenthal, J. J., & Pepper, M. P. (1974). Social class, life events, and psychiatric symptoms: A longitudinal study. In B. S. Dohrenwend & B. P. Dohrenwend (Eds.), *Stressful life events: Their nature and effects.* New York: Wiley.

Nadelson, C., & Sauzier, M. (1990). Intervention programs for individual victims and their families. In M. Lystad (Ed.), *Violence in the home: Interdisciplinary perspectives.* New York: Brunner/Mazel.

Nader, K., Pynoos, R., Fairbanks, L., & Frederick, C. (1990). Children's PTSD reactions one year after a sniper attack at their school. *American Journal of Psychiatry, 147*, 1526–1530.

Narayan, S., Moyes, B., & Wolff, S. (1990). Family characteristics of autistic children: A further report. *Journal of Autism and Developmental Disorders, 20*, 523–535.

Nasser, M. (1986). Comparative study of the prevalence of abnormal eating attitudes among Arab female students of both London and Cairo universities. *Psychological Medicine, 16*, 621–625.

Nathan, P. E., & Niaura, R. S. (1985). Behavioral assessment and treatment of alcohlism. In J. H. Mendelson & N. K. Mello (Eds.), *The diagnosis and treatment of alcoholism* (2nd ed.). New York: McGraw-Hill.

Nathan, P. E., & Skinstad, A. H. (1987). Outcomes of treatment for alcohol problems: Current methods, problems and results. *Journal of Consulting and Clinical Psychology, 55*, 332–340.

National Committee on the Prevention of Child Abuse. (1990). Current trends in child abuse reporting and fatalities: The results of the 1990 annual fifty-state survey. Chicago: Author.

National Institute on Drug Abuse. (1988). *National household survey on drug abuse.* Rockville, MD: Author.

National Institute on Drug Abuse. (1990). *Alcohol and health.* Rockville, MD: Author.

National Institutes of Health Consensus Development Conference Statement. (1985). Electroconvulsive therapy. *Consensus Development Conference Statement*, p. 5.

Nauta, W. J. H., & Feirtag, M. (1990). The organization of the brain. In *Readings from Scientific American.* The workings of the brain, development, memory, and perception. San Francisco: Freeman.

Navia, B. A., Jordan, B. D., & Price, R. W. (1986). The AIDS dementia complex: Clinical features. *Annals of Neurology, 19*, 517–524.

Naylor, H. (1980). Reading disability and lateral asymmetry: An information processing analysis. *Psychological Bulletin, 87*, 531–545.

Needles, D. J., & Abramson, L. Y. (1990). Positive life events, attributional style and hopelessness: Testing a model of recovery from depression. *Journal of Abnormal Psychology, 99,* 156-165.

Nemeroff, C. B., Owens, M. J., Bissette, G., Andorn, A. C., & Stanley, M. (1988). Reduced corticotropin releasing factor binding sites in the frontal cortex of suicide victims. *Archives of General Psychiatry, 45,* 577-579.

Newberger, E. H. (1985). The helping hand strikes again: Unintended consequences of child abuse reporting. In E. H. Newberger & R. Bourne (Eds.), *Unhappy families: Clinical and research perspectives in family violence.* Littleton, MA: PSG.

Newsweek, (1981, January 4), p. 26.

New York State Society for the Prevention of Cruelty to Children. (1990). *Professionals' handbook: Identifying and reporting child abuse and neglect.* New York: Author.

Nihira, K. (1978). Factorial descriptions of the AAMD Adaptive Behavior Scale. In W. A. Coulter & H. W. Morrow (Eds.), *Adaptive behavior: Concepts and measurements.* New York: Grune & Stratton.

Nolen-Hoeksema, S. (1987). Sex differences in unipolar depression: Evidence and theory. *Psychological Bulletin, 110,* 259-282.

Norman, K. (1988). Eating disorders. In H. H. Goldman (Ed.), *Review of general psychiatry* (2nd ed.). Norwalk, CT: Appleton and Lange.

Norris, J. (1988). *Serial killers: The growing menace.* New York: Doubleday.

Norris, P. (1985). On the status of biofeedback and clinical practice. *American Psychologist, 41,* 1009-1010.

Novaco, R. (1975). *Anger control: The development and evaluation of an experimental treatment.* Lexington, MA: Heath.

Nunes, E. V., & Rosecan, J. S. (1987). Human neurobiology of cocaine. In H. I. Spitz & J. S. Rosecan (Eds.), *Cocaine abuse: New directions in treatment and research.* New York: Brunner/Mazel.

Obarzanek, E., Lessem, M. D., Goldstein, D. S., & Jimerson, D. C. (1991). Reduced resting metabolic rate in patients with bulimia nervosa. *Archives of General Psychiatry, 48,* 456-462.

Ochitill, H. (1982). Somatoform disorders. In J. H. Greist, J. W. Jefferson, & R. L. Spitzer (Eds.), *Treatment of mental disorders,* New York: Oxford University Press.

O'Farrell, T. (1989). Marital and family therapy in alcoholism treatment. *Journal of Substance Abuse Treatment, 6,* 23-29.

Ogata, S. N., Silk, K. R., Goodrich, S., Lohr, N. E., Westen, D., & Hill, E. M. (1990). Childhood sexual and physical abuse in adult patients with borderline personality disorder. *American Journal of Psychiatry, 147,* 1008-1013.

Oken, D. (1985). Gastrointestinal disorders. In H. I. Kaplan & B. I. Sadock (Eds.), *Comprehensive textbook of psychiatry* (Vol. 2, 4th ed.). Baltimore: Williams & Wilkins.

Oldham, J. M., & Frosch, W. A. (1986). Compulsive personality disorder. In A. M. Cooper, A. J. Frances, & M. H. Sacks (Eds.), *The personality disorders and neuroses.* New York: Basic Books.

O'Leary, A. (1990). Stress, emotion, and human immune function. *Psychological Bulletin, 108,* 363-382.

Olson, D. H., Russell, C. S., & Sprenkle, D. H. (1979). Circumplex model of marital and family systems: 2. Empirical studies and clinical intervention. In J. Vincent (Ed.), *Advances in family interaction, assessment, and theory.* Greenwich, CT: JAI Press.

Olson, R. P. (1987). Definitions of biofeedback. In M. S. Schwartz (Ed.), *Biofeedback: A practitioner's guide.* New York: Guilford Press.

Olson, R. P., & Schwartz, M. S. (1987). An historical perspective in the biofeedback field. In M. S. Schwartz (Ed.), *Biofeedback: A practitioner's guide.* New York: Guilford Press.

Olweus, D. (1979). Stability of aggressive reaction patterns in males: A review. *Psychological Bulletin, 86,* 852-875.

Opler, M. K. (Ed.). (1959). *Culture and mental health.* New York: Macmillan.

Osborne, A. C., & Glaser, F. B. (1985). Evaluating Alcoholics Anonymous. In T. E. Bratter & G. G. Forrest (Eds.), *Alcoholism and substance abuse: Strategies for clinical intervention*. New York: Free Press.

Overman, W., Jr., & Stoudemire, A. (1988). Guidelines for legal and financial counseling of Alzheimer's disease patients and their families. *American Journal of Psychiatry*, *145*, 1495–1500.

Overmier, J. B., & Seligman, M. E. P. (1967). Effects of inescapable shock upon subsequent escape and avoidance learning. *Journal of Comparative and Physiological Psychology*, *89*, 358–367.

Pagelow, M. D. (1988). Marital rape. In V. B. van Hasselt, R. L. Morrison, A. S. Bellack, & M. Hersen (Eds.), *Handbook of family violence*. New York: Plenum.

Papero, D. V. (1983). Family systems theory and therapy. In B. B. Wolman & G. Stricker (Eds.), *Handbook of family and marital therapy*. New York: Plenum.

Patterson, G. R. (1982). *Coercive family processes: A social learning approach to family intervention* (Vol. 3). Eugene, OR: Castalia.

Patterson, G. R. (1986). Performance models for antisocial boys. *American Psychologist*, *41*, 432–444.

Patterson, G. R., DeBaryshe, B. D., & Ramsey, E. (1989). A developmental perspective on antisocial behavior. *American Psychologist*, *44*, 329–335.

Patterson, G. R., Reid, J. B., & Maerov, S. L. (1978). Development of the family interaction coding system. In J. B. Reid (Ed.), *A social learning approach to family intervention, Volume 2: Observation in home settings*. Eugene, OR: Castalia.

Paul, G. L., & Lentz, R. J. (1977). *The psychosocial treatment of the chronic mental patient*. Cambridge, MA: Harvard University Press.

Paul, R. (1987). Natural history. In D. J. Cohen & A. M. Donnellan (Eds.), *Handbook of autism and pervasive developmental disorders*. New York: Plenum.

Pearlson, G. D., Kirn, W. S., Kubos, K. L., Moberg, P. J., Jarayam, G., Bascom, M. J., Chase, G. A., Goldfinger, A. D., & Tune, L. E. (1989). Ventricle–brain ratio, computed tomographic density, and brain area in 50 schizophrenics. *Archives of General Psychiatry*, *46*, 690–697.

Peele, S. (1989). *Diseasing of America: Addiction treatment out of control*. Lexington, MA: Lexington Books.

Pelletier, K. R. (1979). *Holistic medicine: From stress to optimum health*. New York: Delacorte Press.

Penner, L. A., Thompson, L., & Coovert, D. L. (1991). Size overestimation among anorexics: Much ado about very little? *Journal of Abnormal Psychology*, *100*, 90–93.

Pennington, B. F., & Smith, S. D. (1988). Genetic influences on learning disabilities: An update. *Journal of Consulting and Clinical Psychology*, *56*, 817–823.

Perlmutter, B. F. (1987). Personality variables and peer relations of children and adolescents with learning disabilities. In S. J. Ceci (Ed.), *Handbook of cognitive, social and neuropsychological aspects of learning disabilities* (Vol. 1). Hillsdale, NJ: Erlbaum.

Perls, F. S. (1969). *Gestalt therapy verbatim*. Lafayette, CA: Real People Press.

Perry, D. G., Perry, L. C., & Boldizar, J. P. (1990). Learning of aggression. In M. Lewis & S. M. Miller (Eds.), *Handbook of developmental psychopathology*. New York: Plenum.

Perry, J. C. (1985). Depression in borderline personality disorder: Lifetime prevalence at interview and longitudinal course of symptoms. *American Journal of Psychiatry*, *142*, 15–21.

Perry, S. W. (1990). Organic mental disorders caused by HIV: Update on early diagnosis and treatment. *American Journal of Psychiatry*, *147*, 696–710.

Persons, J. B. (1991). Psychotherapy outcome studies do not accurately represent current models of psychotherapy. *American Psychologist*, *46*, 99–106.

Peters, S. D. (1988). Child sexual abuse and later psychological problems. In G. E. Wyatt & G. J. Powell (Eds.), *Lasting effects of child sexual abuse*. Newbury Park, CA: Sage.

Peterson, C., & Seligman, M. E. P. (1987). Explanatory style and illness. *Journal of Personality, 55*, 237–265.

Petrie, C., & Garner, J. (1990). Is violence preventable? In D. J. Besharov (Ed.), *Family violence: Research and public policy issues.* Washington, DC: AEI Press.

Philips, D. P., & Carstensen, L. L. (1986). Clustering of teenage suicides after television news stories about suicide. *New England Journal of Medicine, 315*, 685–689.

Philips, D. P., & Paight, D. J. (1987). The impact of television movies about suicide. *New England Journal of Medicine, 317*, 809–811.

Phillips, K. A., Gunderson, J. G., Hirschfeld, R. M. A., & Smith, L. E. (1990). A review of the depressive personality. *American Journal of Psychiatry, 147*, 830–837.

Pickens, R. W., Svikis, D. S., McGue, M., Lykken, D. T., Heston, L. L., & Clayton, P. J. (1991). Heterogeneity in the inheritance of alcoholism: A study of male and female twins. *Archives of General Psychiatry, 48*, 19–28.

Pike, K. M., & Rodin, J. (1991). Mothers, daughters, and disordered eating. *Journal of Abnormal Psychology, 100*, 198–204.

Pinel, P. H. (1806). *A treatise on insanity* (D. D. Davis, Trans.). Sheffield, Eng.: W. Todd.

Pitman, R. K., Altman, B., & Macklin, M. L. (1989). Prevalence of post-traumatic stress disorder in wounded Vietnam veterans. *American Journal of Psychiatry, 146*, 667–669.

Pitts, F. N., Jr., & McClure, J. N., Jr. (1967). Lactate metabolism in anxiety neurosis. *New England Journal of Medicine, 277*, 1328–1336.

Piven, J., Berthier, M. L., Starkstein, S. E., Nehme, E., Pearlson, G., & Folstein, S. (1990). Magnetic resonance imaging in autism: Evidence for a defect in cerebral cortical development. *American Journal of Psychiatry, 147*, 734–739.

Piven, J., Tsai, G., Nehme, E., Coyle, J. T., Chase, G. A., & Folstein, S. E. (1991). Platelet serotonin, a possible marker for familial autism. *Journal of Autism and Developmental Disorders, 21*, 51–59.

Pliszka, S. R. (1987). Tricyclic antidepressants in the treatment of children with attention deficit disorder. *Journal of the American Academy of Child and Adolescent Psychiatry, 26*, 127–132.

Plomin, R., DeFries, J. C., & McClearn, G. E. (1980). *Behavioral genetics: A primer.* San Francisco: Freeman.

Plomin, R., Nitz, K., & Rave, D. C. (1990). Behavioral genetics and aggressive behavior in childhood. In M. Lewis & S. M. Miller (Eds.), *Handbook of developmental psychopathology.* New York: Plenum.

Polich, J. M., Armor, D. J., & Braiker, H. B. (1981). *The course of alcoholism: Four years after treatment.* New York: Wiley.

Polivy, J., Heatherton, T. F., & Herman, C. P. (1988). Self-esteem, restraint, and eating behavior. *Journal of Abnormal Psychology, 97*, 354–356.

Pollard, C. A., Pollard, H. J., & Corn, K. J. (1989). Panic onset and major life events in the lives of agoraphobics: A test of contiguity. *Journal of Abnormal Psychology, 98*, 318–321.

Pope, H. G., Hudson, J. I., & Jonas, J. M. (1983). Bulimia treated with imipramine: A placebo-controlled double-blind study. *American Journal of Psychiatry, 140*, 554–558.

Pope, H. G., McElroy, S. L., Keck, P. E., & Hudson, J. I. (1991). Valproate in the treatment of acute mania: A placebo controlled study. *Archives of General Psychiatry, 48*, 62–68.

Pope, K. S., Keith-Spiegel, P., & Tabachnick, B. G. (1986). Sexual attraction to clients: The human therapist and the (sometimes) inhuman training system. *American Psychologist, 41*, 147–158.

Powers, P. S., Schulman, R. G., Gleghorn, A. A., & Prange, M. E. (1987). Perceptual and cognitive abnormalities in bulimia. *American Journal of Psychiatry, 144*, 1456–1460.

Prentky, R. A., Burgess, A. W., Rokous, F., Lee, A., Hartman, C., Ressler, R., & Douglas,

J. (1989). The presumptive role of fantasy in serial sexual homicide. *American Journal of Psychiatry, 146*, 887–891.

Price, R. A., Cadoret, R. J., Stunkard, A. J., & Croughton, E. (1987). Genetic contributions to human fatness: An adoption study. *American Journal of Psychiatry, 144*, 1003–1008.

Prien, R. F., & Gelenberg, A. J. (1989). Alternatives to lithium for preventive treatment of bipolar disorder. *American Journal of Psychiatry, 146*, 840–848.

Prochaska, J. O. (1984). *Systems of psychotherapy.* Chicago: Dorsey.

Purcell, S. D. (1988a). Somatoform disorders. In H. H. Goldman (Ed.), *Review of general psychiatry* (2nd ed.). Norwalk, CT: Appleton and Lange.

Purcell, S. D. (1988b). Dissociative disorders. In H. H. Goldman (Ed.), *Review of general psychiatry* (2nd ed.). Norwalk, CT: Appleton and Lange.

Pynoos, R. S., Frederick, C., Nader, K., Arroyo, W., Steinberg, A., Eith, S., Nunez, F., & Fairbanks, L. (1987). Life threat and posttraumatic stress disorder in school age children. *Archives of General Psychiatry, 44*, 1057–1063.

Quay, H. C. (1986a). Conduct disorders. In H. C. Quay & J. S. Werry (Eds.), *Psychopathological disorders of childhood* (3rd ed.). New York: Wiley.

Quay, H. C. (1986b). Residential treatment. In H. C. Quay & J. S. Werry (Eds.), *Psychopathological disorders of childhood* (3rd ed.). New York: Wiley.

Rabkin, J. G. (1980). Stressful life events and schizophrenia: A review of the literature. *Psychological Bulletin, 87*, 408–425.

Rajfer, J., Aronson, W. J., Bush, P. A., Dorey, F. J., & Ignarro, L. J. (1992). Nitric oxide as a mediator of relaxation of the corpus cavernosum in response to noradrenergic, noncholinergic, neurotransmission. *New England Journal of Medicine, 326*, 90–94.

Rapoport, J. L., & Kruesi, M. J. P. (1985). Organic therapies. In H. I. Kaplan & B. J. Sadock (Eds.), *Comprehensive textbook of psychiatry, IV* (Vol. 2). Baltimore: Williams & Wilkins.

Raz, S., & Raz, N. (1990). Structural brain abnormalities in the major psychoses: A quantitative review of the evidence from computerized imaging. *Psychological Bulletin, 108*, 93–108.

Redmond, D. E. (1985). Neurochemical basis for anxiety and the anxiety disorders: Evidence from drugs which decrease human fear or anxiety. In A. H. Tuma & J. D. Maser (Eds.), *Anxiety and the anxiety disorders.* Hillsdale, NJ: Erlbaum.

Redner, R., Snellman, L., & Davidson, W. S. (1983). Juvenile delinquency. In R. J. Morris & T. R. Kratchowill (Eds.), *The practice of child therapy.* New York: Pergamon Press.

Regier, D. A., Boyd, J. H., Burke, J. D., Rae, D. S., Myers, J. K., Kramer, M., Robins, L. N., George, L. K., Karno, M., & Locke, B. Z. (1988). One-month prevalence of mental disorders in the United States. *Archives of General Psychiatry, 45*, 977–986.

Regier, D. A., Farmer, M. E., Rae, D. S., Locke, B. Z., Keith, S. J., Judd, L. L., & Goodwin, F. K. (1990). Comorbidity of mental disorders with alcohol and other drug abuse: Results from the epidemiological catchment area (ECA) study. *Journal of the American Medical Association, 264*, 2511–2518.

Regier, D. A., Hirschfeld, R. M. A., Goodwin, F. K., Burke, J. D., Lazar, J. B., & Judd, L. L. (1988). The NIMH depression awareness recognition and treatment program: Structure, aims, and scientific basis. *American Journal of Psychiatry, 145*, 1351–1357.

Reich, W. (1972). *Character analysis.* New York: Farrar, Straus, & Giroux. (Original publication 1933)

Reid, W. H. (1986). Antisocial personality. In A. M. Cooper, A. J. Frances, & M. Sacks (Eds.), *The personality disorders and neuroses.* New York: Basic Books.

Reiser, L. W., & Reiser, M. F. (1985). Endocrine disorders. In H. I. Kaplan & B. J. Sadock (Eds.), *Comprehensive textbook of psychiatry* (Vol. 2, 4th ed.). Baltimore: Williams & Wilkins.

Reiss, S. (1985). The mentally retarded, emotionally disturbed adult. In M. Sigman (Ed.), *Children with emotional disorders and developmental disabilities.* New York: Grune & Stratton.

Reitan, R. M., & Wolfson, D. (1985). *The Halstead-Reitan neuropsychological test battery: Theory and clinical interpretation.* Tucson, AZ: Neuropsychologists Press.

Repucci, N. D., & Haugaard, J. J. (1989). Prevention of child sexual abuse: Myth or reality. *American Psychologist, 44,* 1266–1275.

Reus, V. I. (1988). Affective disorders. In H. H. Goldman (Ed.), *Review of general psychiatry* (2nd ed.). Norwalk, CT: Appleton and Lange.

Rice, J., Reich, T., Andreasen, N. C., Endicott, J., Van Eerdewegh, M., Fishman, R., Hirschfeld, R. M. A., & Klerman, G. L. (1987). The familial transmission of bipolar illness. *Archives of General Psychiatry, 44,* 441–447.

Rice, J. K., & Rice, D. G. (1986). *Living through divorce: A developmental approach to divorce therapy.* New York: Guilford Press.

Rich, C. L., Ricketts, J. E., Fowler, R. C., & Young, D. (1988). Some differences between men and women who commit suicide. *American Journal of Psychiatry, 145,* 718–722.

Riddle, M. A. (1987). Individual and parental psychotherapy in autism. In D. J. Cohen & A. M. Donnellan (Eds.), *Handbook of autism and pervasive developmental disorders.* New York: Wiley.

Rie, H. E. (1980). Definitional problems. In H. E. Rie & E. D. Rie (Eds.), *Handbook of minimal brain dysfunction: A critical review.* New York: Wiley.

Rimm, D. C., & Masters, J. C. (1979). *Behavior therapy: Techniques and empirical findings* (2nd ed.). New York: Academic Press.

Ritvo, E. R., Freeman, B. J., Mason-Brothers, A., Mo, A., & Ritvo, A. M. (1985). Concordance for the syndrome of autism in 40 pairs of afflicted twins. *American Journal of Psychiatry, 142,* 74–77.

Ritvo, E. R., Mason-Brothers, A., Freeman, B. J., Pingree, C., Jenson, W. R., McMahon, W. M., Petersen, P. B., Jorde, L. B., Mo, A., & Ritvo, A. (1990). The UCLA-University of Utah epidemiologic survey of autism: The etiologic role of rare diseases. *American Journal of Psychiatry, 147,* 1614–1621.

Roazen, P. (1976). *Freud and his followers.* New York: New American Library.

Roberts, A. H. (1985). Biofeedback: Research, training, and clinical roles. *American Psychologist, 40,* 938–941.

Roberts, L. (1988). Vietnam's psychological toll. *Science, 241,* 159–161.

Roberts, R. N., Wasik, B. H., Costo, G., & Ramey, C. T. (1991). Family support in the home: Programs, policy, and social change. *American Psychologist, 46,* 131–137.

Roberts, S. B., Savage, J., Coward, W. A., Chew, B., & Lucas, A. (1988). Energy expenditure and intake in infants born to lean and overweight mothers. *New England Journal of Medicine, 318,* 461–466.

Robertson, J. R., Bucknall, A. B. V., Skidmore, C. A., Roberts, J. J. K., & Smith, J. H. (1989). Remission and relapse in heroin users and implications for management: Treatment control or risk reduction. *International Journal of the Addictions, 24,* 229–246.

Robins, E. (1985). Psychiatric emergencies. In H. I. Kaplan & B. J. Sadock (Eds.), *Comprehensive textbook of psychiatry, IV.* Baltimore: Williams & Wilkins.

Robins, L. N. (1966). *Deviant children grown up: A sociological and psychiatric study of sociopathic personality.* Baltimore: Williams & Wilkins.

Robins, L. N., Helzer, J. E., Croughan, J., & Ratcliff, K. S. (1981). NIMH diagnostic interview schedule. *Archives of General Psychiatry, 38,* 381–389.

Robins, L. N., & Smith, E. M. (1980). Longitudinal studies of alcohol and drug problems: Sex differences. In O. J. Kalant (Ed.), *Research advances in alcohol and drug problems: Alcohol and drug problems in women.* New York: Plenum.

Robinson, L. A., Berman, J. S., & Niemeyer, R. A. (1990). Psychotherapy for the treatment of depression: A comprehensive review of controlled outcome research. *Psychological Bulletin, 108,* 30–49.

Robinson, N. M., & Robinson, H. B. (1976). *The mentally retarded child: A psychological approach.* New York: McGraw-Hill.

Rodin, J. (1986). Aging and health: Effects of the sense of control. *Science, 233,* 1271–1276.

Rodin, J., & Salovey, P. (1989). Health psychology. *Annual Review of Psychology, 40,* 533–579.

Rogers, C. R. (1961). *On becoming a person.* Boston: Houghton Mifflin.

Rogers, C. R., Gendlin, E. G., Kiesler, D. J., & Truax, C. B. (Eds.). (1967). *The therapeutic relationship and its impact: A study of psychotherapy with schizophrenics.* Madison: University of Wisconsin Press.

Rogers, C. R., & Sanford, R. C. (1985). Client-centered psychotherapy. In H. I. Kaplan & B. J. Sadock (Eds.), *Comprehensive textbook of psychiatry* (Vol. 2, 4th ed.). Baltimore: Williams & Wilkins.

Rogers, R. (1987). APA's position on the insanity defense: Empiricism versus emotionalism. *American Psychologist, 42,* 846–848.

Rohr, J. M., Skowland, S. W., & Martin, T. E. (1989). Withdrawal sequelae to cannabis use. *The International Journal of the Addictions, 24,* 627–631.

Romme, M. A. J., & Escher, A. D. M. A. C. (1989). Hearing voices. *Schizophrenia Bulletin, 15,* 209–215.

Rorschach, H. (1942). *Psychodiagnostics: A diagnostic test based on perception* (P. Lemkau & B. Kronenberg, Trans.). Orlando, FL: Grune & Stratton.

Rose, D. S. (1986). "Worse than death": Psychodynamics of rape victims and the need for psychotherapy. *American Journal of Psychiatry, 143,* 817–824.

Rose, R. J., & Chesney, M. A. (1986). Cardiovascular stress reactivity: A behavior genetic perspective. *Behavior Therapy, 17,* 314–323.

Rosecan, J. S. & Nunes, E. V. (1987). Pharmacological management of cocaine abuse. In H. I. Spitz & J. S. Rosecan (Eds.), *Cocaine abuse: New directions in treatment and research.* New York: Brunner/Mazel.

Rosecan, J. S., & Spitz, H. I. (1987). Cocaine reconceptualized: Historical overview. In H. I. Spitz & J. S. Rosecan (Eds.), *Cocaine abuse: New directions in treatment and research.* New York: Brunner/Mazel.

Rosenbaum, A., & Hoge, S. K. (1989). Head injury and marital aggression. *American Journal of Psychiatry, 146,* 1048–1051.

Rosenhan, D. L. (1973). On being sane in insane places. *Science, 179,* 250–258.

Rosenman, R. H. (1978). The interview method of assessment of the coronary-prone behavior pattern. In T. M. Dembroski, S. M. Weiss, J. L. Shields, S. G. Haynes, & M. Feinleib (Eds.), *Coronary-prone behavior.* New York: Springer-Verlag.

Rosenstein, M. J., Milazzo-Sayre, L. J., & Manderscheid, R. W. (1989). Care of persons with schizophrenia: A statistical profile. *Schizophrenia Bulletin, 15,* 45–58.

Rosenthal, D. (Ed.). (1963). *The Genain quadruplets.* New York: Basic Books.

Rosenthal, D. H. (1970). *Genetic theory and abnormal behavior.* New York: McGraw-Hill.

Rosenzweig, M. R., & Leiman, A. L. (1989). *Physiological psychology* (2nd ed.). New York: Random House.

Ross, C. A., Miller, S. D., Reagor, P., Jonson, L., Fraser, G. A., & Anderson, G. (1990). Structured interview data on 102 cases of multiple personality disorder from four centers. *American Journal of Psychiatry, 147,* 596–601.

Ross, D. M., & Ross, S. A. (1976). *Hyperactivity: Research, theory, and action.* New York: Wiley.

Ross, R. J., Ball, W. A., Sullivan, K. A., & Caroff, S. N. (1989). Sleep disturbance as the hallmark of post-traumatic stress disorder. *American Journal of Psychiatry, 146,* 697–707.

Rossi, E. L. (Ed.). (1980). *The collected papers of Milton H. Erickson* (Vols. I–IV). New York: Irvington.

Rossi, P. H. (1990). The old homeless and the new homelessness in historical perspective. *American Psychologist, 45,* 954–959.

Rounsaville, B. J., Kosten, T. R., Weissman, M. M., Prusoff, B., Pauls, D., Anton, S. F., & Merikangas, K. (1991). Psychiatric disorders in relatives of probands with opiate addiction. *Archives of General Psychiatry, 48,* 33–42.

Rowe, C. J. (1984). *An outline of psychiatry.* Dubuque, IA: Wm. C. Brown.

Roy, A., Adinoff, B., Roerhich, L., Lamparski, D., Custer, R., Lorenz, V., Barbaccia, M., Guidotti, A., Costa, E., & Linniola, M. (1988). Pathological gambling: A psychobiological study. *American Journal of Psychiatry, 45,* 369–373.

Roy, H., Segal, N. L., Cantewell, B. S., & Robinette, C. D. (1991). Suicide in twins. *Archives of General Psychiatry, 48,* 29–32.

Ruderman, A. J. (1985). Dysphoric mood and overeating: A test of restraint theory's disinhibition hypothesis. *Journal of Abnormal Psychology, 94,* 78–85.

Ruderman, A. J. (1986). Dietary restraint: A theoretical and empirical review. *Psychological Bulletin, 99,* 247–262.

Russell, G. (1979). Bulimia nervosa: An ominous variant of anorexia nervosa. *Psychological Medicine, 9,* 429–448.

Russell, G. F. M., Zmuckler, G. I., Dare, C., & Eisler, I. (1987). An evaluation of family therapy in anorexia nervosa and bulimia nervosa. *Archives of General Psychiatry, 44,* 1047–1056.

Rutter, M. (1985). Infantile autism and other pervasive developmental disorders. In M. Rutter & L. Hersov (Eds.), *Child and adolescent psychiatry: Modern approaches.* London: Blackwell.

Rutter, M. (1987). Temperament, personality, and personality disorders. *British Journal of Psychiatry, 150,* 443–458.

Ryan, N. D., Puig-Antich, J., Ambrosini, P., Rabinovich, H., Robinson, D., Nelson, B., Iyengar, S., & Twomey, J. (1987). The clinical picture of major depression in children and adolescents. *Archives of General Psychiatry, 44,* 854–861.

Sachar, E. J. (Ed.). (1976). *Hormones, behavior and psychopathology.* New York: Raven Press.

Sacks, O. (1985). *The man who mistook his wife for a hat.* New York: Harper & Row.

Sadock, V. (1985). Psychosexual dysfunctions and treatment. In H. I. Kaplan & B. J. Sadock (Eds.), *Comprehensive textbook of psychiatry* (Vol. 1, 4th ed.). Baltimore: Williams & Wilkins.

St. George-Hyslop, P. H., Tanzi, R. E., Polinsky, R. J., Haines, J. H., Nee, L., Watkins, P. C., Myers, R. H., Feldman, R. G., Pollen, D., Drachman, D., Growden, J., Bruni, A., Foncin, J. F., Salmon, D., Frommelt, P., Amaducci, L., Sorbi, S., Piacentini, S., Stewart, G. D., Hobbs, W. J., Conneally, P. M., & Gusella, J. F. (1987). The genetic defect causing familial Alzheimer's disease maps on chromosome 21. *Science, 235,* 885–890.

Sameroff, A., Seifer, R., Zax, M., & Barocas, R. (1987). Early indicators of developmental risk: The Rochester longitudinal study. *Schizophrenia Bulletin, 13,* 383–394.

Sanders, B., & Giolas, M. H. (1991). Dissociation and childhood trauma in psychologically disturbed adolescents. *American Journal of Psychiatry, 148,* 50–54.

Sanderson, W. C., Rapee, R. M., & Barlow, D. W. (1989). The influence of an illusion of control on panic attacks induced via inhalation of 5.5% carbon dioxide enriched air. *Archives of General Psychiatry, 46,* 165–169.

Sarrell, D. M., & Masters, W. H. (1982). Sexual molestation of men by women. *Archives of Sexual Behavior, 11,* 117–131.

Saxe, L., Cross, T., & Silverman, N. (1988). Children's mental health: The gap between what we know and what we do. *American Psychologist, 43,* 800–807.

Saxe, L., Dougherty, D., & Cross, T. (1985). The scientific validity of polygraph testing. *American Psychologist, 40,* 355–366.

Saxe, L., Dougherty, D., & Esty, K. (1985). The effectiveness and cost of alcoholism treatment: A public policy perspective. In J. H. Mendelson & N. K. Mello (Eds.), *The diagnosis and treatment of alcoholism* (2nd ed.). New York: McGraw-Hill.

Schachter, S. (1982). Recidivism and self-cure of smoking and obesity. *American Psychologist, 37,* 436–444.

Schachter, S., Friedman, L., & Handler, J. (1974). Who eats with chopsticks. In S. Schachter & J. Rodin (Eds.), *Obese humans and rats*. Washington, DC: Erlbaum.

Schachter, S., & Rodin, J. (1974). *Obese humans and rats*. Washington, DC: Erlbaum.

Schafer, R. (1983). *The analytic attitude*. New York: Basic Books.

Scheff, T. J. (1966). *Being mentally ill: A sociological theory*. Chicago: Aldine.

Schildkraut, J. J. (1965). The catecholamine hypothesis of affective disorders: A review of supporting evidence. *American Journal of Psychiatry, 122*, 509–522.

Schildkraut, J. J., Green, A. I., & Mooney, J. J. (1985). Affective disorders: Biochemical aspects. In H. I. Kaplan & B. J. Sadock (Eds.), *Comprehensive textbook of psychiatry, IV*. Baltimore: Williams & Wilkins.

Schleisser-Carter, B., Hamilton, S. A., O'Neill, P. M., Lydiard, R. B., & Malcolm, R. (1989). Depression and bulimia: The link between depression and bulimic cognitions. *Journal of Abnormal Psychology, 98*, 322–325.

Schmaling, K. B., & Jacobsen, N. S. (1990). Marital interaction and depression. *Journal of Abnormal Psychology, 99*, 229–236.

Schneider, A. M., & Tarshis, B. (1986). *An introduction to physiological psychology* (3rd ed.). New York: Random House.

Schonover, S. C. (1983). The practice of pharmacotherapy. In E. L. Bassuk & A. J. Gelenberg (Eds.), *The practitioner's guide to psychoactive drugs* (2nd ed.). New York: Plenum.

Schreiber, F. R. (1984). *The shoemaker: The anatomy of a psychotic*. New York: Signet.

Schreibman, L., Charlop, M. H., & Britten, K. R. (1983). Childhood autism. In R. J. Morris & T. R. Kratchowill (Eds.), *The practice of child therapy*. New York: Pergamon Press.

Schuckit, M. A. (1987). Biological vulnerability to alcoholism. *Journal of Consulting and Clinical Psychology, 55*, 301–309.

Schuerger, J. M. (1986). Personality assessment by objective tests. In R. B. Cattell & R. C. Johnson, *Functional psychological testing*. New York: Brunner/Mazel.

Schulz, C. G. (1985). Schizophrenia: Individual psychotherapy. In H. I. Kaplan & B. J. Sadock (Eds.), *Comprehensive textbook of psychiatry* (Vol. 1, 4th ed.). Baltimore: Williams & Wilkins.

Schwab, J. J., & Schwab, M. E. (1978). *Sociocultural roots of mental illness: An epidemiological study*. New York: Plenum.

Schwartz, J. L. (1985). *Review and evaluation of smoking cessation methods: The United States and Canada 1978–1985*. U.S. Department of Health and Human Services, National Institutes of Health, NIH Publ. No. 87-2940. Washington, DC: U.S. Government Printing Office.

Schwartz, M. S. (1987). Evaluating research in clinical biofeedback: Caveat emptor. In M. S. Schwartz (Ed.), *Biofeedback: A practitioner's guide*. New York: Guilford Press.

Scientologists fail to persuade FDA on Prozac. (1991, August 2). *The Wall Street Journal*.

Scott, K. G., & Carran, D. T. (1987). The epidemiology and prevention of mental retardation. *American Psychologist, 42*, 801–804.

Scovern, A. W., & Kilmann, P. R. (1980). Status of electroconvulsive therapy: Review of the outcome literature. *Psychological Bulletin, 87*, 260–303.

Selkoe, D. J., Bell, D. S., Podlisny, M. B., Price, D. L., & Cork, L. C. (1987). Conservation of brain amyloid proteins in aged mammals and humans with Alzheimer's disease. *Science, 235*, 873–877.

Selye, H. (1964). *From dream to discovery: On being a scientist*. New York: McGraw-Hill.

Selye, H. (1976). *The stress of life*. New York: McGraw-Hill.

Searles, J. S. (1988). The role of genetics in the pathogenesis of alcoholism. *Journal of Abnormal Psychology, 97*, 153–167.

Sechehaye, M. (1951). *Autobiography of a schizophrenic girl*. New York: Grune & Stratton.

Sedlak, A. J. (1988). Prevention of wife abuse. In V. B. van Hasselt, R. L. Morrison, A. S. Bellack, & M. Hersen (Eds.), *Handbook of family violence*. New York: Plenum.

Semrud-Clikeman, M., & Hynd, G. (1990). Right hemispheric dysfunction in nonverbal learning disabilities: Social, academic, and adaptive functioning in adults and children. *Psychological Bulletin, 107,* 196–209.

Shader, R. I., Scharfman, E. L., & Dreyfuss, D. A. (1986). A biological model for selected personality disorders. In A. M. Cooper, A. J. Frances, & M. H. Sacks (Eds.), *The personality disorders and neuroses*. New York: Basic Books.

Shadish, W. R., Lurigio, A. J., & Lewis, D. A. (1989). After deinstitutionalization: The present and future of mental health long-term care policy. *Journal of Social Issues, 45,* 1–15.

Shaffi, M., Carigan, S., Whittinghill, J. R., & Derrick, A. (1985). Psychological autopsy and completed suicide in children and adolescents. *American Journal of Psychiatry, 142,* 1061–1064.

Shapiro, D. A. (1985). Recent applications of meta-analysis in clinical research. *Clinical Psychological Review, 5,* 13–34.

Shedler, J., & Block, J. (1990). Adolescent drug use and psychological health: A longitudinal inquiry. *American Psychologist, 45,* 612–630.

Sheehy, S. (1983). *Is there no place on earth for me?* New York: Vintage.

Shelton, R. C., Karson, C. N., Doran, A. R., Pickar, D., Bigelow, L. B., & Weinberger, D. R. (1988). Cerebral structural pathology in schizophrenia: Evidence for a selective prefrontal cortical deficit. *American Journal of Psychiatry, 145,* 154–163.

Sherman, L. W., & Berk, R. A. (1984). The specific deterrent effects of arrest for domestic assault. *American Sociological Review, 49,* 261–272.

Sherrington, R., Bynjolfsson, J., Petursson, H., Potter, M., Dudleston, K., Barraclough, B., Wasmuth, J., Dobbs, M., & Gurling, H. (1988). Localization of a susceptibility locus for schizophrenia on chromosome 5. *Nature, 336,* 164–167.

Shlien, J. M., & Zimring, F. M. (1970). Research directives and methods in client-centered therapy. In J. T. Hart & T. M. Tomlinson (Eds.), *New directions in client-centered therapy*. Boston: Houghton Mifflin.

Siever, L. J., & Davis, K. L. (1985). Overview: Toward a dysregulation hypothesis of depression. *American Journal of Psychiatry, 142,* 1017–1031.

Siever, L. J., & Davis, K. L. (1991). A psychobiological perspective on the personality disorders. *American Journal of Psychiatry, 148,* 1647–1658.

Siever, L. J., & Kendler, K. S. (1986). Schizoid, schizotypal and paranoid personality disorders. In A. M. Cooper, A. J. Frances, & M. H. Sacks (Eds.), *The personality disorders and neuroses*. New York: Basic Books.

Silverman, A. J. (1985). Rheumatoid arthritis. In H. I. Kaplan & B. I. Sadock (Eds.), *Comprehensive textbook of psychiatry* (Vol. 2, 4th ed.). Baltimore: Williams & Wilkins.

Silverman, J. M., Mohs, R. C., Davidson, M., Losonczy, M. F., Keefe, R. S. E., Breitner, J. C. S., Sorokin, J. E., & Davis, K. L. (1987). Familial schizophrenia and treatment response. *American Journal of Psychiatry, 144,* 1271–1276.

Silverton, L., & Mednick, S. A. (1984). Class drift and schizophrenia. *Acta Psychiatrica Scandinavica, 70,* 304–309.

Simpson, D. D., Joe, G. W., & Bracy, S. A. (1982). Six year follow-up of opioid addicts after admission to treatment. *Archives of General Psychiatry, 39,* 1318.

Simpson, D. D., Joe, G. W., Lehman, W. E. K., & Sells, S. B. (1986). Addiction careers: Etiology, treatment, and 12-year follow-up outcomes. *Journal of Drug Issues, 16,* 107–121.

Simpson, G. M., & May, P. R. A. (1985). Schizophrenia: Somatic treatment. In H. I. Kaplan & B. J. Sadock (Eds.), *Comprehensive textbook of psychiatry* (Vol. 1, 4th ed.). Baltimore: Williams & Wilkins.

Skinner, B. F. (1969). *Contingencies of reinforcement: A theoretical analysis*. New York: Appleton.

Skinner, B. F. (1974). *About behaviorism*. New York: Knopf.

Smith, D. D., & Robinson, S. (1986). Educating the learning disabled. In R. J. Morris & B. Blatt (Eds.), *Special education: Research and trends*. New York: Pergamon Press.

Smith, E. M., North, C. S., McCool, R. E., & Shea, J. M. (1990). Acute postdisaster psychiatric disorders: Identification of persons at risk. *American Journal of Psychiatry, 147*, 202–206.

Smith, L. W., & Dimsdale, J. E. (1989). Postcardiotomy delirium: Conclusions after 25 years. *American Journal of Psychiatry, 146*, 453–458.

Smith, W. (1989). *A profile of health and disease in America: Mental illness and substance abuse*. New York: Facts on File.

Snyder, S. H. (1976). The dopamine hypothesis in schizophrenia: Focus on the dopamine receptors. *American Journal of Psychiatry, 133*, 197–202.

Snyder, S. H. (1985). Drug and neurotransmitter receptors in the brain. In P. H. Abelson, E. Butz, & S. H. Snyder (Eds.), *Neuroscience*. Washington, DC: American Association for the Advancement of Science.

Sobal, J., & Stunkard, A. J. (1989). Socioeconomic status and obesity: A review of the literature. *Psychological Bulletin, 105*, 260–275.

Solanto, M. (1984). Neuropharmacological basis of stimulant drug action in attention deficit disorder with hyperactivity: A review and synthesis. *Psychological Bulletin, 95*, 387–409.

Soloff, P. H., & Millward, J. W. (1983). Psychiatric disorders in the families of borderline patients. *Archives of General Psychiatry, 40*, 37–44.

Solomon, S. (1985). Neurological evaluation. In H. I. Kaplan & B. J. Sadock (Eds.), *Comprehensive textbook of psychiatry* (Vol. 1, 4th ed.). Baltimore: Williams & Wilkins.

Solomon, Z., Kotler, M., & Mikulincer, M. (1988). Combat-related PTSD among second-generation Holocaust survivors. *American Journal of Psychiatry, 145*, 865–868.

Sonkin, D. J., Martin, D., & Walker, L. E. A. (1985). *The male batterer: A treatment approach*. New York: Springer.

Spanos, N. P., Weekes, J. R., & Bertrand, L. D. (1985). Multiple personality: A social psychological perspective. *Journal of Abnormal Psychology, 94*, 362–376.

Sparr, L. F., & Atkinson, R. M. (1986). Posttraumatic stress disorder as an insanity defense: Medicolegal quicksand. *American Journal of Psychiatry, 143*, 608–613.

Spielberger, C. D. (1983). *Manual for the state-trait anxiety inventory*. Palo Alto, CA: Consulting Psychologists Press.

Spielberger, C. D. (1988). *State-trait anger expression inventory manual*. Odessa, FL: Psychological Assessment Resources.

Spielberger, C. D., Jacobs, G., Russel, S., & Crane, R. S. (1983). Assessment of anger: The state-trait anger scale. In J. N. Butcher & C. D. Spielberger (Eds.), *Advances in personality assessment* (Vol. 2). Hillsdale, NJ: Erlbaum.

Spitzer, R. L. (1991). An outsider-insider's views about revising DSM's. *Journal of Abnormal Psychology, 100*, 294–296.

Spitzer, R. L., & Endicott, J. (1978). *Schedule for affective disorders and schizophrenia*. New York: New York Psychiatric Institute, Biometrics Research Division.

Spitzer, R. L., Skodol, A. E., Gibbon, M., & Williams, J. B. W. (1983). *Psychopathology: A case book*. New York: McGraw-Hill.

Spitzer, R. L., & Williams, J. D. W. (1986). *Structured clinical interview—DSM-III-R*. New York: New York Psychiatric Institute, Biometrics Research Division.

Spohn, H. E., & Strauss, M. E. (1989). Relation of neuroleptic and anticholinergic medication to cognitive functions in schizophrenia. *Journal of Abnormal Psychology, 98*, 367–380.

Sprenger, J., & Kramer, H. (1968). *Malleus maleficarum: The hammer of witchcraft* (P. Hughes, Ed.). London: The Folio Society.

Spring, B., Chiodo, J., & Bowen, D. J. (1987). Carbohydrates, tryptophan, and behavior: A methodological review. *Psychological Bulletin, 102*, 234–256.

Srole, L., Langner, T. S., Michael, S. T., Kirkpatrick, P., Opler, M. K., & Rennie, T. A. (1978). *Mental health in the metropolis: The midtown Manhattan study.* New York: New York University Press.

Stampfl, T. G., & Levis, D. J. (1968). Implosive therapy—a behavior therapy? *Behavior Research and Therapy, 6,* 31–36.

Stanton, M. D. (1981). Strategic approaches to family therapy. In A. S. Gurman & D. P. Kniskern (Eds.), *Handbook of family therapy.* New York: Brunner/Mazel.

Starr, R. H. (1988). Physical abuse of children. In V. B. van Hasselt, R. L. Morrison, A. S. Bellack, & M. Hersen (Eds.), *Handbook of family violence.* New York: Plenum.

Steele, C. M., & Josephs, R. A. (1990). Alcohol myopia: Its prized and dangerous effects. *American Psychologist, 45,* 921–933.

Stein, A., Schleifer, S. J., & Keller, S. E. (1985). Immune disorders. In H. I. Kaplan & B. J. Sadock (Eds.), *Comprehensive textbook of psychiatry* (Vol. 2, 4th ed.). Baltimore: Williams & Wilkins.

Stein, J. A., Golding, J. M., Siegel, J. M., Burnam, M. A., & Sorensen, S. B. (1988). Long-term psychological sequelae of child sexual abuse. In G. E. Wyatt & G. J. Powell (Eds.), *Lasting effects of child sexual abuse.* Newbury Park, CA: Sage.

Steinglass, P., Bennett, L. A., Wolin, S. J., & Reiss, D. (1987). *The alcoholic family.* New York: Basic Books.

Steinglass, P., Westab, E., Kaplan De-Nour, A. (1988). Perceived personal networks as mediators of stress reactions. *American Journal of Psychiatry, 145,* 1259–1264.

Steinmetz, S. K. (1990). The violent family. In M. Lystad (Ed.), *Violence in the home: Interdisciplinary perspectives.* New York: Brunner/Mazel.

Steinmetez, S. K., & Lucca, J. S. (1988). Husband battering. In V. B. van Hasselt, R. L. Morrison, A. S. Bellack, & M. Hersen (Eds.), *Handbook of family violence.* New York: Plenum.

Stephenson, F. D. (Ed.). (1975). *Gestalt therapy primer.* Springfield, IL: Charles C. Thomas.

Stern, J. S., & Lowney, P. (1986). Obesity: The role of physical activity. In K. D. Brownell & P. J. Foreyt (Eds.), *Handbook of eating disorders.* New York: Basic Books.

Stets, J. E. (1988). *Domestic violence and control.* New York: Springer.

Stiles, W. B., Shapiro, D. A., & Elliot, R. (1986). Are all psychotherapies equivalent? *American Psychologist, 41,* 165–180.

Stoller, R. J. (1985). Gender identity disorders in children and adults. In H. I. Kaplan & B. J. Sadock (Eds.), *Comprehensive textbook of psychiatry* (Vol. 1, 4th ed.). Baltimore: Williams & Wilkins.

Stone, A. A., & Neale, J. M. (1982). Development of a methodology for assessing daily experiences. In A. Baum & J. Singer (Eds.), *Environment and health.* Hillsdale, NJ: Erlbaum.

Stone, M. H. (1986a). Borderline personality disorder. In A. M. Cooper, A. J. Frances, & M. H. Sacks (Eds.), *The personality disorders and neuroses.* New York: Basic Books.

Stone, M. H. (1986b). Exploratory psychotherapy in schizophrenic-spectrum patients: A re-evaluation in the light of long-term follow-up of schizophrenic and borderline patients. *Bulletin of the Menninger Clinic, 50,* 287–306.

Strachan, A. M. (1986). Family intervention for the rehabilitation of schizophrenia: Toward protection and coping. *Schizophrenia Bulletin, 12,* 678–698.

Straus, M. A., Gelles, R. J., & Steinmetz, K. (1980). *Behind closed doors: Violence in the American family.* Garden City, NY: Anchor Press.

Strauss, J., & Ryan, R. M. (1987). Autonomy disturbances in subtypes of anorexia nervosa. *Journal of Abnormal Psychology, 96,* 254–258.

Stricker, G. (1991). Ethical concerns in alcohol research. *Journal of Consulting and Clinical Psychology, 59,* 256–257.

Striegel-Moore, R., & Rodin, J. (1986). The influence of psychological variables in obesity. In K. D. Brownell & P. J. Foreyt (Eds.), *Handbook of eating disorders.* New York: Basic Books.

Striegel-Moore, R., Silberstein, L. R., & Rodin, J. (1986). Toward an understanding of the risk factors for bulimia. *American Psychologist, 41*, 246–263.

Strub, R. L., & Black, F. W. (1983). *The mental status examination in neurology.* Philadelphia: F. A. Davis.

Strube, M. J. (1988). The decision to leave an abusive relationship: Empirical evidence and theoretical issues. *Psychological Bulletin, 104*, 236–250.

Stunkard, A. (1986). A tribute to Hilde Bruch. In K. D. Brownell & P. J. Foreyt (Eds.), *Handbook of eating disorders.* New York: Basic Books.

Stunkard, A. J., Foch, T. T., & Hrubek, Z. (1986). A twin study of human obesity. *Journal of the American Medical Association, 256*, 51–54.

Suddath, R. L., Casanova, M. F., Goldberg, T. E., Daniel, D. G., Kelsoe, J. R., & Weinberger, D. R. (1990). Temporal lobe pathology in schizophrenia: A quantitative magnetic resonance imaging study. *American Journal of Psychiatry, 146*, 464–472.

Suddath, R. L., Christinson, G. W., Torrey, E. F., Casanova, M. F., & Weinberger, D. R. (1990). Anatomical abnormalities in the brains of monozygotic twins discordant for schizophrenia. *New England Journal of Medicine, 322*, 789–794.

Sullivan, H. S. (1952). *Schizophrenia as a human process.* New York: Norton.

Sullivan, H. S. (1953). *The interpersonal theory of psychiatry.* New York: Norton.

Susser, E., Struening, E. L., & Conover, S. (1989). Psychiatric problems in homeless men: Lifetime psychosis, substance use, and current distress in new arrivals at New York City shelters. *Archives of General Psychiatry, 46*, 845–850.

Swedo, S. E., Rapoport, J. L., Leonard, H. L., Schapiro, M. B., Rapoport, S. I., & Grady, C. L. (1991). Regional cerebral metabolism of women with trichotillomania. *Archives of General Psychiatry, 48*, 828–833.

Swift, W. J., Andrews, D., & Barklage, N. E. (1986). The relationship between affective disorders and eating disorders: A review of the literature. *American Journal of Psychiatry, 143*, 290–299.

Szasz, T. S. (1974). *The myth of mental illness: Foundations of a theory of personal conduct* (rev. ed.). New York: Harper & Row.

Szasz, T. S. (1986). The case against suicide prevention. *American Psychologist, 41*, 806–812.

Szymanski, L., & Crocker, A. C. (1985). Mental retardation. In H. I. Kaplan & B. J. Sadock (Eds.), *Comprehensive textbook of psychiatry, IV* (Vol. 2). Baltimore: Williams & Wilkins.

Taber, J. I., McCormick, R. A., Russo, A. M., Adkins, B. J., & Ramirez, L. F. (1987). Followup of pathological gambling after treatment. *American Journal of Psychiatry, 144*, 757–761.

Tanzi, R. E., Gusella, J. F., Watkins, P. C., Bruns, G. A. P., St. George-Hyslop, P., Van Keuren, M. L., Patterson, D., Pagan, S., Kurnit, D. M., & Neve, R. L. (1987). Amyloid B protein gene: cDNA, mRNA distribution and genetic linkage near Alzheimer's locus. *Science, 235*, 880–884.

Tariot, P. N., Newhouse, P. A., Mueller, E. A., Mellow, A. M., & Cohen, R. M. (1988). A new scale for the assessment of depressed mood in demented patients. *American Journal of Psychiatry, 145*, 955–959.

Tarnowski, K. J., Prinz, R. J., & Nay, S. M. (1986). Comparative analysis of attentional deficits in hyperactive and learning-disabled children. *Journal of Abnormal Psychology, 95*, 341–345.

Tarter, R. E., & Alterman, A. I. (1988). The neurobehavioral theory of alcoholism etiology. In G. Cludion & D. A. Wilkerson (Eds.), *Etiological theories of alcoholism.* Toronto: Addiction Research Foundation.

Tennant, C. C. (1985). Stress and schizophrenia: A review. *Integrative Psychiatry, 3*, 248–261.

Thaxton, L. (1985). Wife abuse. In L. L'Abate (Ed.), *The handbook of family psychology and therapy* (Vol. II). Homewood, IL: Dorsey Press.

Thoits, P. A. (1986). Social support as coping assistance. *Journal of Consulting and Clinical Psychology, 54,* 416–423.

Thomas, A., & Chess, S. (1977). *Temperament and development.* New York: Brunner/Mazel.

Thomas, A., & Chess, S. (1984). Genesis and evolution of behavioral disorders: From infancy to early adult life. *American Journal of Psychiatry, 141,* 1–9.

Thomason, H. H., & Dilts, S. L. (1991). Opioids. In R. J. Frances & S. I. Miller (Eds.), *Clinical textbook of addictive disorders.* New York: Guilford Press.

Thompson, R. F. (1985). *The brain.* New York: Freeman.

Thompson, T. L. (1985). Headache. In H. I. Kaplan & B. J. Sadock (Eds.), *Comprehensive textbook of psychiatry* (Vol. 2, 4th ed.). Baltimore: Williams & Wilkins.

Thomsen, R. (1975). *Bill W.* New York: Harper & Row.

Thorley, G. (1984). Review of follow-up and follow-back studies of childhood hyperactivity. *Psychological Bulletin, 96,* 116–132.

Tienari, P., Sorri, A., Lahti, I., Naarala, M., Wahlberg, K., Moring, J., Pohjola, J., & Wynne, L. (1987). Genetic and psychosocial factors in schizophrenia: The Finnish Adoptive Family Study. *Schizophrenia Bulletin, 13,* 477–484.

Torrey, E. F. (1974). *The death of psychiatry.* Radnor, PA: Chilton.

Torrey, E. F. (1980). *Schizophrenia and civilization.* New York: Jason Aronson.

Torrey, E. F. (1988a). Stalking the schizovirus. *Schizophrenia Bulletin, 14,* 223–229.

Torrey, E. F. (1988b). *Surviving schizophrenia: A family manual* (rev. ed.). New York: Harper & Row.

Torrey, E. F. (1988c). *Nowhere to go: The tragic odyssey of the homeless mentally ill.* New York: Harper & Row.

Torrey, E. F., & Bowler, A. (1990). Geographical distribution of insanity in America: Evidence for an urban factor. *Schizophrenia Bulletin, 16,* 591–604.

Traicoff, M. E. (1982). Family interventions from women's shelters. In J. C. Hansen (Ed.), *Clinical approaches to family violence.* Rockville, MD: Aspen.

Treffert, D. A. (1988). The idiot savant: A review of the syndrome. *American Journal of Psychiatry, 145,* 563–572.

Treffert, D. A. (1989). *Extraordinary people: Understanding savant syndrome.* New York: Ballantine.

Tross, S., & Hirsch, D. A. (1988). Psychological distress and neuropsychological complications of HIV infection and AIDS. *American Psychologist 43,* 929–934.

Trueman, D. (1984). What are the characteristics of school-phobic children? *Psychological Reports, 54,* 191–202.

Tuma, J. M. (1989). Mental health services for children: The state of the art. *American Psychologist, 44,* 188–199.

Turkat, I. D., & Maisto, S. A. (1985). Personality disorders: Application of the experimental method to the formulation and modification of personality variables. In D. H. Barlow (Ed.), *Clinical handbook of psychological disorders.* New York: Guilford Press.

Turner, S. M., Beidel, D. C., & Costello, A. (1987). Psychopathology in the offspring of anxiety disorders patients. *Journal of Consulting and Clinical Psychology, 55,* 229–235.

Turner, S. M., Beidel, D. C. & Nathan, R. S. (1985). Biological factors in obsessive-compulsive disorders. *Psychological Bulletin, 97,* 430–450.

Turner, S., Calhoun, K. S., & Adams, H. E. (Eds.). (1981). *Handbook of clinical behavior therapy.* New York: Wiley.

Turner, S. M., & Hersen, M. (1981). Disorders of social behavior: A behavioral approach to personality disorders. In S. M. Turner, K. S. Calhoun, & H. E. Adams (Eds.), *Handbook of clinical behavior therapy.* New York: Wiley.

Turner, S. M., Jacob, R. G., Bredel, D. C., & Himmelhoch, J. (1985). Fluoxetine in the treatment of obsessive-compulsive disorder. *Journal of Clinical Psychopharmacology, 5,* 207–212.

Uhde, T. W., Roy-Byrne, P. P., Vittone, B. J., Boulenger, J. P., & Post, R. M. (1985). Phenomenology and neurobiology of panic disorder. In A. H. Tuma & J. D. Maser (Eds.), *Anxiety and the anxiety disorders.* Hillsdale, NJ: Erlbaum.

U.S. Department of Health and Human Services. (1984). The 1984 report of the Joint National Committee on detection, evaluation and treatment of high blood pressure. *National Institute of Health Publications,* No. 84.

U.S. Department of Health and Human Services. (1986). *Smoking and health: A national status report.* Publication No. HHS/PHS/CDC 87-8396. Washington, DC: U.S. Government Printing Office.

U.S. Department of Health and Human Services. (1987). *Report to Congress: Toward a national plan to combat alcohol abuse and alcoholism.* Washington, DC: U.S. Government Printing Office.

U.S. Department of Health and Human Services. (1990). *Alcohol and health.* Rockville, MD: Author.

U.S. Deparment of Justice. (1988). *Drug use and crime.* Rockville, MD: Bureau of Justice Statistics.

Vaillant, G. E. (1983). *The natural history of alcoholism.* Cambridge, MA: Harvard University Press.

Vaillant, G. E., & Perry, J. C. (1985). Personality disorders. In H. I. Kaplan & B. J. Sadock (Eds.), *Comprehensive textbook of psychiatry* (Vol. 2, 4th ed.). Baltimore: Williams & Wilkins.

Valenstein, E. (Ed.). (1980). *The psychosurgery debate: Scientific, legal and ethical perspectives.* San Francisco: Freeman.

Vandenberg, S. G., & Volger, G. P. (1985). Genetic determinants of intelligence. In B. Wolman (Ed.), *Handbook of intelligence: Theories, measurements and applications.* New York: Wiley.

Varley, C. K. (1984). Diet and the behavior of children with attention deficit disorder. *Journal of the American Academy of Child Psychiatry, 23,* 182–185.

Vaughn, C. E., Snyder, K. S., Jones, S., Freeman, W. B., & Falloon, I. R. H. (1984). Family factors in schizophrenic relapse: A California replication of the British research on expressed emotion. *Archives of General Psychiatry, 41,* 1169–1177.

Vincent, J., Varley, C. K., & Leger, P. (1990). Effects of methylphenidate on early adolescent growth. *American Journal of Psychiatry, 147,* 501–502.

Volberg, R. A., & Steadman, H. J. (1988). Refining prevalence estimates of pathological gambling. *American Journal of Psychiatry, 145,* 502–505.

Volberg, R. A., & Steadman, H. J. (1989). Prevalence estimates of pathological gambling in New Jersey and Maryland. *American Journal of Psychiatry, 146,* 1618–1619.

von Bertalanffy, L. (1973). *General system theory: Foundations, development, applications* (rev. ed.). New York: George Braziller.

von Bertalanffy, L. (1974). General system theory and psychiatry. In S. Arieti (Ed.), *American handbook of psychiatry.* New York: Basic Books.

Wakefield, J. C. (1987). Sex bias in the diagnosis of primary orgasmic dysfunction. *American Psychologist, 42,* 464–471.

Walker, L. E. A. (1984). *The battered woman syndrome.* New York: Springer.

Walker, L. E. A. (1990). Psychological causes of family violence. In M. Lystad (Ed.), *Violence in the home: Interdisciplinary perspectives.* New York: Brunner/Mazel.

Wallace, C. J., Boone, S. E., Donahue, C. P., & Foy, D. W. (1985). The chronically mentally disabled: Independent living skills. In D. Barlow (Ed.), *Clinical handbook of psychological disorders.* New York: Guilford Press.

Wallace, C. J., Nelson, C., Liberman, R. P., Atichison, R. A., Lukoff, D., Elder, J. P., & Ferris, C. (1980). A review and critique of social skills training with schizophrenic patients. *Schizophrenia Bulletin, 6,* 42–63.

Wallander, J. L., & Hubert, N. C. (1985). Long-term prognosis for children with attention deficit disorder with hyperactivity (ADD/H). In B. B. Lahey & A. E. Kazdin (Eds.), *Advances in child clinical psychology* (Vol. 8). New York: Plenum.

Wallerstein, J. (1986). Women after divorce: Preliminary report from a ten year follow-up. *American Journal of Orthopsychiatry, 56*, 65–77.

Wallerstein, J. S., & Blakeslee, S. (1989). *Second chances: Men, women and children a decade after divorce.* New York: Ticknor & Fields.

Walsh, B. T., Gladis, M., Roose, S. P., Stewart, J. W., Stetner, F., & Glassman, A. H. (1988). Phenelzine vs. placebo in 50 patients with bulimia. *Archives of General Psychiatry, 45*, 471–475.

Walsh, B. T., Kisseleff, H. R., Cassidy, S. M., & Dantzic, S. (1989). Eating behavior of women with bulimia. *Archives of General Psychiatry, 46*, 54–58.

Wardle, J., & Beales, S. (1988). Control and loss of control over eating: An experimental investigation. *Journal of Abnormal Psychology, 97*, 35–40.

Washton, A. M. (1986). *Cocaine addiction: Treatment, recovery, and relapse prevention.* New York: Norton.

Watson, J. B., & Raynor, R. (1920). Conditioned emotional reactions. *Journal of Experimental Psychology, 3*, 1–14.

Watzlawick, P., & Weakland, J. H. (1977). *The interactional view: Studies at the Mental Research Institute, Palo Alto, 1965–1974.* New York: Norton.

Way, E. L. (1982). History of opiate use in the Orient and the United States. In K. Verebey (Ed.), *Opioids in mental illness: Theories, clinical observation, and treatment possibilities.* New York: *Annals of the New York Academy of Sciences* (Vol. 398).

Wechsler, D. (1981). *Wechsler adult intelligence scale* (rev.). New York: Psychological Corporation.

Weinberger, D. R. (1987). Implications of normal brain development for the pathogenesis of schizophrenia. *Archives of General Psychiatry, 44*, 660–669.

Weiner, H. (1985). Respiratory disorders. In H. I. Kaplan & B. J. Sadock (Eds.), *Comprehensive textbook of psychiatry* (Vol. 2, 4th ed.). Baltimore: Williams & Wilkins.

Weiner, R. D. (1985). Convulsive therapies. In H. I. Kaplan & B. J. Sadock (Eds.), *Comprehensive textbook of psychiatry, IV.* Baltimore: Williams & Wilkins.

Weiner, R. D. (1989). Electroconvulsive therapy. In H. I. Kaplan & B. J. Sadock (Eds.), *Comprehensive textbook of psychiatry* (Vol. 5, 5th ed.). Baltimore: Williams & Wilkins.

Westermeyer, J. (1987). Cultural factors in clinical assessment. *Journal of Consulting and Clinical Psychology, 55*, 471–478.

Weiss, B., Weisz, J. R., & Bromfield, R. (1986). Performance of retarded and nonretarded persons on information-processing tasks: Further tests of the similar structure hypothesis. *Psychological Bulletin, 100*, 157–175.

Weiss, C. J., & Millman, R. B. (1991). Hallucinogens, phencyclidine, marijuana, inhalants. In R. J. Frances & S. I. Miller (Eds.), *Clinical textbook of addictive disorders.* New York: Guilford Press.

Weiss, D.S., & Billings, J. H. (1988). Behavioral medicine techniques. In H. H. Goldman (Ed.), *Review of general psychiatry* (2nd ed.). Norwalk, CT: Appleton and Lange.

Weiss, G., & Hechtman, L. T. (1986). *Hyperactive children grown up: Empirical findings and theoretical considerations.* New York: Guilford Press.

Weiss, J. M. (1977). Psychological and behavioral influences in gastrointestinal lesions in animal models. In J. D. Maser & M. E. P. Seligman (Eds.), *Psychopathology: Experimental methods.* San Francisco: Freeman.

Weiss, R. S. (1979). The emotional impact of marital separation. In G. Levinger & O. C. Moles (Eds.), *Divorce and separation: Context, causes, and consequences.* New York: Basic Books.

Weissman, M. M. (1985). The epidemiology of anxiety disorders: Rates, risks, and familial patterns. In A. H. Tuma & J. D. Maser (Eds.), *Anxiety and the anxiety disorders.* Hillsdale, NJ: Erlbaum.

Weissman, M. M., & Boyd, J. H. (1983). Epidemiology of affective disorders: Rates and risk factors. In L. Grinspoon (Eds.), *Psychiatry update: American Psychiatric Association Annual Review* (Vol. 2). Washington, DC: American Psychiatric Association.

Weissman, M. M., & Boyd, J. H. (1985). Affective disorders: Epidemiology. In H. I. Kaplan & B. J. Sadock (Eds.), *Comprehensive textbook of psychiatry, IV*. Baltimore: Williams & Wilkins.

Weissman, M. M., Leaf, P. J., Bruce, M. L., & Florio, L. (1988). The epidemiology of dysthymia in five communities: Rates, risks, comorbidity and treatment. *American Journal of Psychiatry, 145*, 815–819.

Weisz, J. R., Weiss, B., Alicke, M. D., & Klotze, M. L. (1987). Effectiveness of psychotherapy with children and adolescents: Metaanalysis for clinicians. *Journal of Consulting and Clinical Psychology, 55*, 542–549.

Wekstein, L. (1979). *Handbook of suicidology*. New York: Brunner/Mazel.

Wells, C. E. (1985). Organic mental disorders. In H. I. Kaplan & B. J. Sadock (Eds.), *Comprehensive textbook of psychiatry* (4th ed.). Baltimore: Williams & Wilkins.

Wenar, C. (1990a). Childhood fears and phobias. In M. Lewis & S. M. Miller (Eds.), *Handbook of developmental psychopathology*. New York: Plenum.

Wenar, C. (1990b). *Developmental psychopathology: From infancy through adolescence* (2nd ed.). New York: McGraw-Hill.

Wender, P. H. (1977). The scope and validity of the schizophrenic spectrum concept. In V. M. Rakoff, H. C. Stancer, & H. B. Kedward (Eds.), *Psychiatric diagnosis*. New York: Brunner/Mazel.

Wender, P. H., Kety, S. S., Rosenthal, D., Schulsinger, F., Ortmann, J., & Lunde, I. (1986). Psychiatric disorders in the biological and adoptive families of adopted individuals with affective disorders. *Archives of General Psychiatry, 43*, 923–929.

Werkman, S. L. (1985). Anxiety disorders. In H. I. Kaplan & B. J. Sadock (Eds.), *Comprehensive textbook of psychiatry, IV* (Vol. 2). Baltimore: Williams & Wilkins.

West, M. O., & Prinz, R. J. (1987). Parental alcoholism and childhood psychopathology. *Psychological Bulletin, 102*, 204–218.

Whalen, C. K. (1982). Hyperactivity and psychostimulant treatment. In J. R. Lachenmeyer & M. S. Gibbs (Eds.), *Psychopathology in childhood*. New York: Gardner.

Whalen, C. K., & Henker, B. (1985). The social worlds of hyperactive (ADDH) children. *Clinical Psychology Review, 5*, 447–478.

Whalen, C. K., & Henker, B. (1991). Therapies for hyperactive children: Comparisons, combinations, and compromises. *Journal of Consulting and Clinical Psychology, 59*, 126–137.

Whalen, C. K., Henker, B., & Hinshaw, S. P. (1985). Cognitive-behavioral therapies for hyperactive children: Premises, promises and prospects. *Journal of Abnormal Psychology, 13*, 391–410.

Wheeler, J. R., & Berliner, L. (1988). Treating the effects of sexual abuse on children. In G. E. Wyatt & G. J. Powell (Eds.), *Lasting effects of child sexual abuse*. Newbury Park, CA: Sage.

White, L. K. (1990). Determinants of divorce: A review of research in the eighties. *Journal of Marriage and the Family, 52*, 904–912.

White, L., & Tursky, B. (1985). Commentary on Roberts. *American Psychologist, 41*, 1005–1006.

Widiger, T. A., Frances, A. J., Pincus, H. A., Davis, W. W., & First, M. B. (1991). Toward an empirical classification for the DSM-IV. *Journal of Abnormal Psychology, 100*, 280–288.

Widiger, T. A., Frances, A., Spitzer, R. L., & Williams, J. B. W. (1988). The DSM-III personality disorders: An overview. *American Journal of Psychiatry, 145*, 786–795.

Widiger, T. A., Truci, T. J., Hurt, S. W., Clarkin, J., & Frances, A. (1987). A multidimensional scaling of the DSM-III personality disorders. *Archives of General Psychiatry, 44*, 557–563.

Widom, C. S. (1989). The cycle of violence. *Science, 244*, 160–166.

Wiens, A. N., & Menustik, C. E. (1983). Treatment outcome and patient characteristics in an aversion therapy program for alcoholism. *American Psychologist, 38*, 1089–1096.

Willerman, L. (1973). Activity level and hyperactivity in twins. *Child Development, 44,* 288–293.

Williams, R. B., & Barefoot, J. C. (1988). The emerging role of the hostility complex. In B. K. Houston & C. R. Snyder (Eds.), *Type-A behavior pattern: Research, theory and prevention.* New York: Wiley.

Wilsnack, R. W., Wilsnack, S. C., & Klassen, A. D. (1987). Antecedents and consequences of drinking and drinking problems in women: Patterns from a U.S. national survey. In P. C. Rivers (Ed.), *Alcohol and addictive behavior, Nebraska Symposium on Motivation, 1986.* Lincoln: University of Nebraska Press.

Wilson, G. T. (1986). Cognitive-behavioral and pharmacological therapies for bulimia. In K. D. Brownell & P. J. Foreyt (Eds.), *Handbook of eating disorders.* New York: Basic Books.

Wincze, J., Bansal, S., & Malamud, M. (1986). Effects of MPA on subjective arousal, arousal to erotic stimulation, and nocturnal penile tumescence in male sex offenders. *Archives of Sexual Behavior, 15,* 293–305.

Wing, L., & Attwood, A. (1987). Syndromes of autism and atypical development. In D. J. Cohen & A. M. Donnellan (Eds.), *Handbook of autism and pervasive developmental disorders.* New York: Wiley.

Wise, R. A. (1988). The neurobiology of craving: Implications for the understanding and treatment of alcoholism. *Journal of Abnormal Psychology, 97,* 118–132.

Witkin, H. A., Mednick, S. A., Schulsinger, F., Bakkestrom, E., Christiansen, K. O., Goodenough, D. R., Hirschorn, K., Lundsteen, C., Owen, D. R., Philip, J., Rubin, D. B., & Stocking, M. (1976). XYY and XXY men: Criminality and aggression. *Science, 193,* 547–555.

Woititz, J. G. (1990). *Adult children of alcoholics* (expanded ed.). Deerfield Beach, FL: Health Communications.

Wolfe, D. A. (1987). *Child abuse: Implications for child development and psychopathology.* Newbury Park, CA: Sage.

Wolfe, D. A., Wolfe, V. V., & Best, C. L. (1988). Child victims of sexual abuse. In V. B. van Hasselt, R. L. Morrison, A. S. Bellack, & M. Hersen (Eds.), *Handbook of family violence.* New York: Plenum.

Wolozin, B. L., Pruchinicki, D., Dickson, D. W., & Davies, P. (1986). A neuronal antigen in the brains of Alzheimer's patients. *Science, 232,* 648–650.

Wolpe, J. (1958). *Psychotherapy by reciprocal inhibition.* Stanford, CA: Stanford University Press.

Wolpe, J. (1969). *The practice of behavior therapy* (2nd ed.). Oxford: Pergamon Press.

Wong, D. F., Wagner, H. N., Tune, L. E., Tamminga, C. A., Broussolle, E. P., Ravert, H. T., Wilson, A. A., Toung, J. K. T., Malat, J., Williams, J. A., O'Tuama, L. A., Snyder, S. H., Kuhar, M. J., & Gjedde, A. (1986). Positron emission tomography reveals elevated D2 dopamine receptors in drug-naive schizophrenics. *Science, 234,* 1558–1563.

Wood, W., Wong, F. Y., & Chachere, J. G. (1991). Effects of media violence on viewers' aggression in unconstrained social interaction. *Psychological Bulletin, 109,* 371–383.

Woods, P. J., & Burns, J. (1984). Type-A behavior and illness in general. *Journal of Behavioral Medicine, 7,* 411–415.

Woods, P. J., Morgan, B. T., Day, B. W., Jefferson, T., & Harris, L. (1984). Findings on a relationship between type-A behavior and headaches. *Journal of Behavioral Medicine, 7,* 277–286.

Woody, G. E., McLellan, A. T., Luborsky, L., & O'Brien, C. P. (1987). Twelve-month follow-up of psychotherapy for opiate dependence. *American Journal of Psychiatry, 144,* 590–596.

Wooley, S. C., & Kearney-Cooke, A. (1986). Intensive treatment of bulimia and body-image disturbance. In K. D. Brownell & P. J. Foreyt (Eds.), *Handbook of eating disorders.* New York: Basic Books.

Wooley, S. C., & Wooley, O. W. (1979). Women and weight obsession: Redefining the problem. In P. A. Treichler, C. Kramarae, & B. Stafford, (Eds.), *For alma mater: Theory and practice in feminist scholarship.* Urbana: University of Illinois Press.

Wragg, R. E., & Jeste, D. V. (1989). Overview of depression and psychosis in Alzheimer's disease. *American Journal of Psychiatry, 146,* 577–587.

Wright, L. (1988). Type-A behavior pattern and coronary artery disease: Quest for the active ingredients and the elusive mechanism. *American Psychologist, 43,* 2–14.

Wurmser, L. (1974). Psychoanalytic considerations of the etiology of compulsive drug use. *Journal of the American Psychoanalytic Association, 22,* 820–843.

Wyatt, G. E., & Powell, G. J. (1988). Identifying the lasting effects of child sexual abuse. In G. E. Wyatt & G. J. Powell (Eds.), *Lasting effects of child sexual abuse.* Newbury Park, CA: Sage.

Wynne, L., Singer, M., Bartko, J., & Toohey, M. (1977). Schizophrenics and their families: Research on parental communication. In J. Tanner (Ed.), *Developments in psychiatric research.* London: Hodden & Stoughton.

Yalom, I. D. (1980). *Existential psychotherapy.* New York: Basic Books.

Yankner, B. A., Dawes, L. R., Fisher, S., Villa-Komaroff, L., Oster-Granite, M. L., & Neve, R. L. (1989). Neurotoxicity of a fragment of the amyloid precursor associated with Alzheimer's disease. *Science, 245,* 417–420.

Yaryura-Tobias, J. A. (1977). Obsessive-compulsive disorders: A serotonergic hypothesis. *Journal of Orthomolecular Psychiatry, 6,* 317–326.

Yaryura-Tobias, J. A., & Bhagavan, H. N. (1977). L-tryptophan in obsessive-compulsive disorders. *American Journal of Psychiatry, 134,* 1298–1299.

Yassa, R., Nair, N. P. V., Iskander, H., & Schwartz, G. (1990). Factors in the development of severe forms of tardive dyskinesia. *American Journal of Psychiatry, 147,* 1156–1163.

Youngstrom, N. (1991, July 15). Scientists probe traits of binge eating. *Psychological Monitor.*

Zajonc, R. B. (1980). Feeling and thinking: Preferences need no inferences. *American Psychologist, 35,* 151–175.

Zametkin, A. J., & Rapoport, J. L. (1986). The pathophysiology of attention deficit disorder with hyperactivity: A review. In B. B. Lahey & A. E. Kazdin (Eds.), *Advances in clinical psychology* (Vol. 9). New York: Plenum.

Zigler, E. (1967). Familial mental retardation: A continuing dilemma. *Science, 155,* 292–298.

Zilboorg, G. (1941). *A history of medical psychology.* New York: Norton.

Zilboorg, G. (1969). *The medical man and the witch during the Renaissance.* New York: Cooper Square.

Zubin, J., & Spring, B. (1977). Vulnerability—A new view of schizophrenia. *Journal of Abnormal Psychology, 86,* 103–126.

Zucker, R. A., & Lisansky Gomberg, E. S. (1986). Etiology of alcoholism reconsidered: The case for a biopsychosocial process. *American Psychologist, 41,* 783–793.

Zuckerman, M. (1979). *Sensation seeking: Beyond the optimal level of arousal.* Hillsdale, NJ: Erlbaum.

Zuckerman, M. (1984). Sensation seeking: A comparative approach to a human trait. *Behavioral Brain Sciences, 7,* 413–471.

Zuckerman, M., Ballenger, J., Jimerson, D., Murphy, D., & Post, R. (1983). A correlational test in humans of the biological models of sensation seeking, impulsivity and anxiety. In M. Zuckerman (Ed.), *Biological basis of sensation seeking, impulsivity, and anxiety.* Hillsdale, NJ: Erlbaum.

*P*hoto
Credits

Unless otherwise acknowledged, all photographs are the property of ScottForesman. Numbers in italics are page numbers.

Chapter 1

5 Left, Supreme Court Historical Society; center, A. Archer/Shooting Star; right, Michael Ponzin/Focus on Sports. *6* Top left, David Strickler/The Picture Cube; bottom left, Randy Matusow; right, Loren McIntyre. *7* Rafael Macia/Photo Researchers. *10* Bottom, Spence McConnell/Bruce Coleman Inc. *12* Right, The Granger Collection, New York. *13* By Courtesy of the Trustees of Sir John Soane's Museum. *15* Culver Pictures. *16* Both, The Bettmann Archive. *20* Top, Bob Daemmrich/The Image Works; bottom, Roy Morsch/The Stock Market.

Chapter 2

31 Ann P. Streissguth, University of Washington. *33* Will and Deni McIntyre/Photo Researchers. *38* The Bettmann Archive. *39* Jim Pickerell/West Light. *41* The Bettmann Archive. *42* Association for the Advancement of Psychoanalysis of the Karen Horney Psychoanalytic Institute and Center, New York. *46* Historical Pictures Service. *48* Carl Rogers Memorial Library. *49* Hugh L. Wilkerson. *51* Top, Courtesy of Rollo May; bottom, Popperfoto.

Chapter 3

59 The Bettmann Archive. *60* Courtesy of Professor Benjamin Harris, from Watson's 1919 film *Experimental Investigation of Babies*. *61, 62* David Young-Wolff/ PhotoEdit. *63, 67* All photos, Courtesy of Albert Bandura. *69* Courtesy of Albert Ellis, Institute for Rational Emotive Therapy. *72* Bob Daemmrich/Stock, Boston. *74* Lawrence Migdale. *77* Bob Daemmrich

Chapter 4

87 Stacy Pickerell/TSW, Chicago. *88* Top left, Jim Pickerell/Stock, Boston; top right and center left, Bob Daemmrich/Stock, Boston; center right, Harriet Gans/The Image

Works; bottom left, John Madere/The Stock Market; bottom right, Charles Harbutt/ Actuality. *94* Illustrations from *The Difficult Divorce: Therapy for Children and Families* by Marla Beth Isaacs et al. Copyright © 1986 by Basic Books, Inc. Reprinted by permission of Basic Books, a division of HarperCollins Publishers Inc. *95* Sepp Seitz/Woodfin Camp & Associates. *100* Rick Friedman/Black Star. *101* Archives of the History of American Psychology. *103* From *The Psychiatrist's Guide to Diseases of the Nervous System* by R. L. Lechtenberg. Copyright © 1982 by John Wiley & Sons, Inc. Reprinted by permission of John Wiley & Sons, Inc.

Chapter 5

113 Rick Friedman/Black Star. *115* Alvin H. Perlmutter Inc. *117* Bob Daemmrich/ The Image Works. *120* Courtesy of Professor Benjamin Harris, from Watson's 1919 film *Experimental Investigation of Babies*. *124* James Wilson/Woodfin Camp & Associates. *125* Courtesy of Dr. Joseph Wolpe. *126* Brad Bower/Stock, Boston. *129* The Granger Collection, New York. *133* AP/Wide World. *134* UPI/Bettmann.

Chapter 6

141 Top left, Jim Pickerell/West Light; top right, Bob Daemmrich/Stock, Boston; bottom, Diana Rasche/West Light. *143* AP/Wide World. *144* Top, Pedro Coll/The Stock Market; bottom, AP/Wide World. *147* Walter Reed Army Institute of Research, Washington, D.C. *151* Peter Southwick/Stock, Boston. *152* UPI/Bettmann. *159* Top, Pierre Boulat/Woodfin Camp & Associates; bottom, N. Rowan/The Image Works.

Chapter 7

167 Left, The Granger Collection, New York; right, Ira Wyman/Sygma. *169* Photograph by Dellenback. Reproduced by permission of The Kinsey Institute for Research in Sex, Gender, and Reproduction, Inc. *171* Paul von Stroheim/West Light. *175* James Wilson/Woodfin Camp & Associates. *178* Peter Yates/Picture Group. *181* Ingo Harney/Gamma-Liaison. *183* © Ethan Hoffman/Picture Project. *184* Left, Derek Bayes; right, Bruno de Hamel.

Chapter 8

195 Ron P. Jaffe/Unicorn. *197* Michael Weisbrot/Stock, Boston. *198* Courtesy of Mrs. Frances M. Erdmann. *199* Jose Azel/Contact/Woodfin Camp & Associates. *201* © Copyrighted 1993, Chicago Tribune Company, all rights reserved, used with permission. *203* Ben Gibson/Woodfin Camp & Associates. *204* Richard Hutchings/ Photo Researchers. *208* Ken Kaminsky/The Picture Cube. *211* Mimi Forsyth/ Monkmeyer Press. *215* AP/Wide World. *216* Alcoholics Anonymous World Service.

Chapter 9

224 D. and I. MacDonald/The Picture Cube. *229* Richard Hutchings/Photo Researchers. *232* Left, Rand Hendrix; right, Homer Sykes/Woodfin Camp & Associates. *234* Courtesy of Aaron T. Beck, M.D., Center for Cognitive Therapy. *237* Tony Freeman/PhotoEdit. *238* James Wilson/Woodfin Camp & Associates. *240* P. Chauvel/Sygma. *244* A. Tannenbaum/Sygma. *245* Charles Kenwood/Stock, Boston.

Chapter 10

251 AP/Wide World. *253* UPI/Bettmann. *254* Both, NIMH. *256* Left, Louis Fernandez/Black Star; right, Grunnitus/Monkmeyer Press. *263* All photos, Courtesy of Monte S. Buchsbaum. *264* Cindy Johnson/HarperCollins Publishers Inc. *266* Richard Hutchings/Photo Researchers. *268* Katrina Thomas/Photo Researchers. *271* Courtesy of SILS Program, Los Angeles VAMC. *273* Crandall/The Image Works.

Chapter 11

279 George Goodwin/Monkmeyer Press. *280* Mark Antman/The Image Works. *282* Michael Grecco/Stock, Boston. *286* Rick Friedman/Black Star. *291* Ron Davis/

Shooting Star. *293* Top, Richard Hutchings/Info Edit; bottom, Paul Conklin/ PhotoEdit. *295* Alan Carey/The Image Works. *297* Science VU/Visuals Unlimited. *300* Bouali/Gamma-Liaison.

Chapter 12

307 Left, Steve Schapiro/Sygma; right, William Thompson/The Picture Cube. *309* Arlene Collins/Monkmeyer Press. *313* The Photographers' Library/Uniphoto. *315* UPI/Bettmann. *316* Courtesy of Baylor College of Medicine. *317* Steve R. Krous/Stock, Boston. *321* Matthew Naythons/Stock, Boston. *323* Bob Daemmrich/ Stock, Boston.

Chapter 13

337 Tim Kelly/Black Star. *338* Top left and bottom left, UPI/Bettmann; right, Reuters/Bettmann. *340* The Granger Collection, New York. *344* Jean-Loup Charmet. *345* UPI/Bettmann. *347* Courtesy of Otto Kernberg, M.D. *350* W. W. Norton & Company.

Chapter 14

362 Hank Morgan/Science Source/Photo Researchers. *365* Ida Wyman/Monkmeyer Press. *367* Bill Aron/PhotoEdit. *370* The Granger Collection, New York. *372* Top left, Focus on Sports; bottom left, Culver Pictures; right, Jim Duxbury/Sygma. *373* Plailly/Science Photo Library/Photo Researchers. *375* Nubar Alexanian/Stock, Boston.

Chapter 15

382 Alan Raid/Sygma. *384* UPI/Bettmann. *385* Courtesy of University of Colorado School of Medicine. *386* Ron Sachs/Sygma. *387* UPI/Bettmann. *393* M. Siluk/The Image Works. *395* Mary Ellen Mark/Library. *399* Andy Levin/Photo Researchers.

*N*ame Index

Subject Index